SALTHILL

A History, Part 1

TIMELINES – TALES – THEMES

SALTHILL

A History, Part 1

Paul Mc Ginley

carrowmore.ie

*I gcuimhne ar
mo thuismitheoirí,
Pádraic agus Máire
agus mo dheartháir,
Ciarán.*

*In onóir mo chlainne;
Mary, mo bhean
agus ár muirín,
Brian, Colm, Deirdre agus Paul.*

First published by Carrowmore, 2018

First Edition

Carrowmore Publishing
50 City Quay
Dublin 2
www.carrowmore.ie
@carrowmore101
info@carrowmore.ie

© Paul Mc Ginley, 2018

ISBN: 978-1-9999915-2-4

The right of Paul Mc Ginley to be identified as the
Author of this work has been asserted in accordance with the
Copyright and Related Rights Act, 2000.

All rights reserved. No part of this book may be reprinted
or reproduced or utilised in any form or by any electronic,
mechanical or other means, now known or hereafter invented,
including photocopying and recording, or in any information
storage or retrieval system, without the permission in writing
of the Publishers.

British Library Cataloguing in Publication Data.
A catalogue record for this book is available from the British Library.

Rich in evidence, judicious in its analysis, insightful and written in an assured and engaging style, this study of the origins and development of Salthill is an example of local history at its very best.

Gearóid Ó Tuathaigh,
Professor Emeritus in History,
NUI, Galway.

Extremely well written, this study boasts an extraordinary wealth of information based on great research.

Thomas Boylan,
Professor Emeritus in Economics,
NUI, Galway.

Generously illustrated, this significant and informative book is required reading for anyone interested in the story of Salthill's past.

Ralph O' Gorman,
Rugby historian and Salthill native.

1. Salthill Village c.1870. (Courtesy of National Library of Ireland.)

CONTENTS

	List of Images – Maps – Tables	11
	Salt Hill Timeline to 1901	16
	Reasons for Writing / Acknowledgements	23
	Dónal Taheny – A Tribute	31

Geography of Salthill:
Townlands – Villages – Demesnes – Promenade

1	Salthill's Townlands and Burial Grounds	40
2	Salthill's Villages	47
3	Finding One's Bearings: Maps and Photographs	56
4	Salthill Demesnes of Clanmorris, Persse, O'Hara and Whaley	65
5	Salthill of Walls, Gates and Promenade	81
	Salthill Improvement Committees	94
6	Salthill: What's in a Name?	100

Fishing Heritage

7	Salthill's Fishing Tradition	118

Tourist Attractions and *Fámairí* in 19th Century Salthill

8	Salthill Baths	132
9	19th Century Accommodation and Female Contribution	157

10	*Na Fámairí* and the Lazy Wall	184
11	The Toft Family and Salthill: A Unique Relationship	198
12	Getting to Salthill: Trains, Trams and Horses	217

Famines – Clearances – Landed Society

13	Nineteenth Century Famines and Evictions	230
14	'Improving' Landlords at Salthill's Seafront	245
15	Pollnarooma East of numerous 19th Century Clearances	271
	Marriage Conventions and Choices for Landed Offspring	282
16	Tievegarriff – Cloghatisky – Acres: Famine Experiences	295
17	Salthill's Famine Roads	308
18	A Persse Presence – Row – American connection	330

Townland Data

20	Townland Information from 19th Century	350
	Endnotes	363
	Index	380

LIST OF IMAGES – MAPS – TABLES

1	Salthill Village c. 1870	6–7
2	Dónal Taheny, *Staraí – Oide – Saoi*	31
3	Salthill Townland Map	41
4	O'Hara Burial Ground Headstone	41
5	O'Hara Burial Ground on 19th century map	42
6	Memorial to Eleanor A. Persse at Glenarde	43
7	Flagstone Persse memorial at New Cemetery	43
8	Dominican Cemetery at Taylor's Hill	44
9	*Cillín na bPáistí* memorial stone at Galway Golf Course	45
10	Salthill's 'urban' Villages on 19th century Map	47
11	Griffith's Valuation recording of Salthill & Merrion villages	48
12	Central House, No. 1, Merrion Village	48
13	Thatched cottages at Lower Salthill in early 1900s	49
14	U.S. President, John F. Kennedy, at Lower Salthill in 1963	49
15	Nile Lodge gate and 'bathing box'	50
16	Promenade's Wesleyan Chapel on 19th century map	51
17	Glenorney – originally a Wesleyan Meeting House	53
18	Residence that served as first Post Office on Taylor's Hill	55
19	Salthill Village in 1870s	56
20	Salthill Village, from Ballinasloe House to Ivy Lodge wall	57
21	Salt Hill House – O'Connor's Famous Pub	57
22	Grove View and Kilcorkey Lodge	57

23	Salthill Village, from Prospect Lodge to Seapoint Baths	58
24	Three Salthill Village houses from the past	58
25	Map of Salthill Village and hinterland in 1890s	58
26	Sea View and Barrack Lane in 1890s	59
27	Two saline 'loughauns' on landside of promenade	59
28	Flooding on Rockbarton Road in 1952	60
29	Merrion Village's Eastern end in 19th Century	61
30	Western end of Merrion Village in 19th Century	61
31	Norman Villas	62
32	Map of Kilcorkey – Merrion Village in 1890s	62
33	Salthill's Fine Houses in 1890s	63
34	Traditional townland map showing 2018 street infrastructure	64
35	Map of Clanmorris and Glenarde Demesnes	65
36	Western entrance to 'Chariot' avenue of Glenarde Demesne	66
37	Henry Seymour 'Atty' Persse	68
38	Map of O'Hara's 'Lenaboy' Demesne	70
39	Gated Salt Hill Entrance to Lenaboy Demesne	71
40	Whaley male lineage chart	73
41	Richard Chapell Whaley's family portrait	74
42	Thomas 'Buck' Whaley	75
43	Whaley press advertisement, 1823	78
44	Revagh Road in 2018	81
45	Salthill's 'serpentine' promenade	82
46	Gated entrances to Rockbarton and Cappanaveagh post 1856	83
47	Imposing O'Hara wall at entrance to Salthill Village	83
48	Thomas Grehan of Independent Newspapers, 1921	84
49	The Villa's tall wall at entrance to Lower Salthill	85
50	Dr. Colahan Road sign	85
51	View of Salthill from Taylor's Hill / Kingston	86
52	Tall wall of Monks' Field in 1935	86
53	Start of Salthill's promenade in late 1800s	89
54	Lady with bike on Salthill Promenade	90
55	Samuel Ussher Roberts	92
56	Start of Salthill's promenade post-1934	93
57	*Bóthar Ard* road sign	100

58	*Bóthar Ard agus Bóthar na Trá* map	101
59	Townland name – translation chart	101
60	William Larkin's map of Salthill, 1819	102
61	Chart showing Jones – Conyngham Salthill ties	105
62	Salthill House, Mountcharles, Co. Donegal	106
63	Lady Shea's Plot	108
64	Contrasting Montpel(l)ier signs	109
65	Raleigh Row sign	109
66	Sherwood's Fields – *Seanbhóthar* map	110
67	Tim Shea's public house at Spanish Arch	111
68	San Antonio Terrace	113
69	Monsignor Thomas Mulleady	114
70	Memorials to Fr. Fahy and Fr. Mulleady	115
71	*Morning – Landing Fish at Blackrock,* by Thomas Rose Miles	119
72	Recorder's Quay, 1839	121
73	Bulteel's Marsh	134
74	Dr. Gray's – later Andrew King's – Baths	138
75	King's Hill map	141
76	George Fallon Baths' map	142
77	Seapoint House and Fallon's Baths	143
78	Seapoint corner at Salthill Village c.1870	145
79	Seapoint open-area at Salthill Village c.1930	147
80	Marie Cremen of Seapoint House and Baths	150
81	Hangar – Pavilion Ballroom	155
82	Merville advertisement, 1831	158
83	Three Bathing Lodges; Revagh – Belmore – Brinkwater	159
84	Seafront map of Bathing Lodges	159
85	Cappanaveagh end of Salthill Village	163
86	Fields surrounding Barrack Lane	165
87	Building that narrowed entrance to Barrack Lane	167
88	Lenaboy Avenue Sign	168
89	Behatted man on Promenade's first stone seat	175
90	Mrs. Susan Emerson	177
91	Emerson Avenue sign	178
92	Ryan's Terrace a.k.a. Beach Avenue	180

93	Liam O'Flaherty with daughter, Peggy, at Salthill	186
94	*Fámairí Mná ag an mBalla Fallsa*	188
95	Lazy Wall on Salthill postcard	189
96	Michael Fallon, hero of 1909 rescue	193
97	The Lazy Wall, 1941	195
98	Toft's Fair at Eyre Square	201
99	Atlantic Bar beside Eglinton Hotel	202
100	Toft stalls at Salthill Park, 1933	205
101	Fairground stalls on Maretimo lawn	209
102	Maretimo Bathing Lodge	211
103	Irish Railway map, 1906	218
104	Eglinton Hotel's covered horse-car	219
105	Horse-cars at Salthill during 'Emergency'	220
106	Horse tram at Eyre Square	222
107	Double tram lines at Lower Salthill	222
108	Tram lines to Seapoint House corner	225
109	Salthill's tram terminus at Eglinton Hotel	227
110	Pre – and Post – Famine townland population chart	231
111	Sir William Gregory of Coole	235
112	Fr. Peter Daly's 1865 meeting with Lord Palmerston	237
113	Daly's Place road sign	241
114	Bust and legend commemorating Fr. Peter Daly	244
115	Salthill's sea-front hamlets	245
116	Henry Shaw Jones' advertisement for Cappanaveagh, 1847	250
117	Two 19th century quarry sites at Cappanaveagh	252
118	Rockhill road sign	253
119	Blake Forster Coat of Arms at Salthill and Bushypark	256
120	Attithomasrevagh before it became 'Rockbarton'	257
121	Pillared entrances to Rockbarton and Cappanaveagh	262
122	New road infrastructure at Rockbarton	262
123	Rockbarton Road sign	263
124	Removal of gated entrance at Rockbarton in 1944	265
125	Barton image set	268
126	Rutledge image collection	270
127	Seamount House	275

List of Images – Maps – Tables

128	Fourth Lord and Lady Clanmorris	281
129	Bingham – Persse marriage matrix at Salthill	283
130	Maria Helena Persse, who eloped with Denis Bingham	284
131	Persse Distillery at Nun's Island	289
132	Population / Eviction chart at Pollnarooma East	291
133	Taylor's Hill entrance to Glenarde Demesne	292
134	Large houses at Tievegarriff, 1830s/1840s	296
135	Rose O'Hara at Lenaboy Castle	305
136	Threadneedle Road sign	309
137	Nile Lodge T junction, before the 'New Line' was built	313
138	Two houses at Albert Terrace and St. Mary's College	314
139	Mission School Orphanage and New Line	315
140	Sherwood Avenue sign	315
141	Gothic Mission School design	316
142	Land reclaimed by Grattan Road's construction	320
143	Grattan Road sign	323
144	Grattan Lodge map	325
145	Grattan Lodge postcard	325
146	Martin Conlon	326
147	Celia Griffin and Famine Ship memorials at Grattan Road	329
148	Iconography at Grattan Road, Galway and Murrisk, Mayo	329
149	Timeline of Persse row (1826–1899)	332
150	Burton de Burgh Persse (1779–1859)	334
151	Wilfrid Scawen Blunt	340
152	Residential Persse cluster on Taylor's Hill	341
153	Thomas Moore Persse	345
154	Mount Vernon, Taylor's Hill	346
155	Mount Vernon gate at St. Mary's Terrace	348
156	Mount Vernon on Flaggy Shore, Co. Clare	349
157	Tithe Applotment Books re Salthill, 1834	350–351
158	Griffith's Valuation re Salthill, 1855	359–360

SALT HILL TIMELINE TO 1901

1557   *Capneyvaugh* (Cappanaveagh) – First written record: 'The Mayor and Counsaill have gyvin and graunted the said Wardyn and Vicairs and their successors to be free of all rentes or duties of the pasture and grassing of Cappneyvaugh which they had in yeft (gift) of John Athye.'[1]

1609   *Athey Thomas Reagh* (Attithomasrevagh) – First written record.

1657   *Leneboyes* (Lenaboy), *Pollioomy* (Pollnarooma), and *Cloghahiske* (Clochatisky) – First written records.[2]

1681   'Nicholas Lynch Fitz Marcus of Barney [Barna]…released for the sum of £83 to Ffinyne Hallorane…parts of Pollneromy.'[3]

1691   *Kilcorky* (Kilcorkey) – First written record.

1709   *Tiefgarraff* (Tievegarriff) – First written record.[4]

1756   The Corporation of the Warden and Vicars of King's College, Galway, leased the Cappanaveagh townland to Fielding Shaw.

1797   De Latocnaye wrote of young damsels going 'to refresh their charms in the sea about two miles from the city,' though Salt Hill was not mentioned.[5]

1803   William Skerrett of Poulneroma made an indenture of lease for townland to Constantine Sloper.

1805	'The Warden and Vicars of the King's College of Galway...demised unto Conyngham Jones all that and those the town and Lands of Cappanaveagh situate in the west Liberties of Galway.'[6]
1809	First published record of 'Salt hill near Galway' – identified by this study – in the *Dublin Evening Post* of 7 October, 1809, and in a number of other regional Irish and English newspapers.[7]
1814	First published Directory record of 'Salt-hill Village' – discovered by this study – appeared in Ambrose Leet's Directory, 1814.[8]
1819	'Salt hill' appellation appeared in William Larkin's Galway Map, representing the first cartographic record of that name, at Galway, identified by this study.
1820	1st Lord Clanmorris bought the 'Poulnaroma' townland from Constantine Sloper.
1821	Lieutenant William Hutchinson was in charge of H.M.S. *Plumper* on Galway Bay.[9] The naval officer resided, with his wife Hannah, at Nile Lodge, which he had built following an earlier deed settlement with 'John Whaley of Stephen's Green.' Lieutenant Hutchinson departed Galway in the summer of 1827, following his wife's death in January of that same year.
1828	Next summer 'there will be forty or fifty neat lodges along the sea shore – where there were but two or three a few years since.'[10]
1831	Dr. Gray's Baths opened at bottom of what was later to be called King's Hill.
	Fr. Peter Daly publicly denied 'a most mischievous and most wantonly erroneous report...that serious injury was done by poor peasantry to my house' at Blackrock,[11] as had been recorded in an earlier *Galway Independent* report.[12]
1834	Tithe Applotment Book records re Salt Hill.
1836	When fishing in the bay, a Knocknacarra boat was overturned and several others were damaged on a December Sunday in 1836. The occupants gave no information about their attackers 'partly from fear, and partly from an impression that they were wrong to fish on a Sunday.'[13]

1838	'It is proposed to have a Penny Post established in the village for the convenience of visitors.'[14]
1839	Ordnance Map of Salthill surveyed – engraved in 1840.

John O'Donovan noted that 'a portion of this townland [Lenaboy] on South side of road between the Records Quay and Black Rock belongs to Mr. Whaley, Oran Quay, Dublin and leased to 8 tenants… who have built neat lodges for the Accommodation of Bathers. Lease 1 life or 31 years.'[15]

On the Night of the Big Wind 'scarcely a house in Salt-hill…did not feel the awful effects of the storm.'[16] |
| **1845–1850** | ***An Gorta Mór***

Famine Roads: (a) *Bóthar na Mine,* later known as Threadneedle Road, constructed.
(b) New Line, later known as St. Mary's Road, under construction in 1846 was delayed, and not completed until the early 1850s. |
| **1845** | Dominican Sisters left their Slate Nunnery at Kirwan's Lane and transferred to Seaview on Taylor's Hill – a move not appreciated by their bishop elect, Dr. Laurence O'Donnell.

Henry Shawe Jones leased the Cappanaveagh townland.

Tenant ejectments at Lord Clanmorris' Pollnarooma East. |
1847	'Wholesale clearance' of tenants from Cappanaveagh townland by Mr. Henry Shawe Jones.[17]
1848	Andrew King, and his wife, Jane, took over as proprietors of Dr. Gray's Sea Baths.
1850	Lead mineral discovery at Cappanaveagh, reported by *Galway Mercury*.[18]
1851	**First Dublin train arrived in Galway on 21 July, 1851.**
Salthill Post Office opened.[19] First 'Postmaster' was Ellen Ryan, who lent her name to Ryan's Terrace – Beach Avenue today.
1852	Mr. Thomas Henry Barton purchased, from Lord Oranmore and Brown, the Attithomasrevagh townland that came to be called Rockbarton. Mr. Barton cleared one hundred and twenty nine tenants off his newly purchased landbank,[20] and razed the *Baile Thaidhg Bháin* hamlet to the ground.

Father Peter Daly bought all of Lower Salthill, including Merrion Village, when he purchased the Kilcorkey townland from Mr. Robert Whaley.

Henry Grattan Jnr. bought 'Fairhill & Claddagh' from Robert Whaley.

The Ballynacarrickadoo *clachán* at Blackrock, in the Pollnarooma East townland, was cleared by John Charles Bingham, the Fourth Lord Clanmorris.

'The number of visitors, who are daily congregating Westward may be inferred from the fact, upon some nights there is not a bed unoccupied at the Great Railway Hotel, which contains upwards of seventy sleeping apartments.'[21]

1853 Four Salthill fishermen were each charged on the one day with *being the owner of a certain boat or vessel engaged in fishing…had not the register number assigned to said boat or vessel…painted on the sail of said boat or vessel.*[22]

1855 Griffith's Valuation records re Salt Hill.

1856 First Salthill Improvement Committee – identified by this study – set out to create 'a promenade along the sea shore, separated from the public road by a low parapet wall, which will answer as a seat.'[23]

Captain Francis Blake Forster bought the Cappanaveagh townland, previously owned by Conyngham Jones and Henry Shawe Jones. The Sandymount building was subsequently replaced – on the same site – by the Forster Park residence, which was completed by the early 1860s.[24] Salthill's current Garda Station is housed in that Forster Park residence.

Patent Bill Stickers to her Majesty required 'an additional charge for any Bills to be posted at Salt-Hill or any other locality outside the suburbs of Galway.'[25]

1858 Fr. Peter Daly solicited ejectments against 'eleven tenants in Salthill, whose leases, valid when he bought the property in the court, had run out.'[26]

1859 Dominican Sisters opened a 'Boarding School for Young Ladies' on Taylor's Hill.[27]

1860 **John Gill opened The Eglinton Hotel.**
Daly's Fort under construction for Isaac B. Daly.
'Salt-hill promises to become, ere long, part and parcel of the "city of the tribes".'[28]

1861/'62	Mr. Thomas Moore Persse built Mount Vernon on Taylor's Hill. Lenaboy Castle was built on the site of Lenaboy House for Captain O'Hara. A Mission Church School and Orphanage, for the Irish Church Missions – *Scoil Fhursa* today – was constructed at Nile Lodge.[29]
1862	Wesleyan Chapel / Meeting House opened on the Promenade.[30]
1863/4	Famine Road – *Bóthar na nDeich bPingin* a.k.a. Grattan Road – chiefly financed by Miss Frances (Fanny) Grattan, was constructed.
1864	'A very handsome bathing place for ladies, projected by Mr. Samuel U. Roberts C.E., has been cleared and walled in,' behind 'George's Baths' at Seapoint.[31]
	A Springboard was erected at Black Rock with costs underwritten by John Murphy & John Hogan.[32]
1867	In terms of Village status, the *Galway Vindicator* opined that Salt-hill 'may now fairly lay claim to that appellation.'[33]
1869	A Police Station for Salt Hill was announced following the procurement of suitable premises: 'There will be a constable and four sub-constables at the Station.'[34]
1870	Andrew King's Baths burned down.
1871	First published record of Rockbarton as a Salthill address – identified by this study – appeared in *Tuam Herald*.[35]
	Lower Salthill's Industrial School opened under Patrician Brothers' management.
1872	Salthill's Police Barracks first recorded for rateable exemption.
	Lord Clanmorris sold the Pollnarooma East townland to his brother-in-law, Henry S. Perrse of Glenarde.
1873	Mr. Redmond Burke bought Mount Vernon from Thomas Moore Perrse.
1874	Henry Sadleir Persse cleared five families with children and an aged woman, the remnant of the 'Polnaroma East' tenantry, from his Glenarde Demesne.[36]

1876	Christian Brother Order took over Salthill's Industrial School on being asked to do so.
1879	**Galway – Salthill Tramway began its service.**
1881	Samuel Woods was recorded in Slater's Directory as Salthill's Postmaster. He had been in that postal position for some years and so remained until his death in 1894.
1883	First record of Tofts' Amusements at Salthill.[37]
1885	'Mr. Moon of Galway and some young men of the town,' with Colonel O'Hara's permission, erected a springboard at Blackrock.[38]
1887	Galway's Catholic Diocese bought Mount Vernon as an 'Episcopal Residence' for £1,500.[39] Subsequently changed name to Mount St. Mary's.
1888	Miss Noël Persse (aged 9) died after accident on horse, at the Chariot's entrance gate.[40]
1889	The Cremen family – on replacing Mr. John Parsons – was first recorded at Seapoint House in Cancelled Revision Books.
1892	New Salthill Improvements' organisation held private meeting of prominent citizens on 3 March, 1892.[41]
1894	Mrs. Frances E. Cremen of Seapoint House and her two children, James and Mary, acquired Fallon's Bath premises next door.[42] The Fallon facility had then operated for four decades, or more.
1895	The Townland of Cappanaveagh was auctioned in 10 lots at a High Court Chancery sale. Seventeen acres of that Cappanaveagh land were purchased by prominent citizens under the Salthill Improvements' banner. A public meeting was called to support development plans for the place. The Salthill Improvements' organisation held its first public meeting, which was chaired by Bishop Francis MacCormack, in June 1895.[43] A temporary bandstand was erected on a 'grassy hill beyond the tram line terminus' by the promoters of the Salthill Orchestral Band.[44]
1901	New four storey Dominican Boarding School for girls blessed and opened.[45]

Galway Tennis & Croquet Club opened on Threadneedle Road.

John Tonry and family were running Salthill's Post Office at Elm View.

Census night: 31 March, 1901

REASONS FOR WRITING

The reasons for writing this history are manifold. In the first place, the story of Salt Hill has never been told, and it is a tale that deserves telling.

The place's reputation as a holiday resort has long fed into a sense of seasonal evanescence, where the resort fills and blossoms for the tourist term and hibernates through dull winter months. Ubiquitous 'kiss-me-quick' hats, which were worn at Salthill during the nineteen sixties, epitomized the flighty freedom of holiday transience. That traditional perspective of the place is understandable and differs little from any appraisal of holiday resorts worldwide. In the past, a measure of truth may have been carried in such a conventional view of Salt Hill when less than 250 souls – including Queen's College students – resided at Salthill Village during the resort's downtime. A summer-tourist and winter-student boarding trade was then practiced at the village, and it was not unusual for a number of public houses – and other businesses – to seasonally shut down, in anticipation of lengthening days and sparkling summer sunshine.

But there is more, much more, to the history of the place than summer frolics. During the 19th century the townlands of Salt Hill were cleared of peasant farmers and fishermen, through a combination of periodic famines and 'enlightened' landlords, who were seeking to 'improve' the resort. Outside of the village, Salthill's pre-Famine hinterland was occupied – for the most part – by tenant farmers on small holdings, who were dependent on the landlord of the townland in which they lived and worked. *An Gorta Mór* was to change all that, after which much of Salthill fell into the hands of an emerging commercial and professional class, which co-existed for some decades at Salthill with the rump of a landed elite. Fine new residences, quaintly known as Bathing Lodges, came to join Claremount Lodge and Blackrock House in dotting the land mass that overlooked the sea. Among their number were Glenorney, Gurthard, St. Mary's, Lisgorm and Forster Park. Lower Salthill and Taylor's Hill also featured impressive piles in a hinterland of trophy house opulence, where Lenaboy Castle and Mount Vernon were added to Nile Lodge, the distinctive residence of Lieutenant William and Hannah Hutchinson, who resided there in the 1820s. All of the structures just mentioned still stand.

Many more fine houses have disappeared from sight, the casualties of a structural-social change that was not Salthill specific, but part of a great transformation that was countrywide in its sweep. The sale of the Lenaboy Demesne in 1923 opened the way for the first of many building booms which greatly increased the population of the place, and marked the demise of the landed elite which formerly bestrode Salthill. Once weighty titles that included Lord Clanmorris and Lord Oranmore and Browne, as well as landed names like Whaley, Sloper, Skerrett, O'Hara, Blake Forster and Persse were, over the years, to fade from view. The professional-cum-merchant monikers that followed – including Barton, Rutledge and Hennessy – all had their moments in the Salthill sun, before their holdings were later fragmented to building plot size. Such land splintering opened the place to many more occupants, who would enjoy the advantages of a Salthill residency. Intensive building development, over many 20th century decades, saw to that.

Substantial changes, which were societal, political and economic in nature, meant that the place is now home to few who can trace their Salthill lineage back to the 19th century. While many rural areas take pride in generational family histories, suburban household spans are generally less lengthy. That is not to say that Salthill is totally bereft of some denizens with deep roots in the place. In noting Salt Hill townland tenants from the Tithe Applotment Books, the Conneely and McGrath families of Salthill can boast of a recorded presence at the place from 1834, and most likely from way before that tithe date. In the McGrath case, for example, a press report on the tragic 1909 drowning of Denis McGrath stated that 'he had been born at Salthill, where his family have resided for generations.'[1] 'Feeny' and 'Kain' entries, in the 1834 record, presaged a long Salthill presence for Feeney and Keane families in the area. Fallon is another family name with deep roots in the place. Though the surname was not recorded in the 1834 Tithe record, a George Fallon was born at Salt-Hill in 1788 and Fallon's Sea Baths at Seapoint operated for at least four decades before their sale in the early 1890s. A subsequent and unbroken Fallon presence at Barrack Lane / Lenaboy Avenue continued up to modern times.

In commercial terms, the oldest clan connection with Salthill belongs to the Toft family. On his 1981 election as Mayor of Galway, Councillor Claude Toft spoke of holding family records of amusement ties with the resort from 1883. Claude's Casino still operates today (2018) and the fact that a once seasonal funfair family holds the trading record at the resort tells its own particular tale. That family's first fixed operation began at the Salthill Arcade, under the guidance of Mrs. Florence Toft in 1940, a year after her husband, David (Abby) Toft, had passed away. The Stewart Building

Contracting firm represents the longest running enterprise, throughout the Greater Salthill area, that has operated from the one site since inception. Mr. James Stewart arrived in Galway from Portumna and married his California-born Lower Salthill landlady, Mary Anne Gill, in 1900. Two years later, the longstanding and successful Stewart joinery and building trade was established. One of the seminal developments of the 20th century at Salthill was the 1933 purchase of the Monks' Field by a Castlerea consortium, made up of Francis Hallinan, Patrick Raftery, John Burke and Kate Howley (Dunmore). That purchase facilitated the opening of a south-facing village side to commercial, ecclesiastical and tourism enterprises. Mr. Hallinan first operated a butcher shop in the village, before opening the 13 bedroom Oslo Hotel, which registered with the Irish Tourist Board in June, 1951. The Hallinan family still holds commercial interests at the resort. In terms of one family continuing to run the same business in the same premises at Salthill Village, the O'Connor family at Salthill House has operated its famous bar since 1942. In that year Thomas O'Connor, businessman, bandleader and Fianna Fáil County Councillor, moved to Galway's marine resort, after selling his commercial concerns at Moylough in North Galway.

Some other business families, though no longer trading in the village, spent many years in the place. The Walshe enterprise at the Stella Maris is a good example of such longevity. That tourism business ran for well over eight decades before its 1990 sale. The McAlinney family also enjoyed a good innings at the heart of Salthill. Edward McAlinney, a retired R.I.C. Head Constable, held properties in Salthill before he acquired the Eglinton Hotel in 1897. A family connection with that establishment was to continue for 73 years. Mrs. Susan Emerson, who took over the business in 1929, was Edward's daughter by his first marriage. Further McAlinney tourist trade involvement was to be found at Villa Maria, Atlantic Lodge, The Grand Hotel, Orient Lodge and the Seacrest Restaurant, which operated up to the 1990s. The Finan family's business association with the place was also lengthy. After Castlerea man, Martin Finan, married Mary Ellen Glancy of Salthill in 1907, he was to run the Commercial House for many years. The Finan name was also synonymous with the Bon Bon and more spectacularly with Seapoint Ballroom and Restaurant, which opened in 1949. When Seapoint was sold in 1984, a Finan business connection with Salthill Village had existed for over seven decades.

The great majority of Salthill residents, however, cannot claim a generational link with the area. They belong to the *séideadh isteach* brigade that makes up the great bulk of the place's population. Though the Stewarts can boast of over 110 years' tenure, the Hallinans of eight decades plus, and the O'Connors of over seventy bar-trading years, most other locals lag far behind such longevity. There is, consequently, little communal memory at the resort. While some longstanding families carry local lore of great provenance, such *seanchas* is scarce in Salthill. This book is the first in a history series that will attempt to fill that void, and look at those who trod the trail before the current generation.

Patrick Kavanagh, the Monaghan poet, understood the importance of place and, though he spent the greater part of his life in Dublin, it was the drumlins of his native county that were most mined throughout his poetic odyssey. From that source wondrous words of beauty were crafted that dressed afresh the 'banal' and decorated the 'ordinary.' His 'Epic' sonnet nailed the notion of place, asserted its importance, and celebrated its common beauty. For Kavanagh, the townlands of 'Ballyrush and Gortin' held their own proud place in the world.

Such celebration of place is most often found on sporting fields, where a victorious parish team gives expression to such pride. That same 'delirium' does not always drive town teams. While it is true that some long-settled 'core' urban areas, in common with rural parishes, retain a feral local loyalty, suburban Ireland does not generally experience the same primal ethos. That is understandable, for most Irish suburbs are modern creations, casting people from many counties and countries together in tightly populated pockets. The amorphous nature of city dwelling is, in the main, not conducive to an appreciation of place or a shared history.

Giving the lie to that premise, however, was the unbridled joy of the 2006 crowd that gathered under the Hogan Stand on a cold St. Patrick's Day, when Salthill-Knocknacarra won the All-Ireland Senior Football title. The achievement of such a young club was notable, but what was remarkable was the number of supporters who swarmed onto the Croke Park sward, before the Andy Merrigan cup was presented to team captain, Maurice Sheridan. It was understandable that there were more at that game than at any other played by the club, but on that field were men and women, who had represented and supported Salthill at numerous levels – in various codes and disciplines – over former years. Many of them, in the nature of modern living, had moved away, and their families' ties with Salthill were broken. That cohort embodies a great host of people, who at some time lived by the sea at Galway's first suburb, but became part of the transient tradition that remains a defining feature of the resort. Their pride in the place, nonetheless, was evidenced by their attendance and enthusiasm on a most memorable day.

A further reason for writing this book, if truth be told, is personal. Though not to everyone's liking, history remains a worthy discipline. An essential curiosity about the past has been the dynamic which has driven historical study worldwide, and thereby informed the present. Since coming to reside at Salthill in the early 1960s, a nascent desire to explore the Who? Why? What? of the place's past has grown over time. That personal interest was rewarded through the discovery of a professor 'who couldn't be killed'; two Salthill born Knights of the Realm, one of whom played competitive singles' tennis at Wimbledon; two 'German' Sinn Féiners; military heroes in many conflicts; resolute and independent women of the pre – and post – suffragette era; a pioneering lady professor; the man who first had St. Patrick's Day designated as a national holiday... the list goes on and on. Some of their stories will be covered in this volume, and a future book will deal with the remainder and other personalities yet to be unearthed.

An account of what defined Salthill, throughout its developmental period, will be offered in this edition. For that reason a 19th century focus will distinguish a good part of this book. That time frame demands consideration of the place's fishing tradition; famine times and evictions; landlords and their influence; the development of a tourism product; summer attractions that included a Lazy Wall, as well as the Toft family's contribution to the place. As the timeline of the work is quite loose, some themes will feature coverage that extends well into the 20th century.

For all of that, this study cannot – and does not – promise that it will create an all-encompassing communal memory, or that its prose will do justice to the richness of the place's past, or that its tales will tell the full story of Salthill. Much as it will strive to do so, the achievement of such goals may prove as elusive as the ethereal nature of summer holidays. Having said that, this book represents a first step that will – hopefully – make the reader aware of the diverse history of a locale, many of us are proud to proclaim as our home.

Acknowledgements

This study could not have been completed without the help of a wonderfully supportive family. My wife, Mary, from day one encouraged me to commit to paper all the information I had gathered on Salthill over time. That advocacy was accompanied by steadfast support throughout the research and writing phase. All of my children, Brian, Colm, Deirdre and Paul helped in multifarious ways in getting the book to print. Their collective input included academic advice, graphic design, boundless positivity, and computer expertise. Technological help at public talks has long been the responsibility of the boys of the house, which they have generously given over the years.

Patrick and Máire McGinley, my Donegal parents who reared their family in Galway, imbued in their children a sense of cultural identity that was woven around a shared Gaelic heritage. *Bhí saibhreas cultúrtha agus teangan i dtraidisiúin chlann Mhic Fhionnlaoich as an Fhál Garbh agus muintir Uí Ghallchobhair, Cois Chladaigh, a chruthaigh ionnannas téagartha Gaelach.* History was germane to such identity and it is no surprise that almost all of my siblings share a great interest in the past. The support of Don, Pádraic, Ciarán (R.I.P.) and Cathal, in many spheres across a good number of decades, is much appreciated and here acknowledged.

The Burke family, our close relations and next-door neighbours, are part of a shared Salthill story and I wish to acknowledge the contribution made by my aunt Sarah (R.I.P.), her husband John (R.I.P.), and cousins Margaret (R.I.P.), Joe, Eithne and Denis to the enrichment of that life experience. Ard na Mara is – and has always been – a wonderful place to live among genuine neighbours, past and present.

The supportive direction of Professor Gearóid Ó Tuathaigh and Professor Thomas Boylan is truly valued, as is the academic rigour they brought to the work. Rugby historian Ralph O'Gorman – in his contribution – bore the blessing of a true Salthill native, who appreciates a sense of place. Delivered with wisdom and grace was the counsel of all three mentors, which was not only scholarly but selfless; a manifestation of their commitment to the chronicling of Salthill's past.

I'm also indebted to organisations that offered me a platform for my talks, including the Salthill Active Retirement Association; The Patrick Kavanagh Western Association; *An Taisce*, Galway; *Scoil Íde*; *Coláiste Éinde*; Galway Family History Society West; Salthill Village; Renmore Active Retirement Association; Salthill-Knocknacarra G.A.A.; Knocknacarra Active Retirement Association; Women Graduates of N.U.I.G.; Irish Federation of University Women; Barna I.C.A.; Lower Salthill Residents' Association; Business and Professional Women Galway, and Renmore History Society. A 'Nile to the Sea' guided walk, presented in association with Galway Civic Trust, was also most gratifying. In terms of venues, the Galway Bay and Salthill hotels have always been most accommodating, while Gerry and Joanna Vaughan at the Anno Santo, as well as Anthony and Gráinne Finnerty at Ward's Hotel, were most generous hosts. Renmore Barracks carries the *cachet* of a historical past in its hosting of visiting speakers. Sister Alberta, Archivist at Taylor's Hill, was a most gracious and informative host on my visit to the Dominican graveyard.

The essay, here included, on my former English teacher and later friend, Dónal Taheny, is by way of thanks for the inspiration of his teaching and the wonder he celebrated, not only in literature, but in the glories of the world – across all of the arts. Galway has been well served by its historians and historical enthusiasts in the many societies that seek to make sense of, document, and celebrate what has gone before us. The Galway Archaeological and Historical Society, the Old Galway Society, *Cumann Staire* NUIG, the Renmore History Society and Galway's Museum all offer individual perspectives on subjects that are never constrained by either time or theme. The presence of a University in the town since 1849 has been a great boon, not only to the town in general, but to the many local families who have been lucky enough to have availed of its educational empowerment.

A measure of Galway's interest in local history is the subject's inclusion across all of the local newspapers. The *Connacht Tribune* group boasts a proud tradition in that area throughout its hundred plus years in existence. Father Martin Coen's 'Gleanings' column was both erudite and broad in its range. One time editor, Mr. Jack Fitzgerald, under a *Balor* psuedonym delivered a series of articles, which presented a wonderfully idiosyncratic view of the town he grew to love. Mr. Peadar O'Dowd's stint at the *Connacht Sentinel* seamlessly mixed the old and the new, over many decades, and that newspaper's recent demise was silently lamented by many who valued the local in an urban landscape. The anticipation of a Tuesday name check for footballers as young as ten was one of the joys of growing up in Galway town. Peadar continues his column in the *City Tribune*. The *Connacht Tribune* group of newspapers has provided an invaluable historical archive of the town and county since its 1909 foundation, which was much mined by this study. If the *Irish Times* is lauded nationally as the newspaper of record, then the *Connacht Tribune* deserves such a reputation in a western context, for its contemporaneous noting of events, as they unfolded, provided local context and live immediacy to its reporting. The *Sentinel's* recent passing reflects a fraught and competitive media landscape that is exacerbated by an overarching and pervasive internet presence.

Galway has also been served by two other weekly newspapers, the *Galway Advertiser* and the *Galway Independent*. The former pioneered a successful free-sheet offering that has gone from strength to strength from its 1970 foundation. The *Advertiser's* historical enrichment of the place has been most admirable. That cultural constant was delivered through the writings of Dick Byrne, Tom Kenny and the man who started the entire enterprise, Ronnie O'Gorman. A weekly full page spread on local history is a testament, not only to the scribes, but to the interest of Galway people in the place's past. In more recent times, Willie Henry has delivered a full history page in the *Galway Independent*, as well as producing an array of books, across an impressively broad range of themes. The demise of the *Galway Independent*, as this book is being prepared for publication, is a further example of the unrelenting pressure on the printed word in a fracturing media *milieu*. Where a Galway Town week was – up to very recently – marked by the *Sentinel* on a Tuesday, the *Independent* on a Wednesday, the *Advertiser* on a Thursday and the *City Tribune* on a Friday, the latter two weeklies are all that remain in production.

By contrast, the *Galway Memories'* photographic site, an online Alan Kelly creation, now boasts 20,000 Facebook fans, and features regular historic input from Dick Byrne. The success of its visual Old Galway archive – in a digital age – indicates that the history of the place appeals to Galwegians, across an age span, which stretches from tech-savvy youngsters to more mature history enthusiasts. The *Memories'* site also ensures that the imagery of Galway's past is saved for posterity.

The many scribes referenced in this volume, who have written books on Galway, delivered offerings that ranged from photographic collections to Hardiman's totemic history of the town. In terms of Salthill, Tom Kenny has displayed, in his talks and writings, a great affection for the place of his youth, while the late Tom O'Connor, of NUIG and Gort Ard, had a particular interest in the fine houses of Rockbarton, as part of a much broader historical canvas. I am in debt to all such historians, who have added immeasurably to an appreciation of place, both in our town and county.

Local knowledge was generously given by Mr. William O'Connor, who opened his grocery shop beside the Oslo Hotel in May, 1955. Billy – as he was known to all – was in the vanguard of the Salthill Tourist and Development Association, which elected its first committee in 1960. Billy was chairman of that committee through the seminal Swinging Sixties' decade and the Dunmore native sadly passed away during the writing of this book. Great Ard na Mara neighbours, the late Phyllis and Michael Moroney, Mary Hennelly Flanagan and Professor Pádraig Ó Céidigh all provided insights that aided this study. Piano teacher extraordinaire, Mary O'Connor of Dr. Mannix Road; Gabriel Kearney of San Antonio Terrace; Mick Roche of Dalysfort Road; Liam Sammon of Rockbarton Park; Carolyn Shields of the Wimpey and Oslo; Joe Quinn at the Bon Bon; the Killoran brothers, Tom and James, of the famed Salthill bar; Jarlath Conneely and Paschal Fallon of two of Salthill's oldest families; Seán Treacy of Grattan House; Peter Allen of Threadneedle Road; the O'Farrell family of Claremount Lodge; the late Charlie and Mary Trill of the Claddagh Basin, brothers Colm Powell of the Four Corners and Father Oliver Powell of Gort Ard, Chick Gillen of Dominick Street and Mervue, Mícheál Ó Choinceanainn *as Inis Meáin*, Úna Breathnach *ó chlann cháiliúil Phoblachtánach* and Dr. Máire McGarry of Nile Lodge were all responsible for nuggets of historical gold. I am also indebted to the generosity of Maureen Jennings *agus an t-Ollamh Ó Céidigh, nach maireann*, for the postcards they provided. *Connacht Tribune* photographers, Joe O'Shaughnessy and Stan Shields, who both grew up in Salthill, have been most helpful over many years. Michael Glynn, of the same newspaper, has also been supportive. Lynn Temple, Chairman of Magee Clothing, who was born at Salthill House, Mount Charles, was both generous and gracious in sharing the history of his native heath.

The great repository of knowledge that libraries represent cannot be understated. Galway is indeed fortunate to be well served by such facilities. The principal City Library at what was once Back Street, as well as its satellite operations at Ballybane and West Side, have been information combed throughout this study. The research retreat house that is the ground floor of Island House on Gaol Road has proven to be an oasis of calm and exploration bounty. NUIG's library research room has also presented a happy hunting ground for material across a broad study range. In all of these establishments, advice and assistance were generously given and such guidance is truly appreciated. Staff at a host of other institutions, including the National Library; the National Archives; the Valuation Office; the Registry of Deeds; the General Register Office; the Irish Architectural Archive; Trinity College, U.C.D and Maynooth University Libraries have all been most helpful over years of historical trawling. London researchers, at a number of institutions, were universally co-operative and professional.

Sophie Holford's artistic eye, as designer, added greatly to the presentation of this project, while the leap from raw script to book shelf was made easy through the expertise and supportive guidance of Carrowmore's Publishing Director, Ronan Colgan.

Gabhaim buíochas ó chroí dóibh uilig.
Paul Mc Ginley

DÓNAL TAHENY
Staraí - Oide - Saoi
A Tribute
(1918–2014)

When Dónal Taheny died in October 2014, his Requiem Mass celebrant and long time friend, Fr. Ned Crosby, wondered which character he should speak of. The choices proffered were Dónal Taheny, Mr. Taheny, Dan Taheny or 'Professor Taheeny' – the grand title by which summer-school American scholars addressed him. The Abbey Church congregation recognised all of the personality traits that were evoked by Fr. Crosby's quirky introduction.

Born Daniel Gerard Taheny at Abbey Row, Athenry, on 11 December, 1918, he was to live a long and varied life. Friends and colleagues knew him as Dónal, students of the 'Bish' – over three decades – simply dubbed him Dan. His father, John, was a Mayo native and a member of the Royal Irish Constabulary. In 1901, John Taheney was a single constable, stationed at Cappamore, County Limerick. By 1911 Constable Taheney had wed Limerick born Elizabeth Flanagan, and the Taheney couple with their three children were residing in Limerick City. Promoted to sergeant in 1915, John and his family moved two years later, on transfer, to Galway's

Figure 2.

East Riding. Throughout the bitter War of Independence, Sergeant John Taheney was stationed at Athenry. During that defining conflict, local clashes occurred, including the 1920 Coshla killing of Mr. Frank M. Shawe Taylor. Sergeant Taheney was called to the scene of that particular shooting on 3 March, 1920. The period represented a particularly difficult time for Irish members of the R.I.C., whose position in society had been greatly compromised by the quasi-police force arrival of the dreaded Auxiliaries and Tans.

Kitty Morrissey's memories of the Taheny family, recorded in the book, *Carnaun School Athenry, 1891–1991*, were warm: 'Still remembered fondly by many families in our area, especially the Raftery's of Coshla is a Constable Tahney, whose son Dan, a noted historian, occasionally visits his friends locally.'[1] At the War of Independence's end, however, it was reported that former R.I.C. policemen in the Athenry district were ordered to leave.[2] The Taheney family at that time, whether by choice or compulsion, moved to Galway town and first resided in a flat, at what had previously been the Castle Barracks. Those army buildings are no more, but one tall, white painted section of that structure remains in the memory bank of anyone who recalls the old car park at Corbett's Yard, which featured a Whitehall entrance. It was in the early 1920s that the Taheney family moved to 5 Corrib Terrace, Woodquay, where Dónal was to live for most of his 95 years.

'Taheny' was the surname form used by Dónal, though his father's 1911 census signature – Taheney – boasted an extra 'e,' as did Dan's own birth cert. Surname variations in Ireland were not, of course, unique to the Taheny brand.

Dónal began his schooling at Galway's Patrician national school, locally known as the 'Old Mon' on Lombard Street. That educational establishment predated the current St. Patrick's National School, which today sits on the former Shambles' Barrack site. His second level schooling was enjoyed at Multyfarnham Franciscan College, County Westmeath.[3] Such an educational choice suggests that Dónal may well have considered a religious vocation. Two of his siblings were so called, but they both entered Dominican houses. Dónal was a deeply religious – though not a craw thumping – man, who never mentioned Multyfarnham, nor indeed a possible vocation to this writer. He did, of course, have a great *grá* for the Francisan way of life and a particular affinity with the Abbey Church and its people – both lay and clerical. Those who knew him might consider it a little inappropriate to include the Gaelic word *grá* in a piece about Dónal, for his language leanings tended towards Latin and English. His Arts' degree, however, did include Irish, though the Donegal dialect proved challenging for him on his exam-supervisory forays up north. Those particular summer sorties did supply engaging tales, gleefully recounted with an exaggerated Ulster lilt.

Reflecting Professor Elizabeth Malcolm's prescient observation that R.I.C. constables 'were obsessed with educating their children,'[4] Dónal, on finishing his Leaving Certificate, attended U.C.G., where he graduated with an honours B.A.

in 1939. He also acted as secretary of the Literary and Debating Society in that degree year. University life was much different then, and Dónal fully partook of it. He attended the U.C.G. Garden Party of 1940, for example, which was hosted by the University's Dramatic Society. Theatre boards attracted him and he took part in various local shows and pantomimes, some of which were held at the Empire Theatre, just off William Street. His greatest theatrical review was earned in the lead role of a piece called *Franciscan Spring*, where Dónal played St. Francis of Assisi. A measure of that production's success was that the *Pádraic Pearse Little Theatre* players were invited to perform the drama piece at numerous venues along the western seaboard. It was reprised at a packed Town Hall in 1943 to general and critical acclaim: 'The honours go to Mr. Dónal Taheny as St. Francis. It would be invidious to single out any of the other players as they were all equally good,'[5] said the *Connacht Sentinel*'s review of the production.

Dónal's beloved English and History augmented Irish as his primary university subjects, and he was among the thirty students who were conferred with a B.A. degree, by Rev. Mgr. Hynes, President of U.C.G., in October 1939.[6] Dónal himself recalled that there were only eight students in Professor Mary Donovan O'Sullivan's history class. As one of that number, he was invited to play tennis on Sundays at Lisgorm, the fine stone house on Rockbarton Road, which was then owned by Professor Donovan, and her husband, Major Jeremiah O'Sullivan. Tennis was one of the sports Dónal Taheny enjoyed as a young man, and he represented U.C.G. in both Men's Doubles and Mixed Doubles' matches. A precipitous closing of the foursome tennis custom at Lisgorm presaged the beginning of the Second World War and its 'Emergency' restrictions. It was, incidentally, during that global war period that the Claddagh native and university professor, Mary Josephine Donovan O'Sullivan, published her acclaimed book, *Old Galway: The History of a Norman Colony in Ireland*.

The 'Emergency' years were marked by a scarcity of work, and apart from a temporary stint, or two, at St. Joseph's College, Dónal was unemployed for some time. Ironically enough, the war also delivered an unforeseen teaching opportunity: A number of well-to-do Galwegians, accustomed to educating their families in England, were unable to continue that exclusive schooling practice throughout the war period. Among that cohort was High Street born Dr. Denis Valentine Morris, who operated the Seamount Nursing Home at the western end of Salthill's Promenade. Dr. Morris, whose wife had died some years earlier, was then in residence with his children at Glenina. Dónal Taheny was approached, and the young graduate agreed to tutor the Morris girls in their fine Oranmore Road home. That accommodating arrangement was, alas, not to cover the full span of the war, as the unfortunate doctor died suddenly, at 54 years of age, in July 1941. On the death of their father, Dónal's Glenina pupils were subsequently despatched to a boarding school in County Cork.

Not resting on his laurels, Dónal advertised an Intensive Grinds service in Latin/ English/Irish/ History/Geography, which promised that 'greatest care' would be taken with all pupils. His published 1942 success rate was impressive and the tuition service Mr. Taheny offered covered Intermediate Certificate, degree level, and preliminary solicitors' exams. As it later turned out, Dónal landed his first 'real' teaching job in the De La Salle Secondary school in Macroom. His time in rural Cork during the 1940s represented a learning curve for the urbane young teacher, who was asked to fulfil a range of extra-curricular duties that caught him a little off guard. He also recalled visiting his former Glenina students, on occasion, at their new Cork school. Dónal made the most of his time down south and he played golf locally, being a credible witness to a hole-in-one by the Macroom club captain in 1947.

It was in the following year, 1948, that Dónal rejoined the Patrician fold, on his appointment to a teaching position at Ballyfin College in County Laois. A first year pupil of his, who was to subsequently prosper from an education he deeply valued, remembered making his first train trip to Ballyfin in the company of a teacher he was later to call a 'mentor.' That student's name was Tom Raftery, who found it difficult to secure a secondary school place:

In the spring of 1948 it was decided that I could go to second level in the autumn. All the local colleges, Jarlath's in Tuam, St. Mary's in Galway, and Garbally in Ballinasloe were already fully booked. Mother, as usual, came to my rescue. My parents had a long-time friendship with a Taheny family in Galway. Dónal Taheny, a son who had become a secondary teacher, might be able to help. Dónal had just secured a post in Ballyfin, a Patrician Brothers' College near Port Laois. He phoned the Patricians pleading on my behalf, and I was accepted only because of Donal's pleading and that was a lucky break for me.[7]

That first year pupil went on to become Professor Tom Raftery, Vice President of U.C.C. and a Fine Gael Member of the European Parliament.

The principal at Ballyfin in 1948 was Bro. Valerian, who was later to fill the same role at St. Joseph's, College, Galway. Dónal Taheny transferred from Ballyfin to the 'Bish' in 1951 and he was to spend thirty three years as a member of staff at St. Joseph's College, on Nun's Island. Some months after Dónal's return to Galway, his father, John, died in January 1952 and his mother, Elizabeth, passed away five years later. During his time at the 'Bish,' Dónal filled a multiplicity of roles, including that of Vice-Principal. He was to retire in the summer of 1984.

Given Dónal's interest in Galway and its history, he was disappointed that Paul James O' Connor was not memorialised by the naming of a street in his honour. That Carlow born Patrician brother, who came to Galway town in the late 1820s, recorded his important first step of an educational journey that continues to this day: 'January 15th, 1827 – On this day N.N. and I entered our new monastery after having recited the "Te Deum" in thanksgiving to the Almighty for this new proof of his love…we commenced our labours in the school'.[8] A valued teaching tradition was begun on that January day at what came to be known as the *Old Mon*. It was not schooling alone that Brother O'Connor offered his students, but nourishing food to feed them in hungry times. The Orphans' Breakfast Institute at Lombard Street, Galway was established on 3 May, 1830, 'for the purpose of affording A Daily Breakfast to the poorest of the poor children educated in the Male Parochial Free Schools under the care of the Brothers of St. Patrick'.[9] Henry Inglis, who visited Galway in 1834, was impressed with what he saw at the Presentation Nunnery and the Monks' school: 'In many respects, I found reason to be pleased with these schools: there appeared to be no want of attention on the part of the instructors; the pupils seemed to have profited by their instructions in reading and writing; and one humane regulation particularly pleased me:- a plentiful breakfast of stir-about and treacle is provided for the poor children, before they enter upon their daily tasks.'[10] At the height of the famine in August 1847, the Rev. P.J. O'Brien, of St. Jarlath's College, Tuam, preached a sermon 'in aid of The Male Free Schools, Lombard Street, Galway in which ONE THOUSAND POOR BOYS are gratuitously educated, several hundreds of them provided with a daily breakfast, the most destitute and deserving annually clothed…All are trained up, from the earliest years, in the knowledge of their duty to God and Man under the care of the Brothers of St. Patrick.'[11] Recent rumblings of honouring Che Guevara in Galway only served to highlight for Dónal a local facility for neglecting our own.

In the early 1960s Mr. Taheny campaigned, with his good friend, Professor G.A. Hayes McCoy, for the retention of the Lion's Tower on Eglinton Street. That town-wall tower stood on the Savoy Cinema side of the signature red-bricked Garda Barracks, which ran along the street towards the junction with Daly's Place. In March 1962, Dónal Taheny penned a letter which appeared on the front page of the *Connacht Sentinel*. The importance of the structure under threat was stressed: 'The Lion's Tower Bastion in Eglinton Street must surely be ranked as one of the best examples of medieval walled fortifications extant in Ireland and one must deplore the thought that it is in imminent danger of destruction.'[12] Dónal 'heartily' supported a public subscription campaign, and went even further by approaching, along with Professor McCoy, some business concerns in the town towards that end. Barring a few notable exceptions, both men were disappointed with the response to their pleas, and the tower was eventually replaced by the 1960's concrete block, which today houses the C.A.O. offices.

However, as the gospel Dónal proclaimed fed not the pocket, but the mind and soul, his disappointment did not deter him from continuing to highlight the hidden glories of Galway town and county. This he did in lectures over many decades. His talks were always adorned with colour slides, some of which graphically traced the changes that overtook his beloved bailiwick. Dónal made many appreciate the aura of the local, before such charm was mined for commercial gain. In that very vein, 'History is where you find it' was the title of an Old Galway Society talk, which he delivered at the Imperial Hotel in 1963.

As Dónal's holiday radius lengthened over the years, so did the compass of the lectures he delivered on return. In 1959, for example, 'A Pilgrimage in France, Spain and Portugal' was the theme, while Holland and Belgium featured in 1961. 'This is Scotland' was his 1962 offering. Such colourful talks were delivered in a time that coincided with the arrival of black-and-white Irish television, and they long predated Ryanair's affordable travel-for-all culture. Dónal's slides were ordered and operated by his sister Anne for many years, and his love of photography was reflected in the joy and pride he took from his long involvement with Galway's Camera Club. The Stamp Club he ran at the 'Bish' somehow captured a simpler time, before students began to live their lives through ubiquitous screens, attached to an array of electronic devices. Other involvements included the Old Galway Society, of which he became patron; Galway Archaeological and Historical Society; the Galway Literary Society of which he was Vice-Chairman in 1958–'59; the Patrician Past Pupils' Society; *Cumann Éinde*; and Galway Golf Club. On the golf course he annually contested the President's Cup during the 1950s, and recorded a second round 18th hole victory over T.J. Murphy in 1957.

For all of his pursuits and skills, it was his teaching style that truly marked him. On aged benches Dónal took his place among expectant students, with his long legs – like some contorted willow – curled for comfort beneath him. It was then that the adventure of learning began, and not even he knew where the next forty minutes would take him – or his disciples. For many of his former English students, for example, the poems and plays of class discussion might well have faded from memory, but still recalled is an infectious enthusiasm for learning, and Dónal's deep love of language. It was, ironically enough, at his sister Elizabeth's funeral mass, that Dónal's pedagogical philosophy was succinctly stated: As a teacher 'you bear the responsibility for the future intellectual honesty of the pupils entrusted to your care. You preserve enthusiasm in the face of indifference; you go off on a tangent and open windows of wonder. You do not impart facts – anyone can do that – but a sort of joy and mental inquisitiveness.'[13] His own insatiable curiosity fired the dynamic which drew others in. Among those who were enriched by his distinctive teaching style were the Higher Diploma students of U.C.G., as well as his own pupils.

In talking of Elizabeth Taheny, or Sister Augustine, as she was officially known to her Dominican students, Dónal spoke of her staying lucid to the end. That same blessing became his own gift, for his mind remained razor sharp in old age. So did his tongue, which never lost its cutting edge. The hapless trainee doctor, who was asked to interview 93 year old Dónal for forgetfulness, came to recognise that keenness. When asked to do a simple (100+1) sum, Mr. Dónal Taheny told the young man that he had never been much good at the maths, but wondered if the tyro medic could tell him the pluperfect of the Latin verb *amo*. In the established way of the seasoned school master, Mr. Taheny had to have the last word.

Dónal, of course, was not the only family member with an academic background, or indeed, an interest in history. His older brother, Fr. Luke John Taheny O.P., who joined the Dominican Order at Tallaght in 1927, was the Archivist of the Dominican Order in Ireland, and an acknowledged authority on Irish Dominican history. Father Luke passed away in 1973. Another to join the Dominican fold was Elizabeth Taheny, who became Sister Augustine O. P. in 1939. She was known to legions of her students as 'Gussie' and her teaching subjects were Maths and Science. Sister Augustine served as Principal of the Dominican College on Taylor's Hill, which meant that both 'Gussie' and 'Dan' held leading managerial roles in second level Galway schools. Sister Augustine died in June 2006. Dónal's other sisters were Mary, Christina and Anne. Mary, who married Mr. Peter Clarke of Sandymount in 1942, passed away in January 2006. Miss Christina Taheny, who married George Ruxton in 1946, was widowed seven years later. She subsequently re-married, when she wed Dr. Alun Edwards of Onchan, Isle of Man, who also predeceased her. Christina Taheny (Ruxton-Edwards) died in June 1982. Dónal's Woodquay sibling, Miss Anne Taheny, of 5 Corrib Terrace, passed away in May 2007.

So, post-2007, Dónal represented the last of his tribe in Galway. Following a lifetime of teaching, travelling, reading, researching, photographing, debating, quiz team preparation, acting, golfing, tennis playing, fishing, entertaining, storytelling, commenting, stamp collecting…Mr. Dónal Taheny simply passed away on 21 October, 2014. The one-pint-a-day man knew that he had enjoyed a commendable 'good innings.' He had paid more than his dues and his mark was truly made.

Mrs. Powell, following a December 1967 Old Galway lecture, 'urged Mr. Taheny to write a social history of Ireland, which task, she stated nobody was better qualified to undertake.'[14] Dónal was not to do it, but he did donate his massive slide collection to Galway's Museum, for future generations to learn from, and enjoy. Refusing to give broadcast interviews, Dónal never courted publicity, nor praise. Having said that, an appreciation of recognition was recorded in a 2011 letter to this writer: 'It is nice to be remembered. If you remember your Vergil of old, "forsitan et olim haec meminisse iuvabit". In case you forgot ("perhaps in days to come we shall be pleased to remember these things").'[15]

In honouring that remembrance wish, this essay is presented as a personal tribute to a mentor who deserves gratitude and recognition for his contribution to many people's lives.

Geography of Salthill:
TOWNLANDS – VILLAGES – DEMESNES – PROMENADE

Chapter 1

SALTHILL'S TOWNLANDS AND BURIAL GROUNDS

John O'Donovan (1806–1861), who translated the Annals of the Four Masters, was an Irish speaking scholar and scribe. He became Ireland's Ordnance Survey's principal names' expert and his comprehensive survey was completed in 1846, with over 60,000 townlands on the island being identified and named. A townland, which represents one of the smallest administrative land units in Ireland, can range in size from a few – to thousands of acres. In this study's case, the Acres' townland at just over 4 acres represents the locale's smallest land entity, right beside its largest, Pollnarooma West, at 166 acres. Most townland names are Gaelic in origin, but some did come into existence after the Norman invasion of 1169.

Rural dwellers, in the main, recognise such divisions, but townlands in metropolitan settings have been overtaken by street and district identities. Urban townlands do still exist, but generally only appear in property title deeds. Up to relatively recently, for example, the naming of a townland was required of publicans in alcohol licence applications.

A realisation – and recognition – of local townlands is required in the historical research of Irish places, and Salthill is no exception. Land sales and landlord holdings were almost all identified by townland designations.

For such reasons the accompanying townland map seeks to show the land divisions of former times. Salthill, as defined by this study, lies between *Bóthar na Trá* to the south and *Bóthar Ard* to the north. It stretches from Nile Lodge junction at its eastern tip to the western boundary of Galway Golf Course. The townlands within that geographical span include Kilcorkey (Lower Salthill), Cloghatisky, Lenaboy (incl. Salthill Village), Cappanaveagh, Tievegariff, Attithomasrevagh, Pollnarooma East and Pollnarooma West. Though technically not in Salthill, the Acres townland is also included in the map. That tiny land mass belongs in the Barna District Electoral Division, whereas the Galway South Urban D.E.D. encompasses the eight townlands of Salthill. The reason for Acres' inclusion in this study is to highlight; (a)

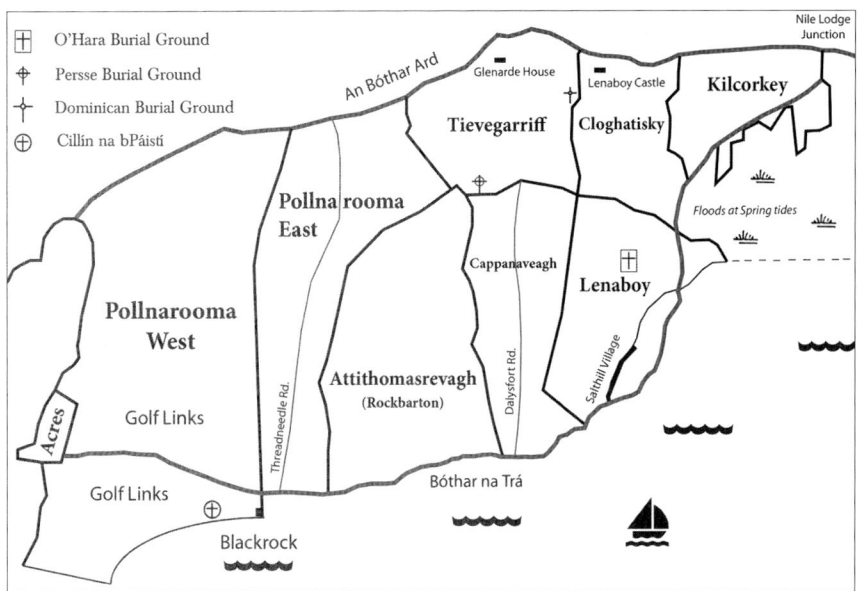

3. Townland map of Salthill, with landmarks indicated to aid orientation. Glenarde House is today the Ardilaun Hotel.

the smallest townland in the general locale; (b) a boundary with the Barna district; and (c) that townland's distinct experience in the famine section of this study.

There are many variations to the spelling of Salthill's townlands and, in seeking consistency; this study will adhere to the forms used in both the 1839 Ordnance Survey map and 1855 Griffith's Valuation record. Indicated above are the ancient townlands of Salthill and also included, for recognition and orientation purposes, are some modern landmarks.

Salthill's Burial Grounds

Salthill was once home to a number of burial grounds, with two of them serving as demesne family plots.

O'Hara Plot

The O'Hara cemetery still stands today, by the pedestrian pathway which links Emerson Avenue with Lenaboy Park. That burial plot was once sheltered and enclosed by a sylvan copse that

4. Sole headstone visible today (2018) above overgrowth at O' Hara cemetery.

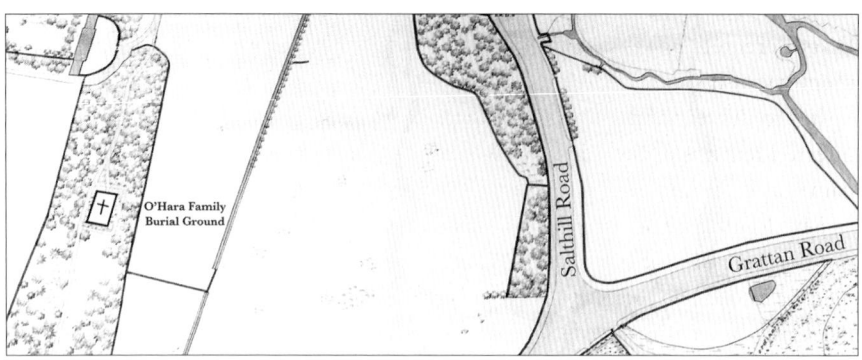

5. O' Hara family burial ground in wooded copse, marked in an early 1870's map, before the King's Hill gate to the O'Hara demesne was in place.

stood close to the Lenaboy Gate, at the foot of King's Hill on the Salthill Road. Like its sister Persse cemetery at Salthill, however, the railed O'Hara plot no longer holds the bodies of the demesne family it was built to hold. The departed of both the Persse and O'Hara septs have been re-interred. Though Canon Jack O'Connor, Parish Priest of Salthill from 1991 to 2000, had hopes of improving the O'Hara burial ground, it stands today overgrown and neglected.

Many reasons might be posited for the cemetery's poor state: (a) It is a little known feature of Salthill; (b) human remains are no longer interred there; (c) no member of the O'Hara family remained in the area after the 1923 sale of the Lenaboy Demesne; (d) the O'Hara family belonged to a minority faith; (e) the same family represented a landlord past. There may, of course, be other reasons but – heedlessly or purposefully condoned – the O'Hara burial ground today stands on raised ground as a telling symbol of a neglected Salthill past.

Persse Plot

The Persse plot lay at the edge of the Glenarde Demesne, right on the border of the Tievegariff and Cappanaveagh townlands. It was on the building of the Glenard housing estate in the 1960s that inhumed Persse remains were re-interred, and the former private cemetery's site today represents the back garden to a Glenard Crescent house. Those buried in the Glenarde burial ground were all related to Henry Sadleir Persse, the last person to have been interred there. They included Henry's sister, Henrietta Burton Persse, and his children: John Beauchamp Persse (5 yrs.); Matilda Theodora Persse (15 yrs.); and Noël Majorie Persse (9 yrs.). Henry's wife, Eleanor Alice Persse, who died in the South of France, was also interred there in 1890. The headstone that once marked her grave was 'carved out of white Sicilian marble,' by Messrs. C.W. Harrison and Sons, 178 Great Brunswick-street, Dublin.[1] Eleanor was also memorialised at St. Nicholas' Collegiate Church in 1891, when Henry Sadleir

Persse 'erected a new bell-frame and two new bells to complete the chime, in memory of his wife.'[2]

It is to the rear of the Protestant chapel at Galway's New Cemetery, that the re-interred remains of the Glenarde Persses now lie. A flagstone memorial lists their names at Bohermore.

Mrs. Matilda Persse (née Persse) – the mother of Henry Sadleir Persse – became the first member of her household to pass away at Glenarde House, when she died in 1862. The Glenarde burial plot did not then exist, and she was interred at her Castleboy family vault.[3] It was following the 1872 formation of the greater Glenarde Demesne, when Henry Sadleir purchased the Pollnarooma East townland to join with his Tievegarriff holding, that the private Persse cemetery at Salthill was developed. It is possible that the 1877 death of five year old John Beauchamp Persse prompted his parents, Henry and Eleanor, to create that graveyard. The burial ground at Glenarde, still recalled by older Salthill locals, was in 'receptive use' for some 22 years, with John Beauchamp being the first in 1877, and his father Henry the last – in 1899 – to have been inhumed there. The 1964 death of Helen Persse at Folkestone saw her ashes return to Galway for burial in the family plot which had, by then, switched to Bohermore after the Glenarde cemetery had been cleared. The inscription for Helen, a daughter to Henry Sadleir and Eleanor Persse, was then

 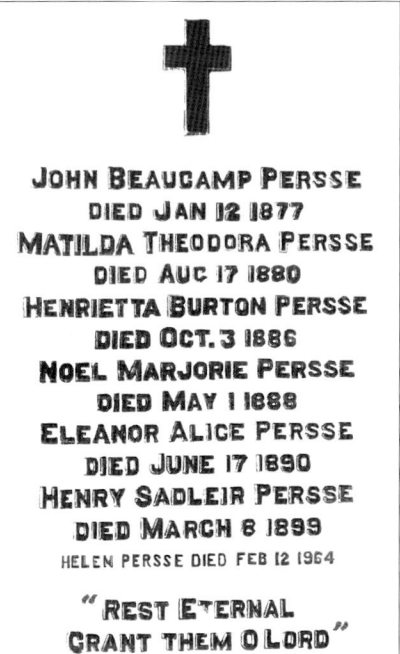

Left 6. Memorial to Eleanor A. Persse at Glenarde. (*Dublin Builder*, 15 July, 1895)

Right 7. Flagstone Persse Memorial at New Cemetery, Bohermore.

added in smaller letters to the New Cemetery's flagstone memorial. Glenarde's elegant marble headstone for Eleanor A. Persse was not transferred to Bohermore, where the name of Eleanor Alice Persse survives on a more prosaic stone tablet.

Lieutenant Cecil De Burgh Persse of the 7th Dragoon Guards, a brother to the Persse children who were re-interred at Bohermore, is memorialised in a Celtic cross inscription at Galway's St. Nicholas' Collegiate Church. Cecil, one of the fallen of the 'Great War,' died in Netley Hospital on 19th July, 1915 'from wounds received at Festubert, 18th May 1915, aged 40 years.' He was buried in the Hospital Cemetery, where his grave is marked by a Celtic cross headstone – 'Erected by his brothers and sisters' – that is not unlike the St. Nicholas' monument.

Dominican Cemetery

8. Entrance to Dominican cemetery, with grotto visible behind railings.

A second Tievegarriff cemetery formed – and yet forms – part of the Dominican Sisters' complex at Taylor's Hill. That second interment site stood to the rear of the original convent and it was in that plot that Mother Bernard Heuston, an older sister to the executed 1916 leader, Seán Heuston, was buried in 1960. Two years later, Mother Dorothy Davis, a sister to Canon Davis who built Salthill Church, was laid to rest in the same cemetery. The Canon is buried in the front lawn of the church he saw dedicated to Christ the King in 1936. The enclosed Dominican burial ground – in marked contrast to Salthill's O'Hara plot – is beautifully presented and maintained.

Cillín na bPáistí

A fourth Salthill cemetery was noted in Ordnance Survey maps as *Kilnapastia (Infants' Burial Ground)*. The *Cill na bPáistí* plot stands above the waterline to the west of Black Rock, and is today marked by a memorial stone near the second tee – along the shoreline pathway – at Galway Golf Club. The stone's inscription reads:

Old Burial Ground. This segment of the foreshore is traditionally known as a burial place. On the early Ordnance Survey map a small rectangular enclosure is marked close to this spot and called Kilnapastia (church of the children). It was a common practice in the past to choose such sites as Killeens for the burial of unbaptised children and strangers. The plaque has been erected by Galway Golf Club to mark the approximate location of this ancient site. Cuireadh iad ar shlí na mara: táid anois ar shlí na fírinne.

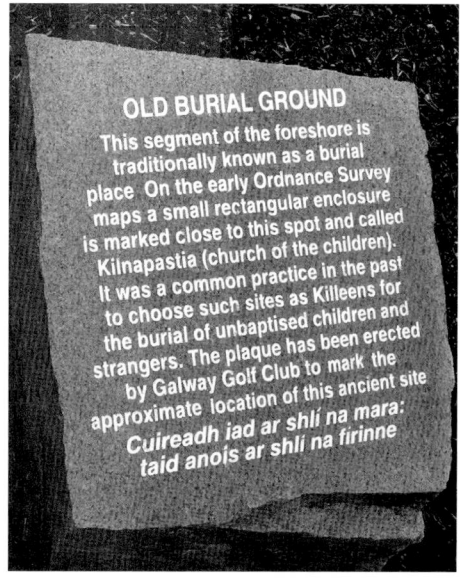

9. Memorial Stone at Galway Golf Course.

It was believed – and taught – in the past that un-baptised babies were bound for neither heaven nor hell. Their eternal destination was a place called *Limbo*. That metaphysical construct was abandoned after 800 years in 2007, when Pope Benedict XVI acted on a Theological Commission report, which found that the concept represented an 'unduly restrictive view of salvation.'[4]

Cappanaveagh Burial Ground

James Hardiman spoke of 'the 40 acres at Cappanaveagh, towards the West (where there is an ancient burial-place but none interred in it for many years).'[5] As Cappanaveagh was in the possession of St. Nicholas College from the 16th century, it is fair to accept the longevity of the site and furthermore assume that those interred in that burial place belonged to the Protestant faith. Hardiman resided, up to the early 1840s, at nearby Tievegarriff and it is unlikely that the 'ancient' cemetery he referenced in 1820 became the Persse plot, which sat on the border of the Cappanaveagh and Tievegarriff townlands. A solitary tree on the Tievegarriff side of the townland border was represented on the 1839 OS map, at the point where the Persse cemetery was later shown in the 1890's edition. While one could speculate that the Persse family might have used/re-used the older site in the second half of the 19th century, the evidence of both Hardiman and Fr. J. Rabbitte offers such speculation little comfort. In the first place, the Persse plot was quite small, in the style of the extant O'Hara cemetery at Lenaboy. Secondly, family plots were carefully guarded by the gentry of old, and Thomas Moore Persse, for example, who built the nearby Mount Vernon and died at Norman Villas, was interred at the New Cemetery at Bohermore, even though he was uncle to Henry Sadleir Persse of the Glenarde Demesne. Fr. J. Rabbitte S.J., writing in the 1920s, recorded that he had 'not met anyone who had heard of an ancient burial ground in Cappanaveagh.'[6] As the graveyard was 'ancient,' in Hardiman's 1820 account, it would be nigh impossible to now pinpoint where it stood.

Kilcorkey Burial Ground

There also appears to have been an ancient burial site in the Lower Salthill townland of Kilcorkey. Fr. J. Rabbitte recorded how he learned of it in the early 1920s: 'A very old man, born and reared in Salthill, tells me there was long ago a burial ground within the Bishop's field and that some of the grave stones were visible when he was a boy. Perhaps at one time there was a church without walls at Kilcorkey.'[7]

Chapter 2

SALTHILL'S VILLAGES

A number of villages, which speckled Salthill's hinterland, fell into two broad categories. In the first instance rural house clusters, or *clacháin* in Irish, were home to the families of peasant farmers and local fishermen, long before more substantial terraced housing lines, which were urban in design, appeared during the 1800s in the Kilcorkey and Lenaboy townlands. The area's quasi-urban centres were Merrion Village at Lower Salthill and Salthill Village further west.

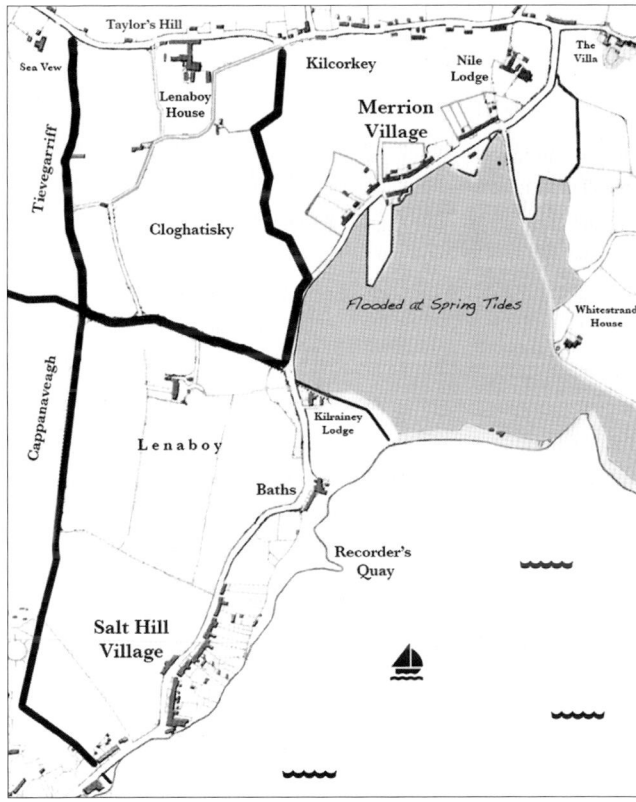

10. The 'urban' villages of Merrion at Lower Salt Hill and Salt Hill to the south-west, which are here represented as they appeared during the 1830s.

Among Salthill's clacháns were the rustic hamlets of Ballynacarrickadoo and *Baile Thaidhg Bháin* (Ballyheigewaun). The positioning of such clusters was generally dictated by local topography, with Fair Tadhg's hamlet being perched on Attithomasrevagh's high ground to prevent flooding. A northern Cappanaveagh cluster availed of the shelter provided by a hill, which later came to be identified with Daly's Fort **(fig.115)**. Such traditional rural enclaves at Salthill were, however, to fall victim to evicting crowbar brigades, which laid them low during the 19th century. Unsurprisingly, the area's dispossession rate accelerated during times of famine and want, and the sorrowful fate of those forgotten hamlets is told in the Famine chapter of this book.

LENABOY—*continued*	KILCORKEY—con.
VILLAGE OF SALTHILL	**VILLAGE OF MERRION**

11. Salthill's Villages as recorded by Richard Griffith in 1855.

Salthill's 'urban' clusters, by contrast, remained on an upward spiral throughout the same period. While it is difficult to be definitive, a reading of an 1839 OS map suggests that Merrion was then marginally bigger than its western sister. Whether or which, Lower Salthill's urban centre was definitely larger than Salthill Village in 1855, when Griffith recorded 50 properties at the 'Village of Merrion,' and 38 holdings at Salthill Village. At the time of Griffith's tally, Number 1, Merrion Village, was Central House, which was felled in 2018.

12. To the left, Central House, No. 1 Merrion Village. On the right, a door/gate in the original Nile Lodge wall, which opened facing Trim's Road – Whitestrand Avenue today.

Salthill's Villages

Not all of the road-hugging terraced housing lines at both Salthill and Merrion were slated, with some buildings initially featuring a thatched roof. The iconic image of American President John Fitzgerald Kennedy, passing through Merrion Village in 1963, shows him passing a thatched dwelling, close to the Bishop's Field gate. A functional and authentic relic of Salthill in former times, that thatched cottage still adorns the terrace of which it remains a part.

13. Thatched cottages at Lower Salthill in early 1900s. (Courtesy of National Library of Ireland.)

14. American President, John F. Kennedy, passing one of Merrion Village's thatched cottages in 1963. (Courtesy of JFK Presidential Library & Museum.)

Merrion's size superiority, during the 19th century, is easily explained. To begin with, Lower Salthill's village was closer to town, thereby facilitating quicker access to facilities, work and commerce. Secondly, it was beside the sea, which encroached on Whitestrand Marsh, before the ocean's inflow was curtailed by the 1860's construction of Grattan Road.

The quizzical folly that is the raised brick hut, which appears above the wall at Nile Lodge, is believed to have been a ladies' bathing box, to be availed of by the lodge's female residents, before a small opening in the house's original wall was traversed to access the beach. That door/gate (**fig.12**) survives opposite the road, which was officially branded Trim's Road, but locally known as McGinty's Lane.[1] The same thoroughfare is today called Whitestrand Avenue.

15. Raised brick building, on the Salthill side of Nile Lodge's gate, believed to have been a bathing box.

The area's resort standing meant that premises at both Lower and Upper Salthill enjoyed the fruits of a boarding trade, which not only catered for summer tourists but served university scholars during darker winter days. That student trade began with the opening of Queen's College, Galway, in 1849. Whereas hungry years dealt a hammer blow to the area's rural hamlets, the place's urban villages avoided a similar fate – for reasons noted in a later description of the Great Famine's effect on Salthill.

Village Status

First recorded as a 'village' in Ambrose Leet's 1814 list of noted places, it was over fifty years later – in 1867 – that a *Galway Vindicator* piece opined that Salthill 'may now fairly lay claim to that appellation.' By that time, Salthill offered 'numerous lodging houses...the "Eglinton," one of the best situated Marine Hotels in Ireland...the "Kyber Pass," a Restaurant, lately opened by Mr. Carr.'[2] Despite such advancements, the newspaper's evaluation may have been a little premature, for Salthill could then only boast a Post Office and Chapel, two of the facilities that unofficially justified village status in Ireland. A Police Barracks, a third branch in the village status tree, was not, however, that far away.

First came a postal presence and Salthill Village warranted – 'for the convenience of visitors' – a Penny Post facility, as early as 1838.[3] Whereas Barna had a Post Office from 1840, Salthill's own office didn't open until 1851,[4] a short time after the Great Famine had wreaked havoc on the land. Ellen Ryan, who lent her surname to Ryan's Terrace – Beach Avenue today – acted as the resort's first 'postmaster,'[5] in a building that was later to be called Ballinasloe House. In a separate 'posting' sense, Salthill's growing importance was reflected in an 1856 announcement that Patent Bill Stickers to her Majesty required 'an additional charge for any Bills to be posted at Salt-Hill or any other locality outside the suburbs of Galway.'[6]

A Place of Worship followed the Post Office, when a Wesleyan Meeting House opened its doors on the promenade. Taking six months to complete, a seaside Chapel was 'dedicated to the worship of Almighty God' on 11 June, 1862. The *Irish Times* reported that 'it was built for the accommodation principally of sea-bathing visitors.'[7] The opening sermon was preached by Rev. John Rattenbury, of London, who was President of the British and Irish Wesleyan Conferences. Despite rain

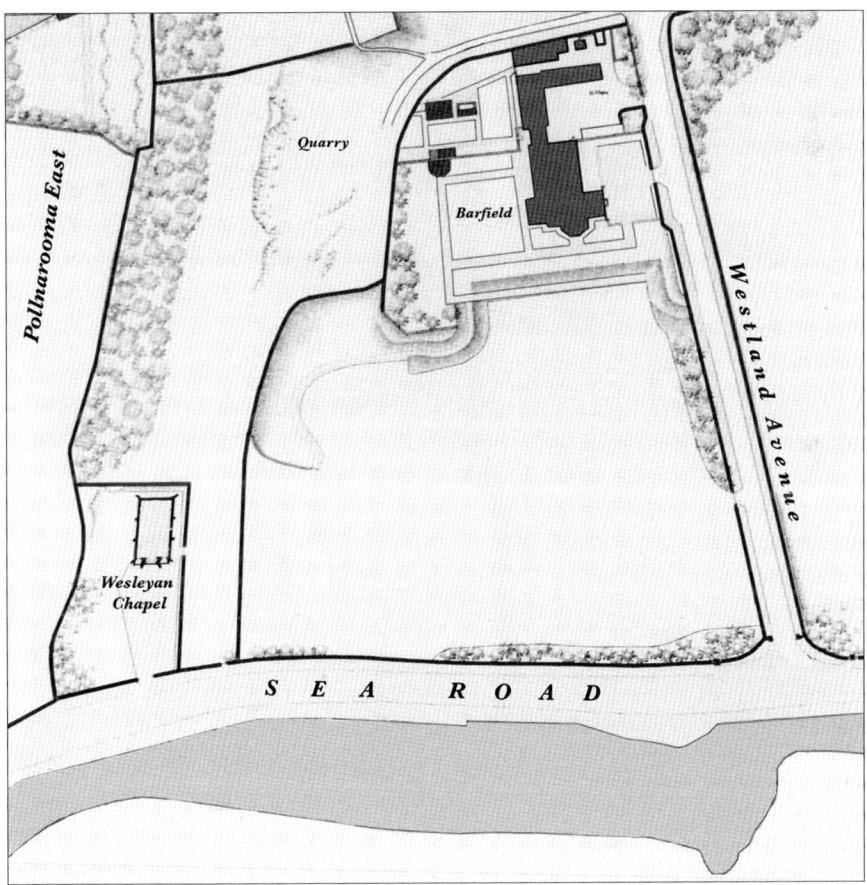

16. Wesleyan Chapel on promenade (Sea Road on map) to the west of Barfield. Westland Avenue is currently called Rockbarton West and the Barfield site is today occupied by the Salthill Hotel.

on the day, a large crowd attended the official opening of a construction that cost £500, with £300 of it being already raised. Seventy of the congregation repaired to the Eglinton Hotel after the opening service, where proprietor John Gill provided a substantial and excellent dinner. Perhaps it was a mark of Wesleyan reserve that no speeches were made at the function. Two votes of thanks, however, were carried; one to Rev. Mr. Rattenbury for travelling from London; and the second to Mr. George Rutledge who gave the site free. The new building was capable of accommodating from two to three hundred persons during Divine Services.

The Wesleyan chapel was not, incidentally, the sole non-Catholic institution in the general area. Slater directories – throughout the later decades of the 19th century – record an Episcopalian Church on Taylor's Hill, with Rev. M.D. Austin (1881) and Rev. Thomas Boland (1894) listed as missionaries. That institution was tied to the Irish Church Mission Orphanage (**fig.139**), sometimes called the Bird's Nest, at the western corner of Sherwood's Fields, in the building that today houses *Scoil Fhursa* at Nile Lodge junction.

The appearance of a Wesleyan chapel at Salthill was not that unusual, for John Wesley – the theologian and clergyman who founded Methodism – had been a regular visitor to the west of Ireland during the previous century. In the course of his twenty one trips to Ireland in the 1747–1789 period, Rev. Wesley visited County Galway on a number of occasions – the first in 1748. It was eight years later that he first called to Galway town, where lodgings were scarce because 'two regiments of soldiers passing through the town had taken up all the inns: however, we procured a private lodging, which was full and agreeable.' A meticulous diarist, John Wesley recorded his visit, and impression of the place:

The town is old, and not ill-built, most of the houses being of stone, and several stories high. It is encompassed within an old, bad wall, and is in no posture of defence, either toward the land or toward the sea. Such is the supine negligence of both English and Irish! Five or six persons, who seemed to fear God, came to us at our lodgings: we spent a little time with them in prayer, and early in the morning set out for Castlebar.[8] Rev. Wesley's Galway followers grew from that small 1756 gathering 'and in 1839 a Methodist Chapel was opened just off Eyre Square at Victoria Place.'[9]

Salthill Chapel becomes a Home

Having thrived through its early years, the Wesleyan facility's star faded at Salthill and the seaside Meeting House was converted into a private residence in 1890. A Cancelled Revision Book note recorded the change: 'Meeting House in process of conversion to dwelling.'[10] John Lynham M.D. became its first residential occupant. The building, which – in the main – retains its original shape, still stands today, to the western side of the Salthill Hotel. It must have been Dr. Lynham who named it Glenorney, for that Salthill address was given in 1894 as the doctor's residence,[11] a mere few years after the premises' function had been changed from devotional to domestic use. The Gaelic provenance of the house title is not surprising for Professor Lynham – 'a distinguished man' – was 'a native Irish speaker.'[12]

As John Isaac Lynham was taking over a Wesleyan facility, there's little surprise that he, and his family, were members of the Methodist faith. John, who married Rebecca Margaret Reed from Galway town in 1880, was Professor of the Practice of Medicine at Galway University, from 1879 to 1912, under both its Queen's and later U.C.G. designations. The university's bursar from 1893, Dr. Lynham also served as Physician to Galway Hospital. He was also a founding member – in 1907 – of the Association of Physicians of Great Britain and Ireland.[13] While in Salthill, his Glenorney gate was once damaged, after which Dr. Lynham sought justice by bringing two men to Galway's Petty Court. It was found that the accused pair did 'unlawfully and maliciously throw down a gate pier.'[14] On his 1912 death, aged 63, the *Connacht Tribune* noted that Dr. Lynham was born in Ballyconneely. However, both of Dr. Lynam's extant census returns record Tipperary as his place of birth. That said, he had strong Ballyconneely connections, for in 1870 John Lynham was fined half a crown for having a licence-less brown terrier in that picturesque Connemara townland.

Though it was only to last some 18 years, and was not sited in the village proper, the creation of a Wesleyan Place of Worship added to the facilities available at Salthill. Primarily a summer amenity, that prom chapel opened, a full seventy four years before a Catholic Church was consecrated at the Monks' Field in 1936. Up

17. Glenorney, a residence on Salthill's promenade, was originally built as a Wesleyan Meeting House.

to that year the Catholic churches closest to Salthill were the Dominican friary at the Claddagh and the Jesuit church on Sea Road. More distant was St. Joseph's, the parish church of Rahoon to which Salthill then belonged. Salthill was not to become a stand-alone parish on the opening of the Church of Christ the King, but it did achieve parochial independence in 1952, with Fr. John Joe Hyland as its first Parish Priest.

The third symbol of village status came into view on the 1869 announcement that a Police Station was to open at Salt Hill, as a suitable premises had been procured for that purpose.[15] First recorded with a rateable exemption in 1872, the resort's police barracks was leased from Samuel Woods, who also acted as the area's postmaster during the 1880s and early 1890s. Samuel must have reacted to an 1884 demand that 'he make drainage from the Police Barracks,'[16] for the barrack building was admirably described eleven years later:

> Ho. and fences all in good repair. Drainage good. Drinking water from pike on premises. Ho. contains 8 rooms & strong room – and occupied by a Segt. & 4 men. Rent fair.[17]

By the time of that 1895 appraisal, Samuel's daughter, Anne Woods, was the station's immediate lessor. Salthill's R.I.C. barracks stood at the back of Bay View Lodge, on a spur off the road that was called Barrack Lane – Lenaboy Avenue today **(fig.26)**.

So, by the early 1870s, the three institutional symbols of a traditional Irish village were in place at Salthill. There were some qualifications, as (a) the land's majority faith was not represented in the resort's place of worship and (b) the chapel lay beyond the village. One could therefore argue that it took a further six decades for the village to be truly made whole. It was in 1933 that a Castlerea consortium – made up of Francis J. Hallinan, Patrick Raftery, John Burke, and Kate Howley (Dunmore) – purchased the Monks' Field, whose frontage ran from Strand House (O'Reilly's Bar & Kitchen today) to the village's junction with Lenaboy Gardens, where optician, Andrea Concannon, currently trades. That 1933 purchase opened up the south facing side of Salthill Village to commercial, residential and ecclesiastical development. Three years later, the Church of Christ the King opened on a central section of that site, and continues to serve the spiritual needs of its Roman Catholic community to this day. The development of the northern side of the village, in tandem with the longevity of its church facility (vis-à-vis its seasonal Wesleyan predecessor), could be used to assert that it was in the 1930s that full village status was truly achieved. Such arguments – however engaging – are little more than conjectural.

Salthill Village was on an upward trajectory from the time the first houses were built at the beginning of the 19th century, on John Whaley's section of Lenaboy. The Police Barracks and Post Office both experienced a peripatetic existence at the place, whereas the Catholic Church has remained rooted at the heart of the village since its foundation. It was following the 1923 sale of O'Hara's Lenaboy Demesne that ribbon roadside development – during the 1920s/'30s – closed the walled pastoral gap that previously separated the urban villages of Merrion and Salthill. That gap was referenced in Michael George O'Malley's description of a walk, from Upper Salthill to Queen's College, Galway, in the early 1900s: 'There was only a blank wall between Upper and Lower Salthill, extending from Ballinasloe House to Woodside House. There were no houses at all along the New Line, as St. Mary's road was then called. We disliked that walk and generally went along Dominick Street West and up the canal.'[18] Woodside House, a few doors from Norman Villas, was the most westerly terraced house in the Lower Salthill townland of Kilcorkey **(fig.30)**.

18. Residence that served as first Post Office on Taylor's Hill.

Though larger in size, at least in the beginning, Merrion Village did not enjoy the same public services as its western sister. From the 1870s, if not earlier, a postal letter box was available at Nile Lodge junction, but it was 1905 before Kilcorkey's first Post Office was opened on Taylor's Hill Road, in premises that yet stand opposite the entrance to Sherwood Avenue. At that time Mr. John Walker was occupier of the house, but by 1911 Mary Ann Glen, wife of army pensioner, William Glen (Glynn), recorded herself as sub-postmistress in the same building. Merrion's proximity to Dominick Street, which featured a Postal Receiving Office from 1853, might have been the reason for a delay in providing Lower Salthill with such a facility. Being within a stone's throw of the Jesuit campus on Sea Road, there was no need for a Merrion church, though a chapel did form part of the Boys' Industrial School complex, which first opened under Patrician Brother management in 1871.[19] Kilcorkey has also been home to the Catholic bishops of Galway since 1887, when the diocese purchased Mount Vernon for £1,500,[20] and changed the name of that fine house, initially built by the Protestant Thomas Moore Persse, to a more suitably denominational Mount St. Mary's.

The urban villages of Salthill and Merrion still thrive today, though the latter name has long disappeared from common currency.

Chapter 3

FINDING ONE'S BEARINGS: MAPS AND PHOTOGRAPHS

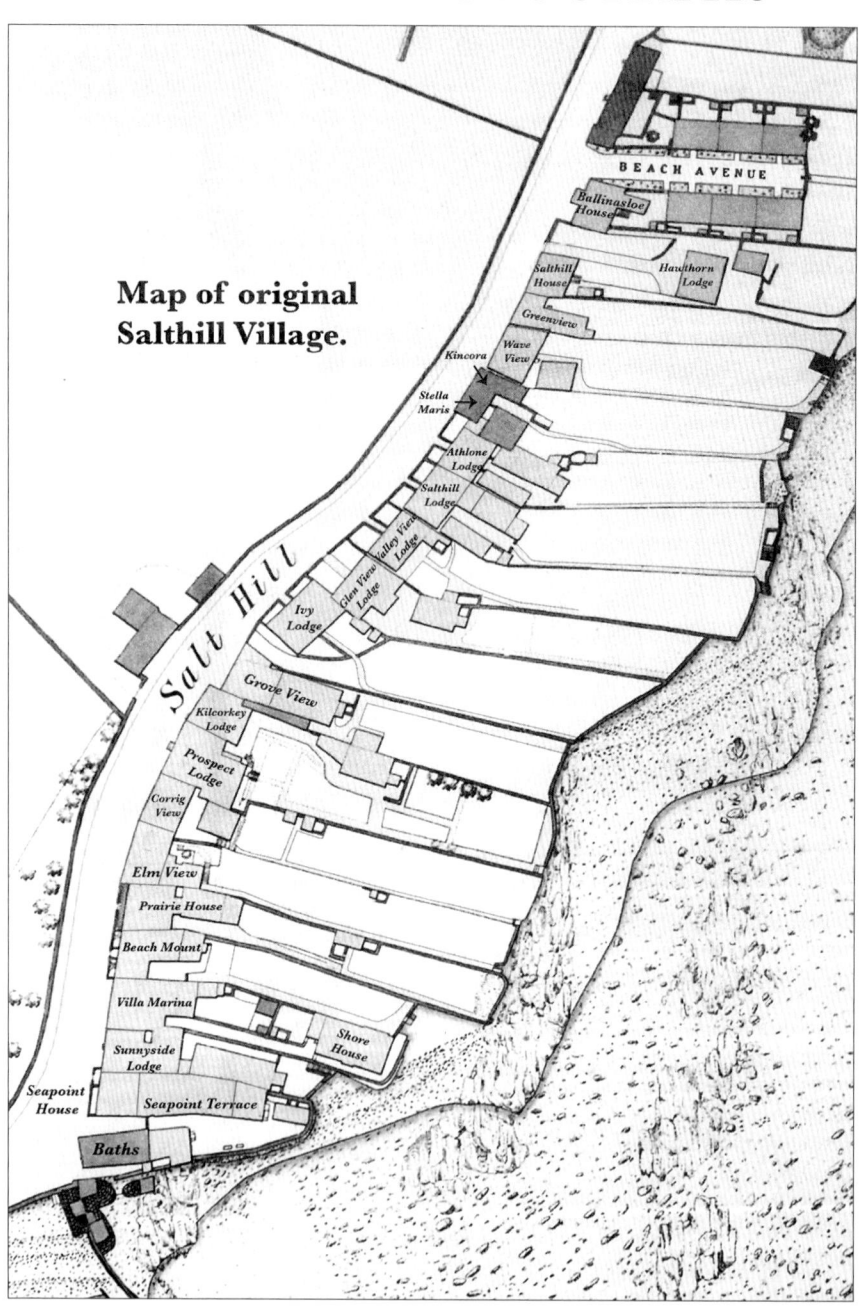

Map of original Salthill Village.

Opposite:

19. Salthill Village in 1870s: Note that the Monks' Field on the opposite side of the main street did not house any significant premises until the 1930s.

This page, from top:

20. Salthill Village from Ballinasloe House (The Bal.) to Ivy Lodge wall.

21. O'Connor's Famous Pub at Salt Hill House, which boasts a bar licence from 1875, has been run by the O'Connor clan since 1942.

22. Between Ivy Lodge and Prospect Lodge stood Grove View and Kilcorkey Lodge. Grove View housed Salthill's Post Office, opposite Salthill Church, from 1946 to the late 1970s.

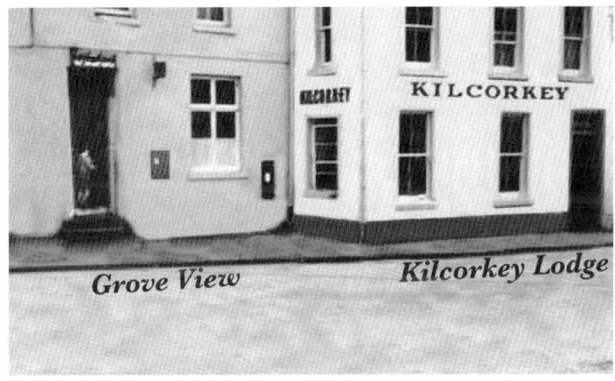

23. Salthill Village, from Prospect Lodge to Seapoint Baths.

24. Three Salthill Village houses from the past.

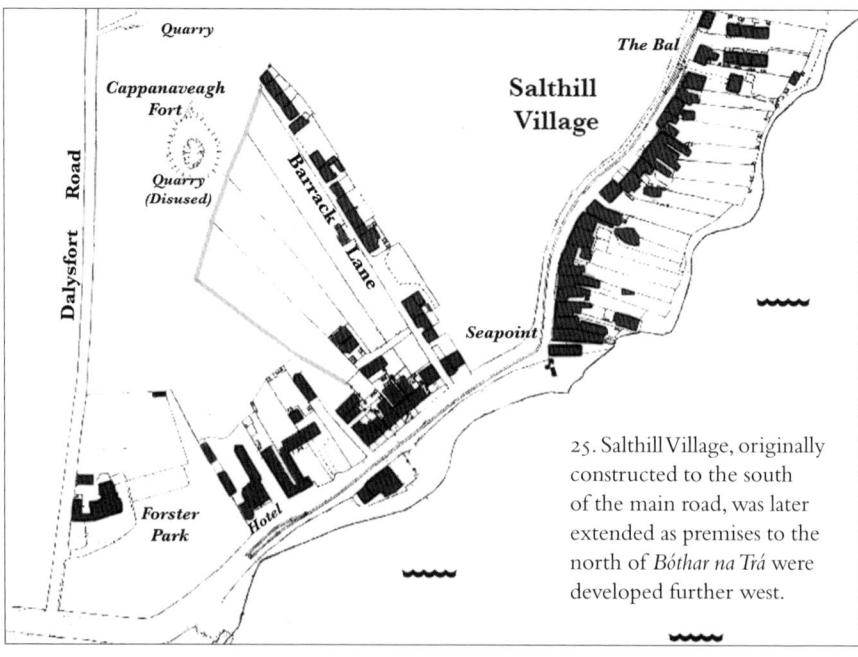

25. Salthill Village, originally constructed to the south of the main road, was later extended as premises to the north of *Bóthar na Trá* were developed further west.

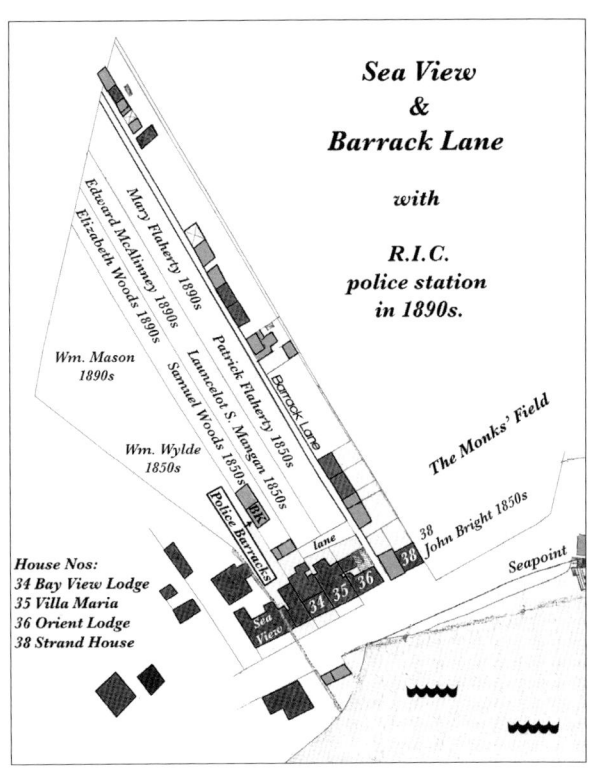

Figure 26.

Sea View and Barrack Lane initially represented the northern wing of Salthill Village, as indicated in the accompanying image **(fig.26)**. Sea View served as a name for (a) the area where Baily Point stands today; (b) a 19th century residence – as indicated – at the western end of a south facing housing line and (c) a later 20th century residence that abutted number 38, Strand House. Bay View Lodge – no. 34 – housed the Post Office during the 1880s/'90s, when Samuel Woods was the local Sub-Postmaster. To the rear of that same building was Salthill's R.I.C. barracks, which was responsible for the street's initial name that was unofficially replaced by its Lenaboy moniker in the early 1920s, following the evacuation and disbandment of the Royal Irish Constabulary. It was 1946 before the Lenaboy Avenue name received official recognition. Note that the entrance to the avenue was not originally restricted, but was subsequently narrowed by a construction that encroached on the thoroughfare. The McAlinney family, of Eglinton Hotel fame, had strong connections with both Villa Maria and Orient Lodge (no. 36). Villa Maria (no. 35) is not to be confused with Villa Marina, which stood two doors from Seapoint House, on the other side of the road.

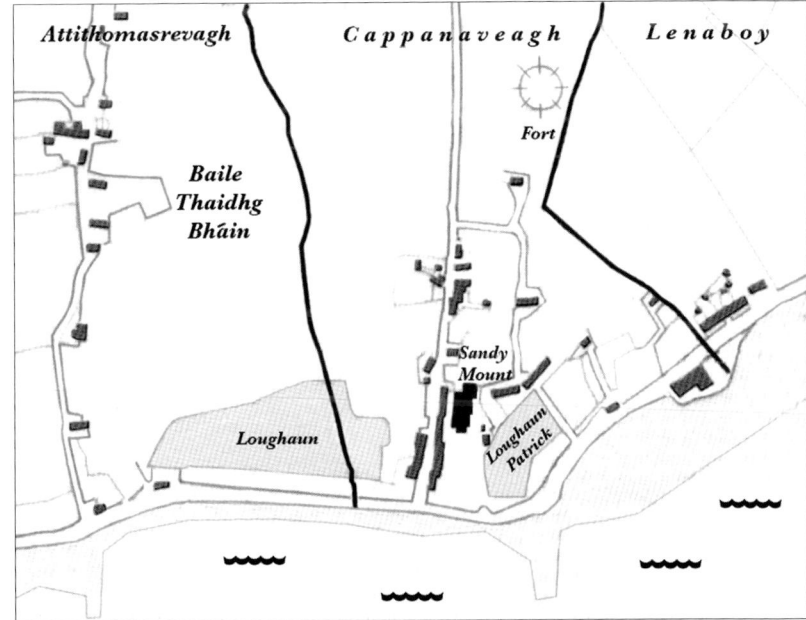

27. Two saline 'loughauns' on landside of promenade.

Two Loughauns: Manifest in the preceding 1830's representation **(fig.27)** is the southern hamlet at Cappanaveagh, which was centred on Sandy Mount, a two storey residence that occupied the site of the present day Garda Station. To the west stood Ballyheigewaun (*Baile Thaidhg Bháin*) at Attithomasrevagh (Rockbarton). Two saline lakes or 'loughauns' were situated on the land-side of the promenade. The western 'Loughaun' primarily belonged to Attithomasrevagh and occupied an area that today stands to the front of the Leisureland site. The eastern portion of that pool, which stood in Cappanaveagh, would today represent the western and low lying frontage of Salthill Park. The smaller Loughaun Patrick, which was – in 1839 – also known as 'Loughaune Phadrick Carter,' ran from today's Atlantic Terrace to Colm's Amusement Centre, previously known as the Salthill Arcade / 'Big Arc.' The presence of that pair of saline pools offers a possible insight into the reason for the Salthill name being adopted in the area, as described in the later 'What's in a Name?' chapter.

The same loughauns also highlight that low-lying terrain's exposure to flooding, which has continued up to the present day. The regular inundation of the same area included flooding in 1926, 1952, 1961 and 2014. In the accompanying image **(fig.28)** from 1952, seawater covered, not only the garden to the front of Maretimo, but the then narrow Rockbarton Road, almost up to the Hangar/ Pavilion Ballroom.

28. Flooding on Rockbarton Road in January, 1952. (Courtesy of *Connacht Tribune*.)

Merrion Village

Situated in Lower Salthill was Merrion Village, a name that has almost vanished from the resort's lexicon. In terms of street outline and structure, however, the Kilcorkey suburb has little changed from previous centuries, with a good number of buildings, from the 19th century, still standing. Among that collection are Nile Lodge, Central House, Spring Lodge, Tandem Lodge, Merrion Lodge (now called St. Joseph's Terrace), the former Boys' Industrial School, Norman Villas, Strand View, the Hillsgrove building and the hotel that traded under a 'Tourist' and later 'Cottage' banner. A thatched cottage on the main street stands testament to a long record of such dwellings on the *Bóthar na Trá* to *Cois Fharraige* route.

Central House was No. 1 Merrion Village. Across the road Spring Lodge, Tandem Lodge and Merrion Lodge stood on the southern side of *Bóthar na Trá*. Ward's Hotel currently sits in the gap between Tandem Lodge and Merrion Lodge – St. Joseph's Terrace in 2018. Trim's Road is now called Whitestrand Avenue. St. Anne's Well was a ritual site that once represented a source of

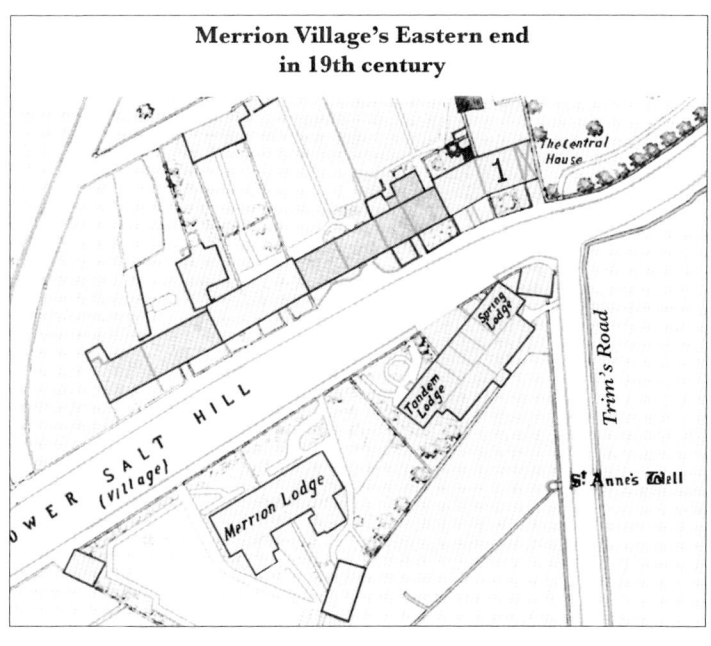

Figure 29.

spiritual significance. It stood on the western side of Trim's Road at a point that corresponds to the current back entrance to Ward's Hotel. No visible trace survives today. Mr. T. O' Connor, of the Ordnance Service, made the following note in an 1839 letter: 'St. Anne's Well, it is said in the Name Book, lies close to Merrion Cottage, a quarter of a mile west of Galway. About this I got no information.'[1]

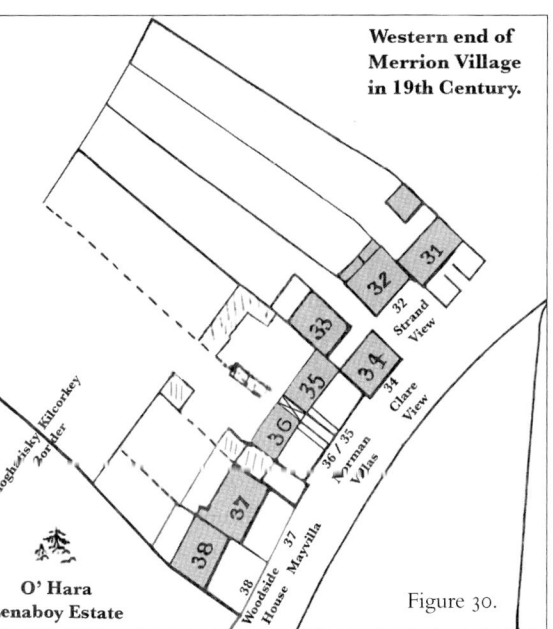

Figure 30.

The most westerly house in Kilcorkey's Merrion Village was Woodside House (no. 38). It was well named because a copse of trees adorned the O'Hara Estate, on the other side of the border wall with Cloghatisky. A high road-hugging O'Hara wall ran to the north of *Bóthar na Trá* from Ballinasloe House (the Bal) to Woodside House up to the 1920s. Norman Villas, which still stand, were numbered 35/36, while both Strand View (no. 32 – PJ. Flaherty's bar today) and the thatched Clare View (no. 34) were licensed premises. The latter licence was voluntarily given up by Mrs. Helly in 1928.

Figure 31.

Norman Villas, whose immediate lessor was Father Peter Daly in 1855, became closely identified with James Davis, a Shop Street merchant and prominent Galway personage, who advertised No. 1 Norman Villa for letting in 1868. When James died in 1894, his son John 'Norman' Davis – an army surgeon – replaced him as lessor. Norman Villas were home, over the years, to occupants whose range of professions included the following disciplines: academia – business – engineering – distilling – seafaring and military.

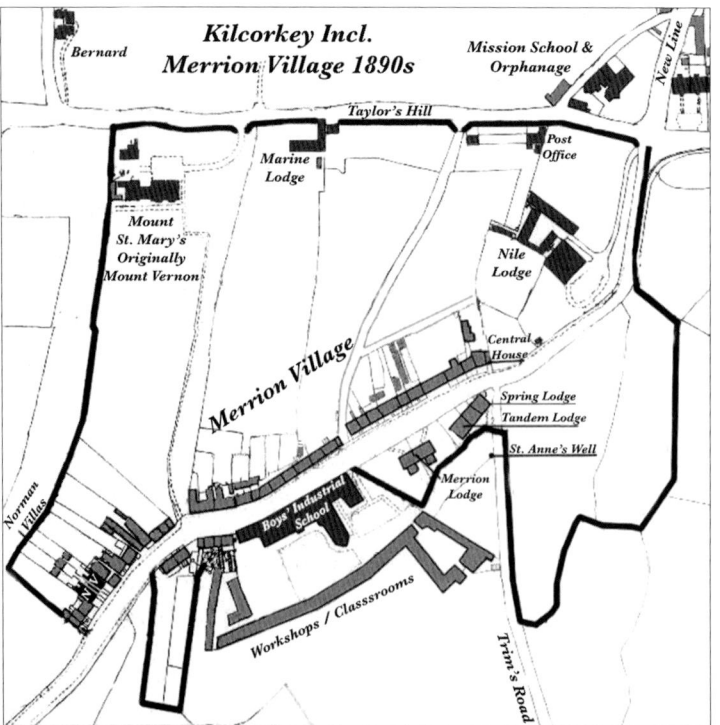

32. An 1890's map of the Kilcorkey townland - within black border - snapshots Merrion Village's progression in the decade before the 20th century dawned.

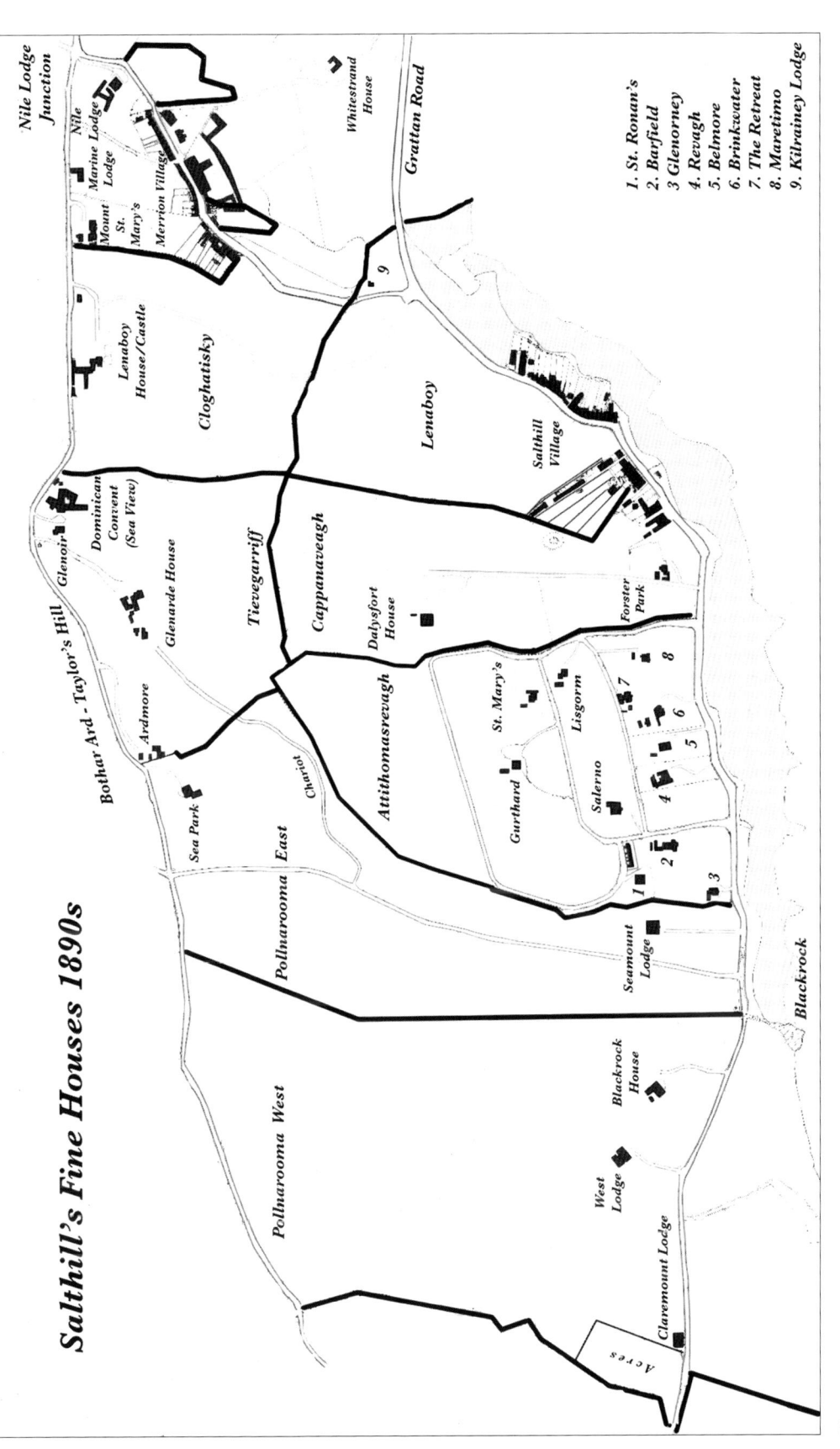
Figure 33.

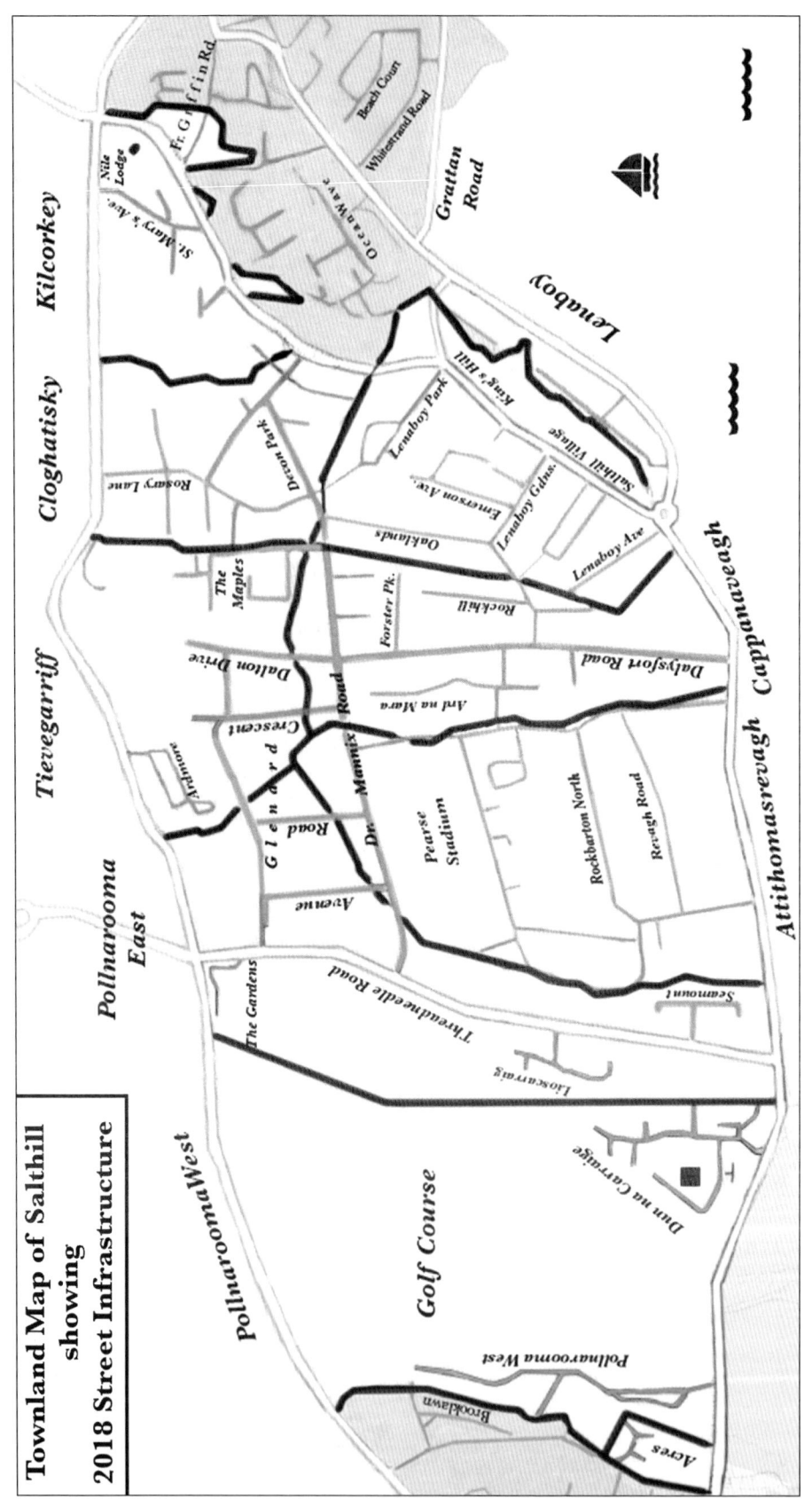
Figure 34.

Chapter 4

SALTHILL DEMESNES OF CLANMORRIS, PERSSE, O'HARA AND WHALEY

Landed gentry, in former times, normally purchased land in significant plot size, with major Salthill landlords generally holding one seaside townland. There were exceptions, of course, with four families at various junctures controlling more than a solitary townland: The Bingham family, under a Lord Clanmorris title, owned – for a spell in the 19th century – both the Pollnarooma East and Attithomasrevagh townlands. That Clanmorris demesne's sea frontage consequently stretched from Blackrock to today's Salthill Park. Despite that, little memory of a Clanmorris Demesne has survived at the place.

Glenarde Demesne

In a local context, demesnes are more associated with the Whaley, O'Hara and Persse families. The latter family, boasting a landed and distilling heritage, produced whiskey at both Newcastle and Nun's Island during the 1800s. A highly reputable product, Persse Whiskey, distilled at Nun's

35. Map of Clanmorris and Glenarde Demesnes at Salt Hill, with 'Chariot' avenue indicated.

Island, was supplied to His Majesty King Edward VII on his 1903 visit to Galway. The family also enjoyed a long 19th century association with Salthill, and Burton de Burgh Persse (1779–1859) was in occupation at Seamount during the 1830s. It was in the early 1860s, however, that Matilda Persse briefly resided in Tievegarriff. On her 1862 death at Glenarde House, she was succeeded by her son, Henry Sadleir Persse of Glenarde and Kiltullagh, who owned the Nun's Island distillery. In 1872, Henry bought the Pollnarooma East townland from his brother in law, Lord Clanmorris, and following that acquisition, the Tievegarriff and Pollnarooma East land banks were joined to form the Persse demesne, which was to enjoy a three decade life span. The Pollnarooma purchase facilitated access to the sea, so that Henry could look from his Glenarde home and know that a stroll to Blackrock could be completed without straying from his own land. To unite the two previously distinct townlands, a pathway from Glenarde House was constructed to connect with the road we now know as Threadneedle. That hedged lane came to be dubbed the Chariot, so titled – it is believed – by youngsters who watched the two Boland sisters – Lory and Maeve – later traverse the route in a pony and trap that was raised to Roman chariot status by imaginative observers. Such metaphorical extravagance, however, might have belonged to an earlier century as a Galway advertisement for a London built coach with 'Eliptic Springs, Lamps, Travelling Boxes &c. in every particular sound and fit for the use of any Nobleman or Gentleman,' was described as early as 1848 as 'A SUPERB CHARIOT.'[1] It was following the 1899 death of Henry Sadleir Persse and concomitant business

36. Lane off Threadneedle Road, which once led to the pillared western entrance gate of Glenarde Demesne's 'Chariot' Avenue.

difficulties that a family of biscuit fame replaced the Persse presence at Glenarde House, during the early years of the 20th century. By 1903 Mr. Patrick J. Boland M.A., a director of Boland's Bakery, was in possession of the property.[2] The Persse creation of the Chariot pathway meant that there were two gated entrances to Glenarde House, one at Taylor's Hill and the other at *Bóthar na Mine*, which came to be called Threadneedle Road.

Salthill's 'Chariot' avenue **(fig.35)** ran from the back of Glenarde House to a pillared end, directly across the road from the current gated entrance to Salerno Secondary School. That Salerno gate, incidentally, had previously serviced *Coláiste Éinde*. A lane, to the immediate north of a four housed Threadneedle Road terrace, still runs to the site of the former 'Chariot' gate, which once stood at the back of Mrs. Mary O'Connor's Dr. Mannix Road home. That house, which fronts onto the Prairie G.A.A. ground, represents the most westerly of the 1960's semi-detached Glenard houses. The O'Connor residence acted as the original show house for the entire estate and Mrs. O'Connor was once told that a girl died following an accident with a horse at the Chariot's entrance. Like most folklore tales picked up by this study, the story has merit, for the *Irish Times* chronicled a tragic accident at Glenarde in May 1888:

Fatal Accident to Miss Persse of Galway: *A very melancholy accident, which terminated fatally, occurred at Glenarde on Wednesday. Miss Noel Persse, daughter of Mr. Henry S. Persse, J.P. and sister of Mr. William Persse, Sheriff of Galway City, an amiable little girl of 10 years, was killed by a fall from a pony. She and her sister went out in the afternoon to take riding exercise, and, when returning to Glenarde, Miss Noel was some distance ahead of her sister, and when she entered the gate at the approach to the house the gate slapped and the pony started, precipitating the poor young lady from the saddle. Her foot caught in the stirrup, and though the pony did not gallop off, she was entirely unable to extricate herself. Her sister galloped up to her assistance, but this had the effect of making the pony start with the poor girl in this awful plight. When assistance arrived she was found to be unconscious, and only lived five minutes afterwards. Miss Noel was a great favourite in the household, and the deepest regret for the sad occurrence is felt by the entire community.*[3]

Dr. Colahan of the Villa was the medical man who attended,[4] and while the *Irish Times* gave '10 years' as her age on death, nine was the figure recorded on the death certificate of Noël Margori (Marjorie) Persse, the youngest of ten children to Henry Sadleir and Eleanor Persse. Though not recorded in the above press piece, it is locally recalled that – in the wake of the accident – Henry shot the horse that was responsible for his daughter's death. Noël was not the only child of that family to die young, for Matilda Theodora (16) and John Beauchamp (5), both expired before adulthood. John died of meningitis at the Lucan Institute in January 1877. That institute was set up by Dr. Henry Hutchinson Stewart in 1856, at what had previously been the Lucan Spa Hotel. Part of the Institute's purpose was to cater for the 'education, training and maintenance' of mentally handicapped children who belonged to the middle class. Four years after John Beauchamp's passing, sixteen year old Matilda Theodora Persse died at Glenarde House of 'primary phthisis,' the term then used to describe consumption-tuberculosis. Dr. Nicholas Clayton of Woodquay, physician at the Fever Hospital, was in attendance at her death. Matilda Theodora was memorialised in glass at St. Nicholas' Collegiate Church on Market Street:

> *The handsome east window, which four centuries ago James Lynch had erected and filled with coloured glass, which long ago had disappeared, was in 1881 put up by Henry Sadleir Persse, in memory of his daughter Matilda Theodora, who died the 18th of August 1881.*[5]

While Henry had that window erected over the church's principal altar in honour of his child, he himself was commemorated after his 1899 death, by his family's erection of a west window in the same building. That resulted in Henry Sadleir Persse of Glenarde being associated with the two most prominent glass features at Galway's Collegiate Church, one over the main door and the other overlooking the primary altar. Not only that, his daughter, Violet Johnson, in May, 1962, presented doors to the church 'in memory of her father and mother, brothers and sisters, all of Glenarde, Galway.' Violet, in contrast to some of her siblings' early deaths, reached 95 years of age before she died in 1968. It was in 1896 that she married Ernest Johnson, and Violet was invested as a Member of the British Empire (M.B.E.) in 1919, because of her wartime work as Donor and Administrator of Ashton Hayes Auxiliary Hospital, near Chester. She subsequently donated a hall to the Women's Institute in the Ashton Hayes area. Violet's sister, Helen Parker Persse, also enjoyed a lengthy life, for she was 86 on her 1964 demise. Helen made her mark in the golfing world through her election as an honorary member of Galway Golf Club, when the local course was sited at Gentian Hill. A scratch golfer, she held the record of her home club, according to 'The Irish Golfer' of June 6th, 1900.

The most famous scion of the Persse family at Glenarde was Henry Seymour Persse (1869–1960), who was universally known as 'Atty' Persse. He described himself as a Distiller and member of the Church of England, while residing at Castleknock in 1901. Ten years later, 'Trainer of Racehorses' was his profession, with Stockbridge as his postal address. Henry married Miss Emily Brooke at Knightsbridge in 1921. She was the daughter of Sir George Frederick Brooke, the Dublin baronet and Chairman of Messrs. G.F. Brooke and Son.[6] Henry's arcane moniker boasted a Salthill origin, for a conjectural local

37. Henry Seymour 'Atty' Persse.

theory traces it to the 'Attythomasrevagh' townland (latterly Rockbarton), which faces onto the promenade. That theory has substance, for a one time Mayor of Galway, Mr. James Redington (1872–1962), whose memories of the town were chronicled in the *Connacht Tribune* during the 1950s, confirmed as much: 'Henry Persse, the well-known English trainer, became known to race goers as "Atty" Persse, the "Atty" being the first part of the name "Attythomas," in Salthill.'[7] It must be pointed out, however, that the Persse family did not own that particular seaside holding, though the neighbouring Tievegarriff and Pollnarooma East townlands both belonged to the landed distillery clan, during the later decades of the 19th century.

Atty's fame sprung from his equine *nous*, which led to his becoming, not only successful, but the oldest horse trainer in Britain at the time of his 1954 retirement from the sport. The script of a *Pathé* newsreel reviewed his sporting life:

At Upper Lambourn in Berkshire lives another 84 year old; Britain's oldest trainer, Atty Persse, who after fifty years at the job, is soon to retire. Born in County Galway, Éire, Mr. Persse, as a young man rode the winner of nearly every important steeplechase in England and Ireland. In 1903 he became a trainer and the initials H.S.P., standing for Henry Seymour Persse, have been a mark to be respected ever since that time. Monarch More [Mór] is one of his pupils at the moment, another is Durante. A painting of Bachelor's Double is among the many souvenirs decorating Mr. Persse's study. But of all the many hundred winners that have passed through his hands, one horse, The Tetrarch, was outstanding. This magnificent creature was unbeaten in the seven races he ran as a two year old in 1913. The only jockey who rode him was the great little Steve Donoghue. Vinegar Hill, winner of the Military Gold Cup in 1911 is another memory for Atty Persse. Although he is giving up training, Atty will stay in the racing game, for as soon as he retires, he intends to buy some thoroughbreds of his own.[8]

The noted Steve Donoghue, stable jockey to Atty Persse, won ten consecutive Jockey Championships in the 1914–1923 period. At a local level, the Galway racecourse committee was proud of Mr. Persse's Sport of Kings' success and – at the time of his 1921 nuptials – delivered an illuminated address to Atty, which paid tribute to his father, Henry Sadleir Persse, for 're-establishing and helping on the Galway Races, which have so continued to flourish.'[9]

Among the other members of the Persse family at Glenarde were Sarah Henrietta, who passed away in 1927 and Eleanora Alice Persse, who was called after her mother, and died in 1937. The eldest, William Henry Persse, who held the Office of High Sheriff of Galway in 1888, married Mary Powlet Cosby in 1893 and died in 1924. So, of the 10 children born to Henry Sadleir and Eleanor Persse, three died before adulthood; one – Cecil de Burgh – was killed in the First World War, and three married, namely William Henry, Violet Seymour and Henry Seymour.

It was in 1890, two years after the death of her youngest child Noël that the family matriarch, Eleanor Persse, passed away at Pau. Aged fifty three, it was on medical advice that she had repaired to the South of France, where her family attended during her final days.[10] Described as 'the soul of benevolence,' Eleanor (née Seymour) Persse was 'the originator of a factory in Galway for the manufacture of straw bottle envelopes, the only one of its kind in the United Kingdom, and by its means helped to support a large number of poor families who had been thrown out of employment by the temporary closing of the Irish jute factory.'[11]

When the Boland family placed the Glenarde property for sale in 1961, it was purchased by Mr. and Mrs. Patrick Ryan of the famed Shop Street drapery store. 'Glenarde House' was subsequently changed to 'Ardilaun House,' which opened its doors as a hotel on St. Patrick's Day, 1962. In the following year, Mr. Patrick D. Ryan had the honour, as Mayor of Galway, of welcoming U.S. President J.F. Kennedy to the *Citie of the Tribes* on an historic day that is still fondly remembered in the town.

O'Hara's 'Lenaboy' Demesne

On the north-eastern side of Salthill Village, the Lenaboy Demesne of the O'Hara sept was made up of the entire Cloghatisky townland and the non-village half of Lenaboy. That particular combination allowed – as late as 1922 – the family patriarch, Lieut. Col. James O'Hara (1865–1928), survey a land bank from his family seat at Lenaboy Castle, which stretched as far as Salthill Village. The walled Salthill road span of that holding ran from Ballinasloe House to Woodside House **(fig.30)**, which stood two doors to the east of what is today Tommy Keane's butcher shop (formerly Gerry Loughnane's). Like Glenarde House, the Lenaboy mansion boasted two gated entrances, one at Taylor's

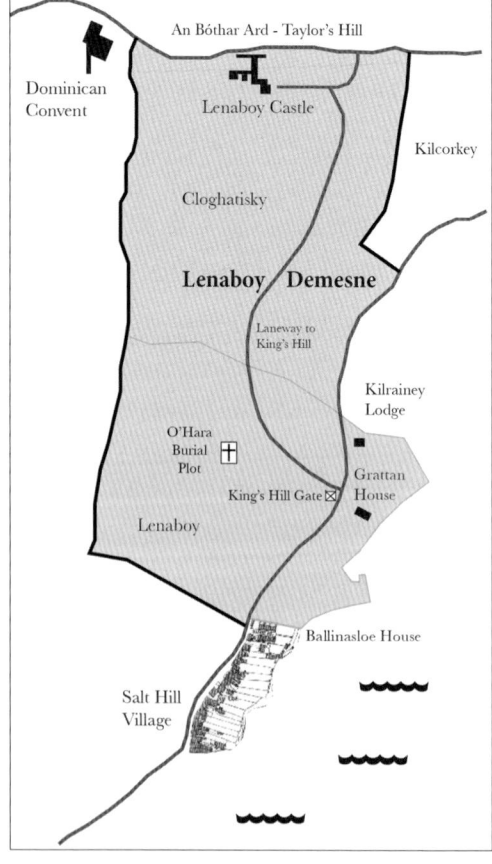

38. O'Hara's 'Lenaboy' Demesne.

39. The gate at the foot of King's Hill, which today marks the entrance to Lenaboy Park, previously represented a Salt Hill Road entrance to the Lenaboy Demesne.

Hill and the other at King's Hill. A private lane, which facilitated access to the sea, ran through the estate to its Salthill entrance at today's Warwick Hotel. While that Lenaboy seat represented the primary O'Hara holding at Salthill, James' uncle, Col. Richard O'Hara, was in residence at the sizable Pollnarooma West townland. It was following Richard's death that his impressive land parcel – which included West Lodge – was purchased by Galway Golf Club in 1924.

The Whaley Demesne

The Whaley surname, of Cromwellian provenance, was notable in Galway over a number of centuries. In relation to Lenaboy, John O'Donovan observed that 'a portion of this townland on South side of road between the Records Quay and Blackrock belongs to Mr. Whaley, Oran Quay, Dublin and leased to 8 tenants who... have built neat lodges for the Accommodation of Bathers. Lease 1 life or 31 years.'[12] The southern location of those lodges indicates that the initial Salthill Village buildings were constructed on Mr. John Whaley's land, in the section of Lenaboy not owned by the O'Hara family. Apart from that Lenaboy holding, the Whaley family was pre-1852, also in possession of Kilcorkey – which housed Merrion Village – as well as the entire acreage of the Claddagh.

An Interesting Lineage

John Whaley, who owned Kilcorkey during the early 1800s, could directly trace his family line to Edward Whalley, the Regicide. One step further back, Edward's mother was Frances Cromwell – aunt to the famed Oliver. The laurel of Regicide – king slayer – was conferred on Edward, for he was the fourth of 59 signatories to the 1649 death warrant on King Charles I. The identity of the masked executioner of that same king still gives rise to historical sleuthing and conjecture. In a local context, some contend that an Irishman, Richard Gunning, did the deed and was rewarded by being granted the property where the 'King's Head' hostelry currently trades on Galway's High Street. Others hold that Colonel Peter Stubbers of Cromwell's army, who captured Galway town after a 1653 siege, was the man responsible. Among that number is historian, Dr. Jackie Uí Chionna, who quotes from a handwritten King Charles II letter, uncovered at the Bodleian Library, which identified Stubbers as 'a Halberdier [an axeman], that assisted at that execrable murder of our Royal Father.'[13] The fact that Peter Stubbers was specifically exempted from a Royal pardon of those implicated in the beheading of Charles I adds further weight to that execution charge.

A familial relationship with Oliver Cromwell provided the backdrop to a pro-Parliament Whaley stance in England's Civil War. Some of the family arrived in Ireland and Sir Edward Sullivan noted that 'Henry Whaley, son of Edward the Regicide, came to Ireland in 1658 with a letter of introduction from Oliver Cromwell to Henry Cromwell, then Lord Deputy.' Oliver's letter began:

Harry Cromwell – I write not often to you. Now I think my selfe ingaged to **my deare Cousin** *Whaley to lay my comands upon you that you shew all lovinge respect to his eldest sonn, by his present Ladye, whom you are to receave in the room of his eldest brother both into his comand and into your affection.*[14]

Whaley fealty to Cromwell delivered Galway land to the family and James Hardiman – in his famed history – made three references to Whaley family holdings:

(a) One was in relation to *an Seoigheach* of Claddagh Ring fame. Purchased in Algiers by a Turkish goldsmith, he later returned to Galway. That Joyce man, according to Hardiman, acquired 'the estate of Rahoon, (which lies about two miles west of the town,) from Colonel Whaley, one of Cromwell's old officers;' (b) 'The Claddagh (an Irish word, which signifies the sea shore) is a village situate on the estate of Mr. Whaley, near the strand;' (c) Mention was also made of Mr. Whalley who had 45 acres at Roscam.[15]

Henry Whalley, M.P. for Selkirk & Peebles 1656–1659, settled in Ireland during the Restoration of the Monarchy and served as Recorder of Galway in 1663. NUIG's Landed Estate database notes that 'John Whaley was granted over 1,600 acres in the county of the town of Galway with additional lands in the baronies of Leitrim, Loughrea, Athenry and Moycullen by patents dated 23 Oct 1667, 6 May 1669 and 3 Aug 1678. Richard Whaley of Newford, Member of Parliament for Athenry, died in 1725 and his son, Richard Chappell Whaley, lived at Whaley Abbey, County Wicklow.'

The latter Richard carried an ominous moniker, for he was known as 'Burn-Chapel' Whaley, a sobriquet that reflected his penchant for incinerating churches, as well as his virulent anti-Catholic *mien*. A widower following the death of his first wife, Catherine Armitage, he was without issue and considered to be mature in age when he reached his fifty ninth year. It was then – in 1759 – that Richard married the eighteen year old, Ann Ward, and when he died a decade

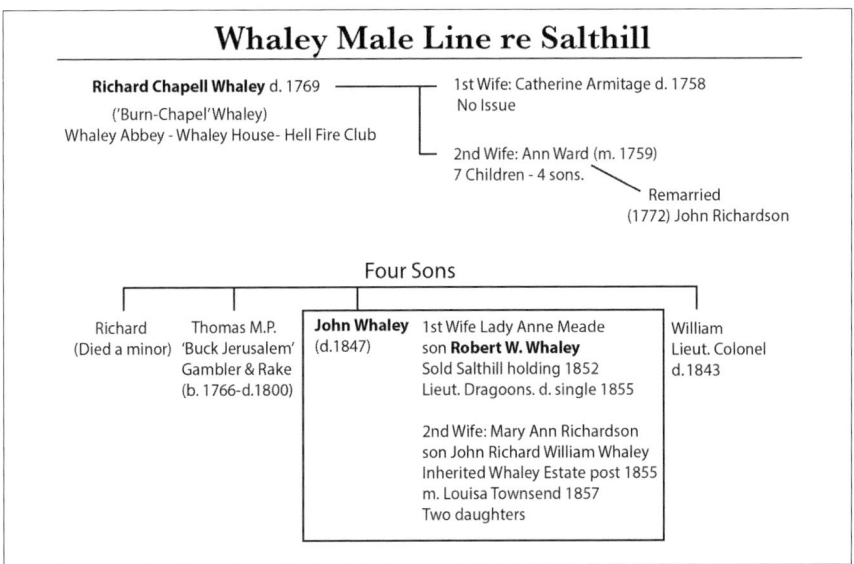

40. An abridged look at the male line in relation to 18th/19th century Whaley ties with Galway/Salthill.

later, Richard Chapell Whaley was survived by seven children – four sons and three daughters.

Richard bought one stone faced house and built another in Stephen's Green, one of which was – ironically enough – to prove pivotal in the development of third level Catholic education in Ireland. In 1754, he purchased 85 St. Stephen's Green South and number 86 was constructed on land adjoining that house. On his death, Richard Chapell Whaley bequeathed number 85 Stephen's Green to his father-in-law, Rev. Mr. Bernard Ward, with number 86 remaining in Whaley hands. Richard's widow, Ann, who remarried when she wed John Richardson M.P. in 1772, was again a widow when she died at Bath in 1826. The *Freeman's Journal*'s record of her passing recalled her first husband's reaction to her bearing him an heir. It noted that Mr. Whaley was 'so highly gratified by that event, that he made her a present of £10,000, for which he is said to have drawn on his banker in the following terms:

Good, Mr. Latouche,
Prithee open your pouch,
And pay my soul's darling,
Ten thousand pounds sterling:
For which this shan't fail ye,
Your servant – M. Whaley.[16]

41. Richard Chapell Whaley's family portrait. (*Irish Arts Review Yearbook,* Vol. 11, 1995)

Such an extravagant response to the arrival of a son is perhaps understandable from a man who was not in the flush of youth, and the reaction was typical of Richard Chapell Whaley, a prominent member of Dublin's Hellfire Club, which did not earn its title *sans raison*. A profligate streak ran in the clan's line. It was only in recent years, that a Whaley family portrait by sculptor, Patrick Cunningham, was discovered during conservation work at Dublin's Newman House. Depicted therein was Richard Chapell with his young wife, Lady Ann, and their seven children in suitably staged poses.

On the left in the Whaley family portrait is the eldest daughter, Susanna, who later married Sir James Stewart of Fort Stewart. Sitting is the young mother, Lady Ann Whaley (née Ward), with her youngest son, William, in her arms. Next stands Richard Chapell Whaley and beside him his eldest son, who bore the same name, and died young. The dancing girl is Anne, who married Hon. John Fitzgibbon, afterwards Earl of Clare and Lord Chancellor of Ireland. Sophia, with fruit in her lap, who went on to wed Hon. Robert Ward, son of Lord Bangor, is to the very right. The two kneeling children are – to the left – Thomas, with a rattle in his hand, and John turning to his sister Sophia. Thomas' toy was a portent of the future for he 'rattled' many cages in adulthood when parading his infamous 'Buck-Jerusalem' persona. John was the man who came to own much of Salthill and all of the Claddagh.

Thomas 'Buck – Jerusalem' Whaley: Gambler and Rake

Reckless extravagance had not a chance to express itself in Richard, the golden boy who prompted his dad's lavish response, for the eldest, who carried his father's name, unfortunately died before coming of age. William, the baby of the portrait, who joined the military and became Lieutenant Colonel W. Whaley, died in 1843.

Thomas, Richard Chapell's second son, bore the colourful handle 'Buck.' Possessed of the family's prodigal peculiarity, a rakish and dissolute personality was described in his naming. He was to win fame, of a sort, over a short lifetime. Four years old when his father died, Thomas, on reaching 16, came into 'an estate of 7,000 pounds a year, besides upwards of 60,000 pounds in money.'[17] He was then despatched to Paris with a tutor, who was unable to curb the young man's ways. On one occasion the young Buck lost £14,000 in one evening's gambling and when bankers were unwilling to honour his cheque, Thomas was forced to flee France. Back in Ireland he was elected M.P. for Newcastle, Co. Dublin,[18] and despite being underage when elected, he served from 1785 to 1790. The boy's wild abandon led to the withering of his inheritance through fanciful flings at fortune.

42. Thomas 'Buck' Whaley.

A measure of the interest taken in Whaley whims is reflected in a 1789 *Freeman's Journal* report of a wager with a fellow, who was later to win fame at the Battle of Waterloo:

> *Last Sunday, in consequence of a wager between the honourable Captain Wesley and Mr. Whaley of 150 guineas, the former walked from the five mile stone on the Bray Road, to the corner of the Circular road at Leeson's Street in 55 minutes: He had one hour to perform it in. A number of gentlemen rode with the walker, whose horses he kept in a tolerable smart trot.*[19]

Captain Wesley, who won the wager, later went by the more courtly title of Hon. Arthur Wellesley, Duke of Wellington. It was in 1798 that Arthur changed the spelling of his surname to the more ostentatious 'Wellesley' and it was 1815 before his greatest victory was achieved with the defeat of Napoleon at Waterloo. Though Mr. Whaley's forename was not given in the newspaper report, it is fair to surmise that it was Thomas who lost the bet. Some Dublin wags were later known to correct those who claimed that Wellesley claimed his first major success in India, reminding all – willing to listen – that the Duke's first triumph was against Mr. Whaley in Dublin.[20]

Thomas Whaley was, however, successful in one outlandish wager which attracted international attention: When asked in 1788 where next he would visit,

Thomas casually replied 'Jerusalem.' Fellow 'bucks' wagered £15,000 that he would be unable to reach the Holy Land, and return within two years. Thomas, true to form, accepted what was then a dangerous challenge and in the company of two friends, Captain Wilson and Moore, headed for the 'Holy City.' Wilson, due to illness, did not make it past Smyrna, but Whaley and Moore returned to Dublin – in February 1789 – to collect Thomas' winnings. The £15,000 pot was not all profit for a considerable sum had been expended on the trip, leaving Mr. Whaley £7,000 to the good. It is hard to believe that the entire caper occurred while he was a Member of Parliament, and his triumphant tour resulted in a further nickname – 'Jerusalem Whaley' – which identified the central figure of Dublin's infamous Hellfire Club. In fact it was Thomas Whaley, in the style of his deceased father, who re-energised the notorious club, which eventually faded on 'Buck's' passing. Among a host of fanciful wagers, one required Thomas to leap from an upstairs window of Whaley House on Stephen's Green into the next passing carriage and kiss its female occupant. The prodigal's debts mounted and after fleeing Dublin's bailiffs, Thomas spent some time with his lady companion in the Isle of Man, having reputedly imported earth from Ireland to win a wager, which proved that he lived on 'Irish soil,' while domiciled abroad. It was at his Manx sanctuary that his memories were chronicled, but 'Buck Whaley's Memoirs' were not published until 1906, a full century after the wild boy's demise. His narrative contains some truthful, if obvious, observations: 'I was born with strong passions, a lively imagination, and a spirit that could brook no restraint. I possessed a restlessness and activity of mind that directed me to the most extravagant pursuits.'[21] It would be difficult to quibble with that self-analysis.

Thomas' domestic situation was, as might be expected, unconventional: Buck Whaley's mistress, Miss Courtney, bore him two sons and a daughter and it was following his partner's demise that Thomas married – some months before his own death.[22] His wife, Mary Catherine Lawless, the daughter of Lord Cloncurry, subsequently raised Buck Whaley's three children as her own. Liver problems caused the profligate's untimely demise – at 33 or 34 years of age – in November, 1800. A court case, which centred on Thomas' age, as entered on a life insurance policy, was heard following his passing. The plaintiff and creditor, Sir John Ferns, held a Sun Insurance life policy on the life of the deceased and was keen to recover 'a sum considerably under what was due to him from Mr. Whaley.' The jury found for the plaintiff and awarded Sir John Ferns the sum of 1,200*l*.[23] Some fourteen months after his obsequies, Buck Whaley remained in the news by featuring in such court reports. Thomas, at the time of his passing, was representing Enniscorthy at Westminster, where he did not always distinguish himself. Inducements were sought to guide his voting on the Act of Union, which was to carry great consequences for Ireland. Promising to vote against the bill, he supported the Union when it came to the floor of the house.

The circumstances of his Westminster appearance for that critical vote were unusual, as the *Freeman's Journal* recorded:

At the period of the Union the late Mr. Whaley, brother in law of Lord Clare, the then Lord High Chancellor of Ireland, was tried and convicted before the present Recorder, for an assault committed by him on a person in very humble life, and was sentenced to imprisonment in the Gaol of Newgate. The Recorder was waited upon by persons of the first rank of influence in the country and solicited to consent to the discharge of Mr. Whaley. The inflexibility of the Judge resisted the application. What followed – Mr. Whaley was suddenly reported ill and his life said to be in danger; the Government discharged him and on the following day, where was he found? – not in the bed of sickness, not breathing the pure air in the vicinity of our city, but in a suffocating, pestilential and corrupt House of Commons, voting away the liberties of the country.[24]

On his passing in 1800, the same newspaper's obituary was, in a gently sympathetic sense, kind to Thomas Whaley: 'Tis well known that Mr. Whaley was blessed with a good understanding, but the whirl and blaze in which he lived, diminished its effect and force in an eccentricity of pursuits; the wide influence of his name and the credit of his estate were without reserve communicated to those ephemeral fashionables, who live like butterflies in the sunshine.'[25] Buck's funeral featured an unusual celebration of his life 'when Mr. Robinson, an Irish-man, who was also a dancing master of that day, danced a hornpipe over the body.'[26]

John Whaley – Salthill interest

A younger brother to Buck Whaley was the man who owned a good part of Salthill. He was Mr. John Whaley, whose inherited division of Richard Burn-Chapel's estate included a number of Galway holdings: The entire Kilcorkey townland, containing all of Lower Salthill, land in Lenaboy where Salthill Village took root, the Claddagh in its entirety, as well as other properties in the town were among the fruits of his bequest. In common with his landed peers, Mr. John Whaley acted through local representatives, and he had a notice – of relevance to Galway – published in May 1800:

Having appointed Thomas Burke Esq. Of Loughrea, my agent, the tenants in the County of GALWAY, and the County of the TOWN of GALWAY, on the Estates of John Whaley, Esq. are desired to pay all Rents and Arrears to Thomas Burke, Esq. and likewise to bring with them the last receipts for Rent paid; Loughrea, 5th May, 1800. John Whaley.[27] The breath of his landed wealth at Galway was glimpsed in a later press advertisement that made reference to: *the several parts of the TOWN OF GALWAY ESTATE of John Whaley, Esq. as follows viz.: Sherwood's Fields, Kilcorkey, Newcastle Fields, Verdon's Fields, The Lanabaties, Fair Hill, Hollaran's Plot, Coach House Fields, and Calf Parks, Killery's Garden, together with the Premises known by the name of Vegge's Plot.* That notice was placed by Hamilton Echlin, Agent and Receiver. In a postscript, prefixed by *Nota Bene*, Hamilton informed those interested that he would attend Connolly's

Inn, in the Town of Galway on the 5th of June, 1823 to receive proposals for the properties.[28]

John Whaley was recorded, from 1818 on, as a resident of 86 St. Stephen's Green South, which was built by Richard, his 'chapel-burning' father. John's wife, Lady Ann, one of ten children, was the eldest daughter of John Meade, Earl of Clanwilliam and Theodosia Hawkins Magill. Caroline Elizabeth Whaley – one of John Whaley and Lady Ann's daughters – married Sir Charles Henry Coote, Bart. of Ballyfin on 26 November, 1814.[29] Their youngest son, Orlando Coote, died at Salt Hill in 1840.[30] It is fair to say that the Whaley family was well connected and while the feckless streak that characterised his brother was not apparent in the man with property interests at Salthill, it must

43. An 1823 *Connaught Journal* - Whaley advertisement on top, with below, John Whaley's signature and seal.

be said that John Whaley did enjoy his fortune. Like many of his class and family, John took a keen interest in racing. In April 1803, for example, Mr. Whaley's horse, 'Buffer' won a cup at the Curragh when beating the Marquis of Donegal's 'Curb.'[31] Greyhound racing also enthused him and his briny bitch 'Weazle' beat Hon. Captain Wodehouse's 'Honesty' at the Curragh Coursing Club in 1838.

For all the fun, life was not without its lows and losses. In September 1828 John Whaley's 27 year old son, Henry, and his 20 year old friend, Christopher St. George Trench Esq., both drowned at Drumsesk Cottage 'in consequence of bathing incautiously.'[32] Four years earlier, Patrick Walker, a young apprentice to the chimney sweep, Blackthorn, 'was unfortunately suffocated when sweeping a chimney in Mr. Whaley's House, Stephen's Green, in consequence of a quantity of rubbish falling down on him.'[33] Another incident in the palatial Stephen's Green residence saw the curtains catch fire when a butler was giving a drink to Mr. Whaley, who was then confined to bed. Though the coachman was severely burned in an effort to rescue his 'master,' Mr. Whaley 'was only slightly "scorched" from the burning embers falling on him.'[34] Two years later – in 1847 – John Whaley died.

Whaley properties were disposed of in the wake of his death. Among them the very fine house that was 86 Stephen's Green South, which was sold by Mary

Anne Whaley (née Richardson), John's second wife and widow. Before that stately home changed hands, the 'Whaley Gallery of Paintings' was auctioned in three portions. Whaley House, which had been erected at a cost of £28,000 by Richard Chapell Whaley was purchased by the Catholic University in 1853 for the 'insignificant sum of £3,000, subject to the nominal rent of £15 per annum.'[35] The reported purchaser was Charles Bianconi Esq., two-time Mayor of Clonmel and public transport entrepreneur. Bianconi was apparently acting as intermediary for Cardinal John Henry Newman who proposed to set up Ireland's first Catholic University at the house.[36] Aware of the distain in which Catholics were traditionally held by the Whaley family, Bianconi served as an agent for the purchaser. The machinations, which whittled the price down to £3,000, remain unclear, but what is certain is that the house built by the virulently anti-Catholic Richard 'Burn-Chapel' Whaley was to become the first home of the Catholic University of Ireland, which later morphed into University College Dublin. The former Whaley residence, with Dr. John Henry Newman as rector and Archbishop Cullen as Chancellor, opened its 'academic' doors in 1854. That Stephen's Green building is today known as Newman House.

Robert W. Whaley

On John Whaley's passing in a black Famine year, his son, Robert, took control of the family estate. It was a time of deep suffering for tenants and great unease for landlords. With landed wealth fast dissipating in the wake of famine years, many were forced to sell their holdings at the Encumbered Estates' Court. Mr. R. Whaley was forced to do the same. He had been ordered by such a court in January 1850 to sell his estate, including Kilcorkey, the Claddagh and Sherwood's Fields.[37] That sale did not happen for two years, but in one day Robert William Whaley sold the Kilcorkey townland of Lower Salthill – which contained 31 acres – for £2,110 to Father Peter Daly; The Townparks' townland that covers 40 acres of Galway town for £2,670 to Mr. McRory; and the Claddagh, which encompassed 29 acres, for £1,710 to Henry Grattan Junior. The day was 13 January, 1852 and the place of sale was a courthouse at 14 Henrietta-Street Dublin. Robert Whaley, as owner, in that same sale disposed of property in the Counties of Armagh, Louth, Carlow, Galway, and Town of Galway. Sir Charles Henry Coote Bart., was Ex parte Petitioner.

After selling such a swathe of land over so many Irish counties, it is hard to believe that three years later Robert Whaley again appeared in court, this time as an insolvent.[38] The man, who followed a family tradition in producing competitive horses at Curragh races, was to die on 5th May, 1855 at his Ranelagh Road residence.[39] A Captain in the 14th Light Dragoons, he was unmarried and the last surviving son of the Lady Anne and John Whaley, late of Stephen's Green. Robert's step brother, John Richard William Whaley, who was the son of John Whaley by his second wife, Mary Anne Richardson, became the heir at law of Robert Whaley.[40]

In 1857 John R.W. Whaley married Louisa Olivia Deane Townsend, daughter of Dr. Townsend, late Bishop of Meath and the couple had two daughters.

In many ways 1852 was a significant year for Salthill, as Cromwellian settlers, after generations in charge of seaside property and holdings in Galway town, had their ties with the place irrevocably severed. From then on it was primarily Irish men who held the land, but, as often occurs, the 'new' differed little from the 'old.' Fr. Peter Daly took over Lower Salthill and Henry Grattan Jnr. took ownership of the Claddagh, with the Grattan influence proving to be more benign. When evictions followed at Salthill in the post-Famine period the 'accursed English' could no longer be blamed. Some in Salthill quickly learned what they probably already knew; the native could be just as callous as the planter.

Chapter 5

SALTHILL OF WALLS, GATES AND PROMENADE

Demesnes and their infrastructures left their imprint on the place. In that context, Revagh Road today represents the closest approximation to what Salthill looked like in the late 19th century. It was to the roads of Rockbarton that summer visitors once retreated from overly warm summer days, for shade from summer sun was offered by the fine walls of Mr. Barton's estate. Respite from clamorous children and a crowded promenade also invited exploration of the local countryside for those who sought a serene stroll.

44. Revagh Road in 2018.

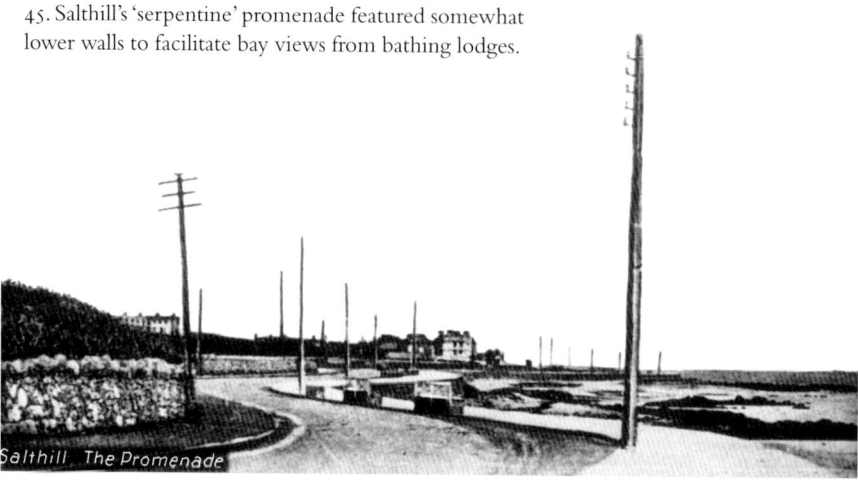

45. Salthill's 'serpentine' promenade featured somewhat lower walls to facilitate bay views from bathing lodges.

Walls and gates delineated demesne and estate properties, and the Bathing Lodges that overlooked Salthill's esplanade were protected by high stone constructions, which not only marked boundaries but assured seclusion for lodge residents. Mr. Barton had a clear vision of what Attithomasrevagh should become and while he favoured privacy, limits were set in his leases. One stated condition was that 'no wall (save such dwelling house) shall be built on the premises exceeding twelve feet in height.' Older and somewhat lower stone screens, which once arced in harmony with a serpentine promenade, facilitated a good view of the prom from the ground floor of seafront villas. Those curved walls were straightened during the road widening of the 1940s, in a development that saw the Prom's older screens being first levelled and then replaced by newer constructions, which moved a little inland to facilitate the broadening of Salthill's sea-boulevard.

The once private exclusivity of Salthill's townlands found expression in the positioning of pillared gates at the entrances to Westland Avenue (Rockbarton West), St. Mary's Avenue (Rockbarton Road), and what came to be called Dalysfort Road. Such barriers, which became casualties of the Prom's 1940's development, were practically always open, except for designated days when a closing custom legally asserted the privacy of guarded grounds. It was the closing of Blackrock on one such day in 1909 that ignited the Bathing Battle of Salthill, which will be described in a future volume of this history.

It was not only at Rockbarton, of course, that tall screens skirted the locale's lanes and roads, for a 'blank wall,' from Ballinasloe House at the eastern edge of Salthill Village to Woodside House (**fig.30**) at the western end of Merrion Village, protected the pastoral exclusivity of the O'Hara demesne, which northerly ran all the way up to Taylor's Hill.[1]

The beginning of that imposing wall can be seen opposite Ballinasloe House in figure 47, which dates from 1911–1914, a decade before the O'Hara Demesne was

Salthill of Walls, Gates and Promenade

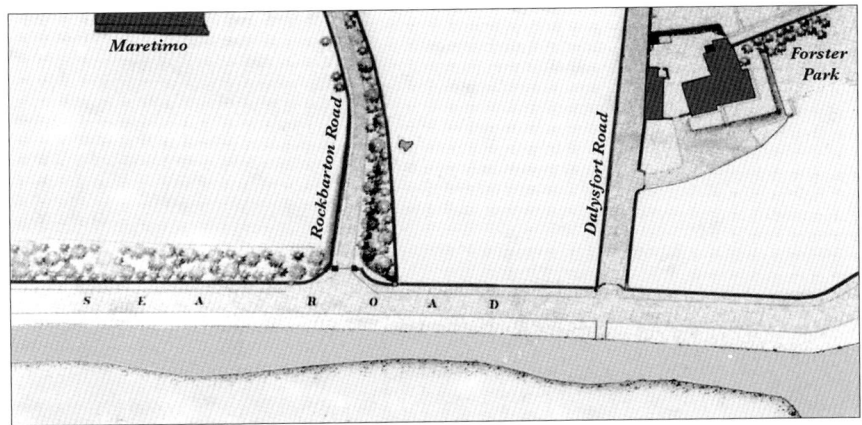

46. Gated entrances marked on post-1856 map, to what became Rockbarton Road and Dalysfort Road. Forster Park today houses Salthill Garda Station. (Some titles added to original map for clarity.)

47. Imposing O'Hara wall, opposite Ballinasloe House, at entrance to Salthill Village.

sold. Confidence in that timeline stems from the 'Flynn's Bar' side banner that is visible on Salthill House. In reality it read 'O'Flynn's Bar,' but the patronym's 'O' prefix – in the above image – lies hidden behind the neighbouring premises. In 1911 a brother and sister, Michael and Margaret O'Flynn from Kilkerrin, replaced a well known Connolly family as licence holders at that public house. Three years later, Margaret married Sligo born Thomas Reginald Scallan and her husband's surname replaced her own over the door. Though twice widowed, Margaret

O'Flynn-Scallan-Ryan made a significant contribution at Salthill, which is detailed in the Boarding chapter of this book.

Beside Salthill House stood the original Ballinasloe House, known to all as 'The Bal.' A Grehan couple, Joseph (from Ballinasloe) and Mary (from Barnadearg), operated that business. Committed Republicans, the Grehan family was obviously skilled at the advertising game. Up to living memory the gable end of that establishment, which marked the eastern end of Salthill Village, carried the punch line command: 'Stop!! This is the Bal' **(fig.47)**. Further evidence of a Grehan facility for promotion was the position held by Joe's brother, Thomas à Kempis Grehan, who was employed from 1909 to 1938 as Advertising Manager with Independent Newspapers. In 1921, Thomas could rightfully boast that he was the 'first Rotary Newspaper Representative in Europe.'[2] One suspects that he might have been the originator of the gable end slogan, which greeted legions of visitors, over many decades, to Salthill Village.

48. Thomas Grehan, Advertising Manager at Independent Newspapers. (*The Rotarian*, May, 1921, XVIII, No.5)

Snatches of other Salthill walls still survive. Beginning at Nile Lodge, standing yet is a small stretch of the wall that enclosed a fine residence, which was built in the early 1800s by a British naval officer, Lieutenant William Hutchinson. That distinctive lodge, which over time lent its name to its immediate hinterland, is among the oldest houses still serving as a private Salthill residence. Across the road, the tall boundary wall of The Villa – up to recently – curved from the Crescent into the principal road entrance to Lower Salthill.

The Villa residence was most identified with a Colahan family of esteemed medical men, whose greatest legacy turned out to be a song. That song was *Galway Bay*, which reached a worldwide audience and earned Bing Crosby a gold record in the late 1940s. The composer, Dr. Arthur Colahan, is today memorialised by the naming of a local road in his honour, and a plaque that features the lyrics of his famed song – in English, Irish, French and Latin – was unveiled during the *Cúirt* International Festival of Literature at Seapoint Promenade on 20 April, 2016 by Councillor Frank Fahy, Mayor of Galway. The man 'who came up with the concept' was Tom Kenny of Kenny's Bookshop.

There are of course other songs which carry a *Galway Bay* title. Songster siblings, Dolores and Seán Keane from Caherlistrane, give voice to a traditional ballad com-

Salthill of Walls, Gates and Promenade

49. The Villa's tall wall (on left behind bus stop), at entrance to Lower Salthill in 1970s. (Photo: Don Mc Ginley.)

posed by Francis Fahy (1854–1935), a Kinvara native. A more modern lyric of the same title was written by Salthill man, Gerry Mulholland, who regularly performed his composition during the 1970s at his family's Hilltop Hotel.

BR. AN DOCHTÚRA MAC UALLACHÁIN
DR. COLOHAN ROAD

Figure 50.

The above sign, which identifies a road that runs through the old Whitestrand Marsh, is positioned at a point not that distant from the southern corner of 'Lady Shea's Plot' **(fig.63)**, within which the Villa residence of the Colahan family was situated. 'Colahan' with middle 'a' was the spelling form used by the family in the census returns of 1901 and 1911. In terms of the sign's Gaelic version, an alternative translation might read: *Bóthar Dhochtúir Mhic Uallacháin*.

At the western end of Salthill, a fine wall that marked the entrance to Blackrock House ran further west as a protective screen to the Pollnarooma townland, which belonged to Col. Richard O'Hara of West Lodge, right up to 1924. Taylor's Hill also featured tall walls which, over time, became perforated by housing and institutional

51. Tall walls at Taylor's Hill / Kingston, overlooking Dalysfort House and Salthill Village.

52. A remnant stretch of the tall wall at the Monks' Field in 1935. (Courtesy of *Connacht Tribune*.)

developments. Remnants do remain on both sides of the rising road, with one good example starting at the Bishop's Palace and running to the turn at Rosary Lane. On the Rahoon side of *an Bóthar Ard,* the curved entrance to Merville Lodge retains a real sense of times past. Figure 51 displays the craftsmanship, as well as the size of Salthill's walls.

The Monks' Field, at the heart of Salthill Village, belonged to the Christian Brothers and ran from the current entrance to Lenaboy Gardens to what was Strand House – O'Reilly's Bar and Kitchen today. After the 1933 purchase of that field by a Castlerea consortium, development was rapid. A 1935 photograph **(fig.52)**, showing the building of the Church of Christ the King, features a remnant of that field's wall still standing to the west of what was then the Kenny sisters' residence and shop – the Galleon Restaurant today.

Other examples remain of Salthill's 'walled' past, but none can compare with the shaded seclusion Revagh Road has retained from previous centuries.

Salthill's Sea-Walls & Esplanade

Bóthar na Trá was – and remains – a scenic sea-skirting route that connects the town to its *Cois Fharraige* hinterland. There's no doubt but that from the time of that road's creation, many people, particularly in summer, enjoyed a stroll to Black Rock. Long before what we now know as Salthill's promenade was ever built, the word 'promenade,' was often used – as verb or epithet – in relation to the resort. An 1837 letter to the press complained about a lack of policemen in the town on a Sabbath day, when two 'poor labourers' were attacked at the Four Corners. The writer opined that such violent conduct was 'too troublesome' for the guardians of the law, because 'it interfered with their toilet, and prevented them from taking their promenade, on Salt Hill, Fort Hill, or some other hill.'[3] Six years later, the Parent Temperance Band 'performed during promenade hours on Sunday...at Salt-hill, to the great pleasure of the inhabitants and visitors.'[4]

The road from the village to Blackrock was ever open to the threat posed by a stormy sea, which did varying levels of damage over many years. It was a thoroughfare that was not neglected during the Great Famine, for County Surveyor, Henry Clements, placed it in the top three Relief Works he projected in March 1846. They were (a) The continuation of the quay from the Claddagh to Nimmo's Pier; (b) Widening of the sea road from Seapoint House to Blackrock; (c) The repair and widening of the road from the top of Bohermore for about three miles towards Tuam.[5] By May, top of the list was the 'widening and protection' of Salt Hill's sea-road, at an estimated cost of £500.[6] That work, which 'was delayed due to the difficulty of hiring carts to move stones,'[7] was to come to nought, following a dreadful storm on Sunday, 24 January, 1847: 'The damage at Salt-hill can scarcely be calculated, for not alone has private property suffered, as is the case of Mr. Delaney [of Seapoint-house] and others, but all public works lately executed from Seapoint-house to Blackrock, have been entirely destroyed. In fact, the shore all this way, and thence to Spiddal, presents one mass of ruin.'[8] That storm was compared to the legendary and severe *Oíche na Gaoithe Móire* of January 1839, which had taken its own grave toll on the region, and was then fresh in living memory. Private enterprise came to the fore in the spring of 1853, when Mr. Thomas H. Barton employed 130 men and 12 horses in the building 'of piers and a sea-wall to make the shoreline suitable for bathing.'[9] That initiative followed Mr. Barton's May, 1852 purchase of the seaside Attithomasrevagh townland, where he built Bathing Lodges, and had in his employ Samuel Ussher Roberts as engineer.

Promenade

Destructive weather struck again in 1856, and in May of that year Mr. Samuel U. Roberts B.E., successor to Mr. Clements as County Surveyor for the County of the Town of Galway, delivered his first report to Galway's Grand Jury. In that account, attention was drawn to a sudden breach 'in the sea-wall near Salthill, on the Barna Road,' which he had repaired 'with the least possible delay.'[10] Primacy was understandably given to the principal thoroughfare that serviced the area. Later in the same year, however, Samuel Ussher Roberts was pivotal to a proposition that would facilitate those who wished to stroll by the sea-front on a proper 'promenade':

It is proposed to apply for a presentment at the next Special Sessions for the County of the Town of Galway for a sum of £50 to complete the sea wall extending along the Salthill road, from the point opposite Captain Blake Forster's residence to the end of the sea wall lately completed by County Presentment. In carrying out this improvement, it is desirable to execute other works, which it is thought will be very advantageous to those who come to Galway for the summer months and for the inhabitants who frequent that road.

The additional works referred to are for the formation of a promenade along the sea shore, separated from the public road by a low parapet wall, which will answer as a seat; and in addition to this it is proposed to form and enclose a space for a band, &c. It is proposed to execute these works by funds raised by subscription, from those who think such an improvement desirable.

The following committee has been appointed for carrying out the above objects – Lord Clanmorris; Anthony O'Flaherty, Esq. M.P.; Lieut.-Colonel French; Very Rev. B. J. Roche V.C.; Rev. John D'Arcy; Capt. Blake Forster; Bernard O'Flaherty, Esq.

Secretary and Treasurer (by whom subscriptions will be received) – S. U. Roberts, Esq.[11]

That 1856 committee, set up to deliver improvements at Salt Hill, is the first group – to have come to this study's attention – that proclaimed such an ambition. There was, undoubtedly, a degree of self-interest in terms of some members of the collective, who owned or occupied property by the sea-front. Secretary Samuel U. Roberts had an interest in a number of Rockbarton properties, having been centrally involved, as architect and engineer, in the building of Mr. Barton's lodges; John Charles Bingham, the fourth Lord Clanmorris, then owned the Pollnarooma East townland; Bernard O'Flaherty occupied West Lodge at Pollnarooma West; Anthony O'Flaherty was in possession of Maretimo; and Blake Forster had – in June 1856 – purchased the Cappanaveagh townland that overlooked the sea. The promenade was to begin from opposite Captain Blake Forster's newly purchased resort residence, which today (2018) houses Salthill's

53. The start of Salthill's promenade, to the front of Forster Park, in the late 1800s. The large house to the right is Maretimo. (Courtesy of National Library of Ireland.)

Garda station. The fact that subscriptions were required indicates that the desired improvement effort was above and beyond what the Town Jury could justifiably deliver. Contributions received by the committee included Lieut.-Colonel French (£6); R.A.H. Kirwan, Esq. (£1); Colonel Geoghegan (£1); William G. Murray (£1); and Thomas M. Persse (£2).

Samuel Ussher Roberts, secretary to the Improvements' Committee in a private capacity, was – in his public role – also proactive in ensuring that Salt Hill's seawall would be strengthened. Storm damage in the December, which followed his autumn 1856 promenade announcement, contributed to Galway's Surveyor allotting four of nineteen work proposals to the sea-side road in May, 1857.

Nos. 8, 9, 10, and 11, are for repairing and coping the Sea-wall on the road from Galway to Barna, by Salthill. I wish here to observe that, during the storm which took place on the 9th December last, very considerable injury was done to a portion of this road; two breaches were made in the sea-wall; large quantities of stone and shingle were thrown upon the road; and the surface was greatly damaged for a considerable portion of its length. I obtained a Magistrates' order for a sum of £10, and had the road made available and safe for public traffic with the least possible delay. The contract which has now been entered into, subject to your approval, is for repairing the damage done by the storm referred to, and for completing and coping 900 lineal feet of the sea-wall, which has been for some years left in an unfinished state. This is, in my opinion a work which is most necessary.[12]

The three hundred yard stretch of sea-wall, then proposed, created a much improved thoroughfare that accommodated a safe pathway along the shore. The experience earned on the completion and coping of Salt Hill's sea-wall would, no doubt, have aided Mr. Roberts' direction of a later promenade at White Strand.

54. The strong sea-wall of Salthill's promenade is visible in the above photograph, which was taken c.1900. The western end of the original promenade's path is shown in the left foreground of this image and indicates that the esplanade initially ran from that western point to its eastern end, opposite Forster Park and the later Rockland Hotel (figs.53 & 56). (Courtesy of National Library of Ireland.)

It would appear from an 1877 Sea Road Committee report that the Salthill promenade was either (a) better built or (b) better taken care of than other local roadway sections. The report found 'the road from the wooden bridge at Dominick Street to Blackrock much neglected, notably as far as the Eglinton Hotel.' Mr. John O'Connor, the contractor responsible for the thoroughfare, was willing to carry out the recommendations of the committee. Furthermore, 'the Borough Surveyor directed to have…the Promenade at Salthill, opposite Forster Park, put in order for the accommodation…of the public.'[13] That recommendation was made some four years after Mr. Samuel Roberts had departed Galway, and taken up a Commissioner post. The breath of Samuel's contribution to the place was reflected in the positions he had held:

He was Surveyor to the West Riding of the County, he was Surveyor to the County of the Town, and he was Surveyor, or, as the technical term, we believe is, Inspector of Highways to the town itself. The first situation he held under the County Grand Jury; the second under the Grand Jury of the County of the Town, and the third under the Town Board.[14]

Mr. Roberts was succeeded in 1873 by Mr. Henry Temple Humphreys, Esq. who transferred from a similar position at Limerick West, to 'take charge of the County Galway West.'[15] The new man, who was London born, was never robust in health and he became 'much shattered by exposure to the cold damp air, and by the fatigue undergone in traversing the long distances of his extensive district.'[16]

During Mr. Humphreys' absence it appears that Richard Newman Somerville C.E., who was a member of the Town and Harbour Boards, dealt with some Surveyor issues, before Mr. Carter Draper C.E. was officially appointed in place of Mr. Humphreys in September 1878.[17] Henry T. Humphreys had resigned his position in January of the same year.

Samuel Ussher Roberts B.E., C.B. (1821–1900)

Samuel Ussher Roberts was an efficient and talented engineer, whose design/engineering pedigree was quite distinguished, for he was the great-grandson of a famed architect, John Roberts (1712–1796). A Waterford native, Samuel was the son of Justice of the Peace, Edward Roberts of Weston. Educated at Burney's Royal Academy, Gosport, the young engineer worked in counties Waterford, Louth, Meath and Monaghan, before taking up employment in Galway. It was at Carrickmacross on 3 May, 1847 that he wed Emily Isabella Forster, eldest daughter of Sir George Forster of Coolderry, Co. Monaghan. A year later, when only in his twenty-seventh year, Mr. Roberts was appointed as a District Engineer in Galway, with responsibility for the Loughs Corrib, Mask and Carra drainage district. That brief 'included the completion of the Eglinton Canal from the port of Galway to Lough Corrib, the improvement of the navigation of Lough Corrib, of the mill power of the River Corrib at Galway and of the Galway salmon fishery. After the completion of these works, Roberts acted as the Board's consulting and inspecting engineer for important drainage schemes all over Ireland.'[18] He was appointed Surveyor for Galway city in August 1855, and two years later became deputy to Mr. Henry Clements B.E., before succeeding Mr. Clements as County Surveyor in 1858. While practicing privately, Samuel was also engineer to the Lough Corrib Drainage and Navigation Trustees and the Galway Harbour Commissioners. He departed Galway in 1873 to take up a position as Assistant Commissioner of Public Works, before becoming Commissioner in 1878. He retired in 1886 and his involvement as Vice-President of the Royal Dublin Society – and judge at the Dublin Horse Show – is still memorialised in the presentation of the Samuel Ussher Roberts' Perpetual Cup for Best Light-Weight Hunter.

In local folk memory, however, Mr. Roberts is generally remembered for his design and delivery of Galway's first water works, which were built at Terryland and opened in 1867. There were, as we have seen, many more strings to the same man's bow, and his imprint on the county, town and Salt Hill was substantial. It was on the western side of the Corrib that he resided, where he regularly changed domiciles, in the style of many of his social ilk. Having arrived during dark famine years, his Galway work was completed during decades that – in turn – delivered promise and despair.

Samuel's sea wall improvement and promenade development was undertaken in the 1850s, when bathing lodge design and construction marked his contribution to the development of Attithomasrevagh, after that seaside land mass had been acquired in 1852 by Thomas Henry Barton. Samuel's architectural flair continued to flower in the following decade, finding expression in his design of Mount Vernon for Thomas Moore Persse; Lenaboy Castle for Col. James O'Hara (1832–1902); the Mission Church School and Orphanage, for the Irish Church Missions at Nile Lodge (*Scoil Fhursa* today);[19] and the Church at Sea Road for the Jesuit order.[20] All four constructions were completed during the early 1860s.

That same period was paradoxically marked at Galway by despair and ambition – ostensibly incongruous bedfellows that benefitted one another: On the one hand, famine once more stalked the land, and inhabitants of the western

55. Samuel Ussher Roberts.

seaboard were hit hard. Town leaders, at the same time, were consumed with the hope of making Galway the hub for Britain's mail connectivity with the New World. That Packet Station ambition triggered a plan to build a Pier, Breakwater and Graving Dock, with the proposed dry-dock earmarked for Mutton Island. In accommodating that project, Mr. Roberts – as County Surveyor – was responsible for building a new line of road from Claddagh Quay to Fair Hill. He furthermore offered his services to Galway's Relief Committee, which was involved in Miss Frances Grattan's famine road, that became an extension of the Pier and Breakwater thoroughfare, by linking Fair Hill to King's Hill at Salthill. Paid 'relief' employment on both schemes saved many from the workhouse, though the ambition that fuelled Galway's great Packet enterprise was not to be fulfilled. Mr. Roberts' earlier experience of constructing and coping Salt Hill's sea-road, would have been advantageous to his direction of Miss Grattan's strand-road enterprise, which was viewed as a great addition to the town's resort. The story of Grattan Road is told in greater detail in the Famine Road chapter of this book.

Mr. Anthony O'Flaherty told a Town Grand Jury meeting in 1864 that Mr. Roberts' £100 salary was too small. That realisation was sharpened when Mr. O'Flaherty learned that the leading engineer in the town was in fact 'nominally' receiving a salary from the Town Commissioners. Payment had been offered him, but Samuel had declined it. The Grand Jury consequently felt it 'a pleasure as well as an act of justice to increase his salary by £90 a year.'[21] Apart from his work on the Claddagh to Salthill line, Samuel U. Roberts was also involved in improving the Headford Road. A far-seeing man, who was most industrious in pursuing Packet Station status for Galway, Mr. Roberts was also behind the delivery of the first Ladies' Beach at Salthill. That facility, constructed behind George's Baths **(figs. 76 & 77)** in 1864, was unfortunately destroyed by a storm five years later.

On a broader canvas, Samuel is recorded as architect/engineer to an 1863 Ballynahinch project, which involved a 'New Tudor Gothic club house, hotel and 4 lodges to be erected.'[22] It is not clear, however, if that work was ever executed.[23] Some years later, Mr. Roberts, along with James Franklin Fuller, was responsible for the building of Kylemore Abbey. While the input ratio of Fuller and Roberts to that stately project is disputed, Anne Lavin, a conservation architect and past-pupil of Kylemore, believes that Roberts was the lead man. In that assertion, Ms. Lavin quotes from the work of local historian, Kathleen Villiers-Tuthill, who, in her 2003 publication, *History of Kylemore Castle & Abbey*, attributed 'the plans and overseeing of construction solely to Roberts.'[24] One of S.U. Roberts' later designs appeared in an 1894 Congested Districts Board tender for a '9-span lattice girder bridge on screw pile piers over Gweebarra estuary with approach roads.'[25] That challenging Donegal construction indicates the breath of Mr. Roberts' architectural reach throughout the country.

During the summer of 1887, Samuel Ussher Roberts, Commissioner of Public Works, Ireland, was 'nominated by Her Most Gracious Majesty the Queen to the Civil Companionship of the Most Honourable Order of the Bath.' Though Mr. Roberts had departed for Dublin, some fourteen years earlier, news of the regal

56. The start of the prom in the post-1934 period, after the Rockland Hotel (on right) and other commercial buildings were built on ground to the front of the then – newly occupied – Garda station. (Courtesy of National Library of Ireland.)

honour was warmly welcomed in Galway, because, as the *Vindicator* observed, Samuel Roberts' name had been 'associated with every important work of improvement connected with out great County and City.'[26] It was in early January, 1900 that Mr. Samuel Ussher Roberts B.E., C.B. died at his home on Pembroke Street, Dublin.

Salthill Improvement Committees

The 1856 committee, of which Mr. Roberts was secretary, did not represent the sole voluntary effort to improve Salthill during the 19th century. A second committee was formed in the early 1890s, which featured a different focus in seeking the same broad goal.

Bright and bad years were experienced at the resort, depending on factors that ranged from weather to the economic climate of the time. Such variations were locally noted and the summer of 1885, for example, appears to have delivered a good trade, when it was reported that 'lodging houses along the beach seem [to be] doing a good business – the only business apparently left now to the good old "City of the Tribes".'[27] A downturn marked the opening years of the following decade, when the resort, which previously had been 'literally crowded from floor to roof, from cellar to attic' was not doing so well. One commentator observed that the 'personality of the denizens seemed entirely changed, no longer was the spirit of fun amongst them...Those who met my gaze on my last visit to Salthill appeared as if they were there merely as a matter of business.'[28] Blame for the decline was placed, in 1891, on an 'entire lack of energy and the right spirit of enterprise on the part of the inhabitants and lodging housekeepers themselves. Again the lodging house-keepers seem to have taken it into their heads that cynical surliness on their own part and slovenliness and dirt and the discomfort caused thereby to their lodgers, are the only means to induce strangers to come to Salthill.'[29]

Publicly described as a 'very neglected watering place,' concern for Salthill was real and resulted in a new movement emerging, which sought to form a company that would enhance the product available at the resort. A meeting, with Bishop Francis McCormack presiding, was held at Mack's Hotel in Eyre Square, on Thursday, 3 March, 1892. Civil Engineer, Mr. Harris, convened the gathering by 'private circular,' thus ensuring that attendees were hand-picked and prominent Galway citizens. Clergymen were to the fore in the list of attendees: 'The Most Rev. Dr. MacCormack, Lord Bishop of Galway; Rev. Father Greaven P.P.; Rev. Father Dooley, P.P.; Sebastian Nolan, T.M. Kenny, solicitor; John J. Kirwan, W.P. Hennessy, Charles Moon, T. Fogarty, George Mack, P. Corcoran, W.H. Halliday.' Letters of apology for inadvertent absence were received 'from Capt. Waithman, J.P., Merlin Park, Dr. Colahan, J.P., the Villa, Major Hackett, J.P., Rutledge Square, Dublin.' The enterprise was commercial in nature, with Mr. Harris predicting 'a dividend of at least 10 percent' from a Limited Liability Company, which was to boast £25,000 in capital. Apart from those who attended the meeting, the following promised cash contributions: B. Connolly, £100; Martin McDonnell, £50; Joseph Semple, £50; Thomas McDonagh £50; P. Grealy, £50; J.W. Blake, £25; John Redington, £25; J. Howse, £50.'[30] Discussions centred on the possibility of procuring land for the building of lodging and boarding houses, as well as a foreshore area for baths at a moderate price. It was after a second meeting at the same venue that the aims of the proposed company were published:

1. To erect suitable lodging houses.
2. To promote better bathing accommodation.
3. To procure land for the purpose of pleasure grounds; and
4. To make provisions for parties building on the sites.[31]

Mr. Harris, who acted as secretary, was confident that a large return would be made from the speculation. Subsequent meetings were held and more money promised. All the while, criticisms of the resort were appearing in the press, with no apparent advances being made.

The reason for inaction was that the Improvement Committee was keen to purchase a parcel of land – with foreshore if possible – and had set its sights on a field between the Forster Park residence and Rockbarton, which was – after many twists and turns – to become Salthill Park. The sale of the Blake Forster Estate, expected to occur in 1893, was awaited, but it did not take place until 1895. When it did, Major Hackett, at the committee's request, made a private bid for the Cappanaveagh land, but the vendors put it to auction. At that public sale, the largest Cappanaveagh lot was purchased for £800, the sum being paid to the credit of the Blake Forster estate by a group that included 'The Right Reverend Francis Joseph McCormack of Saint Mary's…Roman Catholic Bishop of Galway; The Reverend Patrick Lally of New Road…Parish Priest; John Howes of Sea Road… Gentleman; Joseph Semple of Nile Road…Merchant; Michael Hackett of 5 Lower Sackville Street…Dublin, Solicitor; Bartholomew Connolly of Mainguard Street… Grocer; Alexander Moon of Ardmore, Taylor's Hill…Merchant; and John Harris of Saint Francis Street…Engineer.'[32] The latter gentleman, Mr. Harris, was Honorary Secretary to the Improvement organisation, with the others being committee members. The purchased plot contained 'seventeen acres two roods and six and a half perches statute measure or thereabouts.' Following that purchase, a public meeting at Galway's Courthouse was called, to generate support for the venture.

A poor attendance at the subsequent gathering did not bode well for the Salthill Improvements' drive, and speakers were not shy about voicing their reaction – 'shame and surprise' – at the disappointing turnout. There was special reference made to the shortage of shopkeepers present and the Bishop informed the meeting that he expected ten times the number that attended. The provision of suitable accommodation was central to the committee's purpose. Mr. Harris, in outlining plans for a public company spoke of 'the number of bathing boxes to be erected and also the number of lodging-houses with the possibility of a commodious hotel.'[33] A sum of £5,000 was considered adequate for the proposal with shares at £1 each. Mr. H.M.A. Murphy had already been appointed solicitor to the company and other appointments were pending for the 'Galway and Salthill General Improvements Co. Ltd.'

Advancements were made at the resort during the years that bookended the 19th century, despite deflation at the paltry Courthouse attendance of 1895. In the summer of that same year a Salthill Orchestra Band was formed, which also undertook to build a bandstand at Salthill to facilitate their summer recitals. The temporary but impressive structure was erected 'on the grassy hillock beyond the tram-line terminus at Salthill.'[34] Mr. Robertson, organist of the Jesuit Chapel and Hon. Secretary, Mr. James A. Grant, were prime movers in that enterprise. The Orchestra leader was Mr. Sydney Davies, conductor of the Opera House, Cork. Their musical output ranged from works by Gilbert and Sullivan to Bizet and Hermann. Another positive indicator was the June 1896 running of an attractive and inexpensive Dublin to Galway excursion, which allowed enough time for a visit to the town, the Claddagh and Salthill. The 8 a.m. train from Broadstone Station arrived in Galway at noon, and did not depart until seven in the evening.[35] Improvement to the promenade was also delivered in 1896, by the laying down of a 'kind of concrete of tar, sand and stones similar to that used on some of the streets in Dublin and other cities.'[36] An observer in the following year was happy to acknowledge that the esplanade had been 'asphalted,'[37] and Mrs. Power O'Donoghue, writing in the Lady's Pictorial magazine, noted that 'the fine stretch of sea-walk has been improved and rendered enticing…and footpaths, lighting and hotel accommodation improved.'[38] Some stone seats were replaced by those usually found in public parks, and an 1897 report noted a further bathing booth advancement: 'Most comfortable bathing boxes are now placed on the beach for bathers, which can be made available at any state of the tide, as they are on wheels, and a horse and attendant being in waiting to remove them to any position in the sea that the bather may think suitable or desirable.'[39] Such boxes were primarily for lady bathers, as male swimmers were denied comparable comforts, a fact lamented by a 'departing visitor' in 1896, who complained that 'the poor gentlemen visitors have to stand hail, rain and storm on the Blackrock, a pitiable sight of misery sometimes.'[40] In terms of the foreshore, some progress was made – during the 1890s – on clearing 'unsightly heaps of loose and half sunken beds of stone' from sections of the beach.[41]

For all of that, Salthill was not without its limitations and a landed gentleman from the Tuam area wrote to the *Galway Express* to explain that he had to leave the resort in 1896 because of a 'bad smell.'[42] The disgruntled visitor's letter was copied by the *Tuam Herald*, much to the chagrin of Galway's Town Board, which, in complaining about unfair press coverage, drew the opprobrium of both newspapers on itself.[43] The odour at the resort was caused by decomposing seaweed. Salthill was not then considered to be to the forefront of Ireland's marine resorts, and an 1899 report indicated as much: …'there was not even a place of security where a bather could place his or her clothing, and that when dressing, or undressing, they were exposed to the public gaze…not a single house in Salthill had half as many lodgers as they could accommodate. The class of people who come now to Salhill are only those who cannot afford to go…bathing where every consideration is paid to their welfare. In almost every other watering place in Ireland, the comfort of the visitors is looked after, but Salthill is like the forlorn babe in the fairy tale, without a friend to cast a glance of pity on its condition.'[44]

So, it had come to pass that the paltry meeting attendance of 1895 was, indeed, a portent of what was to follow. Despite the efforts of a dedicated committee, made up of leading citizens, public support for its ambitious venture was never sufficient to achieve the goals desired. Subsequent complications stifled progress. The Improvement Committee's land bank was let for grazing, and in 1905 it was jointly purchased by committee members, Mr. T. A. Costello and Mr. B. Connolly, for the original figure of £800. Mr. Costello, in a later *Connacht Tribune* interview, reproached the people of Galway for not improving the facilities at Salthill. The real purpose of his 1909 press contribution was to announce that the former Improvement Committee lands at Salthill, of which he was still co-owner, were for sale. Mr. Costello explained that the committee had worked assiduously for seven years, but that their improvement plans had to be shelved, when the necessary share money did not materialise. In 1909, the Salthill plot was 'available for any private enterprise or speculation in the way of building.'[45]

The owners of the property were men of public standing in the town: Mr. Bartholomew Connolly, a successful merchant, resided for a time at Norman Villas, Lower Salthill, and later at Ely Place, the Crescent. Mr. Connolly, who carried on his business at the Connaught Buildings in Mainguard Street, died at 'Warbracken House' on Sea Road in 1922. Mr. Thomas Abraham Costello, who lived on Taylor's Hill, was a 'Flour Merchant, who traded at Victoria Place,' and was a well known and respected member of the Urban Council. Of Galway pedigree, Thomas was the son of the man who – in 1820 – had started the town's only tobacco factory,[46] 'whose spinners produced a twist tobacco.'[47] Mr. T. A. Costello, who ran unsuccessfully as a Sinn Féin candidate in the local elections of 1920, was father to Captain Costello of the Royal Army Medical Corps and Lieutenant Gabriel Patrick Costello of the Royal Irish Regiment. The latter, Gabriel, was killed in action at the Dardanelles, in Gallipoli, on 16 August, 1915. Though two of his sons wore British uniforms during the

1914–1918 war, another scion, Charles, spent time in jail for his actions against British forces during the War of Independence.[48] It was the Easter Rising of 1916 that prompted the boys' father to follow a Republican path, and up to his death in 1930, Mr. Thomas Costello remained an ardent follower of Éamon de Valera. The Galway merchant was 83 years old on his passing.

Both Costello and Connolly, the joint owners of the Improvement property at Salthill, offered to sell their portion to the other, but agreement was not reached, and Mr. Connolly sold his share to Urban Council trustees in 1912. It therefore turned out that by 1913 the land was owned by Mr. Costello and the Urban Council, with part of it leased to Martin McGrath for £14 per annum.

The creation of a public park at Salthill was an idea long mooted in the town, but eventually acted upon by the Urban Council in the 1912–1914 period. Annually hosted at Eyre Square during Race Week was a summer Bazaar whose proceeds generally went to a chosen charity. On learning that profit from the 1913 event was to be 'devoted to the further development of Salthill as a health and pleasure resort,' the *Connacht Tribune* described the Bazaar of that year as being 'unique.'[49] The purpose was to enhance a place that Father Travers called 'Galway's gold-mine.'[50] In listing advances at the resort, prior to that summer event, the difficulty of congestion on the promenade, particularly during band recitals, was also noted. It was felt that the creation of a public park on the Improvement land would alleviate pressure on the prom, and boost the attraction of the place. Another aim was to provide a pier at Salthill, which turned into an annually debated, but never delivered dream.[51]

The idea of Salthill as a summer fête beneficiary belonged to Mr. Joseph Young. The bazaar that year was initially intended as a fundraiser for a coveted Catholic Cathedral in the town. Bishop O'Dea, however, facilitated the resort's cause by postponing his Cathedral event to the following year. The bishop's consideration extended an Episcopal interest in Salthill's development, by representing a continuation of Rev. Bishop McCormack's role in the 1890's improvement drive. The 1913 Salthill fête was officially opened by Bishop O'Dea, and the contributions of Rev. Father Travers and Stephen Faller were highly valued. The Bazaar Committee was top heavy with people of influence in the town, and its members, under Chairman Mr. Martin McDonogh, included: Rev. Father Travers, Messrs. Crowley, Young, Faller, Donnellan, Campbell, McDonnell, Flaherty, St. George and Dillon. Mr. James Redington was appointed secretary and the following were co-opted onto the working committee: Messrs. M. Tighe, M. Campbell, A.J. Roche, P.J. Byrne, Thomas Kenny, Martin Hynes, P.J. Boland, and T. N. Redington.

The only shadow on the event was Galway's 1913 strike, when builders' labourers demanded 18s. a week in wages and dock labourers asked for a shilling a day rise on their 5s.-6d. *per diem* rate. The Woollen Mills lay idle, Messrs. McDonogh were suffering daily, and ships were held up at the docks. In consequence, over 100 extra policemen were drafted into the town and it was estimated that 600 men were refusing to work.[52] In terms of the Bazaar, the work stoppages 'delayed the project and hampered its progress.'[53] Having said that, the event, which featured a good number of stalls, proved to be a great success. Mr. Toft provided both entertainment and cash, which added to the committee's takings. When Secretary James Redington presented his report, a very credible profit of £521 6s. 1d. had been achieved. Almost every shopkeeper in the town had supported the effort, with the exception of Lipton's, a failure that was duly noted and commented on.

It was the combination of circumstances at play, over the 1912–1914 period, that resulted in pressure being put by the Council on Mr. Costello, one of its members, to sell his portion of the Salthill property. Not happy with the price offered, Mr. Costello refused, and calls were made for compulsory purchase, before costly and detailed arbitration was eventually entered into. Mr. Llewellyn L. Meyrick of the Local Government Board was appointed as arbitrator, and it was in January 1914 that his decision was announced at an Urban Council meeting: The price of the 'Salthill Park' field was fixed at £475, with Mr. Costello to receive £237 and the Council the balance.[54] The award was accepted and the way was cleared to provide a public park at the resort. The development of Salthill Park, however, was to take some time, due to a conflux of early 20th century circumstances, which were both international and domestic in nature. The outbreak of the First World War, in the year of the arbitration agreement, was not to be the sole brake on Salthill's betterment.

Improvement at the resort – throughout the 20th century – was to represent the aim of a litany of organisations, whose sole objective was to make Salthill better. The Salthill Improvement Organisation was to be briefly revitalised in 1909, to be followed by the Salthill Development Association (S.D.A.) in 1934, and a hybrid Galway Corporation – S.D.A. construct; the Salthill Development Committee (S.D.C.), in 1938. Both of the latter groups were joined by the Salthill Citizens' Organisation (S.C.O.) in 1941, leaving three bodies representing the place for a short time. The demise of the S.C.O. in the early 1950s resulted in the setting up of the Salthill Tourist and Development Association, whose initial meeting was held in October, 1959, with officers being elected in January 1960. Galway/Salthill Fáilte was created in 1968 to run the Leisureland project, which opened in 1973. The *bâton* for improving the resort is carried by **The Village Salthill** today; a full 162 years after Salthill's first Improvement Committee began the first leg of an enhancement relay effort that is still running......

A review of the contributions made by 20th century Salthill bodies must await a future volume of this history.

Chapter 6

SALTHILL: WHAT'S IN A NAME?

Salthill, for many, conjures up sparkling images of summer; Blackrock swims, prom strolls, and ice cream cones. The place's very name reflects an ethereal quality, a sense of fleeting joy, and the name, like the village itself, is quite young.

Bóthar na Trá, the area's Gaelic name is older and more easily explained. In the past, as the people of *Cois Fharraige* reached Knocknacarra Cross, they had, as they still do today, a choice of two routes to Galway town. Going straight ahead offered the shortest route along the High Road and part of that road – 'Taylor's Hill' – is still called *Bóthar Ard* as Gaeilge today **(figs. 57 & 58)**. Turning right at the cross presented *Bóthar na Trá*, the beach road skirting the sea to town. It may well have been a one-way system, for laden carts from the west most likely took the more direct downhill route to town, while westbound vehicles would have been inclined to choose the flatter, less challenging – though longer – seaside route home.

The townlands that comprise Salthill also carry rooted identities. Attithomasrevagh, for example, which defines Rockbarton is *the Place of Grey Thomas' house*, Cappanaveagh which includes Dalysfort Road is the *Plot of the Ravens*, while Lenaboy that houses Salthill Village is *the marshy (yellow) meadow*. Such original Gaelic names, some of which only now surface in deed documents, carry little relevance today.

In relation to Salthill's townlands, Dr. T.S. Ó Máille's comprehensive study of 'Place Names from Galway Documents'[1] traced *Capneyvaugh* back to 1557; *Athey Thomas Reagh* (1609); *Leneboyes, Pollioomy and Cloghahiske* (1657); *Kilcorky* (1691) and *Tiefgarriff* (1709). Mr. John O'Donovan – during the late 1830s – gave both the Gaelic form of each townland's name and its translation, in his Ordnance Survey Field Name Books.

Figure 57.

Salthill: What's in a Name?

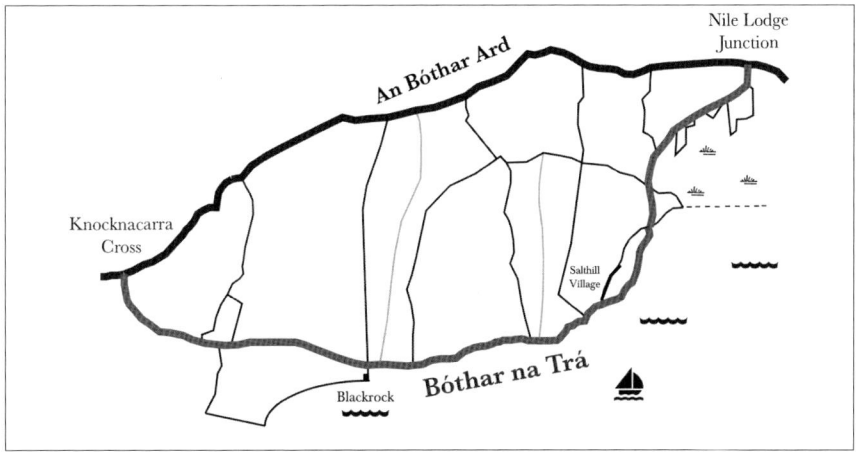

Above 58. *An Bóthar Ard agus Bóthar na Trá.*

Right Figure 59.

Salthill Townlands' Translation

Standard Name.	Irish Form.	Translation.
Attythomasrevagh	Áit Tighe Thomáis Riabhach	Site of Grey Thomas's house
Cappanaveagh	Ceapach na bhFiach	Plot of the ravens
Cloghatisky	Cloch a Toisce	Stone of the treaty
Kilcorkey	Cill Corcaighe	St. Corkey's church
Lenaboy	Léine Bhuidhe	Yellow meadow (wet)
Pollnarooma	Poll na Rúma	Hole of the room or chamber
Teevgarriff	Taobh Garbh	Rough side

It is, indeed, instructive to see well known Galway place names, including *Rahoone*, *Leneboy* and *Shantallow*, appear on Petty's *Hiberniae Delineatio* map, originally published in 1685. The 'Salthill' name cannot boast of such a long legacy, for it is a relatively new entity. According to Ó Máille it was first noted on the Tithe Applotment Books of 1834 and Salthill Village was first recorded in Griffith's 1855 Valuation. Surprisingly, between those particular dates, Salthill merited no mention in Lewis's *Topographical Dictionary of Ireland*, nor indeed in his accompanying Atlas (1837).

This study has found, however, that 'Salt hill near Galway' was noted in October, 1809 as the venue for the marriage of 'the Hon. Charles Ffrench, eldest son of the Right Hon. Lord Ffrench, to Maria, eldest daughter of John Browne, Esq. of Moyne, in the county Galway.'[2] That wedding, which took place on 29 September, 1809 was an all-Galway affair as the groom, Baron Ffrench, belonged to Castle Ffrench in the Kilosolan parish of the Kilconnell barony. The celebrant was the Right Rev. Dr. Nicholas Joseph Archdeacon, Roman Catholic Bishop of Kilmacduagh. A report of that social item, initially carried by the *Dublin Evening Post*, was later relayed by a number of regional British newspapers, and represents the first published record

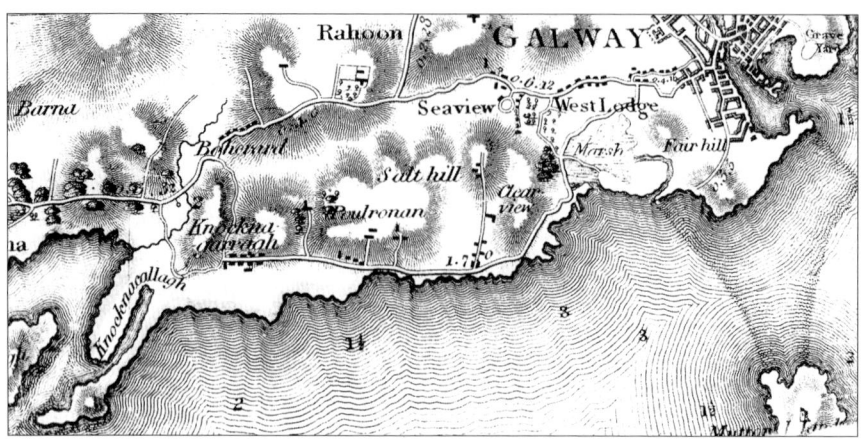

60. William Larkin's Map (1819).

of Salthill – in a Galway context – discovered by this research. While the British Archives retain a document recording that a seafarer, George Fallon, 'was born at Salt-Hill in the County of Galway' in 1788, it is not certain that the place name was in use at the time of George's birth. The reason for uncertainty is that the archived certificate was completed when the 57 year old – black haired and dark skinned – seaman was among the mariners to be 'ticketed in 1845,' the first year of a British ticket system that enabled a seaman carry with him a note of his service and character. Though Salt-Hill was reasonably well established as a name by the time of that mid-nineteenth century British record, it is doubtful that Salt-Hill was in use at the time of George's 1788 birth.

Ambrose Leet was the first to record 'Salt-hill' as a village in his 1814 Directory[3] and the place name's first cartographic record, to be identified by this research, appeared in Larkin's Map of Galway. Salthill's inclusion by William Larkin confirms the name's status in 1819, and its printed position on his map casts fresh light on its origin.

In Larkin's map, the single line of seaside houses that came to identify Salthill village was not represented, indicating that the name predates that building line. The *Salt hill* script, unlike today, was defined by two distinct words, and that particular spelling style persisted throughout much of the 19th century. The handwritten Tithe Books of 1834, however, featured the conjoined version of modern use, reflecting a spelling inconsistency during the early years of the place-name's use in Galway. The *Salt hill* calligraphy – on Larkin's chart – runs from the present Threadneedle Road along by the current Pearse Stadium site, to the left of a byway that is now called Dalysfort Road. The place name is written beneath symbols which Larkin used to describe 'hills and rising ground.' The identity of the 'hill' in Salthill, therefore, represents either the broad incline from *Bóthar na Trá* to *an Bóthar Ard*, or more specifically the hill at Dalysfort, which was not then so called, as landowner Isaac B. Daly did not complete his fine eponymous house until the early 1860s. *Scoil Íde* now stands, atop the hill, on the original site of Mr. Daly's impressive 19th century residence.

An 1867 newspaper piece points to the rise from the sea-front to Boherard as the 'hill' in Salthill: 'The Hill is dotted with villas of great architectural beauty, many of which could be engaged for the season.' The villas in question would have included the fine bathing lodges that then 'dotted' Rockbarton, most of which were 'triumphs of the architectural genius of our eminent local engineer, Mr. Roberts...Looking towards the hill, the Convent of the Dominican Nuns, Lenaboy Castle and the many other seats of our local merchants and gentry, all nicely situated, and the grounds wooded and beautifully laid out.'[4] Such a description, and Larkin's positioning of the *Salt hill* script, strongly suggest that the ascending ground to Taylor's Hill is what is represented in the resort's place name.

Whatever about the precise placing of the hill, the Salt Hill name caught on and came to describe a much wider area. An 1828 *Connaught Journal* report on Galway improvements cited Salthill,[5] while – as Ó Máille recorded – the Tithe Applotment Books included Salthill and Salthill East. The latter pair of 'new' place names appear to have replaced Cappanaveagh and Attithomasrevagh in the Applotment records. This suggests that, in the early 1830s, an area stretching from the present day Burrenmount, beside the Bon Bon, to the Salthill Hotel on the Prom was described as Salthill.

Furthermore, John O'Donovan's Field Books proclaimed that 'Salt Hill is the name given to all those neat Bathing Lodges on the road which is along the sea shore from Galway to Barna.'[6] Ordnance mapped in 1839 was a single row of houses, with their backs to the sea, that spread from the current Post Office, beside the Bal, to Seapoint. That row was later recorded in Griffith's Valuation (1855) as the 'Village of Salthill.' The 'new' name had by then stretched to describe a broader and growing community. Tellingly, a 1909 *Connacht Tribune* advertisement for the sale of Wave View Lodge, described the position of the property 'at Lenaboy now called Salthill,'[7] confirming the relative novelty of the Salthill name as late as the early 1900s.

The Who? and Why? of Salthill's naming.

Salthill is, of course, not an original but an imported name of hitherto unclear origin. There has not been – thanks to the survival of the *Bóthar na Trá* designation – any Galway attempt to forcibly translate Salthill into Gaelic. One suspects that, to a modern sensibility, a corrupted *Cnoc an tSalainn* would not sound – or read – right, even though that particular Irish appellation is employed in the Dublin suburbs. Like Grey Thomas of Rockbarton or Pádraic Carter of Cappanaveagh, the person who – circa 1800 – first named Galway's Salthill has long faded from memory.

This study's first instinct was to surmise that he – or she – might well have hailed from the country that boasts a number of areas, which carry the selfsame place name. England is home to a Salt Hill Cricket club and Salt Hill cider. Berkshire boasts a Salt Hill district to the West of Greater London, with the name derived from Montem Mound, an ancient bank of earth. When the *Irish Times* reported in 1879 that the Countess of Albany and her poet lover, Vittorio Alfieri, 'saw Herschel's observatory at Salthill,'[8] it was the Slough area of Berkshire that was then described. In the North West of England, Salt Hill limestone quarry is to be found in Lancashire. Dublin's Salthill has its own Dart Station, though our suburb unfortunately lost – as World War One closed in 1918 – the most westerly tram terminus in the whole of Europe.

The second of this study's hypotheses focused on the possibility of the Salthill brand arriving – via Dublin – to Galway from English origin, for Ireland's capital city boasted a Salthill area from 1766, if not earlier. Salthill, Merrion Village, Seapoint, Sandymount and Blackrock have long represented neighbouring districts within a neat south-side Dublin cluster. In a local context, Sandymount identified an 1839 two storey house on the site of Salthill's present day Garda Station, while Galway's Merrion Village was recorded at Lower Salthill in 1855. Whatever about the parallel Salthill, Sandymount, Merrion, and Seapoint titles, Ballynacarrickadoo – *Baile na Carraige Duibhe* – identified a house cluster *clachán* from time immemorial, at the end of what became Salthill's Promenade. It is certain that Galway's Blackrock is a translation from native Gaelic – and not a borrowed name.

A Conyngham factor.

Looking north, however, Donegal offers a more compelling source for Galway's Salthill name, for *Tír Chonaill* boasts its own Salthill House at Mountcharles, with wonderful gardens on show. A sizable 650 acre townland, in which the village of Mountcharles is sited, was originally known as *Tamhnach an tSalainn* – a saline field, which, before foreign settlement, described a section of land that retained salt after sea-flooding. During the Plantation of Ulster, that land holding fell into the hands of a Conyngham family of Scottish descent. Rev. Alexander Conyngham, who arrived in the early 17th century, was the first of his family in Ireland and became 'the first protestant minister of Enver and Killymard in the county of Donegal.'[9] It was following the colonisation of the area that English-language place names – Mountcharles and Salthill – gained currency. The Mount Charles designation is believed by some to honour the 1666 knighthood of Sir Albert Conyngham – a son of the pioneering clergyman – by King Charles II. Other folklore takes on the name tie it to the Jacobite Bonnie Prince Charlie of Scotland, or to a local man, 'Charles Conyngham, *tiarna talún*.'[10]

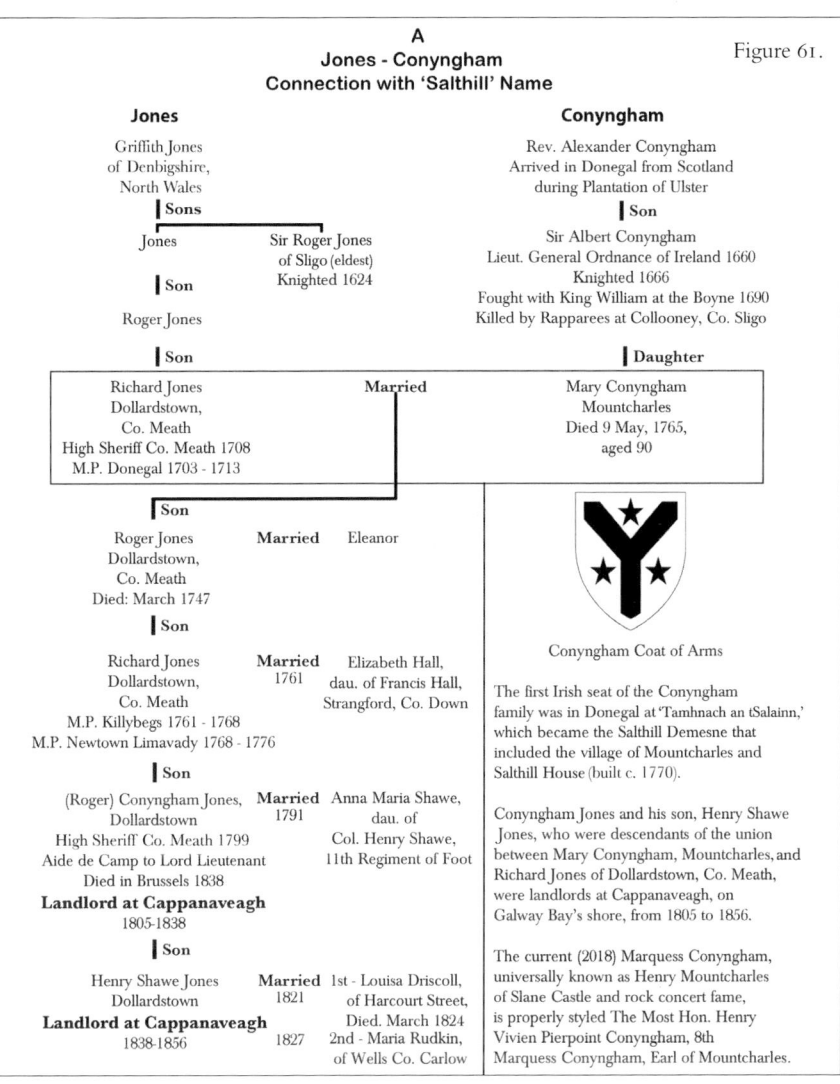

Figure 61.

A fine Conyngham home – built c.1770 – stands on a rise overlooking land that was, betimes, inundated by the sea. That Donegal residence came to be called Salthill House and archival Gaelic records note that '*Tamhnaidh an tSallainn* – Field of the Salt' or 'Tawneytallen'[11] were used to describe Conyngham's Salthill Demesne. The Conyngham family of Mount Charles went on to hold further lands in counties Clare and Meath and by 1876 'the Conynghams owned lands in Co. Donegal (122,300 acres), Co. Clare (27,613acres), Co Meath (7,060 acres) and Kent (9,737acres).' At the present time (2018), the man nationally known as Henry Mountcharles – of Slane Castle and rock concert fame – is properly titled the Most Hon. Henry Vivien Conyngham, 8th Marquess Conyngham, Earl of Mountcharles.

The knighted Albert Conyngham, who had been appointed Lieutenant-General of the Ordnance in the Kingdom of Ireland in 1660, raised – at his own expense – a regiment of dragoons and joined King William at the Battle of the Boyne in 1690. He was subsequently killed by Rapparees near Collooney, Co. Sligo.[12] One of Sir

Figure 62.

Albert's daughters, Mary Conyngham, married Richard Jones of Dollardstown, County Meath,[13] thereby creating a Conyngham – Jones union **(fig.61)**. A Donegal-Meath bond was also created by that marriage, for the groom, Richard Jones, who was High Sheriff for County Meath in 1708, also served as M.P. for Donegal – from 1703 to 1713. Richard's grandson – another Richard – was to later represent Killybegs as a Member of Parliament (1761–1768).

By the early 1800s, Roger Conyngham Jones of Dollardstown, Co. Meath, Lieutenant 4th Dragoons, was landlord at Cappanaveagh, two miles from Galway town. On discarding Roger, his Christian name, Conyngham Jones became his signature title. This shortened moniker highlighted his Conyngham pedigree, in an age when many landed families wished to add prestige to their standing by adding distinguished marriage titles to their own.

It was in 1805 that 'the Warden and Vicars of the King's College of Galway… demised unto Conyngham Jones all that and those the town and Lands of Cappanaveagh situate in the west Liberties of Galway.[14] That conveyance resulted in Conyngham Jones and subsequently his only son, Henry Shawe Jones, filling the landlord role at Cappanaveagh from 1805 to the sale of that holding in 1856. A briny brand had long identified the Conyngham family's Salthill demesne in Donegal, a holding that Conyngham Jones would have been familiar with, for both his father and great-grandfather had, as Members of Parliament, represented Donegal constituencies in which the Conyngham demesne stood. It is plausible, therefore, that on the acquisition of his Cappanaveagh property, Conyngham Jones introduced to Galway the 'Salthill' place name that was identified with his Conyngham heritage. Mr. Thomas Henry Barton would – in a similar fashion – later stamp his surname on the neighbouring Attithomasrevagh townland.

A tight time frame supports the Conyngham naming scenario here presented. While the anglicised 'Tawnaghtallan' (*Tamhnach an tSalainn*) name was noted as early as 1620, it was 1801 before the English 'Salthill' translation was so documented at Donegal.[15] Conyngham Jones became landlord at Cappanaveagh in 1805 and by this research's finding, 'Salthill near Galway' first appeared in print in 1809. It is also significant that the Tithe Applotment Books of 1834 did not list Cappanaveagh and Attithomasrevagh holdings, for those two local townlands were, as earlier indicated, replaced by newly named divisions – Salthill East and Salthill. That renaming occurred during Conyngham Jones' tenure in the place. The Cappanaveagh townland boasted strong connections with the 'Wardyn and Vicairs' of St. Nicholas' Church from 1557,[16] and a church advowson formed part of an 1845 lease renewal by Henry Shawe Jones,[17] who served as a warden at the same church. Such parochial church ties may have played a part in the Tithe records' inclusion of the Salthill name in 1834, a development that gave the 'new' title official church status. A Conyngham-Jones influence cannot, therefore, be discounted in the placing of a name – of Donegal origin – on seaside property at Galway.

Whereas the northern Salthill demesne faced onto Donegal Bay, the western Conyngham Jones' holding overlooked Galway Bay. A feature of Conyngham Jones' Cappanaveagh holding was, as previously detailed, the presence of two saline loughauns on the land-side of *Bóthar na Trá*. The eastern Cappanaveagh pool was described in 1839 as 'Loughaun Patrick' or 'Loughaun – Phadrick Carter,' while its sister pond, which was simply called 'Loughaun,' stretched into Attithomasrevagh. Both of those pools stood on low-lying land at the foot of rising ground, a replica of the Donegal topography which led to the 'Salthill' name being adopted by the Conyngham family at Mount Charles. Figure 27, in the 'Finding One's Bearings' chapter of this book, offers a representation of Cappanaveagh's saline loughauns in areas that are still prone to flooding at Salthill. Just as the honorific 'Mountcharles' title – of Conyngham provenance – travelled from Tirconell's Salthill to Slane in County Meath, might the Salthill place name have been transported southward to Galway?

There is no doubt but that a clear Conyngham connection stretched from Donegal's Mountcharles – through Meath's Dollardstown – to Cappanaveagh in the West Liberties of Galway. The early 19th century adoption of a 'Salthill' brand on the edge of Galway town, during the Cappanaveagh tenure of Conyngham Jones, strongly points to a Donegal source for a name that has, ever since, described Galway's marine resort. Though the salty signature was 'imported' into Galway's hinterland, it is important to remember that – in a Donegal context – the origin of the Salthill name was not a completely alien imposition, but a loose translation of a native Gaelic place name, *Tamhnach an tSalainn*.

It also appears that the Salt Hill name surfaced in Galway around the time that the area first embraced a tourism enterprise. In the great scheme of things, it must be said, that neither the name, nor the village it came to describe, are all that old.

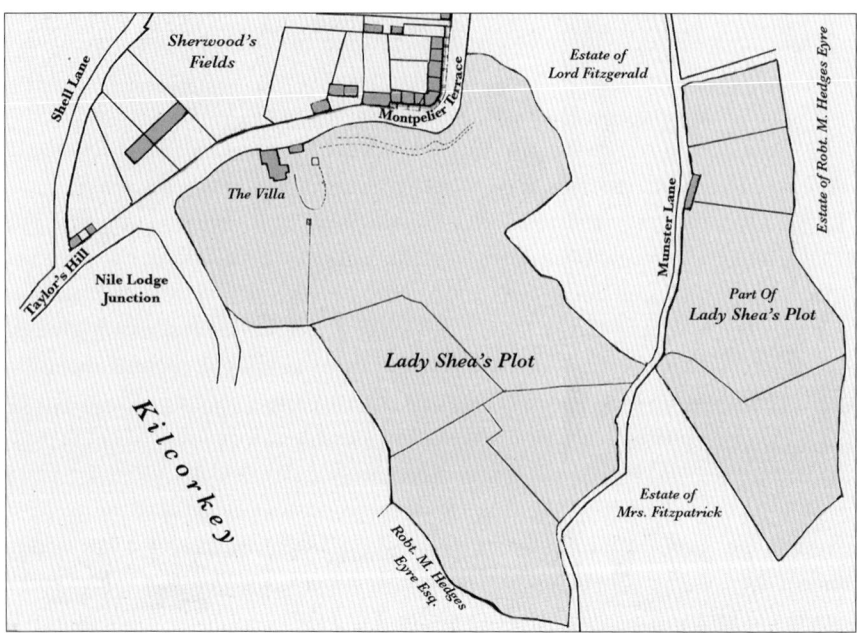

63. Nile Lodge's hinterland featured Shell Lane, Sherwood's Fields, Montpelier Terrace and Lady Shea's Plot.

Curious Place Names in Salthill's Hinterland.

A number of place names at the entrance to Salthill – in Nile Lodge's hinterland – are quite intriguing. A short stroll, from the Jesuit Church to Nile Lodge, requires the traversing of Ely Place, Sea Road, Montpelier Terrace, Devon Place and the Crescent, which included five Albert Terrace premises in 1855, before being officially tagged Palmyra Crescent. Excepting the logical Sea Road naming, which represents an approximate translation of *Bóthar na Trágha*, one wonders if the other titles in that cluster were fanciful adornments, or the product of real connections between property owners / house builders / residents, and the places commemorated in such place names. It is more likely, however, that – similar to Salthill – they were borrowed monikers from another jurisdiction, for not one of the above place names is unique to Galway.

Montpelier or Montpellier?

'Montpelier,' for example, appears to be a curious choice for an 1840's house terrace on the western edge of Galway town, even though similarly named house rows were then to be found at both Cork and Brighton. The terrace at Sea Road was not completed in one lot, for Mr. James Davis, a Shop Street merchant, had two 'new'

Figure 64.

houses bearing the same address, available for letting in June, 1854.'[18] The earliest newspaper reference to Galway's residential row, discovered by this study, was spelt 'Montpelier' in 1848,[19] though a double '**L**' 'Montpellier' form appeared in 1851.[20] That spelling inconsistency has persisted at Galway ever since. Though the disparity arose, most likely, from subjective choices, it does raise the question of whether the terrace was named in honour of 'Montpellier,' the southern French town, or another 'Montpelier' location. Montpelier is the name of: (a) a Galway townland in the parish of Athenry, and (b) a County Limerick village. The same title also identified the Virginia estate of James Madison (1751–1836), the 4th President of America (1809–1817), who was hailed as the 'Father of the American Constitution,' and died during the decade preceding the building of Galway's Sea Road terrace. Is it possible – one wonders – that Mr. John Whaley, who owned Sherwood's Fields where the house row was built, was an admirer of President Madison, in the style of the local Persse family's infatuation with George Washington?

The naming of Galway's Montpelier Terrace may, however, have boasted more banal ties to home, for Dublin's famed Hell Fire Club was sited at Montpelier Hill. Closely identified with that legendary hillside club were members of the Whaley family, and it is, therefore, not inconceivable that a disreputable club for tearaway gentry was memorialised in the naming of Galway's Sea Road Terrace. The definitive truth behind the name choice – despite such conjecture – remains lost to the past.

Whether or which, the 19th century spelling inconsistency has prevailed to the present day, with public signage in 2018 parading 'Montpellier,' and a terrace residence featuring 'Montpelicr.'

Shell Lane

Figure 65.

In a Galway lady's will, which was drawn up on 10 September 1883, some place names that have since faded from local lore, were included. The lady was 'Eliza Killian of Kilcorkey,' who gave and bequeathed 'unto Ada Craughwell of Kilcorkey aforesaid the plot of ground and five small houses thereon at Shell's Lane in the

County of the Town of Galway known as Sherwoods fields held by me under lease.' While Shell Lane may have disappeared from Galway's *lingua franca*, the Gaelic form of that traditional name remains in use on public signage. The older title is believed to have derived from the shells of the lane's hinterland, which were deposited by the sea before the 1860's building of Grattan Road. *Sliogán* is an Irish word for shell. That ancient thoroughfare also bore an older title, according to historian, Rev. J. Rabbitte, who recorded in the early 1920s that 'what is now Shell Lane was called by old people "An tSean-Voher," i.e. the old road.'[21]

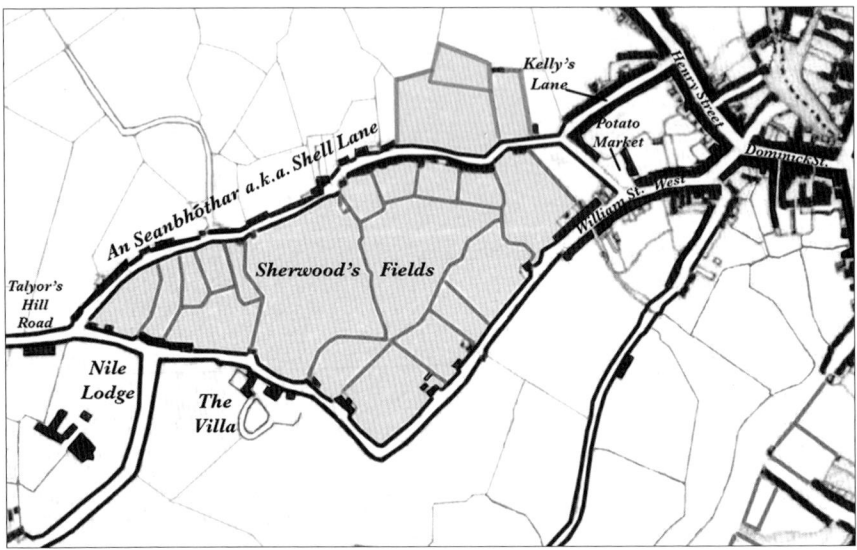

66. *An Seanbhóthar* a.k.a. Shell Lane ran – for the most part – to the north of Sherwood's Fields, which are here shaded. A further three of Widow Sherwood's fields were to the north of Shell Lane, near the point where *An Seanbhóthar* segued into Kelly's Lane – St. Joseph's Avenue today.

When Nile Lodge corner was a T junction – before the construction of the New Line / St. Mary's Road – a*n Seanbhóthar* was quite a busy route. The reason for significant traffic through-flow was that those using *an Bóthar Ard* to reach town – be they locals or *Cois Fharraige* natives – had a choice to make at the bottom of Taylor's Hill. Travelling straight ahead past Nile Lodge junction, and turning left for town at what became Montpelier Terrace, presented both a wide road and somewhat circuitous route. The alternative was to turn left off Taylor's Hill onto Shell Lane and continue on to Kelly's Lane – St. Josesph's Avenue today – before arriving at Henry Street. While that *Seanbhóthar* option was quite narrow, it did offer a sloped and marginally more direct route to town. The same 'sean-voher' was known in the distant past as 'The Highway to Kilcorkey,'[22] which suggests that Shell Lane was a good deal older than the thoroughfare we now know as Sea Road.

Widow Sherwood

Described in 1840 as Widow Sherwood's Fields,[23] the size of figure 66's shaded holding – on the edge of Galway town – would suggest that a family of substance lent its name to it. Thomas Sherwood, for example, was elected Sheriff in place of the deceased George Shaw in 1747 and it was – most likely – the same Thomas who acted as Town Clerk of the Town in 1753.[24] Interred on the grounds of St. Nicholas' Collegiate Church are a number of people bearing the Sherwood patronym, while Michael Sherwood, a shoemaker of Eyre Square, stood guarantor for a Poverty Relief Loan in 1845. The recorded presence of the surname in Galway, as well as the 1840 citing of Widow Sherwood, appears to rule out the fantastically remote possibility of a romantic Robin Hood – Sherwood Forest connection with Galway town.

Lady Shea

Lady Shea's plot **(fig.63)** was not that distant from Sherwood's Fields and the Shea family's lineage was traced by Charles Ffrench Blake Forster 'from O'Shee of county Tipperary, who later moved to county Kilkenny.'[25] An esteemed and not uncommon name in County Galway, there were eleven Tithe Applotment 'Shea' – and two 'Shee' – entries for Galway during the 1826–1830 time period. Other Galway listings of the surname included members of the Irish Constabulary, an Irish Church Missions' clergyman, and a Justice of the Peace, Gartside Shea, who was residing in the Clifden area in 1868. In a Galway town context, Timothy Shea was a resident of Sickeen Lane in 1854, with Elizabeth Shea being recorded by Slater as a Spirit Dealer at Fish Market in 1894. The name over Elizabeth's public house door, however, was 'Tim Shea,' as captured in a late 19th century postcard.

67. Tim Shea's public house at Spanish Arch.

Tim Shea's licensed premises formed part of a building that was later associated with Winston Churchill's cousin, Clare Sheridan, who lived a flamboyantly bohemian and artistic life before her 1947 purchase of the property. She was succeeded at the Spanish Arch – in 1953 – by Major Frederick C. Greenwood of Barna Gardens and *An Bhearna*, Kingshill, who did not tarry long, before selling the premises to solicitor William J.V. Comerford in April, 1954. When Mr. Comerford moved to Dublin on retirement, Comerford House / Spanish Arch House was sold to Galway Corporation in 1970. Galway's Museum was first opened in that building on 31 July, 1972 and served the town up to the 2007 opening of the modern construction to its rear, which now represents Galway's artefact repository. The abutting Spanish Arch, incidentally, did not come into public ownership until Galway Corporation's 1970 purchase of Mr. W.J.V. Comerford's holding, which included both house and Arch.

The honorific 'Lady Shea' moniker points to a titled family as the onetime holder of a plot of land on the north-eastern edge of Salthill. While the lady's identity remains elusive, the chances are that she belonged to one of two Galway families, which boasted knighted Shea patriarchs. She may have been wife to Sir James Shee (Shea), who, on a number of occasions, served as Deputy Mayor of Galway, and became the town's first citizen in 1776. He died in January 1793 and was buried in the grounds of St. Nicholas' Collegiate Church.

Alternatively, though less plausible, it is possible that Lady Shea was the wife of Lord Shee (Shea), of Dunmore, Galway, and of Mudeford House, near Christchurch, Dorset. Three ladies carried that Dunmore 'Lady Shea' title and if one of them gave her title to the land bank on either side of Munster Avenue, the most likely of the trio was Miss Elizabeth Maria Crisp (1764–1838), the wife of the first Shea Baronet. She was the daughter of a remarkable woman, Elizabeth Crisp (née Marsh) 1735–1785, who lived the most fantastically full international life, which became the subject of a celebrated 2007 biography by Linda Colley, entitled *The Ordeal of Elizabeth Marsh – A Woman in World History*.[26] It was in 1783 at Hugli, near Calcutta that Elizabeth Crisp married the first Baronet, Sir George Shee (1754–1825) of Castlebar. Eight years later, Sir George, who enjoyed a successful career in India, purchased the Dunmore estate of Ralph Gore, Earl of Ross. The couple also boasted a Stephen's Green address in 1800.[27] While one of the aforementioned titled ladies, with strong Galway connections, appears likely to have been memorialised in the naming of Lady Shea's Plot, such speculation remains inconclusive.

San Antonio Terrace: Argentina not the Alamo!

San Antonio Terrace represents another intriguing place name, this time at Upper Salthill. Though the Texan *San Antonio* of Davy Crockett and Alamo fame is not memorialised by this house row, the background to its naming is no less intriguing. The story begins with Anthony Dominic Fahy – the son of a Loughrea brewer – who was born at that lakeside town in 1805. Anthony was ordained to the priesthood at Rome, where he stayed until returning to Ireland in 1834. His travels did not then end, because he spent time in Cincinnati before taking up a Rector role at Loughrea in 1836. After spells in Mayo and Kilkenny, where he was Prior of the Black Abbey Dominican community, Father Fahy left Ireland for Argentina, arriving in Buenos Aires in 1844. Three years later, at the height of the Great Famine in Ireland, Fr. Fahy wrote to the Archbishop of Dublin, asking that Irish people be advised to emigrate to Argentina. A sum of £441 was also despatched to Dublin from the Irish Relief Fund, which the Galway priest had set up in his new home town. Within a year, an Immigrant Infirmary to serve those arriving in Buenos Aires had been opened by the Loughrea native.

Father Fahy paid for six Irish seminarians at All Hallows' College to be trained as priests for service in Argentina. Among that number was Thomas Mulleady, the son of James Mulleady and Margaret Bannon of Kilcleigh, Moate. Thomas was baptised on 20 January, 1843 and he was one of the first students to attend St. Mel's Day-school, Longford, which he entered in January 1860 and left in August of the following year, to attend All Hallows in Dublin.[28] Following ordination, Father Thomas Mulleady headed to South America and was installed as a chaplain to the Archdiocese of Buenos Aires in 1867. He was to serve for over thirty years in **San Antonio de Areco, Giles and Baradero**, a little over seventy miles to the North West of Argentina's capital city. Father Mulleady was highly regarded and his area of operation included many of the largest *estancieros* in the entire country. An *estancia* was a large Pampas estate where *gauchos* – cowboys – did the work for an *estanciero* – the ranch owner. Through the years that Father Fahy

Figure 68.

and Fr. Mulleady served in Argentina, tracts of Pampas land were being fenced off to create huge grassland farms, measured in hundreds of thousands of acres. *San Antonio De Areco* was a district where the Irish purchased 'splendid estancias… for a mere trifle' in the 1860s that were worth millions of dollars by 1919. 'One of San Antonio's first wealthy Irishmen was Thomas Donohue, who died in 1866…and owned some twelve thousand sheep.'[29]

Donohue's story reflected the extent of *estancieros'* wealth, and by 1900 almost 300 families owned most of the Argentine Pampas.[30] As would be expected, the greatest migration occurred in the years that followed the Great Famine. Interestingly, many of the Irish emigrants, who took the less travelled route to South America, came from Father Mulleady's home counties in Ireland's midlands, with Westmeath, Longford and Offaly being well represented in that migration cohort.

William Brown (1777–1857) of Foxford, County Mayo, the 'father of the Argentine Navy,' is perhaps the best known representative of an Irish presence in Argentina. Sport also created connections, for hurling was played in that far-distant land from the late 1880s. It was in the 1920s that four clubs created the Argentine Federation of Hurling, and the continued existence of the Hurling Club of Buenos Aires – founded in 1922 – gives a cultural clue to the strong ties that existed between the countries. Though the Buenos Aires club now includes rugby and hockey in a broad sporting portfolio, its hurling team played at Pearse Stadium, Salthill, in 2013 – as part of an inaugural International Hurling Festival. A measure of Father Fahy's status in Buenos Aires is the Loughrea priest's ornate Celtic-cross topped tomb in *La Recoleta* Cemetery. Within the walls of that same Argentine graveyard rest the remains of the 'Spiritual Leader of the Nation' – Eva Perón (Evita), and Mayo native, Admiral Brown.

Father Mulleady did not forget his home country and he contributed $1,000 to aid Irish farmers in 1881. A regular donor to causes, including the Irish Infirmary Fund, he was the first chaplain to raise a contribution for a Sisters of Mercy convent at Mercedes, which opened in 1872. Committed to community work, he founded the College of Our Lady in San Antonio in 1901, with the Irish Brothers of Charity (Misericordia).[31] Father Mulleady retired from his South American ministry in 1903 and returned to Ireland. *Los Capellanes Irlandeses,* Monsignor Ussher's book, indicates that Thomas Mulleady served as pastor to a religious community on

69. Monsignor Thomas Mulleady. (S. M. Ussher, *Los Capellanes Irlandeses…*, 1954.)

his return, and the Diocesan Archivist at Longford, Father Tom Murray, believes that Fr. Mulleady most likely acted as chaplain to the Carmelite Convent in Moate.

It appears that the retired clergyman favoured Salthill as a summer retreat, and Fr. Mulleady built a small terrace of three houses at the northern end of Atlantic Terrace. That row, named after the Argentine parish in which he served, is called San Antonio Terrace. Mr. Gabriel Kearney, who today lives in one of those terraced houses, is guardian of the folklore which recollects a clergyman building 'two and a half houses' there, with the small – 'half' – house being reserved for the priest himself. Gabriel's 'two and a half' description is accurate, as is clear to anyone familiar with the San Antonio housing line **(fig.68)**. Mr. Duffy of Athlone, a nephew to Fr. Mulleady, was the man who built the neat property row. Father Thomas did not have that much time to enjoy his retirement, because he died at his sister's house in Moate on 21 September, 1909. The details of the clergyman's will appeared on the *Irish Independent* some months later, and Father Mulleady's personal estate was valued at £3,664. Among his bequests were Galway properties: 'He left his house at Moate and his effects there and his house in Galway, upon trust for his sister Margaret for life, with remainder to his nephews James and John Duffy; house in Galway and £500 to his sister Mary Duffy; house to his nephew, Michael Duffy.'[32] There is little doubt but that the Moate priest was a wealthy man at the time of his death, but he was not unique in that: 'Fr. Samuel Reilly from Longford went to Argentina about the same time as Fr. Mulleady and amassed a fortune, much of which he left to All Hallows' College.'[33]

Very Rev. Monsignor Mulleady was buried at Rosemount Cemetery, three miles northeast of Moate, where an incorrect year of death appears on his head-

70. On left, one of four seated angels at ornate base to an imposing Celtic Cross in memory of Loughrea's Father Fahy at *La Recoleta* Cemetery in Buenos Aires, with a simpler headstone, on right, for Monsignor Mulleady at Rosemount Cemetery in County Westmeath. (Photo on left - Brian Mc Ginley; on right - Paul McGinley.)

stone. The year of the clergyman's retirement was 1903 and Monsignor Thomas lived, as earlier indicated, for a further six years, during which his Salthill terrace – named in honour of an Argentinian parish – was constructed.

Father Thomas Mulleady was not the sole clergyman to have been identified with the house row, for in 1918 Rev. Arthur J. Murray, late of San Antonio Terrace, Salthill, was ordained sub-deacon by His Eminence Cardinal Pompili at the Church of St. John Lutheran in Rome. Father Murray was the son of Mr. P.J. Murray, 1 San Antonio Terrace, who was – for a number of years – the manager of the Galway Woollen Mills and credited with an improvement in that factory's fortunes. A third priest of the Terrace was Father Joseph Holland, who ministered in Mississippi. He was the son of Patrick, a staff member at U.C.G.'s Natural History Department, and Elizabeth Holland. Joseph shared his place of consecration with the man who built the terrace, when he was ordained in 1921 at All Hallows in Dublin. Father Holland was to spend the rest of his working life in America, though he regularly visited home. Father Joseph served as Pastor of Natchez Diocese, Mississippi.

A later priest to be reared in San Antonio Terrace was Father Seán Foy of the Galway Diocese. Seán was the son of Martin Foy, a national school teacher, and Emma Jane Foy (née Cooke) who ran Foy's Boarding house, before selling it in the mid-1950s. Seán was not the only family member to enter religious life, for a sibling, who served at St. Louis' Convent in Newmarket, England, was known as Sister Marie Martine. The Foy family had a strong association with the Father Griffin Football club and Seán, who was a noted athlete, in both the javelin and shot putt, played with Fr. Griffin's in his youth. He attended St. Mary's College, Galway, and entered Maynooth in 1952. During his clerical career he saw service at Camus, London, St. Patrick's, Salthill and Liscannor, Co. Clare, before he was appointed Parish Priest at Moycullen, where he spent eleven years before his death in 2002. His time in London coincided with the spell that Father Éamon Casey – later Bishop of Galway – spent in England's capital city. Seán's love of sport persisted throughout his life, with golf and cards later replacing the athletic pursuits of his earlier career. Father Seán was made a Canon of the Chapter by Bishop McLoughlin in the year before his death, at the Parochial House in Moycullen.

Father Seán Foy was a clergyman with a great, and sometimes roguish, sense of humour. Salthill native and rugby historian, Ralph O'Gorman, recalls the young man as a clerical student, who happened to be at Blackrock one day when Bishop Michael Browne was taking a dip. Gathering the other lads around him – there were no girls allowed there at the time – Seán advised his rapt audience to observe the bishop approach the Atlantic with the unforgettable poser; 'Will he swim in the water or walk on it?'

Fishing Heritage

Chapter 7

SALTHILL'S FISHING TRADITION

James Hardiman in his authoritative *History of Galway* never mentioned Salthill. That is not surprising for though the seaside spot existed from time immemorial, it only adopted its salty designation some years before Hardiman's tome was published in 1820. Galway town itself, according to the Mayo born historian, 'was but an inconsiderable fishing village' before the arrival of Henry II and 'it was then called *Ballinshruane*, or *the town of the little streams*; because when the winter floods were high in the river, the water flowed through the present site of the town.'[1] In 1762 it was reported that the detailed exactions of the corporation were oppressive, injurious to trade and contrary to law and charter: 'that they greatly discouraged the fishery of the bay and harbour, which was one of the best in the kingdom.'[2] By the 1800s, according to Hardiman, the fishermen of Galway Bay, 'particularly those of the Claddagh village, are very numerous, upwards of 2500 hands being employed in the inner bay alone.' They were, however, 'so wedded to old customs' that they were slow to embrace any improvement in fishing methods. It was estimated that the population of the 'ancient village' exceeded '3000 souls' by 1820.[3] The Claddagh fishermen then viewed 'the bay as their exclusive domain, on which, to use their own words, they never admit any trespasser; and therefore, should a single boat from any other district venture out to fish, without the concurrence of the Claddagh body, it does so at the risk of being destroyed.'[4]

It is clear, therefore, that fishing enterprises on Galway Bay depended on a working relationship with Claddagh boatmen. Such concord depended on observance of the rules laid down, and woe betides those who crossed them. John Cunningham, in his chronicle of 19th century Galway town, described the consequence of disobedience, when quoting one 1820 commentator:

The Galway fishermen will not catch the fish themselves, nor will they allow any others to do it; no, they destroy the nets and assault the crews of the boats which come from other quarters to fish in the bay, as if they had an exclusive privilege to the produce of the ocean…

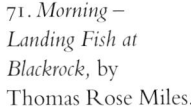
71. *Morning – Landing Fish at Blackrock*, by Thomas Rose Miles.

Thus a Knocknacarra boat was overturned and several others were damaged on a December Sunday in 1836. The occupants gave no information about their attackers 'partly from fear, and partly from an impression that they were wrong to fish on a Sunday.' [5]

One can, from this remove, only wonder if the Claddagh's relationship with Salthill's fisher folk was better than that of the unfortunate Knocknacarra boatmen, who strayed from local sea conventions, as laid down by their town-side neighbours. There is no doubt but that fishing was practiced by the people of Salthill and that lost tradition is captured in a late 19th century painting; *Morning – Landing Fish at Blackrock*.

In a romantically rich image, Thomas Rose Miles, the noted English artist, presents two moored boats unloading their fish at the famed swimming point. Neither remarkable, nor a nod to visual perfection, is the absence of a spring board at the rock, for the board was then but a temporary, seasonal fixture. Red-petticoated women, accompanied by a child, carry the catch away in Miles' evocative image, which also reflects the Claddagh practice of men transferring a haul to their womenfolk. Indeed, the female Blackrock attire of Miles' painting closely resembles that worn by Claddagh women, who were first colour-photographed by Marguerite Mespoulet and Madeleine Mignon, at Galway's famed fishing village in 1913.

A well defined hunter-seller relationship was detailed by Hely Dutton in a piece about Claddagh fishermen and their women folk:

When they are longer at sea than usual, their return is hailed with great joy by their families, ushered into the whiskey shop by their wives, and in a state of intoxication put to bed. The boat is then unladen, and the fish carried to market by the women, who exclusively take possession of it, the husband never interfering, and it is sold to hawkers and women who keep standings in the market. The women pay for every thing, having the complete control of the purse. An instance occurred of a man wishing to keep his own money, but the indignant companions of the wife threatened to burn his house, and actually proceeded to such violence that poor Jerry Sneak was forced to succumb.[6]

To date, there is scant enough documentary evidence of the extent of Salthill's fishing culture, though some newspaper pieces bear testimony to its existence.

An 1861 *Irish Times* report, taken from the *Galway Press*, describes a day of almost biblical bounty on Galway Bay:

> *Large Take of Herrings at Galway.– Our fishermen have benefitted by several large takes of herrings during the week. On Thursday, an immense shoal came in-shore, near Salthill extending from the Baths to Blackrock. The boats of the Salthill Fishermen, who put out to secure the fish, immediately their presence was observed, had the boats filled at the first draft. So close to the shore did the fish come, that the women, by securing baskets to ropes and casting them into the sea, from off Blackrock, pulled them back loaded with fish.*[7]

Such bounty was by times counterbalanced by the sea's ever present danger and a *Tuam Herald* piece recounted the details of a tragic incident off Salthill, when on a stormy October night in 1897 'four men, Peter Doherty and three men named O'Donnell (father and sons) all of Long Walk, were in a boat fishing off Salthill about nine o'clock. The boat was filled with herring, but the men being anxious to take more, commenced to haul in the nets when the craft became overloaded and sank; all hands were drowned.'[8] A *Nenagh Guardian* piece on the same tragedy reported that 'so great is the shoal of herring in the bay that single boats have taken from 26,000 to 30,000 fish in a night.'[9]

Recorder's Quay

Fishing, on any proper scale, required a pier and Salthill organisations throughout the 20th century campaigned for the creation of an adequate berthing facility at the resort. Salthill fishermen of earlier ages, however, used Recorder's Quay for such a purpose. There was a narrow escape for four Claddagh fisherman, who were conveying a new boat 'without ballast' – built at the Claddagh – to Recorder's Quay in 1837. It was the 'third time for one of these four men to escape being drowned'.[10] A late 1830's map of Salthill gives a clear outline of the quay, jutting out from a headland on the seaward side of what was later called King's Hill. That quay's curved head would today stand in the rectangular grassy patch of Claude Toft's public park, somewhere behind the houses that stand to the west of the Galway Bay Apartments. Through time and tide, however, that berthing facility became silted over. Recorder's Quay of official designation also went by a local name; Councillor's Quay. Such divergence between an administrative and colloquial name is not unique in Galway. Locals, for example, never forsook Eyre for the official John Fitzgerald Kennedy name placed on the town's main square. The 'Councillor' title on Salthill's early pier was, ironically enough, invoked by a town Councillor in a 1938 dispute over the ownership of a potential garage site at the bottom of King's Hill, where Kelleher's service station, which opened in the 1950s, currently trades.[11]

Noted as Fair Hill / Recorder's Quay in the Coastguard 'English Head Office Book for Ireland 1845–1862,' it was a busy enough spot during the 19th century.

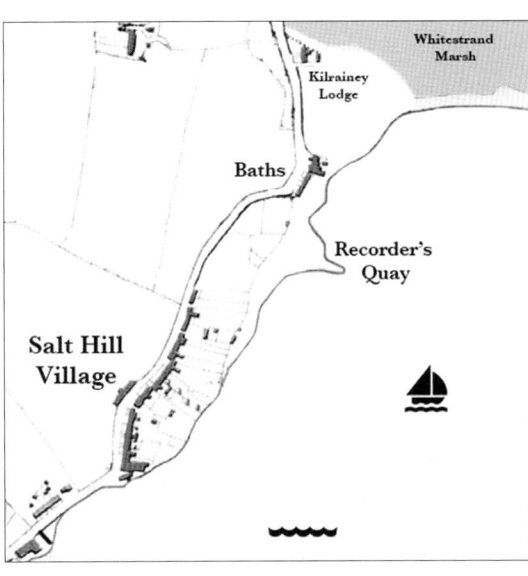

72. Recorder's Quay, 1839.

Serving as a Coast Guard pier, 'Richard Hooper, Esq., Chief Officer of the Coast Guards, Recorder's Quay,' visited men under his charge there in 1843. During that visit, cries were heard of two men who had been thrown into the sea, when their Hooker 'struck on the Black Rock.' The crew members were six hours in the water and Mr. Hooper 'in the most praiseworthy manner immediately had his Boat launched and fortunately succeeded in saving the lives of these poor men.'[12] In June, 1859, a service, which included recreational fishing, was on offer from Salt Hill's quay as a 'convenience for bathers and tourists': 'The Yacht "Black Cat" will be stationed at the Recorder's Quay, Salt Hill, every day from 12 o'clock, Noon, until 9 p.m. for the purpose of conveying persons to any of the towns around the fine harbour. The Yacht is one of the swiftest on the bay. The charges will be moderate so as to afford the people an opportunity of viewing the beauties of the harbour. Fishing gear of every description will be at the command of those on board.'[13] The *Galway Vindicator* described Recorder's Quay in 1861 as 'a place that is visited by many.'[14] That press reference was to the area's attraction as a ladies' bathing haunt.

Records of Salthill's fishing trade

From a fishing perspective, some archival documents do highlight the area's piscatorial tradition. Mr. George Fallon, who was born at Salt Hill in 1788, first went to sea as a fisherman in 1811. A sometime labourer, his 1845 seaman file recorded 57 as his age when 'ticketed.'[15] A September 1853 Petty Court sitting offered further evidence of a vibrant local tradition, when four Salt Hill fishermen were charged with the same offence on the one day. The four were Patt Flaherty, Daniel O'Donnell, Martin Woodhouse and Roger Conneely. The chief boatman of Coast Guards, Anthony O'Flaherty, charged Patt Flaherty with –

> being the owner of a certain boat or vessel engaged in fishing, called the Morning Star, had not the register number assigned to said boat or vessel by the registering officer of the district… painted on the sail of said boat or vessel in figures of such dimensions as the Commissioners

of Public Works in Ireland have in the behalf directed, whereby he has incurred a penalty not exceeding £10-0-0.[16]

The other three were all so charged, with the title of each man's vessel being ascribed: *St. Bridget* was the name of Daniel O'Donnell's boat; *St. Patrick* belonged to Martin Woodhouse, while *The Kate* was Roger Conneely's vessel. All but one paid a five shilling fine for their legal infraction. Roger Conneely's case was dismissed, however, because the fourth Salt Hill fisherman to be arraigned had – by court time – passed away. That 1853 case certainly points to a healthy sailboat fishing industry being practiced at Salthill in the years following the Great Famine.

Ned O'The Hill

In terms of other historical sources, a number of letters – from the 1920s – to the *Connacht Tribune* gives a sense of the fishing trade at Salthill, and the fast submerging Recorder's Quay's role in it. The missives were penned by a man of mystery and learning, who adopted a *Ned O'The Hill* soubriquet. That moniker choice is interesting for a number of reasons. The catchy name derived from the Gaelic *Éamon an Chnoic*, an Irishman of substance, who was dispossessed following Cromwell's Irish campaign, and subsequently took to the hills as a Rapparee. Salthill's epistolary Ned was not a bandit, however, but an erudite individual who had, by his own account, travelled widely.

Furthermore, oral recollections of Lazy Wall *habitués* universally refer to a knowledgeable *Ned O'The Hill* character, who engaged with Salthill's *fámairí* and entertained them in his own distinctive way. Dónal Taheny recalled a tall man sketching images on the ground, surrounded by interested disciples, and the legendary 'Bish' teacher further speculated that Ned may have had a military background. Writing under a *Balor* alias, Mr. Jack Fitzgerald of the *Connacht Tribune* described Ned as a 'very big man, tall and bulky, big boned and firm muscled,' who walked erect and presented an intelligent face. Everyone knew the Lazy Wall regular, but no one very well. He had been a policeman in a Spanish speaking country, according to *Balor*'s reported speculation, and some believed *Conneely* to have been his surname. Salthill's enigmatic figure, according to *Balor*'s account, lodged in a house facing the sea, near the entrance to Lenaboy Avenue.[17] Maurice Semple gave *Connolly* as Ned's putative surname,[18] which is quite close to *Balor*'s *Conneely* designation.

The question is; was the Lazy Wall regular and the cultured letter writer one and the same man?

The learned Ned gave some clues to his background in the text of his writings: He had worked on the great San Pedro breakwater in California, which was created from 1899–1912 by the Utah Construction Company. He had also acted as a 'Spanish correspondent' in a big Glasgow firm, run by Louis Williams, who owned orchards all over the world. The voluble Ned had once been told in

England that Irishmen should go home to their own country, and he appeared to have been very familiar with Australian and Canadian ways. He had 'met several Irishmen, a long way from Tipperary, who, although considered in old Ireland as "well educated" were lacking in the very fundamentals of practical human knowledge; just pitiable...'[19]

By contrast, the range of Ned's own knowledge was remarkable. Quotes were presented in English, Latin, French and phonetic *Gaeilge*: 'Thiginn tu!'; 'Thay shay'; 'Easkeries.' Many scholarly, and some not so scholarly sources were invoked to bolster his various theses, including the Bible, Shakespeare, Euclid, Sir Christopher Wren, Colmcille, Plato, Solon, Columbus, De Lesseps, Lord Macaulay, Edmund Burke, Lord Byron, Copernicus, Cromwell, Mussolini, Pope Gregory XIII and Kepler. Goldsmith's 'Deserted Village' was a favourite which was regularly referenced. Ned's varied disciplines included astronomy, navigation, history, genealogy, etymology, physics, and Greek culture. The breath of the Salthill polymath's geographic knowledge was also most impressive.

Ned O' The Hill, on one occasion, listed academic letters of learning – M.I.A.A. Dip. Comm. – in a 1924 newspaper contribution. Such an appendix appears a little odd in an anonymously penned piece, and it suggests that while the writer wanted to keep his real name off the press pages, he was keen to have his accomplishments recorded. Opinionated in manner, he was not slow to parade his knowledge when expressing views that may not have earned universal approval. His political compass was set so far to the polar right that it struggled to stay on the dial. For him, democracy was 'mobocracy' and Government cost too much. He wrote of hating 'politics' and held that 'native governments should be for the use, not the abuse of its children.' The malaise of state-aided businesses was offered a seasonal and local remedy: 'Well what would we do without our subsidised enterprises...? Well simply let them go where the Salthill fleas go in winter.' Tax collection was another bugbear: 'The only industry in Galway which is working overtime at present is tax-gathering. Custom House clerks (paid of course) work till after supper.' Other areas of government policy also came in for a lash. In censuring 'a derelict educational system,' he was critical of Irish schooling methods and those who made learning 'loathsome.'[20] Ned was also disapproving of Charles Stewart Parnell in facilitating an unfair inclination against 'the little towns who through their greater intelligence and sympathy stuck to him through thick and thin.' That was in reference to an injustice Ned held had been done to town dwellers by the Land Act of 1881, which greatly benefitted rural land holders.

Ned O' The Hill was a true Salthill native, whose grandfather's two-storey thatched house 'stood on the site of the two concrete houses on King's Hill.' Those twin structures, which, up to 2011, housed the *Pointe Boise* nursing home, today trade – on the seaward side of King's Hill – as the Nest Boutique Hostel. The original *ceanntuí* house of Ned's memory 'was demolished by Colonel O'Hara and the large stones heaped on the shore because it obstructed the view of the seascape of Lenaboy Castle.'[21] There was truth in that penned assertion because James O'Hara first knocked a fine Lodge in 1867, which stood on what had once been Dr. Gray's bathing emporium. During the following decade three relatively small houses were also 'downed,' on the seaward side of the rising road that came to be called King's Hill. Dominick and Matthias Burke occupied two of those houses in 1855. The third and largest of the small dwellings, with a rateable valuation of £4, belonged to Denis Conneely, who took possession of the premises in 1869. In that occupation Denis had followed Mary Conneely, who was listed c.1860. That Conneely tenure went back a further generation to another Denis who was *in situ* in 1855.

A reason for the houses' destruction might well have been to improve the sea vista from Lenaboy Castle. As the land from that fine residence to Recorder's Quay was all owned by Captain James O'Hara (1832–1902), the landlord could do as he liked. Another consideration was the transfer of responsibility for Recorder's Quay from O'Hara to the Board of Trade in 1871. A published notice stated that 'the rights and interests of the Crown in the foreshore have, by the Crown Land Acts 1866 been transferred by Captain O'Hara of Lenaboy' to the Trade Board. Part of that notice also sought 'permission to remove and abate the said quay.'[22] Some months later, Captain O'Hara and Michael Hennessy sought £300 to improve Recorder's Quay, which was in bad shape and described as a 'nuisance' by some members of the public. Captain O'Hara produced a plan of the contemplated alterations and affirmed that the place was under the control of the Board of Trade. He had gone to some trouble and expense to impress upon the Board the necessity of complying with the wishes of the people; but the Board would not consent to any alteration unless that a wall with landing steps was built at the place, so that boats could use it.' Others disapproved of the Captain's plans and wanted a landing place 'a little above George's baths, where boats at present land. But as this alteration could not be effected without the approval of the Board of Trade, £50 was allowed to fill up the Recorder's Quay to abate the nuisance.'[23] Disappointment at his genuine efforts to improve the Quay, and a £50 infill at the spot where he had previously held the foreshore rights, may have contributed to a lessening of interest in the area by Captain O'Hara, and a consequent change of plan for the place. One way or another, the neglect of Recorder's Quay was to continue.

As Ned's 1923 account of changes around Recorder's Quay tally with Valuation records of houses knocked in the area by James O'Hara, a more confident reckoning of Ned's identity is possible. Valuation Book evidence strongly supports Jack Fitzgerald's contention that *Conneely* was the anonymous hill man's surname. Maurice Semple's speculation that *Connolly* was Ned's patronym only strengthens Fitzgerald's case, as the surnames, Connolly and Conneely, both fall under the one *Conghaíle* umbrella. Conneely, however, seems to shade the claim for Ned's title. Furthermore, a man named James Conneely, residing in the King's Hill area, was the only person in the entire townland to describe himself as a 'Sailor' in 1911. The 37 year old Galway native was married to Louisa, his 33 year old wife, and the couple kept college students. Indeed the hill of Ned's chosen *nom de plume* may well have been King's Hill, where his grandfather had once resided. Such a speculative jigsaw is not proof of Ned's true identity, but it does offer some insight that might someday positively confirm the name of a bright Salthilll man, who was recognised by everyone, though identified only by an anonymous moniker. This study's best 'guess' is that James Conneely was the local polymath. Oral recollections of his description create the image of a tall erect man of mystique, confidence and intellect.

Because of his affiliation with his grandfather's place of residence, *Ned O'The Hill* took exception to the erection of shore fences, which cut out access to the sea, behind the two iconic King's Hill houses that were built in 1906. In Ned's tirade against the illegality of the fencing action, an insightful précis of Salthill's fishing tradition was given:

In ancient times Salthill (Kilcorkey and Lenaboy) was a fishing village whose inhabitants sustained themselves principally by fishing, entertaining 'Foragies' in the bathing season and cultivating small patches of land in spring and during rough weather. They moored their boats in a fine stone-built harbour known as the 'Councillor's Quay', and which is in good condition yet, if the alluvial sand deposits were dredged. They had an ample roadway all around it to admit carts, etc., to come alongside their boats, to remove the heavy catches of fish, seaweed, etc. That same roadway was also used by bathers from Galway who came to bathe at old Bab's from time out of mind.

Six year's usage constitutes highway (at law). That roadway was used for six thousand years. The roadway around the Councillor's Quay was as much a public domain as the roadway around our New Docks at present… To-day there are garden walls running right down to the very dock walls, so that if one wishes to pass, he has to squeeze by edgeways at high tide and for good measure another fellow has a barbed wire (with barbs like bayonets, mind you), fence set across this six thousand year old highway… It is an unwritten law in all countries that an ample passage (litoral) should be maintained on every seaboard at flood tide for the purpose of supervision of the sea (flotsam, etc.), and also in the interest of coastal defence. An expensive hotel (The Gallface) at Colombo, Ceylon, was built on the seashore a few years ago only on condition that they would get five minutes' notice for its destruction in case of war…

This Councillor's Quay is still in use. Tom Smith uses it yet for his pilot boat and several old natives of Salthill remember fifty-two fishing boats being moored there – a forest of masts. When sailing ships took emigrants across the Western Ocean they used to embark at the Councillor's Quay. Some of those folks who have illegally pirated the domain of the people of Galway, whose grandfathers bathed at Bab's and whose grandfathers made fast their lines to the very pillar stones which are there to this day, and who have even intruded on the domain of Old Neptune himself, would put up some kind of a legal quibbling argument, like the fellow who got up in the middle of the night when the household was asleep and said that they are in possession now, and that that is decimal point 9 of the law.

Ned's letter was concluded with the assertion that 'the evidence of the eldest natives of Salthill and Galway ought to suffice to shift those fortifications which are constructed across the environments of Councillor's Quay.' In a postscript he also disclosed that 'Bonfires used to be lighted at one time on the eve of the 24th of this month (San Juan) at the Councillor's Quay, between which the Corrig Wacha reef lies.'[24]

Hely Dutton's description of that ritual pyro-practice was presented in his 1824 Statistical Survey of County Galway: *On St. John's eve it is the custom to light immense fires of turf, bones, &c. in different parts of the town of Galway; they are surrounded by young people, mostly females, who ask some trifle from each passenger; they are usually armed with bundles of the seed stocks of docks, tied up like small brooms, with which they touch lightly the passengers or lookers on, saying, 'honor to the bonfire,' which every person is expected to do by touching their hat, or if a woman, by a slight courtesy. I have seen some of your mighty sensible people refuse to do this, and I confess enjoyed the touching they received with the dirty brooms.*[25]

Ned O'The Hill, in another press contribution, recorded his dislike of trawling: 'There was a time here in this old town when you would hardly need an alarm clock to rise early. The sound of fisherwomen folk shouting "Fresh plaice, fresh plaice, fresh plaice," was nearly as powerful as a dose of insomnia.'[26] John Freyne's first holiday memory from 1908 was 'waking up in Salthill to the sound of trotting horses and bells ringing and the cry "Fresh Mackerel, Fresh Whiting". The horses and the bells were the horse trams that plied from Galway to Salthill. The women carried baskets of fish on their heads.'[27]

Ned believed that a trawl was a marine plough and that the North Sea was nearly 'combed bald.' Consequently he believed that large trawlers from Belgium, France, England, Scotland, Germany, Holland, etc. were fishing in Irish waters and destroying native fishing stocks. There was truth in Ned's assertion, and at an Irish Fishery Commission hearing at the Courthouse in 1869 the question of Oyster beds had been first raised. 'W. St. George, of Tyrone House, gave valuable evidence on oyster culture, and attributed the falling off in Galway Bay to over-dredging and removing the small oysters. Captain O'Hara spoke of the decline of the fishing village of Claddagh and the poverty of the fishermen, and suggested loans of money to enable them to purchase fishing gear, and he would have no objection to go security for the repayment.'[28] Fishermen's poor financial state reflected a real crisis in the industry and *Ned O'The Hill* recorded how 'Salthill was once a fishing village and some of the old-time Easkeries here could always get a few flat fish when they set their spillards, but now as a Claddagh man said the other day, "You might as well fish in the basin. Trawlers are pirates, pure and simple".' Ned also complained about the three mile limit that was often breached: 'When the

Germans felled the fruit trees of France for timber there was a great howl, and now a great fish-consuming country like Ireland is being cheated out of its supplies by ruthless destruction by French and Belgian, etc.'[29]

A paucity of fish was a reported reality in the early 1870s when a *Freeman's Journal* reporter noted that 'time was, I believe, and fish were numerous in Galway waters, but these are no longer a heaven to the ichthyophagist. Indeed, fish appear to be as scarce and dear here as in Dublin.' The same scribe noted that 'it is interesting to know that the collection of sea weed for manure has grown so profitable an occupation that a large proportion of the fisherman have deserted their nominal occupation for it.' This account was written by a man describing the wonders of Salthill and the 'peasant girls…basket on back, poor toilers of the sea, who live by gathering the refuse of the great waters.'[30] Landlords with holdings open to the sea sought to profit from their beach bounty. In 1852, for example, 'the Seaweed and Shipwreck of the shore of the lands at Attythomasrevagh, at SALT HILL near Blackrock,' were offered to purchasers for one year.[31] Sea weed harvesting at the resort resulted in Mathias Kelly, Michael Burns, Michael Burns Jnr., Martin Molloy and Martin Fallon, all of Salt Hill, being charged in 1860 with 'a breach of the Sabbath by collecting sea weed.' Their case was 'dismissed, it being a case of necessity.'[32] Margaret Ryan, who held a 'Herd's ho[use] off[ice] and land' at White Strand from Henry Grattan Jnr. in 1855, was, according to Griffith's Valuation, responsible for the 'Tolls and customs of White-strand fair,' which was annually 'held on 4th September.' Ten years later in the same area, Bedilia Ryan's 'Right of cutting and selling seaweed' was rateably valued at a sizeable £35 per annum. Mr. James Campbell Esq., J.P. was the target – in 1869 – of an accusatory public letter from Fr. James Corbett, of the 'Arran Isles.' The island curate, in his correspondence, claimed that the Iodine Company, of which Mr. Campbell was Managing Director, operated a monopoly of Arran kelp.[33] Seaweed was also the cargo on the Hooker that 'struck on the Black Rock' as early as 1843 and all such evidence points to the preciousness of the kelp commodity in the 19th century. It is clear, therefore, that the dividend of seaweed harvesting, in tandem with fish volume reduction caused by foreign boat trawling, meant that fishing's financial lure at Salthill was fast fading.

Denuded stocks were not the only impediment to the continuation of fishing at Salthill. Access to the shore was also problematic, for landlords valued seashore ownership. In fact, foreshore rights caused tension and controversy at Salthill right up to the 1940s. Local historian, Tom Kenny, has written of the *Night of the Big Wind*, when Blackrock's fishermen were forced inland after *an ghaoth mhór* of 1839 destroyed their cottages.[34] Galway town was severely affected by the hurricane, which caused many casualties, some of whom were dangerously maimed and bruised, with an expectation that a number would have to 'undergo amputation.' By the bay, the open nature of the hinterland meant 'that scarcely a house in Salt-hill…did not feel the awful effects of the storm.'[35] The Great Famine and its aftermath also hit Salthill very hard. Reflecting a doleful reality, most local townlands suffered a fifty percent – or more – decline in their populations; many residents were evicted, others perished, with emigration facilitating a flight from the place. The story of that population clearance is told in the Famine section of this book.

If there were fishermen, in pre-famine and pre-clearance times, among Salthill's tenant population, many of them were gone by the 1870s. Such a reality is not surprising for that industry's fall from grace was captured in John Cunningham's survey of 19th century census returns: '549 Galway fishermen were enumerated in the 1841 census, this dropped to 504 in 1851. By 1871 the total was a mere 164.' Cunningham also quoted Fishery Commissioner spokesman, John Brophy, who visited the Claddagh in 1868. Brophy reported that 'before the famine of 1846 the Claddagh contained over 3,000 fishermen; now the number of men is not more than 200, and of these the great majority are old and decripid.'[36] Salthill's fishing decline was furthermore reflected in 1901 census returns. Taking the nine townlands of this study, which cover an area from Nile Lodge to the western boundary of Galway Golf Club, only two Salthill men described themselves as fishermen. That represented an amazingly small number for an area perched on the bay. One was Patrick Keane of Barrack Lane and the other was Martin O'Donnell of Kilcorkey, at Lower Salthill. The Keane entry was interesting, for a Richard Keane of Barrack Lane had earlier recorded 'fisherman' as his occupation, at his daughter Barbara's 1884 wedding to Frederick Stiff. A fishing tradition obviously ran in that Barrack Lane family. The O'Donnell clan also clung to the trade they knew, and Salt Hill fisherman, Daniel O'Donnell, who had earlier appeared in the 1853 Court Case, previously described, was most likely related to Martin O'Donnell who filled his 1901 census as a fishing man of the sea.

Claddagh hegemony may also have been a factor in fishing's decline, while Salthill's almost exclusive focus on tourism from the 1800s left little room for another trade. The greatest impediment to a fishing industry at Salthill, however, was the lack of a pier to accommodate boats which would make the enterprise pay. Pilot Tom Smith was among the last to use Recorder's Quay, and he claimed £14 compensation for damage done to his boat, berthed there on 14 February, 1921, after its bottom had been broken with a large stone.[37] The subsequent closing off and neglect of Recorder's / Councillor's Quay sounded the death knell for a trade that most likely had its roots in a far distant past. The need for a pier, following the Recorder's Quay demise, was greatly felt at the resort and a replacement became a primary goal for many Salthill development organisations throughout much of the 20th century. The rationale for a coveted pier, however, had by then changed. No longer was it sought to facilitate fishing vessels, but rather to attract craft that might accommodate, and enhance, the tourism product on offer at the resort.

The deep knowledge of the sea, which was evidenced both in the exploits – and stories – of men like *Ned O'The Hill* and Tom Smith, give credence to a long maritime tradition at Salthill. There were others of course who followed a related sea-trade. Britain's National Archive retains one page of a file on a man called John Murphy, who was born on 26 September, 1870 at Salthill. The hazel eyed 17 year old boy of 'very good' character spent eleven months on H.M.S. *Orwell*, a Britomart-class wooden screw gunboat, from 1 October, 1887 to 1 Sept. 1888, before he requested a return to shore. The briny always beckoned for some and Barrack Lane, also known as Lenaboy Avenue, retained a seafaring tradition through many decades: From fisherman Richard Keane in 1884, through Patrick Keane of the same trade in 1901, to Able Seaman Matthew James Keane, who lost his life on H.M.S. *Onslow* during World War II, on to John McGrath who was – in 1985 – the youngest Irish Naval recipient of a Distinguished Service Medal, the call of the sea along Salthill's shore has retained its power to attract both old and new 'Salts' from Galway's marine suburb. Salthill and the sea which – in so many ways – has nourished it, have forever been inseparable.

Tourist Attractions
and *Fámairí*
in 19th Century Salthill

Chapter 8

SALTHILL BATHS

Salthill's coastal position on the edge of Galway town offered holiday variety, for both the bustle of the town and the serenity of the seaside were available to visitors. That combination was facilitated by an inexpensive horse-drawn transport service, which plied the two mile route that connected Connacht's capital to its marine outpost. Boats, as we have seen in the previous chapter, offered fishing expeditions from Recorder's Quay, as well as trips to towns around the bay. A beautiful view of Burren hills and Galway Bay was augmented by the fresh air of Atlantic breezes. Stolls to Blackrock were accommodated by a sea esplanade that featured stone seats – at intervals – to allow for occasional breaks. Chatty company enlivened a Lazy Wall retreat and summer amusements, available at the Village, attracted the young and young at heart. Lodging facilities, which expanded over time, ranged from the frugal to the flamboyant. The presence of a black umbrella on a sunny day, in the opening image of this book (**fig.1**), indicates that a summer 'tan' was little prized by lady *fámairí* of bygone days. Salthill's beaches were generally stony and swimming during the 19th – and for a good part of the 20th – century, was only practiced by the few, for most vacationers were wary of the sea. A growing appreciation of the health benefits of the briny, however, was reflected in the development of Spa resorts around the Irish coast, with Kilkee and Lisdoonvarna offering attractive facilities in neighbouring Co. Clare. The popularity of Sea Baths, on the rise throughout the 19th century, saw Salthill embrace that health enhancing trade.

'Taking to the waters' – Dr. Gray's Initiative

Though sea water's medicinal value might not then have boasted the depth of scientific data that exists today, most people – who enjoyed the experience – realised that after a bath in the briny, they felt re-energised and radiant. In 1843, for example,

Mr. Hogan of the Baths at Kilkee was satisfied from experience that he had discovered the cure for rheumatism. The *Nenagh Guardian* reported that 'his method is, immediately on coming out of the hot air bath, to put the patient under a cold shower bath, the transition from heat to cold having the best possible effect, and after leaving the shower bath, the person is put into warm blankets, which keep up the perspiration.'[1] Though the stiffening scourge was not eradicated by the Kilkee method, medical men were keenly aware of sea water's benefits. In Galway, Doctor Robert Rogers Gray opened his medicinal Baths on the Salt Hill road in 1831.

Before recording the Longford doctor's contribution to Salthill's Bath culture, it is important to note that the tracing of such bathing facilities, before Dr. Gray's Salthill construction, is constrained by a lack of detailed source evidence. That said, it is clear that the good doctor was not the first to provide such a service in Galway. That was evidenced by his use of the 'NEW' epithet in his Baths' advertisement, and by an anonymous *Well-Wisher* correspondent, who recalled a spell in Bulteel's Baths at the time that Dr. Gray's complex was being built. The facility used by the newspaper contributor was not in Salt Hill, for the scribe walked from Fairhill towards Salt Hill, across the White Strand Marsh, following his dip at Bulteel's.[2] The elder enterprise was also known as the 'Old Baths,' which were always then referenced in relation to White Strand. The General Boundary Surveyor, Richard Griffith, for example, placed his hand-sketched maps of local parishes available for view in July 1837 at 'the Boundary Survey Office on the White-strand, near the old baths.'[3] A child was tragically drowned near those baths during an 1847 gale and 'an Old Bath Road, off the Salt-Hill Road, opposite Mr. John O'Hara's Lodge'[4] was described by a *Galway Patriot* advertisement in 1835. Regular use of the 'old' description indicates that the baths in question were either well aged by the 1830s, or at least older than Dr. Gray's offering.

Bulteel's holdings

Samuel Bulteel Esq. leased the Whitestrand Marsh and Sea Weed shore to 'John Reddington' in November 1819. A section of that seaside ground came to be described in Encumbered Estate land maps as 'Bulteel's Marsh,' which stood on the Fair Hill side of Whitestrand's estuary **(fig.73)**. A baths' facility, bearing the same name, also operated there. Though this study cannot be definitive about the site of the Old Baths, it appears most likely that they stood on the seaward promontory which today represents Celia Griffin Park on Grattan Road. The reason for that assumption is that the closest seaside structure to Bulteel's Marsh, which could operate as a baths' facility, is marked at that headland spot in the Ordnance Survey map of 1839. That same site was later to house Grattan Lodge after Mr. Henry Grattan Jnr. bought the Claddagh's 29 acres from Mr. Robert Whaley in

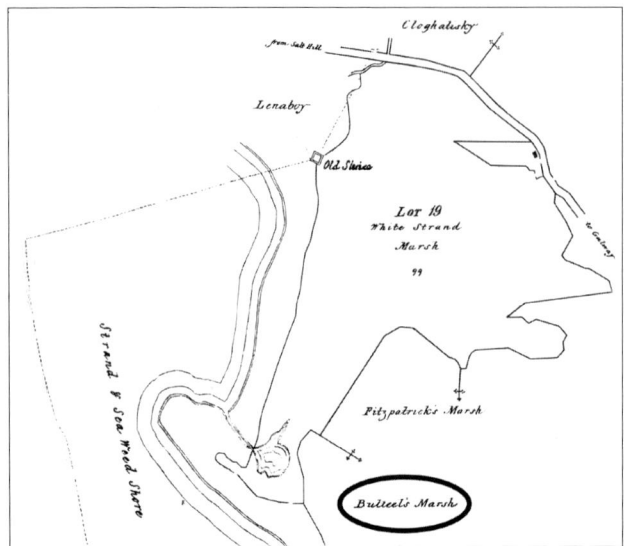

73. Bulteel's Marsh, on Claddagh side of White Strand Marsh, lay opposite the headland – to the lower left – that today is home to Celia Griffin Park. The diamond/square under the 'y' in Lenaboy represents an 'Old Sluice.'

1852. It was Henry's daughter, Miss Fanny Grattan, who was primarily responsible – in an act of great benevolence – for the building of Grattan Road in the early 1860s. Fanny was grand-daughter to Henry Grattan, the famed Irish politician of Grattan's Parliament fame, and daughter to the Henry who purchased the Claddagh. Bulteel was a name with marine connections to Sligo and the lease for 'White Strand Marsh and Sea-Weed Shore' was 'for three lives' of an Irwin family of 'Mountshannon, Sligo.' By the time of the 1834 Tithe collection, it was Mr. Bulteel who appeared in the 'Lenaboy/Kilcurkey' section of that record, though the 42 acres of marsh he held were deemed to be 'untitheable.' Wherever they precisely stood, Bulteel's Baths lay in ruins by 1859.[5]

Many locals identify Seapoint as the epicentre of Salthill's 'Bath' culture, as James Cremen's water emporium – which preceded Finan's famed ballroom – still lives in recent memory. While such recall is absolutely accurate, Dr. Gray's bath facility is often overlooked in local lore. Constructed in 1831, an extensive bathing amenity was then positioned on a one acre plus site, which was later occupied by Grattan House. A modern apartment complex at the bottom of King's Hill, which today bears the Grattan name, sits directly across from the Warwick Hotel's entrance. Dr. Gray's location choice is interesting and probably had something to do with the existence of Recorder's Quay beside his chosen site, and the benefits – engineering or otherwise – of the spot chosen. All maps from the period identify Recorder's Quay, which stood on the seaward side of Gray's Baths. That quay, as earlier indicated, today lies submerged under the reclaimed land of Claude Toft Park. Fishing, leisure and Coast Guard vessels regularly berthed there, so some sea traffic already existed in the locale. More importantly, excepting a Claddagh/Fairhill location, the spot chosen for Dr. Gray's enterprise was the most convenient site to Galway town. Not far from the 'Old Baths,' it occupied a prominent resort position on the Salt Hill road. It must also be remembered that there was no semblance, when Dr. Gray opened his 1831 Baths, of a proper promenade, and Grattan Road was not to be built for another three decades.

The project relied primarily on a tourist and medicinal trade, in a place that was not to benefit from a tram service for nigh on half a century, though horse-car transport did serve the area in 1831. It was to take over a hundred years for the gap between Salthill and its neighbouring town to eventually close. A road-hugging building boom in the 1920s/'30s, which took off after the difficult 1914–1923 decade – and the sale of the Lenaboy Demesne – eventually tied Galway's satellite village to its mother township. Salthill's summer industry was only in its infancy when Dr. Gray opened his bathing business in an area that boasted beaches as stony rough as further out the coast. The *Galway Packet* in 1852 described the local coastline: 'The shore from Sea Point House to the Recorder's Quay is a continuation of rocks and stones which render it most disagreeable, and which could be removed at a small expense.'[6]

When Robert Gray opened his facility in the summer of 1831, he was not reticent about promoting the many and varied advantages of the product on offer:

New Baths, Salt-hill Road, Galway. [Erected in 1831]: Will open for the accommodation of the Public on the First of June instant…the different medicated Bath and the vapour Bath, now so generally recommended by the most eminent Physicians of the day. It is chiefly beneficial in removing Gout in all its forms – Chronic Rheumatism, and Rheumatic pains – and Swelling of the Joints – strengthening the tone of the Stomach, and thereby being so valuable a remedy in Dyspepsia, and all the train of nervous feelings consequent on indigestion. In internal inflammations, as of the liver, lungs, kidneys &c., and from its power of promoting perspiration. It is highly and deservedly recommended for removing dropsical effusions – there is no Bath more in repute for removing the effects of mercury from the constitution and Scrofulous swellings, Ulcers and obstinate diseases of the skin in general yield to a properly medicated Vapour Bath. The plain Warm Baths, Shower Baths, &c. will be given by experienced assistants, and the Medicated Baths under the immediate direction of a Medical Gentleman. May 5, 1831.[7]

Not everyone was as sanguine as Doctor Gray about sea-baths' advantages. Numbered among the doubters was Josephine M. Callwell, who recalled that 'every one bathed in the mornings.' Miss Callwell (1858–1935), whose mother was Maud Martin of Ross Castle, was a famed author of children's books. It was at Kilcummin, Galway, on 2 October, 1856, that Miss Maria Maud Martin married Henry Callwell of Ballycastle, County Antrim. The couple's daughter, Josephine, and son, Charles, both followed literary paths, with history and military biography providing the subject matter for Charles' publications. That latter choice was hardly surprising, for Charles' own military experience led to a knighthood. Major-General Sir Charles Edward Callwell KCB (1859–1928) served during the Second

Boer War and acted as Director of Operations and Intelligence during the First World War. One of Charles' books, *Small Wars, Their Principles and Practice,* became a standard British military manual and 'copies were highly sought after by IRA officers during the War of Independence.'[8] Charles was knighted for his war service in 1917. Neither Charles nor Josephine married and Miss Josephine Callwell died at Glenalla, Ballycastle, County Antrim in February 1935.

Both Callwell siblings would have experienced summers in Salthill in the second half of the 1800s and a patronising glance at some people's faith in the resort's briny benefits was included in Miss Callwell's 1912 *Old Irish Life* publication:

Every summer we, and most other families of our acquaintance, went into the town of Galway, or rather out to the straggling suburb that fronts onto Galway Bay, for some weeks' bathing and sea air. All classes did the same, and indeed it was pathetic to see the faith that the poorer folk had in the 'salt wather' as a cure for all diseases and infirmities, and the struggles that were made and the discomforts endured in order that some ailing member of a family might have the benefit of the health-giving waters of Galway Bay. One poor man carried his wife, who was recovering from a severe illness, nearly fifty miles upon his back, to bring her to the sea, supporting her and the children who accompanied them by begging from house to house along the road. 'Och, but he dearly earned me', said the wife afterwards, when happily she was restored to health and strength.[9]

The final line of Miss Callwell's pen picture indicates that the unfortunate woman's faith was rewarded with a cure, though the author's scepticism, re salt-waters' power, remained stubbornly solid. For some visitors, bathing alone was not enough, as an *Irish Times* piece revealed in 1873: Acting on a value for money principle, 'the peasants who come to Galway seem almost to live in the sea, and, we might add, of the sea. They bathe two or three times a day, and they drink great draughts of the sea-water almost every hour. Morning, noon and night, the peasant visitor to Galway is seen with the small tin vessel from which he takes his doses of salt water. It is not unsafe to conclude that such a line of conduct makes Galway less of a sanatorium to some of its visitors than they imagine.'[10] The drinking of sea-water was practiced a full century before the *Irish Times'* recording of the custom in Galway. A medicinal advertisement, in the *Hibernian Journal*, related one individual's health difficulties: 'On Monday, Sept. 24th, 1774, I was seized with a most violent scorbutic humour...I tried every Means could be thought of, with Bathing, and drinking Sea-Water, without Effect.'[11]

Medical men often prescribed a spell at the sea for patients, and a murder suspect, questioned in connection with an 1882 killing at Parsonstown – also known as Birr – invoked a physician's advice, as part of his alibi, on police apprehension: *As to the statement that he was evading arrest, he states his intention of producing a certificate from Dr. Browne, who ordered him sea bathing, and his assertion is that he was on his way to Salthill, Co. Galway, when he was arrested in Athlone.*[12]

Doctor Robert Gray & Family

The physician who set great store by Salthill's briny was Dr. Robert Rogers Gray. A prominent Galway citizen, Dr. Gray was listed in the Navy List of 1834 as a Surgeon and Agent for the Admiralty. His name appeared, with other public figures, in an 1833 deed related to the Presbyterian Meeting House at Nun's Island. It appears that he lived in that general town locale for a spell, as an 1823 *Connaught Journal* piece noted that, having left Connemara, Dr. Gray had 'taken the House formerly held by Mr. Stephens in Nuns' Island.' The Connemara reference most likely referred to the Clifden area, where Dr. Gray held property, both in the town and at nearby Ardbear. The Gray family also held a large property portfolio in the counties of Longford and Monaghan. Further recorded in the *Journal*'s report was the physician's generosity to the poor of Galway town: 'The Poor will be attended gratis every morning from 8 to 9 o'clock. Diseases of the eyes treated exclusively on Wednesdays. Poor Women in their lying-in will be attended gratis; on their sending a Certificate from their Clergyman of their being unable to pay.'[13] That same year Michael Walsh, a nailer from nearby Bridge Street, who suffered for twelve years with a diseased leg, had his limb amputated by Surgeon Gray. A call was put out to 'the charitable and humane of Galway' for aid contributions towards the recovery of the unfortunate man, who had not worked for several months before his operation.[14] Dr. Gray's benevolence was not transitory, for though he had moved to new premises by 1828, he still gave up 'a few hours each morning to attend a dispensary at his house in Dominick Street.'[15] That free service was to benefit the poor children of the town.

Dr. Gray's public profile was reflected in his being asked to deliver 'an admirable lecture' at the Mechanic's Institute in March 1840, and in his signature being appended to a number of addresses and memorials. One such memorial, in respect of the Fisheries in Galway Bay, was submitted to the Lord Lieutenant of Ireland in the Month of December 1839. The good doctor appeared in a broad range of directories and calendars over the years and Slater's 1846 edition, described him as a Galway surgeon.

In March 1839 Doctor Gray advertised his 'Galway Warm Baths' for letting, after he had installed a new steam boiler and cistern before the summer season, which was to open in May.[16] Nine years later, Dr. Robert Rogers Gray placed his sizable Salthill baths' complex, on the market. That included the April 1848 auction of 'the commodious Bathing Lodge, Kilrea, or the Dairy Lodge, consisting of Parlour, Drawing-room, Store-room, Pantry, Wine Cellar, with Coach-house and Stabling for two horses. This Lodge is close to the Recorder's Quay, near the Baths.'[17] Later in the same year, 'The Interest in the Baths now in complete working order, and Two Bathing Lodges at the Recorder's Quay, Galway' were offered for sale, as was a house in Dominick Street, then occupied by Dr. Browne.[18] Applications were to be

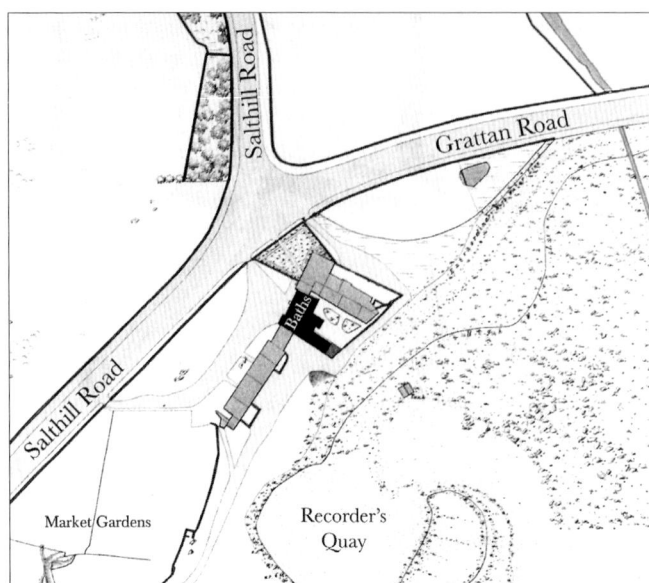

74. Map of Baths' complex, originally built by Dr. Gray and later operated by Andrew King. On lower left are Market Gardens – beside Recorder's Quay – as referenced by Ned O'The Hill.

made to Capt. Clune, Dominick Street, or to Dr. Gray, Clonbalt House, Longford.

In 1844, four years before the Salthill auction, Dr. Gray's eldest boy, Richard Armstrong Gray Esq., of Balton House, County Longford, married Sarah Maria Simpson, the only daughter of Rev. S. Simpson, Blackhall Street, Dublin. Richard was a civil engineer and architect who served as Dublin County Surveyor from 1855 to his retirement in 1896. Just three years into his superannuated years, Richard passed away and was buried in Mount Jerome cemetery. His younger brother, Henry Hugo De Witt Gray, who was born at 4 Dominick Street on 11 July, 1831, followed his brother into the civil engineering trade. In 1868 Henry Hugo boasted a Dublin domicile and a second address at 23 Princess Street, Westminster, London.[19] Henry married Margaret Thompson, the daughter of shipowner, William Thompson, in the Strand district of London during the early 1870s, and they had 11 children; two sons and nine daughters – all of whom were born in England.

Two years after the Lenaboy baths' complex was placed for sale, Doctor Robert Rogers Gray, of Clonbalt, Co. Longford, died intestate in January 1850. Following his death, Elizabeth, his widow, acted for a time as lessor to the Lenaboy property, and she also leased a Dominick Street residence, that was occupied by Maria Brown in 1855. Ten years later, Elizabeth Gray of 7 Upper Sherrard Street, Dublin and her youngest son, Henry Hugo De Witt Gray, of Clonliffe Parade, amicably decided to sell their shares of the Salthill property to the eldest son, Richard Armstrong Gray of 4 Clonliffe Parade, Co. Dublin. On completion of that 1865 arrangement, the property at Lenaboy was sold to Henry Gascoyne of Ballinasloe.[20] It was James O'Hara (1832–1902), however, who replaced Mrs. Gray, as 'Immediate Lessor' of the property, in the post-1855 Revision Book records.

The King Era

Andrew King became occupier of the bath buildings in 1848. He and his wife were to operate a business there for over two decades, with the property valued as 'house, offices and baths.' The eastern environs of the Baths' area deteriorated over the years, particularly at the marsh, which faced onto White Strand. A *Well-wisher* correspondent in 1859 wrote of:

…an ugly, disease engendering swamp between Fair Hill and the Recorder's Quay which, (at least in summer) when the tide is out, is the fruitful source of a most horrible stench, from, I suppose, the decaying of weeds, &c. on it…this really disgusting and loathsome plague-spot, ought to be alluded to be-jure your Town Grand Jury to remedy it, which could be done for little expense, by driving piles along the thirty yards which admits the sea at present [21]

The anonymous scribe's suggestion was a good one and may have been one of the reasons why the owner of the place, Miss Fanny Grattan, soon afterwards followed that counsel. She contributed handsomely to the building of Grattan Road in the early 1860s and the construction of that Famine Relief Road greatly aided many Galway families, through particularly hungry years. Of course, it also helped reclaim the malodorous marsh, which was advertised for letting by P.H. Cullen, West Cottage, Galway, in August 1864. [22]

The abhorrent smell of 1859, however, did have a detrimental effect on the tourist potential of Lower Salt Hill and *Well-wisher* recounted that to his 'certain knowledge, three or four families, who resided both near Nile Lodge and King's Baths, were by this cause alone reluctantly compelled to curtail their pleasures at Lower Salt-hill, this year and go off to other places, not near Galway.' [23] As it eventually turned out, Mr. and Mrs. Andrew King, who ran the baths' operation, had to face greater troubles than a seasonal stink, for their bathing buildings burned down in 1870. A water heating apparatus was the suspected cause of the destructive blaze. A subsequent *Galway Vindicator* piece recorded the King couple's gratitude to their customers and supporters:

Baths Salt Hill; Mr. and Mrs. King – Beg leave to return their sincere thanks to the Clergy, Gentry, Merchants and principal inhabitants of Galway and the surrounding country for the generous support they have accorded to him during the term of thirty-two years he has conducted his Establishment. They take this opportunity of informing the Public that the baths recently burned will, at considerable expense, be in perfect working order during the next Season, when he hopes to merit a continuance of the patronage already extended to him. [24]

The thirty-two year tenure claimed in the press notice appears to have added a decade to the 22 years (1848–1870) the King couple owned their baths' business. It is possible, of course, that the King family were in some way involved with the Gray enterprise before taking full control of it. Of greater interest is the high society nature of the patrons thanked, which indicates that the King establishment was esteemed in Galway at that time. The destructive fire, however, represented a blow to the King venture, with their bath property's valuation falling from a sizeable £16 to a meagre £2-10s. To exacerbate matters, Baths' keeper Mr. Andrew King – aged 56 – who had suffered with heart disease for two years, passed away in early January, 1871. Hopes for the reconstruction of the Baths were consequently never to be realised, and the complex, first constructed by Dr. Gray, was to be further diminished over time.

Apart from his baths' business, Andrew King also sold liquor at his establishment and appeared in court in 1853 for 'having his house and place of sale open for the sale of Beer and Spirits...between the hours of eleven and twelve o'clock at Salt hill...to persons not being travellers, inmates or lodgers.'[25] Though he was fined fifteen shillings for that infraction, Andrew's Salthill premises was not a shebeen. An 1855 Petty Court record noted that he claimed 'a certificate to enable him to get a licence to sell beer,' and spirits. Mr. King did make other court appearances on charges which included permitting three pigs to wander at Upper Dominick Street in 1858, for which he was fined one penny. Andrew King was thrice listed in Griffith's Galway property list, as he was occupier of two neighbouring land banks, amounting to over four acres in the town of Galway, in addition to his Lenaboy holding.

By 1872, Jane King had replaced Andrew as occupier of the reduced property, which was then without the destroyed bath buildings. A map included by Ward & Lock, in their 1890 *Pictorial Guide to Connemara and the West of Ireland,* included the baths at King's Hill, which, by then, had been levelled for well over a decade.[26]

King's Hill naming

There's little doubt but that Andrew King, who followed Dr. Gray into the baths' business at Recorder's Quay, lent his surname to the hill that rises towards Salthill Village. His primary business was widely known as King's Baths and the King family traded on the same Salthill site for over twenty years. While it is possible that the hill's naming had a regal provenance, the presence of a royally surnamed Andrew at its eastern base most likely stamped King's Hill on the rise, which was later to represent the sole climbing challenge to Salthill's tram horses.

There were three impressive holdings on the original Gray site in 1855. The most valuable of them at 3e Lenaboy, included House Offices & Baths, which were occupied by Andrew King. There were, in addition, two other fine lodges then leased by Mrs. Gray. One of them (3c) was occupied by Helen Blake while the other (no. 4) was taken by Paul Rochfort. The latter lodge was recorded as 'down' as early as 1867 and two smaller premises, in the same locale, were later razed during the following decade. *Ned O'The Hill,* as we have seen, believed that such demolitions were designed to facilitate an improved sea view from O'Hara's Lenaboy Castle on Taylor's Hill.[27] A solitary Gray lodge, as it all turned out, survived into the 20th century. That enduring premises went on to be later called Grattan House, so named some time after Grattan Road was completed in the early 1860s.

In the accompanying 1890's representation, tram tracks are indicated on the stretch where a tram-driver was tragically killed in 1914, as described in the 'Trains, Trams and Horses' chapter of this book.

It was in 1946 that Borough Surveyor, Mr. J. S. Carroll, sought to end the confusion presented by a 'muddle of Galway streets.' His assumption, in a prepared report, was 'that the name King's Hill is unofficial,' and he suggested that Salthill Road Lower should extend from Murrays [at Nile Lodge] to the Warwick, with Salthill Road Upper to run from the Warwick to the borough boundary.'[28] It is unsurprising, therefore, that no public signage identified the rise. The name, however, continues to carry currency at Salthill and the 'Kingshill Stores' sign – on image 75 – marked a retail outlet that traded during the 1980s on the corner with Lenaboy Gardens, in a building that currently (2018) serves as the office of Laurence O'Connor & Company, Solicitors. The site of that 1980's Kingshill shop is indicated on the 19th century map above by a 'black V,' opposite the entrance to Beach Avenue.

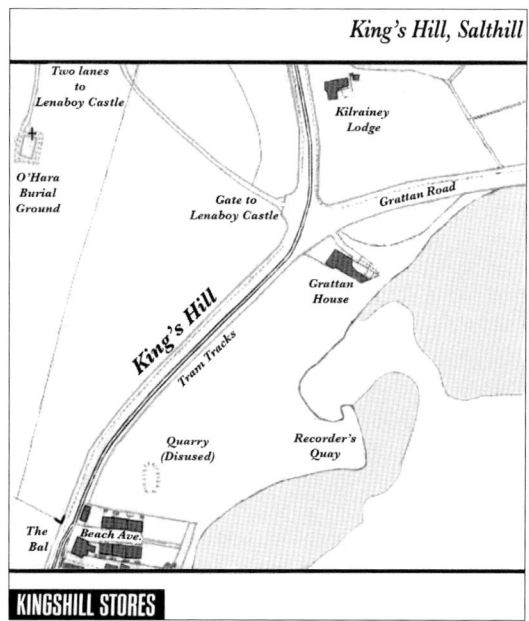

75. Map of King's Hill.

The same map shows Grattan House as the sole surviving Gray building, and taking a century time span – 1855 to 1955 – over twenty individuals have been recorded as occupiers of that residence. Among their number was Mr. Matt Cheevers, who operated a guest house there, before opening the Golf Links' Hotel – at the prom's end – in 1950. The Grattan House premises subsequently became identified with Mrs. Elizabeth Treacy and her family, who later opened the nearby Beach Hotel in 1968. That latter hostelry enjoyed over two decades of custom, and the Treacy clan went on to replace the original Grattan House with an apartment complex, where Seán Treacy today invites patrons to put their feet up and 'relax in comfort.'

Among the more interesting individuals to have stayed at Grattan House was Mr. George Quetelet, a Belgian gentleman, who was arrested – as a spy – by the

R.I.C. at Blackrock, in August 1912.[29] Following a week in Galway Gaol, the innocent captive was released and headed for the safety of Lahinch. Another to note is Frances Elizabeth Cremen, who occupied Grattan House after arriving with her two children, James and Frances Mary, circa 1886. Though the Gray/King baths at the bottom of King's Hill had disappeared by that time, the Cremen surname was to become synonymous with bathing at Salthill over many subsequent decades. After spending three years at Grattan House, Mrs. Cremen moved to Seapoint, where she and her family were to operate what became the most famed of Salthill's bathing facilities. A Seapoint House enterprise, however, had been in operation for some time before Mrs. Cremen arrived at the village's western sea-point.

Seapoint: House and Baths

Seapoint is the spot most identified, in popular memory, with Baths at Salthill. Seapoint House, with Seapoint Baths beside it (**figs.23 & 79**), is an image still recalled by elder Galway citizens. The Seapoint union of boarding house and abutting baths took place under Cremen management, just as the 19th century was drawing to a close. Before that, separate tourism products were on offer, side by side, under various family ownerships. Richard John Griffith did not record a Baths' business at either Seapoint House or George Fallon's neighbouring premises in 1855, though such enterprises were carried out in each establishment before that seminal valuation year.

George's Baths

To begin with the smaller premises (no.27 on Map), which stood on the seaward side of Seapoint House: It was rated at a modest £3 in 1855, though its baths' facility was never noted in that particular record. George Fallon was the man in charge of the bathing operation, which was sometimes referenced in the local press as George's Baths. Such informality reflects the familiarity of Galway's newspaper readership with Mr. Fallon's premises. It appears that George Fallon ran that business from well before 1855, for he was 74 years of age in that valuation year. Born in 1781, Mr. Fallon was described –

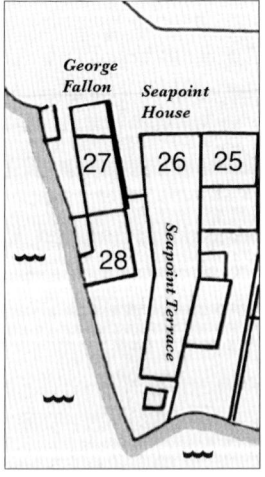

Figure 76

77. Seapoint House to the left, with Fallon's Sea Baths in thatched premises on right. (Courtesy of National Library of Ireland.)

in an 1830 lease – as 'a yeoman,' which then described a freeholder, standing below the status of landed gentry.[30]

George operated his baths' business in a thatched building to the right of Seapoint House. His gable end sign read: *Hot Baths and Bathing, No Refunds.* The Fallon building was to be later bought – and knocked – by the Cremen family of Seapoint House, who developed a more modern baths' facility on the site.

One wonders if George Fallon, in an earlier life, was a man of the sea. A Salt Hill born man of that very name, who was a labourer and fisherman, began his angling career in 1811 and was first ticketed as a Merchant Seaman in 1845. The Bath proprietor's death certificate gives 1781 as his date of birth, while a National Archives' U.K. record notes 1788 as the birth date of George Fallon, the mariner.[31] Allowing for the pre-1864 absence of official birth certification, the seven year difference is not great enough to definitively discount the possibility that the Salthill fisherman later became the local Baths' keeper. However, as the sea-bath businessman was a 'yeoman,' and the mariner a 'labourer' – when not at sea – it is more likely that the two men were related.

George the yeoman was also the lessor, for a number of years, of an abutting Salthill house, (no.28), which stood to the eastern-rear of the baths' premises, and was occupied by Patrick Dea. An 1861 advertisement identified Salthill's Bath proprietor as 'George Fallon, The Baths, Salthill,' and when the first Ladies' Beach at Salthill was created three years later, that Relief Committee construction was built behind Mr. Fallon's Baths. In the description of that beach's destruction by a violent 1869 storm, the area was still described as George's Baths, even though

George Fallon had passed away three years earlier. He was 85 years of age on his death in 1866. George's wife, Bridget, appears to have taken over for a short spell, before James Fallon ran the family business right up to 1893/'4. The Fallon family of Salthill, therefore, operated a baths' business to the seaward side of Seapoint House for the bulk of four decades (1855–1894), and most likely for longer than that. It is also possible – though unproven – that James Fallon, on the selling of his baths in the 1890s, moved across the road to occupy house 44(a) in Barrack Lane, previously occupied by Mary Ward. A Fallon association with Barrack Lane saw that family play its part in the life of Salthill Village over many decades.

Seapoint House

Seapoint House (no.26), which stood on the inland side of George's Baths was – at £23 – the premises with the greatest Salthill Village valuation in 1855. It was its depth, encompassing Seapoint Terrace, which gave the premises its stature. The two-storey Seapoint House abutted a three-storey terrace of Sunnyside Lodge, Villa Marina, Beach Mount and Prairie House. The sole holding in the entire Lenaboy townland to exceed Seapoint's appraisal belonged to James O'Hara (1832–1902), with a rateable valuation of £36. Captain O'Hara's property in that townland, however, only featured a small premises (RV £2-10s), but included over 20 acres of land. It is clear, therefore, that at the time of Griffith's valuation, the highest valued premises in the Village of Salthill was Seapoint House, a position it maintained for many years. Beach Mount's construction (RV £19) and Colman O'Donohue's building of the impressive Prairie House (RV £18) in the same 1855–1861 period did not out-value the older Seapoint premises, even though Beach Mount was described, by its official valuer, as 'a very good house, well situated, offices added.'[32]

Though not the most highly valued, Prairie House was the Village's most striking building during the later decades of the 19th century. Its distinctive American style balcony – and naming – ensured that the boarding house's patrons and general public knew that proprietor, Colman O'Donohue, had enjoyed a successful spell in the Land of Opportunity. The O'Donohue family – which included a clergyman and knighted scion – played a leading role in the place, but as their particular tale better fits a 20th century narrative, that story must await a future volume of this history. 'Michael Horan, Grocer' was the sign above the door at Villa Marina, two doors to the right of Prairie House. Mr. Horan was rateably valued in that premises from 1867 to 1884. The masts of ships at Galway Docks appear to the right in figure 78 and it is also interesting to note that Seapoint House stood at the apex of a tight *Bóthar na Trá* corner.

Seapoint House was primarily a Bathing Lodge that was let out, as was a sister premises, which belonged to the same structure. A *Galway Vindicator* advertisement

78. Seapoint corner at Salthill Village c.1870. Note how the attached Seapoint Terrace stretched almost to the sea, at the rear of Seapoint House. (Courtesy of National Library of Ireland.)

featured Seapoint House, which was to be let furnished for the 1849 Bathing Season: 'This desirable Bathing Residence is commodious and for the immediate Reception of a respectable family. Also, Seapoint Terrace, which is fitted up in a very neat manner, amply Furnished, and capable of accommodating a large family. Both Lodges have Coach Houses and Stabling attached.'[33] The Seapoint House brand had stature for, in December 1857, the *Nenagh Guardian* reported that: 'William Waller, Esq., J.P., Mrs Waller and family have returned to Prior Park, after a sojourn of some months at Seapoint House, Salt Hill, Galway.'[34]

Advertisements for Seapoint House, throughout the later decades of the 19th century, simply offered the premises for letting, with no mention of an on-site baths' facility. That said, the valuation description of the premises in the post-Griffith period was 'House, off(ices), baths & yard.' It was c.1894 that the neighbouring bathing business, which had belonged to James Fallon, was incorporated into the Seapoint complex.

Thomas Delany at Seapoint House

Thomas Delany was the 'occupier' of Seapoint House in 1855. As he was not in residence at Salthill at the time of the 1834 Tithe Applotment tally, his arrival at the resort was in the 1834–1855 timeframe. Mr. Delany owned a number of holdings at Salthill, for in January 1845 he transferred a seaside property to James O'Hara at the resort. That premises had originally been constructed by a builder/carpenter, Ulick Burke, for Thomas' neighbour, 'George Fallon of Salt hill.'[35] The house in question was situated 'on the southside of Salthill between the Recorder's Quay and Cappanaveagh.' That Delany-O'Hara transaction appears to indicate that Mr. Delany operated at Salthill from the early 1840s. A violent 1847 storm, which did great damage in the general resort area, left 'several of the bathing lodges unroofed and the gable of Mr. Delany's handsome lodge at Sea-point flung down.'[36] Some six years later, Thomas Delany of Salt Hill was brought to a Galway Petty Court hearing by Mr. Thomas Mullowney, in an effort to resolve a minor monetary dispute. It appears that Thomas Delany was a single man without a family. The basis for that assumption is an 1855 record, which details a Thomas Delany of Salthill declaring Robert Christopher Barbor as his heir and assignee.[37] Referenced in that succession file was the 'house on the main road to Barna', which boasted a frontage of 30 feet 6 inches. Such a description appears to define Seapoint House. Robert Christopher Barbor was a major landowner with properties in the counties of Dublin, Longford, Leitrim, Roscommon and Fermanagh. Mr. Delany occupied Seapoint House right up to the late 1870s.

John Parsons at Seapoint House

John Parsons succeeded Thomas Delany at Seapoint House circa 1878, and he remained *in situ* up to the late 1880s. The new occupant proved to be an elusive target for this study and the only John Parsons identified in Galway newspapers around that time was an Ennis agent offering emigration to Queensland, Australia. Assisted passage was offered in 1870 to 'eligible persons.'[38] Census returns of 1901 also recorded a John Parsons, and his family, residing at the Gate Lodge of Lenaboy Castle on Taylor's Hill. That gentleman was a 50 year old Church of Ireland, Cornwall born naval pensioner. No relationship between the two individuals, here described, and the man who occupied Seapoint House, throughout the 1880s, has been established.

One way or another, Mr. Parsons was replaced in the Valuation Books by 'Teresa M. Cremmons' in 1889. The 'Cremmons' record of the surname represented one spelling form of a family patronym that came to be identified with Seapoint right up to the mid-1940s, when the premises – house and baths – were sold to Mr. Noel Finan. As 'Cremen' was the spelling style used by the family in census returns and other documents, that variant will be principally used here.

Cremen Family Background

David Cremen graduated as a medical doctor from Trinity College in 1852. He practiced in Dublin and Cork and also lectured on Practical Anatomy at the Cork School of Medicine. As a physician, he contributed papers on Pathological subjects to the Dublin Medical Journal and he resided at 8 Cook Street, Cork in 1858.[39] By 1871, Dr. David Cremen was a 41 year old Physician & Surgeon (not practicing), who lodged at 62 Winchester Street in the parish of St. George, Hanover Square, London. A year later he married a Dublin native, Frances Elizabeth Kelly, and they had two children who were both born in London; James in 1873 and Frances Mary in 1874. In the year following his daughter's birth, Dr. David Cremen, a young man in his forties, died on 6 December, 1875. On David's passing at his Westminster home, his estate, which was valued at under £2,000, was bequeathed to his widow and sole executrix, Frances Elizabeth Cremen. Some years later, Mrs. Frances E. Cremen arrived in Salthill with her two children. The Cremen family first resided at Grattan House for three years, before moving to operate Seapoint

79. Seapoint House and the abutting Seapoint Baths are to the right of this image, which also shows a wide open-area at the Seapoint end of Salthill Village c.1930.

House as a Boarding and Baths' business at the resort. A religious nun, Sister Mary Cremen, who was a 75 year old Cork City native, was recorded as a teacher at the Dominican College on Taylor's Hill in 1901, and it is possible that she was related to the Seapoint House family.

Mrs. Frances Cremen and her two children, James and Mary, were to become synonymous with Seapoint House over the following half-century. After the Fallon baths' business, next door, was taken over by the Cremen enterprise circa 1894, a Valuation note recorded that a 'new bath house was in progress.' By 1898, the Cremen business model included a new Baths and Bathing Boxes' facility which abutted Seapoint House. The house itself had dropped its baths' listing from 1891. The takeover and improvement of the Fallon facility saw the valuation of the newly built Baths' premises jump from a modest £3 to £8-10s.

Photographs from the early 1900s show the improved seaward premises bearing a Seapoint Baths' banner, beside its sister Lodging House. In the image above **(fig.79)**, the horse-drawn cart that stood outside Seapoint Baths – on right – was most likely delivering seaweed. The tight Seapoint corner of the previous image **(fig.78)** had been replaced by a triangular open area. That corner clearance was completed by 1929 and the above photograph was taken before Kenny's Grocery shop at Strand House (O'Reilly's Bar & Kitchen today) was sold to William Sammon in 1934.

Mrs. Frances Elizabeth Cremen continued to let the Seapoint House after her purchase of the property. On census night 1901 it was Rose Adelaide Sheridan, a 69 year old boarding house keeper and widow, who was *in situ* at Seapoint. On the same night Mrs. Frances E. Cremen, whose 'income derived from House Property, Baths dividends,' was not at her Seapoint property, but was recorded as a visitor at the Cappanaveagh home of Mary Josephine Potter. There appears to have been a family relationship between the Cremen, Sheridan and Potter families, with Mary Potter being also recorded, in the early years of the 20th century, as an occupier of Seapoint House for a short spell.

Lily Gertrude Torrens

Miss Lily Torrens, who had briefly resided at the nearby Stella Maris, was also listed as occupier of Seapoint House during the first decade of the 20th century. The daughter of John Torrens, an engineer, Miss Lily Torrens married Thomas Henry Mayne in 1904. There were – in fact – two weddings that year, for the couple first wed in a registry office on 26 April, 1904, before solemnising their union with a wedding ceremony at the Church of St. Nicholas in Galway – on the eve of Christmas Eve – in the same calendar year. The son of a miller, Thomas Mayne was himself a secondary school teacher, who was residing at Chertsey, Surrey, at the time of his marriage to Miss Torrens. Mrs. Lily Mayne, who also occupied Glen View in Salthill Village for a time after her marriage, passed away at Barna in March 1942, with her husband, Thomas, present at her passing.

Mrs. Cremen

By 1911, Mrs. Frances Elizabeth Cremen was again listed as occupier of Seapoint House. She was then a 68 year old Dublin born widow and Lodging House Proprietor, who was living with her two single children; 36 year old daughter Frances Mary Cremen, and 38 year old son, James Cremen – a 'Superintendant of Baths.' Mrs. Frances Cremen appears to have taken an active role in the running of Seapoint House and Baths and in 1906 she brought a Dominick Street gentleman to court for 30 shillings of cash lent within the previous year. In 1913, Mrs. Cremen opposed a £1,200 loan, suggested by Mr. Price, L.G.B. Inspector, for a park and recreation ground at Salthill, claiming that the resort had too many amusements already.[40] Frances Elizabeth Cremen, the family matriarch and widow, who – following the 1875 London death of her husband – had brought her family to Salthill, passed away in 1919.

James and Mary (Marie) Cremen

The family business continued, however, and in June 1919 the seawater baths were open as usual. The following press piece proclaimed both the advantages of the Cremen baths' offering and the geniality of its superintendent:

They constitute an essential feature of holiday pleasures at Salthill and are patronised by practically every visitor who comes to our seaside resort for the summer. The premises have a cleanliness and freshness about them that of itself is invigorating, the attendance is admirable, and they are under the careful management of the courteous proprietor, Mr. J. Cremen.[41]

James Cremen and his sister, Frances Mary Cremen, who was locally known as Mary – or Marie – played prominent roles in Salthill life. Both hit the headlines for different reasons in 1909. It was in August of that year that a dramatic sea rescue saved the life of Paddy Burke, though his Barrack Lane neighbour, Denis McGrath lost his life in the same incident. Miss Cremen was present that day and in the midst of a startled inertia that first gripped putative rescuers, Miss Cremen plucked a life belt from a policeman and cried, 'If no one else tries to save him, I will.' Her daring courage won the admiration of a vocally supportive – though passive – crowd. Her brother, James, also contributed to the rescue of Mr. Burke.[42] That sea rescue was not the sole courageous act carried out by Mary Cremen in 1909, for – some weeks later – she was slightly burned in her efforts to rescue James from a fire at Seapoint baths. The blaze, which followed an engine explosion, did little damage.[43]

Mr. James Cremen's principal brush with local fame revolved around his central role in the 1909 Bathing Battle of Blackrock, which represented a reaction to Colonel Richard O'Hara's refusal to allow swimmers 365 day access to the famed bathing spot. Mr. Cremen – during that fraught year – made fiery speeches, became secretary of the Citizens' Committee which he first proposed, and was one of the six leaders charged with trespass on the rock. Not afraid to voice his opinions in forum or in print, James Cremen's interest in the resort was robustly expressed during his involvement in the Blackrock battle. He also acted as Secretary of the Galway Rate Payers' Association, and served as a committed member of Galway Chamber of Commerce. In that latter capacity he was proactive in having the Chamber co-operate with the Mayor's Fund in 1941.

James Cremen's resort facility, which opened every year in June, suffered badly during the ferocious storm of 1926, which 'crushed in the Seapoint baths at Salthill as though they were egg shells.'[44] By the summer of the following year Mr. Cremen 'had re-erected his baths and bathing boxes and has improved the excellent little bathing pool at the back of Seapoint. He has floated a raft for the accommodation of ladies who desire to dive.'[45] The sole Seapoint Baths' fatality, under Cremen management, unearthed by this research was that of Mr. Mitchell in September 1921. Patrick Mitchell, a 67 year old manager at Messrs. Cloran, Tuam, who was staying at Ballinasloe House, was not in the best of health when he attended the baths and died. An inquest was deemed unnecessary.[46]

A tall man, James Cremen's rallying oratory was not his sole vocal skill, as he was also a talented singer who entertained at various functions. He was known to have sung 'Molly Dooley, Darlin' at a Jesuit Sodality concert, and he also entertained when Galway Chamber celebrated the 1925 wedding of its president, Mr. T.J.W. Kenny. James Cremen was a religious man, committed to his faith, and he was also an active member of the Men's Sodality of the Blessed Virgin Mary, attached to St. Ignatius Church. As a member of the latter group, he visited the Vatican on a 1933 European tour which took in Florence, Venice, Milan, Switzerland and Paris. The Sodality members had 'a special private audience' with Pope Pius XI, who blessed them and gave all Galway pilgrims an

80. Marie Cremen of Seapoint House and Baths. (Courtesy of *Connacht Tribune*.)

opportunity to kiss his ring. In the year following that visit Mr. Cremen pronounced at a meeting, called to facilitate the building of Salthill's own church, that the resort needed a 'moral influence', which a new church would provide.[47] His only three transgressions – identified by this research – were (a) having a black & white terrier without a dog licence in 1896; (b) being fined one shilling in 1920 for riding a bicycle 'without lights after lighting up time'; (c) his non-'bona fide traveller' attendance at Ballinasloe House in 1929. In the local political sphere, James Cremen proposed Susan Emerson, who successfully represented the Salthill Citizens' Organisation in her bid for a Corporation seat in 1942. When he died at Seapoint House in October 1944, Baths' proprietor, Mr. James Cremen, left £2,033 in his will, and was survived by his sister, Mary Cremen.

Within weeks of Mr. Cremen's death, it was reported that Seapoint House and the abutting baths had been sold to a well known Salthill business man for £4,250. It was also announced that the purchaser, Mr. Noel Finan, intended to remodel the baths and continue the business, 'on the most up-to-date lines.'[48] Miss Mary Cremen subsequently sold the entire furniture and effects of the 20 bedroom Seapoint House, which included 'a cottage piano, almost new' and hundreds of pictures. In July 1952, Miss Frances Mary Cremen, aged 78, died at Seamount Nursing Home at the end of the Salthill Promenade, along which she often swam as a young woman. She had taken a keen interest in 'amateur theatricals' during the 1890s and had served for many years as Secretary of St. Joseph's Nursing Society. Her death marked the end of a strong Cremen connection with Salthill that is still recalled today. For well over fifty years Cremen's Baths at Seapoint were central to – and closely identified with – Galway's sea resort.

Salthill Baths' Characters

The bathing box facilities on offer at Salthill, in the immediate post-famine period, were – understandably enough – quite primitive. In 1852, for example, there was 'no such thing as a bathing box for gentlemen at all, and the few miserable ones used by the ladies, are in every way unequal to their purpose.'[49] That said, time brought improvements and there was never any doubt but that Galway's sea resort provided real characters, in the provision of a bathing experience that was rarely forgettable. One such character was Sibby of Salthill.

Sibby as 'high-priestess'

It was in Josephine M. Callwell's memoir that humorous stories appeared, which centred on a lady called Sibby, the one-time matriarch of the Salthill bathing scene. It is difficult to definitively say which bathing emporium, or era, Sibby represented, though it is most likely that she belonged to the 1880s/'90s and that Sibby's service was delivered at a personal facility close to Atlantic Lodge. Salthill's bath lady did provide hot water and she certainly made a strong impression on Miss Callwell:

Sibby was the name of the high-priestess who presided over the bathing rites. She waded out into the sea to give screaming infants the three dips, head downwards, which were the approved method of introducing children to the delights of bathing. Those of more mature growth who were timorous of venturing themselves into the briny deep she encouraged by bidding them seat themselves on the margin and pouring a bucket of sea-water on their heads, as a foretaste of the joys awaiting them. There were but a few bathing-boxes, and if any bathers prolonged their dip beyond what Sibby considered reasonable, she would bestow a resounding smack upon them as they emerged all dripping from the water, accompanying it by a torrent of abuse for having kept the box so long from the others who waited for it. A shower-bath could be had in a shanty hard by, and only the initiated knew that the motive-power needful to raise the water to overhead level was supplied by Sibby's son, who mounted a ladder outside and emptied a pail of water down at the critical moment. Once, indeed, a lady having pulled the string and waiting in vain for the expected douche, heard instead a deep voice overhead – 'A thrifle more to the wesht, I'll trouble ye, me lady'. She rushed forth, horrified and indignant, to confront Sibby, 'Ach, Whist!' said the latter in supreme concern, 'it's only me son, Patsy, and who'd be mindin' him?'

Another time an English lady on a visit to Galway demanded a tepid shower-bath. 'An' what might that be ma'am?' demanded Sibby, to whom such flowers of speech were unknown. 'Tepid? Why, half hot and half cold, to be sure,' was the impatient reply.

The lady undressed and, all unsuspecting, pulled the string. Down came a deluge of scalding water upon her. 'Let me out! let me out!' she screamed in alarm. 'It was a tepid bath that I asked for.' 'Sure ye said that 'twas half hot and half could that t'was to be, an here's the could for ye,' as another pailful was emptied down.[50]

It must also have been Sibby who was recalled by an *Octogenarian* scribe, writing in 1960 of his Salthill memories, for the same 'step a piece west' advice was heard by the correspondent's 'unclothed but still safely purdah' nursery governess before 'a deluge of salt water through a trap door' was delivered in a wooden cubicle by a man overhead. Six pennies represented the tariff for that healthy, if sufferable, service.[51]

Babs of the Baths

Locally known as 'Babs of the Baths,' Barbara Molloy described herself in 1901 as a 79 year old, single, lodging house keeper, who lived in a two room premises at the back of Beach Avenue, or Ryan's Terrace, as it was then still recorded in contemporaneous Revision Books. Barbara's home was one of five dwellings – with a third class rating – in the entire Lenaboy townland at the start of the twentieth century. The *Irish Times*, reporting on a Christmas 1902 tragedy, said that Barbara was 'well known to generations of lady bathers at Salthill, where she had long carried on a private bathing establishment.'[52] When a milk girl, on her regular rounds, called to Barbara's house on Christmas morning, the unfortunate woman was found suffocated, following a fire. A burning bed was quickly thrown out, but 'Old Babs' had, by then, expired. The form of 'bathing establishment', run by Barbara Molloy, was not specified in the *Times*' report, and it may have resembled the bathing-box offerings of the high-priestess Sibby. Eight years later, however, a controversy at Babs Molloy's former patch points to a rental apparel service having being offered at the rear of Beach Avenue. Bab's successor on the site hired out towels, and bathing dresses, to those willing to take to the briny. The same successor did not take too kindly – in 1910 – to ladies bathing on her patch in their own swimming apparel. On identifying those in the water who did not use her services, it was alleged that their clothes were taken and thrown about. At an Urban Council meeting, Mr. Gallagher wondered if the Beach Avenue area was supposed to be a public bathing place. Mr. Binns, in reply, stated that it was a ladies' bathing place and – to laughter – indicated that he never went there. Councillor Gallagher wondered what right the offending woman had to prevent people bathing at the place, and he feared that some would not return to Salthill after a beach experience there. The Council referred the matter to its solicitors.[53]

On the question of rented swimming apparel, Dónal Taheny recalled a rental sign, on the wall at prom's end – for the male swimmers at Blackrock – which read, 'Pants and towel 2d.' John Freyne recorded a similar Salthill memory from 1908: 'The men's bathing place was at the end of the "prom". There was a little stone cottage where towels and bathing suits could be hired.'[54]

Hotel Sea Baths

Sea Baths were considered in the 19th century to have added greatly to hotel facilities in much the same way as swimming pools and spas are valued today. The Eglinton Hotel was opened in 1860 by the pioneering John Gill, who showed commendable enterprise twelve years later when he completed 'at great cost…a suite of Baths in connection with his Hotel, comprising Hot, Cold and Shower.' This additional facility, which was opened to the public on 8 July, 1872, was 'fully equal to the best in the country' and was 'important to tourists, Invalids and others.'[55]

The same baths were to be improved and upgraded over the years. By 1901, with Edward McAlinney in possession, there were a dozen baths, all recently painted and repaired, while seven years later reference was made by the *Galway Vindicator* to the Eglinton Hotel's 'noted vapour baths' which had recently been added 'for the successful treatment of rheumatism and other infirmities.'[56] Not resting on his bathing – or engineering – laurels, Edward McAlinney invented a 'Perfection Heat Concentrator' in 1913, which was fitted to the Bath rooms at his hotel. The new device, which worked in the open and kept the rooms 'cool and perfectly ventilated,' was advertised to relieve rheumatic pains. The sole proprietor of the invention was Mr. McAlinney, who was willing to give particulars free to those who applied. It was reported in that first year of the new baths' development that 'an unusually large number of invalids have come, and those afflicted with rheumatism and like ailments' were benefitting from McAlinney's hot Baths.[57] When the Eglinton Hotel was advertised, in three lots, for auction in 1921, the extent of the hotel's bathing facilities became apparent in press advertisements. Lot 3 represented the baths' emporium, which was housed in a two storey building that contained 14 bathrooms, and included 'Reclining, Shower and Vapour Seawater, equipped with two large iron tanks with a capacity of 8,000 gallons supplied by sea water from pumps driven by steam boiler.'[58]

The hotel was not then sold, but was later purchased in 1929 by Mr. McAlinney's daughter, Mrs. Susan Emerson. Reflecting her father's industrious character, Susan revamped the entire baths' complex, before the Eglinton re-opened for business under Emerson management in June, 1930. Mrs. Emerson was later disappointed that the old Garda Station opposite the Banba Hotel, which she owned, was not developed for public baths during the 1940s, in a controversy that revolved around an Irish Tourist Association offer to grant £55,000 towards the project.

Seawater bathing facilities were also offered by other boarding houses / hotels in the resort, which in some cases simply involved access, from the back doors of their premises to the sea-shore. The Stella Maris represented a good example of a facility that developed its seawater product over time. In 1910, Mrs. D.J. (Mary) Walshe advertised a 'Private bathing strand at back. Perfect and up-to-date sanitary accommodation; hot and cold baths.'[59] Mary was not alone in her private strand offering, for the map of Salthill's original Village **(fig.19)** indicates a back-garden pathway to the sea-shore at almost every premises. A briny Baths' gap in Salthill's facility range followed the Seapoint Baths' 1946 closure, and over a decade later, Mrs. Della Walshe at the Stella Maris advertised that 'Hot Sea-Water and Seaweed Baths' were open to the public.[60] That 1958 development was welcomed by Mayor Ald. P. Greene, who commended Mrs. Walshe's enterprise.[61] Della's initiative meant that the Stella Maris represented the last sea-water baths' facility publicly open to Salthill's tourists, a traditional offering that continued into the 1960s.

A Seapoint Beginning without Baths

It was generally accepted that Seapoint Baths would continue to operate under new management after the 1944 Finan purchase, and a newspaper photo caption in the spring of that year repeated a 'modern lines' improvement, which had been previously promised. That same caption noted that the Seapoint site would also house a concert hall and café. By May of that same year it was announced that the baths' owners had decided to open the existing baths, as the 'new modern' facility would not be completed in time to service the 1945 tourist season. The strictures of the Emergency in Ireland resulted in the proprietors letting it be known that they would be very grateful 'if clients, where possible, would kindly bring Towels.'[62] There was concern about the baths' situation in Salthill a year later, which resulted in a Galway Corporation suggestion that Mr. Finan be corresponded with to ascertain if the baths would be operational in 1946. By May, two positions – boilerman and desk clerk – were advertised to facilitate the re-opening of Seapoint Baths. The famed Gaelic writer from Knocknacarra, Dónall Mac Amhlaigh, 'delivered seaweed by the cartload there in 1946,' the last year the baths opened at Seapoint.[63]

No effort, however, was made in that last year to upgrade the Seapoint Bath facility, a fact that severely complicated the resort's relationship with the Irish Tourist Association. It was the Salthill Citizens' Organisation that had earlier stymied a generous offer of £55,000 from the I.T.A. to build baths on the vacated Garda Station site – across from the Banba Hotel. The reason for refusing the tourist body's largesse was that it would interfere with the private development of Seapoint Baths. The S.C.O.'s rebuff eventually resulted in the Tourist Association's 1947 withdrawal of its offer in favour of the private scheme.

As it all turned out, the third plank of Seapoint's dance hall – restaurant – baths' project never materialised. Though the facility was advertised as 'Seapoint Hydro' in 1949 – the year of its opening – the long sought after baths were never built. As late as 1955 some still hoped that the new Seapoint Baths would be developed, but Claude Toft advised a Galway Corporation meeting in that year that Mr. Finan 'did not intend to go ahead with the baths at present.' Councillor Breathnach remarked that he knew people who had left for Lisdoonvarna when baths were not available at the resort.[64] Four years later – in 1959 – when Alderman Fintan Coogan T.D. raised the Baths' deficit at Salthill, Claude Toft said that 'the Stella Maris Hotel had sea baths which were open to anyone wishing to use them, but he understood that the proprietor was now sorry for having gone to the expense of installing them.'[65] That telling observation indicates that there were genuine reasons in the 1950s for not developing baths at Salthill, a reality not missed by Seapoint's proprietors. The focus was then switching from bathing, to swimming and modern pools. Outmoded baths no longer represented the future. A water feature promised little return, in contrast to the steady cash stream which flowed from ballrooms. Seapoint's entrepreneurs – an amalgam of the Finan and Allen families – had to pay their way, so their energy, understandably, was focused on lucrative dancing. The throngs that Seapoint attracted increased the image and status of Salthill and new businesses flourished to serve patrons' needs, before and after dances. Salthill was on an upward spiral and a bright future – serving young dancing feet, not stiff ageing limbs – beckoned at Seapoint.

Dancing

Salthill, in popular memory, is deservedly associated with dancing, for the resort represented the hub of the town's social scene for many decades. In the past, crossroad dancing – despite church disapproval – featured at Nile Lodge cross,[66] most likely before the Great Famine, when that intersection formed a T junction. Other locales were also used and the famed Knocknacarra and World golfer, Christy O'Connor Jnr., recalled that his father, John, met his wife, Elizabeth Noone from Riverstown, Sligo at a crossroad dance on Taylor's Hill.[67] John and Elizabeth married in the early 1940s.

Organised dancing began at the resort after British forces departed the country. It was in February 1922 that Mr. A.J. Roche, as auctioneer for a Liquidation Commission,[68] sold an R.A.F. Aerodrome at Oranmore – for £515 – to the Urban Council.[69] That structure was then transferred to Salthill Park and became known as the Hangar or Pavilion. The first dance at the venue, organised by Mrs. Young & Mrs. Lavelle, took place on Wednesday, 4 July, 1923, with Mr. Clarke Barry's band providing the music. Both ladies, who were in charge of the Bazaar's dancing saloon at the Square, raised almost £70 at the Hangar's opening night for the Galway Development fund. Galway's Omnibus Company arranged to transport the *Votaries of Terpsichore* from Eyre Square to Salthill, from 10 to 11 p.m., and back again from 4.30 until 5.30 in the morning.[70] Patrons did, indeed, dance the night away in those

81. Hangar – Pavilion Ballroom in Salthill Park.

days, and dancing – for the three to four hundred patrons who attended on opening night – did not cease until the morning clock had struck seven.[71] The potential of the venue was instantly recognised and from then on, the Pavilion became a mecca for dancers who travelled far and wide – many on bicycles – to attend. In March 1943, Salthill's Citizen Organisation entered a £704 lease arrangement with Galway Corporation for the Hangar Ballroom. That initiative, which proved to be a cash cow for the organisation over many years, was of great benefit to the resort and financed the clearing of the foreshore during the 1940s. 'Dancing Feet Make Foreshore Neat' was the catchy promotional slogan of the S.C.O. during that period. The Hangar did not face any local opposition until Florence Toft – following a number of court battles – began hosting dances at her Salthill Arcade in November 1944. Five years later, Seapoint Ballroom made a real statement of intent at the resort and entertained countless hordes of dancers for over three decades, before its 1984 sale. Discos and late bars would also have their day in Salthill, before the epicentre of Galway's night entertainment gravitated to town.

As the dancing story of the resort represents a 20th century phenomenon, a closer look at that tale will be presented in a future volume of this history.

Chapter 9

NINETEENTH CENTURY ACCOMMODATION AND FEMALE CONTRIBUTION

Bathing Lodges – Boarding Houses – and One Hotel

Holiday accommodation at Salthill was multi-tiered and ranged from bathing lodges to boarding houses with one hotel, worthy of that name, on offer through the closing decades of the 19th century, and the revolutionary opening decades of the century that followed. The 1930s arrived before the Eglinton Hotel faced any seaside competition for the prestige clientele Mrs. Emerson then served at the resort's leading lodging facility.

Bathing Lodges

Bathing Lodges represented, for those who took a summer house for the season, the top end of the 19th century status tree. Such residences were a far cry from some seasonal habitations, which might today carry a 'lodge' tag, for Salthill's summer piles were magnificent structures which dominated the landscape. As early as 1831 Father Peter Daly was looking for tenants to take a 'desirable Bathing Residence' that offered 'a dining room, parlour, drawing room and study, 6 bedrooms, a large kitchen, servants' hall, 4 servants' bedrooms, cellars, dairy, &c with coach house and stable for four horses.'[1] The Bathing Lodge on offer was Blackrock House, a massive structure at the end of the promenade which today serves as the headquarters for Ability West. That was not the sole lodge the same clergyman had to offer to discerning and affluent tenants, for Merville House on the crown of Taylor's Hill was also for rent with 'the Lawn extending to the Sea Shore. The HOUSE would be Let as a Bathing Lodge during the summer if not permanently taken.'[2] Such lodges at Salt Hill were being 'rapidly occupied for the Bathing Season, by respectable families from the country' in mid-July 1844.[3] Thirteen years later, spring preparations were well advanced by May for a successful summer season: 'Already

Salt Hill is putting on its livery of gaiety; the lodges have been whitewashed, painted, and prepared by their respective owners in anticipation of a good season.'[4]

Thomas Barton's post-famine clearing of tenants at Attithomasrevagh was to accelerate the building of opulent lodges which included Maretimo, Brinkwater, Gurthard and Salerno. A *Freeman's Journal* reporter observed in 1872 that 'these villas are numerous hereabouts. They are more substantial than showy, and are one and all of comfortable presence and most cosily placed.'[5] Families that occupied such palatial summer residences were accompanied by a retinue of staff – properly known as their 'suite'– to ensure that all needs were catered for during serenely restful days.

82. An 1831 Fr. Daly – *Connaught Journal* advertisement for Merville.

Regularly published over the years were lists of exalted visitors, who leased such bathing lodges at Galway's fashionable watering place. Included in an 1838 *Galway Patriot* summary of late arrivals at Salt Hill were: At Nile Lodge, John O'Hara, Esq., Lady O'Donnell O'Hara, family and suite, from his house, Mountjoysquare, Dublin; Denis Kirwan, Esq. Castlehacket, on a visit to his uncle, Robert Burke, St. Cleran's, Esq.;... the Honourable Mr. Trench of Woodlawn, family and suite.[6] Numbered among a *Galway Vindicator*'s 1869 list were: Burton R.P. Persse Esq. J.P., family and suite; Acheson Ffrench Esq. and Mrs. Ffrench; Mrs. Skerrett and J. Skerrett Esq.; Mrs. Martyn, Tulyra Castle; Shaw Taylor and family; Captain John Eyre and family.[7]

As it turned out, however, the majority of such houses were taken on a more permanent basis, particularly at Rockbarton, where some professors at the new university had taken up Salthill residencies, following the 1849 opening of Queen's College. The Rockbarton lodges, most identified with the town's academics, were constructed post-1852, the year that Thomas Henry Barton purchased the Attithomasrevagh townland. Only three years, therefore, separated the opening of Queen's College, Galway from a major Salthill development, which catered for the housing needs of Galway's professional classes. The Bathing Lodge glory of many such structures was, however, to barely span a century – or less. Changes of use to serve new needs represented the reason for some properties' relatively short 'bathing' existence: Salerno came to house a girls' school, as did Dalysfort House, which previously had operated as a hotel. Mr. Isaac B. Daly's 'splendid house', atop the rising road that took his surname, enjoyed less than forty years of 'bathing' or residential status, for Miss Sarah Jane Galbraith was operating a

83. Three Bathing Lodges overlooking Salthill's promenade, from left; Revagh, Belmore and Brinkwater. The Galway Bay Hotel replaced Revagh and Belmore in the 1990s. (Courtesy of Stan Shields.)

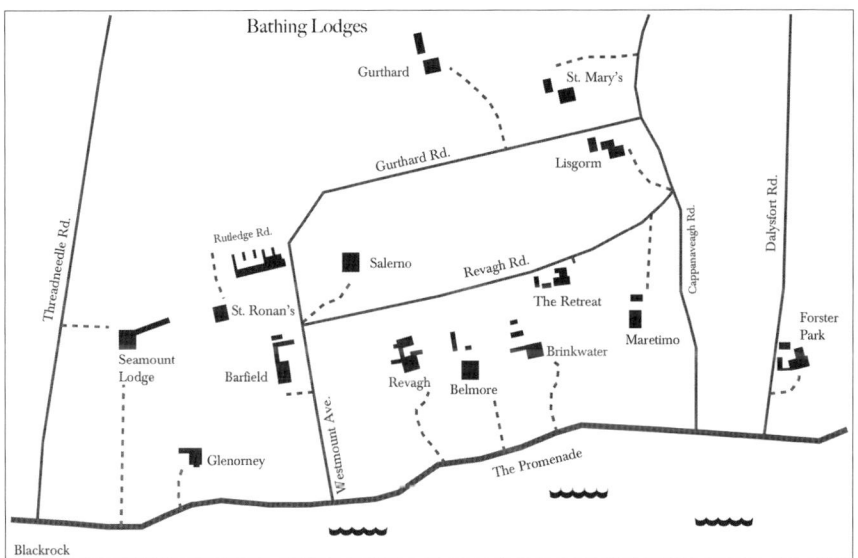

84. Seafront map of 19th century Bathing Lodges.

'First-Class Boarding House and Private Hotel' in the building from the early years of the 20th century.[8]

Samuel U. Roberts' Barfield was, in turn, occupied by landed, commercial and political families, before being purchased by the Munster and Leinster Bank in 1925, for its Lynch's Castle managers. Mr. Francis Mackey, who represented the last of that banking cohort, continued in residence at Barfield for a number of years following his 1958 retirement. On the building's sale, Francis and Margaret Murray opened the Salthill Hotel at Barfield in August, 1963. Maretimo and the Retreat made way for Leisureland, while Seamount served as a Nursing Home before being inevitably knocked for housing development. Gort Ard became an Opus Dei house and two of the prom's primary lodges, Belmore and Revagh, were replaced by the Galway Bay Hotel in May 1998. The majority of Salthill's bathing lodges have now disappeared from the landscape, though a small number do survive: Gort Ard, Lisgorm and St. Mary's at Rockbarton remain as examples of the whimsically titled 'Bathing Lodges' of yore.

Boarding Houses

While the Eglinton Hotel, which opened in 1860, was the first real hotel to be built at Salthill, accommodation – of varying standards – was available at the resort from the initial construction of the curved line of Salthill Village houses. Tourist demand drove the delivery of accommodation as early as 1828, when the *Connaught Journal* reported that *the number of strangers who frequented Galway last season, for the enjoyment of sea bathing, rendered lodgings exceedingly scarce and dear. Houses on the sea road were in great demand, and the owners obtained very high rents, which have induced many persons to erect several neat and comfortable lodges in the direction of the West and Salt hill. This is a good speculation, and we are not aware that money could be more profitably disposed of. Country families will be sure of obtaining every accommodation next summer, as there will be forty or fifty neat lodges along the sea-shore – where there were but two or three a few years since.*[9]

It was ten years later that the proposal to have a Penny Post established in the village further pointed to the resort's significant growth.[10]

Winter student Accommodation
One example of the accommodation range available at the resort was described in Michael George O'Malley's recall of his lodgings at Salthill, on his 1904 entry to Queen's College:

Practically all the students were in 'digs' in Salthill. There were few houses in Lower and Upper Salthill, but they were all lodging houses and empty during the winter except for students. I got digs in Sunnyside Lodge, which was next door to Seapoint House. Both houses are gone and replaced by the Seapoint Ballroom. My two brothers had been in lodgings in Sunnyside fifteen or more years before me. I got a bedroom and sitting room for five shillings a week. If I shared the sitting room the charge was three and sixpence a week. During the summer the houses were full of guests and no student would have been kept…We provided our own food. My father brought me to the shops and established credit for me – groceries, meat coal, etc. I collected the bills once a month and sent them home. Some exhibitions and scholarships kept me in pocket money.[11]

Michael belonged to the O'Malley medical dynasty that boasted strong Connemara roots. He was the sixth son, and last but one of the fourteen children, of Peter James O'Malley, Kilmilkin, Maam and Mary O'Malley, Ballyburke, Westport, Co. Mayo. Michael entered Queen's College, Galway, on a scholarship prize of £20. Considering his two room accommodation – and liberal shop credit – the college student's lodgings were quite comfortable. Seven years after Michael's 1904 college entry, Cusack John O'Malley, a 20 year old Medical student, also stayed at Sunnyside Lodge. Born in Luton, Cusack was the son of Doctor David Joseph O'Malley, a Roscommon native, who practiced medicine in England and the Isle of Man, before returning to Ireland to become the Medical Officer for Glenamaddy. Dr. David O'Malley and his English born wife, Ellen Mary Sansow, reared thirteen children and sent their son, Cusack, to Galway's university.

It is clear that third-level education was not then – and for many still is not – within the economic compass of all Irish families. Such opportunities belonged, in the 19th century, to the fortunate few who could afford what was, in effect, a great luxury. Determination, intelligence, patronage or serendipity sometimes allowed less well off students achieve academic and professional success. One such student was Jamie Mullin, who also qualified, some decades before Michael O' Malley, as a medical doctor at Galway's Queen's College. Throughout his academic journey, Jamie did not quite experience the same standard of comfort enjoyed by the Kilmilkin undergraduate. Taking a most unorthodox educational route, the cart-maker from County Tyrone entered the local Cookstown Academy at 22 years of age, before furthering his academic career at Galway. A combination of luck, hard work, his own genius and his widowed mother's self-sacrifice saw Jamie attain a B.A. degree, before embarking on his medical studies.

In a gem of a book, entitled *The Story of a Toiler's Life,* James described his lodgings at Galway during the 1870s. A steady and sober student from Clare, called O'Brien, advised Mullin that the family of a police sergeant might take him in as a fellow-lodger: *'Accordingly I went there and was shown into a sitting room and bedroom on the top floor, and told that I might share the same with Mr. O'Brien for three shillings per week, the sum to include cooking…The question of food supply, as it may be called in these war times, was the problem I had next to study. It was very simple; I wanted only as much as would keep body and soul together, and for this I calculated about sixpence per day would suffice. I purveyed my food and the landlady cooked it as per agreement. I used to purchase cocoa nibs by the pound and a portion of these prepared in boiling water made an infusion which, taken without sugar or milk, but with dry bread only constituted my breakfast and supper, and cost about four pence. My dinner consisted of a few potatoes and a fried herring, which cost about two pence – the whole day's bill of fare amounting thus to the sum I had calculated on. During the first college term from the end of October till the beginning of the Christmas vacation this was my daily régime, never once broken by the taste of milk, sugar or butcher's meat, and never exceeding sixpence daily – a rate that would make ordinary economy seem the height of extravagance.'*[12]

Mullin's book, published in 1921, was well titled for the author certainly 'toiled' throughout his early days, and whatever rewards came his way were well earned. The Tyrone man became a successful doctor in Cardiff, quite an achievement for a man born into poverty – in 1846 – during the Great Famine. His nationalism was reflected in associations with Fenianism and later with the Irish National League. Though he did not identify the address of the lodgings described above, his accommodation account and diet description captures the fare on offer in Galway-Salthill during the 1870s. Economic circumstances meant that Jamie Mullin did not experience all of the privileges enjoyed by Michael O'Malley. Without shop credit, Mullin's budget was extremely tight and his accommodation was shared with a fellow-student. For all of that, both O'Malley and Mullin did enjoy the luxury of a sitting room, along with sleeping accommodation.

The student-Salthill relationship must have changed somewhat by the 1930s, if one was to heed Mr. Patrick J. Lindsay's recall of his time as a U.C.G. undergraduate during that decade: *There was a great relationship in Galway in those days between landladies and students, except for the Salthill landladies who turfed out their tenants on the first day of May to make way for the more lucrative tourists. We shunned Salthill.*[13] The Mayo man, who – in a 1992 memoir – described himself as an 'unrepentant Blueshirt,' was called to the Bar in 1946, and served as a Fine Gael member of Dáil Éireann (1954–1961 / 1965–1969); Vice Chairman Seanad Éireann 1961–1965; and Master of the High Court 1975–1984.

Frugal Summer Fare

At the lower end of the Lodging House spectrum at Salthill, facilities were much more frugal. In 1910, according to an observation by Urban Councillor McDonagh, as many as six or eight people slept in the one room due to serious overcrowding at the resort. Sir James O'Donohue was quick to react to that inherent criticism of Salthill, where his family occupied Prairie House, a three storey boarding house on Salthill's main street: 'I know that the accommodation Mr. McDonagh refers to applies to only Barrack Lane, and not to the houses in the front, where people can get ample accommodation if they pay for it.'[14] A glimpse of the meagre provisions offered at economy level in the resort was captured in an advertisement for the sale of a boarding house 'at Lenaboy Lane or Barrack Lane, Upper Salthill,' as late as April 1921:

The Premises are held under Lease for a term of 99 years from 1886, at the nominal yearly rent of £1 10s. 0d. The House has a frontage of 30 feet, and contains Kitchen and Three Rooms on ground floor. There is a large room extending full length of house on second floor. In the rere of House are Out-offices used as Bedrooms. The Premises are built with a view to catering for visitors during the summer season, and are admirably adapted for such, capable of accommodating about 30 persons.[15]

A public auction was conducted by A.J. Roche, Auctioneer for the vendor, Mr. Patrick Burke. Sleeping facilities could hardly have been salubrious, with three rooms on the ground floor and one room, running the length of the house, on the upper storey. That description reads like a modern day open-hostel arrangement, without any reference to sanitary or hygiene facilities. Though out-houses served as bedrooms, the one room on the top floor must have catered for the majority of the thirty visitors who lay their heads there at night. Privacy appears to have been of little – or at least secondary – concern in such a scenario, though it must be admitted that maximum use was being made of the available area. The advert boasted of the house being 'admirably adapted' for such accommodation, but it appears unlikely that such summer lodgings could compare with facilities enjoyed by those staying at either Prairie House or Sunnyside Lodge, on the seaward side of the main Salthill road.

A quite colourful – but accurate – description of the boarding standards offered to less well off Salthill visitors was given by J.M. Callwell in her 1912 *Old Irish Life* volume that recalled the author's time at Salthill: *'I'm not one of thim that crowds their houses,' said one woman who catered for this class of lodgers, in lofty scorn of her neighbours; 'I'd niver put them to sleep more nor three in a bed.'*

There was indeed almost a dignified seclusion in such liberal accommodation, since the more general custom was to let each corner of a room to a separate family, who brought their own poor bedding and camped upon the floor as best they could. Even for the better-to-do the arrangements were of a very primitive simplicity, widely different from the luxury that prevails at a fashionable watering-place of the present day, but perhaps our manner of life was to the full as enjoyable.[16]

85. Cappanaveagh end of Salthill Village.

It was not only on Barrack Lane that relatively small houses were furnished to serve many visitors, not all of them human. Geraldine Plunkett Dillon recalled in the Plunkett family memoir – *All in the Blood* – renting 'a small house or two-storey cottage on the beach in Salthill. It had four small rooms and a kitchen in it, but there were beds for fourteen people, feather beds and full of fleas. It belonged to Mrs. Murphy who had a key with which she constantly came in the back door as soon as I went out and abused my unfortunate maid. She had a jar of rotten dripping on the top shelf and was furious when I threw it out.'[17] That residence, which housed Professor Thomas Dillon and family in 1919/'20, was known as *An Teach Beag Bán* and stood on the present Salthill Car Park site, directly across from where the Bon Bon trades today.

An Teach Beag Bán, where the Dillon family resided during the Black and Tan era, is to the right in figure 85. That *teach* is the gabled seaward residence, which faced the gap beyond Finan's Commercial House (Killoran's today). The *bán* adjective of the house's title is explained by the building's whitewashed front façade. The 'beds for fourteen people' within its walls were accommodated over two floors, with twin dormer windows fore and aft at first floor – attic level. Across the road, Martin Donnellan, a grocer and Atlantic Bar licensee, traded to the west of Martin Finan's premises.

A Salthill Street of Many Names

References to Salthill's fleas were not uncommon – even by locals – and the predominance of Barrack Lane's budget boarding facilities led to it being colloquially called 'Flea Lane,' or 'Flay Lane,' over many years. Such a title was not unique to Salthill, for similar handles are yet to be found in places that range from Donegal's Ballybofey to West Yorkshire. A second premise for the root of the avenue's alternative appellation depends on a heavily assonated 'Flay Lane' pronunciation, delivered with a Galway drawl. Anecdotal beliefs hold that 'flay' derives from the word 'flail,' an instrument which was once used for threshing grain at the site. Such a conviction carries currency, for Charlie Adley added the following bracketed codicil to the use of 'Flea Lane' in a 2004 *City Tribune* column; 'my editor informs me this unfortunate moniker evolved from the local pronunciation of its historical title, Flail Lane, dating back to when it led to fields of corn.'[18] That said, the original editor of the *Connacht Tribune*, Mr. T.J.W. Kenny, took no steps to qualify Flea Lane's use in his newspaper's reporting of court hearings, the first of which appeared in 1909, the initial year of the *Tribune*'s existence.[19] The accompanying Lawrence photograph clearly indicates that fields surrounded Barrack Lane, and recent memory recalls fields being farmed by the McGrath family, a clan with deep roots in Salthill. The 'flail' theory, therefore, may have some substance, but it is much more likely that the street's nickname emanated from its boarding past.

Fleas were a scourge to the traveller worldwide and they were not a new irritant to West of Ireland visitors. In 1650, for example, Mrs. Ann Fanshawe, and her husband, Sir Richard, were satisfied – on their arrival at Galway – with a good supper and the cleanliness of their boarding house. Richard, however, awoke in the morning to exclaim, 'My heart, what great spots are these on my legs?' The cause was to be found on the bed he had slept in, which sported 'blankets full of fleas.'[20] Some three hundred years later the same scourge had clearly not been eradicated, for Galway's Town Hall cinema was locally known as the 'Flea House.' Knights of the Realm, university professors and cinema goers were not, of course, the only ones in Galway town to suffer the nips of indigenous insects.

Having said all of that, Barrack Lane residents suffered an understandable sensitivity to the 'Flea Lane' term, which occasionally drew laughter in Galway's court house. When the place was there mentioned in 1914, Mr. Daly, solicitor, played to the gallery with the following rebuke to a witness who uttered the offending street name: 'Now we cannot allow you to make use of filthy language here (loud laughter).'[21] Ten years later, one Salthill reader had clearly grown tired of the clichéd jibe and reacted to another *Tribune* reference to 'Flea Lane.' The offended resident, adopting *Observer* as his *nom de plume*, let fly in a great defence of Barrack Lane / Lenaboy Terrace with a few arrows directed at pretentious foes, at least one of whom – Sir James O'Donohue – had, by then, departed the place. In deference to Barrack Lane denizens over many decades, the published defence, which opened with a Shakespearean quotation, is here presented:

Sir, – *What's in a name?*
 Good name in man or woman dear, my Lord,
 Is the immediate jewel of their soul

86. Fields surrounding Barrack Lane. The house row to the rear is the original Salthill Village line. (Lawrence Collection, Courtesy of National Library of Ireland.)

He who steals my purse steals thrash,
But he who steals my good name
Robs me of that which most enriches me
And makes me poor indeed.

In your last issue I noticed a reference to 'Flea-lane', Salthill. I am a resident of Salthill and do not know where it is. There are four lanes off Salthill road: Beach Avenue, San Antonio-terrace, Dalysfort -terrace and the one (the most important of them all) without a name. In this nameless terrace the houses are of the two-storey, slate type, not like others in the avenues, and cleaner than any other range in the city of Galway. The people who live there are all owners of their own property, not like other localities except the swell ones and those people are farmers, etc., and hold some of the most important posts in town.

I have heard 'Flea lane' jokingly applied to all Salthill, where every house has a high-sounding name to remind some stranger, perhaps, that it is a mansion – bluff! Now the regular old name of this terrace where the property value is greater than most streets in Galway, is Lenaboy, as the rate receipts show, and I think that in this age of bluff nomenclature it is at least entitled to a name from our urban council, which collects a large revenue from it. Not a new name but its own name, – 'Lenaboy -terrace.' Lenaboy is Gaelic. So is Terrace (tir – ground – or – locality). The urban council should protect public property. The entrance to Lenaboy-terrace was encroached upon years ago by a builder, and further invasions are recorded even this present year. Where are our public engineers and solicitors?…It is just as well that this matter came up anyway, and to have our streets properly named. We do not want a name from astronomical Latin nor from any 'View' which does not exist, nor from the ranches of Texas nor from the Lisdoon-Greek mythology. We want no name at all. We have that for thousands of years. All we want is our urban district council to send out its engineer with his map and its painter with his camel hair and write it up, 'Lenaboy Terrace,' the healthiest and most hygienic little street at this side of the river Shannon. OBSERVER [22]

The letter's 'nameless terrace' description was not accurate, for the street was not so much un-named as over-named. Its Barrack Lane handle stemmed from the 1869 sourcing of premises for an R.I.C. Police Barracks in the place. The same street and its hinterland, over the years, carried a number of other titles, which included Bright's Lane – Bright's Road – Brighton Lane – Charlesfield – Woodmount Avenue – Flea Lane – Lenaboy Terrace – Lenaboy Road – Lenaboy Avenue – Lenaboy Lane. Published, public or legal records of the above names have all been identified by this study, though no such contemporaneous reference has been sourced in relation to 'Flail Lane.' One example of the roadway's litany of names is contained in a property agreement between lessor, Sarah Anne Ormbsy, of Commercial Road, Murwillumbah, Sydney, New South Wales, Australia, and lessee, Joseph Keogh, of Barrack Lane, Salthill. Keogh was a professional golfer, who was first employed by the local Galway club in 1907.[23] Jointly signed was a 1911 indenture, in relation to a 'parcel of Land situate at Barrack Lane or Bright's Lane, Salthill, Galway, otherwise known as Charlesfield, otherwise Lenaboy in the parish of Rahoon.'

Observer's Texas reference was directed at what he perceived to be a faux-posh 'Prairie House' appellation on the balconied residence Colman O'Donohue – a returned Yank – had built circa 1860. The scribe's jibe at views 'which did not exist' was aimed at Salthill Village house-names, which boasted of Green/Wave/Valley/Glen/Grove and Corrig vistas before them. Genuine frustration at the narrowing of the street entrance is both palpable and understandable, for the original road had no major access impediment **(figs.25 & 26)**. The narrowed entry at the Upper-Salthill Road end, which still exists today, was created c.1898 by a building on the eastern side of the street. That pinched access is perhaps one of the reasons for the persistent 'lane' tag for, without it, the street's width would have been – in its time – adequate throughout its entire length. Ryan's Terrace at the other end of the village changed to Beach Avenue without any reference to 'lane,' though it was no wider than its Lenaboy equivalent. By *Observer*'s calculation, the encroaching structure at Barrack Lane was constructed a number of years before 1924, the legacy of a building regulation free-for-all, with contemporaneous 'invasions' also of concern in the missive. The offending property was first rateably valued in 1904, with John N. Sleator as immediate lessor. That same house became chiefly identified with Michael 'Esha' Kelly and his wife Bridie. Though he lived at Salthill from 1919 to 1997,[24] the first rateable entry for Michael Kelly – at the house known as Sea View – was in the mid-1930s.

Observer's identification of the Gaelic origin of 'Lenaboy' – *Léana Bhuidhe* – Yellow Meadow – was correct, though the etymological root of 'Terrace' is not native to Ireland, but to Middle French or Vulgar Latin.[25] A Lenaboy brand carried an acceptable *cachet*, as the lane belonged in that townland, and the landed O'Hara family (ad)dressed a 'castle' in the same livery, even though the same 'castle' was built in Cloghatisky. The writer's 'terrace' choice was curious, for a 'Lenaboy

87. The house that narrowed entrance to Barrack Lane in construction c.1898.

ASCAIL AN LÉANA BHÁITE
LENABOY AVENUE

Figure 88.

Avenue' title had been informally used from 1921. When Patrick Burke was selling his thatched cottage in that pre-Independence year, he was obviously not keen to append an (R.I.C.) Barrack Lane to its address, and Lenaboy Avenue was used in his newspaper notice.[26] That advertisement carried the first Lenaboy Avenue reference discovered by this research. Three years later, representatives of the late Patrick Finnerty followed suit, when Renmore Lodge at Lenaboy Avenue was offered for auction in August 1924.[27] Cancelled Revision Books added another version with the following handwritten annotation in 1932: 'Lenaboy Road (formerly Barrack Lane).' So four variants – Lenaboy Avenue/Terrace/Road/Lane – achieved some currency in the post 1920 period, when the people of the place began to use a more acceptable townland derivative. It was some time, however, before Galway Corporation granted one Lenaboy designation official status.

Though Lenaboy 'Terrace' – the suggested title of *Observer*'s 1924 letter – was not adopted in the 1940s, the 'Avenue' designation, already in wider local use, was duly approved. That place name was the subject of a discussion document on housing estate titles in 1946,[28] and survives as the official signature for one of Salthill's most interesting locations. Flea Lane, however, remains part of the Village's *lingua franca* and the current (2018) parish priest, Fr. Gerry Jennings, has been known to reference it on occasion. Just as Flea Markets have achieved chic respectability worldwide, is it possible that Lenaboy Avenue will someday embrace its more bohemian brand or, perhaps, adopt the less-used Bright's Lane banner? Such a scenario is most unlikely, for Lenaboy Avenue – in public use (1921– 2018) for almost a century – has long served as the road's established name.

Whatever about the correct title of the place, it must be recorded that Barrack Lane, over the years, was home to long standing Salthill families, sea-men, fishermen, farmers, policemen, soldiers, heroes, as well as strong women of autonomous *mien* – the very stuff that put the 'salt' into Salthill. One could argue that it was a Republic of independent spirit within the resort. It was at once central to the place and at odds with it betimes. Strong willed and defiant, Barrack Lane made a significant contribution to the Village, anchoring it in the reality of year-round living and connecting it with a more ancient past.

A more detailed account of Barrack Lane's evolution must, alas, await a future edition of this history, to accommodate thematic continuity in the telling of Salthill's story.

Note: Salthill's Barrack Lane was not the sole bearer of that street designation in urban Galway, for another Barrack Lane branched off William Street in Galway town, to where the more recent Edward Square currently stands (2018). Whereas Salthill's barracks housed members of the Royal Irish Constabulary, the town lane was home to members of the British Army at Castle Barracks, the remnants of which stood in what was known as Corbett's Car-Park, before that space became part of the Eyre Square shopping centre. When a Mister John Gallagher, therefore, spoke of Barrack Lane in the early years of the 20th century, it was the town lane he was speaking of, for Gallagher's butcher business was housed in Edinburgh Buildings, where the Treasure Chest now trades. The Castle Barracks' passageway was first called *an Bóthar Dubh* – Dark Lane, later Barrack Lane and Castle Street from the 1940s. That same thoroughfare today represents the entrance to Edward Square.

Premium Boarding at Salthill

The writer, Miss J. M. Callwell, did not herself summer at Salthill's budget boarding establishments, nor – indeed – at the opulent Bathing Lodges on offer. Her top-end boarding experience on Salthill's main street was not without its humorously curious drawbacks:

> *Some of our friends had seaside houses which they occupied during the summer weeks, but for the most part we contented ourselves with such lodgings as the Sea Road afforded, and our difficulties and the shifts to which we were put only afforded merriment to ourselves and our neighbours, with whom we lived in a sort of perpetual picnic…Five o'clock was the recognised hour for dinner in those days, and once, when we had lingered unduly over the meal, I remember the heated and indignant slavey of the lodgings bursting into the room. 'Are yez not done with the plates yit?' she demanded. 'Mrs. Lynch downstairs is waitin' for her turn of them, nor Father Connor can't git his supper till he has the knives.' After dinner every one turned out to walk up and down the Sea Road, and we finished up the day either by bringing our friends home to drink tea with us or by drinking tea with them. If the number of guests at any house exceeded the supply of teacups, some of the invited ran to their own lodgings and brought back a reinforcement from thence.*[29]

In terms of food, Michael 'Esha' Kelly, who lived at the mouth of Barrack Lane up to 1997, described the protocol generally followed by Salthill's boarding population: 'They'd bring their own grub, their own cakes and brown bread, fresh eggs, home cured bacon, and home-made butter. They'd spend ten bob for accommodation and many of them would sleep four to a bed down along Lenaboy Avenue, where most of the Salthill's boarding houses were then located.'[30] Jack Fitzgerald, under his *Balor* pen name, defined the arrival time of *fámairí* at the resort: 'The time of their coming was harvest time on the land. The baths, the meetings with old friends and the making of new friendships! That was their life in Salthill.'[31]

The better boarding houses ran along the original village line, from the eastern Bal and Salthill House, as far as Sunnyside Lodge and Seapoint House to the west. The Stella Maris was a good example of such an enterprise. In 1911, Daniel Joseph Walshe described himself at that establishment as a farmer and lodging house keeper. His wife, Mary (née Curran), hailed from Headford and they had three children, Bridget, Daniel Joseph and Gerard Fursey Walshe. Four boarders, all with educational ties, were included in the April 1911 record. A Professor Patrick O'Madden was one. He was, most likely, the school teacher Patrick O'Madden, who was later arrested at Salthill during the Easter Rising of 1916. Secondary school teachers were, curiously enough, called 'professors' in many Irish secondary schools right up to the 1970s. Three college students lodged at the Stella Maris. They were Aileen Daly, a 25 year old Galway girl; William Matthews, a 24 year old Wicklow man; and 22 year old Arthur McLarchie from Armagh. The male students belonged to the Church of Ireland faith.

The Stella Maris was regularly advertised in the local press as an 'up-to-date private Hotel.'[32] Though the press blurb characterised the premises as an 'hotel,' Daniel Walshe described himself as a 'lodging house keeper.' The Walshe family business at the Stella Maris was to run for a further eight decades from that 1910 promotional pitch. On the same 1911 census night that the Stella Maris hosted four boarders, the Eglinton, generally described as the leading hotel in the resort, housed not one visitor. Éamon Mac Giolla Sheannaigh, wife 'Aina,' family members and a *cailín aimsire* were the only residents there recorded. That seminal tourist enterprise was then fifty one years old.

Salthill's dependence on Tourism

Salthill's almost total dependence on visitor traffic is best illustrated in the Salthill census returns of 1901, when boarding houses made up the great majority of premises in the central Lenaboy townland. Taking that townland, where Salthill Village stood, 61 premises were noted by P. O'Neill, a Roscommon born Constable and enumerator. Of the three score and one premises recorded on 31 March, 1901, a significant forty seven – that's 77% – were recorded as 'boarding houses,' with a mere eight being recorded as private dwellings. Also tallied were four public houses, a police barracks and a solitary Baths' facility at Seapoint. Most of the public houses also kept summer lodgers, so the accommodation premises' percentage was even greater than that recorded. Two of the four pubs were vacant on census night, indicating the seasonal nature of Salthill's bar trade. At the tail end of March, the summer season was still a long way off. Three lodging houses, Seapoint Baths, and one private dwelling were also uninhabited on census night. No hotel was listed at Lenaboy, because the Eglinton, the sole establishment then worthy of that title, belonged to Cappanaveagh, a townland that runs west of the Burrenmount. That solitary hotel, along with two public houses – Kelly's and Collins' – on the main thoroughfare, extended the village beyond Lenaboy.

The 1901 lodging house list at Lenaboy reflected the pervasive accommodation use of premises at the resort. In the 'House and Building Return' section of that year's census tally, the keepers of the 44 occupied boarding houses were given, and were listed in four general areas (a) Barrack Lane; (b) Sea View which represented where Baily Point stands today; (c) The original Salthill Village line; and (d) Ryan's Terrace, which is today known as Beach Avenue.

Reading the census figures of a decade later, some arcane change meant that not one Lenaboy townland house was recorded as a boarding establishment in the 'House and Building Return' of 1911. The overall premises' figure saw a drop of three from the 1901 figure to fifty eight. That number was made up of fifty four 'Private Residences,' three public houses and a police barracks. Though boarding houses were not tallied by Constable Benjamin Goff in 1911, that statistical deficit did not mean that the boarding trade had disappeared from Salthill. Seventeen householders listed Lodging/Boarding House keeper as an occupation in their Lenaboy returns, but the real number of accommodation providers was considerably larger than that. John Kenny at Strand House, for example, described himself as a 'grocer', and that indeed he was. However, he was also an R.I.C. pensioner, and a lodging house keeper. Mrs. Donnellan, who recorded the restaurant trade she ran, also kept summer lodgers to add to the solitary boarder in attendance on census night. Many other Lenaboy householders would have practiced occupations – recorded in census forms – that were augmented by undocumented seasonal tourist trades. A lodging trade represented the heart beat of Salthill's economy.

Collaboration and Regulation

Though competition existed between lodging house operators, co-operation surfaced on occasion. A 1924 meeting of boarding housekeepers was held on a July evening at the Pavilion. An upcoming *Galway Guide Book*, which sought to list the names and addresses of accommodation providers and their tariffs, prompted the gathering. In attendance were Mrs. Kenny, Strand House; Mrs. Donnellan, Salthill Restaurant; Mrs. Kirwan, Grattan House; Mrs. Murphy, Hawthorn Lodge; Mrs. McDermott, 15 Nun's Island, Galway; Mrs. O'Boyle, Burrenmount, Salthill; Mrs. Horan, 2 San Antonio Terrace and Mrs. Holland, 3 San Antonio Terrace. The absence of a boarding house male in attendance suggests that the lodging business was then primarily left to the women of the resort. An earlier tourist advertisement, which appeared in the Dublin press, had drawn a lot of interest from various parts of Ireland and England, and a number of enquiries from the Continent. Prices for Race Week were set at £1 a day (meals included), in an age before such price fixing was outlawed. The meeting was informed that a 500 strong excursion was due on the subsequent Sunday.[33]

There appears to have been little oversight of boarding house standards in the 19th century, and even less civic concern about such matters. That certainly was the case in Galway, if one was to take the reaction of some Town Commissioners to an 1885 Local Government letter, which advised that requisite sanitary conveniences should be provided by accommodation providers. As far as the Commissioner Chairman knew, there was no bye-law enacted in relation to the subject and Commissioner Tierney suggested that the letter be ignored, as he believed the missive to be 'inquisitorial.' Mr. Tierney further wondered if he brought a man to his house at Salthill was he to allow himself be subjected to all that 'humbug.'[34]

Whatever about sanitary regulations, the onset of World War One placed an obligation on boarding keepers to keep a register of visitors at their premises. The first 'registration' case heard in Galway saw Mr. Martin Donnellan, Miss Varilly and Miss Clancy, all of Salthill, being charged under the Aliens' Registration (Amendment) Order 1915. That order 'required every hotel or lodging-house keeper to enter on a register the names, nationalities, etc. of persons over the age of 14 years staying at such hotel or house.'[35] The order was a war-time measure to ensure that no 'alien' escaped the authorities. A real fear of German subterfuge, or infiltration, existed at the time. At the June 1915 court hearing, which involved Salthill's lodging keepers, District Inspector Heard said that he did not seek heavy penalties, as the charges were primarily brought by him 'in order that the public might realise the necessity of complying with the Order.'[36] All three charged were fined one penny for the offence.

Later in the same year, however, Miss Delia Clancy was again in court, this time for failing to register two gentlemen during Race Week. Her earlier oversight was held against her, and her repeat offence resulted in a half crown fine. At that same August hearing, Mrs. McEvaddy, a second Salthill lodging keeper, had solicitor Louis O'Dea in court on her behalf. The lawyer questioned the legality of the registration charge and a legal argument followed which focused on the word, 'alien.' The charge against Mrs. McEvaddy was dismissed and other cases brought by the complainant, Sergeant Reilly, were consequently thrown out on a technicality. The Sergeant had claimed that the sole 'alien' criterion was 'that in order to ascertain whether they are "aliens" or not', was that the official form had to be filled.'[37] Boarding house keepers in the town were also charged with breaches of the Act, including Miss Maude Kyne of Francis Street in 1917.[38]

A First Hotel: The Eglinton

The Eglinton building represented a landmark statement in the development of Salthill for it was the first real hotel at the resort. It was to rank with the best hostelries in the country, but such high standards were not always maintained, for like the seawater that continuously stirred outside – and sometimes inside – its doors, the Eglinton experienced the ebbs and flows of seasonal fortune. The building's early evolution was marked in a Cancelled Revision Book by a simple handwritten note that read: 'Hotel in progress…but the boundary not properly defined. Feby. 1860.'

The man behind the brave venture was a Gort native, John Gill, with Francis Blake Forster as his Immediate Lessor. Mr. Gill's first advertisement for his hotel extolled its advantages:

The Proprietor begs to inform the Public that this large and splendidly fitted-up Hotel will be opened for the reception of Guests and Visitors on Monday, the 16th JULY next. It is beautifully situated on the SEA Road and commands a magnificent view of the Bay. It contains 22 airy and healthful bedrooms, five splendid Sitting-rooms, with other conveniences suitable for a first-rate Establishment. As a picturesque and healthful residence, the Eglinton Hotel can be surpassed by few sea-side summer houses. The WINES, SPIRITS and CUISINE will be in keeping, the charges will be found moderate and the attendance punctual. The Hotel is by permission of that real friend of the Galway Packet Station, called "The Eglinton", as is evidenced by the following letter:- "London 29, Albermarie-Place, June 16, 1860: Sir, I can have no objection to your new Hotel bearing my name, and I trust that the growing prosperity of Galway, will render your investment a profitable one – I am your obedient servant, Eglinton & Winton.[39]

That press announcement made clear that Mr. Gill sought permission from the Earl of Eglinton to have the hotel named in his honour. George Arnulph Montgomerie – the 15th Earl of Eglinton and 3rd Earl of Winton – who served as Lord Lieutenant of Ireland on two occasions, was a man of considerable political influence. On an 1852 visit to Galway, during his first Lieutenancy term, a water channel connecting Lough Corrib to the sea was officially opened. That construction was consequently called the Eglinton Canal. Keen to impress Britain's representative in Ireland, Galway almost fell over itself in prefixing any development of that period with the prestigious Earl's tag. Thus Galway could boast of an Eglinton Canal – Street – Barracks – Buildings – Cricket Club – Racquet Court – Baths – Steamer and Hotel.[40] Mr. Gill served as a Galway Harbour and Town Commissioner and his political *nous* was clear in the name he placed above his hotel's door. The 'friend of the Galway Package Station' referenced in the hotel advertisement, acknowledged Lord Eglinton's support for a local campaign to have trans-Atlantic British mail depart from Galway, an issue that was highly topical at the time. The fact that the 'Eglinton' title yet identifies a good number of enterprises and addresses countrywide suggests that the name choice was not particularly novel. Belfast, for example, boasted an Eglinton and Winton Hotel – colloquially known as the 'Egg and Winkle' – on its High Street.

In 1867, Mr. Gill married Ellen Daly of Douras, a sister of neighbour, Isaac B. Daly, of Dalysfort, Salthill. An 1862 advertisement told how 'the best watering place in the three Kingdoms' had an omnibus which plied between Salt Hill and Galway every half hour.[41] Such a facility preceded the tram service which operated from 1879. An 1864 annotation in the Cancelled Revision Books – 'scarcely any business done here' – must have been penned in the off season, for the *Irish Times* in August of that same year reported that 'The Eglinton Hotel is crowded with tourists.'[42] Such contradictory evidence highlights the perennially seasonal nature of the boarding business at marine resorts. Twelve years after opening, Mr. Gill added a suite of baths to his quality hotel, which were 'comparable to the best in the country.'[43]

Apart from the many civic roles he played, Mr. Gill's contribution to Salthill was manifold: In the first place, his hotel made a confident statement about the resort and its possibilities. The potential to attract a more affluent visitor was presented, and the provision of regular transport to the town was a boon to his prosperous clients. As with the occupiers of Bathing Lodges, a measure of the perceived status of Eglinton guests was that their names were often published in the local press. In August 1871, for example, the list included Mr. Edmund Yates, Telegraph Department G.P.O., London, and Alderman James F. Greene, Charlestown, South Carolina. Of the seventeen guests named in that particular press note, eight were men of the cloth and consequently prefixed with a Reverend designation.[44]

A second advantage of Mr. Gill's construction was that it pulled the village further west, and the Eglinton was later to represent Salthill's horse-tram terminus. Before the Eglinton Hotel existed, village properties only extended to the lane that later separated the Grand Hotel and Burrenmount. That lane is represented today by the access road to Baily Point's car park. Atlantic Terrace, followed by San Antonio Terrace, would later snuggle up alongside the most important commercial building to be built at the resort in the 1800s. The Eglinton retained Salthill's 'most influential' *cachet* for a good spell until Noel Finan, who operated in the hotel's shadow for a spell, took a step eastward and opened Seapoint Ballroom. That was almost ninety years after a Gort pioneer had thrown wide the doors of Salthill's first quality hotel.

Open to debate – perhaps – is the question of whether Mr. Barton's post-1852 Bathing Lodges or the 1860 Eglinton Hotel represented the most significant lodging development at Galway's marine suburb during the 19th century. In terms of longevity, there is no doubt but that the Eglinton enjoyed a lengthier spell servicing Salthill's tourist trade. In their own time and distinctive fashions, Messrs. Barton and Gill certainly contributed to accommodation advancements at the resort. The

89. The Eglinton Hotel, to the left of this postcard image, dragged the village westward after its construction in the early 1860s.

providers of affordable boarding facilities, however, could also justifiably claim that their contribution, in terms of visitor volume, deserves inclusion in any putative or retrospective accolade that might celebrate Salthill's tourist trade evolution throughout the Victorian era.

John Gill's association with the Eglinton Hotel ceased in the mid-1880s, after which a number of names appeared in its occupier column. George Mack, most identified with Eyre Square's Royal Hotel, operated the Eglinton, post-1886, for a short spell. He was followed by Margaret Beatrice and William J.C. Cloherty, before Edward McAlinney – a retired R.I.C. Head Constable – took charge of the resort's leading facility in 1897. The new operator in that year announced that the hotel had changed hands and was then 'an up-to-date establishment' under his personal management. His *Tuam Herald* advertisement boasted that his other private houses at Salthill, *Villa Maria* and *Atlantic Lodge* were 'known as models of comfort to Visitors to Salthill.' Mr. McAlinney's new establishment offered a 'Private Sittingroom for Clergymen' and a 'Special Sittingroom for Ladies.' A range of saltwater baths was also highlighted.[45] The *Irish Times* reported in 1902 that the Eglinton Hotel, which had been tenanted by Edward McAlinney at a yearly rent of £100, was purchased by the tenant for £1,330.[46] Edward's boundless innovation was reflected in his 1913 invention, which improved the baths' heating mechanism at his hotel.[47] Following the death of Edward McAlinney (aged 79) at his residence in late January 1922, his second wife and widow, Anne, continued to operate the business until it was offered for sale seven years later. It was following a February

1929 court case, initiated by creditor, J.T. Miller, that the famed establishment was auctioned – five months later – at the City Arms Hotel, Prussia Street, Dublin. The enterprise, however, remained in McAlinney ownership, for it was purchased for a 'consideration of £3000' by Mrs. Susan Emerson, then a widow.

Susan Emerson

Susan, who had broad experience of the tourism industry, was a daughter of Edward McAlinney by his first marriage. In 1901, at seventeen years of age, Susan McAlinney recorded herself as a Lodging House Keeper at *Villa Maria*, Salthill, one of two boarding houses referenced by her father in the 1897 advert that heralded the inclusion of the Eglinton Hotel into his Salthill boarding portfolio. Susan married a highly qualified Building Trades' and Manual instructor, William Emerson, in 1904. William, who was also a building contractor, had – by 1913 – completed a beautiful Picture and Variety Theatre to the order of Mrs. O'Shaughnessy. Though a July 1913 *Tribune* report placed that facility at Salthill,[48] it was the Court Theatre on Middle Street that was most identified with Mrs. Emily O'Shaughnessy. Mr. Emerson became one of the earliest teachers hired under the South Kensington Board, which operated before the Irish Department of Education came into being. Described as a 'Pioneer in Technical Education,' William taught at the City of Galway Technical School.[49] Mr. and Mrs. Emerson were a most industrious couple and in July 1915, Susan announced the opening of Tea Rooms at 12 Dominick Street.[50] 'Gleann Éinde Tea Rooms' was an interesting name choice for her café, for it re-echoed a McAlinney *grá don teanga* and was – most likely – the genesis of the Hotel Enda title, which was to become identified with Dominick Street for a number of decades. The Éinde/Enda name had close affinities with the McAlinney family, as the Spiddal Church where Susan's brother, Canon Thomas McAlinney, served as parish priest, is known as Cill Éinde.

Not limiting herself to a restaurant trade, Mrs. Emerson let out well furnished accommodation, suitable for business gents,[51] and she capitalised on a stagnant property market in 1920 by offering ten 'airy' rooms at 12 Dominick Street. Her advertisement read: 'As it is impossible to get houses in the City, this affords a great opportunity to people requiring apartments situated in a most central locality.'[52] By 1923, Hotel Enda was up and running and Salthill featured in her advertising copy for a *Connacht Tribune* Tourist Supplement in the following year : '*Admitted by all to be the Best Hotel in the Citie of the Tribes…Within a few minutes' walk of Salthill, Post Office, and Railway Station.*'[53] All then appeared to be progressing nicely for the family, but Mr. Emerson was to suffer 'from a long and tedious illness,' which resulted in his death, at the relatively young age of 52, in December 1926.[54] That loss left Susan Emerson a widow with two sons, William and Enda.

Though purchased in 1929, the Eglinton Hotel did not open under Susan's management until the following year. Facility and baths' improvements occasioned the delay. Both the Eglinton Hotel and Hotel Enda were jointly operated by Mrs. Emerson for a spell and a licence for her Dominick Street property was granted in 1932, before she sold it three years later to Martin Divilly, the well known William Street West butcher, and later Mayor of Galway on two occasions: 1963/'64 & 1970/'71. The Eglinton went on to enjoy great success as a leading Galway hostelry which attracted high-end guests, including Taoiseach Éamon de Valera and Mr. Anthony Eden, before the latter gentleman became British Prime Minister. The Eglinton's only Galway rival – in terms of prestige – over many years was the Railway Hotel on Eyre Square. On the Emerson takeover of the Eglinton, Susan's step-mother, Mrs. Anne McAlinney, and her son, John McAlinney, continued in the tourist trade nearby, where they operated the Grand Hotel.

Mrs. Susan Emerson was to subsequently play a central role, across a number of areas, in the development of Salthill as a thriving resort. A founding member of the Salthill Citizens' Organisation, she won a Galway Corporation seat in 1942, as an S.C.O. representative. Her spats with Miss Maggie Ashe, another lady Councillor, added colour to the Council chamber over a number of years. Having served for two terms, Susan chose not to contest the 1950 plebiscite. Her public profile was further enhanced through her involvement with the Irish Tourist Board and Irish Hotel Federation. Susan attended the 1925 meeting at which the Irish Tourist Association was formed, and became one of its directors. A founding member of the Irish hotel body, she was appointed a permanent director on its board. In a local context, Susan Emerson had the satisfaction of attending the formal opening of a permanent tourism bureau at Galway in the summer of 1955, though she was recovering from illness at the time. She was also a lifelong member of the Patrician Musical Society.

90. Mrs. Susan Emerson, the second female Councillor elected to Galway Corporation in 1942. (Courtesy of *Connacht Tribune*.)

ASCAL mhic eimhiR
EMERSON AVENUE

Figure 91.

When Mrs. Susan Emerson passed away at her Eglinton Hotel residence on 8 April, 1956, tributes were paid to her vitality, professional acumen and achievements at Salthill. Having been centrally involved with Canon Davis in the building of Salthill's church, Bishop Browne of Galway blessed a marble side-altar to her memory at the Church of Christ the King in February, 1958. Designed by leading architect, Michael Scott, the altar was presented by her sons, Enda and William Emerson.[55] Nine years after her passing, Alderman Fintan Coogan T. D. proposed that a new Salthill Road 'be named after the late Mrs. Emerson, who had done a lot for Salthill, and she should not be forgotten'.[56] That proposal was carried and the road, where Seán Kilraine was then building five-bedroom houses, came to be called Emerson Avenue. Though not referenced at the time, one could say that the street naming also paid tribute to the broader McAlinney family – of which Susan was a member – for that family's connection with Salthill, and its tourism trade, had begun in the early 1890s.

A New Era and Salthill's strong Female Influence

Susan Emerson's 1930 re-opening of the Eglinton hotel kick-started a decade that saw a Castlerea consortium purchase the Monks' Field in 1933, and the consecration of the Church of Christ the King in that same field three years later. The south-facing frontage of Salthill Village, from Strand House to the road that services Lenaboy Gardens, was opened up – by that purchase – for ecclesiastical, commercial and residential purposes. Though boarding establishments – including Lucan House and Sarsfield House – opened on that Monks' Field stretch, no hotel appeared thereon during the 1930s. Such enterprises were, however, delivered nearby. The Grand and Banba hotels opened in that decade, as did the Somerset and Warwick at King's Hill. A post-1934 sale of sites to the front of Salthill's new Garda Station facilitated buildings, which included the Rockland, Éire, and Dawn hotels. In terms of lodging facilities, Salthill's hotel stock greatly increased through a seminal decade, and such developments added to the attraction of the place as a resort of quality. A female presence remained a constant in that accommodation development: It was female Monahan siblings who were behind the Somerset and Rockland enterprises, and they were later to donate an altar to Salthill Church, in the same year that the Emerson altar was blessed. Mrs. Annie McAlinney, in the first instance, and later Misses Kate and Winifred Martin operated the Grand Hotel beside the Banba, which was run by a Geraghty sisterhood. In the guesthouse trade, Miss Ann Sarsfield's Lucan House and Sarsfield House, belonging to Mrs. Úna Sarsfield, later combined to create the Sarsfield House Hotel, which subsequently became the Galway International Hotel.

Postmistress Ellen Ryan – Ryan's Terrace – Beach Avenue

The central role of women in the resort's evolution did not begin in the 1930s, and the significance of a female input at Salthill cannot be overstated. While Mrs. Susan Emerson's surname is memorialised in a road name at Salthill, a second lady enjoyed the same honour in an earlier generation. It was in the late 1850s that Ryan's Terrace, now known as Beach Avenue, was built and named after its creator, Ellen Ryan. During the previous decade, 'Ellen Ryan of Salt Hill' did 'promise to pay the Reverend John D'Arcy, Secretary of the GALWAY LOAN, or Order, the sum of Five Pounds,' which was received on 12 June, 1843. The money borrowed from that Poverty Relief scheme was fully repaid by Ellen. Two years earlier, she had acted as guarantor for Mary Clark of Salt Hill, who borrowed three pounds from the same fund.

The mid-century appointment of Ellen Ryan as Salt Hill's first 'postmaster,'[57] not only reflected progress at the village, but Ellen's pioneering presence in the place. Incidentally, in the year of the resort's Post Office opening[58] – 1851 – Mr. Martin Conneely was transferred, from an earlier Galway–Barna route, to a Galway–Salthill messenger position.[59] A number of men, bearing the same Conneely patronym provided a similar service in West Galway over that period, with John B. (Barna–Galway 1848) and Patrick (Galway–Barna 1853) among their number. It was in November 1859 that 'Salthill was brought within the town delivery area and a fourth Letter Carrier was appointed.'[60] Isaac Salter's 1870 Directory included a description of the postal service available at the resort:

Post Office, *Salt Hill, Ellen Ryan, Post Mistress. – Letters arrive from Galway at a quarter past eight and half past three afternoon, and are despatched thereto at half-past ten morning and at half-past seven evening.*[61]

Mrs. Ryan was not simply the first postmistress at the resort, for she was also a significant property holder in the village. Her money – most likely – did not derive from her Post Office position, for £3 was the Salthill sub-postmaster's annual salary in the 1853–1855 period, when her Barna and Moycullen peers were paid £5.[62] It was in 1863 that Mr. Burke of Annagh drew attention to the 'evils of centralisation,' in relation to the Irish postal network, after Post Office authorities had threatened 'to deprive the people of Roundstone of Post-office accommodation, if an eligible official to act for that sum' was not forthcoming: 'Just think of any man, in whom confidence could be placed, undertaking to discharge the duties of Postmaster of such a place as Roundstone…for the munificent salary of £3 a year!'[63] In 1855, Ellen Ryan had an interest in seven Salt Hill Village properties, six as lessor and one as occupier. Her property portfolio was primarily centred to the town-side of the village, with the exception of Ivy Lodge, which she let to lodgers over a long period. House number three was the modest Salt Hill Village property that Ellen occupied at that time,[64] on the very same site where the current postmistress, Esther Daly, operates her Post Office today (2018). Coincidentally therefore, two women – 163 years apart – filled, and now fill, the same role in the same location at Salthill. In between, however, the resort's Post Office occupied a number of sites within the Lenaboy townland, from the area where Baily Point now stands to the bottom of King's Hill.

Though Mrs. Ellen Ryan did occupy the modest number 3 premises in 1855, she was also lessor of the large and neighbouring Plot 4, where she erected a road-side building that subsequently housed her shop and Post Office. That premises was later known as Ballinasloe House (4e). Her six cottage Ryan's Terrace development was completed by 1860. The accompanying map suggests that those cottages were originally thatched. The detached number six house at Salt Hill Village was Hawthorn Lodge. A thatched building (4D, beside number 7) then occupied the road-hugging site that now houses O'Connor's Bar. Ryan's Terrace came to be called Beach Avenue.

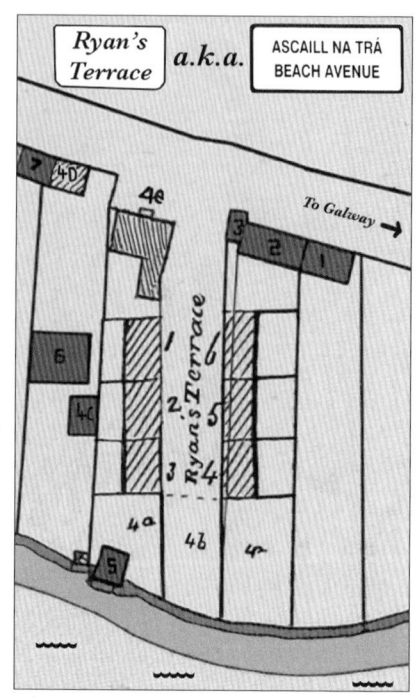

92. Map of Ryan's Terrace, later to be called Beach Avenue.

A mark of Mrs. Ryan's impressive new construction (4e) was that it received a Rateable Value of £14, seven times the rating of the smaller number three premises. Mrs. Ellen Ryan then moved into her larger property, where her grocery shop and Post Office traded for a good number of years. Given the poor remuneration for Ellen's postal duty, her Post Office's ability to attract customers to her grocery trade might have added value to the enterprise. In terms of her retail business, Ellen was charged in 1869 that she 'had in her shop and possession unstamped measures contrary to law,' for which she was fined six pence with costs. Over a decade earlier, at another court hearing, she – as plaintiff – charged a local resident 'for an assault at Salt Hill.' The male defendant was put 'under the rule of bail to keep the peace' and to pay £5 in his own recognisance.[65]

Ever active and progressive, Mrs. Ryan developed a double row of three terraced houses, which faced one another, to the rear of her Post Office. That development was first recorded as 'Ryan's Terrace' on Cancelled Revision Books in 1861. The following annotation was also added: 'These are small cottages built for bathers & let very high altho' in a backward situation.'⁶⁶ Rateably valued at £5-10s. each, Ellen Ryan was lessor to all six properties, which added to the holdings she already possessed in the place. Her six cottage development was to remain a central part of her family's property portfolio for three decades. In 1862, eleven Salthill properties – identified with either Matthew or Ellen Ryan – were offered for letting at the resort, as desirable Bathing Residences. In their promotion, the Ryan's Terrace development was deftly described:

*Six very handsome Cottages, each containing Parlour, two Bed Rooms, Kitchen &c., with two Attic Rooms. The Cottages have been fitted up with the utmost care and attention to the comfort of Bathers. They are situate within 30 yards of the best Bathing shore at Salt Hill, and are equal distance from hot and shower baths. Application to be made to – Matthew Ryan, Tea and Wine Merchant, Eyre-square, Galway or to Mrs. Ellen Ryan, Post office, Salt Hill, Galway.*⁶⁷

Things appeared to be going well at the time, because Matthew was not only a merchant at the town's Square, but also acted as an agent for Australian Packet companies, whose ships offered passage to emigrants.⁶⁸ The year 1864, however, appears to have been a difficult one for the family, as a press report in May declared that 'Matthew Ryan, of Eyre-square, Galway,' was a bankrupt.⁶⁹ Furthermore, a reference to his daughter's wedding, in September of the same year, indicated that Matthew had passed away in the interim: 'At Barna Catholic Church, James Eldest son of the late Patrick Gordon, Esq., of Lisleddy, county Roscommon, to Honor[i]a, only daughter of the late Matthew Ryan, Esq., Salthill, Galway.'⁷⁰ Prior to her wedding, Honoria Ryan had replaced her mother, Ellen Ryan, as lessor of properties at Salthill, which included Ryan's Terrace. Following Honoria's nuptials, her husband, James, took on that lessor role and it was two years after James' death at Nun's Island in 1887 – at the age of 47 – that the impressive portfolio, first developed by his mother-in-law, Ellen Ryan, was placed for auction. Mr. Gordon, who was described in his 1864 marriage certificate as a 'Gentleman,' had 'no occupation' when he died 23 years later. It is possible – though unproven – that in the interim he acted as a Court 'process server,' whose name appeared at the head of a Quarter Sessions' Galway list in 1870.⁷¹ A man of that same name made numerous appearances in an official capacity at court cases in the town during the 1850s and early 1860s.

The 1889 sell-off that followed James Gordon's death came in the wake of a hearing in the Chancery Division of Ireland's High Court. The single lot offered for sale included:

Nos. 1,2,3,4,5 and 6 Beach Avenue, together with a small House in said avenue: The House and Premises known as Ballinasloe House; two small Houses and the Home and Premises known as Scott's Lodge, or Ivy Lodge, all situate in the Parish of Rahoon, and County of Galway; held under lease dated 21st February, 1855, for the term of 999 years from the 25th day of March, 1854, and producing a Net Rental of £100 10s.

Prospective buyers were assured that the houses and cottages were 'let to solvent tenants.'[72] One wonders if a profitable 1854 summer season had prompted Ellen to agree her 999 year lease in February of the following year. A July 1854 news' report points to such a possibility:

'Salt Hill. There is a great influx of strangers already into Salt Hill for the purpose of bathing. – There are but few lodges even now unset. – The rents asked and given are rather high; and it is imagined that this will be the best season experienced by the lodge-owners for years past.'[73]

It was in the 1870s that the short road of Mrs. Ryan's terraced houses came to be called Beach Avenue, a more fashionable name, which supplanted Ryan's Terrace at the resort. Though the auction blurb of 1889 used Beach Avenue, Cancelled Revision Books officially retained the Ryan's Terrace moniker up to 1917. Pioneering Ellen Ryan was succeeded as postmaster by Samuel Woods, who operated from his premises, Bay View Lodge, at the Sea View end of the village, during the 1880s and early 1890s. The Ryan name of postmistress and terrace was, by then, fading from local memory, though the neat avenue Ellen Ryan left to the place still occupies its own quaint corner, at the original entrance to Salthill Village.

Mary Freeman – Bright – Bolton

Mrs. Ellen Ryan was not the only woman of property at Salthill during the 19th century. Another was Mary Freeman. In 1848, Mary – whose father Robert was a Barrack Sergeant – married Joseph Bright, a man of standing, who held property in the Shangort-Knocknacarra area. She was a most enterprising woman in her own right, for whom court house steps held little fear. In an 1864 appearance, she was recorded as a 'Road Contractor' when the County Surveyor, Samuel Ussher Roberts, charged Mary Bright that she did 'neglect to keep in repair a certain road leading from Galway to Barna between the gate at Nile Lodge and the Crossroads at Shangort which roads she is bound by contract to keep in repair.'[74] On the passing of Mr. John Bright – and Joseph, her husband – Mary became a major property owner at Salthill. John Bright was – during the 1850s – not only occupier of what came to be known as Strand House (O'Reilly's Bar & Kitchen today), but immediate lessor to a number of surrounding properties. A perusal of Cancelled Revision Books shows that Mary Bright was recorded in the 1860s as the immediate lessor of every property – bar one – in Barrack Lane, which means that the street's buildings had by then become *de facto* her property. In August 1880, Mary-Freeman-Bright of Blake's Hill, Knocknacarra remarried in the Wesleyan Church of St. Nicholas' parish. Her second husband was Mr. George Bolton, a bachelor 'gentleman' of College Road, who was the son of another 'gentleman,' Henry Bolton. The Bolton family's status also appears to have been land based. Following her second marriage, the name Mary Bolton replaced Mary Bright as lessor of Barrack Lane premises, though the properties' ownership had not changed.

Margaret O'Flynn – Scallan – Ryan

Another entrepreneurial figure at Salthill was Mrs. Margaret O'Flynn-Scallan-Ryan, whose contribution was made during the 20th century. It was following a Connolly tenure that Margaret O' Flynn and her brother Michael, from Kilkerrin, opened for business in early 1911 at Salthill House. Margaret had, by 1914, married Sligo born Thomas Reginald Scallan, a teacher, who passed away in 1923. Their children's names were Gertrude, Ernest and Bernard. In 1929 Margaret remarried, when she wed Michael Ryan, a Garda sergeant, who was then residing at Naas, County Kildare. Salthill House was offered for lease by Mrs. Ryan, in 1937 and 1940, and when both contracts proved troublesome, Margaret took charge of the licence once more. It was in 1942 that she sold her business to Mr. Thomas O'Connor of Moylough, whose family still trades at Salthill House. By the time of that sale, Mrs. Ryan had taken up residence directly across the road in new premises called 'Salthill Stores,' which stood on the Lenaboy Garden corner, where optician Andrea Concannon trades today. There Margaret resided with her daughter Gertrude, who in 1939 had married Mr. Enda Hardiman of the Town Hall family. Mrs. Gertie Hardiman operated the Salthill Stores retail unit, which had living accommodation on the first floor. In the early 1950s an impressive development was in progress at the other end of the village, on a plot of land described in Cancelled Revision records as 'amusement ground.' That ambitious construction contained two lock-up shops at street level with basements under, and three completely self-contained flats, each with front and rere entrances at three floor levels. It was Mrs. Margaret Ryan who built Salthill's first apartment block, which went by the name of Western House. Aptly titled, that development – which today (2018) houses Coco café – still represents the most westerly building on Salthill Village's main thoroughfare. When Mrs. Ryan left Salthill in 1966, she could look back on contributions at the polar points of the village. Her second husband, Michael Ryan, also predeceased her and she passed away, in June, 1974 at St. Vincent's Hospital, Dublin. Through public house, retail and apartment investment, over 56 years at the resort, Margaret O'Flynn-Scallan-Ryan made her mark at Salthill.

The 1933 purchase of the Monks' Field, abutting Barrack Lane, represented a critical phase in the evolution of Salthill Village, and a closer look at that development and its impact will be presented in a future volume of this history. Accommodation offerings were to evolve over time. Such fare, which ran in tandem with hotel development, was to include seasonal B&B, as well as year-round Guest House trades. These, in turn, were to be overtaken by 'cheap and cheery' hostels, followed by modern apartment amenities. Housing booms, as well as social and educational factors, along with government initiatives, were all to play a role in the accommodation fare on offer at Salthill in the post-1930 period.

Chapter 10

NA FÁMAIRÍ AND THE LAZY WALL

Irish coastal tourist resorts, over the years, generally looked the same and offered similar fare; baths, sea, sand, boarding houses, pubs, a dance hall, pleasant views and unpredictable weather. For all of its latent potential, Salthill lagged behind other summer spots, including Tramore and Lisdoonvarna, for much of its existence. Henry Inglis visited Galway in 1834, and remarked that it was 'much resorted to for sea-bathing,' with a 'great many houses' having being built to accommodate strangers. Despite that observation, he believed that 'the situation had nothing to recommend it but the sea: for the country around Galway, and particularly on the western side, is as ugly, as flatness, sterility, and want of wood, can make it.'[1]

Not all reviews were as dismissively cursory, and an *Irish Times* correspondent, writing in the summer of 1867, advised readers to avail of a Midland Railways' excursion and travel West, despite the food distress of that year, as 'every shilling spent by the tourist in the famine districts may be said to be so much contributed towards the relief of the people.' The same journalist's description of a Sabbath day in pre-tram Salthill was warm:

I was very much amused on Sunday in viewing the excursions to Salthill, a very handsome village and bathing place about two miles from this. The road to it is beautiful and level, and there are long vans drawn by two horses always running on it, but Sunday is a great day. I counted in one of the vans eighteen on each side and four in the driver's seat. The fare is one penny and people go in and out without any other business but to enjoy the fresh air and breeze. There is a very excellent hotel at Salt hill and I don't know any place that a tourist could spend a few days more pleasantly.[2]

Not everyone was taken with what Salt Hill had to offer. Effusive exuberance was absent in a 'rambling reflection' by a 1940's *Omnibus* scribe on Salthill's inherent strengths: *It had little more claim to fame than most other sections of foreshore. It was a rocky shore with stretches of shingle and smaller stretches of sand but it had the advantage that it adjoined the city of Galway, and it had the further advantage that its waters were not in danger of being polluted by the town sewage.*[3] Ward & Lock's 1890 *Pictorial Guide to*

Connemara and the West of Ireland was succinct in its sober appraisal of the place: 'It is prettily located, and contains an hotel and some good houses; the beach affords very fair bathing.'[4] Adopting a similarly sober line, an 1896 *Tourist Guide to the West*, which was produced by the Midland Great Western Railway, was less than lavish in its one line assessment of the resort: 'Salthill, the marine suburb of Galway, which is wholesome, but not of particular interest.'[5]

Despite its early limitations and a low to mid-table ranking on the summer retreat pecking order, Galway's resort boasted a distinctive charm that was best personified at the quaintly named Lazy Wall. It was there that visiting *fámairí*, who came to 'take the waters,' passed the time of day along with notable locals, in their own distinctive way.

Na Fámairí

The Gaelic word *fámaire* was used by Salthill locals to describe a particular class of tourist that meant much to the place. By appreciating its advantages and loyally returning on an annual basis, Salthill's regulars not only made a financial contribution, but delivered the foot fall that created a resort of character and charm. It was the country families of Connacht who first valued Salthill as a summer destination and filled the boarding houses and pubs of the seaside village. *Fámairí* proved to be the mainstay of smaller businesses, whose seasonal earnings depended primarily on a provincial rural trade. It was people from the land who 'made Salthill a resort and the Lazy Wall an institution.'[6] In fact, 'many country people "discovered" Salthill before the people of the town recognised that Salthill had possibilities. It was no uncommon thing for farmers and their wives to rear an extra calf or two to be sold off to pay the cost of "taking the water" after the harvest had been put in.'[7]

The *fámaire* expression is interesting, for it carries a variety of dictionary translations, which range from a huge man – or woman – to a large dogfish. Salthill's slang expression defined neither version. The word itself is not an esoteric term, solely used by Galway natives, as it appears in numerous Irish-English dictionaries: Dineen's famed *Foclóir Gaedhilge agus Béarla* (1927) translates the word as: metaphorically a swimmer, a visitor to the seaside (Clare).... *fámaire coirnéil* as a corner boy, a loafer (N. Con): *fámaire mná* as a large (idle) woman. Fifty years later Ó Dónaill's *Foclóir Gaeilge-Béarla* (1977) translated *fámaire* as (a) Stroller, idler (b) Seaside, summer, visitor; sightseer, tourist.

Such lexical definitions hardly do justice to the word's use in Salthill, for language can often be an imprecise medium. Meaning generally depends on context and intent, and verbal subtlety is particularly prevalent in Ireland. The term *fámaire* – which is no longer part of Salthill's *lingua franca* – carried a connotation that reflected a certain attitude to the summer visitor. In resorts worldwide, visitors are welcomed and valued, but seasoned locals often display a tired forbearance towards those who come amongst them. In Ireland for example, humour, *hauteur*, envy and sarcasm can all be evoked by a single term; 'Yank,' a word seldom used in praise, though rarely mean in its mocking. *Fámaire* was similarly nuanced, a local term that, though not quite complimentary was hardly caustic either. Its use asserted the user's worldliness more than the subject's suggested lack of it.

That said, an Irishman who was resident in England indicated – when describing Salthill's 1911 tram service – that not all Galway locals were particularly favourable to *fámairí*: 'There are on every car a number of "deadheads," including off-duty drivers, conductors, stablemen and their friends, who lounge on the platforms of the cars puffing smoke into the faces of despised "formeries," and using language certainly not fit to be used in public, and passing personal remarks on the "formeries," particularly if they happen to be old men or women.'[8]

93. Famed Aran writer, Liam O'Flaherty, with his daughter, Peggy, at the Eglinton Hotel, Salthill, in 1946. (Courtesy of *Connacht Tribune*.)

An *Irish Times* colour piece from 1873 was not – by today's standards – particularly judicious in describing some of the resort's valued visitors as 'peasants,' though the same article did snapshot a time in Salthill tourism's evolution, and also hinted at the locals' patronising view of their visitors: *The peasants who come to Galway during the bathing season, afford a good deal of amusement to the townspeople. The peasant in every country, but the Connaught peasant perhaps more than any other, has this one and foremost principle, that he shall get the fullest value for money.*[9]

It must be said that *fámairí* were better thought of in Salthill than the hapless visitor described in the opening lines of Liam O'Flaherty's ironic book, *A Tourist's Guide to Ireland*:

The tourist is at the mercy of every kind of ruffian. Although every country holds out welcoming hands to him, it is only for the purpose of robbing him of all he possesses, and if he is caught escaping, at the end of his holiday, with even a small coin in his pockets, it's more than likely that the Customs officers are going to fine him to that amount for taking away on his shoes some of the country's mud. And yet, even though the tourist is mulcted in this scandalous manner, in every country, he is always looked upon as a low fellow, an inquisitive, vulgar beggar, a loud-mouthed trot-about, a coarse eater, a foreigner. There are jokes in every literature about his capacity for snoring, about his clothes and about his wife, who seems to be always either very fat or very skinny.[10]

Salthill's Lazy Wall

J.M. Callwell vividly recalled the Lazy Wall – under another soubriquet – and Salthill's summer regulars from the 1800s:

Every one bathed in the mornings, or was supposed to do so, and sundry elderly gentlemen used to establish themselves on the low wall between the road and the beach and exchange salutations from thence to their acquaintance in the water.

'Good day Mrs. D'Arcy, glad to see you,' it used to be, 'I hope you find yourself well this morning, ma'am.' This to a portly matron who was disporting herself in the waves. It was said that all the scandals of the County Galway were hatched at this al fresco club, for which reason the favourite and most frequented coign on the sea-wall was known as Calumny Corner.[11]

Michael 'Esha' Kelly, who lived at Salthill Village for nigh on eight decades,[12] recalled childish roguery with mature ladies who relaxed at the Lazy Wall: 'One trick we used get up to is to go behind their backs and tie the tassels of six or seven shawls together so that when one of the women got up to go, she'd pull six or seven other women's shawls with her. But they took it in good part, the women; it was harmless fun and that was the spirit of it.'[13]

A 1909 description of the type of women who frequented the Lazy Wall and their generic – if overbearing – attire **(fig.94)**, appeared in the *Galway Express*:

Amongst the well-to-do women of the farming class in Ireland a visit to the seaside is considered one of the necessary duties of the year. This visit, be it known, never goes by the name of holiday; it, indeed, forms a sort of sacrificial pilgrimage offered to Hygeia. In their home life they are all dominant, bustling housewives, seeing to the welfare of everything, both within and without, keen of eye, nimble of limb, sharp of tongue; yet when the duty of safeguarding health comes along no business or pleasure is allowed interfere with it…they all dress in their best Sunday clothes, and the very contemplation of their clothes on a very hot day precludes all thought of movement. There is first the shiningly white linen cap with its border of goffered frills and its stiff strings which tie in a capacious bow under the chin; this is generally covered with a heavy woollen head-kerchief – 'to keep off the sun.' Round the shoulders is worn a woollen shawl, heavy and large as a blanket. The gown is made of cashmere, dark red and purple being the favourite colours. The gathered skirts and the plainly cut bodice of early Victorian days still hold sway. The voluminous skirt is generally folded over in a manner to show the heavy fleecy, gay-coloured flannel petticoat beneath, trimmed with a row of black velvet. A large black cashmere apron, a pair of handmade lace boots, and homespun woollen stockings complete an attire suitable for North Pole exploration, but which is borne without

94. *Fámairí Mná ag an mBalla Fallsa.*

a murmur on the hottest day in summer. These elderly ladies sit in rows gazing dreamily out to sea. If they talk to one another it is in the soft, low tones of their native Gaelic, and their voices mingle naturally with the soft gurglings of the sea amongst the rocks. I sat for hours amongst them and I never heard a note of discord in the desultory conversations, nor saw an expression other than one of complete restfulness on any of their faces.[14]

In terms of tourist facilities, it appears that Salthill once housed ladies' salons, which were – it was humorously reported – put out of business by the holistic healthiness of the place: 'We used to have beauty parlours out there, but they have gone out of business – Salthill breezes restore that schoolgirl complexion.' The *Connacht Sentinel* reported in 1943 that there was no barber shop at the resort: 'The place is without a tonsorial parlour where the sturdy agriculturist on vacation can get his whiskers trimmed or his chin scraped.'[15]

Site of Salthill's Lazy Wall

Salthill's quintessential Lazy Wall was a seated line that ran perpendicular to the Grand and Banba hotels – Baily Point's front façade today. The wall's back was next to the gable of shoreline buildings. It was a little cul-de-sac, facing the baths at Seapoint, where the *cul* was the sea shore. The sitters, looking eastward, enjoyed a view of the village and whatever occurred in the space to the front of Seapoint House. In 1924, when a decision was made to erect three wooden seats at the famed meeting place, complaints were made about the destruction of public property.[16] Four years later concern was raised by Mr. Finan about the poor state of the ground at the Lazy Wall, where 'donkeys and carts and everything were left there.'[17] Ladies were that year unable to walk to the abutting bathing strand because of the refuse. Discovered in the water by Lazy Wall *habitué*, Tom Smith, was an exploded shell in 1929. The rusted case, which appeared to be of 'very ancient pattern,' measured 'about eight inches in length and three-and-a-half inches in diameter.'[18] One great advantage of the Lazy Wall was the shelter it afforded. Though the occupants of its long bench sat, direction wise, *tóin le gaoth* – rear to wind – the regular western breezes which blew in from Aran never bothered the sitters, for their *tóins* were protected, not only by the wall, but by the gable of the old Garda Station which stood behind it. Light summer winds were betimes replaced by storms, and huge waves in 1934 and 1940 washed over the tourists' favourite retreat. The 1934 storm was anticipated at the wall and a crowd gathered at Salthill to watch an August Sabbath spectacle: 'The Atlantic was in a black mood on Sunday. Early in the morning the bay looked a bit choppy and the old men sitting on the "Lazy Wall" nodded their heads knowingly....the omnibus which went as far as the golf links got a free

95. Lazy Wall seating runs to the left of the bus in this postcard. Site of buildings to the right is now (2018) occupied by Baily Point.

salt water washing…in the evening Galway residents walked out to Salthill to enjoy the spectacle of the Atlantic in its fiercest mood.'[19]

Lazy Wall – The People's Parliament

In a more measured and restful age, the wall provided a place for friendship, reflection and chat. 'Chat' is probably too small a word to do justice to the place's discourse, for the wall was seen as a People's Parliament where affairs of import were mulled over and discussed. Its membership was made up 'of traditional users and those whose age, interests and way of life'[20] qualified them for a seat at a seaside congress that did not require a ballot. A *Connacht Sentinel* editorial caught the spirit of the scene:

> *It is a place for men who can talk of crops and prices, of matrimonial matches, exchange family stories and tell of the achievements of their children, boast proudly of memories of events of more than half a century ago and talk of all the other things that loosen the tongues of old men with knowledge and imagination. It is a place, too, where women can talk of fowl, eggs and all the other things that make up life in a country kitchen, where they can discuss their families, their neighbours and their illnesses, their own deeds and their neighbour's deeds and misdeeds.* [21]

The same editorial nailed the nexus of Salthill's assembly: 'The Lazy Wall is a parliamentary institution drawing its delegates from the country crossroads.' Salthill could not, of course, boast of hosting the sole Lazy Wall in the land, for the towns of Galway and Ballinasloe had their own versions of such meeting places, as did many other regions. What made Salthill's sittings special was its seasonal assembly of hard working farmers – and their wives – who enjoyed an annual trip to the sea. Salthill's Lazy Wall was a place of happiness. Other walls, nationwide, also served as meeting places, but they were symbolic of hard times when unemployment rates were high. That resulted in the unfortunate and pejorative use of the 'lazy' word, which was less than sympathetic to wall regulars, though it must be said that such spots and their sitters were warmly viewed by a great swathe of the population. A line from a 1959 *Connacht Sentinel* editorial articulated the reality of the decade in which it was written: 'The Lazy Wall[s] of other towns are a reflection on the country and not on the people who man them.'[22]

Lazy Wall Local – Tom Smith

The Lazy Wall assembly was not confined to *fámairí*, for its composition was leavened and sharpened by locals who engaged with summer visitors. One of the best known of the regulars was Tom Henry Smith, who lived a varied, interesting, and at times exciting life. Born in Loughrea, he was first apprenticed to a saddler and worked at that trade in an Eyre Square premises for some time. The job was not to his liking and in 1880 – at age 14 – Thomas ended up in Galway Gaol after being charged with 'absence from business having been indentured an apprentice.' His calendar month sentence was 'commuted & prisoner discharged 9.12.80 – by order of Lord Lieutenant.'[23] The blue eyed, dark haired, fresh faced youngster later took off to sea, without his parents' permission. He was shipwrecked on a voyage to South America and later found employment on a Cleggan fishing boat. During World War II he served on a mine-sweeper in Galway Bay and spent upward of 35 years as a Galway pilot in the same waters. Connected in some way with Barrack Lane, Tom was recorded in the Census years of 1901 and 1911 as a resident at Grove View, where he eventually died. His Grove View home later came to house Salthill Post Office, which opened there in 1946, across from the Church of Christ the King, with Miss Maureen Lynch – later to be Mrs. Maureen Dolan – as postmistress. Tom Smith, who could not swim, was involved in a number of sea rescues: He saved a man called Thomas O'Connor in the wake of a capsized boating incident circa 1889, and on the 19th day of June, 1906, Mr. Smith saved the life of Professor Griffiths of Queen's College, when the university man got into difficulties, while bathing at Blackrock.

The most memorable Salthill rescues with which Tom Smith was identified took place fourteen years apart. The first, which occurred in August 1909, was particularly poignant as it involved the death of a local man and saw a number of Salthill villagers contribute to the rescue of a second native.

Lazy Wall Strand Tragedy

One summer Friday, two Barrack Lane neighbours, Denis McGrath and Paddy Burke, set out for an evening's entertainment. Having enjoyed a few sups, both men asked George Fallon for oars to take a spin in a small boat, used by Mr. George Kemp of Merchant's Road. The plan was to reach Mr. Kemp's yacht, anchored in the bay. Though Mr. Fallon refused their request, the two men sourced a pair of oars and set off in Kemp's row boat, which was beached between Seapoint Baths and Grattan Road. The sea, in a stiff north-westerly wind, was rough and choppy. When the duo were 400 yards from the Lazy Wall, one of the men lost his oar and in an effort to retrieve it, the boat was overturned. Burke, on surfacing, held on to the boat with all of his might, and eventually managed to get onto the keel of the upturned craft.[24]

His friend, Denis McGrath, grabbed the remaining oar and headed for the shore. McGrath's safety strategy was not new to Salthill, for in 1888 two youngsters named Bain, made it to shore after facing similar threatening circumstances. Having being thrown into the sea from their small sailing craft, the older Bain brother was able to swim to safety while his younger sibling hung on to an oar, before being rescued by a combination of Police Sergeant Leonard of Salthill Station, a young gentleman named William Greaves, a Connaught Ranger, and a boy called Burns, who swam out with a ladder to save the struggling youth. The 1888 rescue was greeted with cheers from anxious onlookers.[25] The Bain brothers involved in that earlier Salthill drama were, most likely, the sons of Alexander Bain, who was an agent for the Glasgow, Galway and Limerick Steamers at New Dock.[26]

In 1909, with Denis McGrath in grave danger, a large crowd had gathered on the beach, some of whom railed against the police, who were helpless without a boat to assist them. Sergeant O'Reilly of the Salthill Police Station despatched Constables Leddy and Boyle – on their bikes – to the Claddagh to source a boat, but it arrived too late to be of use. One spirited lady witness made a number of promenade onlookers kneel down and recite the rosary. A boat belonging to Mr. C. O'Malley of Taylor's Hill was procured by Mr. Michael O'Connell of Kilcorkey Lodge. As it had been idle for a year, however, that vessel filled with water on two occasions, when Messrs. James Cremen, Michael O'Connell and Tom Smith used it – in their attempt to reach the men in distress.

In the midst of all the commotion, Miss Marie Cremen, of Seapoint Baths, was the first to venture into the water. She entered one of her own bathing boxes and headed out to sea carrying the Urban Council life belt that she had snatched from the arms of a policeman. 'If no one else tries to save him, I will,' she cried. Her plucky manner and decisive action prompted cheers from onlookers. While in the water, Miss Cremen witnessed Denis McGrath, the man she hoped to save, sink and drown. Mr. McGrath's companion, Paddy Burke, also observed the terrible tragedy from the upturned keel to which he clung. Michael 'Fox' Fallon, a brother of the man who had, earlier in the evening, wisely refused the two men oars, arrived on the scene and dashed into the water. Miss Cremen returned to shore, on seeing Fallon, a strong swimmer, head for the upturned boat that supported Burke. On reaching the craft, Michael Fallon proceeded to tow the vessel shoreward to the acclaim and relief of a shocked crowd. Having re-launched Mr. O'Malley's leaking vessel, Tom Smith and Paddy Burke's father managed to transfer the tiring Burke to their boat and relieve Fallon, who had hauled the lucky victim halfway home.

Mr. Joe Cloherty of Dominick Street, Sergeant O'Reilly, Head Constable O'Keefe and Mr. O'Connell entered the water to render any assistance they could, as they rescued the rescuers. The body of the unfortunate McGrath was found the following day. The only witness to the cause of the boat's upending was Mrs. Grieves, an invalid, who watched from a window in a suite of rooms she occupied at Seapoint House. She was alone at the time, as her maid had gone for a walk. In the end, no blame was attached to any individual by the inquest finding, but the jury strongly recommended the provision of a boat by the Urban Council, and a lifebuoy for such emergencies. Interestingly, it was noted at the time that though a number of others had drowned at Blackrock, and at other parts of the bay, Denis McGrath was the first victim to drown off the Seapoint Baths' area, a fact made more poignant by the realisation that the young man – aged 25 – died within 150 yards of the shore, and 300 yards from his own Barrack Lane home.

The tragedy, though nothing new at Salthill, impacted the area because the victim was local and so were many of the onlookers and rescuers. Though a good number took part in the rescue effort, it was a local man who had saved Paddy Burke. Consequently, 'Mr. Fallon, Salthill, was presented with £5 out of the Carnegie Hero Fund at Galway… in recognition of his bravery in rescuing a man from drowning.'[27] Michael also received a Certificate of the Royal Humane Society.[28]

96. Michael Fallon, hero of 1909 rescue. (Courtesy of *Connacht Tribune*.)

The second major rescue to have involved Lazy Wall regular, Tom Smith, took place in November 1923 when, due to the inclemency of the weather, the *Dún Aenghus* did not sail from Galway to Aran. An Aran shipment of fish was consequently unable to get to market and the crew of the 'Western Star' decided to deliver its consignment to the town. Two passengers, a Garda and a school teacher, travelled on the trawler from the island. Navigation in thick fog proved so difficult that the boat went onto the reef at Mutton Island. With Galway Bay enveloped in an impenetrable haze, the ship's horn was heard from the promenade. When the mist briefly broke, distress rockets were observed and some men on shore took prompt action. They were 'Tom Smith, pilot, Salthill; John Derrane, a 1914 veteran of the Royal Navy and Colonel Murtagh of Rutledge-terrace, a 1914 officer of the Royal Army.' Smith's small boat 'St. Nicholas' was launched and it headed blind into the direction of the distress call. The stricken vessel, which was held 'hard and fast by the stern,' was eventually reached. On board were five of a crew and the two passengers who 'were hanging on to the rail on the windward side.' Using only a pocket compass and a box of matches, all seven were rescued and landed, with their bags and baggage, at the Lazy Wall Strand. The lighthouse keeper was commended for 'shooting his high power rockets towards the corrig watcha in the fog intervals.' The *Connacht Tribune* was loud in its praise of Tom Smith's seamanship: 'The heroism of Smith and his little crew will still stand more illumine the annals of heroism of those "men of the West" who "go down to the sea in ships".' Captain

Meskil, of the *Dún Aenghus*, was later to save the 'Western Star' and bring her safely into Galway Bay, a rather remarkable feat of seamanship.[29]

There's no doubt but that Tom Smith's many tales would have entertained the *fámairí* who shared the Lazy Wall with him. His exploits, however, stretched far beyond the Salthill Village where he lived, or the chatty wall at which he held court. Described as a man who had almost travelled the world, he was colloquially known as an 'Old Salt.' The term describes a raconteur, or teller of sea stories who might sometimes embellish his tales, in the reputational enhancement of the speaker or his colleagues. Like the *fámaire* term, the 'salty' appellation does not exclusively belong to Salthill, though the place of Tom Smith's home added a certain *cachet* to its use in his particular case. Tom Smith was acquainted with ports on both sides of the South Americas. Acquired from such voyages was his peculiar knowledge of what was commonly termed 'Dock Spanish.' His armoury of scriptural quotations was also a particular gift that he employed in the most humorous, unusual and appropriate situations.

On his passing in 1943, Tom Smith was afforded two newspaper eulogies. One was written by a journalist, while the second was penned by a Galway born, Dublin-based businessman, who knew the deceased well:

He was a man of noticeable height, all his long hard life as straight as a rod…Although no college graduate, Tom had a rare, colourful, romantic, tolerably well-informed mind. He had a raciness of expression and a unique breath of outlook, unusual in men of his background. Never a politician, never in all his life a meddler in other people's affairs, Tom's tongue could travel, yet it was never known to hurt.

His anonymous friend spoke of 'The Lazy Wall School of High Nonsense,' in which Tom Smith was the leading light among his voluble peers: *As tongue free, uncensored commentators of the social scene as it passed before their gaze along the Salthill boulevard, they added a great deal to the joy of life of their days. Tom was regarded as the High Professor of the School. Many gems of humour, many bookfuls of character delineations and homely – very homely – philosophy emerged from the Lazy Wall habitués. With Tom gone the School ceases. Its like might never appear again, which is to be regretted.*[30]

The second local character, most identified with the Lazy Wall was *Ned O' The Hill*. Ned's background and character have earlier been described in the fishing chapter of this publication.

Other Lazy Wall tales

The 1909 tragedy was not the sole bathing incident at the Lazy Wall strand. In 1933, Mrs. Kenny of Cloughbrack, Clonbur, began shouting for help on going out of her depth there. A little girl named Lilly Walsh of the Shamrock Concert Company (late of Toft's) swam to her aid, but was dragged down. The distressed

97. The Lazy Wall in 1941. (Courtesy of *Connacht Tribune*.)

victim and her putative rescuer both disappeared, when another young girl, Barbara Stiff of Lenaboy-lane, jumped into the sea. Miss Stiff, a strong swimmer, managed to reach the spot of imminent danger and brought both Kenny and Walsh ashore.[31] In that same year, when Kathleen Geraghty of the Banba Hotel applied for a bar licence, the District Judge asked where her premises was sited. On solicitor Louis O'Dea indicating that it stood near the Lazy Wall, between the Eglinton and Kenny's (at Strand House), Judge Wyse Power responded : 'I don't know where the Lazy Wall is (laughter).'[32] Being neither a local nor a *fámaire*, the Justice was eventually satisfied when he was informed that the Banba was 'near' the Police Barracks at Salthill. The hotel was, in fact, then opposite the Garda Station, which moved premises in the following year to its current position on Dalysfort Road. It was, perhaps, a little surprising that Judge Charles Wyse Power did not know the site of the 'People's Parliament' at Salthill, for he lived for a time at Fort Lorenzo. He certainly knew the Lazy Wall's site in later years for the judge regularly stayed at the Rockland Hotel – following the sale of Fort Lorenzo – on his Circuit Court visits to Galway.

Lazy Wall's End

The road widening, and car park construction, which commenced in the summer of 1959 to rid the resort of a bottleneck at the Banba, necessitated the removal of buildings on the seaward side of the Salthill road. Included in that demolition brief were the premises that housed the Salthill Garda Station up to 1934. The removal of structures to accommodate the omnivorous automobile meant that Salthill's Lazy Wall of lore, laughter, languor and style was to be levelled to the ground. The wall's ethos was neither urbane nor gaudy for it was rooted in the reality of a simpler age, when Salthill played host to *fámairí* who loved the place enough to annually return for the 'taking of the waters' and the chatter of Gaelic *cómhrá*, on a wall that – for some – defined the place. A *Connacht Sentinel* editorial in May 1959 marked its passing: 'No voice will be raised in protest against the passing of the Lazy Wall, but there are many who will regret in silence, for the Wall has a claim on the affection of many.'[33]

It might well be argued that the Wall has never been replaced in Salthill, and many might wonder what its former *habitués* might make of the Baily Point edifice which replaced the more demure Grand and Banba hotels of yore. The truth is that the simplicity of the Lazy Wall's offering had been overtaken by a faster life dynamic, where restful reflection is afforded little time.

The Lazy Wall in Verse

Bearing testament to the reality that the pen somehow out-powers the banishing bulldozer, as well as the battling sword, Séamus O'Kelly's 1918 book of verse, *Ranns & Ballads*,[34] featured a long poem that conserved the poetic spirit of Salthill's Lazy Wall. Its nine sections describe various personages and personalities, who were somehow a part of Salthill's long seat. They were *The Widower*; *An Sean-Fhear*; *The Revolutionary*; *Patsy na Mallacht*; *The Maid of All Work*; *The Tram Horse*; *A Pinch of Snuff*; *The Cockle Sellers*; and *The Seanachie Tells Another Story*. That volume represented the Galway poet's final collection, which he posted to his publisher less than a fortnight before his death. The simple soul of the place, and its long forgotten characters, were captured in O'Kelly's homely verse:

The Widower
Five Black years since I sat here before
Browning my skin by the Salthill shore -
Above all the women on the wall
Sat Ann, a queen in her purple shawl!
How long the days since that bitter May
We laid poor Ann in her House of Clay...

A Pinch of Snuff
...Oh, as to the shop, and trade, and beer.
Thank God we never had such a year!
A good many fine old neighbours died-
(All their wakes we sorrowful supplied).
I've a side-car now...Achah...Oh, Jim?
Well I think I'll make a priest of him.

The Tram Horse

Heigho, back and forth again to go
And I won't get time my wind to blow!
The cobbles are strewn with sand and shells
Over them clang, clang our hateful bells:
Ding-dong, up the hill, keep to the track,
The whip is out when the trace is slack!

Oh, why can't I stand and nod and dream,
For my forty winks in Heaven seem?
To close my eyes and behold Up There
No track, no street, and no moody Square –
But weary old mares in cloaks and shawls
Droning all day upon lazy walls.

A later paean to the Lazy Wall was penned by a lodger at Sarsfield House in 1943:

A Tribute to the Kindness Shown to a Visitor from England

They watch the passing strangers
And their grand new-fangled ways
(The women smile behind their shawls)
And dream of other days,
When they were lads and lassies
Life was sunshine all the way-
They recall it in life's twilight
On the shores of Galway bay.

This grand old village parliament
What tales they all could tell.
Their heads are bowed, their backs are bent,
For me they weave a spell.
The very breath of Ireland
That I've heard of far away-
How proud I am to meet them
By their own dear Galway Bay.

J.K. Sarsfield House.[35]

Chapter 11

THE TOFT FAMILY AND SALTHILL: A UNIQUE RELATIONSHIP

When Mayor of Galway, David Claude Toft, died in office, his 1981 funeral was the last to pass through the town's main thoroughfare, until the cortège of soccer star, Éamonn 'Chick' Deacy, traversed a similar route in 2012. The civic honour accorded to Claude reflected the high point of a long relationship between the Toft Family and the City of the Tribes. That association, full of twists and turns, was never dull, for it was defined by the steely determination of a showbiz family that delivered fun and games through hard and handsome times.

A Lengthy Amusement Tradition

What might broadly be called the amusement industry in the 19th century ranged from cultured theatrical offerings to the opportunist fortune-teller. The *Galway Patriot* newspaper was not overly impressed in 1838 with the diversionary fare on offer in the town. 'Public amusement of late, has been unaccountably trifling in Galway. How differently disposed are our neighbours in Headford.'[1] It appears that the North Galway town was then to the fore in the amusement stakes. On the 1885 arrival of a soothsayer to that same locale, the urbane *Galway Express* opined that there was 'not a place within the rock-grit shores of our lovely Isle more suitable for the deceptive purposes of a fortune-teller than Headford.' A lady, who might have 'distrusted her fair lover,' approached the visiting clairvoyant for guidance. 'However, Jacob Fortune-teller, after making her purse bleed freely, satisfied her as regards her marriage, and its happy consequent results.'[2] Such a service represented one end of a recreational trade that lightened the humdrum of the everyday.

In terms of Galway's theatrical heritage, Richard Martin, also known as *Humanity Dick,* created a theatre at Kirwan's Lane for his wife, Elizabeth, which opened on 8 August, 1783. Revered patriot and father of Irish Republicanism,

Theobald Wolfe Tone, tread the boards in two plays – *All the World's a Stage* and *Douglas* – on opening night at that theatre.[3] In 1835, 'Mr. Samuel Butler, the first Tragedian of the present day, from the Theatre Royal Covent Garden and the American Theatres,' made his Galway debut in Shakespeare's *Hamlet*.[4] Many other touring troupes subsequently visited the town. In the summer of 1869, Mr. Charles Cooke with his 'Great Dramatic Company selected from the Principal Theatres in the United Kingdom' performed at the Eglinton Hotel Ballroom, Salthill, for an entire week.[5] Fifteen years later, in 1884, both Mr. Robert Forsyth's company and Mr. Charles Cooke's ensemble entertained the citizenry. The latter comic thespian played Conn in Boucicault's *The Shaughraun* at Mack's Royal Hotel at Eyre Square in that season. Still recalled in living memory are the travelling shows of the famed Anew McMaster troupe. 'Mr. Anew McMaster's is surely the most unique Shakespearean company that ever achieved the success which his company had undoubtedly done,' was the view of a *Connacht Tribune* critic in 1928.[6] McMaster's touring shows continued into the nineteen fifties and in 1952 a *Connacht Sentinel* scribe praised McMaster's 'dynamic power' in his portrayal of *Othello* at the Town Hall: 'Not far behind the leader came the performance of *Iago*, by Harold Pinter, a splendid and gripping portrayal.'[7] The same Mr. Pinter went on to become a leading English playwright, who won the Nobel Prize for Literature in 2005.

Less refined fare was also offered by travelling troupes, which generally visited during the summer months. In June 1870, for example, 'The Great American Slave Troupe,' which presented 'New and Laughable Burlesques, (Devoid of vulgarity) Plantation Scenes, Songs and Dances,' played, ironically enough, at Black's Hotel in Eyre Square, while both Ginnett's and Batty's circus troupes also entertained the town's folk in that very same month. Batty's show offered something new that season: 'In addition to the usual features of trained horses, acrobats, gymnasts &c...the group of performing hyenas, wolves &c. in the one cage is undoubtedly a marvel.'[8] The Monster Circus that also visited Galway in 1870 featured a Spanish bull fight.[9] Such shows continued to be held at Mahon's Field on Forster Street well into the 20th century.

Galway's audiences were not, it appears, the easiest to entertain. At a concert by Herr Ulle's troupe in 1871 the conduct of Galway's youth was less than cultured and 'simply unbearable. Ladies, notwithstanding their admitted ability, were hooted off the stage; and Fletcher Baker, in that splendid song, "The Death of Nelson" was – anomalous as the expression may seem – "roared" into "silence".' Such a boorish reception was not, it appears, a unique audience reaction, nor indeed confined to Galway youth alone, for on a February night in 1910 visiting students from Belfast and Cork, after enjoying a meal at the elegant Royal Hotel, Eyre Square, headed to the Court Theatre, where they disturbed the performance and riotously took to the stage. 'The students, having the place to themselves, played high jinks on the platform. They danced and they sung, and such singing and such dancing, it is safe to say, was never seen on the stage of the Galway Court Theatre before.'[10]

Amusement fairs, however, generally won greater favour and represented an enterprise that enlivened many long summer nights throughout the land. The Toft family provided one such attraction.

Toft's Fair

Mr. Claude Toft proudly spoke, on his 1981 election as Mayor, of 1883 business links with Salthill, which stretched back to his great grandfather's era.[11] The Toft enterprise of the 1880s provided amusement fairs throughout the country, particularly through the sunshine months. It was a trade that was not universally welcomed and court house visits were an occupational hazard. The Central Hotel Company took a Mr. Toft to court for trading at Exchequer Street, Dublin in 1889, when special reference was made to the noise nuisance of steam organs.[12] The *Irish Times*, in 1893, reported an alleged contempt charge against William Toft for not having obeyed an order of injunction, restraining the continuance of a series of amusement in a field at Fairview.[13] County Galway, as elsewhere, proved challenging in terms of sourcing suitable sites for a travelling trade. Mrs. Alice Leonard of Athenry, for example, complained of Mr. John Toft at a 1901 Petty Session Court, claiming 'wilful trespass' on her pasture. It was alleged that Mr. Toft 'did refuse to leave same when warned to do so by complainant.'[14]

One location that always extended a *fíorchaoin fáilte* to the Toft clan was Galway's Eyre Square, during the town's annual Race Week. Toft's jumping horses, shooting galleries and palmistry tents were all part of a 'TIR-NAN-OGE' atmosphere at an 1895 Galway Fête in the central Town Square.[15] That festival was organised by Father Lally, to pay off the debt on St. Joseph's Church, which had been completed nine years earlier. When a 1913 Bazaar was held at the same venue for the betterment of Salthill, Mr. Toft paid £15 for the rent of the Square and a further £19 for the 'benefit of Salthill.'[16] Toft's enterprises brought the amusement family throughout the country and when the regular postal system did not suit the demands of their travelling trade, it appears that the Toft clan communicated 'by wire.' An 1895 *Freeman's Journal* advertisement read: 'John Toft, Roundabout Proprietor, wanted to communicate by wire with his brother William, Love lane, West, Dublin.'[17]

On the cusp of the 20th century, the majority of newspaper adverts placed by Toft enterprises sought employees. A particular requirement was that applicants should not be partial to alcohol: 'Two or three steady sober Men wanted, used to business. Toft's Galloping Horses, Athenry: drunken men save stamps.'[18] Salthill, with its summer visitors, attracted Toft's amusements for a longer spell than provincial towns, and a Race Week break saw the entire operation traditionally transfer to Eyre Square.

98. Toft's Fair at Eyre Square.

When Salthill Park was purchased as a public space by the Urban Council in 1914, Toft's fair did not immediately move to the new civic site, but remained for some years at its original Salthill setting. That position was behind the Eglinton Hotel, in the general area that today houses San Antonio Terrace. Though not an ideal pitch, it had its advantages in that it was close to the Village, the Lazy Wall and the sea. Not everyone, of course, was pleased with its location. The building of San Antonio Terrace, first rateably valued in 1905, meant that there were more residents to object to its placement, and ten years later complaints were made to the Urban Council 'about the hobby horses at Salthill.' Objecting to Messrs. Toft's presence, a local resident, Mr. Holland, noted the insanitary condition of the field in which the hobby horses were sited. That field abutted the complainant's terraced residence, and 'a continuous drunken brawl which took place there every night' annoyed the Salthill man. The thick smoke from a nearby engine also seriously inconvenienced the Holland household and its seasonal lodgers. A Sanitary Officer, Mr. Waters, inquired into the matter, but he failed to locate either Mister or Mrs. Toft, whose evasive skills proved opportune. Mr. Waters did, however, report that the machine was in the wrong place. Councillor Donnellan suggested that there would have been no complaint but for 'a bit of a brawl that occurred there.' The local politician believed that it was all 'a little bit of "double",' and that he should know as he 'sold some of it.'[19] The councillor's recognition of his own role in the *fracas* that occurred at Toft's amusements drew laughter in the council chamber, for Mr. M.J. Donnellan, who had topped the South Ward poll in January 1914 to become a new Urban Councillor, owned the public house at the corner of Atlantic Terrace, which abuts San Antonio Terrace. The brawlers obviously bought their booze at the Atlantic Bar. It must, therefore, be acknowledged that the publican-cum-councillor was not a disinterested party for Messrs. Toft brought customers his way. The complaint matter was referred to the Medical Officer.

The fare supplied by Toft's amusements evolved through changing times and a 1909 advertisement invited all comers to enjoy a new experience at Galway's summer resort: 'Come, See and Hear the wonderful new cinephone pictures that talk, sing, dance, and play. You will be surprised and delighted. Have you seen the ladies' new game of "Hoop-La?" Great Sport. Toft's Salthill.'[20] A year later, for those who could not travel to Oberammergau, Germany, for the famed Passion Play,

99. Atlantic Bar at opening to Atlantic Terrace, where Martin Donnellan hosted some of Mr. Toft's customers.

the 'courteous and enterprising proprietor' of Toft's amusements had secured at 'enormous expense, a wonderfully faithful and beautifully coloured cinematographic representation of the Passion Play as performed by the Bavarian villagers.'[21] The show was 'patronised every night by crowds of visitors at Salthill.' Two years later, Toft's entertainments at Salthill included 'the famous Dick Turpin series and Shakespeare's masterpiece *Hamlet*.' These pictures were offered in addition to hobby horses, swing-boats and shooting galleries.[22]

William Toft and Mary (Emerson) Toft

The principal in the Toft operation, up to his death in October 1904, was William Toft, who was residing at his Tara Street, Dublin, home in 1901. Born in Wales, William was then a 40 year old Church of England showman who was married to a Scottish born 'show woman.' She was Mary (May) Toft, the daughter of Ellen Emerson, a Galway born actress. It appears, therefore, that a familial Toft-Galway connection stretched well back into the 19th century. William Toft, his wife May, and mother-in-law Ellen, were all – unfortunately – to pass away over a two year period during the first decade of the 20th century. Forty four year old William died at Oxford Lodge, Ranelagh in 1904, and his 36 year old wife passed away in the following year. Some months after May Toft died on 10 May, 1905, her widowed mother, Ellen Emerson – aged 80 – also expired. All three deceased were buried in the same plot at Mount Jerome Cemetery, Dublin. The premature deaths of William and May Toft thrust their Belfast-born eldest son, William Henry (Harry) Toft, at 16 years of age, into the management of the Toft amusement business. The young William married English born, Elizabeth Mary Ashley, in 1908 at St. Peter's Church of Ireland chapel, on Aungier Street, Dublin.[23] It was following a London divorce in January 1934 that William Henry Toft re-married, when he wed Marion MacDonald at the parish Church of St. Jude in Dublin. William's second spouse, Marion, was the daughter of George MacDonald, an amusement caterer. Mrs. Marion (MacDonald) Toft was to later play a central role in the running of the Arcade at Salthill.

Mr. John Toft

Through the closing decade of the 19th century and the opening years of the one that followed, Mr. John Toft was the amusement man most associated with his family's trade in Galway. A Welsh native, his daughter Mary was born in County Galway in 1899, and John was operating at Galway town at the time of the 1909 Abbey Bazaar, when his wife, Annie, passed away at Moate.[24] It was John who was responsible for the passion play event at Salthill and his amusement offerings were presented throughout the county. In 1955, a Roscommon native, John Freyne, then resident in Dublin, penned a memory of his only holiday in Salthill, which he had enjoyed a full forty seven years earlier. Mr. John Toft featured in that reminiscence, which evoked the excitement of boyhood wonder:

By night there was Tofts…Tofts! – the hobby horses, the swing boats, the fun of the fair. I know the Tofts are still going strong (D.G.) but the Tofts of 1908 – that is another matter.

Old Mr Toft – was it John? My first close up of a motor car was the one old Mr. Toft drove out from Galway. I remember he wore a swallow-tail coat like my father. He was regarded as the king of show people. His Fun Fair was part of Salthill. It was there I saw my first moving picture and heard my first Talkies. In 1908: Talkies? Yes, Talkies. The picture showed a lovely girl standing by the sea and a young man singing. A man under the screen sang "Eileen Alanah." There was the picture that "brought down" the house – "The Lady Motor Driver" and a "futuristic" picture, "Parts of 1920," showing pirates robbing a ship at sea from a flying machine.[25]

David (Abby) and Florence Toft

It was David (Abby) and Florence Toft, however, who formed the fairground couple which was – from 1913 – to become most associated with Salthill over many decades. David (Abby) was residing in the Wood Quay, Dublin home of his grandmother, 'Mrs. Emmerson', in 1901 and ten years later was recorded in residence with his Turnball cousins in Belfast. The Turnball family was in the circus business, reflecting the close ties which then connected showbiz families. The 1913 Cork City marriage of David Toft and Florence Piper further highlighted the ties that existed between amusement catering clans throughout the country. Tramore, Co. Waterford, was the address given for Florence and 11 Richmond Hill, Cork was the abode of David Toft, who was then described as being of 'full age.' The couple's wedding ceremony took place in St. Anne's Church, Shandon, according to the rites and ceremonies of the Church of Ireland. The Piper family, which belonged to the Church of England, were show people, most of whose children were London born. Florence, however, was a Dublin native and her parents, William and Emily Piper, were in the Steam Circus business, with Munster representing the geographical axis of the Piper operation.

Toft's ties to Salthill Park

David (Abby) and Florence Toft were a formidable business pair and, as earlier indicated, their amusement enterprise did not immediately transfer to Salthill Park on the Urban Council's 1914 purchase of the place. The Council's plan was to make Salthill Park a place of amusement and recreation, on the lines of Stephen's Green. There were a number of reasons for Toft tardiness in moving west beyond Dalysfort Road to the municipal park. In the first instance, such a prospective move drew opposition from some locals. In 1916, Gerald Cloherty, Walter O'Flaherty and John T. Miller sought an order at the Chancery Division in Dublin, seeking to prevent the Urban Council from letting the public park to the defendant, Mr. David Toft, or to any other person engaged in the same business that involved merry-go-rounds, steam-driven organs or cocoa-nut shies. Mr. Gerald Cloherty, the first named of the complainants, was Clerk of the Crown and Peace, who was then residing at Forster Park, Salthill's Garda Station today. The second was Walter O'Flaherty, a well known Galway contractor, who built the first four houses of what was then known as Dalysfort Terrace, during the years of the 1914–1918 War. The third was Grand Jury member, Mr. John T. Miller, a leading businessman, General Merchant, and Galway-Salthill Tramway director, who resided at Dalysfort House. Justice Gordon made 'no rule' on the injunction motion against David Toft, as delays pushed the sitting out to September, when the summer amusement season was closing.[26]

There were other possible reasons for Toft's delay in occupying Salthill Park: In the first place, World War One resulted in the park being required for allotments, and even as late as 1922, *Feis Mhór na Gaillimhe* – fixed for the venue on 30 July – was postponed and held over until 'favourable political conditions' would prevail.[27] The 1914 –1923 period was blighted with difficulties that defined four conflicts and it was 1923 before Mr. David Toft paid £150 for the use of Salthill Park, and £130 for the use of Eyre Square during Bazaar week. That new arrangement, by way of Urban Council lease or licence, was continued uninterrupted for the following 15 years. The move offered relief to put-upon San Antonio Terrace residents, but little to Surgeon O' Malley the new resident at Forster Park, who had purchased the house from the departing Gerald Cloherty in 1923. In the case of the Forster Park residence, the summer amusement fair simply moved from the house's eastern flank to its western wing.

100. Toft stalls at Salthill Park in 1933, when Lever Brothers (Ireland) Ltd. visited from Dublin – with three hundred of their employees – on a day excursion. (Courtesy of *Connacht Tribune*.)

Not everything ran smoothly in the annual Toft-Council arrangement, however, and in 1926 Councillor Faller wanted to know if Mr. Toft owed the council a sum of £30, which led to a dispute that resulted in a writ being served on the funfair family.[28] Toft's annual Race Week transfer to Eyre Square was faithfully noted by the local Press: 'During the week-end, Mr. A. Toft well known and popular proprietor of Tofts' Amusements, will move his fun fair into Eyre Square, Galway, where it will remain for Race Week. At the end of the week, Mr. Toft will move back to Salthill Park.'[29] Toft's Salthill summer residency continued in that style right up to the late thirties, before some Rockbarton residents organised to clear the park of the resort's Amusement Fair.

The Rockbarton – Toft Amusement Row 1939 – 1941: Round One

An amusement banishment campaign was to have a major impact on the Galway-Toft tale, and the story became a cause célèbre which drew nationwide attention, due to the dynamics of a conflict that placed neighbour against neighbour. Social, as well as other divides, were exposed in the row. The action was triggered in 1939 when it was learned that the Corporation wished to transfer the Toft Amusement Fair from the front – to the rear – of Salthill Park, where the funfair would be a good deal closer to some houses than heretofore. Though not cited in documentation, a Borough Surveyor plan, submitted to Galway Corporation in the previous year, had also included a proposal to build a concrete pitch for amusements at the Park. While the terraced slopes, then suggested for the park by Mr. C.J. O'Callaghan, were most attractive, a concrete amusement facility pointed to a secure future for carnival operators, which would not have appealed to all local residents.

The Corporation received a written complaint from Lisgorm resident, Professor Donovan O'Sullivan, and a further petition from a number of local people, all objecting to Mr. A. Toft's fair at Salthill Park. A loudspeaker, described as a 'refinement of cruelty more worthy of a German concentration camp than that of a progressive corporation like Galway' came in for special criticism. Given the times and what was to follow in Europe, Professor O'Sullivan's war analogy was most unfortunate. The text of the Professor's letter, while reasonable enough, was not to appeal to all of Galway's citizens, because of its strident tone and haughty tenor. Some sections from the Professor's letter are here presented:

........*In the circumstances I feel constrained to write and respectfully ask the Corporation to interfere and prevent the infliction of this new horror on the inhabitants of this district...It cannot be maintained for one instant that it has ever brought a single visitor to Salthill; on the contrary, it has kept many decent people out of it. Its chief result has been to turn this Park every summer into a quagmire and, in more ways than one, to strike a blow at the decencies of this neighbourhood, while it leaves a legacy of tin shacks and such accoutrements to Salthill for the winter which are an eyesore and a disgrace to any self-respecting community...But worse than this is the horrid cruelty of Mr. Toft's loudspeaker. I would remind the members of the Corporation that the loudspeaker goes on continuously every evening from 8 p.m. to 11 p.m., and on Sundays regularly, and sometimes on occasions during the week it is in action continuously from 1 p.m. until nearly midnight and so loud and penetrating is it that it can be heard in the farthest parts of Taylor's Hill and half way, if not wholly, into town...Speaking for myself, I am engaged every year during the months of June and July on a most exacting form of work, University examining, which demands concentrated attention, for at least eight hours per day. Up to the present, owing to the presence of Mr. Toft's entertainment show in the Park, I have been able with difficulty to carry on and then only by retiring to a cellar and plugging my ears to keep out, in some measure, the raucous din.*[30]

To be fair, Professor O'Sullivan was not the sole objector and a good number of her neighbours signed a memorial which was critical of Mr. Toft's enterprise:

'*We, the undersigned, respectfully request the Corporation not to permit the entertainment show of Mr. Toft to be set up in Salthill Park this year, or subsequently: and not to allow any similar show to be installed there at any time....*J. Sullivan, Lisgorm, Rockbarton; Mr. J. Allen, solicitor, Ruttledge Terrace, do.; R.E. Mc Givern, Dalysfort-road, G.M.

Counihan solicitor, do.; M.J. Greally, do.; J.H. Daly, do.; Lilian Johnston, Glenorny, Rockbarton; R. B. Kinneen, Moyveela, do.; M.J. de C. Dodd, Brinkwater, do.; William Cahill, Gurthard, do.; Mary A. McDonogh, Belmore, do.; Dr. Denis V. Morris, Seamount; M.A. Kennedy, The Retreat, Rockbarton; P.Ó Mórdha, St. Mary's, Rockbarton; M. Power, Dalysfort-road; B. Kennedy, do.; James P. Horan, do.; Mary Derrane, Salthill; Walter O'Flaherty, Dalysfort-road; F. Liston, do.; P. McDonogh, do.; Joseph Maher, do.; P. McLean, do.[31]

On receipt of the Rockbarton correspondence, the amusement issue was discussed at a Corporation meeting where the Town Clerk, Mr. Ó Cléaracháin, indicated that Mr. Toft's three year lease was due to expire in October 1940. The councillors were also told that the lease could be terminated on three months' notice. Ald. Ashe pointed out that the Corporation only made £80 per annum on the park. Mr. Lydon supported Toft's position, pointing out that the fair had been coming to Salthill for a number of years and there had never been a previous complaint. That observation was not factually correct, as complaints had been made when Tofts previously operated in the San Antonio Terrace locale, and a court injunction had been sought in 1916 to deny the amusement family access to Salthill Park.

The problem was that the Corporation was to spend £6,000 improving the park and one season of amusements had the potential to destroy much of the work done. Two councillors, Mr. Carrick and Mr Lydon, took Toft's side of the argument. The former claimed that 'the people, particularly the poorer people go out to Salthill to enjoy themselves and we must do something for them,' a view Mr. Lydon shared. One verbal joust pitched Miss Ashe, who said that Mr. Toft was no financial addition to the city, against Mr. Lydon who insisted the poor were entitled to amusements. Ald. Corbett claimed that park revenue at £80 was small and he held that local residents' feelings should be considered. Other venues for Toft's fair were appraised, including South Park and Toft's first amusement pitch close to San Antonio Terrace, but the former option was not in Salthill and the latter site was built-up. After much discussion, it was decided that the Corporation should visit the site, accompanied by members of the Salthill Development Committee.[32]

By early March, the anti-Toft memorial was counteracted by a significant pro-Toft petition, so that the Corporation had both sides of the argument when it reached its decision on the Salthill Park issue. The new memorial in favour of Mr. Toft was signed by ratepayers, residents and business people of Salthill and Rockbarton. It included 'Martin Donnellan, No. 1 Atlantic Terrace, Salthill; Mrs. B. Finan, Salthill; W.J. Sammon, do.; Mrs. S. Emerson, Eglinton Hotel, do.; Miss M.F. Monahan, Rockland Hotel, do.; James Devery, Dalysfort Road: Sarah Judge, Ave Maria, do.; E. Sampson, do.; Miss Annie Brennan, do.; Mrs. D. Powell, do.; Mrs. E.V. Brennan, do.; M. O'Malley, do.; Myles May, do.; George Miller, do.'[33] The pro-amusement points carried validity and the clout of large ratepayers who considered an amusement park, in some form, to be essential to Salthill. Toft supporters asserted that while amusements proved to be a nuisance to some residents, it was a valuable asset to the local business community. In the end the Corporation's decision was to terminate Mr. A. Toft's lease, with the matter being decided on a 5–3 vote.

So, for the first time from 1923 there was no Toft Fair at Salthill Park, and the summer-stay tradition of that resort carnival, which stretched back to the 1880s, was broken and indeed ended. The outcome, which was not universally welcomed, exposed divisions that were not simply of a *Pro* or *Anti*-Toft nature: Salthill versus Town; residents vs. residents; business people vs. residents; and other social status issues all surfaced in press contributions. Letter writers, holding strong views and forthright opinions, described on-the-ground concerns and feelings. One such scribbler – who went by the name *Dominie* – employed wit and wisdom in his take on the amusement issue. Erudite and trenchant comment lent an edge to his *Sentinel* contribution on the 'Banishment of Toft:'

Sir, – It is all very well for those who can dash away to the South of France for sunshine and the balmy breezes of the Mediterranean or for those who can travel to Germany or go skiing in the Alps to get annoyed when they return to Galway because Mr. Abby Toft makes a little noise with his hobby horses and his dodgems, with his pongo and his swing-boats, and the joyous (if vulgar) laughter that accompany them. Toft has been good to Galway, far better than the Corporation, which has treated him so meanly, has deserved. He has never let the priests or the Church down; and he has given more money to charity than anyone who has ever come to Galway. Witness his munificence to the St. Vincent de Paul Society and to other charities in the past.

Therefore, I take off my hat to the Councillors Carrick and Lydon for pointing out to the members of the Galway Corporation (who are such ostriches that they do not know what the "poor ratepayers" want) that Toft's amusements constitute the poor man's sport – in fact, they are the only sport he has, except laying an occasional bob, during the summer months in the arid atmosphere of this burgh…The rich must not have all the pleasure, and the poor all the pain…Dominie'[34]

Another contributor penned a missive expressing *faux*-concern for Professor Donovan O'Sullivan's work schedule: *I hope the Minister of Industry will please note re the lady who is disturbed at her work from 8 p.m. to 11 p.m. after working all day in the University and notify the authorities of same, of the Conditions of Employment Act which allows all employees to work only a 48 hour week…A Galwegian.*[35]

In April, Munster Lane was proposed as a site for Toft's amusements and Corporation members, uneasy perhaps with the depth of reaction to their earlier decision, were informed that it would require a two thirds majority to rescind the Toft ban. In a simmering anti-Corporation atmosphere, Councillors were happy – in May 1939 – to approve plans, submitted by Mrs. A. Toft, for the erection of a Fun Palace at Salthill. The enterprising Florence Toft saw the writing on the wall for her outdoor trade, and quickly adapted to a changing environment by deciding to move indoors. Permanently sited amusements represented the future, so the Toft clan was about to take that particular step in Salthill. On hearing of Mrs. Toft's application, Mr. Cooke said in July 1939 that there were not a hundred people in Salthill, because of the absence of amusements, and the councillor wanted the Fun Palace project to be speeded up.[36]

The Salthill Development Committee, recognising the great loss Toft's fair was to the tourist trade, sought to erect a temporary structure just inside the main gates of Salthill Park, to house indoor amusements. The proposal was shot down by the Borough Surveyor because (a) the plan contravened bye-laws and (b) Mrs. Toft had already been given permission to develop her indoor enterprise.[37] Though barred from Salthill Park, Toft's amusements were in Eyre Square for Race Week in 1939, thereby maintaining a long tradition. In August, Mr. Abby Toft, whose fair was still operating at the Square, agreed to give three benefit nights to the Emmet's Rowing Club for the building of a club-house.

Those who opposed Toft's amusements at Salthill may have enjoyed a quieter summer season in 1939, but their comfort was short lived, when, in August of the same year, a rumour reached Mr. Dodd and Professor O'Sullivan at Rockbarton that Dr. Bartley O'Beirne was going to let the lawn of his Maretimo residence to Mrs. Florence Toft. When the gates of Salthill Park were shut against her, the lawn gates next door, which belonged to the County's Chief Medical Officer, were opened in welcome.

101. Image on left indicates the extensive Maretimo lawn that was offered to Florence Toft, when the adjacent Salthill Park was closed to her. The photo on right shows fairground stalls and equipment on Dr. O'Beirne's Maretimo lawn. (Photo on left courtesy of *Irish Independent* and N.L.I.; image on right courtesy of Peter Allen.)

That lawn would today represent the garden to the front of the Leisureland pool, which features a crazy golf course. A concerned Mrs. O'Sullivan consequently rang Dr. O'Beirne to ask if the rumour was true. 'Not yet' was the neighbouring doctor's pithy reply, and Mrs. O'Sullivan warned her close neighbour that local residents would take legal proceedings against him. This came to pass and when later asked, in court, if he realised that Mrs. O'Sullivan, on calling him by phone, was strongly opposed to the amusement letting, Dr. O Beirne replied that he 'took it as very impertinent of her to ring me up.'[38]

Death of David 'Abby' Toft, 1939

The Rockbarton conflict, which appeared to have been successfully resolved, was then surprisingly re-ignited with a potential burden of costly legal fees. In the midst of all this *brouhaha*, Florence Toft's husband, David 'Abby' Toft, of 10 Villiers Road, Rathgar, passed away at a Dublin Nursing Home in August 1939. He had been ill for some time. Mr. Toft's shows had provided entertainment in most western towns over many decades and he had been a frequent visitor to Galway from 1904. Abby Toft's benevolence was recalled in an obituary reference, which noted that he had never refused requests to allow his show raise finance for churches and various charitable organisations.[39] A 1933 newspaper report captured the spirit of such charity: 'Through the great kindness of Mr. and Mrs. Toft, the boys of St. Joseph's, Salthill, were treated to a delightful evening's entertainment at their popular fair on Thursday evening. For hours the boys took turns on the electric cars, the switch back, moving platform, and on the "Horses".' Mr. Toft allowed all the boys to draw freely for valuable prizes, and at the conclusion Mrs. Toft treated them to a generous supply of fruit and ices. The Superior and Brothers highly appreciate the generosity and thoughtfulness to the boys of Mr. and Mrs. Toft.'[40]

Abby Toft's benevolence and bravery were called upon on another occasion, when, in the summer of 1935, he pulled two Tuam men, Bartholomew Goff and John Nicholson, from a blazing Chrysler car which had been involved in an accident on the promenade. Both men were unconscious.[41]

David 'Abby' Toft was survived by his wife, Florence, and their three children; Maureen, Kenneth and David Claude Toft. Her husband's death, local opposition and the needs of her children, no doubt, focused Florence-Piper-Toft's attention on the best way forward, and such considerations would have contributed to her decision to create an indoor amusement facility, which could operate year round and win wider acceptance within the broader community.

Round Two: 1940 Court Injunction

In early 1940, a request from Mrs. Toft, then a widow, that she be given first choice if Salthill Park was to be leased that summer, sparked a row at Galway Corporation. By March of the same year, however, Dr. O'Beirne had entered a five year rental agreement with Mrs. Toft for the use of Maretimo lands for an amusement fair. Dr. O'Beirne had, by then, obtained permission for the breach of his lease from his landlord, Mr. Dermot Hennessy, who had inherited the Attithomasrevagh/ Rockbarton estate, on the 1935 death of his father, Michael. It was recounted by Dr. O'Beirne that he had previously been approached by Mr. Claude Toft and Mr. Barry, another amusement provider, to let the ground at Maretimo for their shows, but declined, as he did not then have Mr. Hennessy's permission. Dr. O'Beirne also revealed that in honouring his deal with Mrs. Toft, he had turned down an improved monetary offer from Mr. Barry. The O'Beirne – Toft deal was signed in March 1940 and Dermot Hennessy was paid £50 costs for his consent to the agreement.[42]

A third memorial, following the Pro. v. Anti-Amusement petitions of the previous year, surfaced following news of the new deal. The new petition, signed by over four hundred people, sought to have amusements allowed at the back of Salthill Park. It read:

We the undersigned residents of Salthill, after our experience of last season, demand that permanent facilities for amusements in the park be immediately provided by the Corporation and that the levelling of that portion of the Park at the back of the Pavilion be made available for amusements this summer. This is of vital importance to hotel keepers, boarding-house

102. Maretimo on raised ground at site of current Leisureland Centre.

keepers and business people of Salthill, as many of our visitors left last year owing to the fact that no amusements were provided.[43]

In spite of such broad support for amusements at Salthill that summer, an interlocutory injunction, until the trial of the Rockbarton action, was allowed in July 1940. Granted by Mr. Justice Gavan Duffy in Dublin's High Court, the court order forbade Mrs. Toft and Dr. O'Beirne holding the business of an amusement park, or fair, at Maretimo, Rockbarton. That decision was made when dodgem cars, swing boats and other amusement facilities were brought onto Dr. O'Beirne's lawn at Maretimo. Increased sound levels, following a change from steam to electricity, along with the introduction of dodgems and a 'wall of death' were cited as reasons for increased distress to residents. Such a fair was perceived to pose an intolerable nuisance to the plaintiffs, most of whom resided at Rockbarton. The action was served on behalf of Mrs. Mary Donovan Sullivan, Professor of History, U.C.G.; Maurice J. de C. Dodd, retired Land Commission inspector, Brinkwater, Michael McDonogh, medical doctor, Belmore, Mrs. Mary Kennedy, The Retreat, Rockbarton and Robert E. Girvan, Dalysfort-road, Salthill.[44]

Mr. J.H. Daly of the National Bank, who resided at Dalysfort Road, was annoyed when the *Connacht Tribune* mistakenly listed 'Mr. Robert E. Daly' of Dalysfort Road as a plaintiff in the case on 27 July, 1940. That error was explained as a typographical mix-up, which was clarified on the newspaper stating that it was Mr. Girvan, of Dalysfort Road, and not Mr. Daly, who was one of the five plaintiffs.[45]

Supporting Mrs. Toft in an answering affidavit, Mrs. Susan Emerson of the Eglinton Hotel stated that she had never heard a complaint against Toft's fair from any of her guests and that 'Mr. Anthony Eden and his family stayed at my hotel, and while there visited Toft's amusements for a few times.'[46] Mrs. Emerson's reference to a prestigious political guest, who was later to succeed Mr. Winston Churchill as British Prime Minister, added stature to her advocacy of Florence Toft's position. The hotel proprietress further asserted that people had complained the previous year of Toft's absence from Salthill.

Two days after the granting of the court order, Mrs. Toft's fair was transferred to Eyre Square for Galway's Race Week. On 12 August it returned to Maretimo and Messrs. MacDermott and Allen wrote to Mrs. Florence Toft, informing her of her violation of the injunction, and of their intention to take steps to prevent a recurrence of the nuisance. On 3 September the fair was still in place on Dr. O'Beirne's lawn, when Mrs. Toft offered to carry out a test of the noise being complained of. The sound experiment proved troublesome. On the day that Mr. Dodd, at the neighbouring Brinkwater, had gathered his listeners, Florence Toft rang to cancel, as she could not assemble her own auditors at that time. However she turned up, unannounced, at Mr. Dodd's house the following day with her own coterie of witnesses, and 'a little argument' ensued, as Mr. Dodd had no opportunity to have his people present on that occasion.[47]

Round Three: Six Days at High Court in 1941

The Salthill Amusements' Case, as it came to be known, was taken against 'Mrs. Florence Toft, amusement caterer, Thomas Davis street, Dublin and Dr. Bartley O'Beirne, Maretimo, Salthill.'[48] It took six days in Dublin's High Court to complete and attracted national attention, because of the rich mix of characters that ranged from fairground entertainers to university professors, all embroiled in a battle between 'raucous' fun and silent seclusion. On the first court day it was reported that the Wall of Death had not operated at the resort in 1940, though it had been replaced by the 'Blonde Bombshell,' who performed on a motorcycle. Miss Betty Plant, the Bombshell herself, was later to inform Justice Black that 'any noise complained of was not made by any of her motor cycles.'[49] Everyone, it appears, was happy with her performance, which attracted 'a considerable number of people,' even though her 'motor cycle had not got a silencer.'[50]

The scene was set for a colourful case where high profile professionals, a blond lady motorcyclist, and the perceived cream of Galway's social order, took opposing sides at a funfair trial. There was more than the 'Blonde Bombshell' in court with motorised fairground experience, for later Taoiseach, Mr. John A. Costello, K.C. – who was representing Mrs. Toft – told the High Court that 'I may say I have operated the Dodgems myself.' Mr. Justice Black: 'Did you try to collide with anyone?'; Mr. Costello: 'My whole object was to try and prevent other people from colliding with me (laughter).'[51] The Patrick Kavanagh vs. *The Leader* libel lawsuit of 1954 was clearly not the only high profile – and humorous – case that Mr. Costello partook of.

Mr. Dodd, whose Sunday siestas were affected by Toft's fairground noise, contended that the majority of signatures supporting the fair was made up of tourist business operators. The Brinkwater resident denied that he had initiated the petition against the Toft fair at Salthill Park, but said that Mrs. O'Sullivan had brought it to him. The only piece of music he recollected being played at the fair was 'Roll out the Barrel' (laughter). Mrs. Kennedy, widow of the late Mr. M.J. Kennedy, County Surveyor, admitted that she rode on the dodgems at Eyre Square during Race Week, but that if she had thought about it, she would not have done so. When it was put to her that one of her step children achieved first place – and first class honours – in a Universty exam, she agreed, but quicky asserted that he worked hard in the daytime, and that it was brains and work which brought him success. 'And Toft's music' quipped Mr. Ryan, one of Dr. O'Beirne's legal team.[52]

Medical men also took the stand: Dr. Michael O'Malley, Professor of Surgery at U.C.G., informed the court that he had lived at Forster Park, which was very close to Toft's Amusement fair. His wife complained to him that their children could not sleep with the noise from the fair. He found it difficult to get in and out of Forster Park because of the crowded roadway and claimed that one of the reasons he departed his Salthill dwelling was because of Toft's show. Asked whether it was the incursion of the sea in 1926 which brought about that decision, the surgeon said he had forgotten about the sea flooding when he changed residence nine years later. While living at Forster Park he had written to the Urban Council asking to have Toft's Show removed, or its site position changed. The Council refused his request. Dr. W.F. Sandys, the Crescent, Galway informed the court that 'he had a number of patients in Rockbarton and when any of them were ill, the noise of Toft's Show had a deleterious effect.'

Mrs. Mary Donovan O'Sullivan, Professor of History at U.C.G., gave her evidence on the third day. Her recreations involved reading and writing indoors, dancing and playing tennis, while she was also very fond of golf. When asked if she had ever danced to 'Roll out the Barrel,' Mary didn't know if she had. She did say she had suffered physical discomfort because of the noise as she had to work with her ears plugged. Like Mr. Dodd, she was unable to enjoy a sleep on Sunday afternoons.[53]

Mr. James P. Horan, who described himself as 'a gentleman-at-large,' and a Dalysfort Road resident for seventeen year was not discommoded by the loudspeaker's output. He was a member of the party which took part in the disputed audio test at Mr. Dodd's residence, and while he could hear the Fair music from there, considered it to be nothing out of the ordinary. Sergeant Michael Baker of the Dalysfort Road Garda Barracks said that he occupied the quarters there from 1936 and no complaint was ever made to him about the general conduct of the people attending Salthill. The local sergeant also informed the court that there were no prosecutions for disorderly conduct at the amusement park. Mr. William Sammon, treasurer of the Salthill Development Association spoke of the 'quite orderly' crowd he observed at Toft's Amusements and told the court that he was part of a Salthill Development delegation, which had made representations to the Corporation for the continuance of the fair. When Mr. Fitzgibbon, for the plaintiffs, tested the witness; 'I don't suppose you would care to have it under your own window?' Mr. Sammon sanguinely retorted; 'I wouldn't mind.'

On the fifth day of the case, Mr. Fitzgerald, representing Dr. O'Beirne, delivered a searing observation, sodden with sarcasm, when he asked Justice Black 'to take into account the sober, ordinary individual and not the refined sensibilities of a professor, a retired land inspector, or a would-be historian.' The only way Dr. O'Beirne could be held liable – according to Mr. Fitzgerald – was if it could be proven that the use of the park was a nuisance and that O'Beirne should have known it. In his evidence Dr. O'Beirne delivered a précis of his curriculum vitae right up to his appointment as County Medical Officer. A son of the house, Dr. Dónal O'Beirne, said that while pursuing his medical studies at Maretimo, Toft's fair did not interfere with his work. Like the Kennedy undergraduate at the Retreat next door, Dónal achieved first class honours in his exams.

On the final day of the hearing, Mr. McCarthy for Mrs. Toft, advised the Judge that petitions, a combination of which were signed by over five hundred citizens, as against a counter-one signed by just over twenty objectors, should be taken into consideration. On the question of property depreciation, caused by the amusements' presence, it was pointed out that Surgeon O'Malley obtained £5,000 for his Forster Park residence in 1934, having purchased it for £1,900 eleven years earlier.

Justice Black said that Salthill was a well known seaside resort and as regards the residents of such a locality, they could not expect the same degree of quietude as if they were living in a secluded part. The suggestions that the objections were eccentric or based on social snobbery had not been established. However he did allow that 'Mrs. O'Sullivan was an abnormal woman in the sense that she was an intellectual and studious person different from the average person. It might be that she required a higher standard in home requirements.' The Judge believed that the crowd issue was not a serious matter of complaint but the noise output of loudspeakers, dodgem and speedway cars formed the principal plank of the plaintiffs' objections. In delivering his judgement, Judge Black – though he found against her – had kind words for Mrs. Toft.[54]

A summary of the judgement was carried by the *Irish Times*: 'Mr. Justice Black granted an injunction against Mrs. Toft in so far as it referred to nuisance created by noise...He dismissed the action against Dr. O'Beirne with costs...He said he felt very great sympathy with Mrs. Toft because he thought that she had acted in the genuine belief that there would be no nuisance. He did not think that she appreciated that her show would produce the effects on other persons' nervous systems which it did produce, and he thought that she had let herself into entering on her five years' agreement in respect of Dr. O'Beirne's land through a misapprehension.'[55] Mrs. O'Sullivan, Mrs. Kennedy and Mr. Dodd were granted costs in winning the injunction against Mrs. Toft, while the costs of the remaining plaintiffs, Dr. Michael McDonogh and Mr. Robert E. Girvan, who did not appear in court, were not allowed.[56]

So in the end it was Mrs. Toft who was the loser, while the action against Dr. O'Beirne was dismissed with costs. Mr. Claude Toft was later to say that the action cost the family £4,000,[57] a severe blow – though not a fatal one – to their Galway operations.

The Salthill Arcade

Throughout it all, Mrs. Toft was not idle, and the move to indoor amusements was accomplished, when her Arcade opened for business in 1940. Florence Toft's amusement centre was constructed on the town side of the Rockland Hotel, in front of Forster Park, which by then housed the Salthill Garda Station. A turkey was to be won, and Pongo Sessions took place from 8–11 p.m. in November 1940. Comfortable seating and new electric floor heaters were advertised features of Salthill's new fun facility. In 1941, Marvelle, the wonder girl appeared at the Arcade and private interviews could be arranged by appointment, while a year later Madam Ida promised to tell ladies 'Does he love me – yes or no?' Salthill's Arcade annually closed for the winter months, and a Toft Winter Garden opened at William Street West during the resort's seasonal shut down. In 1942 the Arcade opened on Whit Sunday in late May, while Toft's garden opened on 23 October, thus ensuring year round business over two separate locations. Arcade advertisements often carried a closing tag which left no doubt about the ownership of the business: 'Sole Proprietress and manageress: Mrs. Florence Toft.'[58]

Dónall Mac Amhlaigh presented, in a 1968 *Irish Times* piece, his own take on the Arcade vis-a-vis Toft's outdoor funfair at Salthill Park:

Toft's Amusements came to the field in front of the Hangar each summer to our immense delight and the chagrin and annoyance of some of the residents of Dalysfort Road and Rockbarton and some Sundays the Industrial School Boys' Band played heartbreaking marches and melodies like Blaze Away and Over the Waves. Here again you never saw instances of that unashamed loutishness, or clique-consciousness, so many teenagers display publicly today. But Toft's Arcade, when it opened as a permanent proposition, below The Rockland, was no improvement on the fun fair; a forerunner of Bingo was the main attraction here plus a battery of one arm bandits into whose rapacious gizzards shoals of youngsters fought to shove their few pennies. In me it awoke a gambling instinct which I have luckily, since overcome, but for one whole summer the machines claimed my every spare penny and I used lie awake at nights taxing my shaky grasp of figures in a vain effort to think up a winning system.[59]

A further venture at the Arcade meant that the Salthill Park and Maretimo site battles were not the only challenges that Florence Toft had to contend with. Her dance licence ambitions for her Pleasure Palace were also to lead to multiple court appearances. That said, the Toft presence at Salthill was firmly secured by 1940, and was to expand into hotel and casino operations over further decades. The later Toft story at Salthill, most identified with David 'Claude' and Kenneth Toft, must wait for a future edition of this Salthill history series.

Chapter 12

GETTING TO SALTHILL: TRAINS, TRAMS AND HORSES

As Maurice Semple has written of 'Galway's Horse Trams' in his *By the Corribside*[1] publication, and Michael J. Hurley has compiled *The Story of Galway General Omnibus Company Limited*,[2] there is little need for this chronicle to long dwell on the transport connections between Galway and Salthill. What follows here is an overview of the changes that have marked vital transit links to the resort.

Convenient and affordable access is a prerequisite for the success of any tourist destination and Salthill is no different. In that respect, the construction of the Dublin–Galway railway line represented the greatest 19th century infrastructural development to advantage both the town and its marine resort. When the first train arrived from the Capital in 1851, Galway no longer represented a tedious-trek destination. In the second half of the 19th century, far flung populations, from Inishowen's Carndonagh to Baltimore in County Cork, began to be serviced by train transport. A Viceregal 1906 Irish Railways' map **(fig. 103)** presents a labyrinthine web of train corridors, as proof of a time when most areas of the country were within reaching distance of a local station.[3]

Salthill's attraction as a holiday resort was much improved by the railroad advances that followed the Great Hunger. It not only became easier for seasonal tourists to holiday at Galway, but inexpensive rail excursions, particularly at weekends, allowed day-trippers spend time by the sea. The enduring attraction of such excursions continued to bring crowds to Salthill well into the 20th century. Another benefit of rail access was the facilitation of investment from afar, and it was significant that Thomas Barton bought the Attithomasrevagh townland in Salthill at an Encumbered Estates' Court in the year that followed the Dublin train's maiden arrival. Barrister Barton's occupational address was Fitzwilliam-square South, Dublin, so his ability to commute – at intervals – between Dublin and Galway was aided by the rail network's expansion. Galway's location value was undoubtedly inflated by convenient connectivity. Greater motor car ownership, however, which was broadly realised in the 1960s/1970s' era, eventually reduced the number of summer train commuters, as more visitors availed of independent travel arrangements.

Galway's rail connectivity was not, however, universally welcomed in town, for many local enterprises came under severe competitive pressure from the Iron Horse's ability to swiftly and inexpensively deliver goods and commodities to the West. Such pressure, in tandem with the burden of deathly famine years, resulted in many local mills and industries closing during the second half of the nineteenth century. The train's arrival 'changed the wholesale and distribution system irrevocably, with (for example) the enormous warehouses of Merchants Road now surplus to requirements.'[4]

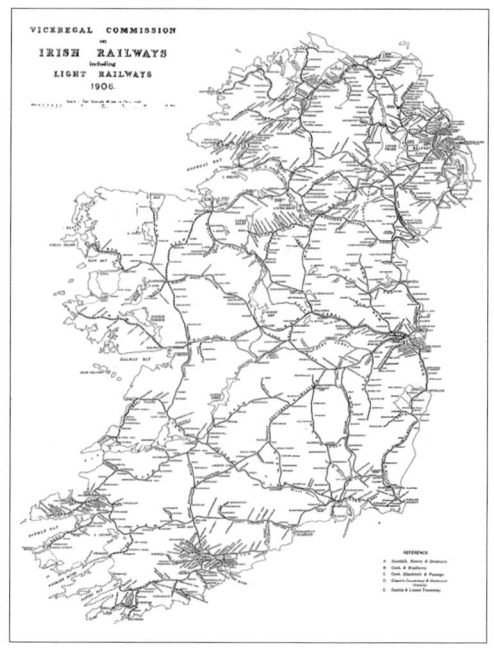

Figure 103.

A Connemara line had been 'mooted from at least 1841,' and Henry Coulter, author of *The West of Ireland: Its Existing Condition and Prospects,* noted – in 1862 – how residents of Oughterard had been 'most anxious to have it carried out.'[5] By November 1871, a newly Incorporated Company planned to bring a Bill to the House of Commons, which would facilitate a Galway–Clifden rail corridor. Of interest in that proposal, from a Salthill standpoint, was the intention to compulsorily purchase land in the townlands of 'Lenaboy, Cappanaveagh, Attathomasrevagh, Pollnarooma East, Pollnarooma West,' and Knocknacarragh.[6] If that enterprise had been successful, the Galway–Clifden train might have merrily puffed alongside Salthill's sea promenade. As it turned out, Connemara's Railway was not to open until 1895, and when it did, a *Cois Fharraige* route was not followed.

Galway – Salthill connections

On alighting at Galway's train station, passage to Salthill was also on offer. Horse drawn cars serviced the Galway–Salthill route from the earliest years of the resort's existence to the early decades of the 20th century. It was in such a car that Galway's young damsels travelled two miles to the sea in 1797, according to De Latocnaye.[7]

Private operators plied the route, primarily during the summer months, and the Eglinton Hotel provided a half hourly omnibus service to town for its own guests. That omnibus 'was dragged to the verge of a precipice' by unruly Queen's College students in 1861, the second year of that hotel's trading.[8] Travel writers' observations suggest that the town-to-prom jaunt was one of the highlights of a visit to Galway. One such scribe described a 'reckless race' in 1873 between passenger laden horse cars, which ensured that a competitive thrill was added to the trip.

Salthill, during the bathing season, is an extremely lively place…On Sunday the 'bus becomes one of the great amusements of the day: shopkeepers, mechanics, servant girls – everybody takes a drive; and to the excitement of the sunshine, and the look of the sea, and the crowds, is sometimes added the stimulants of a reckless race between two or three of the busses. These races are carried on with much noise, and much apparent risk; but somehow or other, no harm seems ever to come of them.[9]

O'Connor's Large Van began its 1857 summer season return-trips to Blackrock at 6 a.m., on Sunday 21 June, from the corner of High Street,[10] whereas 'the cheap and well-appointed 'busses that leave Eyre Square for Salt Hill and Blackrock at seven o'clock every morning' facilitated those who wanted to take an early dip in 1864.[11]

Before the Galway–Salthill horse tram service began on the cusp of the 1880s, there was – it appears – high regard for the traditional horse bus service that preceded it: *The citizens of Galway are very much indebted to the proprietors of the 'busses plying to Salt-hill, who afford a beautiful drive of fully two miles for one penny, wafting the pent-up and hard working people to the seaside to enjoy a mouthful of fresh air from the broad Atlantic; and to the sea-bathing strangers ready and speedy access to the town, to supply*

104. The Eglinton Hotel's covered horse-car prepares to leave for town in the pre-tram era. (Courtesy of National Library of Ireland.)

their wants and pleasures.[12] Such was the view of one 1871 correspondent. During the previous winter, R. Black of the Royal Hotel, at Eyre Square, ran 'a Covered Buss' with fares at 2d. – inside or out. Parcels were also carried, according to size.[13] Indeed, a measure of the popularity of the 'horse bus' service was that the Galway and Salthill Tramway Company 'bought out a number of horse-drawn-bus operators which were threatening their existence,'[14] when the tram line first opened for business in 1879.

One Salt Hill resident who had involvement with pre-tram transport was Matthias Cooke. He appeared in the Tithe Applotment Books of 1834 as occupier of a Salthill holding, measuring 1 rood 37 perches. As that exact measurement was held by four men in a row, it is safe to assume that the four resided in a row of similar houses. Of the nine Griffith entries for Mr. Cooke in 1855, eight were in Lenaboy, with the other at Kilcorkey in Lower Salthill. Mr. Cooke was later a tenant of one of eight cottages in Lower Salthill, according to an 1852 Court Rental record. Matthias Cooke's connection with the place was longstanding, for he was born c.1788, some twenty one years before the Salt Hill name – as it related to the area – was recorded in any document uncovered by this research. He passed away at Upper Salt Hill on 1 June, 1873, with Winifred Lynskey present at his death. A widower, Matthias was 85 years old when he died of 'old age,' and *Car Man* was given as his occupation. Matthias Cooke (1788–1873) saw many changes in a long life spent by the sea.

Horse drawn cars survived well into the 20th century at Salthill, as can be seen from the accompanying 1942 Race Week photograph of such vehicles in the post-tram era. In that image a majority of the cars were gathered outside the Eglinton Hotel, in

105. Horse cars loading at Salthill, *en route* to Ballybrit, during the 'Emergency' years.

an area that represented Salthill's tram terminus up to 1918. The horse-car to the forefront of the picture was loading at Finan's Commercial House, which served as the resort's terminus for the Galway General Omnibus Company, which succeeded the tram service and operated in the 1919–1936 period. The letter font of the bus-stop sign belonged to the Great Southern Railway service, which replaced the Omnibus service in 1936. The Great Southern service itself morphed into *Córas Iompar Éireann* in 1945, and that same lettering style was still in use at Galway bus stops during the 1950s. The photograph was taken during the 'Emergency' years of the Second World War, when fuel was scarce and severely rationed. Press photos of the time show race patrons heading to Ballybrit on any available contraption that was propelled by horse power or pedal power, with other punters forced to rely on shanks' mare.

Horse Tram Service

A horse drawn tram service, which began in 1879, ran from Forster Street in the town – to Salthill's Eglinton Hotel. Though the route was generally flat, an extra horse was attached at the bottom of King's Hill to aid the ascent to Salthill Village. 'Free trips were given passengers for a few days after the opening of the system and on 4th October, 1879, the Board of Trade certificate, which permitted plying for fare, arrived.'[15] The Authorised Capital was £35,000 for a company that was incorporated in 1877 by a Special Act of Parliament, which limited the Director numbers to three. The board trio, on the opening of the service, were Richard N. Somerville, Esq., J.P., Merchant, Town and Harbour Commissioner; W.H. Halliday Esq., Managing Director; and Edward Guilfoyle, Esq., Town and Harbour Commissioner.[16] Among those who followed Mr. Somerville as Chairman were Mr. L.L. Ferdinand; Mr. J. Howse; Mr. Joseph Semple; Mr. H.M.A. Murphy, solicitor; Mr. M. J. Crowley U.D.C.; Mr. Charles Moon; and Mr. J.T. Miller. The promoters of the company were Messrs. Bradjiotte, a Russian Jew ; J.C. Ridley, Newcastle-on-Tyne; and F.C. Winby, a Nottingham engineer, who carried out the engineering work and patented the rails, which he forecast would last for thirty years.[17] The first tramcars, supplied by Starbucks of Birkenhead, were delivered to Galway by sea as low railway bridges out-ruled road transportation. Limestone tramway paving was sourced at Menlo and the Forster Street depot opened in a property, which had previously been owned by Captain Blake Forster.

The public face of the company, over many years, was Mr. Philip McCarthy, who was appointed secretary and manager in 1897. He must have made an impact, for it was recorded in 1900 that 'after many years of ineffectual effort' the Tramway Company had at last 'succeeded in making the line pay its way.'[18] The son of a Tipperary farmer from Thurles, Philip was residing with his wife Ellen, and mother-in-law, Mary Curley, at Lower Salthill in 1901. Ten years later, Philip Joseph McCarthy

106. Horse tram at Eyre Square, heading to Salthill. Note the double track lines, on right, to allow a second tram pass in opposite direction. (Courtesy of National Library of Ireland.)

107. Double tram lines at Lower Salthill.

described himself as a 'Publican & Tramway Manager,' when he and his wife operated a bar, with shop in rear, at premises more recently known as the Cottage, opposite the Lower Salthill headquarters of the Stewart Company. There was doubt about the viability of the tramway at the time of his appointment, but 'in the course of a cursory look through documents,' Philip discovered that a sum of £300 had been deposited as a guarantee for the completion of the line within the original specified time. That deposit was transferred to the company's credit in 1913. Two years earlier, at the time of a strike, relations between the directors and Mr. McCarthy had become strained and the manager 'handed in his resignation, which the directors refused to accept.'[19] It was also reported that 'legal proceedings were instigated…for the purpose of having him removed from office,'[20] though in the end, the company withdrew its case and agreed to pay all costs. Philip McCarthy, whose courtesy and energy were remarked on,[21] continued to work in his managerial position. A newspaper correspondent indicated where opposing sympathies lay during that short 1911 conflict: 'I learned…that a dispute arose recently between the directors of this little Co. and their manager. The latter seems to have bested the former, and the drivers and conductors are, and were during the controversy, on the manager's side.'[22] Incidentally, it was during the 1930s that the premises at Lower Salthill, once occupied by the McCarthy couple, was issued with an hotel licence. That was under the ownership of Michael McLoughlin, who traded as the Tourists' Hotel.

A sense that Galway's star was rising was reflected in the railed cars of the Galway and Salthill Tramway Company, which delivered not only transport but a sense of pride to the place. The single track line, which featured a 3' wide gauge, required passing points to accommodate two-way traffic. Included in the route's double track points were (a) the Eyre Square / Williamsgate Street corner; (b) O'Brien's Bridge; and (c) Montpelier Terrace. The latter bi-way was later transferred to Nile Lodge, where a seating row was laid at the original crossroad entrance to the lodge that was first built by naval Lieutenant William Hutchinson. At the Salthill end, double lines were positioned at points in the road outside: (a) Tommy Keane's present day butcher shop; (b) Ballinasloe House / Salthill House; and (c) the Eglinton Hotel terminus.

The double lines shown in figure 107, which facilitated the passing of Galway–Salthill trams, were situated to the west of Norman Villas, the three storey structure to the left of the image. On the town-side of that same building stood a white-faced thatched cottage with a drinks' licence, called Clare View Bar. That hostelry stood in the space between Norman Villas and another public house, Strand View House, which is today known as P. J. Flaherty's. Captured in the photograph, though difficult to see, is a group of men sitting in conversation on a wall outside the Strand View Bar, to the left of a street lamp. Mrs. Nellie Helly (née Brogan) held licences – during the 1920s – for those neighbouring premises. In 1928 she had the Clare View licence revoked, as her thatched bar was only used during the summer season, and Nellie believed that 'she could do all her business in the one publichouse' – Strand View.[23] That public house was not to be confused with a contemporaneous Strand House at Upper Salthill, where O'Reilly's Bar and Kitchen trades today (2018).

An open-top, double decked tram, which was drawn by two horses, saw service in summer, with a winter trade being adequately serviced by a one-horse-powered, single-decked, closed vehicle. After the tram company's opening, the two penny fare for any portion – or the entire journey – was challenged by the traditional operators, who charged 1d. from town to Nile Lodge, and the same sum from Nile Lodge to the Eglinton. The tram tariff, however, was not reduced, for fear a certain class of passenger would migrate to its service and alienate its regular customers. From the outset, therefore, stiff competition was presented by established bus operators, who had traditionally serviced the route. 'The Company then acquired a controlling interest in these buses.'[24] with the original omnibuses' attraction being manifest in the new provider's expedient purchase. The new trams, which ferried both locals and *fámaiń* to the seashore, added a certain cosmopolitan *chic* to the town – and Salthill. 'The cars had cushioned seats and used oil lamps. Seating capacity was 36, (18 inside and 18 on top). The cars were painted olive green with white panels.' The winter cars – on the other hand – sported battleship grey in harmony with the season through which they ran.[25] It was a Salthill winter tram that was described by Somerville and Ross in their 1906 reflections on Galway: 'Out where the long Sea Road follows the shore of Galway Bay, the great winds press heavily against the windows of Marino Cottage, and the little one-horse trams glide on the desolate shining road like white-backed beetles.'[26]

Like all companies, not everyone was happy with the service provided. Sunday offered its own challenges, for transport schedules did not always tally with Mass times at the Jesuits, the closest tram-connected chapel to the resort. A 1911 visitor's impression gives a glimpse of the service's inadequacies: 'On last Sunday morning, which was a wet one, the Tram Co. provided one car at half-past nine and one at half-past ten to carry upwards of two to three thousand people to Mass. Returning from the Masses it was even worse, as after waiting for a quarter of an hour at the Church door, or under the trees at Nile Lodge, every train would be overcrowded to suffocation.'[27] Tram journeys were not universally trouble-free and a visiting Dublin apprentice sought considerable damages in 1906, following a *contretemps* involving himself and a conductor, which arose from a fare dispute. It was the youthful plaintiff who struck first when he hit the conductor, who promptly responded by knocking the young man 'off the car up against a wall running alongside the line at Nile Lodge.'[28] On another occasion, a man was sentenced to six months' imprisonment for having pickpocketed a sum of money from a lady, while travelling on the Galway – Salthill tram.[29]

Though Mr. Winby's engineered line outlived his three decade prediction, the

Getting to Salthill: Trains, Trams and Horses

108. The horse-tram line, as seen in this post-1879 photo, ran to Seapoint House corner and passed the front doors of the original house row, which first defined Salthill Village. (Courtesy of National Library of Ireland.)

company's financial record of paying out a mere three dividends – over its 39 year existence – told its own tale. The last dividend was paid in 1912, and two years later the onset of – what was termed – the 'Great War' dramatically presaged the company's demise. It was on Tuesday, 4 August, 1914, that Britain declared war on Germany, an announcement that cast a pall over Wednesday's Plate day at Ballybrit, where there was 'nothing like a full attendance.' Horses of a different colour were also affected when all available equine specimens were vetted, with a good many being commandeered by the army for transport purposes: 'The unusual spectacle was witnessed of Messrs. McDonogh's men delivering coal in the "sma' wee hours" while yet the horses remained...In the afternoon, all the tram horses were taken and Galway was without trams. Plenty of cars, however, remained, although some of the drivers intimated that they had been notified to hand over their horses.'[30] Owing to the actions of the military, some tram employees did not turn up for work, and the loss to the war effort of its best horses meant that a restricted service was all that the company could subsequently deliver. Such constraints further contricted revenue flows, and when compensation was sought from the War Office, recompense was refused because the loss was considered to have been a case of 'consequential damages.' It was most likely the loss of its finest animals which led to a prosecution being brought by Constable Kearney against the company in September 1914. The policeman considered a tram horse to have been in an unfit condition when he examined it at Salthill. One explanation posited for the horse's sores was the difficult pull up King's Hill, in a case that was eventually dismissed.[31]

A more melancholy incident at King's Hill occurred on the Friday of the week that the First World War was declared. Half way through its ascent, a tram's swing bar broke and the conductor's brake stopped the vehicle. The driver and conductor then transferred a swing bar from the rear of the vehicle to its front and the horses were re-harnessed. The connecting pin appeared to have been driven home but when the tram recommenced its climb, the pin became detached and the two horses bolted. The driver was not only thrown from the vehicle, but run over by it. Before expiring, he was attended by Fr. Keenan and Dr. Fitzgerald. An 'unshipping of the swing bar' was officially noted by the coroner as the cause of death. The unfortunate victim was James Mulvoy, a 43 year old married man who left a wife and five children to mourn him. Mr. Anthony Clarke was the tram's conductor.[32] The backdrop to the tragedy was noted by the *Connacht Tribune*: 'It should be added that it was only a few days ago that a number of horses were taken over by the military authorities from the Tram Co., when other animals had to be obtained.'[33]

It was not solely the commandeering of its best horses that impacted the company, for World War One also resulted in multiple restrictions, which affected tourist destinations worldwide. When Chartered Accountant, Mr. Crowley, was appointed liquidator in 1918, the sale of the remaining horses represented the first step in the winding up of the firm. There were additional reasons for its closure: Local horse-drawn car operators had continued to undercut the tram company's fares, and motorised vehicles were then becoming more reliable and popular, making a four legged service appear antiquated. As early as 1911, the local press spoke of 'the service to Salthill, which however old-fashioned nowadays, is extremely popular and convenient.'[34] When Salthill's service ceased seven years later, the Galway–Salthill route was taken over by a transport fleet that was no longer drawn by dependable dray horses, but propelled by modern motors. The new Galway General Omnibus Company Limited followed the same Salthill route as its tram predecessor, though its departure point was Victoria Place, and not Forster Street. That route included the town flank of Eyre Square by the Skeffington Arms – Williamsgate Street – William Street – Shop Street – Mainguard Street – Bridge Street – Dominick Street Lower – Dominick Street Upper – William Street West – Sea Road – The Crescent – Nile Lodge – Lower Salthill – King's Hill – Upper Salthill.

That same Galway–Salthill tram route was, therefore, followed by bus operators until one way traffic systems and street pedestrianisation drove vehicles to the north and south of the town's main thoroughfare. After seventeen years plying the route, and expanding to cater for other demands, Galway's Omnibus Company was taken over in 1936 by Great Southern Railways (G.S.R.). That takeover was facilitated by a Government policy, which favoured public transport over private operators. Great

Getting to Salthill: Trains, Trams and Horses

109. Group gathers at Salthill's Eglinton terminus to board the tram to town. (Courtesy of National Library of Ireland.)

Southern Railways mutated to *Córas Iompar Éireann* in 1945 and C.I.E. continued a bus service to Salthill, until the company's 1978 derivative, Bus Éireann, took over the licence. Indeed the figure '1' in the current '401' bus route designation reflects the fact that Galway–Salthill was the first regular and licensed transport corridor in the town. A political *volte-face*, which favoured competition between public and private operators, resulted in a local man, Dónal Joyce, winning a licence to run a private bus service to Salthill. Mr. Joyce's first 'City Direct' bus ran in June 1999.

Motorway

Just as the 1851 Galway–Dublin railway line represented a major transport change in the history of the town, so did the Galway–Dublin motorway link, which opened in December 2009. That latter development offered fresh travel choices, which not only presented opportunities – but challenges to air, rail and road companies. Private bus operators, Citylink and GoBus, for example, currently compete not only with one another on the Galway–Dublin route, but with Bus Éireann and Iarnród Éireann. Galway's airport was to be severely impacted by the competitive speed of access that the motorway offered, not only to Dublin but to its airport. Tourism products also changed to avail of a new order. A one day – 12 hour – excursion, which takes in Galway City and Connemara, is now available from Dublin – proving that a day tripper's radius of discovery has been greatly expanded over time. Low cost air travel in recent years has, of course, also had an effect on Salthill and other Irish tourist resorts. The affordability of foreign destinations has forced Irish tourist centres to readjust to a new reality by presenting novel products in a crowded and competitive sector.

Martin McGrath – A Salthill Man's transport tale

A local man who saw many of the changes that occurred on the Galway–Salthill route was Martin McGrath. A conductor on the horse drawn trams in 1911, he took up driving in 1913. Martin then went on to drive for the Galway General Omnibus Company Limited, followed by a spell with the Great Southern Railways, during that company's Galway term. His driving service was completed with *Córas Iompar Éireann*. Born and reared in Salthill, Martin moved to Henry Street in his twenties, and eventually retired in 1959. He was also the first driver on the Mervue bus route which began on 17 December, 1956. On that fledgling trail he was accompanied by conductor Hyacinth Darcy. Of his early transport years Martin said: 'There was very little traffic in those days, only donkey-carts and side-cars.'[35] Mr. McGrath's safe driving record was praised on his retirement, and it must be said that accidents over the years on the various Galway services were quite rare.

The King's Hill death of tram driver, Mr. James Mulvoy, was not, however, the only fatality to have occurred on the route. A most unusual tragedy occurred on the same transport corridor in 1923, when a male passenger was caught by the rope of an advertising streamer, which hung from Moon's to Dillon's corner, and thrown 'headlong over the bars' to his death. He had been sitting on the last seat of an open-top, double-decked Salthill bound omnibus. The unfortunate victim was Mr. John Doyle, the 53 year old manager of Tyler's boot shop, who left a widow and six children. A resident of Salthill, Mr. Doyle was described as a neighbour of Philip J. McCarthy, the former Tram Company manager. The low hanging streamer had been erected to welcome President Cosgrave and his Dáil Deputies to town. At a subsequent inquest, a *Cumann na nGaedheal* committee member came under intense pressure to say if he knew who had placed the dangerous banner, but the witness – who was without legal representation – refused to give evidence. The coroner's finding on the accidental death read: 'We find that Mr. John A. Doyle met his death by being knocked off the top of the bus while seated as a passenger by a rope stretched across the street from Moon's to Dillon's, bearing a motto.'[36]

Other transport related stories, as they appear in this publication, form part of the fabric of various tales and themes, which are presented in this history series.

Famines – Clearances – Landed Society

Chapter 13

NINETEENTH CENTURY FAMINES AND EVICTIONS

For all of its attractions which brought joy to many, Salthill was also a place of suffering. From Nile Lodge to the western border of Galway's golf course, a great swathe of the area was home to tenant farmers during the 19th century. Vulnerable to the whims of landlords' ambition, their tenure – seldom secure – was greatly compromised during difficult times. Famine delivered dark days and though landed gentry lost wealth during economic downturns, Ireland's tenant class suffered greater loss, be it of their homes, or lives. An emigrant ship oft-time offered the sole chance for long-term survival. More than one famine visited Ireland during the 19th century, but the Great Hunger of the late 1840s is most remembered, for the land and its people were indelibly marked by the devastation wrought by that particularly lengthy calamity. The early 1860s also delivered hungry years along the western seaboard, but that era's blight did not endure as long as its 1840's predecessor. Regular – and at times systematic – clearing of holdings meant that the great bulk of Salthill's tenant farmers were displaced by changing socio-economic forces before the 20th century dawned. On displacement, their homes and villages were razed to the ground, and the cultural lore of Salthill's uprooted legion was lost to memory and time.

An Gorta Mór

Pre-1841 population figures for Salthill are sketchy and the seventy named occupiers in the Tithe Applotment record of 1834 excludes family members, as well as tenants holding less than one acre. However, a comparison of census figures for Salthill's townlands – on either side of the Great Famine decade – gives a good picture of the changes wrought by a disaster that not only delivered death, but influenced the limited life choices of those that survived. The actions of landlords, be they callous or pragmatic, often left tenantry facing *rogha an dá dhíogha*. As *díog* is

Pre - and Post - Famine populations at Salthill's Townlands						
Townland	Population		Inhabited Houses		Total Houses	
	1841	1851	1841	1851	1841	1851
Acres	40	55	6	8	6	8
Attithomasrevagh	118	116	21	23	22	23
Cappanaveagh	171	52	31	6	34	8
Cloghatisky	16	0	2	0	2	0
Kilcorkey	222	311	39	58	45	60
Lenaboy	118	219	30	39	39	54
Pollnarooma East	131	59	20	9	22	10
Pollnarooma West	40	22	5	3	5	4
Tievegarriff	116	34	21	6	24	8
Total	1042	868	175	152	199	175

Figure 110.

a Gaelic word for ditch, one assumes that particular zero-option phrase was coined during a time when a ditch represented the only shelter on offer. A choice between two 'worsts' offers another translation of the same expression. The side of the road, a workhouse, a famine ship would all represent such wretched options. There were many at Salthill who faced dreadful decisions, not only at famine time but in its aftermath. Though Salthill was, even then, a place that promised holiday cheer, not debilitating hunger, many of its townlands' tenants eked out a living from land that was — in many places — less than fertile.

The above table's overall statistics would indicate that the Great Famine's impact on Salthill was not that dramatic: An 1841 population tally of 1042 fell to 868 in 1851, with a concomitant 199 to 175 total house fall. A decrease of 174 persons and 24 residences through the Great Famine decade does not, of course, tell the full story of what happened at the place during a most testing time. Each townland had its own micro-culture, which was tied to its 'urban' or rural make-up, as well as to the character and financial standing of the landlord on whom its denizens were dependent.

Famine impact on Merrion and Salthill Villages

Two of Salthill's townlands were quasi-urban, in so far as they housed distinct and sizable villages. Merrion Village was in Lower Sathill's Kilcorkey townland, which runs from Nile Lodge to the eastern side of Tommy Keane's butcher shop. By housing 222 inhabitants within its borders in 1841, Kilcorkey was more heavily populated than the 188 peopled Lenaboy townland, which incorporated Salthill Village. Ten years later, in the immediate post-famine period, the populations of both townlands had increased; Lenaboy by 31 and Kilcorkey by 89 inhabitants.

That growth was not surprising, for increased post-famine residency numbers were not unusual in urban areas. Galway town experienced a sharp population increase during the *Gorta Mór* period, as it attracted many hapless rural dwellers who hoped for aid in the town, or an opportunity to leave the land of their birth for greener pastures abroad. The town's port represented a route to redemption, with alternative respite choices also available. They included relief works, a soup kitchen, a workhouse, a hospital or – as a last resort – Galway Gaol. In the middle of the Great Famine – on 18 March, 1848 – *The Nation* reported 'that the jail, independently of the hospital was intended to accommodate 110 persons, while on last Saturday it contained no less than 903 prisoners and 34 children! The deaths from the 1st of February to that day were 181 – the number for the week, 44!' In such dire and chaotic circumstances, Salthill's ability to cater for boarders would have attracted some in need of shelter.

Of this study's seven 'rural' townlands, five experienced significant population falls. Pollnarooma West almost halved in population from 40 to 22 inhabitants, whereas Pollnarooma East's fall – from 131 to 59 occupants – represented a 55% decrease. Both Tievegarriff and Cappanveagh underwent a 70% population drop. Cloghatisky's 100 % wipe-out saw that townland's pre-famine tally of 16 inhabitants fall to zero ten years later. The landed O'Hara family of that lightly populated area most likely departed the country – or Salthill at least – during the Great Hunger. The remaining rural townlands, Acres and Attithomasrevagh, appear not to have been severely affected during the dark decade. At Acres, a rise from 40 to 55 inhabitants broke the general 'rural' trend of falling numbers, while Attithomasrevagh stood almost still, with a marginal 118 to 116 population decline.

Each townland, as earlier indicated, boasted its own dynamic and it does not appear that tenants were universally behind with their rents in the general Salthill area. We have already seen that a fishing industry operated out of Recorder's Quay, so some local sustenance must have been available during potato blighted times. Thomas Keneally, in his 'Great Shame' treatise, described shoreline dwellers' reliance on the sea: 'Coastal people in the west dealt with hunger by catching fish, winkles and mussels. They gathered seaweeds named *crother* and *dulaman*, the second of which was not edible until after the first frosts of winter and caused diarrhoea.'[1]

Background to Evictions and its Galway Influencer

Before going into the details of Salthill's eviction culture, it is important to briefly highlight some economic, cultural, and governmental issues which contributed to mid-19th century change at the place. This adjustment was significant. Rural Salthill, in pre-famine times, represented the eastern tip of *Conamara*, where fishing and subsistent farming was carried out by Irish speaking families. In linguistic terms it must be noted that, as late as 1911, Salthill's knighted politician and trader, Sir James O'Donohue, professed himself to be proficient *as Gaeilge*. James' bilingualism was not then unusual, for Nollaig Mac Congáil has pointed out that 82.1% of Galway town's population claimed fluency in Irish at the second census tally of the 20th century.[2]

Ruled by Britain and lacking natural resources that might have fuelled an Industrial Revolution, most of the island's eight million inhabitants were totally reliant on the land and its bounty. In such circumstances, the rural underclass was dangerously dependent on a single root crop, the potato. Tenants with few rights were not only exposed to the vagaries of the weather, but to the humours of landlords. An indigenous succession custom of subdividing land to male offspring made tenancy holdings progressively smaller through generations. Though equitable, in terms of male heirs, that divisional practice was unsustainable. When the potato blight struck, *laissez faire* economic policies meant that adequate relief would not be delivered. A socio-cum-political gulf between a powerful landlord class and a voiceless peasantry exacerbated the situation. The poor become more reliant on their masters than ever before, for it was the landed wealthy who not only peopled local boards and legal benches, but also sat on Relief Committees. Some, as historian John Cunningham has pointed out, sought to profit from the relief works they had charge of.[3] While the Famine hit the poor in terms of life and death, it also struck the gentry, who saw their landed wealth being quickly dissipated. Government Acts were required to deal with the situation and though some measures ostensibly aided the needy, they *de facto* favoured the landlord.

One such adjustment, which made an impact at Salthill, featured a strong Galway input: With the population bursting at the country's seams, emigration offered the greatest room for release. In December 1846 the Marquess of Clanricarde, a prominent Irish landowner, wrote to the British Prime Minister, Lord John Russell; 'nothing can effectively and immediately save the country without an extensive emigration.'[4] Clanricarde's analysis was shared by many. The Poor Inquiry Commission of 1833–1836 had found that 'those who desire to emigrate should be furnished with the Means of doing so in safety, and with intermediate Support,'[5] but that accommodation was little practiced.

Aided emigration was not then a foreign concept with, for example, an Australian Emigration Agent placing an 1838 advert in the *Galway Patriot* offering free passage 'TO SUCH MECHANICS FARM LABOURERS, AND SINGLE FEMALES, AS THE SUBSCRIBER MAY APPROVE OF.'[6] Transport from Cork to join three ships sailing from Plymouth was part of Mr. John Besnard's offer. That initiative was to favour a colonised country, in the far off Southern Hemisphere, which sought to fill specific gaps in its demographic framework. Not everyone was welcome and Australia'a attraction was dimmed in Ireland by; (a) its distance from home and (b) its traditional reputation as a land of cells and convicts. A lack of young females inspired one Irish scheme, which was not very welcome down under:

> Between 1848 and 1850 over 4,000 young women between the ages of fourteen and twenty arrived in Sydney, Melbourne and Adelaide, some of them street-wise kids from Dublin, Belfast and Cork, others from famine ravaged rural districts around Skibbereen, Ballina, Roscrea and Loughrea. Their emigration was the brain-child of Earl Grey, secretary of state for the colonies, and primarily designed to meet an Australian demand for domestic servants and marriageable young women. Grey's own Irish connections may also have prompted him to do something, however small, for famine-stricken Ireland…These were improper women, 'workhouse incapables' who were not carefully chosen migrants and were ill-suited to the needs of the Australian colonies.[7]

Independent America, for the general mass of Irish emigrants, offered a better prospect than a faraway colonised outpost.

The Poor Law Act of 1838 made provision for assisted emigration by providing that 'either guardians or the taxpayers of a Poor Law union could authorise the expenditure of local rates to assist poor persons to emigrate.'[8] It was in 1843 that landlords became responsible for all landholding tax on any tenancy valued at under £4. That decree made the economics of such tenancies – from a landlord's perspective – increasingly burdensome. Government policy in respect of emigration was one of limited intervention until 1847, a year of deepening famine and growing hardship. Amendments in that year to the Poor Law Act delivered a dramatic change to the landlord-tenant relationship.

Gregory's Quarter-Acre Clause

One amendment was known as the 'Quarter Acre' clause, which denied any assistance to those who held over a quarter of an acre of land. That statute placed small landholders in a desperate position. For such tenants and their families to get any government relief, their holdings had to be forfeited. Secondly, any tenant rated at a net value not exceeding £5 was to be assisted to emigrate by the Guardians of the Union, with the landlord not only dropping rent demands, but contributing to his tenant's departure. The resulting template proved to be a perfect blueprint for landlords, particularly unscrupulous ones, to clear their estates of the poor and destitute. The economics of the situation, from a landlord's perspective, were crystal clear, as Lord Lansdowne realised in 1850. A celebrated estate manager, William Steuart Trench, hired by Lansdowne in that year, persuaded his employer 'that the mathematics of emigration were far more attractive than those of maintaining paupers in the poorhouse.'[9]

The man most identified with the watershed amendment of 1847 was Sir William Gregory of Coole. He was later to wed Augusta Persse, who became Lady Gregory on the couple's marriage. The 'Gregory Clause' – regarded as an eviction charter – was unfavourably viewed in Ireland. Historian Christine Kinealy has pointed out that it was after 1847, when 'facilitated by the punitive Quarter-Acre Clause and the soaring burden of poor rates, that some landlords commenced the desired large-scale clearance of their estates.'[10] The Gregory clause's effect was devastating: 'As a rule, not even children were allowed to enter the workhouse until a family's land was surrendered. People had to decide: if we want to eat, we have to give up our land.'[11] Canon John O'Rourke, the parish priest of Maynooth, was caustic in his description of Gregory's contribution: 'A more complete engine for the slaughter and expatriation of a people was never designed.'[12]

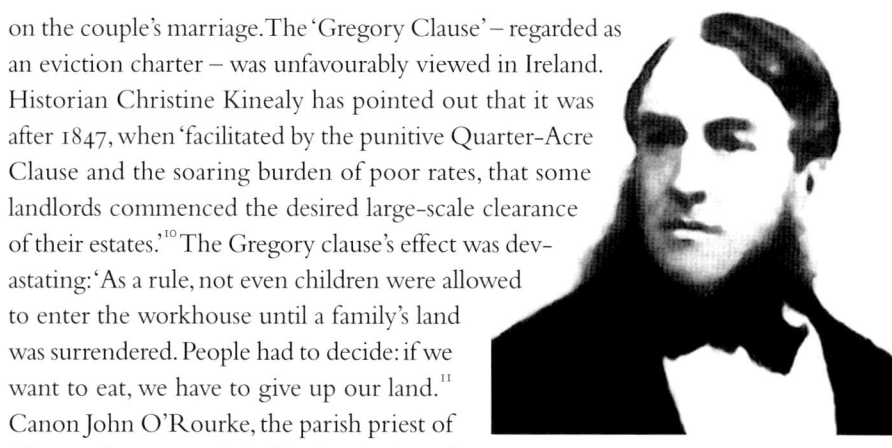

111. Sir William Gregory of Coole.

While there is no doubt about the consequences of the clause, the motive of its proposer has given rise to some discussion. Canon O'Rourke insisted that 'Mr. Gregory's words – the words of a liberal and a pretended friend of the people – and Mr. Gregory's clause are things that should be forever remembered by the descendants of the slaughtered and expatriated small farmers of Ireland.'[13] Another clergyman, Archbishop McHale of Tuam, never forgave the clause's promoter, and the north Galway prelate subsequently referred to him as 'Quarter Acre Gregory.'

A more benign view was presented by Professor Brian Walker of Queen's University, Belfast, at a 2011 gathering at Coole, the onetime seat of William Gregory. Walker holds that Gregory's intentions were charitable in that his proposals were intended to aid those without a future in Ireland: A better life beckoned in America for starving and dying people.[14] Furthermore, by evicting no tenant at Coole, Gregory's famine record would indicate a less than cruel landlord. According to Patrick Melvin, Gregory of Coole was among those landlords who were 'noted for particular kindness and benevolence to their tenants…He did not… raise his rents despite a desperate need for money and his tenants were among "the best housed, best clad, best fed, well-to-do people" in Galway, "living in comfortable cottages with schools and chapels in all directions about them".'[15] Indeed, it was suggested at the time of the 1920 Ballyturin Ambush that Mrs. Margaret Gregory was singularly spared by the I.R.A. because of 'her family affiliation.'[16] That association might be taken as a reference to Margaret's mother-in-law, Lady Gregory, who was a nationalist sympathiser. Alternatively, it could have referred to Margaret's father-in-law's humanitarian treatment of tenants during harsh times. Expressing another view, Pádraig Ó Fathaigh, an I.R.A. operative, suggested that it was Margaret's own disapproving views of Crown force methods during the 1920's Troubles – uncovered in letters intercepted by the I.R.A. – that saved her life.[17]

Encumbered Estates' Court

The strain on landed gentry through famine times also led to the setting up of the Encumbered Estates' Court in 1849, which allowed distressed Irish landlords, or claimants, apply to have a property sold, with the proceeds being used to pay creditors. That legal construct led to a flood of distressed properties being placed on the market over a relatively short period, not unlike the outcome of NAMA,[18] a more recent 21st century Irish asset-management model. As Encumbered Estates' lots were generally sold in townland units, the scheme was only of benefit to the limited few who could afford to buy, and inflate their wealth in the wake of a great disaster. The portmanteau epithet in the 'boomtown rats' coinage of American folk singer, Woody Guthrie, might be flipped to 'doomtime,' with regard to those who profited from Ireland's Great Famine. One effect of the Encumbered Estates' Court system was that many Salthill residents, who had endured the great hardship, were not to survive what followed at the resort.

The Estate Courts' success rate reflected the fallen fortunes of numerous land owners, many of whom were persons of rank in society. In its early years – from 15 November, 1849 to 23 September, 1851 – the number of properties sold amounted to 440, which realised a total of £3,654,500. The status of those availing of the landed court system in 1851 was noted by the *Connaught Watchman*: 'Number of titled persons for the sale of whose estates petitions were presented to the commissioners:- One marquis, 13 earls, three viscounts, five barons, five honourables, twenty baronets, five Knights, seven members of parliament, and five ex-members.'[19]

Fr. Peter Daly and Evictions at Salthill

Evictions, of course, were to play a central part in the story of Salthill and callous ejections in the place long preceded the 1840 decade. Fr. Peter Daly, a controversial clergyman, regarded by some as one of Galway's greatest citizens, is less benignly viewed by others. The Rahoon Parish Priest divided opinion in his lifetime and continues to do so to this day. One truth on which all can agree is that, during the 19th century, he 'was without question the most remarkable priest of the diocese of Galway…From his ordination in 1816 until his death in 1868 he influenced the town of Galway as none other did, lay or cleric.'[20] That opinion was articulated in the opening paragraph of a 1977 series of *Connacht Tribune* articles by historian, Fr. Martin Coen. The conflict-creating capacity of Fr. Daly was also undoubted, and an 1860 fist fight at Eyre Square, which pitched Mr. Launcelot Mangan of Villa Maria, Salthill, against Mr. Blake of the *Galway Vindicator* gave expression to that truth.[21] The pugilistic skills of two of Galway's leading 'gentlemen' were publicly practiced because of their incompatible views of the Rahoon clergyman.

A most capable man, Fr. Daly straddled the civic and spiritual life of the town. On failing to achieve his aim of first becoming Warden and later Bishop of Galway, Peter Daly's energies were channelled into commercial and civic roles, at both Urban Council and Harbour Commissioner level. The cleric's farseeing and brave efforts – throughout the mid-19th century – to win Transatlantic Packet Station status for Galway were dogged by ill luck. Most impressive was his church building record, while his civic leadership on behalf of Galway town was built on purposeful ambition and sharp political *nous*. During his lifetime he visited Pope Leo XII in Rome, presented an Address to Queen Victoria in Dublin, and had the Lord Lieutenant, Earl Musgrave, visit him at Albano Lodge, his Gortacleva home. Father Daly also negotiated with Prime Ministers Lord Derby (1852 & 1858) and Lord Palmerston (1859 & 1861). His fame reached such a pitch that *Punch Magazine* unflatteringly represented his 1861 meeting with Lord Palmerston in a cartoon image, which placed a simian head on the portly Galway priest. That caricature, which appeared only two years after Darwin's 'Origin of the Species' publication, suggested a particularly denigrating image of Galway's leading clergyman.[22]

Father Peter Daly was a very wealthy individual, who placed two fine mansions for rent in 1831; Blackrock House overlooking the bay and Merville House on Taylor's Hill.[23] A sense of tenant dissatisfaction in that same year was suggested when Fr. Daly publicly denied 'a most mischievous and most wantonly erroneous report…that serious injury was done by poor peasantry to my house' at Blackrock,[24] as had been recorded in an earlier *Galway Independent* report.[25] Fr. Daly had previously sued Mr. Connolly of the *Independent* on foot of alleged libels on 31 May, 1828 and 11 June of the same year. That was in the wake of an 1827 trip to Rome, when the Rahoon clergyman was accompanied as far as Paris by a young Dominican nun. Though he sought £1,000 in damages, £200 was the sum awarded to Fr. Daly in the spring of 1829.[26]

In the wake of the Great Famine, Rev. Father Peter Daly bought Lot 25 of Mr.

THE MAN FOR GALWAY.

112. British caricature of Fr. Daly's 1865 meeting with British Prime Minister, Lord Palmerston. Fr. Daly's bag, bearing the word 'SUBSIDY,' is filled with promised votes, while Palmerston's captioned observation reads: "OHO ! Father Daly ! Now I think I understand you." (*Punch Magazine, 16 June, 1865.*)

Robert Whaley's Galway estate, which was sold at an Encumbered Estate Auction on 13 January, 1852. The Kilcorkey townland – in effect the whole of Lower Salthill – was the property purchased by Fr. Daly for £2,110.[27] That sizable sum of money later became an issue of concern to the Sisters of Mercy. Fr. Daly, incidentally, was not the only famed clergyman to have been connected with Kilcorkey: 'In the List of Registered Priests, 1704, "J. Bodkin Fitzpatrick" is mentioned as the "popish priest of Kilcorkey".'[28] The Salthill townland was not the sole property purchased by Fr. Daly in the post-famine period, for he later bought 'The Custom-house and premises in the High-street of Galway' for £810 in 1856.[29]

Charitable work by the Rahoon Parish Priest was recorded during the famine period. 'On Christmas Day, 1846 at Barna, Peter Daly provided each of one hundred families with 'three pounds of beef and a large loaf.'[30] Historian, Fr. Martin Coen, noted that in 1847 'a move to close Blackrock Soup Kitchen was opposed by Fr. Peter Daly. He had himself personally fed 20 or 30 of the most destitute people in Barna. "He imposed on them a slight task of work in return for the trifling quantity of food he was enabled to give them and nothing could exceed the alacrity with which they were earning their miserable pittance".'[31] An insistence on work – slight as it might have been – suggests that the Rahoon Parish Priest was *ad-idem* with the prevailing *laissez faire* economic model of his time, which held that free aid would threaten the concept of private enterprise and make the poor routinely reliant. The Rahoon clergyman had also 'given over Albano Lodge to the Sisters of Mercy who undertook to administer the Government scheme.'[32] Such charitable activism did not exactly chime with other deeds of his.

Of concern to his bishop was the fact that a sizable amount of 'ecclesiastical property was registered in Peter Daly's name.' According to Bishop McEvilly; 'He had been treating the Sisters of Mercy "most barbarously".' In particular it was claimed that 'he had used their money to purchase an estate in Salthill, but that he had refused to admit this…he had expended a very considerable amount of their financial resources in building the chapel adjoining their convent at Newtownsmith.'[33] With regard to the alleged misuse of funds belonging to the Sisters of Mercy, a lawsuit had in fact been initiated on their behalf in February of that year, 1858, but was not proceeded with.'[34] It was following Fr. Daly's death that the Mercy Sisters' issue was resolved because 'as expected his affairs were confused especially in regard to the Convent of Mercy. It took some time for the nuns to secure their title deeds and the money due to them from his estate.'[35]

As previously indicated, Fr. Daly's relationship with the peasantry at Pollnarooma West appears to have been strained in 1831, and his later interaction with Lower Salthill tenants, after his 1852 purchase of the Kilcorkey townland, did not represent much improvement in that regard. It must be acknowledged that Bishop McEvilly was, throughout his Episcopal tenure, at odds with his Rahoon parish priest. Even allowing for such tensions, the bishop's account of Fr. Daly's actions was particularly hard hitting:

Having purchased the estate [Kilcorkey] in question, Peter Daly had cleared it by 'deeds of Landlord persecution,' which he carried out against 'poor people whom he summarily evicted, which if perpetrated by a Protestant Landlord would ring and justly so, from one end of the land to the other. Among other instances I witnessed with my own eyes a poor woman who lived on that property happily for years under a Protestant Landlord summarily evicted by Mr. Daly without a farthing's compensation. Last February in company with the Superior of the Dominican Fathers of this town, Very Rev. Mr. Rush, we witnessed the funeral-like cortege of poor people accompanying her with loud wailing to the train to set out for Liverpool and thence to America. She had five little orphan children, the youngest carried at the breast, and before leaving she on bent knees publicly invoked the curse of her five wandering outcast orphans on her cruel prosecutor…On June 29 (1858) – a church holy-day – he (Fr. Daly) brought two actions in court for ejectment against twenty-one persons…he spent almost the entire day in court evicting tenants and gave me no satisfaction when I wrote to him.'[36]

The previous Protestant landlord, referred to by the bishop, was Mr. John Whaley, who belonged – as we have earlier seen – to a fiercely anti-Catholic family. In 1862, Bishop McEvilly again commented on the Rahoon parish priest: 'He is the greatest tyrant in regard to the poor connected with him, either as parish priest or landlord. Think of a priest with two parishes and countless paupers in his charge giving a ball last year to 150 persons.'[37] Fr. Daly's deeds as landlord were not exclusively recorded by his bishop. The *Nation* newspaper[38] – and later Pádraig G. Lane – both chronicled Rev. Peter Daly's 1858 petitioning of ejectments against 'eleven tenants in Salthill, whose leases, valid when he bought the property in the court, had run out.'[39] Thirteen, not eleven, was the number of Merrion Village tenants to have been so threatened, according to the *Galway Mercury*. They were: **William Connelly; Denis Connelly; Patrick Connelly; Pat Flaherty; Walter Burke; James Rooney; John Donnellan; Michael Quinlan; James Glynn; Michael Reddan; Anthony Collins; Michael O'Brien; and Ellen Burke.**[40] Most were tenants of the Parish Priest on Taylor's Hill Road. All of their houses, with rateable valuations of £1-5s-0d or lower, were small, as were their patches of land, none of which amounted to a rood in measurement. Mr. E. Blake, solicitor for the defendants, said that 'they had laid out hundreds of pounds upon their holdings in this place – upwards of £400. There was about £1-17s. of an arrear now claimed, and his clients were satisfied to let the rev. plaintiff take a decree without costs, but he would not do it. He had got possession of all these unfortunate people's property with the exception of one small house, where the principal defendant had to lock up a small portion of corn; and the whole amount of the difference between the rev. gentleman and his parishioners was, that they were keeping possession of this little house to keep this portion of corn in.'[41] The tenants were ejected and the *Nation* newspaper commented: 'This is pretty work

Father Peter is at. We knew he was great at addresses to the Lord Lieutenant, but we had no idea he was so clever with the crowbar.'[42] The *Galway Mercury* carried the following piece from the *Mail*:

> We make no reflections on the Rev. Peter Daly for the course which he deemed it necessary to adopt towards his tenants. But this we know – if a Protestant landlord had, like Fr. Daly, sought to eject a number of tenants who had laid out hundreds of pounds upon their holdings, and who were only a few shillings in arrears, we should have had no end of diatribes against exterminating monsters, crowbar brigades &c. We commit Rev. Peter Daly to the tender mercies of the League.[43]

The latter reference to 'the League' might explain how Kilcorkey's tenants were legally represented in court, for indigent lessees were rarely so defended. Reports on the Lower Salthill case were carried nationally in columns that opened with opinion pieces on leaseholders' rights,[44] the question on which a Tenant Right League had been founded, in 1850, by Charles Gavan Duffy and Frederick Lucas. Galway hosted a national conference of that Tenant League three years after its foundation,[45] so local knowledge of the movement is undoubted. *Pro bono* representation occasionally contested test cases where critical legal issues were at stake. While judicial considerations do not appear to have been significant in this instance, the fact that it was Galway's most famed and controversial personage – and a clergyman to boot – who was the evicting landlord might have prompted the Tenant Right League – or Mr. Blake as an individual – to plead the case. The paltry arrears' sum at issue further highlighted the callous inequality of the tenant-landlord relationship and attracted publicity, which was vital to those who championed the cause of disempowered lessees.

A second case on the same day pitched Fr. Daly as plaintiff against eight tenants in seeking to recover another portion of the same Kilcorkey lands, with premises thereon. Mr. Rochford, on behalf of Father Daly, said that the person whose life the lease depended on was dead. Lease duration in that era was often fixed to the life span of one or more persons. At that later hearing, however, Michael Connelly swore that it was 'his brother, who was the life in the lease,' and to prove that he was not dead, a handwritten letter was produced, which had been posted the previous October from his sibling in America. That case was dismissed and the following tenants at Lower Salthill were allowed to keep their holdings: **Denis Connelly; Hubert Burke; Mary Martin; Thomas Clarke; Michael Brennan; John Egan; John Wellan; and John Skerrett.**[46] The eight who won their case, along with the 13 who didn't, made up the 21 tenants – referenced by Bishop McEvilly – that Fr. Daly sought to eject from Lower Salthill on the one day.

His undoubted civic achievements allowed Fr. Daly to become more strident both in language and manner as the years passed. In 1859 he criticised the *Galway Vindicator* for not reporting all of his speeches in full. That publication's riposte was sabre-like sharp:

Fr. Daly openly accused this journal of suppressing what the public good demanded. It is not true... But...we plead guilty of one offence – the suppressio veri as regards himself. It was when, in deference to his gown, we did not set him down amongst the chief curse of Ireland – the landlord exterminators. Every man in Galway remembers when he quenched the fires and turned forth the poor from their little holdings in order to add field to field, and accumulate property in an old age...'⁴⁷

Enraged, Fr. Daly brought the *Vindicator* to court seeking £1,000 in damages. At the court hearing several parties, who had been evicted at the suit of Peter Daly, gave evidence to the effect that they had not owed rent; had not received compensation; and had not been permitted to harvest their potatoes, which had been allowed to rot in the ground. The jury found for the *Vindicator*, with the exception of the paragraph which contained the reference to 'landlord exterminators,' for which they awarded the plaintiff a paltry six pence in damages, and the same sum in costs.⁴⁸ Fr. Daly subsequently acquired a local newspaper, the *Galway Mercury*, which had its name changed to the *Galway Press*. Mr. Nicholas Daly, the clergyman's brother, took charge of the new journal.

It must be pointed out that the cases here presented took place in the decade following the Great Famine and were not unique to Kilcorkey or Father Daly. In fairness to the Galway priest, his success as a pragmatic and progressive politician did promote Galway town, whether by dint of his involvement in the 1851 arrival of the first Dublin–Galway train; his work on behalf of the Galway Packet Station; his chairmanship of the Galway Bay Steam Navigation Company; his £1200 investment in the Galway Line; his chairmanship and membership of both the Town Commissioners and Harbour Board; his directorship of the Galway Gas Company; his membership of the Lough Corrib Navigation Trustees; his contract for a Steamer in Lough Corrib named 'Fr. Daly' in his honour; his 1854 development of Lynch's Window at Lombard Street, which some consider to be the first tourist trap in the town. Father Daly's input was, indeed, considered to be of such value that in 1858 the Town Commissioners decided to change the name of Revenue Row at Woodquay to Daly's Place,⁴⁹ which to this day defines the road that connects Eglinton Street with the car park at Barrahalla. An 1859 advertisement described Daly's Place, 'at the corner of Eyre Street and Corrib Street.'⁵⁰

Fr. Daly's skill in revenue collection as well as the fact that he owned the property in question meant that the place was aptly named under either its former or current title. His imposing presence in the local ecclesiastical world was so strong that Dr. McEvilly, who was appointed Bishop of Galway in late December 1856, revealed that

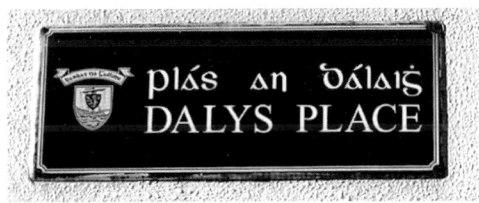

Figure 113.

he had not been the first choice: 'In fact, Dr. Fallon was appointed in 1856 Bishop of Galway and Kilmacduagh but thro' sheer fear of Peter Daly he declined and then I was appointed Bishop of Galway and Kilmacduagh.'[51]

Miss Fanny Grattan v. Rev. Peter Daly

One battle that Peter Daly lost was at Lower Salthill, where a determined female adversary trumped him. The Kilcorkey townland was liable to flooding from the sea, which came across Whitestrand Marsh to the main Salthill Road. Above the waterline of that marsh were the land banks on which (a) Ward's Hotel currently stands and (b) the area where the Stewart family set up their headquarters in the early 1900s. South of the road between those two points was liable to flooding, yet when Peter Daly decided to build a 'Benevolent Home for aged and respectable Females,' it was that very area he chose for his site. A related reason for his choice was that a new road was then under construction. That thoroughfare was to connect the Claddagh's Fair Hill to the bottom of King's Hill at Salthill. In stanching the sea's in-flow, that development was to consequently reclaim much of the foul-smelling marsh. The road building enterprise – not of Fr. Daly's making – was primarily devised to create work for the starving poor. It would, of course, also benefit Fr. Daly's building plans. The big problem was that the land the Parish Priest had chosen for his development was not part of the Kilcorkey townland he had purchased from Robert Whaley in 1852.

Miss Grattan's resolve

At the very same auction where Fr. Daly paid £2,110 for Kilcorkey, Mr. Henry Grattan Jnr., M.P. purchased a Claddagh lot of 29 acres for £1,710. Henry was a son of the renowned politician, Henry Grattan of Grattan's Parliament fame. By the early 1860s, Miss Frances Grattan, daughter of Henry the purchaser, and granddaughter of the famed politician, had succeeded to ownership of the Claddagh. In an act of great kindness she had undertaken to finance the building of a Famine Road that is today known as Grattan Road. Taken aback at seeing a premises being constructed on her private land, which had become more valuable on its reclamation, she brought Fr. Daly to court to prove her title to the site. Few could challenge the most prominent clergyman in the town, but Fanny Grattan showed her forbears' determined leadership in contesting Fr. Daly's claim. In the courthouse, documents were produced which included 'the will of Mr. Henry Grattan [Jnr.], of the 30th December, 1858, devising the lands to Miss Fanny Grattan for her life and the maps.'[52] Miss Grattan won her case and the *Galway Vindicator* later reported on the upshot of the episode: Fr. Daly. 'having built upon ground which the law courts decided belonged to Miss Grattan, that lady having brought an ejectment, succeeded in getting possession of it, and transferred it to the Bishop of Galway for the Industrial School for Boys.'[53] That transfer was made by 'Frances Grattan of Rathgar in the County of Dublin, spinster' to ' Most Rev, John McEvilly R.C. Bishop of Galway, James Martyn of Dominick Street and William George Murray of Salthill called grantees...Those & that part of the lands called the White Strand, in the county of the town of Galway, containing five acres statute measure more or less together, with the messuage or tenement then standing thereon and known as the Benevolent Home.'[54]

Fr. Daly had, on that occasion, met his match and the Boys' Industrial School at Lower Salthill was built on the site that had once been claimed by the Rahoon parish priest. 'On 25th September 1871, "twenty-one poor boys were admitted to the School, Most of them in the lowest state of destitution and misery".'[55] Originally operated – for a few years – by the Patrician Brothers, that institution was first described as St. Patrick's Industrial School, before it later came under the control of the Christian Brothers. That change followed a request from Government Inspector, Mr. John Lentaigne, to the Superior General of the Christian Brothers, asking that his order take over the running of the school in July, 1876.[56] Its patron saint changed when it became known as St. Joseph's Industrial School, by which it was identified right up to 1995. Miss Grattan's munificence is still visible at Salthill in the road that carries her surname, and her contribution to that construction is described in the *Famine Roads'* section of this book.

Fr. Daly's Bequest

When Fr. Peter Daly died in 1868 his family relations, as Fr. Coen recalled, 'profited by his death but later proved to be generous.'[57] That, indeed, was true. Peter Daly's estate was passed to his brother, Patrick Daly, of Newcastle. A mural tablet was placed by Patrick and his daughter, Julia M. Daly, over the place of Fr. Daly's interment at Bushypark. 'The plaque is surmounted by a marble bust of Peter Daly which is considered to be "a good likeness".'[58] When Patrick Daly passed away, the estate transferred to his daughter, Julia, who died – aged 66 – at Lower Salthill in February 1887. Julia's will bestowed property and money on her O'Brien cousins, Emily and Harriet. Mr. Nicholas Daly, her cousin, received £100 along with all of Julia's shares in the National Bank and the Gas Company (Galway Gas Light Company Ltd.). Other Daly cousins, Patrick and Josephine, received some money, while Edward Hill, Julia's 'managing man' was bequeathed two houses with gardens, and her cow. In that respect, Julia Daly was, as Father Coen recorded, quite benevolent. Other endowments included upkeep contributions to Rahoon

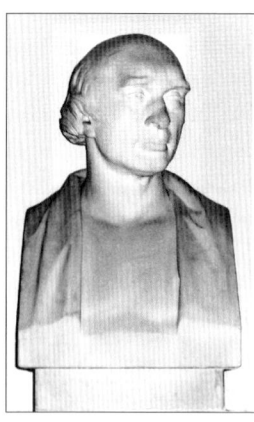

114. Bust of Fr. Peter Daly in Bushypark Church with accompanying legend.

parish churches at St. Joseph's, Barna and Bushypark, as well as annual donations to the Christian Brothers' Industrial School and the Patrician Brothers' Breakfast Institute at Lombard Street.

Julia Daly's greatest munificence, however, was her devising to Dr. Carr, Bishop of Galway, and Fr. Lally, Parish Priest of Rahoon, the lands of Kilcorkey, save those bequests already mentioned. Miss Daly's largesse meant that the Diocese of Galway was given ownership of almost the entire Kilcorkey townland, which had been purchased in 1852 with Sisters of Mercy money by Fr. Peter Daly. The outfall was that Galway Diocese gained access to ground rents from Lower Salthill occupiers, right up to the present time.

It is – judiciously – beyond the remit of this study to adjudicate on the legacy of a man who is now little remembered in the town. Fr. James Mitchell's chronological and meticulously researched profile of Fr. Daly, which appeared in Volume 39 of the *Galway Archaeological and Historical Society Journal* in 1983/'84, represents an even-handed evaluation of Father Daly across the breath of his numerous exploits and many achievements. That study was of great benefit in tracing Fr. Daly's influence on Salthill. It is also worth noting that the two historians to have seriously treated Fr. Peter Daly's intriguing career have been clergymen themselves: Fr. James Mitchell and Fr. Martin Coen.

Chapter 14

'IMPROVING' LANDLORDS AT SALTHILL'S SEAFRONT: SHAWE JONES AND BARTON

Salthill's 19th Century Seafront Hamlets

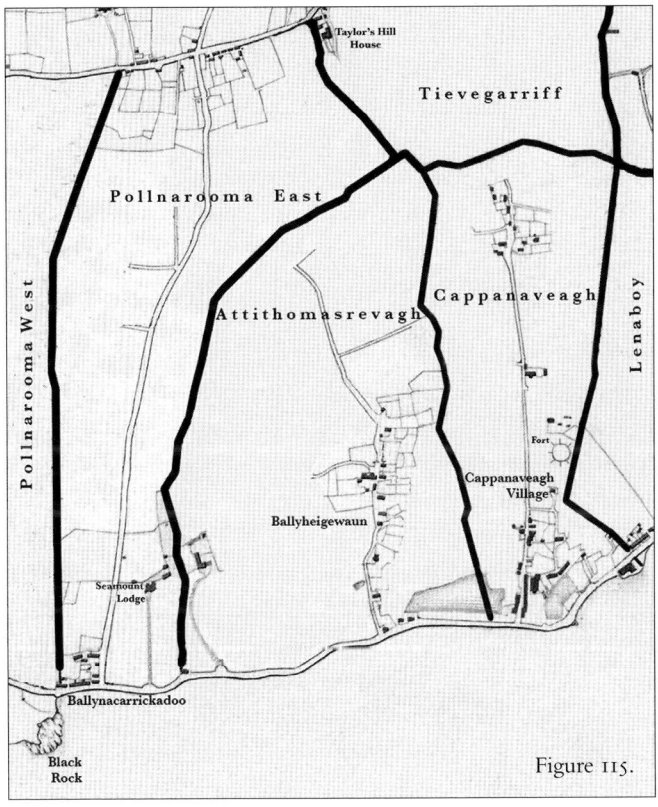

Figure 115.

The above pre-famine representation of three townlands by the sea shows Ballynacarrickadoo (*Baile na Carraige Duibhe*) at Pollnarooma East and houses at the northern end of that same townland, which faced onto Taylor's Hill. All of those premises were cleared. At neighbouring Attithomasrevagh, Ballyheigewaun (*Baile Thaidhg Bháin*) suffered a similar fate. Two distinct

Cappanaveagh algacháns, at the southern and northern borders of the townland, both expired at the hands of the crowbar brigade. The northern Cappanaveagh hamlet stood on the slope – of what became Dalysfort Road – that today runs down to the junction with Dr. Mannix Road and Dalton Drive. This chapter looks at the actions and legacies of two Salthill landlords; Henry Shawe Jones at Cappanaveagh and Thomas H. Barton at Attithomasrevagh.

Henry Shawe Jones at Cappanaveagh

In the 1920s, Fr. J. Rabbitte recorded that 'Irish speakers pronounce the word Cappa-na-viach and say it is the name of the land between Mr. Boland's House (Glenarde) and Upper Salthill.' The same clergyman also sourced a 1557 document which said that; *the Mayor and Counsaill have gyven and graunted the said Wardyn and Vicairs and their successors to be free of all rentes or duties of the pasture and grassing of Cappneyvaugh which they had in yeft (gift) of John Athye.*[1] The Jesuit Father Rabbitte linked the Cappanaveagh townland with the Wardenship of Galway from the 1500s, whereas a 17th century Church-townland connection was the relationship referenced by James Hardiman in 1820: 'In the West franchises a parcel of land called Cappenaveagh... bounded on the South by the highway to the sea' was a possession of St. Nicholas' College in 1637.[2] Hely Dutton in 1824 described Cappanaveagh as a 'Glebe' – cultivable land owned by a parish, church or ecclesiastical benefice.[3] Hardiman further noted that 'The warden is also in possession... of 40 acres at Cappanaveagh, towards the W. (where there is an ancient burial-place, but none interred in it for many years).'[4] As earlier noted in the piece on Salthill's graveyards, it is most unlikely that the burial place referenced by Hardiman had any connection with the private Persse graveyard, which later straddled the Cappanaveagh-Tievegarriff border.

The Cappanaveagh townland was leased – on 8 November, 1756 – to Fielding Shaw by the Corporation of the Warden and Vicars of King's College, Galway. Fielding was succeeded as landlord by Henry Shaw Esq., who had passed away by 1805, after which Conyngham Jones took charge. Four decades later it was Conyngham Jones' son, Henry Shawe Jones, who – on 15 May, 1845, at the yearly rent of £7-7s.- 8d. sterling – signed a forty year renewal of the original 1756 lease. Negotiations on the 1845 deal appear to have been complicated somewhat by a Church Advowson question, which merited both discussion and newspaper coverage.[5] An advowson, in English Ecclesiastical law, is a patronage right which allows the holder 'recommend a member of the Anglican clergy for a vacant benefice, or to make such an appointment.'[6] Such a prestigious power went with the Cappanaveagh townland and was valued by those who held it. Mr. Murray, who 'said he saw improvements making at Cappanaveagh,' urged the immediate sale of the advowson, as he felt the Ecclesiastical Board had no power to prevent it.[7]

In the year of that advowson controversy at Galway, a sectarian spat resulted in Cappanaveagh being referenced in a *Galway Mercury* rebuke to those involved with the Galway Branch of the Hibernian Bible Society. That followed a society meeting in Kilroy's Hotel, where Rev. Mr. Walker stated that the Catholic faith of Irishmen was 'AN AWFUL DELUSION – A GROSS IDOLATRY.' At the same gathering it was decided, as the *Mercury* acerbically put it, 'to invade the cabins of the poor and the mansions of the rich, in endeavouring to thrust a corrupted and mutilated version of the Bible into the hands of Catholics.' The newspaper offered a challenge to the Bible Society's members: 'If the Parsons are the honest men they describe themselves, let them give our people what belongs to them;…let them give back all they have received from us in the shape of Tithes, Corporate property and Church cess; and let them, to come to a recent case, render to the inhabitants an account of the money they put into their pockets for the lands of Cappanaveagh, which they have leased away.'[8] Ten years later, according to Richard Griffith's 1855 valuation, the 'Warden and Vicar of Galway' remained as the 'Immediate Lessor' to fifty acres at Cappanaveagh.

The townland improvements, referenced by Mr. Murray, were evident in an April 1845 advertisement that offered four Bathing Lodges for summer letting at Cappanaveagh. They were The Hotel, Strand Lodge, Green Lodge and Sandymount Lodge.[9] The named Cappanaveagh premises most likely represented a 'few neat lodges,' as referenced by John O'Donovan in his Field Book notes. In that record, 'Cunningham Jones' was listed as the owner of the Cappanaveagh townland, which was 'held by Mr. Richard Lynch of Salthill under lease of 31 years, who sublets it to 30 tenants at will at £5 per acre.'[10] As 'Conyngham' Jones had died at Brussels in 1838,[11] it was his son, Henry Shawe Jones, who agreed the 1845 Cappanaveagh lease.

One Two storey House and Two Villages at Cappanaveagh

A residence, built on the site of Salthill's present day Garda Station, was first called 'Sandy Mount.' That building represented the only two storey house in the Cappanaveagh townland, as recorded by O'Donovan in 1839. A later 1860's building, which replaced Sandymount on the same site, was called Forster Park up to its 1934 sale, after which it became the most recent premises to house the resort's police barracks.

O'Donovan's thirty tenant tally would appear to broadly equate with the 131 pre-famine inhabitants of the townland, as noted in the 1841 census. Two original clacháns in the Cappanaveagh townland were indicated on the 1839 Ordnance Survey map **(fig. 115)**. The larger was at the northern end of the track, which later became Dalysfort Road. There were twelve premises, though it is impossible to say how many, at the end of that track, were outhouses. The most northerly of those houses sat at what is today the junction that connects the Dalysfort and Dr. Mannix roads with Dalton Drive. That means that the northern townland village was perched on either side of a short stretch of today's Dalysfort Road, which currently slopes from the Forster Park housing estate entrance down to Dr. Mannix Road. It was a carefully chosen site, for the village was situated in *An Gleann Ard* or High Glen, and received whatever protection that valley offered. That pre-famine Cappanaveagh *clachán*, which faced Glenarde House on its Tievegarriff northern side, sat on the southern slope of the glen.

The second *clachán* in the townland stood close to the sea and was known as Cappanaveagh Village. That house cluster was sited beside the Sandy Mount building, on either side of the entrance to what would later be called Dalysfort Road. The 1839 OS representation of that southern village's premises suggests cabin/tenement style dwellings. That reading is further strengthened by a later description of roadside 'cabins' being pulled down at Cappanaveagh.[12] Small landholders' homes in the townland were described by O'Donovan in 1839 as 'poor houses stone walls, poor looking.'

There were few premises along the shoreline at Cappanaveagh, for a large *lochán sáile*, or saline lake, sat where Leisureland – and the front of Salthill Park – currently (2018) stand, with a second lake occupying an area from today's Eglinton Direct Provision Centre to Colm's Amusement Centre. That latter lake was identified by O'Donovan as 'Loughaun-Phadrick Carter,' and appeared as 'Loughaunpatrick,' in the 1839 OS map. Like Grey Thomas and Fair Tadhg of former Salthill times, Patrick Carter's name is now rarely recalled, except perhaps when that area's premises are occasionally flooded. It was above the level of Patrick Carter's lake that Sandy Mount / Forster Park were built, though the latter building does appear to have been in some way affected during the storms and floods of 1926.[13] In between the northern and southern Cappanaveagh villages, a fine premises stood in 1839 on the eastern side of the road that divided the townland, directly across from where Eileen O'Brien currently trades at the Hilltop shop.

Cruel Eviction

By the end of the Great Hunger years, many of Cappanaveagh's occupants would be gone and *ocras* alone did not drive them out. On Tuesday, 24 August, 1847, at the height of a dreadful time, a particularly cruel eviction took place:

Evictions in Galway: It gives me much pain to state, that under a habere at the suit of Mr. Jones, a lessee of the Warden and Vicars of Galway, the Sheriff was engaged on yesterday protected by a large posse of the police, and a considerable force of the 49th infantry, and a troop of dragoons in the eviction of the tenants on the lands of Cappanaveagh at Salt-hill. The reason for this wholesale clearance we have not heard – whether it was for rent and arrears of rent, or to make way for "improvements." But whatever may have been the reason it is unfortunate that so many wretched creatures at a period like this should be thrown houseless upon the world…If to the miseries of starvation and disease the crowning one of extermination is to follow, all that we can say is, God help the poor.[14]

Conneely lore

The family lore of Cappanaveagh's Conneely family preserves the story of that Jones' eviction. An ancestor, Thomas Conneely, who was born before the Great Famine, was a victim – as a child – of that dreadful clearing. Thomas recalled an evicting troop – which included police and military – turn up, at what became Dalysfort Road to drive them from their home. Contemporaneous reports of the sad event confirm what Thomas Conneely had always affirmed: Those evicted from Cappanaveagh were not behind in their rents, but were arbitrarily dispossessed by Henry Shawe Jones. Mr. Thomas Barton's subsequent clearing of Attithomasrevagh for Bathing Lodge development was not highly thought of by Mr. Conneely, whose family experienced first-hand the pain of such a heartless act. It is a tribute to the Conneely clan that the family, whose Salthill roots go back beyond the Tithe Applotment records of 1834, remain *ag baile,* representing an unbroken Salthill connection, which has long outlasted the landlord masters of ephemeral property privilege. The Conneely clan was back at Cappanaveagh in the autumn of 1851, when Thomas' father, Mr. John Conneely, leased a small holding from Henry Shawe Jones, the man who had – four years earlier – evicted John and his family from the same townland. Mr. Thomas Conneely, who lived for almost a hundred years at Salthill, died in August 1941, 'at his residence, 4 Lenaboy Avenue.'[15] He recalled how his family, on eviction, went west in 1847 and paused to gather themselves, and some supplies, in the Seamount area. Again that lore has merit for it was most likely at Blackrock, beside the Ballynacarrickadoo hamlet, that supportive aid was offered. A Relief Committee soup-kitchen had been set up at Blackrock some three months before the Jones' eviction at Cappanaveagh[16] and it was from that source, or possibly from the people of Ballynacarrickadoo themselves, that support was given.

Reasons for Eviction?

There's little doubt but that the draconian Gregory clause, already discussed, was a stimulant for action at Cappanaveagh. That initiative, adopted by the government in June 1847, was viewed as a weapon which would allow landlords 'clear their estates of pauperised smallholders who were paying little or no rent.'[17] Historian, James S. Donnelly Jnr., has pointed out that while not all 'consequences of the quarter-acre clause were fully appreciated in advance, its enormous potential as an estate clearing device was widely recognised in parliament.'[18] Such potential was neither overlooked – nor wasted – at Galway, and the *Vindicator* in the month of the clause's enactment opined: 'It is not at all unlikely but that Gregory's quarter-acre test will ere long occasion an extensive depopulation of the rural districts.'[19] Within a month of that local report appearing, Mr. Jones placed the following advertisement in the *Galway Mercury*:[20]

SALT HILL.

TO BE LET for the Season, Unfurnished, the HOTEL and THREE LODGES at Salt Hill, the property of Henry Shaw Jones, Esq., who will Sell a quantity of his adjoining property on lease, for Building, the favourable situation of which for Bathing Lodges requires no comment. Also, TO BE LET, THREE HOUSES or the Church-yard.

For particulars, apply to Mr. Michael Perrin, Mary street.
June 29th, 1847.

116. Henry Shaw Jones' 1847 advertisement for Cappanaveagh.

The *Mercury* notice tells a tale. By offering land for building, Mr. Jones was to the fore in recognising the investment opportunity that Salthill Bathing Lodges offered – some five years before Mr. Barton bought the neighbouring townland for the same purpose. For both men 'improvement' was euphemistically equated with tenant clearances. The unfurnished nature of the advertised 'Hotel' indicates that premises to have been a bathing lodge, or boarding house of some description, which operated in the townland, at least thirteen years before John Gill opened his landmark Eglinton Hotel at Cappanaveagh in 1860.

Not wasting any time in availing of a new opportunity, Mr. Jones's Cappanaveagh evictions occurred within three months of the Gregory Clause becoming law. There is no doubt but that his plans, which required the removal of rent compliant small tenant holders, appear heartless. Mr. Shaw Jones was patently aware of the Gregory clause's import, as it related to increased landlords' power, and his pioneering spirit focused on being among the first to avail of those same powers. As already noted, that same spirit was also reflected in his identification of Bathing Lodges as an investment opportunity during the darkest of famine days. His entrepreneurial vision was formed a full two years before the introduction of the Encumbered Estate system. That said, Mr. Jones was later forced to avail of the same Landed Court facility.

A Lead Mine at Cappanaveagh

A further issue was to surprisingly come into play at Cappanaveagh. In November 1850, news broke that a lead mine had been found in the townland. Such a scenario might suggest that Mr. Jones knew of wealth 'in them there hills,' and decided to clear tenants in an effort to expedite a harvesting of his mineral find. The *Galway Mercury*'s report of the Salt Hill find, however, discounts such a theory:

> About a mile distant from this town at Salt Hill, there were a number of cabins on the road side, all of which have been thrown down some time since by order of the landlord, a Mr. Jones of Dublin, who holds those lands under the Warden of Galway. Some of the peasantry being lately employed in clearing one of the foundations, discovered what he thought to be a quantity of silver ore mixed in the stone. The story soon spread; a number of the country people came and commenced operations in their rude way, of course quite unproductive. A captain of a mining company at Scariff, was sent for, who came and examined the mine or ore and declared it an excellent rich lead mine, taking samples of it to Dublin, where he now is in treaty with Mr. Jones.[21]

The newspaper account confirms that it was the post-eviction knocking of evicted tenants' cabins which led to the mineral discovery. The clearing of unsightly cabins, as we have already seen, was to enhance the townland and facilitate the creation of Bathing Lodges.

The significance of the mineral find at Cappanaveagh was reflected in the story being carried as far away as Warwickshire, where the *Royal Leamington Spa Courier* carried a terse one-liner: 'Discovery of a Lead Mine. – A Galway paper states that a lead mine has been discovered at Salt Hill near Galway.'[22] The story moved on rapidly, and before month's end, the *Leinster Express* described the interest taken in the discovery, as well as the extent of the find: 'Our article last week, on the above subject, has, we perceive, drawn the attention of several strangers to this locality at Salt Hill and on further investigation it is now satisfactorily proved that the mine, or ore extends all through the lands of Cappanaveagh. We hope soon to have to announce the working of it by some company possessed of adequate capital.'[23]

The *Freeman's Journal* also picked up a local report on developments: *It gives us much pleasure now to state that the recently discovered lead mine at Salt-hill near this town, will soon be operated upon by a practical gentleman who has just concluded a treaty with Mr. Jones, the present lessee of the ground. Mr. Jones has, we are informed, written to his man of business here, to say that over 100 men will be put to work on the mine in the beginning of January next.*[24]

By January 1851, the mine was, indeed, up and working: *It now gives us much pleasure in stating that it is fully at work, and several persons employed on it; but owing to the very rainy weather, little progress can be made with the work. We are glad to hear it is of a most promising appearance.*[25]

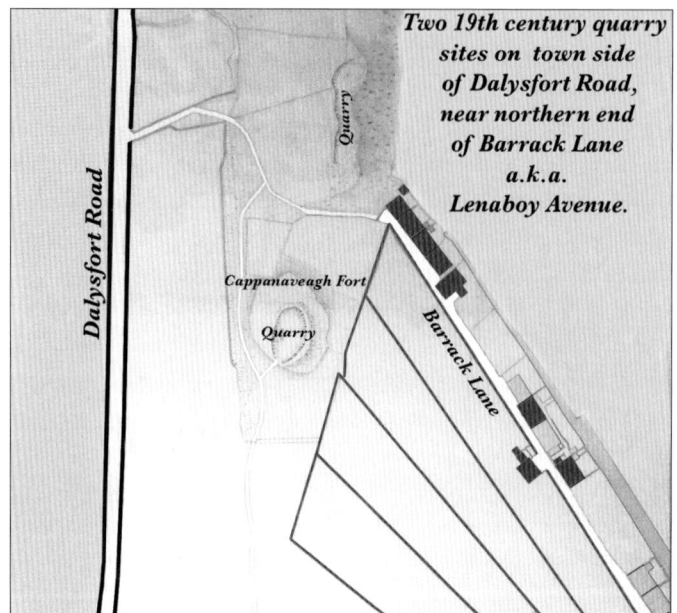

117. The southern quarry site was positioned in the ancient 'circular enclosure,' known as Cappanaveagh Fort.

Ordnance Survey Maps point to the areas which were most likely mined for lead. The 1839 O.S. Map of Salthill marked 'Cappanaveagh Fort' as a symmetrically circular feature, which was more recently noted under 'Unclassified Enclosures and Earthworks,' in the 1993 Archaeological Inventory of County Galway:

Cappanaveagh Fort indicated on Ordnance Map stands at raised end of Lenaboy Avenue. It is described as a 'Circular Enclosure: On S-facing slope, now part of the suburbs of Salthill, Galway City. Marked on OS maps as a circular enclosure (D. 30 m), No visible surface traces of which survive.'[26]

A later map featured 'Quarry (Disused)' in the Cappanaveagh Fort area with a second 'quarry' designation a little north of that point. That second 'quarry' location today represents the vacant site that stands behind the last terraced house on Dalysfort Road – just before the junction with Rock Hill. The O'Reilly family – of Strand House and latterly O'Reilly's Bar and Kitchen – recall the 'Quarry' moniker being used to describe that locale. The same place was also known as the 'Rocks' by those who took a Sunday shortcut through that area, *en route* to Salthill Church in the 1960s. Rockhill, which retains the craggy appellation, delineates that hinterland today.

The lead mine venture was not to last. In fact, the boast that the entire townland was rich in lead was not trumpeted, when Henry Shawe Jones placed the Cappanaveagh townland for sale six years after the mineral find was first declared. It was the place's desirability 'for villa residences,' which was promoted at auction time, when it was also pointed out that 'there had been recently a considerable outlay upon these lands.'[27] Such a sales pitch was not surprising, for it continued the investment strategy of Mr. Jones, and Thomas Barton was, by then, leading the way in such developments at the abutting Attithomasrevagh townland. According to the Cappanaveagh auction brochure, there were only three tenants and six residences in the townland at the time of its 1856 sale. The tenants were William Wylde with two properties; John Conneely with one; and owner, Henry Shaw Jones, with three residences and land. The total house tally was then six, quite a drop from thirty four – with 31 inhabited – which had stood in 1841. The destruction of up to 28 residences, over a fifteen year period, captured the scale of 'improvement' visited on the townland. A population fall at Cappanaveagh from 171 inhabitants in 1841, to 52 ten years later, was mirrored in a drop from thirty tenants in 1839 to three in 1856. Such figures reflect the significant impact of Mr. Jones' deeds at Salthill. There's no doubt but that the arbitrary 1847 removal of tenants and their cabins represented the greatest 'advance,' which had been made at Mr. Jones' seaside holding. An indigenous community, whose rooted period at the place is unknown, was expelled and forced to face an uncertain future. Though the Conneely clan returned to the place, the identity and fate of their erstwhile Cappanaveagh neighbours remain unknown.

118. The Rockhill road sign is today positioned on the edge of the more northern Cappanaveagh quarry site. Bereft of an appended 'e,' the Gaelic version of the name should read *Cnoc na Carraige*.

While legal, Mr. Shaw Jones' actions, through difficult years at Cappanaveagh, were less than charitable. The Cappanaveagh chief was, undoubtedly, not unique among landlords. As a man identified with a townland, which boasted longstanding and close ties to the Church of St. Nicholas – where he served as a warden,[28] Mr. Jones' evictions are difficult to ethically rationalise. It must be acknowledged, however, that evictions did cross both religious and clerical divides, with Rahoon's Parish Priest, Fr. Peter Daly, being a regular landlord attendee – as earlier noted – at ejectment hearings.

Shaw(e) Jones' family background

The Shaw surname had standing in Galway over many generations and Hardiman recorded a post-Aughrim meeting between the Williamite General Ginkle and 'Mr. Shaw, a merchant of the town,' who had escaped from Galway with some other Protestants on 17 July 1691.[29] Another account told how information from Shaw had aided the Williamite capture of Galway town.[30] Hardiman further emphasised the prominence of the Shaw family by placing it among 'the several leading families of Eyre, Shaw, Staunton and Fitzpatrick,' who 'successively commanded the representation, and directed the affairs of the town.'[31] Robert Shaw, for example, was Town Clerk in 1679 and Recorder of Galway in both 1718 and 1737,[32] while Croasdall Shaw of Dominick Street was recorded in *Pigot's Provincial Directory* as a member of the town's Nobility/Gentry in 1824. A Shaw family also held land in the Salthill area, for when Thomas Shaw placed Galway holdings for sale in 1758, among the 24 lots were forty acres at Shantalla, and 26 acres at Lenabaty (Lenaboy): 'These Lands lie in the West Liberties of the Town of Galway, and are let very cheap.'[33] Andrew Lynch was the Lenabaty tenant at the time of that 18th century sale. A Shaw(e) presence of some description, as earlier described, enjoyed the lion's share of a century's tenure at Cappanaveagh in the 1756–1856 period.

Both of his parents' patronyms were combined in the surname of Henry Shaw Jones. The first was variously spelt 'Shaw' or 'Shawe.' It was at Dublin in July 1791 that Conyngham Jones of Dollardstown, Co. Meath, 'lieutenant in 4th reg. dragoons, and aide-du-camp to the Lord Lieutenant,' married Miss Anna Maria Shawe, daughter of the late Colonel Shawe of the 11th regiment of Foot.[34] During the 1820s, Conyngham Jones retained a Stephens' Green address, and in 1821, at Dublin, Henry Shaw Jones Esq., only son of Conyngham Jones of Dollards-town, Co. Meath married Louisa, youngest daughter of T. Driscoll of Harcourt Street Esq., one of his Majesty's Counsel at Law.[35] That marriage was short-lived, for in March 1824, Louisa passed away 'of a premature accouchement,' at her father in law's Dollardstown seat.[36] Her widowed husband, Henry, fought a duel in the following year, though the reason for his pistol engagement is unclear:

> At six o'clock on the morning of Saturday the 26th inst., a meeting took place on the Strand at Sandymount, near Dublin, between Henry Shawe Jones, Esq., seconded by George Armstrong, Esq. and Ambrose Upton Gladstones Esq., when Mr. Gladstones having received Mr. Jones fire, discharged his pistol in the air. The parties were then taken off the ground by their seconds without effecting a reconciliation.[37]

In 1826 Ensign Henry Shawe Jones from the 81st Foot became 'Lieutenant of Infantry by purchase.'[38] A year later – on 26 July, 1827, Henry remarried, when he wed Maria Rudkin, daughter of Gilbert-Pickering Rudkin, Esq. of Wells, Co. Carlow, an Army Captain who had served in 1808 as High Sheriff of that county.[39] The Shaw Jones family appear to have spent some years – during the 1830s – in Italy, where two sons; Gilbert (at Florence), and Henry (at Naples), were born. In 1838 at Brussels, Henry's father, Conyngham Jones Esq. of Dollardstown, Co. Meath and Stephen's Green, passed away of 'apoplexy.'[40] It was subsequent to his father's death that Henry and family returned to Ireland, and in 1845 the lease for the Cappanaveagh townland was taken up. Henry was proactive, during his time in Galway, in trying to 'improve' his Salthill holding and he also served on Galway's Grand Jury. He was not afraid of any person or institution that was less than honest in their dealings with him. In 1846, for example, two notices were served on the Town Commissioners for trespass on his property at Tankerville's Plot,[41] a holding Henry owned at Church Lane in Galway town, which had been in the possession of Mrs. Tankerville, widow, in 1831. Henry S. Jones also brought a seasonal tenant, Roscommon magistrate John J. Sullivan Esq., to court in 1855 for unpaid rent, and damage done to the Salthill lodge he had taken.[42] Mr. Thomas Heher was also summoned to court by the Cappanaveagh land owner in 1852 for 'looting potatoes at Salthill on the 13th inst.'[43]

It was at Devonshire in March, 1867 that Captain Henry Shawe Jones of Dollardstown, late 33rd Regiment & Royal Westmoreland Militia, passed away.[44] His son, Gilbert Pickering R. Shaw Jones, a Captain of Militia and Landlord to 500 acres, was residing with his mother Maria, a retired Officer's widow, at Bristol in 1871. Four years later, Gilbert married Marie E. J. Bond at Tenby in South Wales, and died on 7 August, 1901 at Merrion Road, Dublin. He was buried at Mount Jerome cemetery.

Blake Forster at Cappanaveagh

The Jones' receivership sale of 1856, 'indemnified ... by the Lands of Dollardstown,' in County Meath,[45] resulted in the Cappanaveagh townland being sold at auction for £1810. The 'Blake Forster' name then replaced 'Jones' as the landed authority at Cappanaveagh. Boasting a lengthy and illustrious lineage, the new arrivals could trace their ancestry back to Anacher, the great Forester of Flanders, who died in 837.[46] The incoming family's Coat of Arms was placed on a new residence, which replaced Sandy Mount on the same site during the early 1860s. That new house's name was Forster Park and the Blake Forster logo is still visible on the premises, which today serves as Salthill's Garda Station. An effort was also made – à la Barton – to have the Cappanaveagh townland name changed to Forster Park, for when Captain Francis Blake Forster's son, Francis O'Donnellan Blake Forster, was himself forced to sell his Salthill holding in 1895, the description given was 'the Lands of Cappanaveagh, now called Forster Park.'[47] While both names remain part of Salthill's *lingua franca*, they represent different entities today: Cappanaveagh is the name of an apartment complex in the Lenaboy townland, while Forster Park identifies a residential street at the northern end of Dalysfort Road.

By way of history, fate or coincidence, the Latin motto of the Blake Forster family – *Audaces Fortuna Juvat* – Fortune Favours the Brave – appears perfectly fitting in its unobtrusive presence on the front facade of Salthill's Garda Station.

The same ensign figures prominently on Blake Forster headstones at the townside gable of Bushypark Church, where a number of family members are buried. That Roman Catholic chapel was built in the 1830s by Father Peter Daly, Parish Priest of Rahoon. The same clergyman was in the chair at a Town Commissioners' meeting – in August 1858 – when a Galway road was named in honour of the Forster family. The following motion was then presented to the Town Board:

119. To the left, Blake Forster Coat of Arms featuring an *Audaces Fortuna Juvat* motto, on front façade of Forster Park, today Salthill's Garda Station. The same ensign and motto, on right, is to be found on three headstones at the town-side gable of Bushypark Church.

> *We, the undersigned inhabitants of the place recently known by the name of 'College Road,' would feel obliged if the Town Commissioners would be pleased to change the name of that to 'Foster Park' on their map, inasmuch as the Foster family for four or five hundred years, were residents in the County, and had also property in the Town, as well as being members of the old Corporation, and having at all times identified themselves with the People, and very often at a great sacrifice of their own interests.*
>
> *In consequence of the great inconvenience experienced not alone by strangers but by the inhabitants of the town, from the confusion that results from another road at the opposite end of the town having lately acquired that name, since the erection of the Queen's College, and the establishment from which the above locality derived its name being only a Grammar School, under the Governors of Erasmus Smith, the undersigned, therefore, respectfully request, that the name of the locality be changed to that of 'Foster Street.'*[48]

In a lexical context, the 'Foster' spelling of the surname was the most common published variant in Galway newspapers of the 1850s, comfortably outnumbering its 'Forster' equivalent. On the residents' 1858 motion being unanimously passed, Captain Blake Forster, a member of the Commissioner Board, thanked his colleagues 'for the compliment therein conveyed to himself and his family.' The Captain owned 'some fee simple property in that neighbourhood' and it was reported that 'in the days of the penal laws, when the nuns were hunted out of Galway, it was his family, who were then Protestants, that gave them [Dominican order] the slate nunnery, the title deeds of which he still had in his possession.' It turned out, therefore, that the thoroughfare from Moneenageisha to the Square, once simply known as *an Bóthar Beag*, ended up with a further two monikers; College Road and Forster Street. All three handles remain in use today, with *TG4* rugby commentators being largely responsible for the current currency of the original Gaelic title.

Thomas Henry Barton at Attithomasrevagh

Though Fr. Peter Daly is sometimes recalled, in terms of evicting landlords at Salthill, Henry Shaw Jones is generally forgotten. Regularly and unknowingly referenced, however, is a third property owner, whose surname is articulated every time his prized holding is mentioned. That landlord is Thomas Henry Barton, who bequeathed his name to a place he called Rockbarton. The original name of the townland was Attithomasrevagh, which he purchased in 1852, the same year that Fr. Peter Daly acquired Lower Salthill's Kilcorkey. Barton's impact on Salthill was considerable, but before we look at his influence, it is important to set the scene for his arrival.

The Attithomasrevagh name represents a corrupted Anglicisation of *Áit Tighe Thomáis Riabhach*. John O'Donovan, in his Field Name Books, translated the name as 'the site of Grey Thomas's house,' while P.W. Joyce later chose the word 'swarthy' to describe the man's complexion.[49] Though we now realise that distinctive colouring distinguished Thomas, we know little else about the man who lent

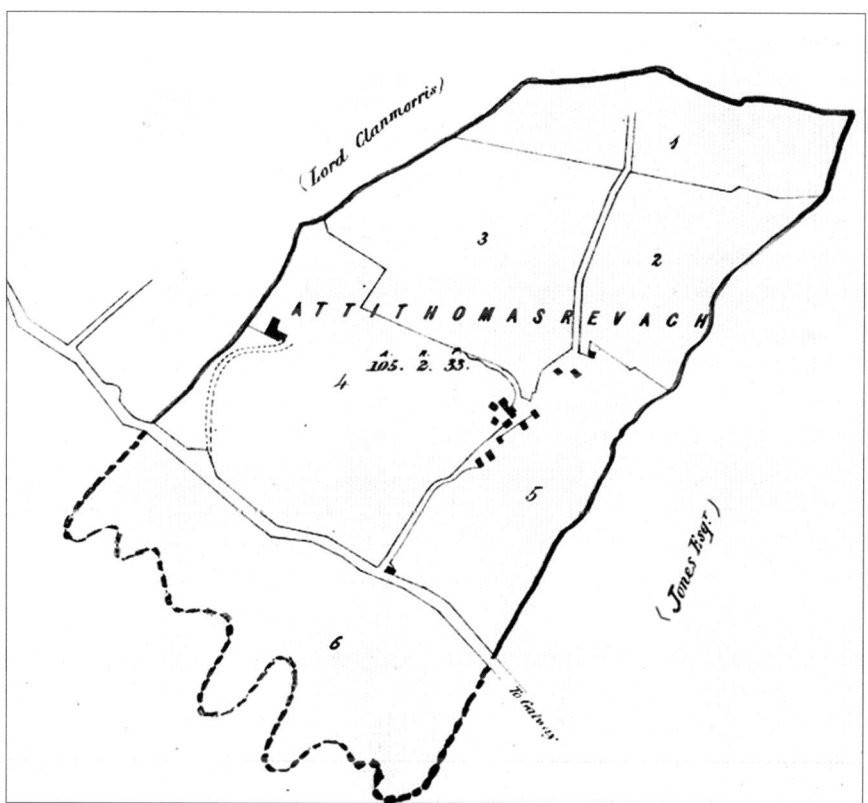

120. A land map of Attithomasrevagh, before it became Rockbarton, which shows the *Baile Thaidhg Bháin* hamlet and the shore rights that went with the townland.

his name to a land mass that neatly sits in the middle of Salthill's promenade. T.S. Ó Máille noted that the name 'Athey Thomas Reagh' was first recorded in 1609,[50] so it is most likely that Thomas' true identity is forever lost to the past. The place name is little used now, except by *Raidio na Gaeltachta* commentators who recall Tomás, when identifying the townland in match reports from Pearse Stadium. *Bailte fearainn* might well be redundant in urban areas, but they still resonate with those whose traditions remain rooted in place.

Within that townland in 1839 stood a *clachán* – hamlet that was known as Ballyheigewaun or *Baile Thaidhg Bháin*. Another Anglicised spelling was 'Ballynagarvane.' That particular house cluster was centred on high ground, opposite the current entrance to *Gort Ard*. Might the Fair Tadhg who lent his name to the *clachán*, be the same man as Grey Thomas who is recorded in the townland's title? Though possible, it is unlikely that such a connection will ever be fully established. The identities of Thomas and Tadhg are, alas, lost to history by time and many Salthill tides. The eastern side of the access road to Tadhg's *clachán* featured a number of 'cabins.' That south-north pathway opened at the seafront, just to the east of the current gated entrance to the Galway Bay Hotel. It not only gave access to the townland's village, but ran further north into the marshy ground that later came to house Pearse Stadium. The land map **(fig. 120)** above also shows the extent – number 6 on map – of the townland's sea shore rights, which were to come into focus in 1930, at the time of the building of two outdoor pools at Ladies' Beach.

Denis Arthur Bingham, the third Lord Clanmorris of Newbrook, Co. Mayo, was the Attithomasrevagh landlord in 1839. Denis, a famed horseman, also owned the bordering Pollnarooma East townland. O'Donovan recorded that a Patrick Reily, Claregalway was the agent for Lord Clanmorris who let the Attithomasrevagh land out to 19 tenants at will, for £4.10s. per acre. A Field Book's cogent description of the place ran; *Soil a light moory nature, producing potatoes, bad oats and onions. This land all rocky, except a few acres joining Salt Hill Road – houses stone walls (poor cabins). Mr. Kelly of Barna Lodge receives the rent of this townland at present. This village is called Ballynagarvane. There is a small long house called [unable to read].*'[51] The stand alone 'long house' to the west of the townland, as indicated in the 1852 auction map, featured its own private avenue.

Famine outcome at Attithomasrevagh

The Attithomasrevagh townland, by the time of the Great Famine, was in the possession of Lord Oranmore and Brown. Though townlands – Pollnarooma East and Cappanaveagh – on either side of the place suffered greatly during the *Gorta Mór*, its effect was not as severely felt at Dominick Brown's Salthill holding. Population figures, from the 1841 and 1851 census returns, show a drop of two persons from

118 to 116 in the townland, and a slight rise in total house numbers from 22 to 23. It appears that the inhabitants of Attithomasrevagh were somehow spared the worst effects of the great catastrophe. They were not, however, to survive what followed.

Lord Oranmore and Browne was ordered, in December 1849, to sell his Salthill properties among many other holdings.[52] Consequently Right Hon. Dominick Brown sold Attithomasrevagh on 25 May, 1852, as Lot 2 of twenty three holdings in an Encumbered Estate sale. The auction brochure spiel ran:

Lot 2 – *Consisting of the Lands of Atty-Thomas-Revagh is in the Parish of Rahoon, and Barony of Galway, convenient to the Town, and adjacent to the fashionable Watering-place of Seapoint. This townland possesses great capabilities and facilities for the erection of Bathing-Lodges, having an extensive shore frontage, and will become of great value by completion of Railway, intended Packet Station, and inland communication through Lough Corrib.* Newspaper adverts gave other details: *Lot 2 – Attythomasrevagh, or Salt Hill with rocky shore, 105A 2R 33P statute measure; net yearly value, 67l valuation of Messrs. Brassington and Gale, 81l 2s 5d.*[53]

The first offer was for £1000, and the *Freeman's Journal* recorded the purchaser as Mr. Thomas Courtney, who paid £1850 for the townland. The man who, in fact, came to own Attithomasrevagh was Thomas Henry Barton. Mr. Courtney, a solicitor, who regularly purchased properties at auction, boasted an address at Fitzwilliam square-East, just around the corner from Mr. Barton, whose office as barrister lay on the southern side of the same fashionable Dublin Square. The Salthill holding was bought 'in trust' for Mr. Barton.[54] The sale of the 23 lots realised £49,935 for Lord Oranmore, equal to 16 ½ years' purchase on the rental.

Less than three weeks after the purchase of the townland, a June advertisement in the *Galway Mercury* indicated the purchaser's plans for the area to which he was to append his name. Mr. Barton's desire to have his name identified with his Salthill property became clear quite quickly, as is obvious from that early newspaper notice. The new owner's ambitious vision for the place was also indicated in the same piece:

Barton Lodges, *Galway Bay. To Be Let, on Building Leases. Plots of various sizes, commanding fine Sea views. The property (lately Lord Oranmore's) is situated close to Salt Hill, and one mile from Galway. It has been laid out for Marine Villas upon a plan by Frazer. For particulars, apply to T.H. Barton, Esq. 6 Fitzwilliam square, South Dublin.*[55]

In the way of all catastrophes and recessions, the Great Famine's destructive impact on the hordes created opportunities for the handful. Heavily tenanted land had become a burden for landlords who were already heavily indebted. On such holdings being sold at Encumbered Estate Auctions, purchasers saw no profit in persisting with a subsistent farming model on their lands. 'Improvement,' in the main, became a byword for clearing holdings of people and replacing them with grass and animals, thus creating grazier estates, which drew the ire of land-starved farmers and the dispossessed. Alternative schemes were also enticing, as Henry Shaw

Jones had identified at neighbouring Cappanaveagh. The great attraction of Mr. Barton's land bank was its seaside position and potential as a Bathing Lodge centre.

The terminus for the Midland Great Western Railway stood beside the town's Square, on the opening of rail 'traffic from Dublin to Galway on the 1st August, 1851.'[56] That major infrastructural boost, which occurred just 10 months before the townland was purchased, meant that Mr. Thomas Henry Barton could easily spend time in Galway, away from his legal work in Dublin. Though Barton hailed from a landed Tipperary family, his plans for Attithomasrevagh had nothing to do with agriculture. He set out to make it 'one of the most scenic places in Ireland.' That ambition had been favourably accommodated by the legal framework which followed the Gregory Clause's 1847 adoption.

The *Galway Packet* newspaper became a cheerleader for what the new landlord set out to achieve. It must be stressed that Barton's methodical approach to bathing lodge construction was to come at a cost, and the townland's peasantry were obliged to pay it: On Monday, 16 August, 1852, just three months after Mr. Barton had purchased Attithomasrevagh, one hundred and twenty nine persons were evicted from the townland. The *Galway Packet* told how 'the Sheriff and a party of police preceded to the lands of Attythomasrevagh, for the purpose of ejecting some tenants.' The newspaper was quite tolerant of Barton's actions for it went on to state that 'however much we might condemn a system which deprives a fellow creature of his home, we cannot, in this case, charge the proprietor with any degree of harshness. The evicted all owed large arrears, in many instances amounting to seven years' rent, yet he gave £3 to each householder, and allowed him to take away his crop.'[57] The *Nenagh Guardian* carried a similar report of the eviction.[58] Barton's clearing policy was coldly clinical, yet it was not, in both newspapers' view, completely callous. What hard economics dictated, the law facilitated and it must be acknowledged that Barton was more generous to his lessees than Henry Shaw Jones had been at nearby Cappanaveagh. Despite that, the people of Attithomasrevagh, who managed to survive the Great Famine, were not to survive Barton's ambition.

While local lore in Salthill's urban setting is today quite scant, it is not Barton's bounty that is generally recalled. The scale of 'social engineering' that took place at Salthill's sea-front was quite significant. Taking Griffith's Valuation data of 1855 and census figures on either side of it, it is clear that house numbers in the townland fell – after the great 1852 eviction – from 23 in 1851 to a mere 2 four years later. By 1861, they had rebounded to 15. The population fell from 116 in 1851 to 52 a decade later. It is evident, however, that the 52 inhabitants of 1861 were 'new' residents of the townland. The 116 persons who had lived there a decade earlier were scattered to destinations unknown.

The *Galway Packet*'s forbearance towards the evictions of August 1852 was followed in the following month by a detailed and glowing account of Barton's plans for his newly purchased property:

We are deeply gratified to perceive that operations have been already commenced for effecting a very great improvement in the vicinity of this town, by converting a district, rugged and neglected, with one of the most picturesque spots of which this country can boast. The large tract of ground between the village of Salthill and Black Rock, which has been lately purchased in the Encumbered Estates Court by Mr. Barton of Dublin, is now in the process of being laid out in building plots, under the superintendence of Mr. Frazer, the eminent landscape gardener. This spacious piece of ground possesses the highest natural capabilities, and when properly planted and built upon, will not be surpassed by any of the most celebrated scenery in Ireland… We have heard that several parties, even in Dublin, have already manifested very great anxiety to obtain building plots there. We hope the operations will be pushed on with vigour; that the grounds will be cleared and put to rights before the winter sets in; and that before the commencement of the next bathing season, several villas shall have arisen to receive the rapidly increasing influx of visitors to our attractive watering place.[59]

Doubtless, Salthill lacked sufficient lodge accommodation of Mr. Barton's standard, and the new landlord was keen to keep an eye on developments at his Galway holding. On Thursday, 2 December, 1852, for example, he arrived at mid-day by train from Dublin, *accompanied by Mr. Frazer…and having called on S.U. Roberts, Esq., C.E. they drove to the grounds purchased by Mr. Barton…and after examining the works now executing under the superintendence of William Molloy, Esq. C.E., he expressed himself well pleased at the manner in which they had been carried out…You can hear the constant click of the hammer, from seven in the morning until five in the evening of somewhat over 200 men and boys breaking stones, for the new roads…each labourer receives 5s. for his week's work, this being at the rate of 10d. per day…The grounds are to be beautifully and tastefully planted, with forest-trees and ornamental shrubs. A contract has been entered into with Mr. Francis Madden, of Ballinasloe…Mr. Barton has left this morning by the 8 o'clock train a.m. for Dublin.*[60]

A Gated and Designed Demesne

Two months later – in February, 1853 – improvements at Attithomasrevagh were again noted, with the *Packet* detailing the construction of two gated entrances at Barton's Salthill holding:

There will be two grand entrances – one at the east, or townside, and the other at the west, or Blackrock side. The piers which are in the course of erection stand one hundred feet apart. The material is massive limestone, rock face, chisel dressed and beautifully moulded. They will be twelve feet high and four and a half feet square. The pier caps have six mouldings, finely chiselled; they are five feet six inches square, and will consequently project six inches over the piers.[61]

The townland's design involved the creation of an access road system, which did not include the old path to *Baile Thaidhg Bháin*.

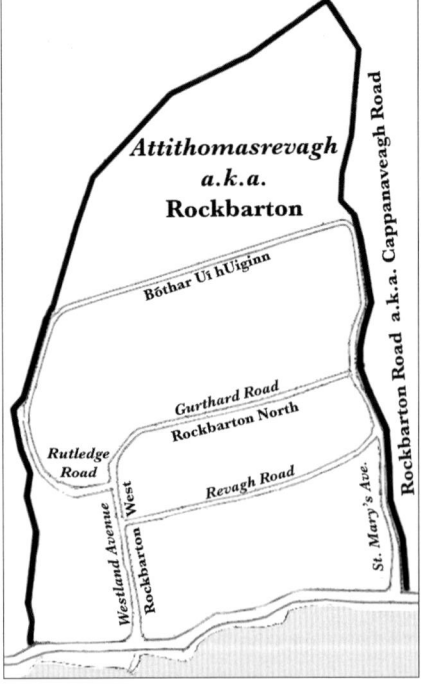

121. The tall four-pillared entrance to Mr. Barton's estate, at what is now Rockbarton Road, towers over the strolling shawled women, and dwarfs the more sober white-capped pillared entrance to what is now Dalysfort Road at Cappanaveagh.

122. An elegant road layout was designed and constructed at Mr. Barton's newly purchased townland – in the early 1850s – to accommodate the building of Bathing Lodges. A mixture of road names is here added, with 19th century designations appearing in italics.

Two parallel south-north roads, opening at the seafront, were constructed. That pair still exist today. The westerly roadway at the current Salthill Hotel is now called Rockbarton West, though it was known in 1875 as Westland Avenue.[62] The easterly roadway, by Leisureland today, was built along the border with Cappanaveagh and follows the contours of that particular boundary. That pathway was, for a time, described as St. Mary's Avenue, for it served – and yet serves – as an access route to St. Mary's bathing lodge. Mr. Gerald Bartley, T.D., a Fianna Fáil Government minister and long-standing bungalow resident on that particular road, which skirted neighbouring townlands, always gave his address as Cappanaveagh Road. It was in 1958 that Galway Borough Council announced the 'extension of Rockbarton Road at Cappanaveagh – 143 lineal yards.'[63] That proposal was published in the year following the opening of Pearse Stadium, and the extended road would (a) eventually join with Dr. Mannix Road, and (b) facilitate the construction of the house row, which now overlooks the eastern main-gate boundary wall of the stadium. When a discussion ensued on the naming of the road, a local plebiscite opted for the 'Rockbarton' option. However, a compromise – of sorts – is enshrined in today's road signs where that particular thoroughfare is identified as Rockbarton Road *as Béarla* and *Bóthar Cheapach na bhFiach* (Cappanaveagh) *as Gaeilge*.

123. Road sign at Leisureland before 2014 storm.

Rockbarton's principal access routes were complemented and crossed by three parallel west-east roads that are today represented by (a) Revagh Road, (b) Rockbarton North (once called Gurthard Road), and (c) Bóthar Uí hUiginn, the road that borders the southern – seated stand – wing of Pearse Stadium. The elegant alignment of those same boulevards was described in 1853: *The roads leading from the two entrances are thirty feet wide. After gradually ascending to the highest level of the villa grounds, they wind with a gentle curve round the entire, and form a beautiful circular road nearly two English miles in length. There are three parallel roads intersecting the grounds at convenient distances…The works are being rapidly pushed on to completion, under the able superintendence of Mr. Molloy, C.E., who has displayed great skill and taste laying out the several plots, and an energy and activity truly wonderful in pushing on the works through the very unfavourable weather.*[64]

Bóthar Uí hUiginn – a 20th century naming

While the Cappanaveagh name can be traced to 1557 and Rockbarton to the mid-19th century, *Bóthar Uí hUiginn* is a more recent coinage. That road – which abuts the southern side of Pearse Stadium – was named in honour of Michael O'Higgins. It was while watching the 1964 All Ireland Football final on television that Councillor Mícheál O hUiginn passed away at his Taylor's Hill home. Mícheál was himself a double All Ireland winner. Having captained Galway to senior football glory in 1934, that successful side became the first Galway team to visit the United States. Mícheál's second Celtic Cross was won in 1938. He enjoyed Sigerson Cup success with U.C.G. and also represented Connacht in the capturing of Railway Cup medals in 1934, 1936 and 1938. In a local context, Michael O'Higgins was a founding member and loyal supporter of St. Michael's G.A.A. club. His sporting stature and the proximity of an un-named road to a new G.A.A. stadium contributed to the designation of *Bóthar Uí hUiginn*. Michael was also centrally involved in the business and political life of the city. A principal in the wholesale and manufacturing firm of *Tomás Ó hUiginn agus a Chomh. Teo.* on Rahoon Road, Mícheál Ó hUiginn won a Corporation seat for Fianna Fáil in 1955 and was still serving at the time of his premature passing, at the age of fifty one.[65] He was a member of the Chamber of Commerce, and his family's love for all things Irish is still reflected in the Gaelic signage that today (2018) adorns the company's Shantalla premises. His son, also Mícheál, subsequently served on the Borough Council and was elected Mayor of Galway on three occasions – in 1972, 1979 and 1995. *Bóthar Uí hUiginn* was reported to have been 'in very bad repair' in March, 1967, when renovative work – costing £1,000 – was proposed by Alderman Thomas Tierney, who, later in that same year, became the first Labour Mayor of Galway.[66]

Mícheál Ó hUiginn was not the only famed footballer to die watching the 1964 All Ireland final, for Mr. Michael Donnellen T.D. of the legendary Dunmore sporting dynasty – who was sitting in the Hogan Stand – also passed away that day. Mick Donnellan was a member of the first Galway team to win a senior All Ireland in 1925, and he captained the first Connacht Team to win the Railway Cup in 1934. He also captained Galway in the 1933 football final, his last big game in Croke Park. The pathos of the circumstances surrounding the 1964 death of Michael Donnellan was captured in a *Connacht Tribune* report: 'His son, the Galway Captain John was unaware of the tragedy until the final cheers had died away some time after the last whistle. His second son, Pat, a team substitute, was also unaware of his father's death until after the game.'[67] A farmer, Mr. Michael Donnellan first entered politics in 1927, when he became a member of Galway County Council. Twelve years later he founded *Clann na Talmhan*, a political movement that represented the views and needs of small farmers in the West of Ireland. He was first elected to Dáil Éireann in 1943 and went on to win six successive General Election contests, over his 21 years in the *Oireachtas*. He served as Parliamentary Secretary to the Minister for Finance in the 13th (1948–1951) and 15th Dáil (1954–1957).

Two of Michael Donnellan's sons, John and Pat, were part of Galway's famous three-in-a-row 1960's success, while his grandsons, Michael and John, also claimed

Celtic crosses. Michael won All Ireland senior medals with Galway in 1998 and 2001, with his brother, John, earning his reward – as a playing squad member – during the successful 2001 campaign. Michael subsequently starred for Salthill-Knocknacarra in the County Final victory of 2005 and the All-Ireland Club success of the following year.

Promenade Gates Knocked

Rockbarton's imposing gated entrances of 1853 stood sentinel guard right up to the 1940s, when they were eventually knocked at the straightening – and widening – of the promenade. The neighbouring Cappanaveagh townland, not to be outdone, boasted a gated entrance at what came to be called Dalysfort Road. Such gates, which appear in old maps of the place, indicate the private nature of the estates they guarded and were, most likely, annually closed on designated days to assert that privacy.

The 'massive cut stone gate piers' at Westland Avenue a.k.a. Rockbarton West, that led to Barfield (Salthill Hotel), stood directly across from the first shelter on Salthill's promenade, the sloped roof corner of which is shown – to the right – in figure 124. This 1944 *Connacht Sentinel* photograph was taken at the time of the promenade's widening, when the pillared entrances to Rockbarton were cleared away. Under construction, further inland, was a new promenade wall that is visible to the left.

While Mr. Barton, as purchaser and financier, was undoubtedly the man behind the 'Rockbarton' enterprise, the expertise of four other men – Messrs. Roberts, Molloy, Frazer and Madden – was employed to deliver the new land-

124. Construction of a new prom wall to the left, before Mr. Barton's pillars and wall were demolished in the 1940s, to accommodate a widening of Salthill's promenade. (Courtesy of *Connacht Tribune*.)

lord's vision. Mr. Frazer was the landscape gardener, who was supplied with trees and shrubs by Mr. Madden. The on-site overseeing presence was civil engineer, Mr. William Molloy, and Mr. Roberts' architectural flair was reflected in the building of bathing lodges, which were also described as marine villas. 'All the beautiful villas which adorn the place owe their origin to his fertile mind' was the 1864 *Irish Times'* record of Mr. Samuel U. Roberts' contribution to the beautification of Salthill.[68] Two 1857 *Galway Vindicator* advertisements – on the one page – provide an example of the pervasiveness of Mr. Roberts' involvement in Bathing Lodge development at the place. To be let or sold was St. Mary's, 'lately built by T.H. Barton Esq.,' while The Retreat, which 'had been lately built on the property of Thomas H. Barton Esq.' was available for letting. One of the people to be contacted in the latter case was S.U. Roberts, Esq., C.E., at the neighbouring Brinkwater lodge.[69]

Though built as Bathing Lodges to cater for tourists, Rockbarton's fine houses were principally occupied by professors from the new Queen's College, which had opened a mere three years before Thomas H. Barton purchased his Salthill holding. Value for money was offered by Encumbered Estate auctions; the 1851 completion of a Dublin–Galway train line facilitated his investment; the law of the land supported his evictions; and the opening of a university, at the tail end of the land's greatest famine, provided Salthill's new landlord with top class tenants.

Mr. Thomas Henry Barton

Thomas Henry Barton was born in 1816, the youngest son of High Sheriff Dunbar Barton and Elizabeth Riall of Rochestown, Co. Tipperary. The family owned a substantial land bank in the Premier County. Thomas, who was called to the bar in 1844, married Hon. Charlotte Plunket, the daughter of the 3rd Baron Plunket of Newton on 6 January, 1853. Number 6 Fitzwilliam-square South was the barrister's Dublin address in 1858, which changed some years later to 7 De-vesci Terrace, Kingstown. He subsequently resided at Longford Terrace in Monkstown. In 1866, the third edition of *The New Practice of the Civil Bill Courts,* by T.H. Barton A.M., Professor of Constitutional and Crown Law at the King's Inns, was extensively advertised for sale.[70] In that same year the Lord Chancellor appointed Thomas as Chairman of the Kildare October sessions and he became Divisional Magistrate for Dublin in the following year. According to an 1876 landowners of Ireland list, Thomas H. Barton, with an address at 22 Longford-terrace, Dublin, owned 679 acres in Co. Tipperary, with a valuation of £495.

During his relatively short Galway enterprise, Mr. Barton became involved in local affairs. He was a delegate member of 'noblemen and gentlemen' received by the Lord Lieutenant in May 1861 on the subject of a Galway postal subsidy.

In a dramatic incident at Salt Hill, in July 1856, Thomas Barton showed courage and humanity when saving a woman, who was seen to sink beneath the waves. Despite 'labouring under temporary lameness from an accident,' Thomas 'at once plunged into the sea and with the assistance of Constable Quinn, of Galway, succeeded in pulling the half-dead lady ashore.' Three doctors – Croker, King and England – who were near at hand, rendered aid and after 'two hours of suspended animation she eventually recovered.'[71] Large crowds of 'country men' who were standing about had refused Barton's request to enter the sea. Their reluctance prompted different reactions in two press reports of the incident. The *Nenagh Guardian* focused on the courageous conduct of Mr. Barton and Constable Quinn, in contrast to the passivity of rustic onlookers. No allowance was made for the dilemma of the spectators. The *Galway Vindicator*, on the other hand, adopted a more charitable view of the countrymen's inaction, stating that 'they were only sojourners for the time being from the inland country for the benefit of bathing, and they entertain a great dread of the sea to which they are unaccustomed, especially when it rolls and swells as it did yesterday during the accident,'[72] The Tipperary newspaper report, for the most part, was word for word consistent with the Galway telling of the event, so it is clear that the Nenagh editor lifted the story from the *Vindicator*, but excised any excuse for the hesitant countrymen. As Barton originally hailed from the Premier County, the local man had to be properly fêted. 'Spin' might be a modern media term, but nuanced reporting is certainly not new.

On home soil Mr. Barton contested, as a Conservative, the General Election of 1852 for the Clonmel Borough, but was easily defeated, taking a mere 84 votes to 182 for the Honourable Cecil John Lawless, who won the seat for the Liberal Party.[73] Barton's national profile increased when he supported the cause of William Smith O'Brien, the Young Ireland leader who was jailed in Tasmania. During Smith's imprisonment abroad, Barton became one of his most loyal supporters, acting as one of four secretaries who organised an 1852 memorial to the Lord Lieutenant; 'to entreat the royal clemency on behalf of William Smith O'Brien and his Companions in penal exile.'[74] In 1858 when the Pacific, a 'noble steam ship' sailed on its first voyage from Galway to New York, carrying the mails, a 'party arrived at the dock whose presence elicited enthusiasm and every demonstration of respect.'[75] The members of that party were William Smith O'Brien, accompanied by Francis Comyn Esq. and T.H. Barton Esq. A statue to William Smith O'Brien stands on O'Connell Street, Dublin, today.

The eldest of Thomas Henry's children, Right Honourable Dunbar Plunket Barton, first and last Baronet, was invested as King's Council (Ireland); served as an Irish Unionist M.P. for Mid-Armagh from 1891 to 1900; and was both a High Court Judge and Judge of the Chancery Division. Dunbar also held the office of Senator at the National University of Ireland from 1909 until his death in 1937.

125. The signatures of Thomas Henry Barton and Charlotte Plunket on 6 January, 1853; the day of their marriage. To the right their eldest son, Sir Dunbar Plunket Barton (1853-1937), M.P. for Mid-Armagh (1891-1900), as caricatured by *Spy* (Leslie Ward) in *Vanity Fair*, 7 April, 1898.

Thomas Henry Barton LL.D. died at the age of 62, on 19 April, 1878, at his Monkstown residence. The *Freeman's Journal* noted in its obituary piece that Barton was a 'brother-in-law of the present Lord Plunket.'[76] An *Irish Times* piece referenced his friendship with the Lord Chief Justice Whiteside. In fact, James Whiteside was Barton's witness at his marriage to Charlotte Plunket in 1853. The *Irish Times*' report also opined that the lingering illness to which Thomas Henry had succumbed 'displayed itself in his countenance, and many erroneously attributed to...a haughty disposition that which was principally occasioned by weakness of constitution, and that disinclination for a display of warmth of manner which is often more effusive than genuine.'[77] Tribute was further paid to his 'equable temperament' and 'anxiety to administer justice impartially.' He may not have been so fondly remembered by displaced Attithomasrevagh tenants.

Having said that, Thomas Barton is still recalled in the surname he left to the place. His desire to be identified with his new land mass was evident, as we have seen, in the early naming of Barton Lodges. Rockbarton was poised, as early as March 1862, to replace Attithomasrevagh as the townland's name. In a property deed involving Barton and George Johnston Allman, a parcel of land was described as being situated 'in the Townland of Rockbarton, otherwise Attithomasrevagh.' The fact that Rockbarton, as a Galway townland, was so soon entered into a legal document indicates that it was lawyer Thomas Henry himself who titled the place. Other Salthill purchasers sought to emulate Barton by having their names attached to their properties, including the Blake Forster family at Cappanaveagh. It was on 5 August, 1871, that Thomas Barton's place of residence was given in the *Tuam Herald* as 'Rockbarton,' the first public use of that Salthill address to have come to this study's attention. The new place name was then becoming established in Galway and Grey Thomas' slide into obscurity had begun. *Bhí Áit Tighe Thomáis Riabhach ag sleamhnú ó chuimhne na ndaoine.* Another *Tomás*, Mr. Thomas Henry Barton, had usurped him.

The Rutledge Legacy

George Rutledge was a second man to frank his name on Attithomasrevagh. His family's success can be traced back to a James Rutledge who left Mayo for France in 1691 with 'the defeated Irish troops. Like many army officers, he later made the transition to trade in order to survive.' The Rutledge fortune was made at Nantes, where other Galway family names also featured in trading triumphs; Joyce, French and Browne.[78] In 1858, George Rutledge, a significant landowner in a number of counties, was renting Revagh on the Salthill sea-front from Thomas Barton. He must have been pleased with his investment, for in the following year George leased – for 999 years – a parcel of land centred on the site of today's Salthill Hotel. He – like Mr. Barton – may have been aware of an 1852 *Galway Packet* article, which advised that the area might be 'divided into small lots or terraces somewhat after the manner of Kingstown, Killiney, Dalkey, Tramore, Kilkee, or the Cork river.'[79] It was on his second parcel of leased land that Rutledge built the elegant five house terrace, which retains his surname to the present day. St. Ronan's was the name given to the detached residence he built nearby. George Rutledge was – as we have earlier seen – the man who donated a promenade site for the building of Salthill's Wesleyan Church / Meeting House in 1862.

Mr. Rutledge's principal Galway trade was as an ironmonger and seed merchant at 11 High Street and Eyre Square.[80] He also opened a new Coach Factory at Victoria Place in 1855,[81] and served as a Grand Jury member in 1861. Interested in racing, one of his horses, Colleen Bawn, ran at the Castlebar meet in 1868. It was in December of that same year that he died, at 50 years of age, after 'an illness in fever of about a fortnight.' Tribute was paid to George Rutledge on his passing: 'He was a most industrious and respectable man and erected many of the handsomest buildings in the suburbs'[82] Not only was he considered a loss to his wife and family, but to the town itself. Mr. George Rutledge was interred in the very neat little cemetery that adjoined the Wesleyan Chapel on Victoria Road.

His widow, Mrs. Rebecca Rutledge, continued to run the family's ironmonger trade on High Street[83] and a seed enterprise at 22 Shop Street.[84] It was in November 1875 that she placed her Salthill holding for sale in three lots at a Landed Estate Court. Michael Hennessy purchased Lot 1 – Revagh for £585, with James Campbell acquiring Lot 2 – which included Barfield – for £650. Rebecca held

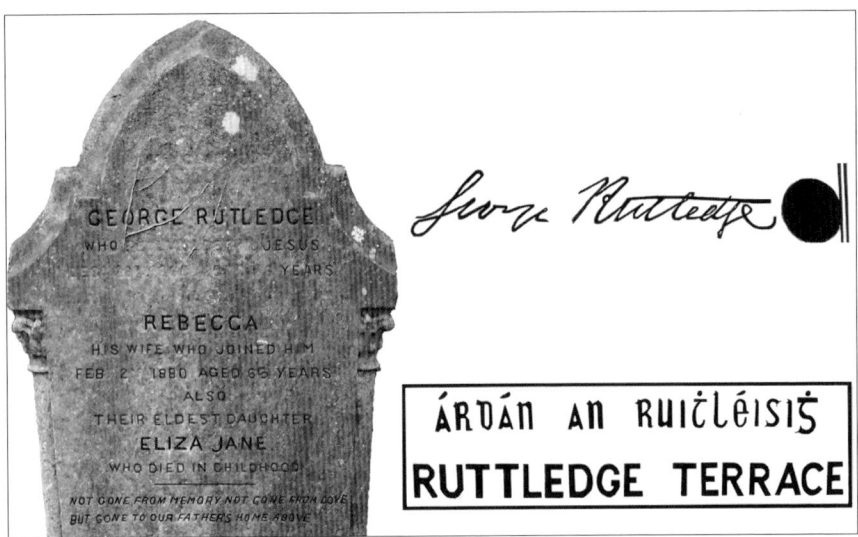

126. Rutledge headstone at rear of present day (2018) United Methodist Presbyterian Church at Queen Street, with George Rutledge's signature to an 1861 indenture, and public signage at Rockbarton.

on to Lot 3, Rutledge Terrace, and was occupier of one of the residences up to her death, at 65 years of age, in 1880. The Rutledge name, however, survives in the stylishly terraced residences she and her husband left to Rockbarton. While public signage and Google Maps today include a double 't' in the spelling of 'Ru**tt**ledge Terrace,' the shorter – single 't' – form was the one used by the couple who developed the house row, as can be seen in the accompanying headstone image and signature. That spelling inconsistency is not new, for 'Ru**tt**ledge Road' appeared in a number of 19th century maps of the area.

Chapter 15

POLLNAROOMA EAST OF NUMEROUS 19TH CENTURY CLEARANCES

The townland's name has many spellings and its earliest written appearance, according to Dr. T. S. Ó Máille, was as 'Pollioomy' in the Terrier to Petty's 1657 Map.[1] James Hardiman noted that 'One of the ancient Irish sept of the O'Hallorans...were the original proprietors of the entire district' which included the 'the estate of Poulnaromhy,' before the Skerrett family purchased it.[2] That was true for Finyn Halluran, who was admitted to the freedom of Galway on 11th July, 1688 at Mr. Mayor's house...had lands mortgaged to him in 1680 by Roderic O' Flaherty, the author of *Iar-Connacht*. 'Nicholas Lynch Fitz Marcus of Barney [Barna]...released for the sum of £83 to Ffinyne Hallorane in 1681 parts of Pollneromy.'[3] The Skerrett family, which succeeded the O'Halloran clan at Pollnarooma was 'established in the barony of Clare from the 17th century. Three sons of Dominick Skerrett, Mayor of Galway in 1642, founded the Skerrett families of Carnacrow, Dangan and Ballinaduff...In the 1870s the Skerretts owned 3,733 acres in county Galway and 969 acres in county Dublin.'[4] Burke's *Landed Gentry of Ireland* 1899 states that the Skerrett family 'was originally settled in Galway and formed one of the thirteen tribes of that ancient town.'[5] O'Halloran initially, and Skerrett secondly were the principal Pollnarooma landholder families, before names like Sloper, Persse and Lord Clanmorris laid claim to the place. The Skerrett family did not depart the locality on selling the townland in 1803, for Anthony Skerrett was in residence at nearby Kingston House in 1845.[6]

The Pollnarooma townland was at some stage split in two and an 1812 census recorded returns for 'Poulnaromhy' and 'Skerrett's Poulnarohmy.' Skerrett's half was to become Pollnarooma East by 1855, as confirmed by an early 19th century transaction which involved an 1803 lease made between 'William Skerrett of Poulneroma ...Galway, Gentleman, of the one part and Constantine Sloper of Galway...Merchant, of the other part.'[7] That agreement related to land in what was later described as the Pollnaroooma East division.

The Sloper Family

Before moving further with the story of Pollnarooma East, it is important to look at the Sloper family's involvement with the area. Having taken charge of Pollnarooma East in 1803, the family's interest in the townland was sold seventeen years later to Lord Clanmorris. Sloper ties with the place, however, did not cease on that sale, for the family continued to occupy a two acre plot on the Taylor's Hill side of Pollnarooma East. Family members were major stakeholders in the general *Bóthar Ard* hinterland, and a Sloper involvement was most important to the tale of nearby Tievegarriff. The Slopers represented a leading merchant-cum-political presence, both in the town, and on Taylor's Hill, where they developed many fine residences. A succession of men named Constantine Sloper operated in Galway throughout the 19th century. It was the first of that century's Constantine line who purchased Pollnarooma East at Salthill in 1803 from Mr. Skerrett. Among the residences identified with Sloper occupiers – or lessors – were; Sea View at Tievegarriff, which was later purchased by the Dominican Nuns; a Pollnarooma East house that came to be called Sea Park; Mount Eaton at Tievegarriff, as well as Rahoon Lodge; Wellfield; and 'Bath Lodge, otherwise Rape Park, otherwise Kingstown House and Demesne, in the County of the Town of Galway.'[8] Bath Lodge and Kingstown House stood on the northern side of the current Kingston Road, and the Patrician monastery currently occupies the original Kingstown House site. The Sloper family's business empire was centred on the Galway dock area and an 1818 deed of lease, between Constantine Sloper and Robert Hedges Eyre of Macroom Castle, gave Sloper 'the ground with warehouse and stone house on the north side of Merchant's Road leading from the Square to the Long Walk including the site of the town wall.' On a Sunday evening in the autumn of 1824, Mr. Constantine Sloper passed away 'at his house in Flood Street... the integrity of whose life and amiable disposition have rendered his death a matter of very general regret.'[9]

The three youngest of Constantine's sons were named William, Richard, and Constantine. It appears that it was the latter pair who became most involved in Galway trading circles, and the Sloper family's involvement with trans-Atlantic passenger transport preceded the Great Famine. In 1840, for example, when *Midas* was advertised as the first spring ship for America, Constantine Sloper was the man to contact.[10] As an Ireland–New World passenger trade was primarily a one-way journey at that time, the custom was to ferry goods home on the return leg. Constantine, unhappy in 1840 with the charges levied on him for landing timber at Forthill, raised the issue with the Harbour Commissioners.[11] Five years later the timber laden *Midas* was lost near Stromness in Scotland, and though the 'Captain and crew endured the greatest privations...providence spared their lives.'[12] That ill fated vessel was returning from St. John's, New Brunswick.

It was in 1844 that Constantine Sloper of Galway wed 'Jane, second daughter of the late William Grieves, Esq. London.'[13] Mr. Sloper was not to enjoy a long marriage, for Constantine's death was announced in December, 1848: 'At his residence, Back-street, of fever, in the 46th year of his age, Constantine Sloper, Esq., Merchant, and a Member of the Board of Town Commissioners. In his general intercourse through life he secured for himself the respect and esteem of his fellow-citizens, from his urbanity of manners and strict adherence to honor and integrity.'[14] Mr. Sloper's death from fever – at a young age – gave proof to the fact that it was not only the poor who fell prey to the horror of famine times. Following Constantine's death, Richard Sloper of Kingston offered for letting the dwelling house, stores and yard at Merchant's Road and Back Street, where the 'well established General Mercantile Business of the late Proprietor' included an extensive Timber and Iron trade.[15]

Richard Sloper Esq. owned a shop and warehouse at the 'corner of Cross-street and Bridge-street, Galway,' where 'superior Port and Sherry Wines,' directly imported from Cadiz and Oporto were on offer in July 1836.[16] By the following year that business in wine and grocery, which had operated for sixty years, was offered for rent.[17] In 1861 Nicholas J. Bodkin, Esq., eldest son of Walter Bodkin, Esq. of Omey, Clifden married Marcella Josephine, daughter of Richard Sloper Esq. of Sea View, Galway.[18] That Bodkin-Sloper union created a strong connection with Connemara and resulted in at least one Sloper appearance at a Clifden Petty Court Session, which centred on a minor monetary issue.[19]

Richard Sloper's residencies were ever changing, a feature of well heeled families at the time. His wife gave birth to a daughter at Sea View in 1845; Bath Lodge was his abode from August 1848; the 1860s were spent at what later became Sea Park, while Wellfield was the address recorded on his 1879 death. A small geographical area encompassed all of those residences in the Boherard-Kingston locality. Wellfield stood on the same – northern – side of the Taylor's Hill road as Merville Lodge, and a short distance closer to town than the impressive Merville, a residence that still stands today on Boherard **(fig.152)**. Richard Sloper, like his father before him, served for many years as a Town Grand Jury member. At an 1871 meeting he gave rise to some amusement, by speaking in favour of an amendment and then voting against it.[20]

The *Galway Vindicator*'s record of Richard Sloper's 1879 passing read:

We regret to announce the death of Richard Sloper Esq. which melancholy event took place at his residence, Wellfield, near the city on the 18th inst. – after a short illness, during which he was fortified by the rites of holy Church. Mr. Sloper was much respected by all who knew him as an upright honest man. Yesterday his remains were interred in the family vault at the West Cemetery. The deceased gentleman was in the 75th year of his age. – R.I.P.[21]

A son of Richard Sloper, Taylor's Hill, Galway, died in January 1902.[22] He was Doctor Constantine William Sloper, who appears to have been twice recorded in the census returns of the previous year. There were five returns nationwide by people with a Sloper surname in 1901. Two entries were uncanny in their similarity. One listed 'Cornealus,' while the other noted 'Cornelius' Sloper. Both identified a Roman Catholic Medical Practitioner, aged 55, who was born in Galway City. One was recorded at his Dublin home, while the second entry listed Cornelius as a visitor to the home of a medical doctor, Patrick Charles Gorham at Main Street, Clifden. Though a discrepancy in the Christian name spelling exists, that divergence might easily be explained by the Connemara entry being filled by the visitor's Clifden host. It appears plausible that the same doctor was doubly listed – on either side of the island. If that is true, then the total number of people with a Sloper surname – in the entire country – amounted to four in 1901. It is salutary to note that a family of substantial Galway merchants, throughout a good part of the 1800s, no longer held sway at the century's end. Their time and memory had faded.

Doctor Constantine was 56 years old when he died in 1902, while his father, Richard, had lived a lengthier three quarters of a century. Though Richard reached a good age for the 19th century in which he lived, one of his employees – who hardly enjoyed a merchant's comforts – easily surpassed Mr. Sloper in the longevity stakes. The *Tuam Herald* recorded Mr. Michael Hennessy's passing in 1894:

> An old man named Michael Hennessy, a native of William Street West, Galway has just died at the Workhouse Hospital at the patriarchal age of 107 years. The deceased has been for over 46 years in the employment of the late Richard Sloper, Taylor's Hill Galway. Up to a few months ago this old resident of Galway had been in the best of health, and in possession of all his faculties, and could tell stirring tales of the days of his youth, having a clear recollection of the deeds of the first Napoleon and the bitter days of '98. At the beginning of the present year he got an attack of influenza, which he at first treated as an ordinary cold, but his frail system was not able to cope with the severe complaint from which he was suffering, and although he received the best care and attention while in hospital from Dr. Lydon and the good nuns of the institution, he succumbed to the attack, and ended his long life within the walls of the workhouse.[23]

Population falls at Pollnarooma East

In terms of tenant clearances, Pollnarooma East was to suffer more than any other Salthill townland. Hardiman claimed that 1812 census returns offered the most accurate estimate of the population of Galway at that time. By that census tally there were then 30 families, of which 27 were involved in agriculture, living in 30 inhabited houses at 'Skerrett's Poulnarohmy.' No families were employed in Trade Manufactures or Handicraft, and the community was made up of 112 males and 126 females, which amounted to a sizable population of 238 inhabitants.[24] The

127. Seamount Lodge, a hospital – nursing home during the 20th century.

Tithe Applotment record of 1834 listed a mere seven landholders in 'Poulnarooma,' but that tally did not; (a) include family members; (b) account for any landholder under one acre nor (c) distinguish between the East and West townland divisions.

That East-West divide was noted in 1839, when there was still a solid population in the Pollnarooma East townland. At that time John O'Donovan recorded 14 tenants and 10 cottiers paying £2-2s. per acre for land described as 'light, moory and some parts gravel[l]y, producing potatoes, oats and flax.' Inhabitants were described as poor with only one two storey house situated in Pollnarooma East. That was Seamount Lodge, which was then occupied by Burton Persse, Esq. (1779–1859). Though Seamount and its attendant outbuildings represented the place's predominant structural feature; clacháns at the northern and southern boundaries of the townland are worth noting (**fig.115**). Facing the sea on the southern – *Bóthar na Trá* – side was a village called Ballynacarrickadoo, a name that represented a bowdlerised Anglicisation of *Baile na Carraige Duibhe* or Blackrock Village. A line of buildings ran, from a site once occupied by the Craughwell family, which stood on the present day vacant plot that directly faces the diving board, to the corner of what became known as Threadneedle Road; in other words along the line of the present day Ocean Towers' apartment block. Other buildings stood behind that line. A second house cluster stood at the northern end of the townland. Five premises, facing onto Boherard, ran in a row east of the junction which connects the present day Threadneedle Road with Taylor's Hill. Four other buildings stood behind them. To the west of that same junction three well spaced dwellings faced *an Bóthar Ard*. Apart from road-hugging dwellings/cabins at the polar – northern and southern – ends of Pollnarooma East, the rest of the townland was totally free of buildings, with the notable exception of Seamount Lodge.

There is no surprise in the presence of a Persse family member at Seamount in 1839, as the townland was, for the greater part of the 19th century, identified with two closely linked landed families: Bingham and Persse. Burton de Burgh Persse, the man who occupied Sea Mount in 1839, was the son of Burton Persse (1746–1831) and Sarah Pennefather. Master of the Moyode estate, Burton, who was closely identified with the Newcastle Distillery, was also central to a Persse family row that spanned the greater part of the 19th century, and is later described in this narrative. Patrick Melvin has noted that Moyode's Burton Persse gave reductions of 20-30% on his Galway, Roscommon, Kilkenny and King's County estates during the Great Famine.[25] Burton's son, Henry Sadleir Persse, was not, alas, to replicate his father's generosity in 1870's dealings with his Salthill tenants.

Bingham – Lord Clanmorris Line at Salthill: One to Five

The Bingham surname might not be as well known as the Persse appellation, for it was usually hidden under a Clanmorris title. John O' Donovan's Field Books record the owner of the Pollnarooma townland as Lord Clanmorris, New Brook, Co. Mayo. That lordly designation was first created in 1800 for John Bingham of Foxford, whose family held extensive lands, principally in the counties of Mayo and Galway. In 1876, a total of 12,337 acres in County Mayo, 5,295 acres in County Galway and 479 acres in the town of Galway belonged to the Bingham estate. As the title belonged to the Peerage of Ireland, Lord Clanmorris was not entitled to a seat in the House of Lords at Westminster. Four men held the Lord Clanmorris title during the Bingham tenure at Pollnarooma.

First Lord Clanmorris (1800–1821)
– JOHN BINGHAM (1762–1821)
The first was John Bingham. Having represented Tuam from 1797 to 1800, he exchanged his seat in 'that rotten borough' for £8,000 and an Irish peerage.[26] Mr. John Bingham became the first Baron Clanmorris of Newbrook on 31 July, 1800. A score of years later, some months before he died, he bought a seaside townland called 'Poulnaroma' for £1,400 from Constantine Sloper, a Galway merchant.

Second Lord Clanmorris (1821–1829)
– CHARLES BARRY BINGHAM (1796–1829)
'The Handsomest Man in Ireland'
John Bingham was followed by his eldest son, Charles Barry Bingham, who was only twenty five years old on becoming the 2nd Lord Clanmorris. Reputed to be 'the handsomest man in Ireland,'[27] Charles passed away at Plymouth on board his

yacht *Watersprite* in June 1829. With less than nine years to enjoy the benefit of his title, Charles Barry Bingham died without issue.

Third Lord Clanmorris (1829–1847)
– DENIS ARTHUR BINGHAM (1808–1847)
Famed Horseman

As Charles died without an heir, the lordly Bingham responsibility fell to his brother, Denis Arthur, who became the Clanmorris baron referred to by O'Donovan in his Field Book reports. Born in 1808, Denis Bingham was a young man of 18, who was implicated in the murder of Jeremiah O'Sullivan, a father of three, which took place during riotous 1826 election behaviour at Eyre Square. As Mr. James Daly was assured of winning the first seat of an upcoming Parliamentary ballot, the real contest was between Richard Martin (Humanity Dick) and James Staunton Lambert, who were seeking to fill the second position. Dr. John Cunningham has documented how 'intimidation and a degree of violence' were central features of Galway plebiscites,[28] with paid mobs looking to advance their candidates' chances. In this instance, a house was burned with the loss of one life and some days later, near Kilroy's Hotel at Eyre Square, Thomas Dillon Lambert, a brother of candidate James, shot and killed Mr. Jeremiah O'Sullivan, a Richard Martin supporter. At the subsequent trial, 'which excited an interest unparalleled in the annals of this county,' it was alleged that 'the said Denis Arthur Bingham and the several other prisoners arraigned, were then and there aiding and assisting the said Thomas Dillon Lambert.'[29] The accused cohort was acquitted and though James Lambert lost the election, he succeeded in having the result overturned. That was on petition to the House of Commons, 'because of the tactics employed and the close outcome.'[30] A Parliamentary Enquiry into that plebiscite chronicled the fierce and fiery tenor of Galway's election culture.

Three years after that court scare, Denis Arthur reached his majority and took up the Clanmorris title, which he held until his own demise in 1847. Denis Arthur was considered to have been a great sportsman and a passage from an 1895 *Daily Telegraph* article, by the Hon. F. Lawley, recalled the third baron's prowess in the equine world:

> At that time Lord Clanmorris possessed the best stud of hunters and steeplechasers that Ireland contained. Amongst them were included that celebrated steeplechaser Jerry, so well known in England, and Lancet, whom Lord Clanmorris regarded as better than Jerry. It was notorious that he had again and again refused a thousand guineas (then a great sum) for each of these grand chasers.[31]

Denis Arthur Bingham, whose 1825 marriage was twice solemnised (**p.284**), died on 24 February, 1847 at Rugby, Warwick in his 39th year.

Fourth Lord Clanmorris (1847–1876)
– JOHN CHARLES BINGHAM (1826–1876)
The man who cleared Ballynacarrickadoo and sold Pollnarooma East

John Charles Bingham, who was born in 1826, became the fourth Baron when he attained his majority in November of the year of his father's demise. Though John Charles' elevation occurred in the middle of the Great Famine years, it was reportedly greeted with great festivity in Mayo: 'The town of Foxford presented a gay and animated scene of rejoicing a few nights since, caused by the arrival of Lord Clanmorris, who on his coming of age hastened to visit his tenantry in and about Foxford.'[32] John Charles, despite his youth, was soon appointed Deputy Lieutenant for County Mayo.[33] Great difficulties, however, were experienced by tenants through dark times which impacted on landlords countrywide. Whatever about civic appointments and reported celebrations, the Westport court sessions of 1847 witnessed the serving of a large number of civil bills for non-payment of rent against occupying tenants on the Bingham estate in Mayo. In the following year, Thomas Warren White Esq., who was executor to the third Baron's will, attempted to deliver decrees for rent in County Mayo. However a mob greeted Lord Clanmorris' agent and he was assaulted, his portmanteau opened, and all documents therein destroyed. Mr. White recuperated from his injuries at the residence of Rev. M. Green.[34] John Charles, the man who cleared Ballynacarrickadoo, was also the last Bingham landlord of the townland, which he sold in 1872 to his brother-in-law, Henry Sadleir Persse for £1,400.

Fifth Lord Clanmorris (1876–1916)
– JOHN GEORGE BARRY BINGHAM (1852–1916)
Pollnarooma born but never a landlord at Salthill

John Charles' eldest son, John George Barry Bingham, became the fifth Lord Clanmorris on his father's 1876 passing. Though John George was born in August 1852 at Seamount in Pollnarooma East,[35] he was not to become landlord to the townland of his birth, for – as earlier noted – that property had passed to Persse hands four years before his accession to the family's title. That particular land transfer facilitated the expansion of a Persse presence at Salthill, by allowing Henry S. Persse of Glenarde House add the Pollnarooma East townland to his original Tievegarriff holding, thereby creating an extended and 'delightful' Glenarde Demesne, which was to span three decades.

The Salthill born Etonian and fifth Lord Clanmorris, John George Barry Bingham, who married Matilda Catherine Maude Ward of Bangor, County Down in 1878, was A.D.C. to the Duke of Malborough, Viceroy of Ireland, 1876–1878, and Master of County Galway Foxhounds (The Blazers) 1891–1895.[36] He was refused a motion to annul his bankruptcy in September 1899 at the Belfast Bankruptcy Court,[37] and died in November 1916 at Bangor Castle, Co. Down. Two of his sons fought in the First World War: Lt. Col. John Denis Yelverton Bingham, who was awarded a Distinguished Service Order (1918), was also decorated with the award of Legion of Honour. Another son, Rear-Admiral Hon. Edward Barry Stewart Bingham was awarded the Victoria Cross for his actions at the Battle of Jutland, where he had been taken prisoner. Edward B.S. Bingham was later invested into the Order of the British Empire (O.B.E.), and served as naval Aide-de-Camp to H.M. King George V in 1931.

Famine times at Pollnarooma

The Clanmorris-Bingham estate was under some pressure even before the Great Famine struck, and numerous court cases attest to a strain on resources. Captain Robert Bayly, late of the 60th Rifles, who had won judgement in 1833 for the payment of £2,000 from Denis Arthur Bingham, was still awaiting payment seven years later. An 1840 court sitting was told that Lord Clanmorris 'sought to evade payment of this debt on the grounds that the money for which the bond was passed was won from him at play.' A game of Hazard had been lost in 1833 by Clanmorris, and his counsel, Mr. Brewster Q.C., cited legal Acts which banned excessive gaming, in excusing his client's refusal to pay his bond.[38] Denis Arthur Bingham's £2,000 bet in 1833 was £600 greater than what his father had paid for the Pollnarooma townland thirteen years earlier. That wager represented an example of capricious profligacy, for which some landlords were noted. Perhaps unsurprisingly, an 1843 Chancery Court case – with Denis Arthur as defendant – resulted in several Towns, Lands, Tenements and Premises in the Mayo Demesnes of Newbrook and Kilmain being placed for sale.[39]

Mayo was not the only place where Lord Clanmorris' authority affected tenants. At Salthill the population of Pollnarooma East fell from 131 to 59 during the hungry 1841–1851 decade, with the house count dropping from 22 to 10. It is unlikely that tenants went of their own volition, given a combative Clanmorris approach in Mayo and elsewhere. Two men held the Lord Clanmorris title over the 1845–1850 period, with Denis Arthur Bingham doing so up to his February 1847 death. A pair of ejectment cases in the summer of 1845 highlighted Lord Clanmorris' Galway difficulties. The prosecution of a case involving Lord Clanmorris as plaintiff against 'Egan & several others' by 'the Solicitor for the Receiver, Mr. Wallace' told its own story. A fraught non-payment of rents' backdrop told another. Mr. Wallace, acting 'under the order of the master' said that 'if the parties would pay the rent, possession would not be demanded of them.' Mr. Bath, who was concerned for the defendants, declined under those circumstances to contest the ejectment.'[40] The Clanmorris position appears to have been equitable in that case, though it is unlikely that the defending tenants had the wherewithal to clear their arrears and avoid eviction.

The second case, 'Clanmorris v. Lee,' on the same day, was a little different and quite quizzical. The case centred on the defendant's son, a married man who had – for twelve years – occupied a property, which had originally been let to his father, Mr. Lee. The rent continued to be paid by the father, who was recompensed with an eight shillings annual payment by his son. An ejectment was requested in the case and granted to Lord Clanmorris as plaintiff, despite there being no arrears.

More interestingly, in the hearing of that second case some broader points arose: Though the first Lord Clanmorris purchased the Pollnarooma East lease in 1820 from Constantine Sloper for £1,400, Mr. Sloper was still entitled to an annual £56 stipend. By 1845, the third Lord Clanmorris had to likewise pay a yearly sum to Constantine's successor, Richard Sloper. Denis Arthur Bingham, however, had not paid his annual fee to Sloper, the 'Fee Simple Proprietor,' who was described in court as the 'head landlord.' That indeed he was, for as late as 1855 Richard Sloper was immediate lessor to 53 of the 81 acres in the townland, where he 'occupied' a further two. Richard, who was present at the 1845 hearing, unsuccessfully sought to explain the situation. Mr. Wallace – for the Receiver – then accused Sloper of interfering in the case and suggested that the tenants had 'been induced to withhold payment of their rents.' Mr. Bath, for the defendants, claimed that 'the rent was refused to be taken from us.'[41]

If all the hurled accusations were true, the situation was curious: (a) Mr. Richard Sloper, the 'head landlord' had not been paid by the landlord Clanmorris. (b) Sloper, in turn, was accused of advising the townland's tenants not to pay Clanmorris. (c) The tenants tried to pay Clanmorris but their money was refused. It was a mess and the court evidence did not appear to stack up. The only certain thing was that Mr. Lee was evicted. Though Pollnarooma East was not specifically referenced in reports of the cases described, the Sloper-Clanmorris relationship fits that Salthill townland. Mr. Martin Egan, who was recorded as a tenant of Lord Clanmorris at Salthill in 1834, was most likely the defendant in the 'Clanmorris v. Egan & Others' case of 1845. If not, the man seeking to defend his holding was a relation. It is also highly likely that the evicted Mr. Lee was in some way connected to Mr. James Lee who was accused by Lord Clanmorris – in October, 1852 – of having committed a 'wilful trespass...at Poulnaroma...after being warned to leave same' and did 'unlawfully and forcibly enter and take possession of complainant's house at Poulnaroma last on the 11th inst.'[42]

By 1852 of course, it was the fourth Lord Clanmorris who brought the case, as John Charles Bingham was enjoying the fifth year of his lordly tenure in that year. Aware of Mr. Barton's ambition at neighbouring Attithomasrevagh, the young Clanmorris decided to follow suit in terms of tenant clearing at Pollnarooma East. Though the latter townland's population had fallen to 52 post-famine, there was perceived scope for another tenant clear-out. The *Packet* newspaper, in praising Barton's ambition and enterprise, was also urging Clanmorris to replicate Barton's policy of developing bathing lodges. That investment opportunity was considered by John Charles, for an 1851 advertisement for Seamount Lodge also offered 'about Forty Acres of Land, which might be laid out in plots as desirable sites for Building ground.'[43] Though that particular option was not pursued at Pollnarooma East, an 1852 tenant clearance policy was certainly enforced: 'Forty persons were evicted, this week, for non-payment of rent for their tenements on the Salt Hill road, on the property of Lord Clanmorris. Many of the parties owed as much as six years' rent, besides poor rates and taxes. This property is adjoining Mr. Barton, and we trust it will be laid out in a similar manner.'[44] The reference to tenements on the Salt Hill road indicates that it was John Charles Bingham who delivered

128. Fourth Lord and Lady Clanmorris, photographed in 1865 at Clonbrock House. (Courtesy of National Library of Ireland.)

the final blow to Ballynacarrickadoo, the *clachán* that once stood at Blackrock. How long it stood there has not been ascertained by this study but one suspects that the hamlet boasted a rich history, not in terms of prosperity, but in the wealth of its people and lore. *Baile na Carraige Duibhe* at Pollnarooma East suffered the same sad fate as *Baile Thaidhg Bháin* at Tievegarriff.

John Charles Bingham, photographed above, was the man who cleared the Ballynacarrickadoo hamlet at the prom's end in 1852. The seated Lady Clanmorris' maiden name was Sarah Selena Persse, the daughter of a Persse father and mother. A sister to Henry Sadleir Persse of the Glenarde Estate, she gave birth to the fifth Lord Clanmorris, John George Bingham, at Seamount in August 1852, the year of the neighbouring clearance.

The fourth Lord Clanmorris 'improved' other Galway holdings around the time that he was evicting people at *Bóthar na Trá*. In 1853, for example, he employed Mr. John Madden of Prospect Nurseries, Castleblakeney to effect improvements upon his Claregalway estate, through the planting of a forest and fox cover at Kiniska.[45]

It was to the Bingham family's Galway seat at Gregclare, near Ardrahan, that John Charles' remains were brought when he died at Lismany, Clontuskert in April

1876. A special Athenry–Ardrahan train was run to accommodate the crowds that attended the funeral of a 'lamented Nobleman,' so called by the *Tuam Herald*, which also stated that Lord Clanmorris 'was deservedly esteemed in Galway.' The same newspaper's account of the obsequies described the high regard in which Lord Clanmorris was held by his tenants: *Before the hearse a Procession of the Tenantry of the Estates in Mayo and Galway, and their sons composed of about 800 men was formed four deep and walked to the cemetery in white shoulder scarfs and hat bands. The men had all a well-to-do appearance, were evidently respectable members of the farming class, and all appeared deeply grieved at the serious loss they had sustained in the lamented death of Lord Clanmorris, who without exception was one of the most generous and kind-hearted landlords in Ireland.*[46]

That published paean might well have been disputed by a number of *Bóthar na Trá* evictees. John Charles had been a prominent member of the Galway Blazers and was considered to be 'a capital sportsman and devoted to hunting – he was a great loss to everyone, but especially to the hunt, as he was our best supporter.'[47]

Marriage Conventions and Choices for Landed Offspring

Bingham – Persse Marriage ties

The accompanying chart highlights the marital ties that connected the Bingham and Persse families at Pollnarooma East: Three Bingham landlords of the townland were married to ladies bearing a strong Persse heritage. The fourth Lord Clanmorris' wedding – in 1849 – represented the greatest example of that familial bond, for John Charles Bingham, the son of Maria Helena **Persse**, married Sarah Selina **Persse**, whose mother was Mrs. Matilda **Persse** – née **Persse** (1793–1862), and whose father was Burton **Persse** (1779–1859).

The Bingham-Persse marriage matrix suggests a restricted spouse range within the limited gene pool of Ireland's landed gentry. In a major family row, which ran over decades (1826–1899), the selfish requirements of a Persse father and son to unite the Roxborough and Castleboy estates, pointed to a potential vulnerability for younger siblings. High society daughters and non-elder sons were not always well placed to make 'good' marriages, which might add standing and worth to the family line. Burton De Burgh Persse (1779–1859), for example, fathered 15 children – 8 sons and 7 daughters – over two marriages. Eight of Burton's children married. Of the seven who remained single, two didn't reach adulthood. Four daughters and one son – of marriageable age – never wed. Such large families were not unusual in the Persse line, with Dudley Persse fathering sixteen children over two marriages. One of Dudley's children was Isabella Augusta Persse (1852–1932), considered to have been the 'plain one' among her sisters. In 1880, she became the second wife to widower, William Gregory, a

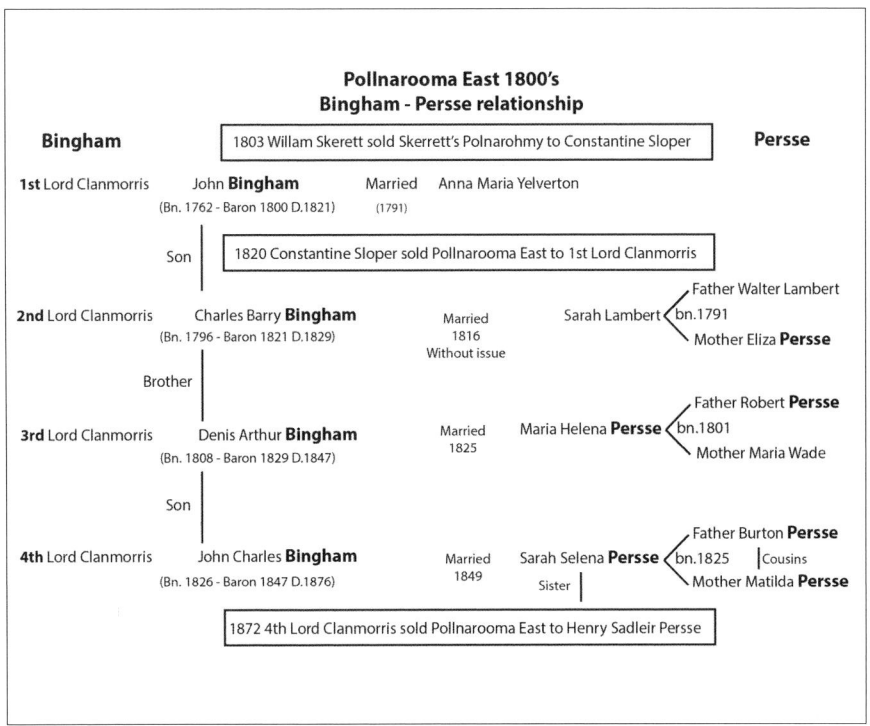

Figure 129.

former Member of Parliament and Governor of Ceylon, who was 35 years her senior. A passing reference to that union, which she subsequently edited out of her *Seventy Years'* biography, was candid in Lady Gregory's forthright recall: 'My mother [was] never quite sure he [Sir William] had not married me as a compliment to her.'[48] The life decisions of landed daughters may, of course, have simply been personal choices, without reference to any of the considerations here discussed, for as Patrick Melvin – in his study of the marriage machinations of landed gentry – has noted, 'daughters certainly appear in many cases to have minds of their own in matters of marriage and remained single if they failed to find a suitable match.'[49]

Advantageous marriages were particularly important to the Persse family, whose origins are not all that clear, despite a family tradition of claiming kinship with a Percy line, which boasted a number of Earls of Northumberland. That connection was paraded in the Persse family's use of the Percy motto: *Esperance en Dieu* – Hope in God.[50] Clergymen appear to have been the early representatives of the family in Ireland, with Rev. Robert Persse arriving in 1602. His grandson, Dudley Persse (1625–1699), who became Dean of Kilmacduagh in 1660, was the founder of the family's fortunes.[51] Having acquired large estates by the mid-18th century, increased prestige – rather than wealth – became important in marital affairs.

The enhanced status of favourable unions was represented in the Persse family's adoption of spouses' surnames, which included Stratford, Brooke, Blakeney, Seymour and Parsons.

Elopement

An amorous marriage of personal choice was represented in a youthful romance, which preceded two 1825 nuptials involving the third Lord Clanmorris. As a minor, Denis Arthur Bingham first eloped with Miss Maria Helena Persse to Scotland, where they wed. On learning of it, Dowager Clanmorris – mother of the groom – refused to recognise the union and headed to the courts, after which the young lovers were placed in confinement. Some time later, the Lord Chancellor 'was pleased to permit them to go at large, on their own recognizances, to make their appearance when called on; and in the mean time not to meet or cohabit together.'[52] A few days later, the marriage was recognised at the Chancery Court and Lady Dowager's case was dismissed. His Lordship, however, 'was also pleased to order that the parties should again go through that ceremony, which accordingly took place on Saturday...the 23d instant, in St. Anne's Church.' The minor Denis Arthur, twice church coupled, was 'allowed an annuity of £2,000 per annum, until his minority shall have ceased.'[53] That doubly-bonded union produced nine children, before Denis Arthur died, aged 39, in 1847.

130. Maria Helena Persse, who eloped with Denis Arthur Bingham to Scotland in 1825. She became Baroness Clanmorris in 1829.

Breach of Promise

The course of true love did not always run true, a reality that no social class – including the gentry – could evade. In December 1867, Rupert George Brady of Myshall, Carlow, a Captain in the 2nd Regiment of Foot, proposed to Sarah Belinda Persse of Mount Vernon on Taylor's Hill. She was daughter to Thomas Moore Persse, who had built the residence that was to later become home to the Catholic Bishops of Galway. Rupert broke off the engagement the following February, and Sarah sued for Breach of Promise, seeking £5,000 in damages. Captain Brady brought the issue to the Court of Queen's Bench in Dublin, seeking to have the case heard anywhere but Galway, where he believed a fair trial was impossible. The reason for Rupert's concern centred on 'the great influence the Persse family had among the special jurors of the county,' particularly as 'strong observations' had been made upon the defendant's conduct at a dinner of the club hunt, where the plaintiff's father was an elder member. In response, Mr. Thomas

Moore Persse said that he only spoke of the court action 'to his family, to his legal advisers, and a few friends.'[54] Despite that Persse assurance, the Chief Justice decided that the hearing be held in Dublin.

Judge George presided some weeks later, when nineteen year old Sarah Persse sued 'by her next friend, Henry Sadleir Persse, against Captain Rupert George Brady.' A 'next friend' protocol was employed when a person represented another, who in Common Law was unable to maintain a suit on his or her own behalf. Sarah's legal 'friend' was her relation and neighbour, Henry Sadleir Persse of Glenarde House. At the Breach of Contract hearing it was explained 'that a day was fixed for the ceremony; that a reasonable time for marrying the plaintiff had elapsed, and that the contract was left unperformed by the defendant.'[55] Responding, 'the defence did not deny the contract to marry, but averred that it was conditional, and not to be carried out until the defendant had obtained the rank of Major in the army, or the consent of his father, J. Beauchamp Brady, and that neither of these events had yet happened.' Following negotiations, a settlement was reached, with plaintiff's counsel making it clear that the action was not taken by Sarah Belinda Persse in pursuit of money, but 'in order to set herself and her family perfectly right in the eyes of the public.'[56] Captain Brady was then required to pay £200 to each of two charities chosen by Miss Persse, and he also had to pay all costs. Two years later – in July 1870 – the 21 year old Miss Sarah Belinda Persse did marry, when she wed Colonel Francis Knatchbull in Dublin. The couple reared three Knatchbull children and Sarah was aged 98 when she died at a Southbourne nursing home in 1947. Her one time *beau*, on the other hand, did reach the rank of Major, but Rupert George Brady 'died in January 1873 at Belgaum Bombay,' two and a half years after his former fiancé had married her Colonel.

Alternative Choices

For society ladies who, through chance or choice, did not marry, church ministry offered an alternative lifestyle. A religious vocation, for some Catholic families, offered unwed daughters protection and comfort through life. A wedding dowry, in some instances, was then supplanted by a sizeable contribution to a chosen convent. Issues of status and economics were at play in that commitment, with substantial dowries allowing Society entrants become 'Choir Nuns' as distinct from 'lay nuns,' who were more accurately described as 'servant sisters.' Members of the latter caste, lacking the wherewithal to muster a dowry, were further disadvantaged by being poorly educated. Camillus Metcalfe, who exposed the culture of convent life in her 2005 publication, *For God's Sake: The Hidden Life of Irish Nuns*, highlighted the hierarchical nature of a veiled order: 'At dinner, you had the superiors at the top table, then the senior sisters, then the ordinary, then the novices. The lay sisters never ate in the community. They had to dine separately.'[57] 'There was a social class system in operation in the convent that designated the lay Sisters, as second class and discriminated against them, by assigning them to the lowliest tasks, while the Choir Sisters were educated and afforded opportunities to work with the public.'[58] The Cultural resources of the institution and its leadership positions were exclusively reserved for the higher order of religious female.[59] In a local context, Frances Grattan, of Grattan Road renown, failed to join the Poor Clare Sisters at Drumshanbo, though her sister, Marian, was successful. While not quite matching a priest in the family, a nun in the clan did carry its own *cachet*.

Protestant ladies, without nunneries, were not without a denominational alternative for, unlike their Catholic sisters, they could wed men of the cloth. That choice was made by members of the O'Hara family, with Emily O'Hara, a sister to Col. O'Hara (1832–1902) of Lenaboy, marrying the Trinity educated Rev. James O'Sullivan of Kerry in the early 1870s.[60] The couple first lived at Palymra Terrace, before moving to Blackrock House a number of years later. In 1890, Dr. James O'Sullivan D.D. was elected the Church of Ireland Bishop of Tuam, Killala and Achonry, which resulted in the couple leaving Blackrock House for The Palace, Tuam. On Mrs. Emily O'Sullivan departing Blackrock House, she was replaced by her elder sister, Anne (Anna) O'Hara, whose married name was Mrs. Lancaster. Anne, like Emily, had also chosen a clergyman, when she married Reverend James Lancaster M.A. in 1856. An O'Hara alliance with clergymen and their families was, of course, nothing new in Galway, for in 1823 'in the Cathedral of Tuam, James O'Hara, Esq. [1796–1838] of West Lodge' wed Anne Le Poer Trench, daughter of the last Archbishop of Tuam.[61] Longstanding O'Hara attachments to the Church of Ireland were perhaps best exemplified in Mrs. Emily O'Sullivan (née O'Hara), when, on her 1904 death, she 'entered into rest in the Palace, Tuam – under the same roof where she was born when her grandfather, Dr. Le Poer Trench, was Archbishop of Tuam.'[62]

It appears that Protestant churchmen were generally considered to be a safe option for daughters, because of the security and status they offered. Not every clergyman, however, found it easy to find a spouse. Clerical rank and location would have been issues worthy of consideration by potential partners. Such matters were important, and one man of the cloth – in search of a soul mate – was keen to point out that any prospective spouse of his would be allowed retain her property assets. The clergyman's location, reputedly beautiful, does appear to have been lightly populated. His 1827 newspaper advertisement, which long preceded online dating sites, read: *A Beneficed Clergyman of fifty, a resident in a beautiful part of the country (but where the object he has now in view is exceedingly difficult of attainment) is really desirous of being introduced to an educated and ladylike woman, of suitable age, whose property may continue at her own disposal. – Address,"* &c.[63]

Courtship and marriage etiquette were undoubtedly different in the past, with a lady's dowry generally playing a central role in most matches. It was not only clergymen, however, who could forego such financial concerns for some suitors placed greater emphasis on other factors, as can be discerned from the following 1873 *Freeman's Journal* advert: **Matrimony** – *A young Gentleman, of prepossessing appearance, aged 27 years, residing in the County Galway, wishes to communicate with a view to matrimony, with a young Lady of engaging manners; she must be young, good looking, and pretty well accomplished; fortune not the slightest object; handsome young widow not objected to; cartes carefully and confidentially returned if not approved of. Address Zed, Post Office, Galway.*[64]

Though the outcome of *Zed*'s quest is uncertain, there is little doubt about the young man's cavalier confidence.

In a secular man's world, the financial situation of sons was not as acute as that of daughters, with other options on offer, including church or military positions. Army life appealed to some landed families, while in the Perrse line, that family's commercial involvement – particularly in the distilling trade – offered a range of good positions to male offspring. Some, however, did choose a military path, including Captain Robert Persse (1833–1921) of the Royal Canadian Rifles, and Lieutenant Cecil De Burgh Persse of the 7th Dragoon Guards, who lost his life in the 1914–1918 war. Others found employment in civil service positions with, for example, Henry S. Persse Jnr. (1818/'26) and Robert D. Persse (1829/'50) serving as postmasters at Galway, and Neptune Persse (1831/'52) filling the same role at Athenry.[65] Status and influence would have contributed to the procurement of such positions. In the case of Mr. Parsons Persse, for example, British postal records have noted that his appointment followed this instruction: *Appoint Mr. Parsons Persse in office in charge of British Mails sent through Foreign Countries, if qualified, on the recommendation of myself. Clanricarde.*[66] That personal 1849 endorsement came from Ulick John de Burgh, Marquess of Clanricarde, who was British Postmaster General (1846/'52), and Lord-Lieutenant of County Galway (1831/'74). Henry Stratford Persse (1769–1833), on the other hand, did not crave civil service roles for his family. Emigration was a career option he favoured, and in 1821 'sent three of his sons to America as he saw no future in Ireland for them.'[67]

Henry Sadleir Persse – New Landlord but same policy at Pollnarooma East

Following the Bingham family's tenure, Mr. Henry Sadleir Persse took charge at Pollnarooma East. The new landlord's plan for his seaside acquisition was to further 'improve' the place and he first sought to have the land cleared. 'Notices to Quit' were served on the peasantry in May 1873, with instructions to vacate by the following November. Possession was not ceded, so ejectment notices were brought to the January 1874 sessions, where Mr. Persse obtained 'overholding' decrees against his 'new' tenants; they being of long standing but he being the latest landlord. The tenants, who were vulnerable against the powerful forces that were ranged against them, included:

Michael Flaherty, 13 ½ acres; rent £23-10s-6d a year. Flaherty, who had a large family, lived in comfortable circumstances. He had a public house and spent forty years *in situ* at his Salthill holding. He was given possession of the place 'as a marriage portion with his wife, the daughter of a man called Mannion.' A contemporaneous Petty Session record noted that 'Michael Flaherty of Tailor's Hill, Galway' was charged that he did 'on the 21st day of July 1873 at Spiddle Fair… unlawfully sell and expose for Sale, by retail intoxicating liquor, without being duly licensed to sell same.'[68] The case against him on that occasion was dismissed; **Peter Gannon**: 2 acres; rent £6-10s a year. He was born in the cottage he resided in and his father, who was the tenant, died after the ejectment decree was served; **Thomas Grogan**: 2 ½ acres; rent £5 a year: a married man who was born in the place and had a family of four; **Michael Grogan**: 1 ¼ acre; rent £2-6s. a year. Also born in the place, he was a married man with a family of six; **Charles Quirk**: 1 ½ acres; rent £3-10 a year. Charles was married with five children and received his holding as a marriage portion with the daughter of a man named Connelly; **Sally Burke**: An aged woman who was given a house by Lady Clanmorris, for which she paid no rent.[69]

The listed six tenant cohort, and their families, represented the remnant of the 'Polnaroma East' tenantry which had been 'very populous up to the bad times,'[70] and all – bar Michael Flaherty – had fully paid up their rent. Flaherty furthermore attested that he was willing at any time to settle with the landlord.

Salthill's looming dispossessions were highlighted in January 1874 when an anonymous letter writer alerted *Vindicator* readers to a 'whimsical' ejectment at Boherard where an 'entire village are about to be evicted and thrown on the roadside, numbering about thirty souls.'[71] The newspaper received 'a heap of letters' on the Taylor's Hill evictions but chose not to publish them, opting instead to first investigate the situation at Pollnarooma East. It found that Richard Sloper, the 'Fee Simple Proprietor or Head Landlord,' disagreed with Mr. Persse's decision, but was powerless to stop the evictions. The *Vindicator,* following its analysis of the Salthill townland's story, opined that Mr. Persse was mistaken in making a 'very unpopular' decision. The same newspaper did, however, imply that Henry Sadleir Persse; 'being one of the largest and most liberal employers in Galway, should be one of the most popular men in our city.' Also highlighted – by way of contrast – was the Pollnarooma peasantry's respect for the previous landlord family.[72]

Whereas the *Galway Packet* had acted as cheerleader – two decades earlier – for the evicting actions of both Barton and Clanmorris, the *Galway Vindicator* of 1874 defended the tenantry's position in a full column exposition of the case. Irate at the audacity of a local journal to question him, Henry S. Persse put pen to paper in a public reply. He believed that he was fully within his rights to force people, who had resided at Pollnarooma since birth, to leave and allow him improve the value and appearance of his recent acquisition. Henry explained that he had offered his tenants a two option choice; (a) a three year lease or; (b) a two-man arbitration on compensation if they chose to cede possession. Mr. Persse first chose two gentlemen, Mr. Pierce Joyce, Mervue, and Mr. George Morris M.P., to act as arbitrators, but agreed to a request for a tenant representative, Mr. Thomas Kearns. By Persse's account, the tenantry almost immediately reneged on the arbitration agreement 'so the ejectments went on before Mr. Henn, the Chairman early in January, and decrees were obtained against them.' Subsequent to that, Henry Persse offered five years rent if they would give up possession. Though that proposal satisfied some tenants, the remainder, with one exception, offered up possession if they were offered seven years rent. Mr. Persse did allow that tenants 'were paying more than their holdings are worth,' and pleaded an unwillingness to disturb them. He did not, however, wish to leave the place as 'a perfect wilderness.' Having explained his position, Mr. Persse took aim at the *Vindicator*:

I am really at a loss to understand why or by what authority you take it on yourself to endeavour to arbitrate between me and my tenants. Perhaps your next step will be to arrange the scale of wages between the labourers and tradesmen employed by me in my distillery…I can safely say that I never did a harsh or unkind act in my life. I have always endeavoured to be as charitable as my position would allow me, and whether in this instance I settle amicably or otherwise, I will not be debarred from improving the place by fear of becoming unpopular through the Galway Vindicator.[73]

The letter's tetchy closing betrays irritation at being questioned. His own appointment of 'landed' arbitrators appeared totally reasonable to him, even though

131. Persse Distillery at Nuns' Island, as seen from the West Bridge, known as O'Brien's Bridge from 1899. (A. Barnard, *The Whiskey Distilleries of the United Kingdom*, 1887)

he was agreeable to allow a third – minority opinion – partake in deliberations. Mr. Persse's final sentence, replete with personal pronouns that never strayed from the first person singular, articulated a sense of entitlement that brooked no questioning. The *Vindicator*, defending its journalistic right to comment, hit back:

Upon every principle of moral law these poor people have a perfect right to remain in occupation of their holdings, so long as they pay their rent. And they have the rent paid up to the day… Evidently the place occupied by those poor people of Polnaroma East must have been once – and at no distant day – a barren rock. What labour must have been expended on it to bring it into the state in which it is in at present! But Mr. Persse wishes to 'improve' the place; and his idea is to 'improve' the people off the land and turn it into a grass farm. There has certainly been too much of this kind of 'improvement' in Ireland.

Henry S. Persse, like the fourth Lord Clanmorris before him, did not choose to develop Bathing Lodges, as Mr. Barton had done at Attithomasrevagh. The grass farm concept, which he chose to pursue, placed landlords' rights above tenants, who were to be replaced by livestock. That particular policy led to numerous attacks on grazier holdings, with East Galway in the vanguard of such onslaughts. The *Vindicator* offered Mr. Persse some advice: 'We would suggest to Mr. Persse, in the kindest spirit, that to take an interest in the people, to keep them in their Cottages, and to teach them to improve their humble residences, would be a species of real "improvement," which, in the end, would afford him more solid gratification than if, after depopulating Polneroma East, he made it at great expense, as smooth and velvety as the lawn at Glenarde.'[74] The *Nation* and *Freeman's Journal* covered the Salthill saga with the latter publication referring to the 'unmelodious name' of Pollnarooma East. Both papers supported the *Vindicator*'s stance on the issue, with the *Freeman* stating that 'it is the bounden duty of a public writer to throw over tenants the broad shield of journalism.'[75]

Mr. Henry Persse's clearing of a hamlet, at the Boherard end of Pollnarooma East, took place over twenty years after the seaside Ballynacarrickadoo *clachán* had been razed to the ground. The earlier eviction at Pollnarooma East was recalled by the *Galway Vindicator* in 1874, when it stated that 'about 1848 there were some seventeen houses in the village, the occupants having being ejected for non-payment of rent. There is still a lively recollection of "Sam Cross," who was the principal instrument in those exterminations. He was a bailiff and a tax collector who afterwards went to America, and seems to have being lost sight of in the crowd on that "go-a-head" Continent.'[76] The 'about 1848' date – recalled from memory – for the Pollnarooma East ejectments, could refer to either the 1845 or 1852 eviction cases, earlier described. However, Petty Court records of the period show that Samuel Cross, the referenced poor rate collector, was most active in the early 1850s, and that same revenue enforcer was among the men to be contacted re the letting of Lord Clanmorris' Seamount House in 1851.[77] Such time correlations make it almost certain that the seventeen houses to have been demolished belonged to

Ballynacarrickadoo, the seaside *clachán* that was cleared in 1852. A contemporaneous *Galway Packet* report, as earlier noted, stated that the forty evictees, cast out in September of that post-famine year, were expelled from 'their tenements on the Salt Hill road.'[78] On Clanmorris land at Salthill, during the early 1850s, such sited dwellings were only located at Ballynacarrickadoo. When cleared, it took a long time for that beautifully positioned spot to re-invent itself.

Considering the fact that the Fourth Lord Clanmorris was landlord at the time of that Ballynacarrickadoo clearance, the *Vindicator*'s 1874 reportage of local praise for Lord and Lady Clanmorris appears curious. One explanation might be that those evicted in 1852 did not – or could not – pay their rents. Mr. John Charles Bingham's retention of paid up tenants, who remained at Pollnarooma East, would have been appreciated by that compliant cohort, which resided at the Taylor's Hill end of the townland. As responsible tenants, who were quite comfortable, the arbitrary dispossession strategy of their new landlord, Mr. Persse, would have outraged them in the early 1870s. Lady Clanmorris' generosity to Sally Burke would also have been recognised in the place. In the case of the Fourth Lord Clanmorris, the *Tuam Herald* – on his 1876 death – did say that the one-time Pollnarooma lessor, was a 'generous and kind-hearted' landlord.[79]

Mr. Persse was not the only land holder to pursue an 'improvement' policy, and his attitude to tenants – as aired in his *Vindicator letter* – exposed the broad, unbridgeable social chasm that divided landlord and tenant. Mr. Persse was a wealthy man and the positions he held reflected his status in society: He was a Landlord, a Distiller, a Magistrate; a Town and Harbour Commissioner; Treasurer of the County Infirmary; and a Member of the Board of Guardians of the District Lunatic Asylum, Ballinasloe. He was also, for some time, Master of the 'Galway Blazers' and owner of the famed horse, 'Stella.'

It was to become clear over time that Mr. Persse succeeded in his ambition, for nowhere in Salthill was a clearance policy as successfully implemented as it was

Year:	Population/Evictions at Pollnarooma East
1812:	Inhabitants: 238
1839:	Inhabitants: 14 Tenants; 10 Cottiers
1841:	Inhabitants: 131
1845:	Evictions granted by court - Number unclear
	Great Famine
1851:	Inhabitants: 59
1852:	Evicted: 40 people - 17 houses razed
1874:	Evicted: 5 Families with children and an aged woman - 'Numbering about thirty souls.'
1893:	Inhabitants: Three Households: Persse, Holmes, Walsh (coachman's house)
1901:	Inhabitants: 25 people in two households: Persse (Seamount) and Holmes (Sea Park)
1911:	Inhabitants: 8 people in one household: Mr. Peter Condon – coachman.

Figure 132.

133. Taylor's Hill gateway to Henry S. Persse's Glenarde Demesne, which today serves as the entrance to the Ardilaun Hotel.

at the Prom's end. Taking a few key dates, Pollnarooma East's population decline was appreciable.

At Pollnarooma East, the Great Famine's ejections-cum-tenant attrition was followed by the 1852 clearing of peasantry by the fourth Lord Clanmorris. Unlike Thomas Barton, however, John Charles Bingham did not develop Bathing Lodges at the place. Over twenty years later – in 1874 – Henry S. Persse delivered another 'improvement' scheme which did not deliver any discernible enhancement to the area, except to clear it of peasantry. In one hundred years, the population of Pollnarooma East fell from 238 to 8, a reflection of the focused success of various landlords' shared ambition. A culture built upon a great divide between landed gentry and subsistent peasants accommodated that depopulation. There was little shared – but bitter tension and deep suspicion – between polarised social classes. One famine story, lifted from the *Wexford Guardian* by the *Tuam Herald* in 1848, defined a deep chasm. It told of *a poor woman, the wife of a poor aged man, who was 30s. in debt for rent, when clinging to her wretched cabin, had her arm dislocated by the landlord, who was tried at Dungarvan Quarter Sessions …The Jury convicted. Sentence – To be imprisoned until he would pay the woman the enormous damages of ten shillings!!! Why, a peasant's son would be fined £10 for throwing a stick at a landlord's hare.*[80]

Courts were administered, for the most part, by those with landed backgrounds, who carried their particular view of the world into the court house. Incremental property law changes, however, and a number of conflicts – of both local and global dimensions – were poised to deliver major changes during the early decades of the 20th century.

Henry S. Persse died in 1899 and the Nun's Island distillery he owned was in receivership by 1906. Glenarde House and its attendant lands were occupied by Mr. Patrick Boland in 1903. Three years later, Henry Persse's trustees sold the Pollnarooma East townland in four lots. The glory days of the Persse era were over, and the Glenarde demesne faded from view and memory.

Sea Park – A significant second house at Pollnarooma East

Before leaving Pollnarooma East, it is important to note a second 19th century house – of stature and status – in the townland. Whereas Seamount overlooked the sea at Blackrock from the early decades of the 19th century, a second residence – built close to Boherard in the 1860s – did likewise from a higher vantage point. First called Sea View, that fine Sloper pile, which was part of a local building boom, featured a curved entrance avenue off Taylor's Hill. Its name was to later change from Sea View to Sea Park.

An earlier Sloper house at Tievegarriff had also been called Sea View, where Richard Sloper's wife delivered a daughter in 1845,[81] the same year that the house was sold. The Dominican Nuns, on purchasing the premises, set upon developing the St. Rose Convent in the place. Some fifteen years later, in 1860/'61, Richard Sloper built another large house, this time on a two acre site at Pollnarooma East, which the family had retained from its ownership of that townland. That new home was also branded Sea View. Such a choice was not surprising for landed and mercantile families liked to retain house names. The O'Hara family's town seat, for example, which was West Lodge in the early 1800s, was not the same West Lodge – again of O'Hara provenance – that was acquired by Galway's Golf Club in 1924. Richard Sloper left the second Sea View residence in the mid-1870s, before transferring to the nearby Wellfield Cottage (**fig.152**), on the northern side of Taylor's Hill, where he died in 1879.

Following Richard Sloper into the Pollnarooma East Sea View residence was Maria Smith, who remained there for over a decade, before that house came into the ownership of the Holmes' clan. On 18 September, 1890, a daughter, Anna, was born at Sea Park to Mrs. Holmes, wife of Captain Harry William Holmes,[82] with a son, Noel, arriving in December of the following year.[83] Though it might well have been Maria Smith who changed the house name, there is documentary proof that it was called Sea Park from 1890, under Holmes' occupation. One of the reasons for changing from the Sloper 'Sea View' name might have been a Holmes' desire to place their own moniker on a fine Taylor's Hill pile. Another reason may have been to differentiate their home from a Sea View area – and similarly named house therein – at Salthill Village. A third consideration was that an earlier Sea Park name at Salthill, which had been identified mid-century with Mr. William Buckley of the *Galway Packet* newspaper,[84] was no longer in use at the resort.

The Holmes' family at Sea Park

Harry William Holmes Esq. married Anna Concannon, a member of a famed legal family from Tuam, in 1882. The Holmes' tale is a most interesting narrative that embraces a strong military tradition; sacrifices in the 1914–1918 War; decorations and a knighthood following World War II; raids on their Rockwood home; a Davis Cup and Wimbledon competitor; another fine house at King's Hill and the development of Lenaboy Park. As the contribution of the Holmes' family to Salthill is generally recalled in terms of their second coming, when Greenmount House – where the Warwick Hotel stands today – was built, their story will be told in greater detail in a future volume of this history.

The Holmes' family left Sea Park after the 1905 death of Harry's brother, Robert, and that Taylor's Hill residence was subsequently occupied, in turn, by John P. Gunning, Patrick J.B. Daly and James Wilson. The longest incumbent of the three appears to have been Daly – a famed Land League lawyer – who took the house in 1907, but was living at 2 University Road in 1911. Mr. Daly placed Sea Park on the market in both 1910 and 1914. One advertisement noted that it offered 'stabling for two horses, coach house, coal house, wash house, and piggery with a lawn and large fruit and vegetable garden attached. There is a right of way from the house across the Glenarde demesne to the sea.'[85] The man most identified with Sea Park over subsequent decades was Dr. Séamus O'Beirn, who resided there with his family from the mid-1910s until his death in 1935.

Seamount and Sea Park, the two large houses that adorned Pollnarooma East from the 1860s no longer stand. The former served for a number of 20th century decades as a nursing home / hospital, but both of the townland's signature premises were knocked in relatively recent times for residential development. After Seamount was razed to the ground in 1977, Mr. Matthew J. Hanley applied for planning permission to build a residence at 1 Seamount, Pollnarooma East, in the following year. Planning for apartments at Sea Park was requested in the early years of the new millennium, and those apartments today occupy a site, which was previously identified with a merchant Sloper clan, and later with a Holmes' family that produced a knighted scion.

Chapter 16

TIEVEGARRIFF – CLOGHATISKY – ACRES: DISPARATE FAMINE EXPERIENCES

Tievegarriff

A 70% population drop – over the 1840s – in the Tievegarriff townland certainly points to a significant tenant clearance. That high percentage rate represented a significant 21 to 6 inhabited house reduction, along with a 116 to 34 dweller drop. The development of two new residences and gardens – Glenarde House and Mount Eaton (later Glenoir) – appears to have contributed to the changes that occurred at Tievegarriff during the Great Hunger decade.

At the time of the Tithe collection, Richard Sloper – 2 acres; James Hardiman – 13 acres; James O'Hara (1748– 1838) – 17 acres; Mrs. Browne –16 acres; and John Sweeney – 2 roods, were the 'paying' occupiers of the place. The Tievegarriff townland, like Cloghatisky beside it, was primarily an O'Hara holding in 1834. Five years later, two large houses were noted at *Taobh Garbh* – Taylor's Hill House and Sea View. When John O'Donovan stayed at Taylor's Hill House in the 1830s, the *logainm* expert and Irish scholar recorded two 'farmers' in Tievegarriff. One was Constance Sloper, whose Sea View house was then occupied by Richard Lynch, Esquire. The second was his scholarly host, James Hardiman, who had – in an earlier role as Sub-Commissioner for Public Records – employed O'Donovan to copy Irish manuscripts in 1826. The two academics were, therefore, well acquainted.

Taylor's Hill House – James Hardiman's residence of changing names

Two homes carried a 'Taylor's Hill House' tag during the 19th century. The first was in Tievegarriff, on the Salthill side of Taylor's Hill Road. That fine abode was called Theevgarrive Lodge or Taylor's Hill House, according to John O'Donovan, and the latter name featured in the 1839 Ordnance Survey Map. It was then home to Mr.

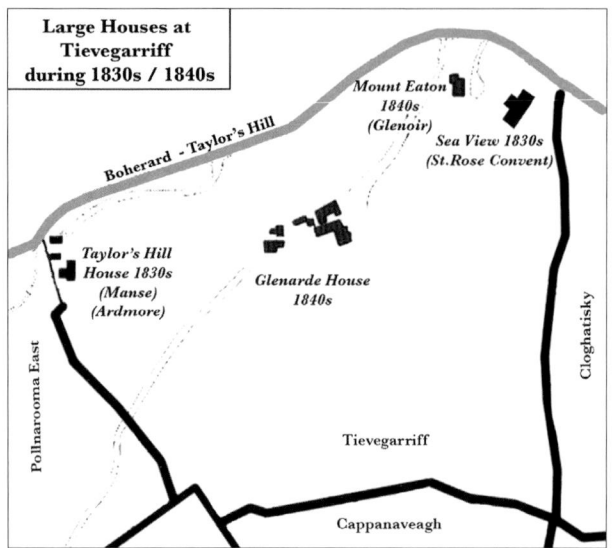

134. Sea View and Taylor's Hill House of the 1830s were joined at Tievegarriff by Glenarde House and Mount Eaton, during the Great Famine decade.

James Hardiman, who had resided at Tievegarriff from at least 1834, when he was recorded in a Tithe Applotment record. Following the historian's 1841 departure, that Taylor's Hill House came to be briefly called 'The Manse' and later 'Ardmore,' a name it retains to this day. It was under the Ardmore title that the residence was advertised in 1847.

With the 'Taylor's Hill House' name no longer in use, the same handle was subsequently used to describe an equally old house on the northern Rahoon-side of Boherard. That latter residence, which stood directly across the road from the Gate Lodge to Glenarde House, was knocked in the 1950s and replaced by a new home in the same location. The large site of the second named Taylor's Hill House is today home to a pitch and putt course, on the hill after which the residence was called.

Mr. Hardiman was described as a farmer by O'Donovan. Such a description, in terms of Field Book demands, was accurate, but more than a little understated. True, Hardiman held land in both Mayo and Galway, but it was as a scholar, historian and librarian that he is yet remembered. Hardiman's *History of Galway* – his *magnum opus* – was published in 1820, and his contribution as librarian at Queen's College, Galway is today memorialised in the naming of the Hardiman Library, which sits at the heart of N.U.I. Galway's expanding campus. Mr. Hardiman's scholarship and benevolence were recognised locally in 1842, not long after he departed Taylor's Hill, and some seven years before he began working at the university:

Jas. Hardiman, Esq., late of Taylor's Hill, Galway, the eminent Historian and Antiquarian, in addition to his many munificent donations to the public, and especially the tenantry on his estate in Mayo, has threshed all his corn & purchased an additional quantity at market, and given it to his tenants for seed. He has also distributed among them all his potatoes, at the instance of his Agent, Mr. O'Flaherty, who represented to him their distressed state, owing to the failure of their crops last harvest. Would to God that many of the landed proprietors in this and the neighbouring counties would follow the noble example!* [1]

Hardiman's reputation and generosity, however, did not serve to leave his Galway property outrage free: *On Sunday night last, a sheep, the property of James Hardiman Esq. was maliciously killed and carried off the lands at Taylor's Hill, the ruffians leaving the head only behind. We are informed that two more sheep were shorn upon the same lands, on the same evening. The police have found no clue to the perpetrators of this wanton outrage upon the property of a gentleman so universally esteemed and respected.* [2]

James Hardiman's time at Galway's university was quite short, for though he worked at Queen's College in 1849, its opening year, he was to pass away six years later. Warm tributes were paid on his 1855 demise, with many publications in Ireland and England carrying a *Galway Vindicator* résumé of his life:

Mr. Hardiman, in early life, practiced as a solicitor, but on receiving his appointment in Dublin Castle, as Commissioner of Records, he seems to have given up the profession. It was whilst engaged in this congenial employment that he became acquainted with many curious and valuable manuscripts relating to Irish history and families, of which he subsequently availed himself. The History of Galway will long remain a monument to his patient research and historical accuracy. It is chiefly on this history that his fame will depend and his future character be appreciated. To the lovers of natural poetry, his Bardic Remains of Ireland will continue to be a desideratum. He was also the translator of the Statues of Kilkenny; but the last work he gave the country was a History of Iar Connaught, originally written by O'Flaherty in Latin, translated by Mr. Hardiman, and published by the Archaeological Society. Since he gave up his appointment as Commissioner he has chiefly resided in Mayo and Galway. On the establishment of the Queen's Colleges in 1849, Mr. Hardiman was appointed to the office of Librarian, a post which he continued to fill with urbanity, and to the satisfaction of the Professors, up to the time of his lamented demise. He endowed a monastery in Mayo, built by the Franciscan Monks, with ten acres of land for ever and during the famine of '47 and '48, his charity was displayed in feeding the children daily who attended the schools. To him the Galway Institute mainly owes its existence. He was instrumental in procuring its charter, and subsequently bestowed on its library a donation of one thousand volumes. [3]

The Galway Institute referenced in Mr. Hardiman's obituary was a precursor of Galway's Chamber of Commerce, and the university library that bears his name notes – on its website – that Hardiman 'declined the chair of Irish' on taking up his librarian position. Mr. James Hardiman's funeral Mass was held at the Parish Church of St. Nicholas and he was buried in the Abbey Cemetery.

Taylor's Hill House – the Manse – Ardmore

James Hardiman's Taylor's Hill House, one of the townland's original fine piles, underwent change during the 1840s. It was on 20 November, 1841 that Mr. Hardiman transferred his residence and land to Reverend Joseph Fisher, who remained there until 1845, when it was again placed on the market. The property was, on that occasion, advertised by Rev. Fisher as 'The Manse, Taylor's Hill,'[4] for a house and land occupied by a religious minister was then so described. Next up was Resident Magistrate, J.B. Kernan Esq., who spent some time in the dwelling before offering the 'House and Lands called Manse, or Ardmore,' for letting in March 1847.[5] It is clear, therefore, that it was Mr. Kernan who first named the property Ardmore, before departing for the neighbouring Glenarde residence. Mr. Kernan was followed at Ardmore by Samuel Ussher Roberts, whose influence as borough engineer was most significant in terms of both Galway and Salthill. Mr. Roberts, whose wife delivered a son at Ardmore in 1850, chose to leave Taylor's Hill the following year.[6] Though Mr. Roberts was not responsible for the name change, one wonders if he 'improved' Ardmore during his time there. A cartographic comparison between the 1839 OS map and its 1890's equivalent shows three broadly similar shapes, though the principal structure seems to have been extended somewhat over time. Roberts' record of house residencies and constructions at Salthill was prolific, as he was the principal architect on the 1850's Bathing Lodges created by Thomas Henry Barton at Rockbarton. Roberts furthermore built Barfield (Salthill Hotel) for himself, and he lived at Brinkwater among other Rockbarton Lodges during his time in the place. In the Taylor's Hill area alone, Mr. Roberts was architect/engineer on (a) the Mission Church School and Orphanage at Nile Lodge (*Scoil Fhursa* today), (b) Mount Vernon (the Bishop's Palace) and (c) Lenaboy Castle (James O'Hara's Boherard pile).[7] It is hardly idle to speculate that Roberts improved his Taylor's Hill home during his spell there, even though his family's occupancy was quite short. According to its 1851 sale's blurb, Ardmore boasted a 'Cow House, Sheds and Piggery' as well as 'a large GARDEN, walled, and stocked with new Trees of the best description.'[8] Thomas Moore Persse became the recorded Ardmore occupier in 1855, and he remained there throughout the second half of that decade. Indian corn was grown on Mr. Persse's holding in 1859 that 'looked as rich and as healthy as if it grew in the most fertile fields of America.'[9] The same Thomas Moore Persse was, in that year, contemplating building what became his Mount Vernon mansion, a little closer to town on Taylor's Hill.

Sea View – A Sloper house that became a Dominican Convent

The Sloper family's original Sea View House represented the second landmark residence at *Taobh Garbh* in 1839. It had been occupied prior to 1841 by Richard Lynch, who was followed at the house by Patrick Marcus Lynch, a Guano and Flax Seed Merchant at Back Street and Director of the Provincial Bank of Ireland. When offered for lease in October 1844, that three storey residence featured 'stabling for six horses, coach houses, cow-house, &c.' Also boasting five acres of 'Meadow and Pasture,' application was to be made to Richard or Constantine Sloper.[10] By the following summer new lessees were to occupy that house, but before they did, 'the lady of Richard Sloper' gave birth to a daughter at Sea View in February, 1845.[11] Five months later, the Dominican Order of Nuns moved into Mr. Sloper's impressive Sea View residence, and that community, which set up house at Taylor's Hill on the cusp of the Great Famine, continues to reside in – and serve – the area to this day.

The nuns' original plan had been to depart their ill-suited Kirwan's Lane Slate Nunnery for Dangan, but circumstances saw them take up residence *ar an mBóthar Ard*. That change of plan did not best please their neighbour and Bishop elect, Dr. Laurence O'Donnell, who believed that the sisters had acted *ultra vires*, a charge the sisters denied. In October of the year of the nuns' transfer, Dr. O'Donnell was consecrated at the Parish Chapel 'as Bishop of his native town.'[12] On the Monday preceding that ceremony, Dr. O'Donnell hosted a dinner for five bishops 'at his lodge, Fort Lorenzo.' Unhappy with the Dominican nuns' move, Dr. O'Donnell declared their newly occupied residence 'to be henceforth under a Canonical Interdict until you return with your Community to some place within the precincts of the town.'[13] An unseemly stand-off then ensued, which engaged Roman Church interest in the Galway affair. As Eucharistic celebration at their new convent was prorogued by Episcopal edict, the nuns were obliged to go out in all weathers to Mass. Following a nine month impasse, the Bishop visited Sea View and lifted the Interdict, but only after insisting that the sisters 'go back to the old Nunnery and stay there for the space of eight days.' There was a touch of autocratic posturing in such a pointless demand, which was replicated in the bishop's later statement that he was 'satisfied with your submission and atonement,' after the nuns had carried out his order by temporarily returning to Kirwan's Lane. The bishop's facility for imperious impudence was neither lost on – nor forgotten – by the Taylor's Hill nuns. That truth is discernible in a pithy commentary on Bishop O'Donnell's ways by Dominican historian, Sister Rose O'Neill, who observed that 'it is significant that he actually named his episcopal residence FORT Lorenzo.'[14] It was in 1994 that Sister Rose published *A Rich Inheritance; Galway Dominican Nuns, 1644–1994,* a history of her Order's time in Galway. Though the nuns set up home at Taylor's Hill in 1845, the property was purchased outright in 1867 when 'possession was handed over formally by old Mr. Sloper who took a sod from the lawn and placed it in the hands of the prioress.'[15]

Hunger and Tragedy on Taylor's Hill

Sister Rose's comprehensive account also records the hardship of the famine years that coincided with the nuns' arrival at Tievegarriff: *Their convent being situated on the direct route from Connemara proved a refuge to the stricken crowds of hungry people who daily thronged into the town in the hope of obtaining some relief. In conjunction with the other Religious of the town, the nuns set up a kitchen to provide food for the famine-stricken, but many died by the roadside before they could reach the friendly gate. The children required to be clothed, as well as fed, and often the nuns laboured far into the night on this work of charity.*[16]

The mortal effect of hunger in the area was evident at an 1847 inquest, chaired by Mr. Perrin, which described the fate of a woman called Lawless of Rahoon, 'who was taken suddenly ill on the Taylor's hill road, near the convent of the Dominican Nuns. She had been…in a weakly state, though she received some assistance at the soup kitchen of the neighbourhood, yet was on Friday added to the list of victims.'[17] A year later, three year old Mary Keady, who lived at Taylor's Hill 'died of starvation.' The girl's mother, Catherine Keady, explained the terrible circumstances of her child's death: The family had been refused relief for a fortnight and the inquest found 'that the death of the child is attributable to the party whose duty it was to transfer the names from the books of the relieving officer to those of the storekeeper, but failed to do so in this instance.'[18] Bureaucratic incompetence at that time resulted in death for the voiceless and penniless poor. An earlier 1842 disaster showed that hunger was not the sole threat to the life of the young: 'Yesterday at Taylor's Hill, a woman in the act of drying Flax set fire to a cabin, when melancholy to relate, four young children perished in the flames.'[19]

At the time of such tragedies occurring, John Connolly of Taylor's Hill won a mathematical prize in the *Belfast Almanac*, and Nicholas Smyth of Abbeygate-street did likewise in England's *Ladies' Diary*.[20] The Taylor's Hill man's undoubted scientific acumen was exhibited in an 1847 *Vindicator* letter on nautical tides. Newton and Keplev were among those referenced in Connolly's treatise, which sought to explain 'spring tides' among other phenomena.[21] Mr. Connolly's scientific contributions to newspapers was longstanding for a letter he wrote to the Editor of the *Dublin Evening Post* in 1841 on the 'Occultation of Venus' was also carried by the *Freeman's Journal*: 'The observation was made by the writer of this *annonce* with a telescope attached to a repeating circle, and a sidereal clock whose error and rate were previously determined.'[22]

Of relevance to the development of Boherard was an 1844 letter which 'was read by the chairman [of the Town Commissioners] containing an attack upon the motives of some gentlemen respecting the making of a footpath on Taylor's Hill.' In response to that criticism, Constantine Sloper proposed a motion that a sum not exceeding £5 should be paid 'in compensating the owners of two houses whose property would be encroached on.'[23] Road works were also carried out on Taylor's Hill during the famine and in 1847 it was announced that 'the cutting on Taylor's Hill is nearly completed.' Not everyone was happy with the work, with occupiers of 'some cabins' and more modest 'tenements' complaining of being 'incommoded by the filling opposite their doors.' Mr. Henry Clements, County Surveyor, said that 'the only way to remedy all the inconveniences complained of was to raise the houses proportionally as the road has been raised.'[24] Such development, however, was welcomed by those who found work on it, but the discommoding of tenement dwellers as well as the questioning of motives for public works on Taylor's Hill is noteworthy.

Two new Houses at Tievegarriff: Glenarde House and Mount Eaton

In 1841, Tievegarriff was home to 116 residents in 21 houses. The majority of those residents lived in humble abodes, which were variously described as cabins or tenements. Most of those cabins were to disappear during a decade where the big house tally was to double to four. It appears most likely that the 'improvement' of Tievegarriff, through the development of large new residences and their grounds, contributed to the disappearance of small holders' dwellings.

Glenarde House

Of the pair of new villas, the Glenarde residence appeared first. Though not appearing in the 1839 OS map, the third residence of character in the townland was completed by 1842, when its creator, Richard M. Lynch, described his 'most desirable residence' as 'quite new.'[25] The Glenarde name – derived from *an Gleann Ard* or 'High Glen' within which it is situated – was recorded during the house's first occupancy. A Salt-hill resident in 1837, Richard Mark Lynch, Esq., Glenarde, was listed by Slater in 1846 as a member of the nobility and gentry of Galway. Mr. Richard Marcus Lynch also inherited an estate in the parish of Ballynakill, barony of Killian, County Galway, from his father, who was leasing some of the estate from the Bellew family. A Merchant at Back Street in 1837,[26] Richard, who acted as Treasurer to the County Infirmary in 1845,[27] also served as a Poor Law Inspector and a Special Commissioner for Income Tax.[28] Over Glenarde's early years, the house was occupied by various members of the landed Lynch family and let out when not required by a member of the proprietary clan.

'The House of Glenarde' which 'commands an extensive view of the sea.'[29] was taken in 1846 by the family of John B. Kernan, West Galway's Resident Magistrate, who received that commission in 1843. In that house move, the Kernan clan moved but a few short steps from neighbouring Ardmore. On 15 April, 1847, a wedding was celebrated 'at Glenard, the residence of the bride's father, by the Right Rev. Laurence O'Donnell, Bishop of Galway.' The groom was Bernard O'Flaherty, Esq., Ardville, in the County of the Town of Galway,' who married 'Anne Jane, second daughter of J.B. Kernan Esq., R.M. of the County of Galway.'[30] The Kernan family remained in residence for a number of years and on 25 September, 1854, 'at her residence, Glenard, after a very protracted illness, Maria, the beloved wife of John B. Kernan Esq.', passed away.[31] In September of the following year it was announced that John B. Kernan Esq., R.M. 'had arrived at Glenard from Germany…in the enjoyment of excellent health and spirits.'[32] A Kernan affiliation with the Lynch family was created when John's son, Hubert Prendergast Kernan of Cabragh, Co. Monaghan married Kate, the daughter of James Lynch Esq. of Windfield, Co. Galway, in 1857.[33]

Mr. Theobald Blake J.P. was in residence at Glenarde for some four years before it was occupied in the early 1860s by a man with whom it was to enjoy a long association. He was Henry Sadleir Persse, who, as earlier referenced, was to form the Glenarde Demesne in 1872, by uniting the neighbouring Tievegarriff and Pollnarooma townlands.

Mount Eaton, a second 1840's Tievegarriff residence – later called Glenoir

With Richard Sloper as immediate lessor, a 'neat and commodious new house' called Mount Eaton was completed by 1844. That residence was available for letting in that year with applications to be made to the Rush and Palmer office.[34] It was occupied in 1846 by Mrs. Eliza Rush,[35] and when Eliza died at Mount Eaton in early January 1855, the press noted that she was 'relict to the late James Rush Esq., and mother of Ambrose Rush, Esq. J.P.'[36] That well known family was part of the Rush and Palmer company, which owned mills at Nun's Island and Bridge Street, as well as a baking outlet at Dominick Street in 1846.[37] Mount Eaton stood close to – and west of – Sea View, which had been leased by the Sloper family to the Dominican nuns in 1845. The townland's newest dwelling, Mount Eaton, which boasted 7 acres of land, was to play host to a good number of subsequent occupiers that included Coast Guard Officer George Clarke; immediate lessor Richard

Sloper; Rev. John Lewis of the Congregational Church on Sea Road; and William King, Professor of Mineralogy and Geology, Queen's College, Galway. The house name, Mount Eaton, had – by 1875 – been replaced by Glenoir and was so recorded when 'Margaret Galvia King, daughter of William King, Sc.D., Glenoir', married Even Maberly Durand Byrde, H.M. Civil Service, Ceylon, at Nuwara Elyia.[38] The Glenoir residence, which was marked in an 1890's Ordnance Survey map, was to become identified for a good part of the 20th century with Mr. William Faller and family.

Before leaving the newly built Glenarde and Mount Eaton residences, it is important to note that both were completed and occupied before the Great Famine took full effect. The Nuns' occupation of the existing Sea View also fell within that same pre-famine timeframe. The Dominican Sisters soon added to their Taylor's Hill abode: 'Owing to the smallness of the house... a new wing was built facing south over the Bay. This cost twelve hundred pounds, considerably more than was realized by the sale of the old Nunnery.'[39] That significant sum, which was expended 'on their chapel and great wing of a house,' never touched 'a penny of their funded means.'[40] To put that £1,200 cost into perspective, Fr. Peter Daly acquired the whole of Lower Salthill – including Merrion Village – when he purchased the Kilcorkey townland for £2,110 in 1852.

Tievegarriff Résumé

So, through the 1840's decade, two new residences – and improvements at Sea View – were completed at Tievegarriff. Each of the townland's four fine houses had land banks and it is notable that the Nuns' acreage in 1845 was in pasture, while Ardmore's nine Irish acres were described in 1851 as being 'well fenced and cleared, in good order for crop, hay or grass.'[41] Both Glenard and Ardmore were referenced in 1853 as exemplars in a sale advertisement for another Salthill townland, which pointed out the potential of what could be achieved by improving tenants, who were willing to expend considerable capital on the development of impressive residences.[42] Such a commendation indicates that the clearing of townlands for superior seaside villas was practiced at Tievegarriff, just as it had been at Cappanaveagh and Attithomasrevagh.

A dramatic population decrease at Tievegarriff, over a ten year period, tallies with such a policy practice. However, as no single townland intervention, like the 1845 and 1852 evictions at Pollnarooma East; the sizable 1847 Cappanaveagh clearance; or the 1852 ejections at Attithomasrevagh, has come to this study's attention, it might be reasonable to assume that the undisputed clearance of the Tievegarriff townland occurred piecemeal over a decade, with a good part of it being accomplished by 1845. At the end of *an Gorta Mór*, the inhabited house count at Tievegarriff stood at six, quite a fall from twenty one occupied homes in 1841. As four of the six surviving houses were large villas, only two 'small homes' stood in the entire townland in 1851, where such cabins numbered at least eighteen ten years earlier. Tievegarriff's population had fallen from 116 inhabitants to the 34 tally of 1851. Four years later, Richard Griffith recorded NO small dwelling in the entire townland, when its residential occupiers were the Dominican Nuns at Sea View; Elizabeth Rush at Mount Eaton; John B. Kernan at Glenarde; and Thomas Moore Persse at Ardmore. One could surmise that hunger, and the tenantry's search for a better future, might well have contributed to a flight from the place, but it is more plausible that the development and improvement of the townland made the greatest contribution to that peasantry's scattering. A complete subsistent farming clearout – by 1855 – points to a policy driven strategy. One way or another, the cleansing of a peasant population during the 1840s was most successful at Tievegarriff. Anne O'Hara and Richard Sloper were listed in Griffith's 1855 Valuation as the immediate lessors of almost the entire 40 acres of the townland.

Cloghatisky Famine Wipe-out

A Cloghatisky townland wipe-out, from sixteen occupants to none, over a famine decade most likely resulted from a confluence of factors. In the first place, James O'Hara (1748–1838), Recorder of Galway, and his son James O'Hara (1796–1838) Member of Parliament, both died within a month of each another in the winter of 1838. James O'Hara (1832–1902), the successor to the Lenaboy estate, was then six years old and would not reach his majority until 1853. The young James was educated at Eton and subsequently joined the Dragoon Guards, (Queen's Boys). Lenaboy House, as it was then, was most likely little used by the O'Hara family and it was not unusual for members of that household to spend time in England and elsewhere. The Etonian James, who took over at Lenaboy in 1853, married his bride, Blanche, eldest daughter of Rev. Sebastian Gambier, Vicar of Sandgate, at the Parish Church of St. James in Piccadilly, London in 1864.[43] His grandfather, James O'Hara (1748–1838), had moved to Cheltenham for a few summer months, during his final illness in 1838, before returning to Lenaboy where he died.[44] It is most likely, therefore, that a fraught environment in Ireland would have resulted in landed families taking time away from their holdings in a country ravaged by hunger and disease.

The return to Lenaboy of Mrs. O'Hara, 'accompanied by her amiable family... after an absence of many years,'[45] in the summer of 1850 indicates that such a course of action had been taken by the O'Hara clan. She was relict of James O'Hara Esq., and in the years that followed, annual press reports appeared on the quality of the potatoes grown in her garden. As there was no one present on 1851 census night at

135. Rose O'Hara in the garden of the family seat, Lenaboy Castle. (Courtesy of National Library of Ireland.)

Cloghatisky, where Lenaboy House stood, it appears that the O'Hara family and suite had, once more, temporarily left for another habitation. Because that 1851 head count was taken on 30 March, it is possible that members of the O'Hara clan would have returned to Lenaboy House during brighter summer months.

It must be acknowledged that members of the broader O'Hara family were not adverse to tenant evictions, and one man, who was to the fore in that regard, was John O'Hara Esq., the Under-Sheriff for the County. John regularly attended, in an official capacity, at numerous ejections. They included taking 'possession under a civil bill ejection decree, of several unfortunate wretches, tenants of Bishop Daly' in October 1847,[46] and attending at the dispossession of thirteen families in the Athenry area during the following year.[47]

That said, this research has found little evidence of O'Hara evictions at the Lenaboy Demesne. At the 1853 'rejoicings at Lenaboy' when James O'Hara reached adulthood, James H. Burke, Esq. said that the young man was 'determined to pursue the same kind and liberal course of treatment towards his tenants, that has guided his ancestors…and of this you have the best proof, by forgiving large arrears due on his attaining his majority.'[48] O'Hara's Salthill seat was not, however, eviction free and in 1855 'Mr. Cullen (Sanitary Officer) reported that he had been served with notice to the effect that two families were about to be evicted off the property of

James O'Hara Esq., of Lenaboy.'⁴⁹ On the other hand, it must be remembered that the same James O'Hara (1832–1902); (a) supported the famine-time building of Grattan Road in the early 1860s,⁵⁰ and (b) was willing to go security for Claddagh fishermen's loans towards the tail end of that same decade.⁵¹

Acres' Famine Story

It is clear that tenants throughout Salthill suffered through famine times. In that context, a fifteen person inhabitant rise – from 40 to 55 – at the bordering Acres townland appears odd. That healthy population statistic in a four acre area, belonging to Barna's District Electoral Division, might be explained by a policy adopted by Nicholas Lynch of Barna House, the man who owned Acres. He was Chairman of the Relief Committee and 'the *Vindicator* accused Nicholas Lynch of issuing work tickets to "comfortable tenantry upon his own property to enable them to pay rents to him with more facility, [while he] had withheld them from squatters and other needy people on his estate".'.⁵² Lynch admitted giving tickets to his tenants who 'had corn in their haggards,' but claimed that the corn was his and not theirs, while some of the lessees' cows had been bought with credit from him. 'I got fifty tickets to distribute – of those I gave thirty-seven among my tenantry, and when I could not give relief tickets to the remaining who stood in need of them, I came into Galway, and I bought sixty hundred of meal for them.'⁵³ Galway historian, John Cunningham, believes that Lynch's rebuttal of the charge of prioritising his own needs – through his tenants' relief tickets – was 'not convincing.'⁵⁴ The same Mr. Lynch of Barna came in for further criticism at the tail end of the Great Famine years. In 1849 there was concern at a suggestion that the Boundary Commission was going 'to separate Barna and Carrowbrowne from the electoral division of Galway...and by that means to throw the support of the paupers cleared off these estates and that took refuge in Galway, on the rates of the town...Mr. Lynch first cleared his estate [Barna] of paupers and then attempted to have his estate separated from the rest of the union and by that means get rid of the liability of supporting them at the workhouse.'⁵⁵

Tenant clearing not unique to Ireland

There is no doubt but that Salthill, from Pollnarooma's Blackrock to Kilcorkey's Nile Lodge, experienced many evictions in the combing clear of subsistent landholders. The crowbar brigade sought to add profit to landed property. Though some landlords desired grazing and manicured demesnes, others invested in the development of bathing villas. Both ambitions took a heavy toll on small tenant holders – who stood in the way of profitable investment. That voiceless cohort became the dispossessed.

Tenant evictions during the 19th century, however, were not unique to Ireland. An 1847 *Galway Mercury* article, which detailed contributions towards famine relief on either side of the Irish Sea, was headlined 'The Famine in Ireland and Scotland.'[56] *Fuadach na nGaidheal* represented a parallel forced displacement of indigenous Gaelic tenants in Scotland, except that in *Albain* the purpose was to clear the way for sheep grazing. That Caledonian *fuadach* has not been forgotten, and yet rankles with some. Left wing Scottish troubadour and activist, Dick Gaughan, sings a Brian McNeill song which chronicles *Clíora Mór na hAlban*:

Farewell to the heather in the glen
They cleared us off once and they'd do it all again
For they still prefer sheep to thinking men
Ah, but men who think like sheep are even better
There's nothing much to choose between the old laird and the new
They still don't give a damn for the likes of me and you
Just mind you pay your rent to the factor when it's due
And mind your bloody manners when you pay! [57]

Townland improvements at Salthill, however, were represented by Bathing Lodges in the Barton style or pasture in the Persse model. The former pointed the way to a tourism product, while grass and the land on which it grew would – over time – become most valuable as sites for 20th century building booms. An entire Salthill generation and its culture were lost in the 19th century clearing of subsistent peasant farmers. On their going, the Salthill villages of Ballynacarrickadoo, *Baile Thaidhg Bháin* and Cappanaveagh were razed to the ground and erased from local memory. Some Salthill families, who can boast of surviving such dreadful times, still reside at *Bóthar na Trá*. They, however, represent a great minority in a place that is not renowned for deep rooted denizens.

Chapter 17

SALTHILL'S FAMINE ROADS

One of Salthill's great ironies is that though it has long been viewed as a salubrious settlement to the west of Galway town, three roads that more or less book-end the place are famine roads, built to give work to the poor and destitute. Those thoroughfares are Threadneedle Road, St. Mary's Road and Grattan Road. Though not in Salthill, Grattan Road and St. Mary's Road – a.k.a. the New Line – were also constructed during famine times and offered greater access to the place. Famine Roads throughout the country still give expression to the *laissez faire* economic model of a time when free aid was viewed as a template that would make the Irish 'habitually dependent' on the British Government. Gratuitous relief to the starving posed a threat to 'all private enterprise,' in the rigid reading of a policy that held sway at the time. Work had to be done to 'earn' aid, but the work provided was meaningless, for many of the roads were going nowhere. That verity was voiced in Eavan Boland's perceptive description of relief-work constructions in her famed *Famine Road* poem:

............................*The Relief*
Committee deliberated: 'Might it be safe,
Colonel, to give them roads, roads to force
From nowhere, going nowhere of course?'[1]

Threadneedle Road and St. Mary's Road are products of *Gorta Mór* Relief Schemes, while the later Grattan Road resulted from the benevolence of a charitable and independent lady, whose familial political heritage was most impressive.

Bóthar na Mine – Threadneedle Road

Bóthar na Mine, the road's traditional Gaelic name, bears greater meaning and boasts deeper roots than Threadneedle, its more chic Anglo-*parvenu*. *Min* is the Irish word for meal; a coarse powder ground from grain. Charity cereals of famine times are memorialised in the thoroughfare's 'Meal Road' name. Constructed during the dark famine years of the mid-19th century, those that worked on the road were given grain as sustenance in hardy times. Indian meal was then the staple offering of Relief Committees nationwide. The Galway committee in May 1847 'allocated three tons of rice and Indian Meal between the several soup kitchens in the district.' Listed among eight charity kitchens was 'Clybane Soup-kitchen, Taylor's Hill' whose record of daily rations read: *Gratuitously to 280 persons: Sold to 1,961 persons*. That 2241 person total represented the second greatest daily throughput, behind the Central Soup Kitchen at Back Street (St. Augustine Street), which catered for over 2,700 attendees. The Taylor's Hill facility, however, far exceeded all other kitchens in terms of those paying for their rations. It was announced at a Friday committee meeting in May 1847, during which the above relief statistics were given, that the Board of Works had declared that 'no relief is in future to be given under the provisions of the Labour Rate Act, but under the "Temporary Relief Act".' On the following Monday, sixteen depots under the Temporary Relief Act were placed under sub-committees. Among that tranche of feeding facilities, which doubled the previous number, Clybane-Taylor's Hill was retained, and a new kitchen – number 14 – was set up at Blackrock.[2]

The track that became Threadneedle Road, which did not appear in Larkin's 1819 map of Galway, was subsequently represented in the 1839 Ordnance Map. It is clear, therefore, that the pathway which was to divide the Pollnarooma East townland was created during a twenty year (1819–1839) time frame. In 1832, 'the grand jury gave [John] Logan, the very fine surveyor and mapper...the sum of ninety shillings for a "map survey of the new line of road from Thos. Pear's house at the turn of the road to Rahoon [i.e. Kingston Cross] passing through Pollnarooma to meet the Galway–Barna Road at the Black Rock." This is now Threadneedle Road.'[3] The track of that road can accordingly trace its roots back to the early 1830s.

As part of famine relief works in Galway, one of the roads to have meal offered to its weakened workers was the proposed Dangan–Salthill

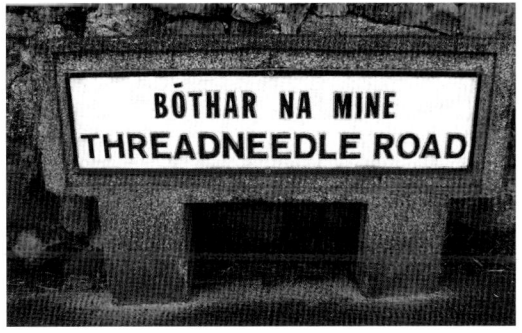

Figure 136.

Road of 1846: 'Improving new line of road from the Dangan Road to the sea, commencing at Lady French's, £500.'[4] The Honourable Dowager Lady Ffrench resided at Glenlo, where she died in December, 1849.[5] While it was already possible – in the 1840s – to travel by road from Salthill to Dangan, that route was quite circuitous for Nile Lodge corner then constituted a T junction, as St. Mary's Road did not then exist. It was during the Great Famine years that the New Line – between Nile Lodge and Leetle Street – which became St. Mary's Road, was first begun. That new road created a more direct Blackrock–Salthill–Newcastle–Dangan thoroughfare. In that context, a second Blackrock–Dangan artery was certainly not of major infrastructural significance, and a 'going nowhere' quality marked the Pollnarooma East project.

Historian, John Cunningham, in his comprehensive history of Galway town, 1790–1914, delivered an 1846 description that tallies with the *Bóthar na Mine* story: *Some work did begin in mid-May, when the Board of Works hired 175 to build a road linking Dangan with Salthill. But a new sea front road between Seapoint and Blackrock was delayed due to the difficulty of hiring carts to move stones. Those hired included army pensioners – not the most destitute of the people. The destitute presented their own problems. Of Bartholomew Keedy, who was sacked because his inertia gave bad example, it was later asserted that he had got 'weak on his spade' due to hunger. And malnutrition rather than drink was found to explain the shambling gait of another would-be worker. Responding to such reports, the committee ordered that meal be made available to destitute workers, with the cost to be deducted on pay-day.*[6]

Origin of the road's English Name?

The naming of Threadneedle Road is curious. It could simply have been coined because the pathway it represented was 'threaded' through the Pollnarooma East townland that it still divides. Some suggest a punned 'tailor-needle' relationship with Taylor's Hill, to which the famine road is joined. Though possible, that explanation appears unlikely. Thomas Taylor, Mayor of Galway in the late 1760s, is the man celebrated in the naming of the Boherard hill which towers over *Bóthar na Trá*.[7] The Taylor family settled in Galway at the beginning of the 18th century, with 'Walter Taylor acting as Mayor in 1731, Anthony Taylor as Sheriff in 1735 and Thomas Taylor as Mayor in 1768.'[8] Taylor's Hill was noted in Field Book notes by John O'Donovan who – during his survey time at Galway – stayed at Taylor's Hill House, with his host James Hardiman. As the letter *y*, not *i*, was used in the presentation of 'Taylor's Hill Ho.' on the 1839 Ordnance map of the area, it is unlikely that two eminent academics would have mistaken 'Taylor' for 'Tailor' in that spelling. That said, a Petty Court recording clerk did note 'Tailor's Hill' as an address for Michael Flaherty of Pollnarooma East in 1873.[9]

Though various suggestions have been made for the English name choice, there is general agreement that the name was borrowed from Threadneedle Street, its illustrious London relative. The Bank of England is sited on that 'street', whereas Salthill's suburban thoroughfare is more prosaically described as a 'road.' The etymology of the original English version is also disputed with one explanation being based on the Anglo-Saxon word, *thrydda* or *thrydde*, meaning 'third.' Another Anglo-Saxon word, *threadn*, meaning 'to prosper' is also proffered, while *Thrig-needle* from the three needles present in the emblem of the Needlemaker's Company has also been considered. It might be argued that the triad symbolism in Salthill's case represents one thoroughfare connecting two others – the Promenade and Kingston – but numerous roads serve such a purpose without adopting such a name.

Just as the Salthill name is a cloned construct, Threadneedle was also imported by those who, in Donagh Mc Donagh's words, 'look to the East for a sign.'[10] The name at Salthill is not old and was almost certainly the choice of an Anglophile. As Pollnarooma East was cleared of peasant farmers to the point where only two townland houses were occupied during the first census tally of the 20th century, it is fair to presume that the thoroughfare was named by a member of those households, or at the Tennis and Croquet Club which was newly opened on the road. That club's pavilion represented the only building on the townland's rising road for many years, and that same facility was primarily frequented by those who boasted distinctive names of a double-barrelled, military, or titled nature. It is, therefore, plausible to assume that the road name emanated from that sporting source. If not, a member of the Perrse or Holmes' households in the townland's principal piles – Seamount and Sea Park – might have come up with 'Threadneedle.' The occupants of those two dwellings, who later saw family members perish – wearing British uniforms – during the 1914–1918 War, were great supporters of their local tennis club. William Henry Persse's aversion to Gaelic League activity, as evidenced in a postscript to a 1901 letter, which offered grounds for the club,[11] suggests that he would have favoured 'Threadneedle Road' to *Bóthar na Mine*. The word Threadneedle did not appear in that particular missive and its absence suggests that the road was not then so described.

It has not been possible to be definitive about the year in which the road was named, except to say that it was so labelled during the opening decades of the last century. The Tennis Club's address for the early years of its Pollnarooma tenure was generally given as Salthill. By the summer of 1920, however, some newspaper reports of an arson attack on the pavilion gave 'Thread Needle' Road as the club's location.[12] The same split version of the road name was used by the *Connacht Tribune* as late as 1926,[13] after which it appears to have settled into its portmanteau 'Threadneedle' form, thus bringing it into spelling harmony with its Old Smoke sister. The name did not appear in Cancelled Revision Books until the early 1930s, and local newspaper references to the road multiplied throughout that decade, when a mini-building boom began to take root in the area. By that time, of course, construction had begun on what was, eventually, to become *Coláiste Éinde*, and fine houses were beginning to appear on Threadneedle Road, particularly along its eastern stretch.

Famine times, and the trauma that once gave life to its *Bóthar na Mine* construction, had by then faded from memory. Such forgetfulness, particularly in Pollnarooma, is understandable for current household residencies in the townland all began post-1911. Earlier evictions, famines, land clearing, and fate dictated that the place had to start afresh from then. The collective memory of the entire townland had been wiped clean, for its lore and legend vanished with its 19th century inhabitants. Though some fortunate denizens of that departed cohort moved voluntarily, many more were driven out and forced to find their fortune elsewhere.

New Line a.k.a. St. Mary's Road

Though not in Salthill, a second Great Famine road not only provided access to the resort, but also freed up an area that was to later house St. Mary's College. Prior to its building, Nile Lodge corner was a T junction, with no direct route to Newcastle. Furthermore, the construction of what became St. Mary's Road created a triangular site that is today home to *Scoil Fhursa*.

Like many new avenues of the past, the roadway that tied Lower Salthill to Newcastle was first called the 'New Line,' and officially retained that generic soubriquet until 1913. On the week ending 18 November, 1846, ninety seven men were working on that development.[14] Galway's 'Scrutiny Committee' wrote to the Board of Works in the following month, seeking 'to obtain an order for the completion of the road leading from Newcastle to Nile Lodge, for which only 150*l* was sanctioned, the sum granted at Sessions being 250*l*.' It was at that time that Mr. Clements, as Borough Surveyor, 'resigned to the Board of Works the care of the relief works in the district' which he 'could not conscientiously retain the charge of any longer.'[15]

Through the famine years of the new line's construction, progress was slow and in 1849 the road was not only incomplete, but the subject of a legal case. Mr. Clements at a court hearing complained against Mr. Dooley for a breach of the Road Act. The road had not been opened 'by reason of some cabins not being given up at one end of it. A man of the name of Ryan lived at [the] Nile Lodge end of the road, who got no compensation for his ground. He afterwards sold his interest to Mr. Dooley, who it appeared is about building on the site of the road.' Lawyers appearing for Mr. Dooley 'contended as the road was an abandoned one, and never was intended for more than to give temporary employment to a parcel of poor people, that Mr. Dooley had every right to it now, particularly

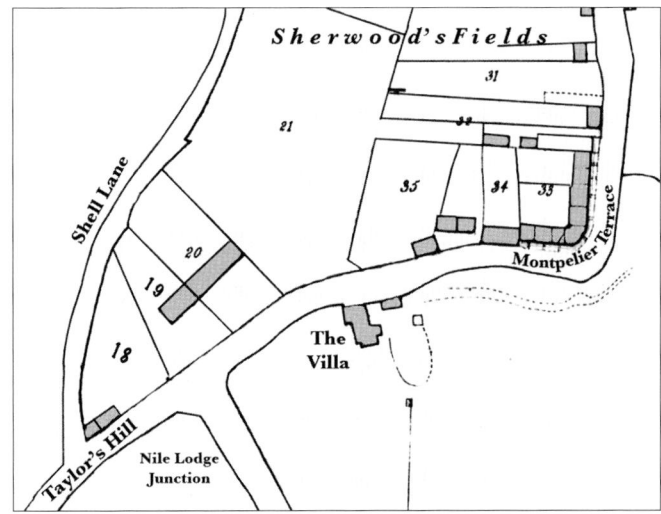

137. Nile Lodge T junction and Garden no. 19, before the 'New Line' was built.

as he got no compensation.'[16] Such evidence confirmed that the New Line was perceived to be work of no real value for the starving poor. That road was – in its time – of the 'going nowhere' variety. At a Town Commissioner meeting in late November 1849, the board was informed 'that the County Surveyor summoned Mr. Dooley for stopping up the new line of road between Nile Lodge and Dangan, and that the matter being referred to the Board of Works, that body in reply stated that they were ready to give the Grand Jury a loan to complete the works.'[17] Mr. Clements was still unhappy in October, 1850 that 'Mr. Dooley had intruded on the new line of road,'[18] and on the last day of that same month it was announced that 'a sum of £200 was lodged' for the Nile Lodge to Dangan road.[19] Board of Works' road money, in relation to the New Line, was being discussed as late as 1851.[20]

The men accused of holding up the road were firstly Mr. Ryan and later Mr. Michael Dooley, after the latter had purchased the former's holding. William-street, Galway, was the address of Mr. Dooley, who identified himself at an 1845 Court sitting as being in the employment of Lord Fitzgerald, who owned land on the southern side of Sea Road.[21] Four years later, the wife of 'M. Dooly' delivered a baby at Montpelier Terrace, which overlooked a tract of Lord Fitzgerald's holding.[22] Mr. Michael Dooley was also recorded as a tenant holding Garden no. 19 at Sherwood's Fields, which held 'two good slated dwellings, Offices and Garden' in 1852.[23]

The 'slated' reference from a contemporaneous auction brochure affirms Mr. Dooley's construction of two fine houses – at his no. 19 plot – which stood in the way of the new road. That new line of road was to divide Shell Lane and leave the triangular number 18 plot for the Irish Church Mission Orphanage and School – *Scoil Fhursa* today.

138. On left, two 'Albert Terrace' houses built by Michael Dooley in the mid-19th century, with St. Mary's College, on right, which opened on the New Line in 1912.

At the time of Griffith's 1855 Valuation, Michael Dooley was the immediate lessor to Samuel Ussher Roberts, Galway's Borough Engineer, and John S. Kirwan, of a well known and landed Galway family. Those two gentlemen resided in a pair of impressive houses, in what Richard Griffith called Albert Terrace, but was also known – from the early 1850s – as Palmyra Terrace. The latter address was noted when Samuel Roberts' wife, Emily, home-delivered a daughter in April, 1851.[24] Mr. Kirwan lived in the last house of the row, abutting the new road, while the Roberts' household resided next-door. Mr. Dooley's two premises still stand today and represent the western terrace-end of what we now know simply as the Crescent. According to Richard Griffith, there were five houses in Albert Terrace in 1855 and the New Line between Nile Lodge and Newcastle had definitely been completed by then. The placement of Mr. Dooley's pair of slated houses, in the path of the proposed Newcastle – Nile Lodge road, ensured that the new line would not be completely straight, and a curved kink – which still exists towards the Nile Lodge end – was forced on the builders: The famine road had to run by the gabled end of one of Mr. Dooley's two leased houses, as it still does to this day.

When completed, the new roadway from Newcastle that opened onto Nile Lodge junction created a triangular plot of land, which became a site for the Protestant Mission School that today is home to *Scoil Fhursa*. Defining the three sides of that triangular site today are short sections of Taylor's Hill and St. Mary's Road, with Sherwood Avenue *ar chúl na scoile*. The latter avenue name is not surprising for Shell Lane skirted the northern end of Sherwood's Fields, which once covered an area from the present day *Scoil Fhursa* site as far as Ernie Deacy's Vegetable shop, near the Small Crane. Those fields' southern-eastern border was the road that today runs from the entrance to Sherwood Avenue, along by The Crescent to Devon Place before turning left by Montpelier Terrace, on past Ely Place, and almost as far as the Small Crane, which housed a potato market in 1852 **(fig.66)**.

The westerly section of the divided Shell Lane, which ran behind the Mission School and Orphanage, became a subject of debate in 1863. Two efforts to have that short stretch closed up were made in that year, as Messrs. John Harrison and

Right 139. A triangular site, created by the New Line, housed the Taylor's Hill Mission Church, School and Orphanage, with Shell Lane (now Sherwood Avenue) to its northern rear, and the New Line (now St. Mary's Road) to its front. That site today (2018) houses *Scoil Fhursa*.

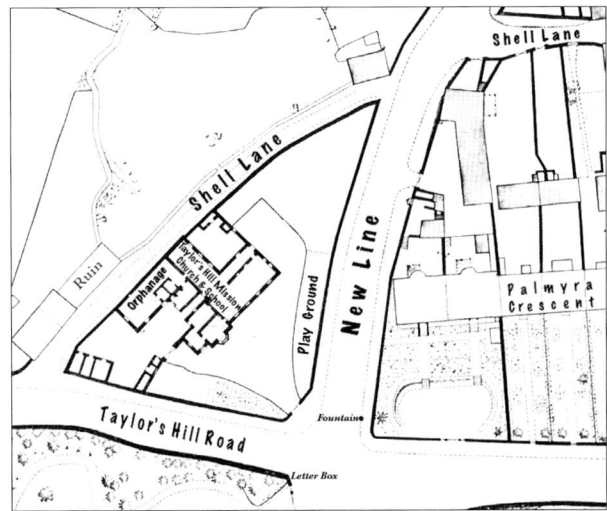

Below Figure 140.

James Forbes considered it to be in bad repair and a nuisance. Their first application was rejected by the Grand Jury on the grounds 'that a portion of the lane was inhabited and was a public thoroughfare.' It was suggested at a second discussion on the issue that 'Mr Harrison was so deeply interested in this matter because it was intended to transform the passage into a play-ground for the children attending the Taylor's-hill school.'[25] An extended playground, however, was not provided, for it was decided to improve and repair the road that is now known as Sherwood Avenue.

Taylor's Hill Mission Orphanage, Church & School – The Bird's Nest

The Irish Church Missions' Society, founded by Rev. Alexander Dallas, was virulently opposed to 'the errors of Romanism,' and sought to convert Irish Catholics to the Protestant faith. Active in West Galway and South Mayo during the Great Famine, those that converted were disparagingly known as 'Jumpers'– from the Gaelic verb *iompaigh* (to turn) – and 'Soupers,' who accepted the sustenance that saved them from starvation. The Society built orphanages at Kingstown, Dublin (1859) and Nile Lodge junction, both of which were colloquially known as the 'Bird's Nest.' Other orphanages were also operated by the Society, including one at Aasleagh and *Nead na Farraige* at Spiddal. The story of the Connemara Mission is comprehensively told in Mirriam Moffitt's 2008 book, *Soupers and Jumpers, The Protestant Missions in Connemara 1848–1937*.[26]

141. Mr. Roberts' Gothic Mission School design – Scoil Fhursa today.

Mr. Samuel Ussher Roberts was architect on the Church Mission building at Galway. He and his family, as earlier noted, lived nearby for a time at the residence to the right in the Albert Terrace image above **(fig.138)**. Samuel's design of the Irish Mission Church and School was described by the *Dublin Builder* in 1862: *The style is Gothic, the rubble of walls being in alternate courses of granite and local marble, the windows having pointed arches, the roof high pitched, and one portion of the building two storeys high for teacher's residence, committee &c.*[27]

Cáit Ní Ríordáin, in her 1988 publication, *Bhí mé i Scoil Fhursa,* tells the story of the school's opening:

The Missionaries felt that a new Mission School house and Dormitory were needed in Galway, and through the generosity and help of Captain George Wale, who was in the Coastguard service in Galway at the time, the premises known as 'Sherwood Fields' Orphanage' was built in 1862. It was opened by Mr. Dallas, and was to be under 'the superintendence of Reverend E. Ellis and was given the Bishop's 'license,' which meant it could be used as a place of worship. It also contained a dwelling house…The Irish Church Missions understood the value of using the Irish language when it was the vernacular of the children and they were very careful to appoint teachers with a knowledge of Irish.'[28] Unsurprisingly, the Church and Mission School at Nile Lodge was viewed with suspicion by some members of the majority faith in Galway.

It was not Mr. Robert's medieval stone construct, however, that caused concern among citizens, but the proselytising reputation of the new establishment's patrons. That led to the 'Bird's Nest' becoming an object of distrust among Roman Catholic locals, who were wary of whatever occurred at the place. As early as 1866, an 'alleged outrage at "The Mission School",' led to an inquiry being conducted by Mr. Starkie R.M. and Captain Blake Forster. When the 'outrage' story first broke in March, it was explained that the schoolhouse was used 'as the parochial church of the parish of Rahoon,' and that during a Sunday evening service, 'some malicious person climbed on the roof, and threw a packet of gunpowder down the chimney.' It was thought that the intended target was the fireplace of the vestry, which was behind the pulpit, but that the powder was diverted by a flue into the fireplace of 'an adjoining apartment, in which two children of the schoolmaster, Mr. St. George, were at the time playing.' An explosion took place, which 'burned very severely the elder of the two children,' who was described as being in a very precarious position.[29] The story was picked up by newspapers nationally and the *Vindicator* took umbrage, on behalf of its readers, that 'a calumny' against the 'character of the locality' had been circulated, which the Rector of Rahoon, Rev. John Treanor, did not correct. The same organ was also annoyed that Mr. Starkie R.M. had offered a reward 'for the discovery of the perpetrator of an outrage that no one believes ever was committed.'[30]

There was agreement that the explosion was caused by gunpowder, but the delivery of – or source of – the powder was disputed. The school teacher and vicar held that it was maliciously dropped down a chimney, while a second opinion pointed to explosive material being housed at the school, because 'blasting operations' had been 'carried on [at] the premises lately.'[31] The testimony of two individuals was published in the press. The younger witness, Francis Jackson, who was then an apprentice at the *Express* office, was 'out of the dormitory' for over a year. Francis claimed that he had seen powder in the Mission premises, during the previous twelve months, and explained that powder was hanging up in a bag at the school master's kitchen. Mr. St. George rejected that charge and denied having any powder on the premises. Master Jackson did not believe that the gunpowder had been thrown down the chimney, but if it had, he suspected a boy called Egan to be the culprit.

Mr. Jack Toohey, the school watchman, who had been in the employ of the Irish Church Mission Society for eighteen years, explained how on nights of Divine Service he would 'walk occasionally from the gate to the end of the church, lest any offensive characters might enter for the purpose of causing a disturbance about the place.' Such strict surveillance pointed to the protective policy of a facility, which was in its infancy at Nile Lodge corner, in a less than welcoming environment. On the clear Sunday night of 25 March, 1866, Mr. Toohey did not see any person on the roof and it was believed that the burning episode was an accident. The fact that the injured boy burned his hand was presented as proof that a youthful daredevil was the victim of his own foolishness, 'when putting the powder into the fire.'[32] The school authorities did not come well out of the affair.

Almost half a century later, the Mission School at Nile Lodge again drew local attention. That was during the 1913 Dublin Lockout, which pitted workers behind trade union leader, James Larkin, against employers led by William Murphy, the proprietor of the *Irish Independent*. The suffering of poor Dublin children during that industrial dispute was severe and Pádraig Yeates has recorded how their plight prompted 'Madame Dora Montefiore, a member of a prominent liberal Jewish family, to provide temporary foster homes for strikers' children in Britain. Dr. Walsh (Archbishop of Dublin), who had been relatively sympathetic towards the strikers, denounced the scheme for putting the Catholic faith of the children at risk. He also believed it would expose them to the higher living standards of Britain and leave them discontented with their lot when they returned home. Catholic clergy mobilised 'vigilance' committees in Dublin and Dún Laoghaire, which prevented all but a small number of children from leaving the city. The supply of children rapidly dried up when the Murphyite press began publishing the names and addresses of parents. The tremendous effort put into preventing the children leaving Dublin was not paralleled by similar efforts to look after them at home.'[33]

Galway also experienced industrial unrest that year, which, as we have seen, had an impact on the organisation of the 1913 Bazaar, whose proceeds were destined for the improvement of Salthill. A rumour circulated locally that some children of Dublin's striking workers had been sent to Galway, and the *Connacht Tribune* reported on the story:

A considerable amount of sensation was caused in Galway during the week end by the rumour that fifteen children of the Dublin strikers had been secretly sent to Galway to be lodged at what is locally known as the 'Bird's Nest.' The report also gained credence that close upon a dozen children had been sent to a home in Clifden. The affair caused no small sensation and vigilant members of Galway Ladies' Auxiliary of the A.O.H. [Ancient Order of Hibernians] were speedily on the track of the alleged proselytisers. No facts, however, came to light, although it was stated positively by certain people who said they had witnessed the transportation of the children, that a number of them had been taken out on the Galway and Salthill trams, and had actually been seen entering the home. Our representative has investigated the matter carefully, and called recently at Taylor's Hill Church Missions School, where the children were said to have been brought. In an interview with Mr. Bane, the head master, he emphatically stated that there was not the smallest scintilla of foundation for the sensational rumours that had been going about. 'We have not received any of the Dublin strikers' children here,' he added in reply to further inquiries. Asked if it was not true that children had recently been received into the school, he replied that only one Protestant child had come there during the last six weeks, and it is a native of a western county.[34]

It was also in 1913 that the New Line – on which the Mission School stood – was renamed. In June of that year, Mr. Stephen Faller of the Crescent officially proposed a St. Mary's moniker for the road, a motion that was unanimously approved by the Urban Council.[35] There was sense in that naming, for by then St. Mary's College had been built on the New Line, and that imposing building still proudly overlooks the thoroughfare, which borrows its patron's name. The predominance of St. Mary's as a name in the area stemmed from the renaming of Mount Vernon, when that house was acquired – for £1,500 in 1887 – as the bishops' residence and rebranded as Mount St. Mary's. A house terrace; an avenue; a school; and a road were all subsequently styled under the same title.

Bóthar na nDeich bPingin – Grattan Road

While Threadneedle Road and St. Mary's Road were both the products of *Gorta Mór* relief works, their sister Famine Road was a later construction. Grattan Road was built during the early 1860s, when the western seaboard, in particular, suffered greatly through hungry years.

Miss Frances Grattan was the granddaughter of Henry Grattan, of Grattan's Parliament fame, and daughter to Henry Grattan Jnr., the man who bought the Claddagh in 1852 for £1,710. She and her sister, Marian, were both religious and single ladies, who contributed to the 1864 formation of a Poor Clares' Convent in Drumshanbo. Both siblings wished to join the congregation but their 'mother was so against Marian Grattan joining that she went to Rome to get an edict from Pope Pius IX to stop her entering the convent. The elder Fanny was too sick to join, but in April 1865, Marian's dream came true and she entered the convent in Drumshanbo, under the name of St. Mary. When Mother St. Joseph died in June 1879, Mother St. Agnes (Marian Grattan) became abbess and stayed in that position for thirty-three years, until her death on 29 May, 1912. She was aged seventy-two and had suffered a long illness.'[36] Though Fanny was unable to fulfil her wish to join the order she 'generously supported the community by giving all her inheritance.'[37]

Long before Frances Grattan's inheritance helped the Sisters of St. Clare, the people of Galway had been enriched by the same lady's great generosity. She was devised, in late 1858, the entire Claddagh land bank which her father, Henry, had purchased six years earlier. Incidentally, in that same year, 1858, Frances' sister, Pauline Grattan, married Thomas Arthur Bellew, Esq., of Mount Bellew, thus creating a further Grattan-Galway connection.[38] The year 1862 was particularly distressful for the people of Galway town, and the Catholic Bishop, John McEvilly, penned a letter to the *Irish Times* on behalf of a local Relief Committee, made up of men of every religious denomination, who worked cordially together in the administration of relief to 1,300 families. The bishop noted that 'in this number are

142. Land reclaimed by Grattan Road's construction is shown inside white border. (Courtesy of *Irish Independent* and N.L.I.)

not included 100 families of Claddagh fishermen, who, in consequence of stress of weather, are unable to go to sea, and are thrown a burden on the town. I believe the benevolent lady who owns the Claddagh, Miss Fanny Grattan, has expended in this relief more money in one year than she has received from them for years together.'[39]

Miss Grattan's charitable work continued into 1863, when her idea of building a famine relief road through her seaside property first materialised. It is impossible to say if a suggestion by a *Well-wisher* correspondent in 1859, the year that she came into possession of her Galway property, played any part in Fanny Grattan's enterprise. The anonymous scribe advocated the driving of 'piles along the thirty yards which admits the sea at present,' which would reclaim the malodorous White Strand Marsh.[40]

In terms of that marsh's historical background, Father J. Rabbitte believed that 'The Whyte Strand…through which the Grattan Road was made' was the scene of a famed battle of old: 'In Hardiman's [edition of O'Flaherty's] *Iar-Connacht,* p. 384, we read that the Earl of Clanricarde with his people were defeated at Trabane, white strand, by Murrough O'Flaherty. Hardiman assumes that this Trabane was the one near Barna but as the account says that "most of the Earl's people were drowned in the sea and river," the Trabane would appear to be the one at Salthill.'[41] That battle was fought in 1564 and Roderic O'Flaherty's account ran: 'The earl's people were forced to turn their backs and the most part of them drowned in the sea and river of Galway…some got over the river but such was their apprehension of death, they knew not how.'[42]

Making her own history, it was Miss Frances Grattan who was to the fore in financing an 1860's road, which connected the Claddagh's Fair Hill to the foot of Salthill's King's Hill. In 1863, the *Vindicator* reported that 'half the population of our ancient city were in a state of destitution,' and a Relief Committee was in place to offer aid to the distressed poor. That committee was presided over by Bishop

McEvilly 'and composed of our leading gentry and merchants and the clergy of all denominations.'[43] Galway, at the same time, was striving to become the departing port for Britain's mail to the New World. As a Graving Dock (dry-dock) was considered essential to the delivery of Packet Station status,[44] Mutton Island was identified as the site for that proposed structure. To facilitate that development, County Surveyor, Samuel Ussher Roberts, took charge of the creation of a new line from Claddagh Quay to Fair Hill, which was initially known as the Breakwater Road. In tandem with that development, Miss Grattan undertook to build a road from Fair Hill to King's Hill. The Claddagh road to Fair Hill was to begin 'behind Donelan's house at Ball's Bridge,'[45] while Grattan Road was to end at the Baths, which stood at the foot of King's Hill. Work on the Headford Road was also prioritised by Mr. Roberts at that time.

In early 1863 'Mr. Roberts tendered his very valuable services to the Relief Committee,' which meant that Galway's public and charitable agencies co-operated on joint schemes. The Committee had been furnished with plans 'of the proposed Pier and Breakwater and Graving Dock' by the County Surveyor, who also announced that – for that public project – he could 'make the labour …in the shape of relief.'[46] The Claddagh–Fairhill Road, in the direction of the intended Pier and Breakwater, was started in January 1863. A line to Fairhill had previously been mooted – seventeen years earlier – by Mr. Roberts' predecessor, Mr. Clements, C.E., who considered such a development 'most useful and calculated to serve Galway very much, namely a continuation of Dominick street direct to the sea at Fairhill.'[47] That project was priced at £1,200 in 1846.

The *Dublin Builder* reported on the later 1863 enterprise and stated that it was 'progressing under the direction of Mr. S.U. Roberts C.E. and "400 men are employed thereon who would otherwise be starving, or inmates of the workhouse".'[48] A decision had been made, earlier in the same year, that no two members of the same family would be employed on a relief scheme, to ensure that whatever aid was available would be spread as widely as possible.[49] It was in June, 1863 that Miss Grattan laid the first stone on her strand road, which was a continuation of the Claddagh–Fairhill line.

The Galway Contract… June 10, 1863… On this day fifty or sixty of our idle population were put to work at a new line of road some time since projected by Miss Grattan to run through her property, which borders on the sea shore, leading to the marine little town of Salthill, so well known as a bathing-place. She, with a most benevolent disposition has come forward in this, the most trying season for the poor man to help him over it by giving extensive employment. It is expected that 500 will be employed before a week is over.[50]

Though the worker numbers projected, and those later reported, did not always tally, it was clear that many were saved from the workhouse by Miss Grattan's initiative. In August, the *Vindicator* reported on progress, which was being supervised by Miss Grattan's local agent, Mr. Cullen:

> The embankment being built at the marsh by Miss Grattan is at present giving considerable employment. There are over a hundred men employed, including labourers and masons, under the superintendence of Mr. Cullen at an expense of £100 a week…There is, therefore, a good prospect for the labouring classes in that direction. The Grattan Road will be a great advantage to the town, as it will open up one of the pleasantest suburbs of our city both as a promenade, and for building purposes. The improvements to be made in the bay in that neighbourhood will have the effect of making the town grow in that direction.[51]

The same newspaper returned in October to the road development. It first announced that Miss Grattan proposed building 'several marine residences' on her reclaimed land before reporting that the road would not be completed that year, owing to the Grand Jury's solicited £800 loan being unavailable. Despite that delay, an optimistic view of the project was presented:

> The completion of the Grattan Road will add much to the beauty and salubrity of the handsomest of our suburban districts. The embankment being made by Miss Grattan will reclaim 28 acres of land, which is now a swamp, but which will become, with a little cultivation, some of the most fertile ground in the neighbourhood…In the past season of distress Miss Grattan has given great employment to the poor of that neighbourhood in making this road and embankment. Since June last up to the present time, there have been over 200 labourers employed and from 12 to 14 masons regularly. Over £1,200 have been expended by Miss Grattan's agents in carrying out this great work. It will, when finished, completely alter the appearance of Salt Hill, and contribute much to make that favourite watering place one of the nicest localities in the Kingdom.[52]

There was further delay in the following year, with the Grand Jury's £800 loan again at issue. In March, Mr. Roberts explained that 'an omission in the presentment of the sum provided for interest' resulted in a refusal by her Majesty's Treasury to sanction the loan. The works were consequently suspended.[53] The problem was rectified at Presentment Sessions, where the loan was approved, and Mr. Roberts re-commenced the works on Grattan Road,[54] which continued into the summer of 1864. In June, the *Irish Times* reported that 'The Grattan Road is in steady progress; there are over fifty men, between masons and labourers, employed on it.'[55] In January 1865, money was subscribed to complete the Grattan Road,[56] a task that was duly accomplished. The following year saw tenders being sought 'to make 14 perches of a protection wall on the South East side of the road from Fairhill to Salthill, between the sluice at the end of the Grattan Road, and the gable end of the house lately occupied by Miss Nally, the expense of same not to exceed £1 per perch.'[57] Miss Jane Nally had occupied a substantial house, with a rateable valuation of £13 10s., beside Andrew King's Baths' complex at the bottom of King's Hill.

In relation to Eavan Boland's perspective on the futility of famine roads, it must be acknowledged that a 'going nowhere' characterisation of Miss Grattan's construction would not be completely true. At the time of the road's creation, however, its western destination was quite modest, for the gently sloping line of thatched and slated houses that made up Salthill Village was then less than sixty years old – and quite small. A more sheltered path to the fledgling resort already existed in *Bóthar na Trá*. The new road's construction did, however, have two advantages. Firstly, it provided paid work for starving men and their families. Secondly, its creation reclaimed a smelly and unsightly marshy area, which was, according to the 1839 Ordnance map, 'Flooded at Spring Tides.'

Figure 143.

Whatever about Ireland's debt to her famed forbear, Fanny Grattan – in her very own right – is worthy of Galway's gratitude, for she contributed £1,200, a massive sum at the time, to the building of her famine relief road. In her gallant kindness to the poor of Galway, Miss Grattan paid an enormous sum to aid unfortunate people from whom she received no benefit. It might be argued that the building of Grattan Road delivered reclaimed land to the Grattan Estate, a fact not missed by a rate setting official, whose Revision Book note recorded that Miss Grattan's land was 'well enclosed in 1863 & protected from sea.'[58] While her road construction added value to the land she held, its cost went way beyond what Miss Grattan could have bought for the same £1,200 sum. To put Fanny Grattan's munificence in context, her father had purchased the 29 acres of the Claddagh, which included the Whitestrand Marsh, for £1710 a decade earlier, while Fr. Daly had purchased the whole of Lower Salthill at the same time for £2110. Miss Grattan, as we have earlier seen, also donated five acres of her reclaimed land for the building of an Industrial School for Boys. Though not matching Miss Grattan's personal philanthropy, the town's Grand Jury committed £800 towards the new road, and a combination of the Relief Committee and Captain O'Hara (1832–1902) added a further £300 to the project.[59]

The *Vindicator* accounts of 1863 were prescient in predicting Galway's urban westward spread, and the creation of Galway's first suburb. It is also clear that the road was publicly named before its construction began,[60] and that its English name, 'Grattan Road,' was not preceded by its colloquial Gaelic title: *Bóthar na nDeich bPingin*. Agreed in February 1863 was a proposal by Mr. Roberts that – on relief work – 'less able bodied men be paid nine pence a day, and those who were better able to work a shilling.'[61] Those remunerative scales do not appear to have been disbursed at Grattan Road, for a ten-penny-a-day rate is enshrined in the Gaelic *Bóthar na nDeich bPingin* name, which was – most likely – coined by Gaelic speaking labourers who hard-earned those same coppers. The Irish and English versions still appear today on official road signs.

Grattan Lodge a.k.a. Moon's Lodge

A black and white postcard picture of Grattan Lodge, Salthill, recalls a time when Miss Grattan retained a residence on the seaside promontory, which is now home to Celia Griffin Park. That same Lodge enjoyed connections with a broad range of people, including parliamentarians on either side of the Irish Sea.

This study has earlier surmised that Bulteel's Baths, which were described as old in the early 1830s, may have been sited on the same promontory, which then abutted Bulteel's Marsh. Those baths lay in ruins by 1859. Following Grattan Road's construction in the early 1860s, that triangular headland stood to the seaward side of Miss Grattan's famine thoroughfare. The same foreland was part of the 1852 purchase of the Claddagh by Henry Grattan Jnr. and a herd's house was sited there. That was before Henry's daughter, Frances (Fanny) Grattan, took charge of the place, following her father's 1859 death. A larger building, rateably valued at £6 was erected on the site in 1865 by Miss Grattan, not long after the completion of *Bóthar na nDeich bPingin*. The new Lodge was leased for a spell by Frances Grattan, before she was replaced as Immediate Lessor by the Honourable Charles Langdale, whose son – also Charles – had married Frances' sister, Henrietta Grattan, in 1852. The Honourable and elder Charles Joseph Langdale (1787–1868) was regarded 'as the Nestor of the old English Catholics,' who claimed 'on behalf of his religion, the right of political emancipation.' On its eventual concession, 'he was one of the first English Catholics to enter the first Reformed Parliament of 1833–'34.'[62] It was around the beginning of the 1870's decade that noted draper, Alexander Moon, became the recorded occupier of the seaside Grattan Road residence. An age-old and persistent nuisance of coastal living was to irritate Alexander, who brought a Mincloon man to court on the following charge:

> That deft. did on the 29th day of January 1873 at Grattan's Lodge in said county unlawfully steal, take and carry away a quantity of sand, complainant's property at Grattan's Lodge aforesd.[63]

On Mr. Moon taking up residency, during the mid-1880s, at Ardmore on Taylor's Hill, the seaside lodge was again let out. Replacing Alexander Moon as occupier was Monica Whammond (née Oliver), who had married James Whammond in 1855, and Monica was followed by Sybilla L. Warren, who was, one suspects, connected to the brush making family of that surname at Dominick Street.

Hermina Dacies, who was fined for having a licence-less white poodle at Grattan Road in 1894, was the next occupier, before John Flynn and family took up a residency there in the following year. John, a Limerick born widower, described himself as a 'Const.[able] Pensioner' on his census form, when residing with his daughter Marian, on Grattan Road in 1901. John was followed by Martin Rhatigan of Creagh, Ballinasloe, who had joined the Connaught Rangers in January 1888, and saw service in India and Egypt during his initial 23 year army term. Giving

Salthill's Famine Roads

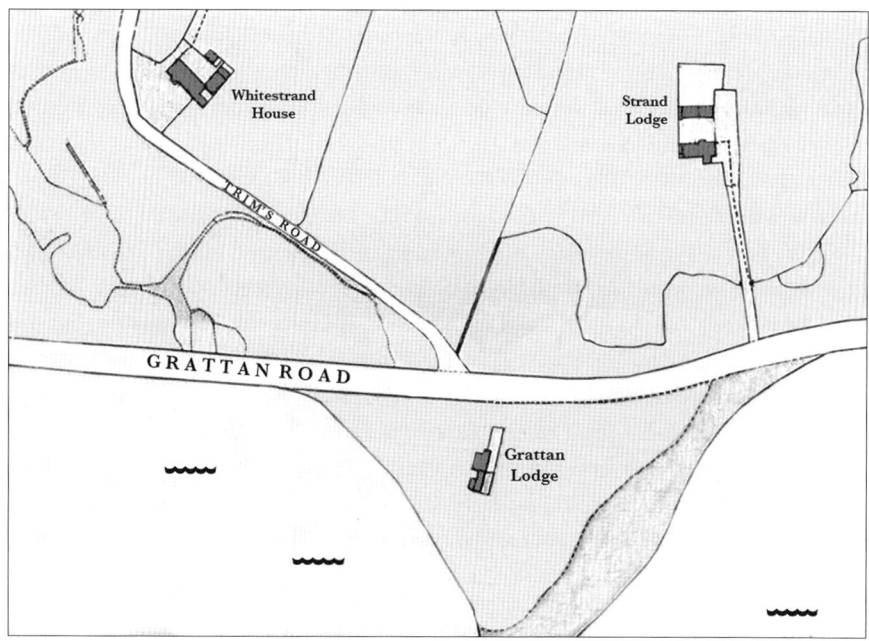

144. Nineteenth century representation of Grattan Lodge, on seaward side of Grattan Road.

145. Grattan Lodge postcard.

his trade as Game keeper, Martin left the service as a Colour Sergeant in 1912, but subsequently signed up for First World War – short service – duty on 27 November, 1914. Then aged 47, his address was given as 84 Lower Salthill. Following the war, Martin's army pension address was the Post Office at Taylor's Hill.[64] A married man, Martin had wed Mary Anne (O') Flynn at St. Joseph's Church in February, 1905.

Following Mr. Rhatigan at Grattan Lodge was George Lyons, who had tied the knot in the very same year as his predecessor, when he married his Scottish born *beau*, Mary Jean Mowatt Milne, at Galway's Presbyterian Church. A Fishery Inspector, George and family were in residence at Grattan Lodge in 1913, but did not tarry long before they were replaced by Claire Millard, who may have been the 'Miss Millard' who succeeded Miss Clancy as Manageress of the Railway Hotel in 1923.[65] Next up was Mr. John Kelly, who divided the Lodge into two houses before selling the property to Leo Leonard, a plumbing contractor, who had married Margaret O'Neill of Clybaun, Barna, in 1928. After a short time at Grattan Lodge, the Leonard family moved, and following their later arrival at Lower Taylor's Hill, Mrs. Leonard became postmistress of the local Post Office, after the 1939 death of neighbour Mrs. Glynn, who had held that position for many years. Mr. Leo Leonard became best known in the town, following his appointment as Water Inspector to Galway Corporation in 1953. A son of that Leonard household, also Leo, who today (2018) resides at Taylor's Hill, was born at Grattan Lodge.

It was a Conlon presence of political pedigree that replaced the Leonard occupancy on Grattan Road. Martin Conlon, the son of a farmer, who was born at Kilmore, County Roscommon in 1879, was to live a most interesting and revolutionary life. Martin married Margaret (Peig) Concannon of Glenamaddy in 1910 and both were committed Republicans. A fluent Irish speaker, Peig was an early *Cumann na mBan* recruit, who 'marched in uniform in the O'Donovan Rossa funeral,' and delivered a message of Rebellion, hidden inside the sole of her stocking, to Mícheál Thornton at Spiddal during Holy Week, 1916. In the course of the Rising, which began some days later, Peig served 'by giving assistance all round, nursing the sick and preparing food for them.'[66] She opened a shop at 342 North Circular Road in 1918.

Peig's husband Martin, a Gaelic Leaguer and Sinn Féiner, was a leading member of the Irish Republican Brotherhood, who served in a

146. Martin Conlon, in centre, at the time of the pivotal O'Donovan Rossa funeral. Bottom right is Countess Markievicz.

reconstituted IRB Supreme Council after the Rebellion. On arriving in the Capital as a young man, he had taken up a position with the Rates Department of Dublin Corporation and fought in the Church Street area of the city during the Rising, before escaping to England in its wake. Martin became a great friend to Michael Collins, who was a regular visitor to the Conlon home at Cabra Park, which was a noted refuge for men 'on the run.' It was in that house that Bulmer Hobson was 'detained' in the days before Easter Monday 1916.[67] Three years later, during the War of Independence, the men who set out to kill Lord French, the British Viceroy, left Conlon's Cabra home. Among them was Martin Savage, who ate his last meal at a Conlon table, before being killed in that attack. Dan Breen was injured in the same engagement. Never arrested himself, Martin Conlon went on to represent Roscommon as a Cumann na nGaedhael T.D. in Dáil Eireann (1923–1933), and was later a member of the third Seanad (1938–1943). Two of Martin's brothers had connections with Galway, with Father Michael Conlon O.P. serving as Prior at the Claddagh up to 1933, before transferring to the Dominican House at Tallaght. Another brother, James Conlon, a Salthill resident, was a Commercial Traveller, who was found dying on O'Connell Street in 1934. Though a tramcar driver was charged with causing the fatality,[68] insufficient 'evidence to show how he came by the injuries' was noted on Mr. Conlon's death certificate.

Mr. Martin Conlon set up his own Auctioneering firm, with business addresses at Dublin and Galway's Grattan Lodge in the 1930s. Though their principal residence was in Dublin, the Conlon couple spent time at Grattan Lodge, with their summer stays being occasionally announced in the local press, as it was in 1936.[69] Summer lettings were regularly advertised, with four chalets also available on the site. The lodge's position was topographically problematic, with climatic and human influences proving troublesome. In 1941, for example, Martin wrote to Galway Corporation complaining about immense quantities of gravel and sand being removed from the site,[70] a longstanding problem that had irritated Alexander Moon sixty eight years earlier. A short stretch of wall – which still stands – was erected along the pathway in 1943 to prevent sand from accumulating in the roadway. It was in 1957 that Mrs. Peig Conlon, of Grattan Lodge, brought a claim against Galway County Council 'in respect of damage to a house and four adjoining bungalows at Grattan Road.' The damage was done following a bad storm when the house was 'swamped by the high seas and the tenants had to evacuate. The house was then boarded up but was broken into and considerable damage was caused.'[71] Fifty five pounds was paid in compensation. In that same year – 1957– the house was described as a 'ruin,'[72] and its ultimate demise followed the destruction wrought by Hurricane Debbie in 1961. Two years later, Mrs. Peig Conlon of North Circular Road passed away and her husband, Martin, died in 1965. Martin's papers today form part of U.C.D.'s Archive collection.[73]

Residents of Grattan Road's promontory carried – and yet carry – happy memories of the place. During the research period of this study, Mrs. Phil Moroney of Ard na Mara – a relative of Martin Conlon – passed away. She liked to recall the first months of her marriage in 1951, when her new house at Ard na Mara was not completed in time. While waiting for contractor Malachy Burke to finish her home, she and her husband, Michael, resided in a chalet on Grattan Road's headland, where Mrs. Moroney began each day with a bathe in the briny. John and Eileen O'Shaughnessy also resided at Grattan Road for a time before moving to Mayvilla at Lower Salthill, where they reared their family of photographic and rowing renown.

'Grattan Lodge' and 'Moon's Lodge' represented alternative house titles that were not coined without cause. As Miss Grattan built the residence in 1865, her surname was appended to it and 'Grattan's Lodge' was the house-name noted at the court case pursued by Alexander Moon in 1873. That said, recorded Moon ties to the lodge – as occupier or lessor – stretched from the late 1860s to the early 1930s, even though Alexander Moon had passed away in 1902. The Grattan connection was also considerable as Henry Grattan (Jun.) M.P., and his daughters, Fanny and Henrietta (Langdale), also boasted strong ties with the place. Frances' altruistic contribution to the area was truly remarkable, through her generosity to the Claddagh people, as well as her donation of a site for a Boy's Industrial School, not to mention her bounty in financing a famine road, which saved many from starvation during the early 1860s. Miss Frances Grattan, unable to join the Poor Clares at Drumshambo because of ill health, personified a Christian philosophy throughout her secular interactions with Galway and its people.

Those here chronicled were not the only people to have lived on the Grattan Road headland, for many unrecorded tenants would have occupied premises on that site, which has not been free of human habitation since 1961. Throughout subsequent decades, youngsters have seasonally pitched their tents at a place, which offers a great vantage point for a Colahan-Crosby moment, where one can joyously watch 'the sun go down on Galway Bay.' One wonders if a man of mystery, who has spent over a year in a self-made, minimalist tent on the ocean's edge during 2015/'17, has any idea that in occupying a patch of seaside Galway ground, he has shared links – however tenuous – with worthy British Parliamentarians and feisty Irish Rebels, as well as a host of other colourful characters.

Celia Griffin Park

Celia Griffin Park, on that same land patch, today memorialises a tragic and unfortunate young girl who, as a six year old child, perished in March 1847 – during the Great Hunger. Celia is representative of so many victims of starvation and suffering.

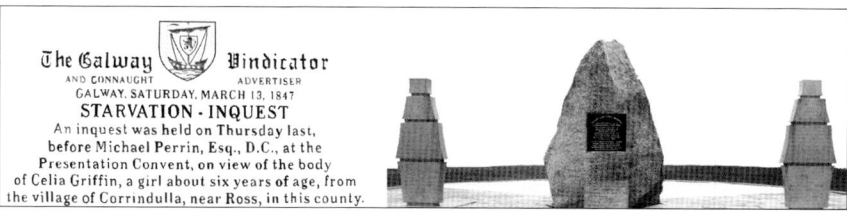

147. To the left, the opening section of a *Galway Vindicator* report on the inquest into the tragic death of Celia Griffin, which is cut in stone at Grattan Road. To the right, a memorial to the famine ships that departed Galway *le linn an Ghorta Mhóir*.

148. Inscription – to the left – at Galway's Famine Memorial Park, where the names of famine ships are recorded on Grattan Road. Skeletal image of a famine ship – to the right – as represented in sculptor John Behan's National Famine Monument at Murrisk, Mayo.

A monument, featuring a press report of her plight, pays moving tribute to Celia and those she represents.

In listing transatlantic vessels of the period, other standing monuments at Celia Griffin Park pay individual tribute to the ships, their captains and crews that carried countless thousands from Galway Bay to a New World. The act of naming was raised to an exalted level by the poet Patrick Kavanagh in the line: *Naming these things is the love-act and the pledge.*[74] In that reverential context, respect is paid and thanks given by Galway's Grattan Road memorial to the crafts that ferried fleeing West of Ireland families, and individuals, to more promising American shores.

At the foot of Croagh Patrick, on the other hand, a ghostly vessel, evoking the coffin ships of popular memory, represents Ireland's National Famine Monument. Distinctly different perspectives are represented in contrasting memorial iconography at Galway's Grattan Road, and Murrisk's road to Louisburgh.

Chapter 18

A PERSSE PRESENCE – ROW – AMERICAN CONNECTION

The life of gentry's gents was betimes enlivened by wagers, which were often profligate, in diversions that ranged from horse racing to card playing. Thomas 'Buck' Whaley's gambling spirit, as earlier described, was much broader in its range – to the point of the bizarre. Members of Salthill's landed elite enjoyed many luxuries that included sailing yachts and the opportunity to travel abroad for recreational purposes. Despite such grandeur and opulence, life was not without its travails in the world of romance, as experienced by Sarah Belinda Persse, and health, with landed families losing family members to the maladies of the day. Familial friction was not unknown in landed society, and one family – with strong Salthill ties – experienced such strife.

A Persse presence was almost pervasive – during the 19th century – in the general Salthill area, as family members enjoyed ties with numerous residences in the place. Blackrock House, Seamount, Glenarde House, Ardmore, Mount Vernon, Nile Lodge, Norman Villas, The Croft, St. Helen's and number 2 Beach Avenue were all home, at some time, to a Persse occupant. Some stays were quite short. In the mid-1860s, for example, when Nile Lodge was briefly home to Henry Sadleir Persse, he was replaced by Anne O'Hara as occupier at Glenarde. Henry subsequently returned to Glenarde, where he resided up to his 1899 demise. Another Persse gentleman enjoyed the luxury of Blackrock House and the comfort of a Beach Avenue cottage during his time at the resort. That antipodal residency experience was the upshot of a family row, which was as bitter as it was lengthy.

Persse Family Row

Sibling tensions in landed families could be acute, particularly as the financial stakes were especially high. The Persse family did not escape such divisions and members of three estates, Roxborough, Castleboy and Moyode, became involved in a complex dispute, which resulted in judgement hearings being held in settings that ranged from Galway's court house to the House of Lords.

The Persse dispute in outline: The primary Roxborough seat was originally united with a smaller Castleboy holding. That situation became complicated, however, when the single man in possession of Castleboy was errant in his ways. In 1828, the owner of Roxborough chose to prove that the Castleboy master was a 'lunatic.' On his death the unmarried man – proven to have been of unsound mind – left the Castleboy estate to his two sons by a local woman. Irate, the Roxborough master subsequently succeeded in reuniting the Roxborough and Castleboy estates. In his own will, however, the same master of Roxborough once more separated the two estates by leaving Roxborough to his eldest son and Castleboy to a younger scion. Unhappy with that bequest, the elder son, whose case to have the two estates re-merged went all the way to the House of Lords, later evicted his younger brother from the Castleboy Estate. The sibling evicted from Castleboy came to live at Black Rock House in Salthill.

Burton De Burgh Persse of Moyode was implicated in the tangled tale, by his accompaniment of the wayward Castleboy man to a Dublin hospital in 1826, for which he was well rewarded. The eldest son of Roxborough, who should have been the travelling companion, lamented his failure to do so and that regret also contributed to the conflict. It was the Moyode master who seasonally lived at Seamount in Salthill. The family rift was to run – in terms of law suits and pamphlet publications – from the 1820s to 1899.

The proliferation of Persse names, because of the family nature of the dispute, and the sheer complexity of the story, require a timeline diagram as a skeletal reference point for the reader:

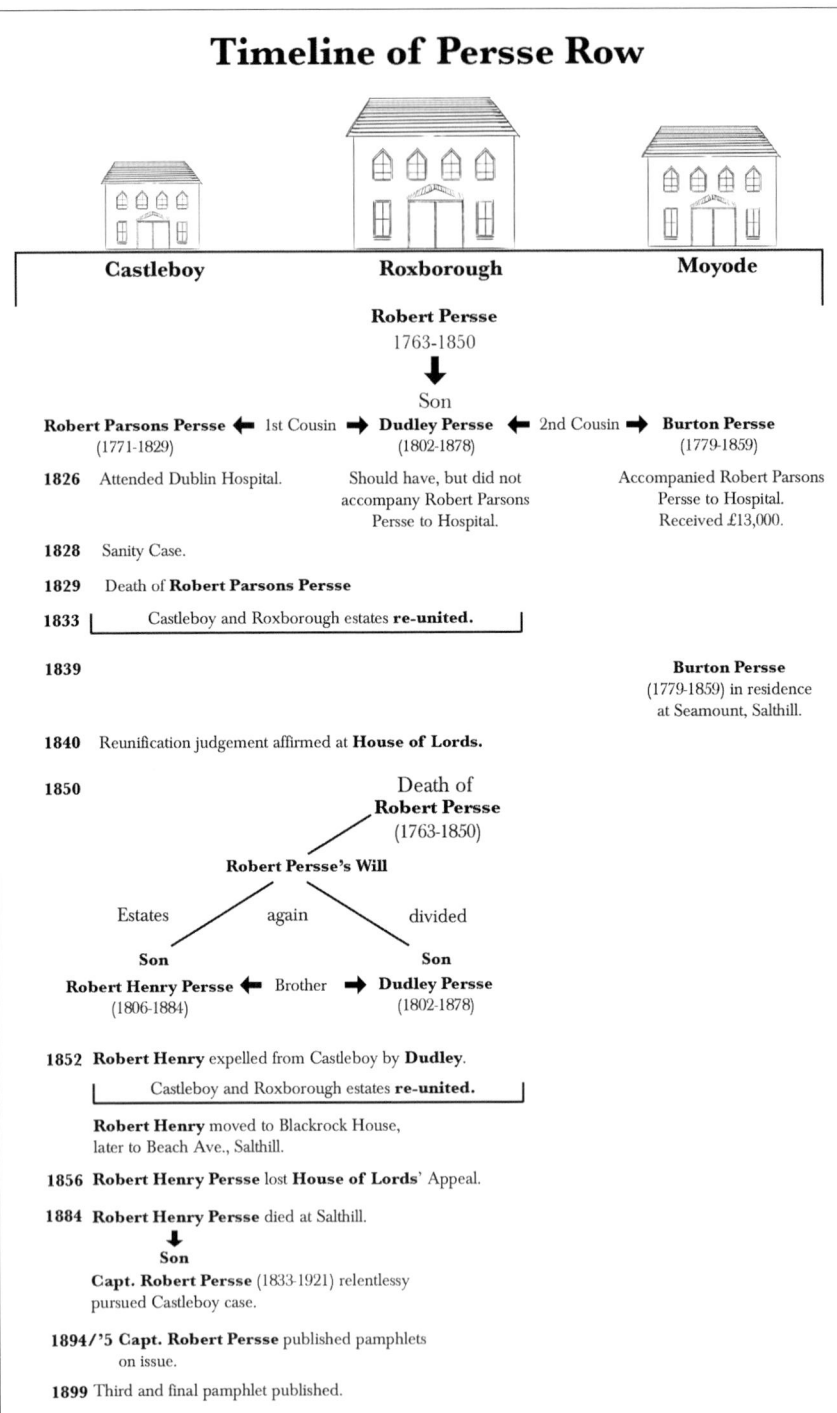

Figure 149.

A more detailed telling of the tale: The oddly fascinating story of Robert Parsons Persse (1771–1829), an unmarried man who occupied the Castleboy seat, was to play a pivotal role in the Persse row. Though single, Robert had fathered a number of children, and when he 'died in 1829 without lawful issue...He left the bulk of his property to his illegitimate children Patrick and George Persse by Brigid Coen, a local woman.'[1] Also mentioned in Robert's will were children of his by Jane Meheron, Mary Knee, Honora Fahey and Mary Calnon.[2] The Castleboy man, who was central to the formation of the County Galway ('Blazers') Hunt, followed an unconventional and dissolute lifestyle, which had previously caused enough concern to have him become the subject of an 1828 lunacy commission. Burton Persse (1779–1859) of Moyode – and also of Sea Mount – was central to that *de lunatico inquirendo* case, which sought to determine the sanity – or otherwise – of Robert Parsons Persse.

Burton de Burgh Persse, Esq. (1779–1859) – Salthill connection

Burton, as earlier noted, was involved with the Newcastle Distillery, whose most recognisable legacy to the place is Distillery Road, which has – over time – become enveloped in an ever expanding NUIG campus. Burton was the man to contact in 1823, when advertised for letting was 'the extensive Brewery, Malt-House, and Concerns at NEWCASTLE, within half a mile of the Town of Galway, situated on the banks of Lough Corrib, which is navigable to the extent of forty miles; and this Brewery supplies Porter, Ale and Beer to several towns on its borders, and the Boats in return bring Fuel and Corn.'[3] The partnership operating that distillery was dissolved 'by mutual consent' in September 1832, after which the business was carried on by 'BURTON PERSSE solely.'[4]

Twice married, Burton first wed Anchoretta Eyre, daughter of Colonel Giles Eyre and Anne Daly, in January 1820. They had four children before Anchoretta passed away in April, 1824. Burton remarried in the following year when he wed his cousin, Matilda Persse (1793–1862), daughter of Henry Stratford Persse and Anne Sadleir. Eleven children were born to that second union, one of whom was Henry Sadleir Persse, who resided at Glenarde House for over three decades. Burton Persse also retained a seasonal residence at Salthill, and was recorded as occupier of Sea Mount, at the prom's end, in 1839. Burton Persse, Esq., J.P., D.L., died 'at his residence, Moyode Castle,' at the age of 77 in August 1859.[5]

During the 1820s, Burton's support for the alleged lunatic, Robert Parsons Persse, was questioned in the courthouse by the Roxborough side. Fifteen days of a 'Very Singular Case' represented 'the longest time known to have been occupied in this country in any similar proceedings.'[6] The Roxborough branch of the family, recognising the danger inherent in their Castleboy relation's domestic situation – and mental state – had taken action after Mr. Parsons Persse was removed to Dublin in 1826 for medical treatment. The 'decay of understanding of Mr. P. Persse was produced by intemperance' and it was Robert Persse (1763–1850) of Roxborough, 'heir-presumptive of Robert Parsons Persse,' of Castleboy who initiated the sanity case. While Roxborough's Robert was nominally the litigant, it was Dudley Persse (1802–1878), 'the son, at his own expense, and in the name of his father,' who pursued the action.[7] Looking to the future, Dudley wished – like his father – to have the estates united. At the 1828 hearing, it was relayed that a cousin, Burton Persse of Moyode, had

150. Burton de Burgh Persse Esq. (1779–1859).

travelled to Dublin two years earlier with the patient, though it was Roxborough's Mr. Dudley Persse, who – by right – should have done so. The responsibility was Dudley's for he was the eldest son of 'the lunatic's heir apparent.' Unable to travel because of his marriage to Katherine O'Grady in November 1826, Dudley came to realise – and regret – the great cost of his oversight.

Burton de Burgh Persse (1779–1859), the man who accompanied the Castleboy master to Dublin, was to profit by his action. It was alleged at the sanity hearing that 'from the moment he stepped into his carriage until the present time, Mr. Burton Persse had exclusive control and dominion' over Robert Parson Persse's affairs. Of concern to the plaintiff was an investment fund of £13,000 which had come under Burton Persse's control. Dr. Mahony, who had forsaken his medical practice at Loughrea to attend to the bed ridden Mr Parsons Persse in Dublin, was the witness who verified the transfer of that large sum to Burton Persse: 'On the 20th of March, 1827, Dr. Mahony authenticated the document by which 13,000*l* was irretrievably transferred.'[8] The recipient, Burton Persse, claimed it was a voluntary gift and that he was under no obligation to refund it, even if Robert Parsons Persse was to die. The jury found in 1828 that Robert Parsons Persse was of unsound mind, and was so incapacitated from 17th Nov. 1826. It was also confirmed that the (nominal) petitioner, Robert Persse (1763–1850) of Newcastle Lodge (and Roxborough), was heir at law.

A multiplicity of court cases followed, including a Coen v. Persse case at Galway Assizes in 1833, which centred on the legitimacy of wills made by Robert Parsons Persse: 'Never having married, he had no legitimate issue; but he had a considerable number of natural children, the eldest of whom was called Patrick Persse.'

By that stage Patrick was dead, though George, the younger son mentioned in the disputed legacies, was still alive. It was estimated that Robert Parsons Persse's personal property, chiefly in funds, amounted to £30,000. On a Galway jury failing to reach a verdict, the heir-at-law, Captain Robert Persse of Roxborough, came into possession of the Castleboy estate.[9] Further litigation – including Irish Court of Chancery hearings – followed, before Dudley Persse brought the case to the House of Lords on 13 February, 1840, after which Roxborough's claim on Castleboy was affirmed.[10]

An Ironic Sequel

Robert Persse, who declared in December 1827 'that the Roxburgh and Castleboy estates should never be separated,'[11] lived to see them rejoined. However, on his 1850 death at Newcastle Lodge, Robert's own will divided the holdings once more: The larger Roxborough seat was bequeathed to his eldest son, Dudley Persse, with the smaller Castleboy estate going to Robert Henry Persse, a younger scion. Dudley, the first born, was irate at the dilution of his inheritance by his father's separation of the Roxborough and Castleboy holdings, particularly as he (Dudley) had been to the fore in fighting – and financing – the battle to have them united. Once more ascending court house steps, Dudley succeeded in winning possession of the smaller holding, after which his younger brother Robert Henry and family were put out of Castleboy in 1852.'[12] Four years later the House of Lords was revisited when the evicted Robert Henry Persse (1806–1884), 'of Rock House, in the County of the Town of Galway,' appealed against the dispossession 'decree of the Court of Chancery in *Ireland*, of the 12th of June 1852.' Not only was the evicted petitioner's claim dismissed, but Robert Henry had to 'pay or cause to be paid to the said Respondents the Costs incurred in respect of the said Appeal.'[13] Dudley Persse Esq., the Respondent and victor, who had failed to travel with his 'unsound' cousin to hospital, and later drove a younger brother from the smaller family holding, was the father – by a second marriage – of Lady Augusta Gregory (née Persse).

One wonders what drove Dudley to such lengths to have Castleboy re-united with the Roxborough estate. Might it have been his oversight, in not escorting his ailing relation, Robert Parsons Persse, to Dublin in 1826, that contributed to a desire to right some perceived wrong? Alternative reasons were also at play: On the death of his father, the effort and expense of Dudley's litigious efforts appeared to have come to nought, when his brother Robert Henry was bequeathed the Castleboy holding. Further battles then required further effort. There's little doubt but that there was no love lost between Dudley Persse of Roxborough and Burton Persse of Moyode, the man who did travel in 1826. That enmity appears to have been both constant and caustic, for in 1855 it was reported that 'Dudley Persse, Esq., of Roxborough, accompanied by Jos. McDonnell, Esq., Sub-Sheriff, attended on Thursday last, at Newcastle, Galway, by virtue of an injunction from the Court of Chancery, and placed Mr. Persse in possession of the extensive distillery concerns formerly in possession of Burton Persse Esq.'[14] It is also possible that Burton Persse's taking sole charge of the Newcastle distillery in 1832 may have been in some way connected to the family squabble.

Two of the male characters entangled in that Persse row spent time at Salthill: Moyode's Mr. Burton de Burgh Persse (1779–1859), who profited from the saga, was resident at Seamount in 1839. On the other hand, the unfortunate Robert Henry Persse, who was evicted by his own brother from Castleboy in 1852, subsequently came to reside at Blackrock House, with a Salthill address being given at his House of Lords' appeal in May, 1856:

You are the Appellant in the case of Persse V Persse?
I am.
Where do you live?
At Galway – within Two Miles from the Town – Rock House.'[15]

While Blackrock House was a fine residence, Robert Henry Persse's London quarters, at the time of court hearings, were not universally hospitable: Due to an alleged costs' liability from an earlier court case, he was arrested on 9 May, 1856, at his lodgings at 125 Albany Street, and held at Whitecross Street Prison until his 26th May appearance at the House of Lords' Appeal hearing. Following the loss of that petition, Robert Henry was to return to Salthill, where he resided for the best part of three further decades. Not all of those years were spent in the luxury of Blackrock House, for in the mid-1870s Robert Henry Persse replaced James Gordon as tenant of house number 2 Beach Avenue, a terraced residence on a short laneway off Salthill Village, which still stands today. Robert's dramatic fall from Master of Castleboy, to a Blackrock House tenancy – a spell in Whitecross prison – and his final years' occupation of a terraced Salthill cottage, must have been hard on a man, who was in his 78th year on his passing.[16] His long held grievance would have been exacerbated by the fact that it was his own brother, Dudley Persse, who was primarily responsible for his fall. The Beach Avenue address, which headed an 1879 letter from Robert Henry Persse to Lord Dunsandle, was to represent his home until his demise on 3 April, 1884.[17] The funeral of Robert Henry Persse Esq. J.P. left Salthill at 10 a.m. on Tuesday, 8 April, for 'Castle Boy,' the estate from which he was evicted in 1852, and for which he, and his son, Captain Robert, spent two lifetimes fighting. It was Robert Henry's son, Captain Robert Persse (1833–1921), who arranged to have his father interred at Castleboy.

Of note is Patrick Melvin's sharp observation that 'Lady Gregory's idealistic efforts to bridge Anglo-Irish and Irish Ireland overshadowed memory of the somewhat unpopular Persses.'[18] The division at the heart of the lengthy Persse squabble resulted in a public and rancorous rupture, which was well publicised throughout its convoluted and long running cycle. That cycle extended beyond the 1856 House of Lords' decision, with cases being contested on an allegedly suppressed 1807 deed, which purportedly negated the covenant on which Dudley won his claim to the disputed estate. The latter cases were pursued by Captain Robert Persse (1833–1921), the eldest son of Robert Henry Perrse, the evicted Castleboy master. Robert, like his father, deeply resented the loss of Castleboy, which he believed was his by right. Educated at Cheltenham, he was appointed to the Royal Canadian Rifles and married Ann O'Hara of Raheen at York, Toronto, in 1860. Robert's focus on what he considered to be the suppressed 1807 deed was unrelenting, and in his sights were those he believed contributed to the document's suppression. It was not solely Lady Gregory's father who was the subject of Captain Robert's outrage. Also implicated by the Captain was Augusta Gregory's mother, Mrs. Frances Persse (née Barry), who was accused of having been party to a 'conspiracy' and 'swindle,' which was perpetrated against him (Captain Robert) and his father (Robert Henry). Sharply accusatory and forthright 1893 letters, communicating such conspiratorial charges, were posted to Mrs. Persse at the Croft, her Taylor's Hill residence. Captain Robert believed that she had discovered the 1807 deed, and 'her skill and diplomacy' were deemed by him to be central to the denial of his entitlement.[19] Mrs. Persse therefore represented a third family member – resident in the general Salthill area – who was putatively embroiled in the sad affair.

Captain Robert's former solicitor and friend, James Galbraith Esq., was another identified as a foe. Of Williamite stock, the Galbraith family held large land tracts in Galway, with James Galbraith of Cappard owning 4,636 acres in the county during the 1870s. A Galbraith-Persse connection stretched back to the marriage of Major Hugh Galbraith and Catherine, the eldest daughter of the Rev. Dudley Persse, Archdeacon of Tuam (1662–1699).[20] Captain Robert Persse (1833–1921) was informed by his own mother that she had the 1807 deed delivered to James Galbraith in 1862, after which Robert approached James for the document. Though Robert testified that Galbraith showed him the paper-wrapped deed, which had been delivered by Martin Fox, from Mrs. Persse of Blackrock House to Cappard House, he (Robert) had not been given access to it. The reason given was that it was only to be transferred on the passing of his father. In the wake of Robert's father's 1884 demise, James Galbraith was again approached for the elusive document. First claiming he could not find it, Captain Robert's request was subsequently put off on a number of occasions, after which an 1888 *Persse V Galbraith* court hearing was held. At that hearing Galbraith was accused of perjury by Capt. Robert and Galbraith claimed that Captain Persse 'had got a craze.'[21] The result, once more, went against the Captain, who was additionally burdened with costs.

Beaten, but unbroken, Captain Robert Persse privately published pamphlets which described the injustice he believed had been done to his family. The first entitled, *A Deed of Settlement Suppressed in a Court of Justice,* appeared in two parts, the first in 1894 and the second in the following year. In 1897, Robert pursued an ejectment action against all parties he considered to have been 'wrongfully' in possession of the Castleboy Estate, a case he again lost, with costs awarded against him. Captain Robert's final defiant act was the publication of *An Appeal to Parliament– Persse V Persse* in 1899.

It is significant that *Burke's Landed Gentry of Ireland* in that same year, 1899, did not include Robert Parsons Persse, or any of his children in its genealogical records. Deep seated fratricidal enmity, born out of disputed legacy claims and entitlements, along with family embarrassment about Robert Parsons Persse's errant ways and sanity case, were most likely responsible for the omission. It was somehow decided that Robert Parsons Persse's place in the family tree was best erased. If one was to identify the 1826 attendance at a Dublin Hospital of Robert Parsons Persse as the beginning of a saga of division and strife, and Captain Robert Persse's 1899 pamphlet as its bitter end, then the entire affair marked three generations of a famed Galway family over the course of 73 hostile years. One might well surmise that – in some cases – the fall of Ireland's landed gentry was not simply a product of external climatic and political forces, but the result of its own avarice and profligacy, which ultimately delivered a quite precipitous end. A comprehensive account of the entire *Persse V Persse* saga forms part of Gerry Kearney's 2016 book, *The Persse family of County Galway: Genealogy and History, 1554–1964*.

Bloody Bodkin story

Though the Persse row was undoubtedly bitter, it pales into insignificance when placed against the 18th century tragedy that befell the landed Bodkin clan. It was in September 1740 that an internecine family massacre took place at Carrowbrown House, some four miles from Tuam. The victims included Oliver Bodkin Esq., his second wife, Margery, and their son Oliver, along with Marcus Lynch Esq., a visiting merchant from Galway. Also killed, as reported by *Pue's Occurrences,* were five of the house's employees. Two, of the three hanged for the crime, were members of the Bodkin family: Dominick Bodkin was the brother of – and John Oliver the son by a first marriage of – Oliver Bodkin, the murdered man of the house. Also hanged for the heinous deed was Shane Ryeevagh, a shepard. To compound the tragedy, the condemned John Oliver Bodkin alleged at the gallows that an undetected fratricide had earlier occurred. Succession rights lay at the heart of all these tragedies which earned the family a *Bloody Bodkin* soubriquet. That fearful story is told in historical novel form by Paul McNulty in his 2015 publication; *A Story of the Bodkin Murders* and by Jarlath O'Connell on Galway Library's website. The callous brutality of such deeds makes explicitly clear that Ireland's landed class was not free from familial tensions.

Galbraith – Persse ties at Salthill

A Galbraith-Persse family connection, which played its part in the Castleboy affair, appears to have survived into the 20th century at Salthill, for in October 1911, Anchoretta Maria Persse, a half-sister to Henry Sadleir Persse of Glenarde, passed away at Dalysfort House. That fine pile was then functioning as a hotel under the watchful eye of Sarah Jane Galbraith. Anchoretta Persse, a single woman, who was buried at Aughrim, had recorded herself – in the year of her passing – as an 86 year old lady of 'independent means.' Her £344-12 s. effects were bequeathed to her niece, Anchoretta Maria Wade – with whom Miss Persse had resided at St. Helen's, Taylor's Hill – and Dorothea Matilda Wade. Members of the Wade family had also played a role in the long running Persse row.

Miss Galbraith, though born in Edinburgh, belonged to an old County Galway family. She was the first to operate Dalysfort House as an hotel, having had an earlier interest in Maretimo, which she occasionally advertised for letting.[22] As proprietress of Dalysfort, Sarah Galbraith regularly promoted in the *Irish Times* her 'First-Class Boarding House and Private Hotel,' which was 'open all the year.'[23] A loyal supporter of the Connaught Rangers, she helped collect, in association with Mary A. Lawson, donations and clothing for members of that force, which was stationed at Natal in 1900. Sixteen pairs of socks represented her own contribution.[24] When she died in 1913, Miss Galbraith's funeral to Loughrea was attended by the servants of Dalyfort House.[25] Bequeathed to one of her chief mourners, Miss Sarah J. Russell, were Sarah Jane Galbraith's effects, to the value of £649-1s.-6d.

A Papist poet at Taylor's Hill

During the late 18th century, the Roxborough tenants of William Persse (1728–1802) were mainly Catholics, a situation that later changed when, as Lady Gregory pointed out, 'a colony was formed on the estate of Protestants imported from the North.'[26] Staunch Protestantism – by the 1880s – certainly marked the faith of the Persse family, a fact revealed in one dinnertime story of the past. It is generally accepted that Lady Gregory enjoyed a close relationship with Wilfrid Scawen Blunt, an English poet, womaniser, breeder of purebred Arabian horses and anti-colonist. The latter political conviction resulted in Mr. Blunt becoming embroiled in Ireland's Land War affairs, for which he spent time in Galway Gaol. On learning of his imprisonment, Lady Gregory, who was in Italy at that time, 'wrote to her relative, Henry S. Persse, one of the visiting magistrates, who lived at Glenarde, Taylor's Hill. He both called to see Blunt on several occasions and wrote, unavailingly, on his behalf…to the General Prisons Board.'[27]

Local lore recalls that Scawen Blunt was entertained to dinner by Lady Gregory's mother some time after his release from prison. One such folklore version, recalled by eminent local historian, the late Dónal Taheny, placed the dinner at Taylor's Hill. Wilfrid was a Roman Catholic and the story goes that when the poet blessed himself before dining, a surprised Mrs. Frances Persse remarked that he was the first Papist to sit at her table. While Papists – to borrow the lady of the house's description – did not 'sit' at her table, Roman Catholics had continued to 'serve' on Persse estates. A perusal of Persse census returns in 1901 confirms as much.

151. Wilfrid Scawen Blunt as a young man in the 1860s.

Though a whiff of legend colours the 'Papist' tale, it has merit, for Scawen Blunt in his 1912 book, *The Land War in Ireland*, confirmed such ardent Persse religious fervour. His own version of the dinner affair was related in the same narrative: 'We made other visits too, among them one on Mrs. Persse, Lady Gregory's mother, a fine old lady who talked to us of Jesuit intrigues and Popery generally. [N.B.– Mrs. Persse was a typical Irish Protestant of the old school. Lady Gregory had had some difficulty in persuading her to receive our visit; she had never had a Papist under her roof before.]'[28] Mr Blunt's record of the dining engagement not only confirms the truth of the oral telling, but also notes the dinner date as 19 June, 1888. At that time Mrs. Frances Persse was, as we have seen, in residence at the Croft, so the Taylor's Hill venue of local lore is also accurate. The home of Rev. J. D'Arcy in 1839, that fine house was initially called Vicar Croft and simply the Croft in later years. It was in that house that the 80 year old Frances Persse passed away on 22 March, 1896. The same dwelling still stands today on the Rahoon side of *an Bóthar Ard* and is included in Ireland's National Inventory of Architectural Heritage.

The Scawen name was not unknown in Galway, for Sir William Scawen, a London financier and army clothing contractor, at one time owned the Galway estate of Moyode and Castleboy. William sold that holding to James Ruck, a London merchant, who, in turn, sold it to Robert Persse (1689–1781) in 1741.[29] A tangential Scawen-Persse connection therefore existed long before Lady Gregory's 19th century friendship with the campaigning and charismatic Wilfrid.

Glenarde House, most identified with Henry Sadleir Persse, was in the possession of the famed distilling family from the 1860s to 1903. Thomas Moore Persse resided at Ardmore before he built Mount Vernon – a little lower down on Taylor's Hill – during the early 1860s. Mrs. Frances Persse, wife of Dudley Persse and mother to Lady Augusta Gregory, resided at the Croft (Vicar Croft), where she

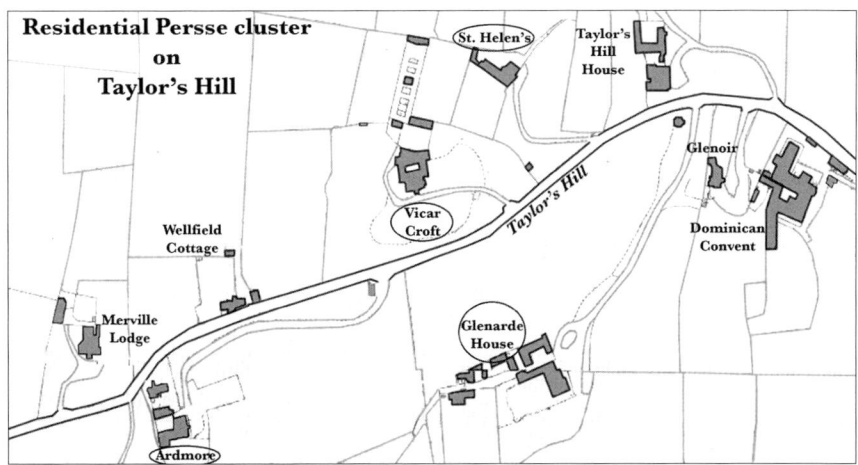

152. Vicar Croft, which lies on the northern side of Taylor's Hill, was part of a house cluster that featured a strong Persse presence.

hosted a dinner for Wilfrid Scawen Blunt in 1888. Miss Anchoretta Persse was in residence at St. Helen's with her niece, Anchoretta Maria Wade, at the time of the 1911 census. The building in the above image, which is titled Taylor's Hill House, was – as previously described – the second residence to use that name in the 19th century.

A Galway – American connection

Galway's Persse family enjoyed strong ties with America that stretched back to the 1780s. It was in the months before he became first President of the United States that George Washington exchanged letters with Colonel William Persse (1728–1802) of Roxborough, a great-grandfather to Lady Augusta Gregory, and grandfather to Thomas Moore Persse, who resided for a good number of years in the Salthill area.

William Persse's military rank was adopted when he formed the Roxborough Volunteers in 1777 – during the period of the American War of Independence (1775–1783). British army personnel were withdrawn from Ireland at that time in an effort to thwart an American drive for sovereignty, in what was then a British colony. In a less fortified Ireland, the threat of invasion, along with a need to maintain order, prompted landed proprietors to raise local Volunteer corps. At a seminal 1782 Ulster Volunteer Convention at Dungannon, an inclusive resolution was passed: 'As men and as Irishmen, as Christians and as Protestants, we rejoice in the relaxation of the Penal Laws against our Roman Catholic fellow-subjects.' A subsequent convention at Ballinasloe carried similar motions, which included the following: 'That no power on earth has a right to make laws to bind this kingdom, except the King, Lords and Commons of Ireland, and that we will resist, with our lives and fortunes, the execution of any other laws, as we consider to be governed by a foreign legislature over which we have no control.'[30]

A month later Mr. Henry Grattan Snr. delivered on his promise to declare 'the right to a legislative independence' for Ireland. That was done on 16 April, 1872 in College Green, with rows of Volunteers in attendance. What resulted was the formation of Grattan's Parliament, which required royal assent and an Act of Repeal. The Roxborough Volunteers and their leader, Colonel William Persse, were loud in their praise for what had been achieved by the Volunteer movement, and by Mr. Grattan, who was duly elected an honorary member of Colonel Persse's corps. When the 1783 Act of Renunciation – giving legislative independence to Ireland – was passed at Westminster, a memorial bridge was erected by Colonel Persse at Roxborough, which commemorated the Volunteer contribution to Irish parliamentary independence. Despite Mr. Grattan's initial success, political reform did not follow and disillusionment with the new order set in.

Symptomatic of that despair was a dwindling of Volunteer numbers that was exacerbated by the 1783 end of the American war, which removed one of the primary reasons for the force's existence. Ten years later, the passing of a Militia bill by government effectively put an end to the Volunteer organisation. Perhaps the most telling indicator of the failure of Grattan's Parliament was Colonel Persse's support for a 1799 resolution that called for the passing of an Act of Union with Britain, which occurred in the following year. That put an end to a short-lived, though long-coveted Irish Parliament, which the Colonel had previously supported and championed.

Sir Edward Newenham, M.P. Enniscorthy (1769–1776) and Dublin (1776–1797), was a colleague of William Persse in the Volunteer movement. Their friendship became familial in 1787, when Newenham's son, Edward, married Elizabeth, William Persse's eldest daughter. Fervent admirers of George Washington, both the knighted Newenham and Colonel Persse saw personal parallels with the American leader in a shared desire for liberty. All three men were also interested in agriculture, an enthusiasm that Washington exhibited in the great care taken in developing his Mount Vernon estate in Virginia. In August 1787, Newenham wrote to Washington, informing him that he was prevented from making a trip to America. In that same missive Mr. Persse, who was to forward some plants to Washington, was introduced to the American leader. Two of the letters, which formed part of a Virginia-Galway correspondence, are here quoted. Colonel Persse's initial – 1788 – correspondence, which is preserved in the Library of Congress, was unearthed by esteemed local historian, Rev. James Mitchell, in the early 1960s.

> Roxburrow,
> Near Loughrea,
> Ireland.
> Oct. 11th. 1788.

Dear Sir,
Some time ago I mentioned to Sir Edward Newenham my intention of sending you some gooseberry plants of a remarkable fine kind, which I now send you by a ship from the port of Galway, which is but sixteen miles from my place. I intended sending you some grass seeds, but our Summers are so uncertain I could not get any this season fit to send.

It would give me particular pleasure to have it in my power to contribute to your rural Amusements; it is the kind of life I take the greatest pleasure in, and feel for those that delight in so beautiful and pleasing a study – it would make me feel extremely happy if you would mention to me any kinds of corn or seeds you would wish to have: I could send them to you with the greatest ease.

Plant the gooseberries in a rich deep soil, put a good deal of rotten dung into each hole before you plant them, keep them open in the middle, don't allow too many branches on a tree, and the fruit will be very large and fine – I have them as large as walnuts. Give them a North aspect and as little sun as you can but not great shade of trees: I fear your climate is too hot.

Sir Edward, Lady Newenham and Family are now here, also Mr. Wallace, who often mentions your name with the greatest gratitude; he often entertains me with the beautiful situation of your place.

Sir Edward and I often talk of visiting America but I fear the attention of our families won't permit us, tho' our wishes are to see it; it is the country of all on earth I long most to see: it would give me new life and vigour to see the upright and honest men of America.

Give me leave, dear Sir, to assure you I have been, in the worst of times, your well-wisher and a sincere friend to the liberties of America.

I have the honour to be, dear Sir, your sincere and affectionate

> Humble servant,
> Willm. Persse [31]

The reply from George Washington arrived some months later and read:

> Mount Vernon,
> March 2, 1789.

Dear Sir,
Your polite letter, dated the 11th of October last, has been duly received and merits my particular acknowledgement. I have also to thank you very sincerely for the gooseberry plants, which have arrived safely at Baltimore, from whence I have not yet been able to obtain them on account of ice in our rivers. I shall have your directions as to the mode of culture particularly observed, and hope the plants may succeed as happily as in your climate. For you may be assured the greater care of them will be taken, because it is a natural circumstance for us to feel

a predilection for whatever comes from one whose ordinary pursuits and political principles are consonant to our own!!!

I am not without hopes that Sir Edward Newenham and yourself will find time, at some period in your lives, to make a visit to America, for which you have both witnessed so ardent an attachment.

I cannot conclude this letter without expressing my great obligations for your kind offers of contributing, by the transmission of other natural productions of your country, to my rural amusement: and assuring you that I have the honour to be, with great consideration, Sir, your most obedient servant.
GEORGE WASHINGTON
To Colonel William Persse.[32]

While Colonel William espoused the American cause of freedom from England, one of his brothers, Henry Persse (1740–1805), was an officer in the British forces that sought to deny independence to that country. Henry was Captain in the 46th – an Irish Regiment of Foot – which was sent in 1775 to assist Britain in America at the time of the Revolutionary War. Captain Henry Persse retired two years later, and was commissioned in the Galway Militia in 1793. He died aged 65, at Aughnacloy, Co. Tyrone, in 1805.

President Washington was not the only famous man to be acquainted with Colonel William Persse, for Rev. John Wesley, the Anglican clergyman, theologian and founder of Methodism, was also known to him. Persse households were visited, on at least two occasions during many visits, made to Ireland by Rev. Wesley in the 1747–1789 period. John Wesley dined as a guest of the 'Colonel' at Roxborough on 17 May, 1785[33] and two years later, the same cleric 'had much conversation with Mrs. Persse, a woman of many sorrows' at Castleboy.[34]

Thomas Moore Persse and Mount Vernon

Though Colonel William Persse did not make it to America, some of his grandsons did emigrate there. On their going, William's son, Henry Stratford Persse (1769–1833), reminded his boys of their grandfather's love of that faraway place: 'I dare say how warmly attached my father was to the American Cause and how sincere his Friendship for General Washington.'[35] A copy of one of Washington's letters to Roxborough was also forwarded by Henry Stratford to his sons in America. One of those sons, who returned home, made his mark on Salthill. He was Thomas Moore Persse, a resident for a good number of years at Galway's marine resort. Though he chose to return to Ireland, Thomas – a naturalised American citizen – retained a great affection for the Land of Opportunity. Attached to the Persse distillery at Newcastle, he was to lose his eldest son, Henry Stratford Persse (1841–1843), not three years old, when the toddler fell into the Corrib while playing outside Newcastle House in 1843. A negligent servant was thought to have been responsible.[36]

Thomas Moore Persse had married Margaret Hickman, daughter of Dublin Crown solicitor, Edward Shadwell Hickman, three years earlier. Of their eight children, three sons – Henry Stratford (aged 2), Henry Thomas (aged 5) and Burton Washington (aged 4) – all died in childhood. The Washington forename of the third boy symbolised a continuation of the family's fascination with the first President of America. One of Thomas M. Persse's children did emigrate stateside. She was Georgina Henrietta Persse, who married Dr. Joseph Persse Smith at Limerick in 1877, and died a widow in Illinois – at the age of 84 – in 1936.

153. Thomas Moore Persse, United States' Consul at Galway.

Thomas Moore Perrse J.P. served as High Sheriff of Galway town in 1850 and was Town Commissioner chairman, as well as thrice filling the role of United States Consul at Galway. In the latter capacity, for example, he placed an 1859 advertisement in the *Galway Vindicator*, seeking to identify the 'kin of Roger McGrath.'[37] Thomas' position became compromised during the American Civil War (1861–1865), and Mr. William H. Seward, U.S. Secretary of State to President Abraham Lincoln, was instrumental in having him replaced as consul: 'William West was appointed to Galway due to Seward's "influence...friendship [and] sympathy for all foreigners and Irishmen" and amid complaints of disloyalty against the incumbent Thomas Moore Persse who was also a Justice of the peace and 'can't serve two masters".[38] The masters in question were America and Britain, for Thomas Moore Persse had sworn allegiance to the Queen on becoming a Galway Magistrate, and to America on becoming a U.S. citizen in 1834. Despite the forfeiture of his consul position, it was Thomas Moore Persse who was to the fore in leading Galway's reaction to the 1865 assassination of Abraham Lincoln:

> It will be seen...that a most influential meeting of the people of Galway, called together by the respected Chairman of the Town Board, Thomas M. Persse Esq., was held on Thursday last in the Town Court House. The resolutions adopted, and the speeches delivered on the occasion must be gratifying to the American people...It will gladden our countrymen in America that the voice of Old Galway has been so eloquently raised in detestation of one of the cruellest crimes, one of the most diabolical deeds that disgrace the annals of the world's history.[39]

Such rhetoric from the mid-1860s confirms that the voicing of Galway opinion on international affairs is not a new phenomenon, and – given the family's fondness for America – it was unsurprising that it was a grandson of Colonel

154. Mount Vernon on Taylor's Hill, originally built by Thomas Moore Persse, was later called Mount St. Mary's, but is locally known as the Bishop's Palace.

William Persse who led Galway's response to the assassination of the 16th President of America, three quarters of a century after his forebear had corresponded with the first holder of that esteemed office.

The three Salthill residences associated with Thomas Moore Persse were Ardmore, Mount Vernon and Norman Villas. Two were leased and the third was built by him. Mr. T.M. Persse followed engineer, Samuel Ussher Roberts, into Ardmore in 1855 and entertained Lord Dunkellin there three years later, following the latter's return from India, where he had served as Military Secretary to the Viceroy.[40] In the following year – 1859 – it was reported that Indian corn was grown on Mr. Persse's Taylor's Hill holding that 'looked as rich and as healthy as if it grew in the most fertile fields of America.'[41] The occupant of Ardmore was, in that year, contemplating building what became his Mount Vernon mansion, a little closer to town on Taylor's Hill.

The new residence was 'approached by two entrance gates, one leading to the Salthill-road with the other opening on the Taylor's Hill side.'[42] Both of those gates still exist today and the Salthill Road yet features the southern entrance gates to both the Perrse built Mount Vernon, and Lenaboy Castle of O'Hara provenance. Both buildings were constructed during the same period, with the *Dublin Builder* recording in April 1862 that 'two costly mansions' were 'recently erected,' one of which, Mount Vernon, cost £4,000 and Lenaboy Castle £3,500.[43] Both were built by Mr. Semple, with Samuel U. Roberts as engineer. T.M. Persse's creation was 'a granite building with limestone dressings' which was briefly called North Villa.[44]

Its more enduring Mount Vernon name memorialised the longstanding Persse affinity with George Washington, and Thomas Moore Persse was in residence at his new pile in 1861.[45]

The quality of the build at Mount Vernon was remarked on in a Cancelled Revision Book annotation; 'This house is built in the first style,' and that assessment was re-echoed in more recent times by Andrew Caddell, a descendant of Thomas Moore Persse who has recorded online that 'Thomas Moore Persse built a fabulous mansion, which he called "Mount Vernon" after Washington's home, and which is based on it, even down to the cherry wood used in the interior and brought by boat from Virginia.'[46] An Irish-American connection is therefore embodied in the very fabric of Mount Vernon. Given the provenance and lavish nature of the residence, it is surprising that Mount Vernon is not included on the online National Monuments / Architectural Heritage map, as it pertains to Salthill, when the neighbouring Lenaboy Castle and Glenarde House / Ardilaun House Hotel are both noted on the Department of Arts, Heritage and Gaeltacht site.

Thomas Moore Perrse's ability to spend £4,000 on his new Taylor's Hill home indicates a successful spell in America after which he invested heavily in the Newcastle distillery, with which he became identified. An agent of Lloyd's of London, his mercantile career involved trading in corn, coal and guano, which made use of extensive stores and yards that extended along Forster Street. He was also the owner of the barque 'Bonito.' Despite his broad commercial involvement, the majestic villa he built on Taylor's Hill was listed in 1873, as the second of two lots for auction at the Landed Estates' Court. The 'plot of land containing 3a 3r 38 p, with dwelling houses and offices, known as Mount Vernon'…held under lease for 999 years' was sold to Mr. Redmond Burke for £905.[47] Mr. Thomas Moore Persse Esq. saw a poor return on the £4,000 he had expended on the property some twelve years earlier.

Redmond Burke, with an address at Annagh, Gort in 1868,[48] was a Magistrate and large landowner in South Galway. A man of that name was also recorded as a 'furniture broker' at Upr. Abbeygate Street in 1870.[49] Mr. Burke continued his judicial functions while resident at Taylor's Hill and he occupied Mount Vernon for fourteen years, before making a healthy profit on selling the original Persse mansion – in 1887 – to Galway's Catholic Diocese for £1,500. That purchase coincided with the Episcopal appointment of Dr. Francis McCormack, who succeeded Bishop Thomas Carr, following the latter's appointment as Archbishop of Melbourne.

The *Tuam Herald* carried the rationale for that ecclesiastical purchase:

It was long felt that an Episcopal Residence should be provided for the Chief Pastor of the Dioceses of Galway, Kilmacduagh, and Kilfenora, and the advent of His Lordship, The Most Rev. Dr. McCormack was deemed by our Catholic Community as an opportune time for the accomplishment of so laudable a purpose…Recently a Mansion in every possible respect most

155. Mount Vernon gate at St. Mary's Terrace residence on Taylor's Hill.

suitable, situated in the most suburb of our City, was offered for sale, and has been secured for this purpose at a cost of £1,500. This amount is considered most reasonable when we take into account the position, suitability, and elegance of Mount Vernon the name by which the residence is known…It was determined at a public meeting of the inhabitants of Galway that our bishop should have no pecuniary liability in the transaction.[50]

The last sentence of the above quotation made clear to Galway's inhabitants that the purchase price of the new residence would not fall on the bishop. What the people of Galway may not have known was that the Lower Salthill townland, in which Mount Vernon stood, had come into the possession of the Diocese in the same year that the house was acquired. It was in February 1887 that Julia Daly, a niece of Fr. Peter Daly, passed away, and her will bequeathed the Kilcorkey townland – almost in its entirety – to the Galway Diocese. That meant that Bishop McCormack became what was then termed the 'head landlord' of almost every property in the townland, and consequently received payment from all immediate lessors who leased property in the place. Julia Daly's generous bequest might have contributed to a decision to have the bishop's residence sited in a townland, which had just come into the possession of the diocese.

Mount Vernon was later changed to Mount St. Mary's, after which a naming pattern was established in the area that is preserved today in St. Mary's Terrace, St. Mary Avenue, St. Mary's College and St. Mary's Road. The Mount St. Mary's tag never really caught on, for Mr. Persse's construction is colloquially known – up to the present day – as the Bishop's Palace. It was in the year of its purchase that the *Galway Vindicator* had the 'pleasure in announcing that it…will in future be known as the Palace of the Lord Bishop of Galway.'[51] The Mount Vernon name, however, did not totally disappear from view on Taylor's Hill, for a St. Mary's Terrace house is identified by that title, in the residence's wrought iron gate. It was at Mount St. Mary's on Taylor's Hill that Bishop Éamon Casey hosted a lunch for Pope John Paul II, on 30 September, 1979, during the pontiff's memorable visit to Galway. On that visit the Pope was conferred with the Freedom of Galway and the page he signed, on becoming a Freeman of Galway City, 'was specially prepared for the occasion by Carol Ann Moroney of Ard na Mara [Salthill], a qualified commercial artist. She also prepared the illuminated scroll which was presented to the pontiff.'[52]

Before leaving the story of Taylor's Hill's Mount Vernon, it is important to note another house of the same name on the Flaggy Shore, at the edge of the Burren in Co. Clare. That Mount Vernon residence preceded the Salthill construction, for it was built in 1788 for Colonel William Persse, the man with whom George Washington was then corresponding. During the late 19th century, it served as the summer house for Sir Hugh Lane, a nephew of Lady Gregory, whose 1915 death on board the Lusitania was followed by a dispute as to whether Dublin or London should have ownership of his Continental painting collection. A sharing of the art works was agreed in 1959. On Augusta Gregory coming into possession of the Burren's Mount Vernon, it was visited by many lights of the Irish Cultural Renaissance, including W.B. Yeats, Æ (George Russell), Seán O'Casey, J.M. Synge and George Bernard Shaw. The house was presented by Lady Gregory as a wedding present to her son, Robert Gregory, but the unfortunate Robert was to perish during the First World War and is memorialised in Yeats' poignant poem; *An Irish Airman Foresees his Death*. The Flaggy Shore's Mount Vernon today offers hospitality and accommodation as an historic private house. Thomas Moore Persse, the man who built his impressive pile on Taylor's Hill, passed away on 15 May 1884, at Norman Villas in Lower Salthill, within clear sight of his Mount Vernon creation. Thomas was interred at the New Cemetery in Bohermore.

Though prominent Persse personages resided in many Salthill / Taylor's Hill residences, Mount Vernon is the sole one to have been built by a member of the family. The other homes were constructed and occupied before they became identified with the Persse brand.

156. Mount Vernon on Flaggy Shore, Co. Clare.

Chapter 19

TOWNLAND INFORMATION FROM 19TH CENTURY

Townland	Names of Occupiers	Quantities in detail			Quality
		A.	R.	P.	
Acres	Patrick Creaghan & Partner	6	0	8	1
Cloughatisky	Jas. O' Hara Esq.	32	1	23	1
East Salthill	Willm. Kelly Esq.	31	2	0	1
		45	1	16	2
		T. 76	3	16	
Lenaboy and Kilcurky. The Estates of W. Whaley and Jams. O'Hara Esqs.	Willm. Conneely	1	1	20	1
	John Connor	1	1	20	1
	John Feeny	1	1	20	1
	Denis Feeny	1	1	20	1
	Michael Burke	1	1	20	1
	Widw. Mary Clougherty	1	1	20	1
	Bryan Connor	1	1	20	1
	Math(ia)s Cooke	1	1	20	1
	Patk. Kennedy			29	1
	Rodger Conneely			29	1
	Michl. McDonagh		1	18	1
	Thos. Scanlon			37	1
	Den(i)s Connelly		1	0	1
	John Connelly		1	0	1
	Widw. Judith Woodhouse		1	37	1
	Math(ia)s Cooke		1	37	1
	John Burke		1	37	1
	Barthw. Costello		1	37	1
	John Connor	1	0	39	1
	Ww. Mary Flaherty		2	20	1
	Ww. Mary Connor		2	20	1
	Ww. Mary McDonogh		2	20	1
	Martin King		2	37	1
	Mr. Bulteel	42	0	18	(untitheable)
	Mrs. Austin			29	1
	John O'Hara Esq	3	0	28	1
	Wm. Flaherty		3	27	1
	Wm. Connelly		3	27	1
	Patrick Lean			30	1
	Jas. O' Hara Esq.	25	3	34	1
	Jas. McGrath	9	1	27	1
	Domk. Burke & Pr.	1	1	33	1
	Mr. Robert Grey	1	2	19	1
		T. 62	0	11	

Tithe Applotment Books for Salthill

signed by *James Ffrench...Nov. 29th 1834*

Townland Information from 19th Century

Townland	Names of Occupiers	Quantities in detail A. R. P.	Quality
Poulnarooma	Jas. O'Hara Esq.	47 3 31	1
	Widow King	13 2 10	1
	Mr. Pat King	25 3 26	1
	Mr. Wm. Clarke	9 2 21	1
	Den(i)s. Clarke Esq.	24 1 33	1
	Presentation Nuns	8 1 30	1
	Rev. P. Daly	4 0 33	1
		T. 134 0 24	
Salthill	Lord Clanmorris	7 3 30	1
	Patk. Laffy	1 3 11	1
		2 0 35	2
	Martin Egan	3 25	1
		1 0 34	2
	Patk. Joyce	3 25	1
	John Doherty	1 2 20	1
	Patk. Lee	3 25	1
		3 1 16	2
	James Laffy	2 35	1
		2 1 11	2
	Michl. Gannon	2 35	1
		1 3 11	2
	Widw. Darby Laffy	2 35	1
	Mich. Laffy	2 0 35	1
	Patk. McGrath	3 0 38	1
	Math(ia)s. Flynn	4 0 0	1
	William Mannion	2 0 3	1
	Patk. Mannion	3 0 38	1
	Martin Kain	1 0 12	1
	Barthw. Connor	3 1 16	1
	Barthw. Hynes	3 1 16	1
	Mark Flynn	3 1 16	1
	Michl. Grogan	3 1 16	1
	David Hanley	3 1 16	1
	John Walsh	3 1 16	1
	Widw. Clougherty	1 2 28	1
	Michl. Conneely	1 2 28	1
	Robt. Persse Esq.	7 2 16	1
	Mr. P. Reily	3 0 38	1
		T. 77 1 0	
Theeve Garriffe	John Sweeny	3 9	1
	Mr. James Hardiman	6 0 36	1
		7 1 5	2
	James O'Hara Esq.	17 0 26	1
	Mrs. Browne	16 0 10	1
	Mr. R. Sloper	2 1 2	1
		T. 49 3 8	

Figure 157

John O'Donovan's Field Name Books.
1838/'9

Acres Townland

Standard Name: Acres (belonging to Barna Electoral District).

Variants and sources: Acres : Clerk of the Peace
Acres : Sketch Map
Acres : The Revd. P. Daly, P.P.

Description:
'Proprietor Nicholas Lynch, Esq., Barna. Agent Martin Morris, Esq. Galway. The townland is held by 6 tenants at will. Rent £4.11s. per acre. Soil light and gravelly producing potatoes and a little onions. This townland is free from stones. Houses stone cabins. Inhabitants poor. Nothing remarkable on it.'

Attithomasrevagh Townland

Standard Name: Attythomasrevagh

Irish Form of Name: Áit Tighe Thomáis Riabhach

Translation: Site of Grey Thomas's house
'Site of swarthy Thomas's house.' (P.W. Joyce)

Variants and sources: Attythomausreevagh : Clerk of the Peace
Atty Thos. Reagh : Quit Rent Ledger
Attythomasreevagh : Rent Ledger
Attythomausreevagh : Sir V. Blake, Menlo
Attythomausreevagh : Sketch Map
Attythomausreevagh : The Revd. P. Daly, P.P.

Description:
'Proprietor Lord Clanmorris, New Brook, Co. Mayo. Agent Patrick Reily, Claregalway. This townland is held by 19 tenants at will. Rent £4. 10s. per acre. Soil a light moory nature, producing potatoes, bad oats and onions. This land all rocky, except a few acres joining Salt Hill Road – houses stone walls (poor cabins).

Mr. Kelly of Barna Lodge receives the rent of this townland at present. This village is called Ballynagarvane. There is a small long house called [unable to read].'

Cappanaveagh Townland

Standard Name: Cappanaveagh

Irish Form of Name: Ceapach na bhFiach

Translation: Plot of the ravens

Variants and sources:
Cappanaveeagh	:	Clerk of the Peace
Capaghneveagh	:	Down Survey
Cappanaviogh	:	Freehold Registry 1832
Cappanaviogh	:	Rent Ledger
Cappanaveeagh	:	Sir V. Blake, Bart
Cappanaveeagh	:	Sketch Map
Cappannaveeagh	:	The Rev. P. Daly, P.P.
Cappanaveeagh	:	Tithe Applotment Book

Description:
'Proprietor Cunningham Jones, Dublin. This townland is held by Mr. Richard Lynch of Salt Hill under lease of 31 years, who sublets it to 30 tenants at will at £5 per acre. Soil light sandy clay. Producing potatoes, bad oats and spots of onions. This townland is rocky and poor houses stone walls, poor looking. There are a few neat lodges which are set to bathers during the Summer season. There is a small Fort called Cappanaveagh. There is one two stor[e]y high house called Sandymount.'

Cloghatisky Townland.

Standard Name: Cloghatisky

Irish Form of Name: Cloch a Toisce
Cloch an Choiscthe (logainm.ie) *Coiscthe* from verb *cosc* – check / prevent.

Translation: Stone of the treaty.
   Cloch Scoilte – split stone.

Variants and sources: Coghathisky : Clerk of the Peace
   Cloghhiskey : Down Survey
   Cloughskeltha : Mr. Kelly of Barna, Agent
   Cloghathiska : Rent Ledger
   Cloghathisky : Sir V. Blake, Bart
   Cloghathisky : Sketch Map
   Coghathisky : The Rev. P. Daly, P.P.

Description: 'This townland belongs to James O'Hara, Esq., Recorder of Galway and is a part of the Demesne of Leanaboy.'

Kilcorkey Townland

Standard Name: Kilcorkey

Irish Form of Name: Cill Corcaighe

Translation: St. Corkey's church

Rev. J. Rabbitte :'The first part of the name may be from *cill*, a church; the second part from Corcach, gen. corcaighe, a marsh; or the 2nd part may be a proper name: there is a curcach Cille Curcaige in the Martyology of Donegal which has been identified with the Parish of Kilcorkey, barony of Ballintubber, diocese of Elphin. The late Dean Kelly in his notes on this diocese says Corcaige is the name of an Irish Saint of old.' **Prof. Tomás Ó Máille :** Kilcork(e)y: 1691 part of the west lib. and suburbs...1720 Kilcorkey...in the West...; 1686 the wett piece of ground mearing on the highway to Kilcorky and the Lenaboys. **P.W. Joyce**: Kill alone is the name of more than a score of places in various counties: in most cases it stands for cill, a church: but in some it is for *coill*, a wood.

Variants and sources: Kilcorky : Clerk of the Peace
   Killcorkey : Down Survey
   Kilcorkey : Freehold Registry
   Kilcurkey : Rent Ledger

Kilcorky	: Sir V. Blake, Bart
Kilcorky	: Sketch Map
Kilcorky	: The Rev. P. Daly, P.P.
Kilcurky	: Tithe Applotment Book

Description:
'Proprietor Mr. Whaley, Ormond Quay, Dublin. This townland is occupied by 43 tenants in small plots. Lease of 21 years. Rent £6 per acre. County Cess 2s. 6d. per £1. The following lodges are in this townland. Nile Lodge of two stor[e]y high, the residence of John O'Hara, Esq. Treasurer, Merrion Cottage. There are a few more respectable in this townland which bear no name. In general the houses are very respectable.'

Lenaboy Townland

Standard Name: Lenaboy

Irish Form of Name: Léine Bhuidhe

Translation: yellow meadow (wet)
'Lena signifies a marshy meadow.' (P.W. Joyce.)

Variants and Sources: Leanaboy	: Alteration by Mr. Burke 24th Feb. 1838
Leanaboy	: Clerk of the Peace
Leanaboy	: Freehold Registry 1823
Leneboy or Lenebatha	: Rent Ledger
Leanaboy	: East Sketch Map
Leanaboy	: The Rev. P. Daly, P.P.
Leanaboy	: Tithe Applotment Book

Description:
'Proprietor James O'Hara, Esq., Recorder of Galway. The greatest portion of this towland is held by Proprietor who lives in Leanaboy House of two stor[e]y high with suitable offices and a good garden and Demesne beautifully planted and free from rocks. The Baths built by Doctor Grey are in this townland. A portion of

this townland on South side of road between the Records Quay and Black Rock belongs to Mr. Whaley, Oran Quay, Dublin and leased to 8 tenants who has given their [unable to read] term to [unable to read] who have built neat lodges for the Accommodation of Bathers. Lease 1 life or 31 years.'

The *Dublin Evening Mail* reported in January, 1849 that Michael Morris Esq. Lenaboy, was appointed as High-Sheriff for the Town of Galway. Michael went on to become the 1st Baron Killanin and died at Spiddal in 1901.

Pollnarooma East Townland

Standard Name: Pollnarooma East

Irish Form of Name: Poll na Rúma

Translation: hole of the room or chamber

Variants and sources: Poulnarooma East : Clerk of the Peace
Poulronan : County Map
Poulnaruma : Freehold Registry 1823
Poulnaroma : Rent Ledger
Poulnarooma East : Sketch Map
Poulnarooma East : The Rev. P. Daly, P.P.
Poulnarooma E. : Tithe Applotment Book

Description:
Proprietor Lord Clanmorris, New Brook, Co. Mayo. Agent Mr. Pat Reily, Claregalway. This townland is held by 14 tenants and 10 cottiers. No lease. Rent £2. 2s. per acre. Soil light moory and some parts gravel[l]y, producing potatoes, oats and flax. Last Cess 4s. per acre. This townland is both bad and rocky. Houses of stone walls. Inhabitants poor. In this townland there is a two stor[e]y high house with offices and called Seamount Lodge, now occupied by Burton Persse, Esq.

Pollnarooma West Townland

Standard Name: Poulnarooma West

Irish Form of Name: Poll na Rúma

Translation: hole of the room or chamber

Variants and sources: Poulnarooma W. : Clerk of the Peace
Poulronan   : County Map
Poulnaruma   : Freehold Registry 1823
Poulnaroma   : Rent Ledger
Poulnarooma W. : Sketch Map
Poulnarooma W. : Tithe Applotment Book

Description:
Proprietor James O'Hara, Esq., Leanaboy House, Galway. A part of this townland is held by 4 tenants at will. Rent £3.18s. 9d. per acre. Soil a light moory nature producing potatoes, oats and flax. Last Cess 5s. per acre. Black Rock Lodge two stor[e]y high was built by Rev. Peter Daly, R.C.P. and now occupied by Charles Lynch, Esq., Claremont Lodge built by the late Denis Clark of Galway is two stor[e]y high with suitable offices ? to each of the townland lodges. Claremount Lodge is at present unoccupied. This townland is bad and rocky.

Tievegarriff Townland.

Standard Name: Teevgarriff

Irish Form of Name: Taobh Garbh

Translation: rough side
rough hill-side (P.W. Joyce)

Civil Parish: Rahoon

Variants and sources: Taobh Garbh : Clerk of the Peace
Thievegorriff : Rent Ledger
Theevegorriff : Sir V. Blake, Bart
Theevgorriv   : Sketch Map
Theevgorriv   : The Rev. P. Daly, P.P.

Description:
This townland is occupied by two farmers. The first is James Hardiman, Esq., who has a neat two stor[e]y high house with suitable offices and garden neatly planted. It is called Theevgarrive Lodge or Taylor Hill House. The 2nd is Seaview House of three stor[e]y high with offices and garden and a handsome plantation occupied by Richard Lynch, Esq., Galway. This part of townland is the property of Constance Sloper of Galway.[1]

Note: The townland information above is taken from the Galway Library website, available [online] @: http://places.galwaylibrary.ie/place

GRIFFITH'S VALUATION 1855

Salthill's Townlands.

WEST WARD—PARISH OF RAHOON.

No. and Letters of Reference to Map.	Names.		Description of Tenement.	Area.	Rateable Annual Valuation.		Total Annual Valuation of Rateable Property.
	Townlands and Occupiers.	Immediate Lessors.			Land.	Buildings.	
	ACRES. *(Ord. S. 94.)*			A. R. P.	£ s. d.	£ s. d.	£ s. d.
1 a	Barbara Connor,		House and land,		1 6 0	0 5 0	1 11 0
b	Mary Hopkins,		House and land,		1 6 0	0 7 0	1 13 0
c	Thomas Crane,	Nicholas Lynch,	House and land,	4 3 27	0 13 0	0 10 0	1 3 0
d	Martin Madden,		House and land,		0 13 0	0 6 0	0 19 0
e	John Flaherty,		House and land,		0 13 0	0 5 0	0 18 0
f	William Halloran,		House and land,		0 13 0	0 10 0	1 3 0
			Total,	4 3 27	5 4 0	2 3 0	7 7 0

No. and Letters of Reference to Map.	Names.		Description of Tenement.	Area.	Rateable Annual Valuation.		Total Annual Valuation of Rateable Property.
	Townlands and Occupiers.	Immediate Lessors.			Land.	Buildings.	
	ATTITHOMAS-REVAGH. *(Ord. S. 94.)*						
1			Land,	26 1 24	22 0 0	—	
2	Thomas H. Barton,	In fee,	Land,	12 2 31	12 0 0	—	57 0 0
3			Land,	11 0 8	13 10 0	—	
4			Land,	7 0 5	9 10 0	—	
5	George Rutledge,	Thomas H. Barton,	House, office, and land,	1 3 18	2 10 0	23 0 0	25 10 0
6	Thomas H. Barton,	In fee,	Land,	14 3 39	18 0 0	—	18 0 0
7	Samuel Roberts,	Thomas H. Barton,	Land,	2 2 31	3 10 0	—	3 10 0
8	Anthony O'Flaherty,	Same,	House, offices, and land,	4 1 23	5 10 0	22 0 0	27 10 0
			Total,	81 0 19	86 10 0	45 0 0	131 10 0

No. and Letters of Reference to Map.	Names.		Description of Tenement.	Area.	Rateable Annual Valuation.		Total Annual Valuation of Rateable Property.
	Townlands and Occupiers.	Immediate Lessors.			Land.	Buildings.	
	CAPPANAVEAGH. *(Ord. S. 94.)*						
1 a		Warden and Vicar of Galway,	Houses, offices, & land,	50 0 5	62 0 0	19 0 0	
— b	Henry S. Jones,		House and office,	—	—	4 0 0	86 5 0
— c			House and office,	—	—	3 5 0	
— d	Michael Byrne,	Henry S. Jones,	House,	—	—	0 10 0	0 10 0
— e	William Glynn,	Same,	House and office,	—	—	1 10 0	1 10 0
— f	Vacant,	Same,	House,	—	—	0 15 0	0 15 0
— g	John Conneely,	Same,	House and garden,	0 1 0	0 10 0	4 15 0	5 5 0
— h	William Wylde,	Same,	House, office, back-ho., and yard,	0 1 8	—	21 0 0	21 0 0
— i	Oliver Dobbyn,	William Wylde,	House and yard,	—	—	12 0 0	12 0 0
— j	William Wylde,	Henry S. Jones,	House and yard,	—	—	6 10 0	6 10 0
— k	William Wylde,	Same,	House and yard,	—	—	14 0 0	14 0 0
			Total,	50 2 13	62 10 0	87 5 0	149 15 0

No. and Letters of Reference to Map.	Names.		Description of Tenement.	Area.	Rateable Annual Valuation.		Total Annual Valuation of Rateable Property.
	Townlands and Occupiers.	Immediate Lessors.			Land.	Buildings.	
	CLOGHATISKY. *(Ord. S. 94.)*						
1	James O'Hara,	In fee,	House and land,	33 1 13	58 10 0	40 0 0	98 10 0
			Total,	33 1 13	58 10 0	40 0 0	98 10 0

No. and Letters of Reference to Map.		Names.		Description of Tenement.	Area.	Rateable Annual Valuation.		Total Annual Valuation of Rateable Property.
		Townlands and Occupiers.	Immediate Lessors.			Land.	Buildings.	
		KILCORKEY. (Ord. S. 91.)						
1		Edward C Burke,	Mark Lynch,	House, offices, and land,	6 1 27	11 0 0	36 0 0	47 0 0
2		James O'Hara,	Rev. Peter Daly,	Land,	10 3 4	16 0 0	—	16 0 0
—	a	Anne Dunne,	James O'Hara,	Ho., offs., & sm. garden,	—	—	17 0 0	17 0 0
—	b	William Heron,	Anne Dunne,	Ho., off., & sm. garden,	—	—	12 0 0	12 0 0
		VILLAGE OF MERRION. SEA ROAD.						
3	1	Lodgers,	Anne Coyle,	Ho., off., yard, & garden,	0 0 24	0 10 0	16 0 0	16 10 0
—	2	John Dolan,	John Creane,	House, yard, & garden,	0 0 17	0 5 0	2 5 0	2 10 0
—	3	John Creane,	Rev. Peter Daly,	Ho., off., yard, & gardens,	0 1 17	0 15 0	4 0 0	4 15 0
—	4	John Bohen,	Cecilia Conneely.	House, yard, & garden,	0 0 15	0 5 0	2 5 0	2 10 0
—	5	James Corry,	Mary Jones,	House, yard, & garden,	0 0 15	0 5 0	2 5 0	2 10 0
—	6	Miss Ryan,	Peter Sweeny,	Ho., off., yard, & garden,	0 0 20	0 10 0	12 10 0	13 0 0
—	7	Owen Quirke,	Immediate Lessor,	House and yard,	—	—	8 10 0	8 10 0
—	8	Lodgers,	Edward D. Burke,	House,	—	—	1 10 0	1 10 0
—	9	Michael Kearns,	Same,	House and yard,	—	—	3 0 0	3 0 0
—	10	Edward D. Burke,	Rev. Peter Daly,	Garden (in rere),	0 0 25	0 10 0	—	0 10 0
—	11	Thomas Lane,	Same,	Ho., off., yard, & garden,	0 1 20	0 15 0	2 15 0	3 10 0
—	12	Patrick Flaherty,	Same,	Gardens (in rere),	0 0 38	0 12 0	—	0 12 0
—	13	Michael Donnell,	Denis Conneely,	House and yard,	—	—	3 0 0	3 0 0
—	14	Patrick Conneely,	Rev. Peter Daly.	Ho., off., yard, & garden,	0 3 17	2 10 0	3 10 0	6 0 0
—	15	Bartholomew Costello,	Same,	House, yard, & garden,	0 1 16	1 2 0	2 3 0	3 5 0
—	16	Bartholomew Burke,	Same,	House, yard, & garden,	0 1 22	1 5 0	2 0 0	3 5 0
—	17	Mary Connell,	Same,	House, yard, & garden,	0 1 36	1 5 0	2 0 0	3 5 0
—	18	Mary Meledy,	Mary Connell,	House and yard,	—	—	2 0 0	2 0 0
—	19	Matthias Cooke,	Rev. Peter Daly.	Ho., off., yard, & gardens,	0 1 36	1 5 0	2 15 0	4 0 0
—	20	Martin Woodhouse,	Same,	Ho., off., yard, & gardens,	0 1 35	1 5 0	3 15 0	5 0 0
—	21	Judith King,	Same,	Ho., off., yard, & sm. gar.	—	—	3 10 0	3 10 0
—	22	Michael Keane,	Same,	House, yard, & garden,	0 0 17	0 7 0	1 13 0	2 0 0
—	23	Hubert Burke,	Same,	House, yard, & gardens,	0 1 10	1 0 0	4 0 0	5 0 0
—	24	Denis Conneely,	Same,	Garden (in rere),	0 2 25	2 0 0	—	2 0 0
—	25	Mary Martin,	Denis Conneely,	Ho., off., yard, & sm. gar.	—	—	3 0 0	3 0 0
—	26	Mary Clarke,	Same,	House and yard,	—	—	1 5 0	1 5 0
—	27	Michael Brennan,	Hubert Burke,	House, yard, & garden,	0 0 12	0 5 0	1 5 0	1 10 0
—	28	Michael Mahon,	Same,	House, yard, & garden,	0 0 26	0 10 0	2 15 0	3 5 0
—	29	Mrs. Halley,	Patrick Conneely,	House, yard, & garden,	0 0 28	0 10 0	3 10 0	4 0 0
—	30	John Skerrett,	Denis Conneely,	House (in rere),	—	—	1 0 0	1 0 0
—	31	John Magrath,	Rev. Peter Daly,	House, yard, & garden,	0 0 13	0 5 0	3 0 0	3 5 0
—	32	Thomas Davern,	Same,	House (unfinished) & gar.	0 0 13	0 5 0	—	0 5 0
—	33	John Morris,	Same,	House (in rere),	—	—	2 5 0	2 5 0
—	34	John Morris,	Same,	House, yard, & garden,	0 0 10	0 5 0	2 10 0	2 15 0
—	35	Roger Conneely,	Same,	House, yard, & garden,	0 0 18	0 7 0	2 3 0	2 10 0
—	36	Patrick Kennedy,	Same,	House, yard, & garden,	0 0 35	0 12 0	1 3 0	1 15 0
—	37	Mary O'Kelly,	Hubert Burke,	Ho., offs., yard, & sm. gar.	—	—	8 0 0	8 0 0
—	38	John O'Reilly,	Mrs Conneely,	Ho., yard, & sm. garden,	—	—	3 0 0	3 0 0
—	39	Martin King,	Rev. Peter Daly,	House, yard, & garden,	0 1 23	1 0 0	3 5 0	4 5 0
—	40	Peter King,	Same,	Ho., off., yard, & garden,	0 0 32	0 12 0	3 13 0	4 5 0
—	41	Martin King,	Same,	Ho., off., yard, & garden,	0 0 37	0 12 0	3 3 0	3 15 0
—	42	Lodgers,	Martin King,	House,	—	—	1 10 0	1 10 0
—	43	Lodgers,	Same,	House, office, and yard,	—	—	2 10 0	2 10 0
—	44	Denis Doovally,	Burton Persse,	House, office, and yard,	—	—	11 0 0	11 0 0
—	45	Lodgers,	Honoria O'Dea,	Ho., off., yard, & garden,	0 0 18	0 10 0	14 10 0	15 0 0
—	46	Captain Richardson,	Same,	Ho., off., yard, & garden,	0 0 16	0 10 0	17 0 0	17 10 0
—	47	Lodgers,	Same,	Ho., off., yard, & sm. gar.	—	—	11 0 0	11 0 0
—	48	Captain Richardson,	Same,	Coach-house and stable,	—	—	4 0 0	4 0 0
—	49	Lodgers,	Same,	House,	—	—	7 0 0	7 0 0
—	50	Vacant,	Same,	House,	—	—	1 0 0	1 0 0
		TAYLOR'S-HILL ROAD.						
—	1	Walter Burke,	Denis Conneely,	House, yard, & garden,	0 0 28	0 10 0	1 5 0	1 15 0
—	2	Denis Conneely,	Rev. Peter Daly,	Building-ground,	0 0 23	0 10 0	—	0 10 0
—	3	Lodgers,	William Conneely,	House, yard, & sm. gar.	—	—	1 10 0	1 10 0
—	4	Lodgers,	Same,	House, yard, & sm. gar	—	—	1 10 0	1 10 0
—	4a	William Conneely,	Rev. Peter Daly,	Garden (in rere),	0 0 37	0 15 0	—	0 15 0
—	5	Patrick Conneely,	Same,	Building-ground,	0 1 0	0 15 0	—	0 15 0
—	6	John Donnellan,	William Conneely,	House, yard, & garden,	0 0 12	0 5 0	1 5 0	1 10 0
—	7	Mary Kenny	Same,	House, yard, & garden,	0 0 12	0 5 0	1 5 0	1 10 0
—	8	Patrick Conneely,	Rev. Peter Daly,	Building-ground,	0 0 25	0 10 0	—	0 10 0
—	9	James Glynn,	Denis Conneely,	House, yard, & garden,	0 0 11	0 5 0	1 5 0	1 10 0
—	10	John Redden,	Same,	House, yard, & garden,	0 0 11	0 5 0	1 5 0	1 10 0
—	11	Anthony Collins,	Same,	House, yard, & garden,	0 0 12	0 5 0	1 5 0	1 10 0
—	12	Nicholas Fleming,	Thomas Conneely,	House, yard, & garden,	0 0 12	0 5 0	1 5 0	1 10 0
—	13	Maryanne Bermingham	Patrick Flaherty,	House, yard, & garden,	0 0 12	0 5 0	1 10 0	1 15 0
—	14	Mary Wade,	Patrick Conneely,	House, yard, & garden,	0 0 12	0 5 0	3 0 0	3 5 0
				Waste under houses, yards, streets, and small gardens,	4 2 13	—	—	—
				Total,	31 0 17	54 9 0	280 18 0	335 7 0

Griffith's Valuation 1855

No. and Letters of Reference to Map.		Names.		Description of Tenement.	Area.	Rateable Annual Valuation.		Total Annual Valuation of Rateable Property.
		Townlands and Occupiers.	Immediate Lessors.			Land.	Buildings.	
		LENABOY. (Ord. S. 94.)						
1		James O'Hara,	In fee,	Offices and land,	26 2 6	33 10 0	2 10 0	36 0 0
2		James M'Grath,	James O'Hara,	House, offices, and land,	10 2 6	19 0 0	3 10 0	22 10 0
3	a	Denis Conneely,	Same,	House, offices, & land,	1 2 35	1 10 0	4 15 0	6 5 0
	b	Dominick Burke,	Same,	House, offices, & land,		1 10 0	4 10 0	6 0 0
—	c	Matthias Burke,	Same,	House and office,	—	—	0 10 0	0 10 0
—	d	Helen Blake,	Mrs. Grey,	House and offices,	—	—	13 0 0	13 0 0
—	e	Andrew King,	Same,	House and offices,	—	—	16 0 0	16 0 0
4		Paul Rochfort,	Same,	House, offices, and land,	3 2 26	1 10 0	14 0 0	15 10 0
		William Conneely,				0 15 0	—	0 15 0
		John Feeny,				0 15 0	—	0 15 0
		William Feeny,				0 7 0	—	0 7 0
		Denis Feeny,				0 7 0	—	0 7 0
		Matthias Cooke,				0 7 0	—	0 7 0
5		Martin King,	John Whaley,	Land,	3 1 17	0 7 0	—	0 7 0
		Dominick Burke,				0 15 0	—	0 15 0
		Patrick O'Flaherty,				0 7 0	—	0 7 0
		Mary Rush,				0 7 0	—	0 7 0
		Bridget Laffey,				0 15 0	—	0 15 0
		John Gunning,				0 15 0	—	0 15 0
—	a	James O'Dea,	John Gunning,	House,	—	—	0 15 0	0 15 0
		VILLAGE OF SALTHILL.						
6	1	William Feeny,	John Whaley,	House and garden,	0 0 26	0 10 0	1 15 0	2 5 0
—	2	Vacant,	Ellen Ryan,	House and garden,	0 0 25	0 10 0	2 5 0	2 15 0
—	3	Ellen Ryan,	Matthias Cooke&others,	House and garden,	0 0 26	0 10 0	2 10 0	3 0 0
—	4	Vacant,	Ellen Ryan,	House and garden,	0 0 26	0 10 0	1 10 0	2 0 0
—	5	Mary Malley,	Same,	House (in rere),	—	—	1 0 0	1 0 0
—	6	Patrick Conneely,	John Whaley,	House, office, & garden,	0 0 28	0 10 0	9 10 0	10 0 0
—	7	Patrick Lynch,	Ellen Ryan,	House and garden,	0 0 14	0 5 0	1 5 0	1 10 0
—	8	Vacant,	Same,	House and garden,	0 0 14	0 5 0	7 15 0	8 0 0
—	9	John Feeny,	John Whaley,	House and gardens,	0 1 12	1 0 0	3 0 0	4 0 0
—	10	Bridget Laffey,	Same,	House, office, & garden,	0 0 39	0 15 0	3 0 0	3 15 0
—	11	Martin Kane,	Same,	House and garden,	0 0 18	0 5 0	4 5 0	4 10 0
—	12	William Conneely,	Same,	House and garden,	0 1 3	0 15 0	4 15 0	5 10 0
—	13	Margaret Carroll,	Dominick Burke,	House and garden,	0 0 13	0 5 0	4 5 0	4 10 0
—	14	Bridget Hurley,	Catherine O'Connor,	House, offices, & garden,	0 0 15	0 5 0	10 15 0	11 0 0
—	15	Lodgers,	Ellen Ryan,	House, office, & garden,	0 0 28	0 10 0	8 10 0	9 0 0
—	16	John Gunning,	Matthias Cooke&others,	Office,	—	—	2 0 0	2 0 0
—	17	Patrick Conneely,	John Whaley,	Offices & small garden,	—	—	2 5 0	2 5 0
—	18	Lodgers,	John Grealy,	House,	—	—	4 0 0	4 0 0
—	19	Lodgers,	Same,	House and garden,	0 0 13	0 5 0	13 5 0	13 10 0
—	20	Michael Feeny,	John Whaley,	House, office, & garden,	0 0 10	0 5 0	2 10 0	2 15 0
—	21	Maria Nugent,	Same,	House, office, and yard,	—	—	10 10 0	10 10 0
—	22	Catherine O'Connor,	Same,	House, office, and yard,	—	—	4 5 0	4 5 0
—	23	Sarah M'Carthy,	Matthias Cooke&others,	House, offices, and yard,	—	—	4 5 0	4 5 0
—	24	Catherine Kearney,	Same,	House, office, & garden,	0 0 16	0 5 0	5 5 0	5 10 0
—	25	Maria Nugent,	Same,	Ho., offs., & sm. garden,	—	—	4 5 0	4 5 0
—	26	Thomas Delany,	Same,	House, offices, and yard,	—	—	23 0 0	23 0 0
—	27	George Fallon,	Same,	House and office,	—	—	3 15 0	3 15 0
—	28	Patrick Dea,	George Fallon,	Ho., & sm. gar. (in rere),	—	—	0 15 0	0 15 0
—	29	Patrick Flaherty,	John Whaley,	Gardens (in rere),	0 0 11	0 5 0	—	0 5 0
—	30	Matthias Kane,	John Bright,	House (in rere),	—	—	0 10 0	0 10 0
—	31	Martin Lydon,	Same,	House,	—	—	0 15 0	0 15 0
—	32	John Bright,	John Whaley,	Offices,	—	—	0 15 0	0 15 0
—	33	Vacant,	William Wylde,	House & small garden,	—	—	12 10 0	12 10 0
—	34	Samuel Woods,	John Whaley,	Ho., offs., & sm. garden,	—	—	14 0 0	14 0 0
—	35	Launcelot S. Mangan,	Same,	Ho., back-ho., & sm. gar.	—	—	15 0 0	15 0 0
—	36	Patrick Flaherty,	Same,	House, offices, and yard,	—	—	5 5 0	5 5 0
—	37	Nathaniel Kane,	Same,	Garden,	0 0 6	0 3 0	—	0 3 0
—	38	John Bright,	Same,	Ho., off., & sm. garden,	—	—	6 0 0	6 0 0
				Waste under houses, yds., streets, & strand,	2 1 37	—	—	—
7		James O'Hara,	In fee,	Waste land at shore,	1 1 14	—	—	—
				Total,	52 1 4	70 15 0	260 5 0	331 0 0

No. and Letters of Reference to Map.	Names.		Description of Tenement.	Area.	Rateable Annual Valuation.		Total Annual Valuation of Rateable Property.
	Townlands and Occupiers.	Immediate Lessors.			Land.	Buildings.	
	POLLNAROOMA, EAST. (Ord. S. 94.)						
1 A	Lord Clanmorris,	Richard Sloper,	House, offices, and land	13 2 10	13 10 0	21 0 0	} 57 10 0
– B			Land,	49 3 17	23 0 0	—	
– a	Michael Grogan,	Lord Clanmorris,	House and land,	0 3 10	0 12 0	0 8 0	1 0 0
– b	Patrick Grogan,	Same,	House and land,	1 2 19	1 4 0	0 8 0	1 12 0
– c	Patrick Broderick,	Same,	House and land,	0 3 10	0 15 0	0 10 0	1 5 0
– d	Martin Conroy,	Same,	House and land,	0 3 10	0 15 0	0 10 0	1 5 0
– e	Michael Flaherty,	Same,	House, offices, and land	2 1 29	2 0 0	1 0 0	3 0 0
– f	Mary M'Grath,	Michael Flaherty,	House,	—	—	0 8 0	0 8 0
– g	Nicholas Walsh,	Same,	House,	—	—	0 10 0	0 10 0
– h	Michael Gannon,	Lord Clanmorris,	House and land,	0 3 10	0 15 0	0 10 0	1 5 9
– i	Martin Donohoe,	Same,	House,	—	—	0 5 0	0 5 0
– j	Barthw. Cannovan,	Same,	House,	—	—	0 5 0	0 5 0
2	Edmund Duffy,	Same,	Land,	7 2 25	8 10 0	—	8 10 0
3	Richard Sloper,	In fee,	Land,	2 2 37	2 10 0	—	2 10 0
			Total,	81 0 17	53 11 0	25 14 0	79 5 0

No. and Letters of Reference to Map.	Names.		Description of Tenement.	Area.	Rateable Annual Valuation.		Total Annual Valuation of Rateable Property.
	Townlands and Occupiers.	Immediate Lessors.			Land.	Buildings.	
	POLLNAROOMA, WEST. (Ord. S. 94.)						
1			Land,	16 2 35	8 10 0	—	
2			Land,	4 3 30	3 5 0	—	
3			Land,	11 0 15	6 10 0	—	
4			Land,	10 1 10	7 0 0	—	
5	Anne O'Hara,	In fee,	Land,	8 2 25	4 10 0	—	} 109 5 0
6			Land,	6 3 15	4 0 0	—	
7			Land,	10 1 35	8 0 0	—	
8			Land,	8 0 0	5 15 0	—	
9			Herd's ho., offs., & land,	19 1 5	28 0 0	3 0 0	
10			Land,	41 0 33	30 15 0	—	
– 9 b	Rev. George Brownrigg,	Anne O'Hara,	House,	—	—	11 0 0	11 0 0
– 10 a	Vacant,	Same,	House,	—	—	1 5 0	1 5 0
11	Edward O'Flaherty,	Same,	House, offices, and land,	16 0 30	16 10 0	27 0 0	43 10 0
12	Robert H. Persse,	Superioress of Presentation Convent,	House, offices, and land,	7 3 35	11 0 0	35 0 0	46 0 0
13	Rev. Peter Daly,	Same,	Land,	4 2 23	6 10 0	—	6 10 0
– a	Michael Folan,	Rev. Peter Daly,	House,	—	—	0 6 0	0 6 0
			Total,	166 1 16	140 5 0	77 11 0	217 16 0

No. and Letters of Reference to Map.	Names.		Description of Tenement.	Area.	Rateable Annual Valuation.		Total Annual Valuation of Rateable Property.
	Townlands and Occupiers.	Immediate Lessors.			Land.	Buildings.	
	TIEVEGARRIFF. (Ord. S. 94.)						
1	Rev. John D'Arcy,	Anne O'Hara,	Land,	0 1 30	0 10 0	—	0 10 0
2	Elizabeth Hynes,	Rev. John D'Arcy,	Land,	0 1 25	0 10 0	—	0 10 0
3 a	Superioress of Convent,	Richard Sloper,	House, offices, and land,	7 1 25	12 0 0	30 0 0	42 0 0
– b	R. C. Chapel,	Same,	Convent R. C. Chapel (no rent)	—	—	8 0 0	8 0 0
4	Elizabeth Rush,	Same,	House, offices, and land,	6 0 30	10 10 0	20 0 0	30 10 0
5	John B. Kernan,	Anne O'Hara,	House, offices, and land,	18 1 15	23 0 0	40 0 0	63 0 0
6	Thomas M. Persse,	Same,	House, offices, and land,	13 3 10	17 0 0	29 0 0	46 0 0
			Total,	46 2 15	63 10 0	127 0 0	190 10 0
			EXEMPTIONS: Convent R. C. Chapel	—	—	8 0 0	8 0 0
			Total, exclusive of Exemptions,	46 2 15	63 10 0	119 0 0	182 10 0

Figure 158.

ENDNOTES

Salt Hill Time Line to 1901:

1. J. Rabbitte, 'Galway Corporation MS. C.,' *JGAHS,* Vol. 14. (1928-1929), p. 2
2. T.S. Ó Máille, 'Place Names from Galway Documents,' *JGAHS,* Vols. 23-24 (1948-1951)
3. J. Rabbitte, 'Galway Corporation MS. C.,' *JGAHS,* Vol. 14. (1928-1929), p.4
4. T.S. Ó Máille, 'Place Names from Galway Documents,' *JGAHS,* Vols. 23-24 (1948-1951)
5. C. De Lactocnaye, *A Frenchman's Walk Through Ireland 1796-97,* Dublin 1917, p.150
6. Memorial of Indenture of Assignment, 23 July, 1841
7. *Dublin Evening Post,* 7 Oct. 1809; *Belfast Commercial Chronicle,* 9 Oct. 1809; *Hampshire Chronicle,* 16 Oct., 1809
8. A. Leet, *A Directory, to the Market Towns, Villages, Gentlemen's Seats and Other Noted Places in Ireland,* Dublin 1814, p.346
9. *Freeman's Journal,* 8 Nov., 1821
10. *Connaught Journal,* 18 Dec., 1828
11. Ibid., 28 April, 1831
12. *Galway Independent,* 27 April, 1831
13. J. Cunningham, *'A town tormented by the sea': Galway 1790-1914,* Dublin 2004, pp. 80-81
14. *Galway Patriot,* 27 June, 1838
15. J. O'Donovan*, O'Donovan's Field Name Books, 1838/'39,* Galway Library, [online] @: http://places.galwaylibrary.ie/place/11261
16. *Tuam Herald,* 12 Jan., 1839
17. *Galway Vindicator,* 25 Aug., 1847
18. *Galway Mercury,* 16 Nov., 1850
19. J. O'Connor, 'Aspects of Galway Postal History 1636-1984,' *JGAHS,* 44 (1992), p. 157
20. *Galway Packet,* 18 Aug., 1852
21. Ibid., 25 Sept., 1852
22. Galway Petty Court Record, 1853
23. *Galway Vindicator,* 4 Oct., 1856
24. Cancelled Revision Book annotation, 1864
25. *Galway Mercury,* 16 Feb., 1856
26. *Nation,* 24 July, 1858
27. *Galway Vindicator,* 19 March, 1859
28. *Nenagh Guardian,* 19 Sept., 1860
29. *Dublin Builder,* 15 April, 1862
30. *Irish Times,* 13 June, 1862
31. Ibid., 3 Aug., 1864
32. *Galway Vindicator,* 23 July, 1864
33. Ibid., 26 June, 1867
34. Ibid., 20 Oct., 1869
35. *Tuam Herald,* 5 Aug., 1871
36. *Galway Vindicator,* 10 Feb., 1874
37. *Connacht Sentinel,* 30 June, 1981
38. *Connacht Tribune,* 17 Jan., 1986
39. *Tuam Herald,* 4 Nov., 1887
40. *Irish Times,* 5 May, 1888
41. *Galway Vindicator,* 5 March, 1892
42. Cancelled Revision Book record, 1894
43. *Galway Express,* 8 June, 1895
44. Ibid., 6 July, 1895
45. R. O'Neill, *A Rich Inheritance,* Galway 1994, p. 128

Reasons for Writing / Acknowledgements:

1. *Connacht Tribune*, 28 Aug., 1909

Dónal Taheny, A Tribute:

1. K. Morrissey, 'From the Fireside,' *Carnaun School Athenry, 1891-1991*. Ed. F. O'Regan, Galway 1991, p. 96
2. *Connacht Tribune*, 6 May, 1922
3. Ibid., 31 Oct., 2014
4. E. Malcolm, *The Irish Policeman 1822-1922: a life,* Dublin 2006, p. 67
5. *Connacht Sentinel*, 13 April, 1943
6. *Connacht Tribune*, 29 Oct., 1939
7. T. Raftery, *My Life,* 2013, p. 32: [online] @: https://proftomraftery.files.wordpress.com/2013/09/dadsbookv2.pdf
8. 'The Patrician Brothers' Schools,' *Galway Reader*. Ed. S.J. Maguire, Volume 3, Nos. 1 and 2, 1950, p. 55
9. *Galway Mercury,* 30 May, 1846
10. H. Inglis, *A Journey throughout Ireland during the Spring, Summer and Autumn of 1834,* London 1838, p. 216
11. *Galway Mercury,* 14 Aug., 1847
12. *Connacht Sentinel,* 20 March, 1962
13. *City Tribune,* 30 June, 2006
14. *Connacht Tribune,* 22 Dec., 1967
15. Personal letter

Chapter 1. Salthill's Townlands and Burial Grounds:

1. *Irish Builder*, 15 July, 1895
2. J. Fleetwood Berry, *The Story of Saint Nicholas' Collegiate Church*, Galway 1989, pp. 81-82
3. *Galway Vindicator*, 25 June, 1862
4. *Irish Times*, 21 April, 2007
5. J. Hardiman, *The History of the Town & County of the Town of Galway*, Dublin 1820, p. 250
6. J Rabbitte, 'Galway Corporation MS. C', *JGAHS*, Vol. 14 (1928-29), p. 3
7. Ibid., *JGAHS*, Vol. 12 (1922-1923), p. 26

Chapter 2. Salthill's Villages:

1. *Connacht Tribune*, 6 May, 1911
2. *Galway Vindicator*, 26 June, 1867
3. *Galway Patriot,* 27 June, 1838
4. J. O'Connor, 'Aspects of Galway Postal History 1638-1984,' *JGAHS*, Vol. 44 (1992), p. 176
5. *Post Office Directory*, 1858
6. *Galway Mercury,* 16 Feb., 1856
7. *Irish Times*, 13 June, 1862
8. J. Wesley, *The Journal of the Rev. John Wesley, A.M.,* Vol II., London 1827, p. 323
9. United Methodist Presbyterian Church, Galway. *History,* [online] @: http://unitedchurchgalway.ie/welcome/history/
10. Cancelled Revision Book annotation, 1890
11. *Slater's Directory*, 1894
12. M.G. O'Malley, 'Memories of Queen's College, Galway, 1904-1906,' *JGAHS*, Vol. 50 (1998), p. 115
13. J. Murray, *Galway: A Medico-Social History,* Galway 1994, p. 237
14. Galway Petty Court Record, 1896
15. *Galway Vindicator*, 20 Oct., 1869
16. Galway Petty Court Record, 1884
17. Cancelled Revision Book annotation, 1895
18. M.G. O'Malley, 'Memories of Queen's College, Galway, 1904-1906,' *JGAHS*, Vol. 50 (1998), p. 116
19. Justice S. Ryan, 'St. Joseph's Industrial School, Salthill ("Salthill"), 1870-1996,' *Ryan Report* 2009, p. 523
20. *Tuam Herald*, 4 Nov., 1887

Chapter 3. Finding One's Bearings- Maps and Photographs:

1. J. O'Donovan & others, *Letters... Antiquities of the County of Galway... Ordnance Survey in 1839* - Vol. 1., p.133

Chapter 4. Salthill Demesnes of Clanmorris, Persse, O'Hara and Whaley:

1. *Galway Vindicator*, 14 June, 1848
2. *Tuam Herald*, 16 May, 1903
3. *Irish Times*, 5 May, 1888
4. *Galway Vindicator*, 2 May, 1888
5. J. Fleetwood Berry, *The Story of St. Nicholas' Collegiate Church*, Galway 1989, p. 81
6. *Connacht Tribune*, 2 July, 1921
7. Ibid., 9 April, 1955
8. *Pathé News*' audio report, 1954
9. *Connacht Tribune*, 2 July, 1921
10. *Cork Constitution*, 20 June, 1890
11. *Dublin Daily Express*, 19 June, 1890
12. J. O'Donovan, *O'Donovan's Field Name Books, 1838/'39*, Galway Library, [online] @ : http://places.galwaylibrary.ie/place/11261
13. J. Uí Chionna research quoted [online] @: http://www.thekingshead.ie/about/
14. T. Whaley, *Buck Whaley's Memoirs*, Ed. Sir E. Sullivan, Bart., London 1906, Preface.
15. J. Hardiman, *History of Galway*. Dublin 1820, (a) p. 15; (b) p. 292; (c) Appendix No. VII. p. xxxvi
16. *Freeman's Journal*, 4 Sept., 1826
17. T. Whaley, *Buck Whaley's Memoirs*, Dublin 2006, p 12
18. P. M. Geoghegan, 'Buck Whaley, dissipation and destruction,' *History Ireland*, Issue 2, Volume 15., March/April 2007
19. *Freeman's Journal*, 18 Sept., 1789
20. *Anglo Celt*, 1 Dec., 1852
21. T. Whaley, *Buck Whaley's Memoirs*, Dublin 2006, p. 230
22. *Freeman's Journal*, 8 Nov., 1800
23. *Finn's Leinster Journal*, 10 Feb., 1802
24. *Freeman's Journal*, 23 Dec., 1818
25. Ibid., 8 Nov., 1800
26. *Irish Times*, 13 Dec., 2016
27. *Freeman's Journal*, 10 May, 1800
28. *Connaught Journal*, 22 May, 1823
29. *Freeman's Journal*, 5 Dec., 1814
30. *Tipperary Clans' Archive*, Jan., 1840
31. *Finns Leinster Journal*, 11 May, 1803
32. *Freeman's Journal*, 5 Sept., 1828
33. Ibid., 1 Oct., 1824
34. Ibid., 22 March, 1845
35. Ibid., 5 Feb., 1853
36. *Irish Times*, 21 Feb., 2015
37. *Galway Mercury*, 27 April, 1850
38. *Freeman's Journal*, 14 Feb., 1855
39. *Nation*, 12 May, 1855
40. *Freeman's Journal*, 8 Feb., 1856

Chapter 5. Salthill of Walls, Gates and Promenade:

1. M.G. O'Malley, 'Memories of Queen's College, Galway, 1904-1906,' *JGAHS* Vol. 50 (1998), p. 116
2. *The Rotarian*, May, 1921, Chicago, p. 267
3. *Galway Patriot*, 17 May, 1837
4. *Galway Vindicator*, 16 Aug., 1843
5. *Galway Mercury*, 7 March, 1846
6. Ibid., 2 May, 1846
7. J. Cunningham, *'A town tormented by the sea: Galway 1790-1914*, Dublin 2004, p. 130
8. *Galway Mercury*, 30 Jan., 1847
9. J. Cunningham, *'A town tormented by the sea': Galway 1790-1914*, Dublin 2004, p.169
10. *Galway Mercury*, 17 May, 1856
11. Ibid., 4 Oct., 1856
12. Ibid., 23 May, 1857
13. *Galway Vindicator*, 9 June, 1877
14. Ibid., 13 Dec., 1873
15. Ibid., 12 Nov., 1873
16. *Directory of Irish Architects 1720 -1940*,

17. *Galway Vindicator*, 14 Sept., 1878
18. *Directory of Irish Architects 1720 -1940*, [online] @: http://www.dia.ie/architects/view
19. *Dublin Builder*, 15 April, 1862
20. *Directory of Irish Architects 1720 -1940*, [online] @: http://www.dia.ie/architects/view
21. *Galway Vindicator*, 9 March, 1864
22. *Directory of Irish Architects 1720 -1940*, [online] @: http://www.dia.ie/architects/view
23. *Historical Report*, Ballynahinch Castle, [online] @: http://www.ballynahinchcastle.com
24. K.Villiers-Tuthill, *History of Kylemore Castle & Abbey*, Connemara 2002, p.73 & *Irish Times*, 27 Oct., 2015
25. *Directory of Irish Architects 1720 -1940*, [online] @: http://www.dia.ie/architects/view
26. *Galway Vindicator*, 29 June, 1887
27. *Tuam Herald*, 5 Sept., 1885
28. Ibid., 15 Aug., 1891
29. Ibid., 12 Sept., 1891
30. *Galway Vindicator*, 5 March, 1892
31. *Tuam Herald*, 12 March, 1892
32. Memorial of Lease, 1895
33. *Galway Express*, 8 June, 1895
34. Ibid., 6 July, 1895
35. *Tuam Herald*, 27 June, 1896
36. Ibid., 7 March, 1896
37. Ibid., 17 July, 1897
38. Ibid., 11 July, 1896
39. Ibid., 31 July, 1897
40. *Galway Express*, 3 Oct., 1896
41. *Tuam Herald*, 31 July, 1897
42. *Galway Express*, 26 Sept., 1896
43. *Tuam Herald*, 10 Oct., 1896
44. Ibid., 5 Aug., 1899
45. *Connacht Tribune*, 5 June, 1909
46. Ibid., 6 Dec., 1930
47. Ibid., 11 Dec., 1954
48. Galway Gaol Record, 23 Sept., 1920
49. *Connacht Tribune*, 13 June, 1913
50. Ibid., 7 June, 1913
51. Ibid., 21 June, 1913
52. Ibid., 5 April, 1913
53. Ibid., 27 Sept., 1913
54. Ibid., 3 Jan., 1914

Chapter 6. Salthill: What's in a Name?:

1. T.S. Ó Máille, 'Place Names from Galway Documents,' *JGAHS*, Vols. 23-24 (1948 -1951)
2. *Dublin Evening Post*, 7 Oct., 1809
3. A. Leet, *Directory to the Market Towns, Villages, Gentlemen's Seats, and Other Noted Places in Ireland*, Dublin 1814, p.346
4. *Galway Vindicator*, 26 June, 1867
5. *Connaught Journal*, 18 Dec., 1828
6. J. O'Donovan, *O'Donovan's Field Name Books, 1838/'39*, Galway Library, [online] @: http://places.galwaylibrary.ie/place/11754
7. *Connacht Tribune*, 29 May, 1909
8. *Irish Times*, 1 Jun., 1879
9. J. Burke, *A General and Heraldic Dictionary of the Peerage and Baronetage of the British Empire*, Vol. 1., London 1831, p. 280
10. *Logainm.ie*, [online] @: https://www.logainm.ie/ga/1416621
11. Ibid.
12. *The Gentleman's and London Magazine: Or Monthly Chronologer, 1741-1791*, London, Jan., 1791, p.392
13. *The Peerage of England, Scotland and Ireland*, Volume III, London, 1790, p.299
14. Memorial of Indenture of Assignmen*t*, 23 July, 1841
15. *Logainm.ie*, [online] @: https://www.logainm.ie/en/14227?s=Salthill+Demesne
16. J. Rabbitte, 'Galway Corporation MS. C.,' *JGAHS*, Vol. 14. (1928-29), p. 2
17. *Galway Vindicator*, 10 May, 1845
18. *Galway Mercury*, 1 June, 1854
19. Ibid., 11 Nov., 1848
20. *Galway Vindicator*, 14 June, 1851
21. J. Rabbitte, 'Galway Corporation MS. C.,' *JGAHS*, Vol. 12 (1922-1923), p. 27
22. Ibid., p.26

23. *Dublin Evening Post*, 16 June, 1840
24. *The London Magazine and Monthly Chronologer,* 1853, p. 167
25. NUIG Landed Estates' Database, [online] @: http://landedestates.nuigalway.ie/LandedEstates/jsp/estate-show.jsp?id=1015
26. L. Colley, *The Ordeal of Elizabeth Marsh – A Woman in World History,* New York 2007
27. *Freeman's Journal,* 22 Mar., 1800
28. Ardagh and Clonmacnoise Diocesan Archives
29. T. Murray, *The Story of the Irish in Argentina,* New York 1919, p.229
30. *Encyclopaedia Britannia,* [online] @: http://www.britannica.com/EBchecked/topic/193282/estancia#ref90911
31. S. M. Ussher, *Los Capellanes Irlandeses en la Colectivdad Hiberno-Argentina Durante el Sigle XIX,* Argentina 1954, P. 187
32. *Irish Independent,* 22 Apr., 1910
33. Ardagh and Clonmacnoise Diocesan Archives

Chapter 7. Salthill's Fishing Tradition:

1. J. Hardiman, *History of Galway*, Dublin 1820, p. 2
2. Ibid., p. 186
3. Ibid., p. 292
4. Ibid., p. 294
5. J. Cunningham, *'A town tormented by the sea': Galway 1790-1914,* Dublin 2004, pp. 80-81
6. H. Dutton, *A Statistical and Agricultural Survey of the County of Galway,* Dublin 1824, p. 199
7. *Irish Times,* 7 Oct., 1861
8. *Tuam Herald,* 16 Oct., 1897
9. *Nenagh Guardian,* 13 Oct., 1897
10. *Freeman's Journal,* 13 Oct., 1837
11. *Connacht Tribune,* 26 Nov., 1938
12. *Galway Vindicator,* 14 April, 1843
13. *Galway Mercury,* 25 June, 1859
14. *Galway Vindicator,* 24 Aug., 1861
15. National Archives U.K., BT File 113/73; Register ticket 145,028
16. Galway Petty Court Record, 1853
17. *Connacht Tribune,* 27 March, 1981
18. M. Semple, *Some Galway Memories,* Galway 1973, p.114
19. *Connacht Tribune,* 31 May, 1924
20. Ibid., 7 March, 1925
21. Ibid., 7 July, 1923
22. *Galway Express,* 18 Feb., 1871
23. Ibid., 10 June, 1871
24. *Connacht Tribune,* 7 July, 1923
25. H. Dutton, *A Statistical and Agricultural Survey of the County of Galway.* Dublin 1824, p. 200
26. *Connacht Tribune,* 15 Dec., 1923
27. ibid., 31 Dec., 1955
28. *Galway Express,* 4 Sept., 1869
29. *Connacht Tribune,* 15 Dec., 1923
30. *Freeman's Journal,* 23 May, 1872
31. *Galway Mercury,* 11 Sept., 1852
32. Galway Petty Court Record, 1860
33. *Galway Vindicator,* 21 Aug., 1869
34. *Galway Advertiser,* 17 May, 2012
35. *Tuam Herald,* 12 Jan., 1839
36. J. Cunningham, *'A town tormented by the sea': Galway 1790-1914,* Dublin 2004, p. 234
37. *Connacht Tribune,* 30 April, 1921

Chapter 8. Salthill Baths:

1. *Nenagh Guardian,* 4 Oct., 1843
2. *Galway Vindicator,* 14 Sept., 1859
3. *Galway Patriot,* 15 July, 1837
4. Ibid., 8 Aug., 1835
5. *Galway Vindicator,* 14 Sept., 1859
6. *Galway Packet,* 25 Aug., 1852
7. *Connaught Journal,* 5 May, 1831
8. 'Small Wars by Colonel C.E. Callwell: a Military Times Classic.' *Military History Monthly,* 11 Nov., 2010
9. J. M. Callwell, *Old Irish Life,* Edinburgh 1912, p.345

10. *Irish Times*, 6 Oct., 1873
11. *Hibernian Journal*, 21 June, 1775
12. *Irish Times,* 21 Aug., 1882
13. *Connaught Journal*, 30 June, 1823
14. Ibid., 10 July, 1823
15. Ibid., 20 Oct., 1828
16. *Galway Patriot*, 13 March, 1839
17. *Galway Vindicator*, 29 March, 1848
18. Ibid., 18 Nov., 1848
19. *Thom's Directory*, 1868
20. Registry of Deeds' record, 1865
21. *Galway Vindicator*, 14 Sept., 1859
22. Ibid., 24 Aug., 1864
23. Ibid., 14 Sept., 1859
24. Ibid., 10 Dec., 1870
25. Galway Petty Court Record, 1853
26. Ward & Lock, *Pictorial Guide to Connemara and the West of Ireland*, London 1890, p.36
27. *Connacht Tribune*, 7 July, 1923
28. *Connacht Sentinel*, 13 Aug., 1946
29. *Connacht Tribune*, 24 Aug., 1912
30. Registry of Deeds' record, 1830
31. National Archives U.K., BT 113/73
32. Cancelled Revision Book annotation, c.1860
33. *Galway Vindicator*, 30 June, 1849
34. *Nenagh Guardian*, 16 Dec., 1857
35. Registry of Deeds' record, 1845
36. *Galway Vindicator*, 27 Jan., 1847
37. Registry of Deeds' record, 1855
38. *Galway Vindicator*, 20 July, 1870
39. *Medical Directory for Ireland*, 1858, p. 33
40. *Connacht Tribune*, 27 Dec., 1913
41. Ibid., 7 June, 1919
42. Ibid., 28 Aug., 1909
43. Ibid., 4 Sept., 1909
44. Ibid., 6 Nov., 1926
45. Ibid., 16 July, 1927
46. Ibid., 24 Sept., 1921
47. *Connacht Sentinel*, 19 June, 1934
48. Ibid., 24 Oct., 1944
49. *Galway Packet*, 25 Aug., 1852.
50. J. M.Callwell, *Old Irish Life,* Edinburgh 1912, p. 347
51. *Irish Times*, 30 Aug., 1960
52. Ibid., 27 Dec., 1902
53. *Connacht Tribune*, 24 Sept., 1910
54. Ibid., 31 Dec., 1955
55. *Freeman's Journal*, 9 July, 1872
56. *Galway Vindicator*, 18 July, 1908
57. *Connacht Tribune*, 19 July, 1913
58. Ibid., 6 Aug., 1921
59. Ibid., 23 July, 1910
60. Ibid., 8 Nov., 1958
61. Ibid., 26 Sept., 1959
62. Ibid., 23 June, 1945
63. Ibid., 3 July, 1981
64. Ibid., 3 Sept., 1955
65. Ibid., 26 Sept., 1959
66. G. Ó Tuathaigh, ' "…the air of a place of importance," Aspects of Nineteenth-Century Galway,' *Galway Town & Gown 1884-1984*, Ed. D. Ó Cearbhaill, Dublin 1984, p.143
67. *Irish Examiner*, 7 Jan., 2016
68. *Connacht Tribune*, 4 Feb., 1922
69. Ibid., 8 April, 1922
70. Ibid., 30 June, 1923
71. Ibid., 7 July, 1923

Chapter 9. Nineteenth Century Accommodation and Female Contribution:

1. *Connaught Journal*, 16 May, 1831
2. Ibid., 9 May, 1831
3. *Galway Vindicator*, 17 July, 1844
4. *Galway Mercury*, 16 May, 1857
5. *Freeman's Journal,* 23 May, 1872
6. *Galway Patriot*, 27 June, 1838
7. *Galway Vindicator*, 25 Sept., 1869
8. *Irish Times*, 23 Nov., 1907
9. *Connaught Journal*, 18 Dec., 1828
10. *Galway Patriot*, 29 June, 1838
11. M. G. O'Malley, 'Memories of Queen's College, Galway, 1904-1906,' *JGAHS* Vol. 50 (1998), pp.112-117
12. J. Mullin, *The Story of a Toiler's Life.*, Ed. Patrick Maume, Dublin 2000, p.100
13. P. J. Lindsay, *Memories*, Dublin 1992, p. 51
14. *Connacht Tribune*, 13 May, 1911
15. Ibid., 23 April, 1921
16. J.M. Callwell, *Old Irish Life*, Edinburgh 1912, p.345

17. Geraldine Plunkett Dillon, *All in The Blood,* Ed. Honor Ó Brolcháin, Dublin 2006, p.292
18. *City Tribune,* 27 Feb., 2004
19. *Connacht Tribune,* 18 Dec., 1909
20. C. Kelly, *The Grand Tour of Galway,* Cork 2002, p. 8
21. *Connacht Tribune,* 19 Sept., 1914
22. Ibid., 17 May, 1924
23. J. Cunningham, M. Mac Sweeney, *The History of Galway Golf Club,* [online] @: http://www.galwaygolf.com/
24. *City Tribune,* 11 April, 1997
25. *Etymology Dictionary,* [online] @: http://www.etymonline.com/
26. *Connacht Tribune,* 30 July, 1921
27. Ibid., 2 Aug., 1924
28. *Connacht Sentinel,* 13 Aug., 1946
29. J.M. Callwell, *Old Irish Life,* Edinburgh 1912, p.348
30. *City Tribune,* 7 Sept., 1990
31. *Connacht Tribune,* 24 April, 1981
32. Ibid., 23 July, 1910
33. Ibid., 12 July, 1924
34. *Galway Vindicator,* 13 June, 1885
35. *Connacht Tribune,* 26 June, 1915
36. Ibid.
37. Ibid., 14 Aug., 1915
38. Ibid., 6 Oct., 1917
39. *Galway Vindicator,* 20 June, 1860
40. J. Cunningham, '*A town tormented by the sea': Galway 1790-1914,* Dublin 2004, p. 171
41. *Irish Times,* 18 Aug., 1862
42. Ibid., 3 Aug., 1864
43. *Freeman's Journal,* 9 July, 1872
44. *Galway Express,* 5 Aug., 1871
45. *Tuam Herald,* 28 Aug., 1897
46. *Irish Times,* 30 Jan., 1902
47. *Connacht Tribune,* 19 July, 1913
48. Ibid., 12 July, 1913
49. Ibid., 1 Jan., 1927
50. Ibid., 10 July, 1915
51. Ibid., 8 June, 1918
52. Ibid., 13 March, 1920
53. Ibid., 8 March, 1924
54. Ibid., 1 Jan., 1927
55. Ibid., 15 Feb., 1958
56. Ibid., 23 Jan., 1965
57. *Post Office Directory and Calendar,* 1858
58. J. O'Connor, 'Aspects of Galway Postal History 1636-1984,' *JGAHS,* 44 (1992), p. 157
59. British Postal Service Appointment Books, 1851
60. J. O'Connor, 'Aspects of Galway Postal History 1636-1984,' *JGAHS,* 44 (1992), p. 144
61. *Slater's Directory,* 1870
62. J. O'Connor, 'Aspects of Galway Postal History 1636-1984,' *JGAHS,* 44 (1992), p. 190
63. *Galway Vindicator,* 31 Jan., 1863
64. Griffith's Valuation, 1855
65. Galway Petty Court Records, 1869 & 1856
66. Cancelled Revision Book annotation, 1861
67. *Galway Vindicator,* 26 April, 1862
68. *Galway Mercury,* 11 Dec, 1858 & *Galway Vindicator,* 3 Aug., 1864
69. *Dublin Evening Mail,* 11 May, 1864
70. *Waterford Mail,* 3 Oct., 1864
71. *Tuam Herald,* 30 July, 1870
72. *Daily Express,* 4 May, 1889
73. *Galway Mercury,* 15 July, 1854
74. Galway Petty Court Record, 1864

Chapter 10. *Na Fámairí* and the Lazy Wall:

1. H. Inglis, *A Journey throughout Ireland during the Spring, Summer and Autumn of 1834,* London 1838, p. 217
2. *Irish Times,* 20 June, 1867
3. *Connacht Sentinel,* 10 Aug., 1948
4. Ward & Lock, *Pictorial Guide to Connemara and the West of Ireland,* London c.1890, p.44
5. *Connacht Sentinel,* 29 July, 1958
6. Ibid.
7. Ibid., 10 Aug., 1948
8. *Connacht Tribune,* 12 Aug., 1911
9. *Irish Times,* 6 Oct., 1873
10. L. O'Flaherty, *A Tourist's Guide to Ireland,* London 1929, p. 5
11. M. Callwell, *Old Irish Life,* Edinburgh

1912, p. 346
12. *City Tribune,* 11 April, 1997
13. Ibid., 7 Sept., 1990
14. *Galway Express,* 9 Oct., 1909
15. *Connacht Sentinel,* 17 Aug., 1943
16. *Connacht Tribune,* 7 June, 1924
17. Ibid., 7 July, 1928
18. Ibid., 27 April, 1929
19. *Connacht Sentinel,* 28 Aug., 1934
20. Ibid., 26 May, 1959
21. Ibid., 3 Sept., 1957
22. Ibid., 26 May, 1959
23. Galway Gaol record, 1880
24. *Connacht Tribune,* 28 Aug., 1909
25. *Nenagh Guardian,* 29 Aug., 1888
26. *Slater's Directory,* 1881
27. *Freeman's Journal,* 8 Dec., 1909
28. *Connacht Tribune,* 11 Dec., 1909
29. Ibid., 1 Dec., 1923
30. Ibid., 12 June, 1943
31. Ibid., 23 Sept., 1933
32. Ibid., 10 June, 1933
33. *Connacht Sentinel,* 26 May, 1959
34. S. O'Kelly, *Ranns & Ballads,* Dublin 1918, pp. 26–34
35. *Connacht Tribune,* 24 July, 1943

Chapter 11. The Toft Family and Salthill: A Unique Relationship:

1. *Galway Patriot,* 27 June, 1838
2. *Galway Express,* 13 June, 1885
3. P. Phillips, *Humanity Dick: The Eccentric Member for Galway,* Kent 2003, pp.65-66
4. *Galway Patriot,* 7 Oct., 1835
5. *Galway Vindicator,* 10 July, 1869
6. *Connacht Tribune,* 14 Jan., 1928
7. *Connacht Sentinel,* 30 Sept., 1952
8. *Galway Vindicator,* 11 June, 1870
9. *Galway Express,* 10 Sept., 1870
10. *Galway Observer,* 26 Feb., 1910
11. *Connacht Sentinel,* 30 June, 1981
12. *Freeman's Journal,* 25 April, 1889
13. *Irish Times,* 26 July, 1893
14. Galway Petty Court Record, 1901
15. *Freeman's Journal,* 7 Aug., 1895
16. *Connacht Tribune,* 27 Sept., 1913
17. *Freeman's Journal,* 6 July, 1895
18. Ibid., 4 Sept., 1895
19. *Connacht Tribune,* 21 Aug., 1915
20. Ibid., 14 Aug., 1909
21. *Galway Observer,* 17 Sept., 1910
22. *Connacht Tribune,* 24 Aug., 1912
23. *Irish Times,* 6 Nov., 1908
24. *Connacht Tribune,* 31 July, 1909
25. Ibid., 31 Dec., 1955
26. *Freeman's Journal,* 2 Sept., 1916
27. *Connacht Tribune,* 15 July, 1922
28. Ibid., 7 Aug., 1926
29. Ibid., 24 July, 1937
30. Ibid., 25 Feb., 1939
31. Ibid.
32. Ibid.
33. Ibid., 4 March, 1939
34. *Connacht Sentinel,* 14 March, 1939
35. *Connacht Tribune,* 18 March, 1939
36. Ibid., 15 July, 1939
37. Ibid., 29 July, 1939
38. Ibid., 31 May, 1941
39. *Connacht Sentinel,* 29 Aug., 1939
40. *Connacht Tribune,* 9 Sept., 1933
41. *Irish Times,* 27 Aug., 1935
42. *Connacht Tribune,* 31 May, 1941
43. Ibid., 2 March, 1940
44. *Connacht Sentinel,* 9 July, 1940
45. Ibid., 21 Sept., 1940
46. *Irish Times,* 25 July, 1940
47. *Connacht Tribune,* 24 May, 1941
48. *Irish Times,* 29 May, 1941
49. *Connacht Tribune,* 31 May, 1941
50. *Irish Times,* 26 July, 1940
51. *Connacht Sentinel,* 27 May, 1941
52. *Connacht Tribune,* 24 May, 1941
53. Ibid.
54. *Connacht Tribune,* 31 May, 1941
55. *Irish Times,* 30 May, 1941
56. *Connacht Tribune,* 31 May, 1941
57. Ibid., 17 Nov., 1956
58. Ibid., 23 May, 1942
59. *Irish Times,* 4 March, 1968

Chapter 12. Getting to Salthill: Trains, Trams and Horses:

1. M. Semple, *By the Corribside,* Galway 1981, pp. 16-19
2. M J. Hurley, *The Story of Galway General Omnibus Company Limited,* Galway 2014.
3. *Viceregal Commission on Irish Railways, including Light Railways.* 1906.
4. J. Prunty, P. Walsh, *Irish Historic Towns Atlas,* No 28, Dublin 2016, p. 8
5. H. Coulter, *The West of Ireland: Its Existing Condition and Prospects,* Dublin 1862, p. 131
6. *Dublin Evening Mail,* 4 Nov., 1871
7. C. De Lactocnaye. *A Frenchman's Walk Through Ireland 1796-97,* Dublin 1917, p. 150
8. *Irish Times,* 30 Oct., 1861
9. Ibid., 6 Oct., 1873
10. *Galway Mercury,* 30 June, 1857
11. *Galway Vindicator,* 16 July, 1864
12. *Galway Express,* 5 Aug., 1871
13. *Galway Vindicator,* 29 Oct., 1870
14. M.J. Hurley, *The Story of Galway General Omnibus Company Limited,* Galway 2014, p. 3
15. *Connacht Tribune,* 1 June, 1918
16. *Belfast Newsletter,* 2 Oct., 1879
17. *Connacht Tribune,* 1 June, 1918
18. *Tuam Herald,* 21 April, 1900
19. *Connacht Tribune,* 8 April, 1911
20. Ibid., 1 June, 1918
21. Ibid., 8 April, 1911
22. Ibid., 12 Aug., 1911
23. Ibid., 20 Oct., 1928
24. M. Semple, *By the Corribside,* Galway 1981, p. 17
25. Ibid., p. 16
26. E. Somerville & M. Ross, *Some Irish Yesterdays,* London 1906, p. 10
27. *Connacht Tribune,* 12 Aug., 1911
28. *Irish Times,* 29 Oct., 1906
29. Ibid., 14 Aug., 1909
30. *Connacht Tribune,* 8 Aug., 1914
31. Ibid., 26 Sept., 1914
32. Ibid., 15 Aug., 1914
33. Ibid., 8 Aug., 1914
34. Ibid., 8 April, 1911
35. *Connacht Sentinel,* 21 July, 1959
36. *Connacht Tribune,* 21 July, 1923

Chapter 13. Nineteenth Century Famines and Evictions:

1. T. Keneally, *The Great Shame,* London 1999, p. 129
2. N. Mac Conghráil, 'An Ghaeilge agus *The Connacht Tribune*,' *JGAHS,* Vol. 61 (2009), p. 210
3. J. Cunningham, '*A Town tormented by the Sea*': *Galway 1790-1914,* Dublin 2004, p. 136
4. J. J. Percival, *The Great Famine,* London 1995, p. 191
5. Third Report of The Commissioners... Condition of the Poorer Classes in Ireland, London 1836, p. 8
6. *Galway Patriot,* 14 Nov., 1838
7. T. McClaughlin, 'Lost Children,' *History Ireland,* Volume 8, Issue 4, Winter 2000
8. Poor Relief (Ireland) Act, 1838
9. T.P. Coogan, *The Famine Plot,* New York 2012, p. 197
10. C. Kinealy, *This Great Calamity,* Dublin 1994, p. 23
11. C. Tóibín, 'Erasure,' *London Review of Books,* Vol. 20. No. 15, 30 July, 1998
12. Canon J. O'Rourke, *The Great Irish Famine,* Dublin 1989, p. 171
13. Ibid.
14. *Galway Advertiser,* 29 Sept., 2011
15. P. Melvin, *Estates and Landed Society in Galway.* Dublin 2012, pp. 207-8
16. P. Ó Fathaigh, *War of Independence,* Cork 2000, p. 28
17. Ibid., p. 75
18. National Asset Management Agency, 2009
19. *Connaught Watchman,* 8 Oct., 1851
20. *Connacht Tribune,* 19 Aug., 1977
21. *Irish Times,* 9 Jan., 1860
22. *Punch,* 15 June, 1861
23. *Connaught Journal,* 9 May, 1831

24. Ibid., 28 April, 1831
25. *Galway Independent*, 27 April, 1831
26. *Connaught Journal*, 6 April, 1829
27. *Freeman's Journal*, 14 Jan., 1852
28. J. Rabbitte, 'Galway Corporation MS. C.,' *JGAHS*, Vol. 12 (1922-1923), p. 27
29. *Dublin Evening Post,* 11 Nov., 1856
30. *Galway Vindicator,* 30 Dec., 1846
31. *Connacht Tribune,* 18 April, 1975
32. Ibid., 9 Sept., 1977
33. J. Mitchell, 'Father Peter Daly (c.1788-1868),' *JGAHS*, Vol. 39 (1983-1984), p. 70
34. Ibid., p.72
35. *Connacht Tribune,* 23 Sept., 1977
36. J. Mitchell, 'Father Peter Daly (c.1788-1868),' *JGAHS*, Vol. 39 (1983-1984), pp. 71-2
37. Ibid., p.89
38. *Nation*, 24 July, 1858
39. P.G. Lane, 'The General Impact of the Encumbered Estates Act of 1849 on Counties Galway and Mayo.' *JGAHS*, Vol. 33 (1972-1973), p. 49
40. *Galway Mercury*, 3 July, 1858
41. *Nation*, 24 July, 1858
42. Ibid.
43. *Galway Mercury*, 10 July, 1858
44. *Dublin Evening Mail*, 7 July, 1858
45. *Galway Mercury*, 3 Sept., 1853
46. Ibid., 3 July, 1858
47. *Galway Vindicator*, 24 Dec., 1859
48. Ibid., 11 Feb., 1860
49. J. Mitchell, 'Father Peter Daly (c.1788-1868),' *JGAHS*, Vol. 39 (1983-1984), p. 72
50. *Galway Mercury*, 25 June, 1859
51. J. Mitchell, 'Father Peter Daly (c.1788-1868),' *JGAHS*, Vol. 39 (1983-1984), p. 69
52. *Galway Vindicator*, 5 Aug., 1863
53. Ibid., 4 Jan, 1873
54. Memorial of lease, 1873
55. S. Ryan, 'St. Joseph's Industrial School, Salthill ("Salthill"), 1870-1996,' *Ryan Report* 2009, p. 523
56. Ibid.
57. *Connaught Tribune*, 23 Sept., 1977
58. J. Mitchell, 'Father Peter Daly (c.1788-1868),' *JGAHS*, Vol. 39 (1983-1984), p. 114

Chapter 14. 'Improving' Landlords at Salthill's Seafront:

1. J. Rabbitte, 'Galway Corporation MS. C.,' *JGAHS*, Vol. 14. (1928-29), p. 2
2. J. Hardiman, *History of Galway*, Dublin 1820, p. 244
3. H. Dutton, *A Statistical and Agricultural Survey of the County of Galway,* Dublin 1824, p. 505
4. J. Hardiman, *History of Galway*, Dublin 1820, p. 250
5. *Galway Vindicator,* 10 May, 1845
6. *Oxford Dictionary*
7. *Galway Vindicator*, 10 May, 1845
8. *Galway Mercury*, 16 Aug., 1845
9. Ibid., 26 April, 1845
10. J. O'Donovan, *O'Donovan's Field Name Books, 1838/'39,* Galway Library, [online] @: http://places.galwaylibrary.ie/place/11011
11. *Freeman's Journal*, 28 Nov., 1838
12. *Galway Mercury*, 16 Nov., 1850
13. *Connacht Tribune*, 24 May, 1941
14. *Galway Vindicator*, 25 Aug., 1847
15. *Connacht Tribune*, 30 Aug., 1941
16. *Galway Vindicator,* 12 May, 1847
17. J.S. Donnelly, *The Great Irish Potato Famine,* Dublin 2008, p.102
18. Ibid.
19. *Galway Vindicator*, 5 June, 1847
20. *Galway Mercury*, 10 July, 1847
21. Ibid., 16 Nov., 1850
22. *The Royal Leamington Spa Courier*, 23 Nov., 1850
23. *Leinster Express,* 30 Nov., 1850
24. *Freeman's Journal*, 19 Nov., 1850
25. *Galway Mercury*, 18 Jan., 1851
26. *Archaeological Inventory of County Galway.* Vol. 1: West Galway, Dublin 1993, p. 45
27. Landed Estates' Auction Documentation, 1856
28. *Galway Mercury*, 2 April, 1853
29. J. Hardiman, *History of Galway*, Dublin 1820, p. 157
30. *Political State of Great Britain*, London 1717, p. 332

31. J. Hardiman, *History of Galway*, Dublin 1820, p. 187
32. Ibid., p. 230
33. *Pue's Occurrences*, 29 July, 1758
34. *Bath Chronicle and Weekly Gazette*, 14 July, 1791
35. *Dublin Weekly Register*, 22 Dec., 1821
36. *Dublin Evening Mail*, 26 March, 1824
37. *Belfast Commercial Chronicle,* 30 March, 1825
38. *Southern Reporter*, 5 Sept., 1826
39. *Belfast Commercial Chronicle,* 8 Aug., 1827
40. *Freeman's Journal*, 28 Nov., 1838
41. *Galway Mercury*, 28 Nov., 1846
42. Ibid., 24 March, 1855
43. Galway Petty Court record, 1852
44. *Saunder's Newsletter*, 14 March, 1867
45. Landed Estates' Auction Documentation, 1856
46. *Galway Vindicator*, 20 Oct., 1866
47. *Irish Times*, 21 Feb., 1895
48. *Galway Vindicator, 21 Aug., 1858*
49. P.W. Joyce, *The Origin and History of Irish Names of Places*, Dublin 1875, p. 278
50. T.S. Ó Máille, 'Place Names from Galway Documents,' *JGAHS*, Vol. 23 (1948-1949), p. 96
51. J. O'Donovan, *O'Donovan's Field Name Books, 1838/'39*, Galway Library, [online] @: http://places.galwaylibrary.ie/place/10831
52. *Galway Mercury*, 27 April, 1850
53. *Freeman's Journal*, 27 May, 1852
54. *Galway Vindicator*, 26 May, 1852
55. *Galway Mercury,* 11 June, 1852
56. *Slater's Directory*, 1856
57. *Galway Packet*, 18 Aug., 1852
58. *Nenagh Guardian*, 25 Aug., 1852
59. *Galway Packet*, 11 Sept., 1852
60. *Galway Vindicator*, 4 Dec., 1852
61. *Galway Packet*, 12 Feb., 1853
62. Landed Estate Court map, 1875
63. *Connacht Tribune*, 22 Nov., 1958
64. *Galway Packet,* 12 Feb., 1853
65. *Connacht Tribune*, 3 Oct., 1964
66. *Connacht Sentinel*, 7 March, 1967
67. *Connacht Tribune*, 3 Oct., 1964
68. *Irish Times*, 28 April, 1864
69. *Galway Vindicator*, 27 May, 1857
70. *Dublin Evening Mail*, 6 Jan., 1866
71. *Nenagh Guardian*, 23 July, 1856
72. *Galway Vindicator*, 16 July, 1856
73. *Catholic Telegraph*, 24 July, 1852
74. *Freeman's Journal*, 12 May, 1852
75. Ibid., 27 Aug., 1858
76. Ibid., 20 April, 1878
77. *Irish Times,* 20 April, 1878
78. L.M. Cullen, 'Galway Merchants in the Outside World,' *Galway Town & Gown 1884-1984,* Ed. D. Ó Cearbhaill, Dublin 1984, p.69
79. *Galway Packet*, 11 Sept., 1852
80. *Galway Vindicator*, 26 Feb., 1859
81. *Galway Mercury*, 7 July, 1855
82. *Galway Vindicator*, 30 Dec., 1868
83. *Slater's Directory*, 1870
84. *Galway Vindicator*, 26 Feb., 1870

Chapter 15. Pollnarooma East of numerous 19th Century Clearances:

1. T.S. Ó Máille, 'Place Names from Galway Documents,' *JGAHS*, Vol. 24 (1950-1951), p. 137
2. J. Hardiman, *History of Galway*, Dublin 1820, p.20
3. J. Rabbitte, 'Galway Corporation MS. C.,' *JGAHS*, Vol. 14. (1928-29), p.4
4. NUIG Landed Estates' database, [online] @: http://www.landedestates.ie/LandedEstates/jsp/family-show.jsp?id=116
5. B. Burke, *A Genealogical and Heraldic History of the Landed Gentry of Ireland*, London 1899, p.412
6. *Galway Mercury*, 22 Nov., 1845
7. Memorial of lease, 1803
8. Landed Estate Court Rentals' documentation, 1848
9. *Connaught Journal*, 4 Oct., 1824
10. Ibid., 6 Feb., 1840
11. Ibid., 27 Feb., 1840
12. *Cork Examiner*, 12 Feb., 1845

13. *Freeman's Journal*, 23 Jan., 1844
14. *Galway Mercury*, 30 Dec., 1848
15. Ibid., 10 Mar., 1849
16. *Galway Patriot*, 30 July, 1836
17. Ibid., 11 Mar., 1837
18. *Galway Vindicator*, 8 June, 1861
19. Galway Petty Court Record, 1899
20. *Tuam Herald*, 18 Mar., 1871
21. *Galway Vindicator*, 19 Nov., 1879
22. *Saturday Herald*, 11 Jan., 1902
23. *Tuam Herald*, 12 May, 1894
24. J. Hardiman, *History of Galway*, Dublin 1820, p.284
25. P. Melvin, *Estates and Landed Society in Galway*, Dublin 2012, p. 207
26. *Burke's Peerage, Baronetage, and Knightage*, 107th edition, Ed. C. Mosley, Delaware 2003, Volume 1, p. 794
27. Ibid.
28. J. Cunningham, '*A Town tormented by the Sea*': Galway 1790-1914, Dublin 2004, p. 115
29. *Drogheda Journal*, 2 Aug., 1826
30. J. Cunningham, '*A Town tormented by the Sea*': Galway 1790-1914, Dublin 2004, p. 112
31. *Daily Telegraph*, 24 Dec., 1895
32. *Galway Mercury*, 6 Nov., 1847
33. *Dublin Post*, 4 Mar., 1848
34. *Freeman's Journal*, 28 Sept., 1848
35. *Galway Mercury*, 28 Aug., 1852
36. *Who's Who*, London 1914, p. 396
37. *Freeman's Journal*, 26 Sept., 1899
38. *Dublin Evening Post*, 30 Apr., 1840
39. Ibid., 17 Jan., 1843
40. *Galway Mercury*, 21 June, 1845
41. Ibid.
42. Galway Petty Court record, 1852
43. *Galway Vindicator*, 14 June, 1851
44. *The Packet*, 18 Sept., 1852
45. *Galway Mercury*, 26 Mar., 1853
46. *Tuam Herald*, 15 Apr., 1876
47. B.M. Fitzpatrick, *Galway Hounds & Jolly Boys*, Dublin 1878, pp.143-4
48. T.S. Napier, 'Lady Gregory's "Emigrant's Notebook".' Lisa e-journal, Vol. 3, 2005, [online] @: https://lisa.revues.org/2473
49. P. Melvin, *Estates and Landed Society in Galway*. Dublin 2012, p. 172
50. G. Kearney, *The Persse Family of County Galway*, Galway 2016, p. 8
51. P. Melvin, *Estates and Landed Society in Galway*. Dublin 2012, p. 39
52. *Belfast Commercial Chronicle*, 23 May, 1825
53. *Dublin Evening Post*, 28 July, 1825
54. *Belfast News-Letter*, 28 May, 1868
55. *Dublin Evening Post*, 10 July, 1868
56. Ibid.
57. *Irish Examiner*, 24 Nov., 2014
58. C. Metcalfe, *For God's Sake*, Phd. thesis, University of East London, April 2011, p. 153
59. G. Grace, 'Sisters behind the grille,' *Times Higher Education*, 9 Mar., 2007, [online] @: http:timeshighereducation.com
60. *Tuam Herald*, 24 May, 1890
61. *Westmeath Journal*, 1 May, 1823
62. J. Fleetwood Berry, *The Story of St. Nicholas' Church*, Galway 1989, p. 83
63. *Belfast Chronicle*, 21 March, 1827
64. *Freeman's Journal*, 24 Jan., 1873
65. J. O'Connor, 'Aspects of Galway Postal History 1638-1984,' *JGAHS*, Vol.44 (1992), pp. 178-180
66. British Postal Service Appointment Book, 1849
67. G. Kearney, *The Persse Family of County Galway*, Galway 2016, p.195
68. Galway Petty Court Record, 1873
69. *Galway Vindicator*, 18 Feb., 1874
70. Ibid., 10 Feb., 1874
71. Ibid., 17 Jan., 1874
72. Ibid., 18 Feb., 1874
73. Ibid., 21 Feb., 1874
74. Ibid.
75. *Freeman's Journal*, 3 Mar., 1874
76. *Galway Vindicator*, 18 Feb., 1874
77. Ibid., 14 June, 1851
78. *Galway Packet*, 18 Sept., 1852
79. *Tuam Herald*, 15 Apr., 1876
80. Ibid., 22 July, 1848
81. *Connaught Telegraph*, 19 Feb., 1845
82. *Freeman's Journal*, 23 Sept., 1890
83. *Nenagh Guardian*, 30 Dec., 1891
84. *Galway Mercury*, 1 Jan., 1853
85. *Connacht Tribune*, 13 Aug., 1910

Chapter 16. Tievegarriff - Cloghatisky - Acres: Disparate Famine Experiences:

1. *Tuam Herald*, 22 July, 1842
2. *Dublin Morning Register*, 20 May, 1842
3. *The Weekly Telegraph*, 17 Nov., 1855
4. *Galway Mercury*, 14 Feb., 1845
5. *Galway Vindicator*, 24 March, 1847
6. *Galway Mercury*, 4 Jan., 1851
7. *Dublin Builder*, 15 April, 1852. p.74
8. *Galway Mercury*, 4 Jan., 1851
9. Ibid., 1 Oct., 1859
10. Ibid., 11 Oct., 1844
11. *Connaught Telegraph*, 19 Feb., 1845
12. *Cork Examiner*, 5 Nov., 1845
13. R. O'Neill, *A Rich Inheritance*, Galway 1994, p. 48
14. Ibid., p. 47
15. Ibid., p. 104
16. Ibid., p. 51
17. *Freeman's Journal*, 24 May, 1847
18. *Galway Vindicator*, 22 April, 1848
19. Ibid., 21 Sept., 1842
20. Ibid., 25 March, 1848
21. Ibid., 25 Sept., 1847
22. *Freeman's Journal*, 31 March, 1841
23. *Galway Mercury*, 20 Dec., 1844
24. *Galway Vindicator*, 20 March, 1847
25. Ibid., 6 July, 1842
26. Fictitious Votes' Report, 1837
27. *Pettigrew & Oulton Dublin Almanac*, 1845
28. NUIG Landed Estates' database, [online] @: http://landedestates.nuigalway.ie/LandedEstates/jsp/estate-show.jsp?id=1230
29. *Galway Vindicator*, 11, April, 1846
30. *Galway Mercury*, 17 April, 1847
31. *Dublin Evening Post*, 30 Sept., 1854
32. *Galway Vindicator*, 12 Sept., 1855
33. Ibid., 18 Feb., 1857
34. *Galway Vindicator*, 17 July, 1844
35. *Slater's Directory*, 1846
36. *Galway Vindicator*, 10 Jan., 1855
37. *Slater's Directory*, 1846
38. *Freeman's Journal*, 23 March, 1875
39. R. O'Neill, *A Rich Inheritance*, Galway 1994, pp. 50-51
40. Ibid., p. 56
41. *Galway Mercury*, 4 Jan., 1851
42. Ibid., 7 May, 1853
43. *Morning Post*, 21 Dec., 1864
44. *Galway Patriot*, 4 July, 1838
45. *Galway Mercury*, 10 Aug., 1850
46. Ibid., 23 Oct., 1847
47. *Galway Vindicator*, 7 Feb., 1848
48. *Galway Mercury*, 15 Oct., 1853
49. Ibid., 17 Feb., 1855
50. *Galway Vindicator*, 5 Aug., 1863
51. *Galway Express*, 4 Sept., 1869
52. John Cunningham, '*A Town tormented by the Sea*,': *Galway, 1790-1914*, Dublin 2004, p. 136
53. *Galway Mercury*, 14 Nov., 1846
54. John Cunningham, '*A Town tormented by the Sea*,': *Galway, 1790-1914*, Dublin 2004, p. 136
55. *Galway Mercury*, 6 Oct., 1849
56. Ibid., 16 Jan., 1847
57. B. Mc Neill, *No Gods (and Precious Few Heroes)*, Greentrax Records, 1995

Chapter 17. Salthill's Famine Roads:

1. E. Boland, 'Famine Road,' *The War Horse*, London 1975
2. *Galway Vindicator*, 12 May, 1847
3. P.J. Kennedy, 'The County of the Town of Galway.' *JGAHS*, Vol. 30 (1962-63), pp. 98-99
4. *Galway Mercury*, 7 March, 1846
5. Ibid., 8 Dec., 1849
6. J. Cunningham, '*A Town tormented by the Sea*': *Galway 1790-1914*, Dublin 2004, p. 130
7. S. Spellissy, *The History of Galway City & County*, Limerick 1999, p.105
8. J. Dalton, *The History of the County of Dublin*, Dublin 1838, p. 296
9. Galway Petty Court Record, 1873
10. D. MacDonagh, 'Dublin Made Me,' *Oxford Book of Irish Verse*, Oxford 1958

11. P. O'Dowd, *Galway Lawn Tennis Club; A History*, Galway 2005, p. 5
12. *Galway Express*, 3 July, 1920
13. *Connacht Tribune*, 27 Feb., 1926
14. *Galway Vindicator*, 21 Nov., 1846
15. *Galway Mercury*, 5 Dec., 1846
16. Ibid., 10 Nov., 1849
17. Ibid., 1 Dec., 1849
18. Ibid., 19 Oct., 1850
19. Ibid., 2 Nov., 1850
20. Ibid., 5 April, 1851
21. Ibid., 17 May, 1845
22. *Galway Vindicator*, 11 July, 1849
23. Landed Estate Auction Catalogue, 1852
24. *Galway Vindicator*, 16 April, 1851
25. Ibid., 7 Feb., 1863
26. M. Moffitt, *Soupers and Jumpers, The Protestant Missions in Connemara 1848-1937*, Dublin 2008.
27. *Dublin Builder*, 15 April, 1862, p. 74
28. C. Ní Ríordáin, *Bhí mé i Scoil Fhursa*, Galway 1988, p.10
29. *Dublin Evening Mail*, 28 March, 1866
30. *Galway Vindicator*, 7 April, 1866
31. Ibid., 31 March, 1866
32. Ibid., 14 April, 1866
33. P. Yeates, 'The Dublin 1913 Lockout,' *History Ireland*, Issue 2 (Summer 2001), Volume 9.
34. *Connacht Tribune*, 25 Oct., 1913
35. Ibid., 28 June, 1913
36. Drumshanbo (Murhaun) Parish, [online] @: http://drumshanboparish.ie/content.aspx?par=118&ContentId=63
37. Poor Clares, *Our Story*, [online] @: http://poor-clares.com/history
38. *Tuam Herald*, 11 Sept., 1858
39. *Irish Times*, 26 Feb., 1862
40. *Galway Vindicator*, 14 Sept., 1859
41. J. Rabbitte, 'Galway Corporation MS. C.' *JGAHS*, Vol. 12 (1922-1923), p. 27
42. R. O' Flaherty, *West or h-Iar Connaught*, (original 1684). Ed. J. Hardiman, Dublin 1846, pp. 384-5
43. *Galway Vindicator*, 31 Jan., 1863
44. Ibid., 7 Feb., 1863
45. Ibid., 4 Feb., 1863
46. Ibid., 31 Jan., 1863
47. *Galway Mercury*, 3 Oct., 1846
48. *Dublin Builder*, 1 March, 1863, p. 43
49. *Galway Vindicator*, 4 Feb, 1863
50. *Irish Times*, 11 June, 1863
51. *Galway Vindicator*, 5 Aug., 1863
52. Ibid., 24 Oct., 1863
53. Ibid., 9 March, 1864
54. Ibid., 12 March, 1864
55. *Irish Times*, 15 June, 1864
56. *Galway Vindicator*, 28 Jan., 1865
57. Ibid., 6 June, 1866
58. Cancelled Revision Book annotation, 1863
59. *Galway Vindicator*, 5 Aug., 1863
60. Ibid., 30 May, 1863
61. Ibid., 4 Feb., 1863
62. *Wexford Independent*, 9 Dec., 1868
63. Galway Petty Court Record, 1873
64. British Army WWI Pension Record.
65. *Connacht Tribune*, 12 May, 1923
66. Bureau Military History, WS. 419
67. Ibid., WS. 798
68. *Irish Independent*, 1 June, 1934
69. *Connacht Tribune*, 11 July, 1936
70. Ibid., 4 Oct., 1941
71. *Tuam Herald*, 19 Oct., 1957
72. Cancelled Revision Book annotation, 1957
73. U.C.D. Archives, Ref.: IE UCDA P97
74. P. Kavanagh, 'The Hospital,' *Collected Poems*, London 1972, p. 153

Chapter 18. A Persse Presence - Row - American connection:

1. P. Melvin, *Estates and Landed Society in Galway*, Dublin 2012, p. 185
2. G. Kearney, *The Persse Family of County Galway*, Galway 2016, p. 98
3. *Dublin Evening Post*, 20 Sept., 1823
4. Ibid., 2 Oct., 1832
5. *Connaught Watchman*, 9 Sept., 1859
6. *Dublin Morning Register*, 23 May, 1828
7. *Cases Heard and Determined by the House of Lords; 1839, 1840 & 1841*, London 1842,

p. 120
8. *Dublin Morning Register,* 23 May, 1828
9. *Dublin Mercantile Advertiser,* 12 Aug., 1833
10. *Cases Heard and Determined by the House of Lords; 1839, 1840 & 1841,* London 1842, p. 110
11. Ibid., p. 120
12. P. Melvin, *Estates and Landed Society in Galway.* Dublin 2012, p. 185
13. *Journals of the House of Lords,* Volume 88, London 1856/1857, p. 226
14. *Cork Examiner,* 30 May, 1855
15. *Journals of the House of Lords,* Volume 88, London 1856/1857, p. 189
16. *Daily Express,* 8 April, 1884
17. G. Kearney, *The Persse Family of County Galway,* Galway 2016, p. 252
18. P. Melvin, *Estates and Landed Society in Galway,* Dublin 2012, p. 401
19. G. Kearney, *The Persse Family of County Galway,* Galway 2016, p. 243
20. B. Burke, *A Genealogical and Heraldic History of the Landed Gentry of Ireland,* London 1899, p. 559
21. *Irish Times,* 23 April, 1888
22. Ibid., 26 June, 1895
23. Ibid., 23 Nov., 1907
24. Ibid., 8 Feb., 1900
25. *Connacht Tribune,* 31 May, 1913
26. J. Mitchell, 'Colonel William Persse,' *JGAHS,* Vol. 30 (1962-1963), p. 75
27. J. Mitchell, 'The Imprisonment of Wilfrid Scawen Blunt in Galway: Cause and Consequence.' *JGAHS,* Vol. 46 (1994), p. 90
28. W.S. Blunt, *The Land War in Ireland,* London 1912, p. 443
29. P. Melvin, *Estates and Landed Society in Galway,* Dublin 2012, p. 39
30. J. Mitchell, 'Colonel William Persse,' *JGAHS,* Vol. 30 (1962-1963), pp. 55-56
31. Ibid., p. 80
32. *Connaught Journal,* 18 Oct., 1830
33. J. Mitchell, 'Colonel William Persse,' *JGAHS,* Vol. 30 (1962-1963), p. 51
34. J. Wesley, *The Works of the Reverend John Wesley, A.M.,* Vol. IV, London 1829, p. 376
35. J. Mitchell, 'Colonel William Persse,' *JGAHS,* Vol. 30 (1962-1963), p. 84
36. G. Kearney, *The Persse Family of County Galway,* Galway 2016, p. 208
37. *Galway Vindicator,* 17 Sept., 1859
38. B. Whelan, *American Government in Ireland 1790-1913,* Manchester 2010, p. 106
39. *Galway Vindicator,* 6 May, 1865
40. Ibid., 27 March, 1858
41. *Galway Mercury,* 1 Oct., 1859
42. Landed Estates' Auction brochure, 1873
43. *Dublin Builder,* 15 April, 1862
44. Landed Estates' Auction brochure, 1873
45. *Dublin Evening Mail,* 30 Nov., 1861
46. A. Caddell letter re Persse Family, 2001, [online] @: http://www.genealogy.com/forum/surnames/topics/persse/14/
47. *Freeman's Journal,* 19 April, 1873
48. *Thom's Directory,* 1868
49. *Slater's Directory,* 1870
50. *Tuam Herald,* 4 Nov., 1887
51. *Galway Vindicator,* 2 July, 1887
52. *Connacht Sentinel,* 9 Oct., 1979

Chapter 19. Townland Information from 19th Century:

1. J. O'Donovan, *O'Donovan's Field Name Books, 1838/'39,* Galway Library, [online] @: http://places.galwaylibrary.ie/place

INDEX

Alfieri, Vittorio, 104
Allen, family, 154
Allen, J(ohn), 206
Allen, Peter, 209
Anacher, Forester of Flanders, 255
Archdeacon, Nicholas Joseph (Dr.), 101
Armitage, Catherine, 72
Armstrong, George, 254
Ashe, Margaret (Maggie)(Ald.), 177, 207
Ashley, Elizabeth Mary, 203
Athye, John, 16, 246
Austin, M.D. (Rev.), 52
Bain, Alexander, 192
Bain, brothers, 191
Baker, Fletcher, 199
Baker, Michael (Sgt.), 214
Balor (Fitzgerald, Jack), 122, 124, 169
Bane, Mr., 318
Bannon, Margaret, (Mulleady), 113
Barbor, Robert Christopher, 146
Barry, Clarke, 155
Barry, Frances, 337
Barry, Mr., 211
Bartley, Gerald, T.D., 263
Barton, Dunbar (High Sheriff), 266
Barton, Dunbar Plunket M.P., 267–268
Barton, Thomas Henry, (Professor, Barrister), 81–82, 87–88, 92, 106, 158, 174, 217, 245–246, 249–250, 252, 255, 257, 259–260, 261–262, 265–269, 280–281, 288, 290, 292, 298, 307
Bath, Mr., 279, 280
Bayly, Robert (Capt.), 279
Behan, John, 329
Bellew, family, 301
Bellew, Thomas Arthur, 319
Benedict XVI, Pope, 45
Besnard, John, 233
Bianconi, Charles, 79
Bingham, Charles Barry, 276–277
Bingham, Denis Arthur, 258, 277, 279, 280, 284
Bingham, Edward Barry Stewart (Rear-Admiral), 279
Bingham, John Charles, 88, 278, 280–282, 291–292

Bingham, John Denis Yelverton (Lt. Col.), 279
Bingham, John George Barry, 278, 281
Bingham, John, 276
Binns, Mr., 152
Black, Justice, 213–215
Black, R., 220
Blake, E. (Solicitor), 239–240
Blake, Helen, 140
Blake, J.W., 95
Blake, Mr. (*Vindicator*), 236
Blake, Theobald J.P., 302
Blunt, Wilfrid Scawen, 339–341
Bodkin, Dominick; John Oliver; Margery; Oliver Jnr.; Oliver, 338
Bodkin, Nicholas J. & Walter, 273
Boland, Eavan, 308, 322
Boland, family, 70
Boland, Lory & Maeve, 66
Boland, Patrick J. (P.J.), 67, 98, 246, 293
Boland, Thomas (Rev.), 52
Bolton, George, Henry & Mary, 182
Bond, Marie E.J., 255
Boyle, Constable, 192
Bradjiotte, Mr., 221
Brady, J. Beauchamp, 285
Brady, Rupert George (Capt.), 284–285
Breathnach, Councillor, 154
Breen, Dan, 327
Brennan, Annie & E.V., 207
Brennan, Michael, 240
Brewster, Mr. (Q.C.), 279
Bright, John, Joseph & Mary (Freeman - Bolton), 182
Brooke, Emily & George Frederick (Sir), 68
Brophy, John, 128
Brown, William (Admiral), 114
Brown, Dominick, (Lord Oranmore & Brown) 258–259
Brown, Maria (1855), 138
Browne, Dr. (1848), 137
Browne, Dr. (1882), 136
Browne, Maria & John (1809), 101
Browne, Michael (Bishop), 116, 178
Browne, Mrs. (1834), 295
Buckley, William, 294

Burke, Dominick & Matthias (1855), 124
Burke, Ellen (1858), 239
Burke, Hubert (1858), 240
Burke, James H. (1853), 305
Burke, John, 54
Burke, Malachy, 328
Burke, Paddy (1909), 149, 191–193
Burke, Patrick (1921), 163, 168
Burke, Redmond, 347
Burke, Robert (1838), 158
Burke, Sally (1873), 288, 291
Burke, Thomas, 77
Burke, Ulick,(pre-1845), 145
Burke, Walter (1858), 239
Burns, boy (1888), 192
Burns, Michael & Michael Jnr.(1860), 127
Butler, Samuel, 199
Byrde, Even Maberly Durand, 303
Byrne, P.J., 98
Caddell, Andrew, 347
Cahill, William, 207
Callwell, Charles Edward, (Sir, Major-General), 135
Callwell, Henry, 135
Callwell, Josephine M. (J.M.), 135–136, 151, 163, 169, 187
Calnon, Mary, 333
Campbell, James (J.P.), 127, 269
Campbell, M. (1913), 98
Carr, Mr. (Restaurant, 1867), 50
Carr, Thomas, (Bishop, Dr.), 244, 347
Carrick, Cllr., 207, 208
Carroll, J.S., 141
Carter, Patrick (Phadrick- Pádraic), 60, 103, 107, 248
Casey, Éamon (Bishop), 116, 348
Charles I, King, 71
Charles II, King, 72, 104
Cheevers, Matt, 141
Churchill, Winston, 111–212
Clancy, Delia (Salthill), 172
Clancy, Miss (Railway Hotel), 326
Clanmorris, Dowager, 284
Clanmorris, Lady, 281, 288, 291
Clanmorris, Lord, 65–66, 88, 258, 271–272, 276–282, 284, 290–292
Clanricarde, Earl of (1564), 320

Index

Clanricarde, Marquess of (1840s), 233, 287
Clark, Denis (1839), 357
Clark, Mary (1841), 179
Clarke, Anthony (1914), 226
Clarke, George (Coast Guard), 302
Clarke, Thomas (1858), 240
Clayton, Nicholas (Dr.), 68
Clements, Henry, 87–88, 91, 301–313, 321
Cloherty, Gerald, 204–205
Cloherty, Joe, 192
Cloherty, William, J.C. & Margaret Beatrice, 175
Cloran, Messrs., 149
Clune, Capt., 138
Coen, Brigid, 333
Coen, Martin (Fr.), 236, 238, 243–244
Colahan, Dr. Arthur (1884-1952), 84
Colahan, Dr. (Nicholas Whistler), 67, 94
Collins, Anthony, 239
Collins, Michael, 327
Comerford, William J.V., 112
Comyn, Francis, 267
Concannon, Andrea, 54, 183
Concannon, Anna (1882), 294
Concannon, Margaret (Peig), 326–327
Conlon, James, 327
Conlon, Martin, 326–328
Conlon, Michael, (Fr. O.P.), 327
Conneely, Denis & Mary, 124
Conneely, James, 124–125
Conneely, John (1851), 249, 253
Conneely, John B. (1848); Martin (1851); Patrick (1853), 179
Conneely, Louisa, 125
Conneely, Roger, 121–122
Conneely, Thomas, 249
Connelly, Denis, 239–240
Connelly, Michael, 240
Connelly, Patrick & William, 239
Connolly, B. (Bartholomew), 95, 97–98
Connolly, John (1841/'47), 300
Connor, Father, 169
Conyngham, Albert (Sir), 104–105
Conyngham, Alexander (Rev.), 104
Conyngham, Charles (landlord), 104
Conyngham, Henry Vivien (Earl of Mountcharles), 105
Conyngham, Mary, 106
Coogan, Fintan (Ald. & T.D.), 154, 178
Cooke, Charles, 199
Cooke, Cllr. (1939), 209
Cooke, Matthias (1788–1873), 220
Coote, Charles Henry (Sir), 78–79
Coote, Orlando, 78
Corbett, Ald., 207
Corbett, James (Rev. Fr.), 127
Corcoran, P., 94
Cosby, Mary Powlet, 69
Cosgrave, President, 228

Costello, Captain, 97
Costello, Charles, 98
Costello, Gabriel Patrick (Lieut.), 97
Costello, John A., K.C., 213
Costello, Thomas Abraham (T.A.), 97, 98–99
Coulter, Henry, 218
Counihan, G.M., 207
Courtney, Miss, 76
Courtney, Thomas, 259
Craughwell, Ada, 109
Craughwell, family, 275
Cremen family, 146
Cremen, David (Dr.), 146
Cremen, Frances Elizabeth, 142, 146–148, 150
Cremen, Frances Mary/Marie, 148–150, 192
Cremen, James (J.), 134, 147–150, 192
Cremen, Mary (Sister), 147
Crisp, Elizabeth (née Marsh) (1735–1785), 112
Crisp, Elizabeth Maria (1764–1838), 112
Crockett, Davy, 113
Croker, Dr., 267
Cromwell, Frances, 71
Cromwell, Henry (Harry), 72
Cromwell, Oliver, 72
Crosby, Bing, 84, 328
Cross, Sam(uel), 290
Crowley Mr. (Bazaar 1913), 98
Crowley, Mr. (Liquidator 1918), 226
Crowley, M.J. (U.D.C.), 221
Cullen, Archbishop, 79
Cullen, Mr. (Agent), 321–322
Cullen, Mr. (Sanitary Officer), 305
Cullen, P.H., 139
Cunningham, John (Dr.), 118, 128, 233, 277, 306, 310
Cunningham, Patrick, 74
Curley, Mary, 223
Curran, Mary, 170
D'Arcy, John (Rev.), 88, 179, 340
D'Arcy, Mrs., 187
Dacies, Hermina, 324
Dallas, Alexander (Rev.), 315–316
Daly, Aileen, 170
Daly, Anne, 333
Daly, Bishop, 305
Daly, Ellen, 174
Daly, Isaac B., 103, 158, 174
Daly, James, 277
Daly, Julia M., 243, 244, 348
Daly, Mr. (Solicitor, 1914), 165
Daly, J.H., 207, 212
Daly, Robert E., 212
Daly, Nicholas, 241, 243
Daly, Patrick & Josephine, 243
Daly, Patrick J.B., 294
Daly, Peter (Rev. Fr.), 62, 79–80, 157–158, 236–244, 253, 255, 257, 303, 323, 348

Daly, Esther, 180
Darcy, Hyacinth, 228
Davies, Sydney, 96
Davis, John 'Norman,' 62
Davis, Mother Dorothy, 44
Davis, James, 62, 108
Davis, Canon (Rev.), 44, 178
de Burgh, Ulick John (Clanricarde), 287
De Latocnaye, 218
De Valera, Éamon, 98, 177
Dea, Patrick, 143
Deacy, Éamonn 'Chick,' 198
Deacy, Ernie, 314
Delany, Thomas, 145, 146
Derby, Lord, 237
Derrane , John, 193
Derrane, Mary, 207
Devery, James, 207
Dillon Thomas (Professor), 164
Dillon, Geraldine Plunkett, 164
Dodd, Maurice (M.) J. de C., 207, 209, 212–215
Doherty, Peter, 120
Dolan, Maureen (née Lynch), 191
Donnellan, John (Galway Capt., 1964), 264
Donnellan, John (1858), 239
Donnellan, Martin (Cllr. M.J.), 98, 164, 172, 201–202, 207
Donnellan, Michael & John (Footballers 1990s-2010s), 264–265
Donnellan, Mick, T.D. (Footballer 1920s/'30s), 264
Donnellan, Mrs., 171
Donnellan, Pat (Footballer 1960s/'70s), 264
Donnelly, James S. Jnr., 250
Donoghue, Steve, 69
Donohue, Thomas, 114
Dooley, Father, 94
Dooley, Michael (1840s/'50s), 312–314
Doyle, John, 228
Draper, Carter, 91
Driscoll, Louisa and T., 254
Duffy, Charles Gavan, 240
Duffy, James, John, Margaret, Mary & Michael, 115
Duffy, Justice Gavan, 212
Dunkellin, Lord, 346
Dunsandle, Lord, 336
Dutton, Hely, 119, 126, 246
Éamon an Chnoic, 122
Eden, Anthony, 177, 212
Egan, (boy), 317
Egan, John, 240
Egan, Martin, 280
Eglinton, Earl of, 173
Ellis, E. (Rev.), 316
Emerson, Ellen ('Emmerson'), 202, 203, 204
Emerson, Susan (Cllr.), 150, 153, 157, 176–179, 207, 212

Emerson, William(Jnr.) & Enda, 176, 178
Emerson, William, 176
England, Dr., 267
Eyre, Anchoretta, 333
Eyre, Giles (Col.), 333
Eyre, John (Capt.), 158
Eyre, Robert Hedges, 272
Fahey, Honora, 333
Fahy, Anthony Dominic (Rev. Fr.), 113–115
Fahy, Francis, 85
Fahy, Frank (Cllr. Mayor), 84
Faller, Stephen (Cllr.), 98, 205, 319
Faller, William, 303
Fallon, Bridget, 144
Fallon, Dr., 242
Fallon, George (1909), 191
Fallon, George (Baths), 142, 143, 144, 145
Fallon, George (Mariner), 102, 121, 143
Fallon, James, 144, 145
Fallon, Martin (1860), 127
Fallon, Michael 'Fox', 192, 193
Fanshawe, Richard (Sir) & Ann, 165
Ferdinand, L.L., 221
Ferns, John (Sir), 76
Ffrench, Acheson & Mrs., 158
Ffrench, Charles. 101
Ffrench, Dowager Lady, 310
Ffrench, Lord, 101
Finan, Martin, 164, 189
Finan, Noel, 146, 150, 154, 174
Finan, Mrs. B., 207
Finnerty, Patrick, 168
Fisher, Joseph (Rev.), 298
Fitz Marcus, Nicholas Lynch, 271
Fitzgerald, Dr., 226
Fitzgerald, Jack (*Balor*), 122, 124, 169
Fitzgerald, Lord, 313
Fitzgerald, Mr. (Solicitor), 214
Fitzgibbon, John, 74
Fitzgibbon, Mr. (Solicitor), 214
Fitzpatrick, J. Bodkin (Rev.), 238
Flaherty, Michael, 288, 310
Flaherty, P.J., 61, 223
Flaherty, Pat, 239
Flaherty, Patt, 121
Flynn, John, 324
Flynn, Mary Anne (O'), 326
Fogarty, T., 94
Forbes, James, 315
Forster, Charles Ffrench Blake, 111
Forster, Emily Isabella, 91
Forster, Francis Blake (Capt.), 88, 173, 221, 255–256, 317
Forster, Francis O'Donnellan Blake, 255
Forster, George (Sir), 91
Forsyth, Robert, 199
Fox, Martin, 337
Foy, Martin & Emma Jane, 116
Foy, Seán (Rev. Canon), 116

Frazer, Mr., 259, 261, 265–266
Freeman, Mary (Bright- Bolton), 182
French, Lady, 310
French, Lieut. Colonel, 88–89
French, Lord, 327
Freyne, John, 126, 152, 203
Fuller, James Franklin, 93
Galbraith, James, 337
Galbraith, Major Hugh, 337
Galbraith, Sarah Jane, 158, 339
Gallagher, Cllr., 152
Gallagher, John, 169
Gambier, Blanche & Sebastian (Rev.), 304
Gannon, Peter, 288
Gascoyne, Henry, 138
Gaughan, Dick, 307
Geoghegan, Colonel, 89
George V, King, 279
Geraghty, Kathleen, 195
Geraghty, sisterhood, 179
Gill, John, 52, 152, 173–175, 250
Ginkle, General, 253
Girvan, Robert E., 212, 215
Gladstones, Ambrose Upton, 254
Glynn (Glen,) Mary Ann, 55, 326
Glynn (Glen,) William, 55
Glynn, James, 239
Goff, Bartholomew, 210
Goff, Benjamin (Constable), 171
Gordon, James, 181, 336
Gordon, Justice, 204
Gordon, Patrick, 181
Gore, Ralph, 112
Gorham, Patrick Charles, 274
Grant, James. A., 96
Grattan, Frances (Fanny), 92, 134, 139, 242–243, 286, 319–324, 328
Grattan, Henrietta (Langdale), 324, 328
Grattan, Henry (Jnr., M.P.), 79–80, 127, 133, 242, 319, 324, 328
Grattan, Henry (Snr., M.P.), 134, 242, 319, 342
Grattan, Marian & Pauline, 319
Gray, Dr. Robert Rogers, 124, 132–135, 137–138, 140
Gray, Henry Hugo De Witt & Richard Armstrong, 138
Gray, Elizabeth, 138, 140
Greally, M.J., 207
Grealy, P., 95
Greaven, Father, 94
Greaves, William, 192
Green, M. (Rev.), 278
Greene, James F. (Ald.), 174
Greene, P. (Ald. Mayor), 153
Greenwood, Frederick C. (Major), 112
Gregory, Augusta Lady (née Persse), 234–235, 282–283, 335–337, 339–341, 349
Gregory, Margaret, 235
Gregory, Robert, 349

Gregory, William (Sir), 234–235, 282
Grehan, Joseph & Mary, 84
Grehan, Thomas (à Kempis), 84
Grey, Earl, 234
Grieves, Jane & William, 273
Grieves, Mrs., 192
Griffin, Celia, 133–134, 324, 328–329
Griffith, Richard (John), 48, 133, 142, 247, 304, 314
Griffiths, Professor, 191
Grogan, Michael & Thomas, 288
Guilfoyle, Edward, 221
Gunning, John P., 294
Gunning, Richard, 71
Guthrie, Woody, 236
Hackett, Michael (Major J.P.), 94–95
Halliday, W.H., 94, 221
Hallinan, Francis (J.), 54
Halluran, Finyn (Hallorane, Ffinyne), 271
Hanley, Matthew J., 294
Hardiman, Enda, 183
Hardiman, Gertie (Scallan), 183
Hardiman, James, 45–46, 72, 118, 246, 253, 271, 274, 295–298, 310, 320
Harris, John C.E., 94–96
Harrison, C.W. & Sons, 42
Harrison, John, 314, 315
Heard, District Inspector, 172
Heher, Thomas, 255
Helly, Nellie (née Brogan), 61, 223
Henn, Mr., 289
Hennessy, Dermot, 211
Hennessy, Michael (d.1894), 274
Hennessy, Michael, 124, 269
Hennessy, W.P., 94
Henry II, King, 118
Heuston, Bernard (Mother) & Seán, 44
Hickman, Edward Shadwell & Margaret, 345
Hill, Edward, 243
Hobson, Bulmer, 327
Hogan, Mr. (Kilkee), 133
Holland, Elizabeth (Mrs.), 116, 171
Holland, Joseph (Rev. Fr.), 116
Holland, Patrick, 116
Holmes, Anna (b.1890), 293
Holmes, Anna (née Concannon), 293–294
Holmes, Harry William (Capt.), 293, 294
Holmes, Noel (b.1891), 293
Holmes, Robert, 294
Hooper, Richard, 121
Horan, James P., 207, 214
Horan, Michael, 144
Horan, Mrs., 171
Howley, Kate, 54
Howse, J., 95, 221
Humphreys, Henry Temple, 90, 91
Hurley, Michael J., 217
Hutchinson, William (Lieut.), 84, 223
Hyland, John Joe (Rev. Fr.), 54

Hynes, Martin, 98
Ida, Madam, 216
Inglis, Henry, 35, 184
Irwin, family, 134
Jackson, Francis (Master), 317
Jennings, Gerry (Rev. Fr.), 168
John Paul II, Pope, 348
Johnson, Violet (née Persse), 68
Johnston, Lilian, 207
Jones, Henry (S.) Shaw(e) (Capt.), 106–107, 245–255, 257, 260
Jones, Gilbert Pickering R. Shaw(e), 254–255
Jones, Henry Pickering R. Shaw, 254
Jones, Maria (Rudkin), 254–255
Jones, Richard (M.P. 1703 – 1713), 106
Jones, Richard (M.P. 1761–1768), 106
Jones, Roger (Conyngham / Cunningham), 106–107, 246–247, 254
Joyce, (*an Seoigheach*), 72
Joyce, Dónal, 227
Joyce, Pierce, 289
Joyce. P.W., 257
Judge, Sarah, 207
Kavanagh, Patrick, 213, 329
Keady, Mary & Catherine, 300
Keane, Barbara, 128
Keane, Dolores & Seán, 84
Keane, Matthew James, 129
Keane, Patrick, 128–129
Keane, Richard, 128–129
Keane, Tommy, 70, 223, 231
Kearney, Constable, 225
Kearney, Gabriel, 115
Kearney, Gerry, 338
Kearns, Thomas, 289
Keedy, Bartholomew, 310
Keenan, Fr. (Rev.), 226
Kelly, Bridie, 167
Kelly, Frances Elizabeth (Cremen), 146
Kelly, John, 326
Kelly, Mathias, 127
Kelly, Michael 'Esha,' 167, 169, 187
Kelly, Mr. (Barna), 258
Kemp, George, 191
Kennedy, B., 207
Kennedy, John Fitzgerald (President), 49, 70, 120
Kennedy, M.J., 213
Kennedy, Mary (M.A.), 207, 212, 213, 215
Kenny, John & Mrs.(Strand Ho.), 171
Kenny, Mrs. (Clonbur), 194– 195
Kenny, sisters, 87
Kenny, T.J.W. (*Conn. Tribune*), 149, 164
Kenny, T.M. (Solicitor), 94
Kenny, Thomas, 98
Kenny, Tom (Bookshop), 84, 127
Keogh, Joseph, 166
Kernan, Anne Jane, Hubert Prendergast, & Maria, 302
Kernan, John B. (J.B.) R.M., 298, 302, 304
Killian, Eliza, 109
Kilraine, Seán, 178
Kinealy, Christine, 235
King, Andrew, 138, 139, 140, 322
King, Dr., 267
King, Jane, 140
King, Margaret Galvia, 303
King, William (Professor), 303
Kinneen, R.B., 207
Kirwan, Denis, 158
Kirwan, John J., 94
Kirwan, John S., 314
Kirwan, Mrs., 171
Kirwan, R.A.H., 89
Knatchbull, Francis (Col.), 285
Knee, Mary, 333
Kyne, Maude, 172
Lally, Patrick (Rev. Fr.), 95, 200, 244
Lambert, James Staunton & Thomas Dillon, 277
Lancaster, Ann (née O'Hara), 286
Lancaster, James (Rev.), 286
Lane, Hugh (Sir), 349
Lane, Pádraig G., 239
Langdale, Charles Joseph & Charles Jnr., 324
Langdale, Henrietta (Grattan), 324, 328
Lansdowne, Lord, 234
Larkin, James, 318
Larkin, William, 102–103, 309
Lavelle, Mrs., 155
Lavin, Anne, 93
Lawless, Cecil John, 267
Lawless, Mary Catherine, 76
Lawless, Ms. (Rahoon), 300
Lawley, F., 277
Lawson, Mary A., 339
Leddy, Constable, 192
Lee, James & Mr.(1845), 280
Leet, Ambrose, 50, 102
Lentaigne, John, 243
Leo XII, Pope, 237
Leonard, Leo; Leo Jnr.; & Margaret, 326
Leonard, Alice (Athenry), 200
Leonard, Sergeant (R.I.C.), 192
Lever, Brothers, 205
Lewis, John (Rev.), 303
Lincoln, Abraham (President), 345
Liston, F., 207
Lydon, Cllr. (1930s), 207–208
Lydon, Dr., 274
Lynch Marcus (d. 1740), 338
Lynch, Andrew, 254
Lynch, James & Kate (1857), 302
Lynch, James (1400s), 68
Lynch, Maureen (Dolan), 191
Lynch, Mrs., 169
Lynch, Nicholas, 306
Lynch, Patrick Marcus, 299
Lynch, Richard M. (Marcus), 247, 295, 299, 301
Lynham, John Isaac (Professor, Dr.), 52–53
Lynskey, Winifred, 220
Lyons, George, 326
Mac Amhlaigh, Dónall, 154, 216
Mac Congáil, Nollaig, 233
Mac Giolla Sheannaigh, Éamon & 'Aina' (Mc Alinney), 170
MacDermott & Allen, Messrs., 212
MacDonald, George & Marion, 203
Mack, George, 94, 175
Mackey, Francis, 159
Madden, Francis, 261, 265–266
Madden, John, 281
Madison, James (President), 109
Magill, Theodosia Hawkins, 78
Maher, Joseph, 207
Mahony, Dr., 334
Mangan, Launcelot, 236
Markievicz, Countess, 326
Marsh, Elizabeth (Crisp), 112
Martin, Elizabeth, 198
Martin, Kate & Winifred, 178
Martin, Maria (Maud), 135
Martin, Mary, 240
Martin, Richard (Humanity Dick), 198, 277
Martine, Marie (Sister), 116
Martyn, James, 243
Martyn, Mrs., 158
Marvelle, 216
Matthews, William, 170
May, Myles, 207
Mayne, Thomas Henry, & Lily (Torrens), 148
McAlinney, Ann(i)e, 177, 178
McAlinney, Edward, 153, 175–176
McAlinney, family, 59, 178
McAlinney, John, 177
McAlinney, Susan (Emerson), 176
McAlinney, Thomas (Canon Fr.), 176
McCarthy, Ellen, 221
McCarthy, Mr. (solicitor), 215
McCarthy, Philip J. (Joseph), 221, 223, 228
McCormack, Francis (Mac) (Bishop), 94–95, 98, 347–348
McDermott, Mrs.171
McDonagh, Donagh, 311
McDonagh, Thomas, 95
McDonnell, Jos., 336
McDonnell, Martin (1892), 95
McDonnell, Mr. (1913), 98
McDonogh, Martin (Cllr. 'McDonagh' 1910), 98, 162
McDonogh, Mary, A., 207
McDonogh, Michael (Dr.), 212, 215
McDonogh, P., 207
McEvaddy, Mrs., 172
McEvilly, John (Bishop), 238–241, 243, 319, 321
McGivern, R.E., 207

McGrath, Denis, 149, 191–193
McGrath, John, 129
McGrath, Martin (1913), 98
McGrath, Martin (Driver 1911–1959), 228
McGrath, Roger (1859), 345
McHale, Archbishop, 235
McLarchie, Arthur, 170
McLean, P., 207
McLoughlin, Bishop, 116
McLoughlin, Michael, 223
McMaster, Anew, 199
McNeill, Brian, 307
McNulty, Paul, 338
McRory, Mr., 79
Meade, John, 78
Meheron, Jane, 333
Melvin, Patrick, 235, 276, 283, 336
Meskil, Captain, 194
Mespoulet, Marguerite, 119
Metcalfe, Camillus, 285
Meyrick, Llewellyn L., 99
Mignon, Madeleine, 119
Miles, Thomas Rose, 119
Millard, Claire, 326
Miller, George, 207
Miller, John T. 176, 204, 221
Milne, Mary Jean Mowatt, 326
Mitchell, James (Rev. Fr.), 244, 342
Mitchell, Patrick, 149
Moffitt, Mirriam, 315
Molloy, Barbara ('Babs of the Baths'), 152
Molloy, Martin (1860), 127
Molloy, William, C.E., 261, 263, 265–266
Monahan, M.F., 207
Monahan, siblings, 178
Montefiore, Dora (Madame), 318
Montgomerie, George Arnulph, 173
Moon, Alexander, 95, 324, 327–328
Moon, Charles, 94, 221
Moore, Mr., 76
Moroney, Carol Ann, 348
Moroney, Michael & Phyllis (Phil), 328
Morris, Den(n)is Valentine (Dr.), 207
Morris, George M.P., 289
Mulholland, Gerry, 85
Mulleady, James, 113
Mulleady, Margaret, 115
Mulleady, Thomas (Msgr. Fr.), 113–116
Mullin, Jamie, 161–162
Mulvoy, James, 226, 228
Murphy, H.M.A. (Solr.), 96, 221
Murphy, John (b.1870), 129
Murphy, Mrs. (Hawthorn Lo.), 171
Murphy, Mrs. (landlady), 164
Murphy, William, (1913 Dublin), 318
Murray, Arthur J. (Rev. Fr.), 116
Murray, Francis & Margaret, 160
Murray, Mr. (1845), 246–247
Murray, P.J., 116

Murray, Tom (Rev. Fr.), 115
Murray, William George (G.), 89, 243
Murtagh, Colonel, 193
Nally, Jane, 322
Ned O'The Hill, 122–126, 129, 138, 140, 194
Newenham, Edward (Jnr.), 342
Newenham, Edward (Sir) & Lady, 342–344
Newman, John Henry (Cardinal), 79
Ní Ríordáin, Cáit, 316
Nicholson, John, 210
Nolan, Sebastian, 94
Noone, Elizabeth, 155
Ó Cléaracháin, Mr. (O'Callaghan, C.J.), 206–207
Ó hUiginn, Mícheál (O'Higgins) (Cllr., d.1964), 264
Ó hUiginn, Mícheál (O'Higgins) (Cllr. Mayor), 264
Ó hUiginn, Tomás, 264
Ó Máille, Tomás, (Dr. T.S.), 100–101, 103, 258, 271
Ó Mórdha, P., 207
O'Beirn, Séamus (Dr.), 294
O'Beirne, Bartley (Dr.), 209–215
O'Beirne, Dónal (Dr.), 214
O'Boyle, Mrs., 171
O'Brien, Eileen, 248
O'Brien, Emily & Harriet, 243
O'Brien, Michael (1858), 239
O'Brien, Mr., 161
O'Brien, William Smith, 267
O'Callaghan, C. J. (Ó Cléaracháin), 206–207
O'Casey, Seán, 349
O'Connell, Jarlath, 338
O'Connell, Michael, 192
O'Connor, Christy Jnr. & John, 155
O'Connor, Jack (Rev. Canon), 42
O'Connor, John, 90
O'Connor, Laurence & Co., 141
O'Connor, Mary, 67
O'Connor, Thomas (1889), 191
O'Connor, Thomas (Cllr. & Publican), 183
O'Dea, Bishop, 98
O'Dea, Louis, 172, 195
O'Donell, Daniel, 121–122, 128
O'Donnell (father and sons), 120
O'Donnell, Laurence (Bishop), 299, 302
O'Donnell, Martin, 128
O'Donoghue, Power (Mrs.), 96
O'Donohue, Colman, 144, 167
O'Donohue, James (Sir), 162, 165, 233
O'Donovan Rossa, 326
O'Donovan, John, 71, 100, 103, 247–248, 257–258, 275, 277, 295–296, 310
O'Flaherty, Anthony (Coast Guard), 121
O'Flaherty, Anthony M.P., 88, 92

O'Flaherty, Bernard, 88, 302
O'Flaherty, Liam, 186
O'Flaherty, Mr. (Agent), 297
O'Flaherty, Murrough, 320
O'Flaherty, Peggy, 186
O'Flaherty, Roderic, 297, 320
O'Flaherty, Walter, 204, 207
O'Flynn (Scallan - Ryan), Margaret, 83–84, 183
O'Flynn, Michael, 83
O'Gorman, Ralph, 116
O'Grady, Katherine, 334
O'Halloran, clan, 271
O'Hara, Ann (Raheen), 337
O'Hara, Anne ('Anna' Lancaster), 286
O'Hara, Anne, 304, 330
O'Hara, Emily (O'Sullivan), 286
O'Hara, James (1748–1838), 295, 304
O'Hara, James (1796–1838), 286, 304
O'Hara, James (Col.) (1865 –1928), 70
O'Hara, James (Col., Capt.) (1832–1902), 92, 123–124, 126, 138, 144, 286, 298, 304–306, 323
O'Hara, James (1845), 145
O'Hara, John, 133, 158, 305
O'Hara, Lady O'Donnell, 158
O'Hara, Mrs., 304
O'Hara, Richard (Col.), 71, 85, 149
O'Hara, Rose, 305
O'Higgins, Michael (Ó hUiginn, Mícheál) (Cllr., d.1964), 264
O'Higgins, Michael (Ó hUiginn, Mícheál) (Cllr. Mayor), 264
O'Keefe, Head Constable, 192
O'Kelly, Séamus, 196
O'Madden, Patrick, 170
O'Malley, Cusack John & David Joseph (Dr.), 161
O'Malley, Michael George (Professor, Surgeon), 55, 160, 162, 207, 213, 215
O'Malley, C., 192
O'Malley, Peter James and Mary, 161
O'Neill, P. (Constable), 170
O'Neill, Margaret, 326
O'Neill, Rose (Sister), 299
O'Reilly, family, 252
O'Reilly, Sergeant, 192
O'Rourke, John (Rev. Canon), 235
O'Shaughnessy, Emily, 176
O'Shaughnessy, John & Eileen, 328
O'Shee, 111
O'Sullivan, Emily (née O'Hara), 286
O'Sullivan, James (Bishop Dr.), 286
O'Sullivan, Jeremiah (d.1826), 277
O'Sullivan, Jeremiah (J.) (Major), 206
O'Sullivan, Mary Josephine Donovan (Professor), 206, 208–210, 212–215
Oranmore and Brown, Lord, 258–259
Ormsby, Sarah Anne, 166
Palmerston, Lord, 237
Parnell, Charles Stewart, 123
Parsons, John, 146
Pennefather, Sarah, 276

Percy, family, 283
Perón, Eva (Evita), 114
Perrin, Mr., 300
Persse, Anchoretta Maria, 339, 341
Persse, Burton (1746–1831), 276
Persse, Burton de Burgh
  (c.1779–1859), 66, 275–276, 282,
  331, 333–336
Persse, Burton Robert Parsons (R.P.)
  J.P. (1828–1885), 158
Persse, Burton Washington, 345
Persse, Cecil De Burgh (Lieut.), 44,
  69, 287
Persse, Dudley (1625–1699), 283
Persse, Dudley (1802–1878), 282,
  334–337, 340
Persse, Dudley (Rev. Archdeacon)
  (1662–1699), 337
Persse, Eleanor Alice (A.) (d.1890),
  42–44, 67, 69–70
Persse, Eleanora Alice (d.1937), 69
Persse, Elizabeth (Newenham), 342
Persse, Frances (née Barry)
  (1810–1896), 337, 340
Persse, George, 333, 335
Persse, Georgina Henrietta, 345
Persse, Helen (Parker), 43, 68
Persse, Henrietta Burton, 42
Persse, Henry (Capt.) (1740–1805), 344
Persse, Henry S. Jnr. (P.O. 1818/'26),
  287
Persse, Henry Sadleir (1832–1899),
  42–43, 46, 66–69, 276, 278, 281, 285
  287–293, 302, 330, 333, 339–340
Persse, Henry Seymour 'Atty,' 68, 69
Persse, Henry Stratford (1841–1843),
  344
Persse, Henry Stratford (c.1769–1833),
  287, 333, 344
Persse, Henry Thomas, 345
Persse, Isabella Augusta (Lady
  Gregory), 234–235, 282–283,
  335–337, 339–341, 349
Persse, John Beauchamp, 43, 67–68
Persse, Maria Helena, 282, 284
Persse, Mary Catherine, (née Lawless), 76
Persse, Matilda (née Persse)
  (1793–1862), 43, 66, 282, 285
Persse, Matilda Theodora, 42, 67, 68
Persse, Matilda, (c.1793–1862), 333
Persse, Mrs. (Castleboy, 1787), 344
Persse, Mrs. (mother of Capt. Robert
  [1833–1921]), 337
Persse, Neptune (P.O. 1831/'52), 287
Persse, Noël Majorie (Margori),
  42–43, 67
Persse, Parsons (1849), 287
Persse, Patrick, 333–335
Persse, Robert (1763–1850), 334–335
Persse, Robert (c.1689–1781), 340
Persse, Robert (Capt.) (1833–1921),
  287, 336–338
Persse, Robert (Rev. 1602), 283

Persse, Robert D. (P.O. 1829/'50), 287
Persse, Robert Henry (1806–1884),
  335–337
Persse, Robert Parsons (1771–1829),
  333–335, 338
Persse, Sarah Belinda, 284–285, 330
Persse, Sarah Henrietta, 69
Persse, Sarah Selena, 281–282
Persse, Thomas Moore (M.), 46, 55,
  89, 92, 284–285, 298, 304, 340–341,
  344–349
Persse, Violet Seymour (Johnson),
  68–69
Persse, William (Col.) (1728–1802),
  339, 341–344, 346, 349
Persse, William Henry (Sheriff)
  (1863–1924), 67, 69, 311
Pinter, Harold, 199
Piper, Florence, William & Emily, 204
Pius IX, Pope, 319
Plant, Betty, 213
Plunket, Charlotte, 266, 268
Plunket, Lord, 268
Pompili, Cardinal, 116
Potter, Mary Josephine, 147
Powell, Mrs. D. (Dalysfort Rd.),
  207–208
Power, Charles Wyse (Judge), 195
Power, M., 207
Price, Mr., 148
Quetelet, George, 141
Quinlan, Michael, 239
Quinn, Constable, 267
Quirk, Charles, 288
Raftery, Patrick, 54
Rattenbury, John (Rev.), 51–52
Reddan, Michael, 239
Reddington, John (1819), 133
Redington James (1872–1962), 69,
  98–99
Redington, John (1892), 95
Redington, T. N., 98
Reed, Rebecca Margaret, 53
Reilly, Samuel (Rev. Fr.), 115
Reilly, Sergeant (O'Reilly), 172, 192
Reily, Patrick, 258
Rhatigan, Martin, 324, 326
Riall, Elizabeth, 266
Richardson, John M.P., 73
Richardson, Mary Anne (Whaley), 79
Ridley, J.C., 221
Roberts, Edward & John, 91
Roberts, Samuel Ussher, 88–89,
  90–94, 103, 159, 182, 261, 265–266,
  298, 314, 316, 321–323, 346
Robertson, Mr., 96
Robinson, Mr., 77
Roche, A.J., 98, 155, 163
Roche, B.J. (Rev. Fr.), 88
Rochford, Mr., 240
Rochfort, Paul, 140
Rooney, James, 239
Ruck, James, 340

Rudkin, Gilbert-Pickering & Maria,
  254
Rush, James & Ambrose, 302
Rush, Eliza, (Elizabeth) 302, 304
Rush, Mr. (Rev.), 239
Russell, George (AE), 349
Russell, Lord John P.M., 233
Russell, Sarah J., 339
Rutledge, George, 52, 269, 270
Rutledge, James & Rebecca, 269
Ryan, Bedelia, 127
Ryan, Ellen, 51, 179–182
Ryan, Honor(i)a, 181
Ryan, Margaret (1855), 127
Ryan, Margaret (O'Flynn-Scallan),
  84, 183
Ryan, Matthew, 181
Ryan, Michael (Garda Sgt.), 183
Ryan, Mr. (Sherwood Fields), 312–313
Ryan, Mr. (solicitor), 213
Ryan, Mr. and Mrs. Patrick (D.), 70
Ryeevagh, Shane, 338
Sadleir, Anne, 333
Sammon, William (W.J.), 147, 207, 214
Sampson, E., 207
Sandys, W.F. (Dr.), 214
Sansow, Ellen Mary, 161
Sarsfield, Mrs. Úna & Miss Ann, 179
Savage, Martin, 327
Scallan, Gertude, Ernest & Bernard,
  183
Scallan, Thomas Reginald, 83, 183
Scawen, William (Sir), 340
Scott, Michael, 178
Semple, Joseph, 95, 221
Semple, Maurice, 122, 124, 217
Semple, Mr. (Builder 1862), 346
Seoigheach, An (Joyce), 72
Seward, William H, 345
Shaw, Anna Maria; Colonel; &
  Croasdall, 254
Shaw, Fielding, 246
Shaw, George Bernard, 349
Shaw, George, 111
Shaw, Henry, 246
Shaw, Mr. (Merchant, 1691), 253
Shaw, Robert, 253
Shaw, Thomas (1758), 254
Shea, Elizabeth & Gartside, 111
Shea, Lady, 85, 108, 111–112
Shea, Tim(othy), 111–112
Shee (Shea), Lord; George (Sir); James
  (Sir), 112
Sheridan, Clare, 112
Sheridan, Rose Adelaide, 147
Sherwood, Michael & Thomas, 111
Sherwood, Widow, 110–111
Shields, Stan, 159
Sibby of Salthill, 151–152
Simpson, S. (Rev.), 138
Simpson, Sarah Maria, 138
Sisters of Mercy, 114, 238, 244
Skerrett, Anthony & Dominick, 271

Skerrett, J. & Mrs., 158
Skerrett, John, 240
Skerrett, William, 271–272
Sleator, John N., 167
Sloper, Constantine (Constance) (d.1848), 272–273, 295, 299, 301
Sloper, Constantine (d.1824), 271–272, 276, 280
Sloper, Constantine William (Dr.) (d.1902), 273–274
Sloper, Marcella Josephine, 273
Sloper, Richard (d.1879), 273–274, 280, 288, 293, 295, 299–300, 302–304
Smith, Eramus, 256
Smith, Joseph Persse (Dr.), 345
Smith, Maria, 293
Smith, Tom (Henry), 125, 128–129, 189–194
Smyth, Nicholas, 300
Somerville and Ross, 224
Somerville, Richard Newman, 91, 221
St. George, Mr. (Mission School), 98, 317
St. George, W. (Tyrone Ho.), 126
Starkie, Mr. (R.M.), 317
Stewart, Henry Hutchinson (Dr.), 67
Stewart, James (Sir), 74
Stiff, Barbara, 195
Stiff, Frederick, 128
Stubbers, Peter (Col.), 72
Sullivan, Edward (Sir), 74
Sullivan, John J., 255
Sweeney, John, 295
Synge, J.M., 349
Taheny, Dónal (Dan), 122, 152, 340
Tankerville, Mrs., 255
Taylor, Shaw, 158
Taylor, Anthony; Thomas; & Walter, 310
Thompson, Margaret & William, 138
Thornton, Mícheál, 326
Tierney, Commissioner, 172
Tierney, Thomas (Ald. Mayor), 264
Tighe, Mr., 98
Toft, Annie (d. 1909), 203
Toft, Claude (David) (Cllr. Mayor), 120, 134, 154, 198, 200, 210–211, 215–216
Toft, David A. (Abby), 99, 204–210
Toft, Florence - Mrs. A(bby) (née Piper), 156, 204, 208–213, 215–216
Toft, John (d.1912), 200–201, 203
Toft, Kenneth, 210, 216
Toft, Marion (née MacDonald), 203
Toft, Mary (May) (née Emerson), 202–203
Toft, Maureen, 210
Toft, William (d. 1904), 200, 202–203
Toft, William Henry (Harry), 203
Toohey, Jack, 317
Torrens, John & Lily Gertrude (Mayne), 148
Townsend, Bishop & Louisa Olivia Deane, 80
Travers, Father, 98
Treacy, Elizabeth & Seán, 141
Treanor, John (Rev.), 317
Trench, Anne Le Poer, 286
Trench, Archbishop Le Poer, 286
Trench, Christopher St. George, 78
Trench, Mr., 158
Trench, William Steuart, 234
Turnball, family, 204
Uí Chionna, Jackie (Dr.), 72
Ulle, Herr, 199
Ussher, Monsignor S.M., 114
Wade, Anchoretta Maria, 339, 341
Wade, Dorothea Matilda, 339
Waithman, Capt., 94
Wale, George (Capt.), 316
Walker, Brian (Professor), 235
Walker, John, 55
Walker, Patrick, 78
Walker, Mr. (Rev.), 247
Wallace, Mr. (1788), 343
Wallace, Mr. (Solicitor, 1845), 279–280
Waller, William and Mrs., 145
Walsh, Archbishop, 318
Walsh, Lilly, 194–195
Walsh, Michael, 137
Walshe, Bridget; Daniel Joseph (Jnr.); & Gerard Fursey, 170
Walshe, Daniel Joseph, 170
Walshe, Della, 153
Walshe, D. J. Mrs. (Mary, née Curran), 153, 170
Ward, Ann, 72
Ward, Bernard (Rev.), 73
Ward, Leslie, 268
Ward, Mary, 144
Ward, Matilda Catherine Maude, 278
Ward, Robert, 74
Warren, Sybilla L., 324
Washington, George (President), 109, 341–344, 347, 349
Waters, Mr., 201
Wellan, John, 240
Wellesley, Arthur, Duke of Wellington, 75
Wesley, Capt., 75
Wesley, John (Rev.), 52, 344
West, William, 345
Whaley, John (1667), 72
Whaley, John (d. 1847), 54, 71–74, 77–79, 109, 239
Whaley, Ann (Lady-née Ward), 73–74
Whaley, Anne (Fitzgibbon), 74
Whaley, Caroline Elizabeth, 78
Whaley, Col. W. (William) (d.1843), 73–75
Whaley, Colonel (1600s), 72
Whaley, Henry (d. 1828), 78
Whaley, Henry, (1658), 72
Whaley, John (1667-1669), 72
Whaley, John (d. 1847), 54, 71–72, 77–78, 109, 239
Whaley, John Richard William, 79–80
Whaley, Mary Anne (née Richardson), 79
Whaley, Richard Chapell ('Burn-Chapel') d.1769, 72–74, 79
Whaley, Richard Chapell (died young), 73–74
Whaley, Richard M.P. (d.1725), 72
Whaley, Robert W. (William), 73, 79, 133, 238, 242
Whaley, Sophia & Susanna, 74
Whaley, Thomas 'Buck' Jerusalem, 73–77, 330
Whalley, Edward the Regicide, 71
Whalley, Henry M.P. (1656-1659), 72
Whalley, Mr., 72
Whammond, James & Monica (née Oliver), 324
White, Thomas Warren, 278
Whiteside, Chief Justice, 268
Williams, Louis, 122
Wilson, Captain, 76
Wilson, James, 294
Winby, F.C., 221, 225
Wodehouse, Captain, 78
Woodhouse, Martin, 121–122
Woods, Anne, 54
Woods, Samuel, 54, 59, 182
Wylde, William, 253
Yates, Edmund, 174
Yeates, Pádraig, 318
Yeats, W.B., 349
Young, Joseph, 98
Young, Mrs., 155